J. Gresham Machen

J. GRESHAM MACHEN
At about forty-five years of age

J. Gresham Machen

A Biographical Memoir

by

NED B. STONEHOUSE

THE BANNER OF TRUTH TRUST

THE BANNER OF TRUTH TRUST
3 Murrayfield Road, Edinburgh EH12 6EL
P.O. Box 621, Carlisle, Pennsylvania 17013, U.S.A.

★

First Edition, Wm. B. Eerdmans Publishing Co. 1954
Reprinted 1955
Second Edition, Westminster Theological Seminary
1978
Third Edition, Banner of Truth Trust 1987

★

ISBN 0 85151 501 0
Library of Congress Number 54-6236

★

Printed by PARK PRESS
South Holland, Illinois U.S.A. 60473
1987

To
MARILYN
ELSIE
and
BERNARD

GREATHEART. But here was great odds, three against one.

'Tis true," replied Valiant-for-truth; "but little or more are nothing to him that has the truth on his side..."

Then said Great-heart to Mr. Valiant-for-truth, "Thou has worthily behaved thyself; let me see thy sword." So he showed it to him.

When he had taken it in his hand, and looked thereon a while, he said, "Ha, it is a right Jerusalem blade."

VALIANT. It is so. Let a man have one of these blades, with a hand to wield it, and skill to use it, and he may venture upon an angel with it. He need not fear its holding, if he can but tell how to lay on. Its edge will never blunt. It will cut flesh and bones, and soul and spirit, and all. Heb. 4:12.

GREATHEART. But you fought a great while; I wonder you was not weary.

VALIANT. I fought till my sword did cleave to my hand; and then they were joined together as if a sword grew out of my arm; and when the blood ran through my fingers, then I fought with most courage.

GREATHEART. Thou hast done well; thou hast resisted unto blood, striving against sin. Thou shalt abide by us, and go out with us; for we are thy companions.

Then they took him and washed his wounds, and gave him of what they had, to refresh him; and so they went away together.

-*Pilgrim's Progress*

Preface to the First Edition

Although seventeen years have gone by since the passing of J. Gresham Machen, the luster of his life has not dimmed for those who knew him well. He remains Mr. Valiant-for-Truth *par excellence,* still vibrant in their memories, though he has long since gone up over the Delectable Mountains and across the river into the city of God. But memories falter and generations pass on, and it is well that a record should be made where reminiscences, gathered up and joined with other knowledge, may be stored so as to inform and quicken the faith and life of those to whom he may be little more than a name.

Machen's place within the history of our times, and especially of the twenties and thirties, has been so conspicuous that his life will continue to be of interest so long as men reflect upon the religious and ecclesiastical developments of the first half of the twentieth century. Even writers whose viewpoints were antithetical to his own—including the caustic sceptic H. L. Mencken, the idealistic but agnostic Pearl Buck and the penetrating Unitarian Albert C. Dieffenbach—acknowledged that he towered above his contemporaries in strength of character and fidelity to principle. There were also those who could mark the deeper channel of his life such as Caspar Wistar Hodge, his colleague and friend at Princeton, who characterized him at the time of his death as "the greatest theologian in the English-speaking world" and "the greatest leader of the whole cause of evangelical Christianity." Machen will continue to attract attention, however, not only because of his place in the history of recent decades. For by his deeds and words he set in motion spiritual forces which have not spent their strength. And if, as one observer who is to speak forth in these pages said, he was "a saint of God who loves truth, seeks truth, finds truth, and upholds truth against all adversaries, however mighty," his witness cannot perish. As a testimony to the truth it may still serve to arouse the consciences of men of this day and may break forth with fresh intensity and power in the future.

Though he was one of the most publicized men of his day, he got, on the whole, an astonishingly poor press. His doctrinal position, for example, was often designated as that of "extreme fundamentalism," when as a matter of fact he was not precisely described as a fundamentalist at all. Frequently pilloried as bitter and bigoted, he was in truth a man of profound humility and of rare sympathy and fair-mindedness. The concern to disclose what manner of man Machen really was has been one of the factors affecting the disposition of this biography.

Selectivity has been demanded for another reason. Though some details had to be searched out with a microscope, in the main the biographer has suffered from an embarrassment of riches so far as sources are concerned. The books, articles, reviews, sermons, addresses, newspaper and magazine stories, for the most part well known or readily accessible, give all the information that a student of his life might fairly ask for. But there were also his letters, copies of letters and miscellaneous papers and memoranda, thousands upon thousands of them, cramming some thirty drawers of his filing cabinets. And among the letters, there was as precious and memorable a collection as a biographer could ever hope to peruse, those exchanged between Machen and his mother over a period of nearly thirty years. During the earliest stages of this undertaking, a decade or so ago, a somewhat different scope was in view. But when Machen's letters to his mother were found in Baltimore a few years ago, to be integrated with her letters to him found in his files, the story could not be other than a personal one, although of course the public aspects of his career could not be neglected.

The maturing of Machen's thought and the development of his scholarly labors are extensively illumined in these pages, but an exhaustive evaluation of his significance as a theologian has not been undertaken. Nor has it proved practicable to dwell at length upon the history of the institutions with which Machen's name was prominently associated. Their backgrounds and beginnings, the principles involved and the motive forces which were operative are reflected upon, but the developments of the final years, which are otherwise most fully documented, are presented here only in summary fashion. Hardly any aspect of his life fails to find at least brief mention, but countless details which in the telling would have required another volume or two have been passed over. In sharpest contrast is the fulness with which his years abroad in 1905-06 and 1918-19 are treated, the periods when, lacking the opportunity of face to face conversations with family and friends, he most completely reveals his mind and heart.

Regrettably I could not bring to this undertaking the skill of a professional man of letters, but every other advantage has been mine, including the sympathetic understanding possible only in a friend and associate. To mark the point where personal observations began, it may be noted that it was in the fall of 1924 that I first entered his classes in Princeton. A growing admiration of his life and labors and the beginnings of personal friendship were to characterize the student years that followed. Our relationships were to become far more intimate, however, in the year 1929 as association in the same department of the Seminary and the larger aspects of academic and ecclesiastical life was entered upon. Those seven and one-half years were far too few from my point of view but, crowded as they were with delightful and satisfying contacts, my cup of thanksgiving continues to overflow at the remembrance of them.

A very special expression of gratitude is due the Machen family—especially Dr. Machen's brother, the late Arthur W. Machen, and Mrs. Machen, but also their children, Miss Mary Gresham Machen and Mr. Arthur W. Machen, Jr. Not only was I given complete freedom in the use of letters, papers and the scrapbooks prepared by his mother's loving hands, but my every inquiry was patiently and helpfully answered. Though the labor involved has been exacting, and its completion seemingly long delayed, their confidence and encouragement have been most refreshing. Gratifying also has been their response to *God Transcendent* and *What is Christianity?*, offered as earnests of the larger undertaking.

It is my pleasure to express here also my deep appreciation of the encouragement of many others, including the trustees, faculty, alumni and friends of the Seminary. The generosity of the trustees and of my colleagues in support of and adjustment to a term's leave of absence, granted to expedite the completion of the biography, must be singled out for particular thanks. In this as in all other matters I am also deeply grateful for the unfailingly heartening support of my wife.

A few notes, the minimum that seemed required, appear at the close. They are mostly bibliographical, but there is also a necessary one on the correct pronunciation of J. Gresham Machen. The notes also offer the opportunity of making particular acknowledgment of the courtesy of a number of publishers in permitting quotation of certain copyrighted materials.

Preface to the Second Edition

The present edition is revised only to the extent of a few minor changes in details and the elimination of typographical blemishes. It is a privilege also to add here an expression of cordial appreciation of the generous reception given the book since it first appeared a few months ago and of the publisher's anticipation of continued interest.

N.B.S.

CONTENTS

ILLUSTRATIONS

J. Gresham Machen

1

MACHENS AND GRESHAMS

John Gresham Machen was born in Baltimore on July 28, 1881, the second of three sons in the family established on February 13, 1873, when Arthur Webster Machen was united in marriage with Mary Jones Gresham in Macon, Georgia, the home of the bride. At the time of the marriage Mr. Machen was forty-five years of age, having been born on July 20, 1827, while Miss Gresham, whose natal day fell on June 17, 1849, was in her twenty-fourth year.

At the birth of Gresham, as he was called in the family, his father accordingly had just entered upon his fifty-fifth year, and there may have been those who predicted that the paternal influence would likely prove negligible. In any case, the providential ordering of events accomplished a quite different result. For Arthur W. Machen lived until December 19, 1915, and the interval of more than thirty-four years following Gresham's birth was for him a period of extraordinary physical and mental vigor. He rejoiced to see the day when his son, after a period of agonizing heart-searching and disquiet, had come to find sure ground under his feet and had embarked upon his career as an ordained minister of the gospel and a duly installed professor in Princeton Theological Seminary.

Although the influence of the father upon his son was remarkable, that of the mother naturally enough excelled. She survived her husband by nearly sixteen years. When she passed away on October 13, 1931, Dr. Machen was fifty years of age and had attained a position of world-wide influence and fame. Her son was to survive her by only a little more than five years, and thus she remained in intimate contact with him throughout nearly his entire life. Physical well-being of an enduring kind was never her good fortune in her adult life, but there was a compensation of extraordinary mental and spiritual force to the end of her life span of eighty-two years. And it was her rare intellectual alertness and accomplishments, reinforced by a profound and childlike Christian faith, which made those fifty years of motherly devotion and comradeship an extraordinary feature of his life. The fact that Gresham Machen never married was evidently a contributing factor in these relationships, for though he enjoyed the companionship of women, and was plainly not a bachelor of set purpose, as matters turned out his mother was the one woman who decisively influenced his life. No one ever seriously rivalled her in her capacity to satisfy his need of deep spiritual sympathy or in her hold upon his affection and admiration.

These considerations suggest the propriety of treating our subject's ancestry at some length in this opening chapter. Quite apart from one's knowledge of his forebears Machen's life would be fascinating, and in view of its dynamic—one might almost say meteoric—character, he might be classed with those who have "no need of ancestors." To neglect his ancestral background would, however, result in a grave impoverishment of our knowledge of his life. Machen was the child and heir of parents whose religious, cultural and social outlook conditioned his life and thought to a considerable degree. His life was so deeply rooted in ancestral soil and so intimately intertwined with the mature stock from which it sprang that inquiry into his family background serves to illumine many aspects of his life and career. Memorial volumes prepared by loving hands bring to light many heroic figures on both sides of the family, but attention will be focussed here chiefly upon his father and mother.

THE MACHENS

Arthur Webster Machen was the son of Lewis Henry Machen and Caroline Webster Machen, who were married in the City of Washington in the year 1816. Miss Webster was a native of New Hampshire who had been residing with her father in Washington for a number of years. The Machens, however, were Virginians of English ancestry, and the influences of the South were to be dominant in the history of the family. Although Lewis Machen was born in Maryland, and spent brief periods, including the last year of his life, in that state, and although he lived in Washington for more than thirty years, ties of ancestry and affection bound him to Virginia. He maintained his residence there for nearly twenty years towards the end of his life.

When his father Thomas Machen, who had been born in Virginia in 1750, died in 1809, young Lewis, then only nineteen years old, was compelled to undertake the support of his widowed mother and three sisters. He soon found employment as a clerk in the office of the Secretary of the United States Senate, a connection he was to maintain for nearly fifty years. To one with his mental vigor and capacity this position was never completely satisfying. He undertook it, as he said, only because he was prompted by a "strong moral necessity . . . for the benefit of those who had a claim to my protection and exertions." This sense of duty marked the man in all of his life, and indeed was one of the distinguishing qualities of his son Arthur and his grandson Gresham.

Though the position in the Senate office did not afford the most congenial employment, there were solid compensations for one who was a spirited patriot. After a few years he received a spectacular opportunity to prove his patriotism, for he was responsible for preserving the archives and secret documents of the Senate in the year 1814. They would have fallen into the hands of the British or have been consumed in the fire which destroyed the Capitol had not Lewis Machen, acting with foresight, energy and courage in the panic which had developed at the approach of the British, arranged for and overseen their removal into the country. The fifty years of his activity in the office of the Senate brought him into intimate contact with many of the great men of the day, and, for one as intellectually and morally alert as he was, it was inevitable that he should be actively interested in public affairs. He was a Whig rather than a Democrat, and in 1828 wrote a series of vigorous articles in opposition to the election of Andrew Jackson.

The articles, which were published in the *National Intelligencer*, appeared under an assumed name no doubt due to the precarious nature of his own position, but his authorship was generally recognized. When his superior in the Senate office indicated his decided disapproval of this political activity, Lewis Machen defended his rights as a citizen with characteristic eloquence and courage.

> Upon entering the public office, I engaged to perform, to the best of my ability, a known and prescribed duty; to conform to the instructions of the head of the office relating to that duty; and to receive as an equivalent for the services thus rendered, not as a consideration for rights abandoned, the compensation which might be allowed by law. But I never did engage to become an automaton or a machine; to look on unmoved, or without effort, when I should see the republic institution of my country in danger, or to surrender a single right of an American citizen.
>
> In the office and during the hours devoted to its duties, I acknowledge and obey an official superior. When my official duty has closed, I stand on an equal footing with any man that breathes. In the hours of relaxation from the toil and drudgery of office, my thoughts shall wander as discursive as the air; my opinions, uncontrolled by human authority, shall be embodied in any form my judgment shall approve; and while others are extinguishing life in dissipation, or permitting their faculties to grow torpid from disuse, it shall be my endeavor to treasure up these precious

fragments of existence, and devote them to objects which I may deem beneficial to my family or society, and pleasing to that Being who has the time of all at his command.

It would be a mistake to suppose, however, that Lewis Machen was an extremist. That there was nothing provincial about his outlook is indicated, for example, by his advocacy of the Whig party, and in particular by his enthusiasm for the views of Daniel Webster. While not an abolitionist, he did regard slavery as an evil which would disappear from natural causes more happily than from sudden emancipation. Although concerned to preserve the rights of the States, his loyalty to the union was such that he regarded those who about 1850 "seriously concocted and traitorously planned the dissolution of this Confederacy" as worthy of being visited with "the severest moral retribution."

Not all "the hours of relaxation" were taken up with political interests. He was intensely devoted to his growing family. After residing for a few years in a rented dwelling, he had erected a commodious home on Maryland Avenue, in Washington, where the family lived from 1822 to 1843. Arthur W. Machen was born in this home in 1827, one of seven children of whom only three survived infancy or childhood, the others being a sister Emmeline, born in 1817, and a brother James, born in 1831.

The home was a place of culture of a very exceptional kind. Although Lewis Machen was denied the advantage of a college education, interest in learning welled up within him so spontaneously that he gained a far wider culture than is common today among those who are under compulsions of one sort or another to acquire an education or an education of a sort. His love of literature extended beyond the English classics to works in Latin, French and Spanish which he read with ease. He inculcated a love of these good things in his children, not only by specific instruction but also by the acquisition of a remarkable library. The library contained not only his own favorite writings, but he also acquired others such as the Greek classics that his sons might be tempted to read them. The library grew as he added items, to the extent that modest income allowed, from the sale of the private library of Thomas Jefferson and of the famous Kloss collection. Collectors' items, including examples of the famous presses of the early centuries of printing, found a place in the library, as did also books chosen for their fine bindings and artistic illustrations. In this home therefore, under parental tutelage and example, a passionate love of books and a deep but unaffected love of learning and beauty were part of the atmosphere breathed by the children. Arthur Machen was to inherit many of these books, and they formed the foundation for the establishment of his own distinguished library. Of more importance still he acquired a taste for these fine things in his early years that was to develop in later life into solid and mature appreciation and knowledge.

Still another quality (besides patriotic ardor and intellectual appetite) distinguished that Washington home, a quality that was to prove an even more basic influence for the future. The home in which Arthur Machen was reared was characterized by a robust piety. His mother was also remembered for the purity and strength of her religious faith, but the father fulfilled his task as head of the family in matters religious in his characteristically virile way. It was a family where the Bible was honored and read as the Word of God; where family prayers were part of the routine without being merely routine exercises; where membership in and attendance upon the services of the Christian church were regarded as sacred obligations and genuine privileges.

The faith of Lewis Machen had not come without consideration of the appeal made by rationalism and infidelity. When it came, however, it found expression in a childlike faith in Christ as the crucified Redeemer; it likewise embraced the comprehensive unity of Biblical truth. Although he was brought up as an Episcopalian, he joined the Presbyterian Church in early manhood out of deliberate preference, soon became an elder, and to the end of his life was an ardent believer in Presbyterian doctrine. At the time of the division of the Presbyterian Church into the Old School and New School in 1837, he was an elder in the Fourth Presbyterian Church of Washington. In the course of developments, the other members of the session and a large majority of the congregation cast in their lot with the New School, but Lewis Machen sent a brief letter to the session in which he demanded his dismissal to a congregation maintaining without dilution the Calvinistic doctrine of the Westminster Confession. A longer formulation of his point of view, although not actually sent, is especially illuminating as to the clarity and vigor of his Christian faith. It included the following:

> The manifestation of opinion, in the recent election of the Pastor of the Church, leaves me no room to doubt the prevailing sentiment. By the choice which they made they distinctly ratified the acts of the Session, and gave their adhesion to the New School Assembly. To remain longer in their communion would neither conduce to the benefit of the Church, nor to my own spiritual improvement. If I attempted, while remaining, to check by reason, persuasion, or remonstrance, the force of the prevailing error or misapprehension, I should be regarded only as a refractory member, daring to resist the will of a majority and to think for

himself. If I remained a silent and passive spectator, this apparent acquiescence would make me a participator in their acts, or, at least, render me a very equivocal supporter of the cause which my conscience approved.

I have therefore been compelled, by a sense of what is due to others as well as to myself, to retire from your communion.

It cannot be disguised that the Presbyterian Church is rent into two parties, differing essentially from each other on fundamental points; the one maintaining the Calvinistic doctrines of the Confession of Faith according to their obvious meaning; the other, either denying them altogether, or so explaining them as to make them in effect Arminian or Pelagian. Twenty years ago I assented to the Doctrines of the Confession of Faith, not without hestitation, but after the best examination in my power, and with a conviction of their conformity with the divine will, revealed in Scripture. Subsequent reflection and experience have furnished no cause for recantation. I shall adhere, then, to the standards of the Church, and to that division of its members which shall most unequivocally, and consistently, maintain them.

In pursuing this course, I am actuated by no unfriendly spirit, and I have felt the difficulties which surround the points in controversy. To reconcile the foreknowledge of God, and his absolute control over all events, with that free agency of man which makes him accountable for the moral conduct upon which these events apparently depend, is not the work of human reason. The brightest intellect has never yet penetrated the mysterious cloud which envelopes this subject. Taught by experience the fallibility of my judgment, I bow with submission to that Divine Word which represents God as the moral governor of the world and the absolute disposer of events; operating by his spirit upon the hearts of men; and, according to the councils of his own will, making some of the fallen posterity of Adam vessels of wrath, and others vessels of mercy. I do not impugn the sincerity, the purity of motive, or the ability, of those engaged in the propagation of opinions which many, equally sincere and pure and able, have deemed erroneous or pernicious. But forced by circumstances to take a position on one side or the other, I prefer submitting to any inconvenience, and sharing any obloquy, to a negative support, or actual abandonment of the cause of truth and vital Christianity. In adopting an alternative which at best is painful, I can only pray the Great Head of the Church so to influence the hearts and guide the determination of his professing followers as to banish all discord, error, and self-delusion, and hasten his reign of universal righteousness and peace.

I remain,

Your affectionate brother in Christ,

L. H. Machen,

Late Elder in the 4th Presb. Church.

ARTHUR WEBSTER MACHEN

At the time that this letter was written, young Arthur was twelve years old, and thus at an age when his father's Christian faith, not to speak of other qualities, would long before have begun to make a deep impression upon him. His early education was received in private schools, the last being Abbot's Select Classical Seminary, a school conducted by a Mr. Abbot, a New Englander, from which he was graduated in 1842. Such records as have been preserved from those days indicate that, in addition to English and Algebra, the curriculum was largely made up of French and Greek and Latin, in all of which he did excellent work. It also appears that he had developed a talent as a story-teller, an accomplishment which won him first prize in class competition, and was afterward to provide some helpful income as well as diversion.

Following graduation he entered Columbian College (the forerunner of George Washington University) and studied there for at least one year. But the plan to continue there so as to prepare for Harvard was not realized, for in 1843 Arthur Machen interrupted his academic career because of rather delicate health, and was not to resume it until 1849. The interruption coincided with the removal of the family from the Washington residence to a farm of some 725 acres near Centreville in Fairfax County, Virginia, about twenty-five miles from Washington. One of the reasons for the purchase of the farm, named "Walney," was the father's purpose to improve the health of the family. Since Lewis Machen was detained by duties in Washington during a considerable part of the year, the management of the farm fell largely upon the shoulders of Arthur and his younger brother James. There was more than supervision, however, for the boys engaged in the actual labor too, with solid rewards accruing in the form of greatly improved health. But for Arthur Machen the farm did not bring an end to intellectual pursuits. The winter season brought some opportunity for concentration upon classical and other studies, but even in going to market with cattle he had available in his pocket some intellectual pabulum. This habit of carrying books in his pockets was one that carried over into the next generation, for Gresham Machen never went anywhere, it seemed, without having immediately at hand a large supply of reading matter, and even specified that his top coats should be tailored with spacious additional inside pockets for this purpose.

At long last, in 1849, in his 22nd year, Arthur Machen's plan to enter Harvard was realized, but not without some modification of the original program. For now he decided to dispense with the arts degree which had been in view and to enter the Harvard Law School at once. The two-year course, leading to the bachelor of laws degree, however, whetted his appetite for more academic training, and he remained for a year of graduate study. That his academic attainments at Harvard were of an exceptional kind is shown by the consideration that he enjoyed the respect and confidence of his professors to an unusual degree. Professor Parsons, engaged in the preparation of a book on Contracts, sought and secured his aid, not only in the preparation of notes for the volume but also in the contribution of a chapter on slavery. His academic success may also be measured somewhat from the fact that his thesis won the prize in the class competition for the year 1851.

Though he remained for a year of graduate study, the reader should not conclude that this was made possible by the affluence of his father. The fact is that Lewis H. Machen could ill afford to contribute financially to the support of the son. Arthur Machen was, however, so independent and energetic that he largely earned his own way. The occasional assistance of Professor Parsons provided some pecuniary returns. But a more substantial and steady income resulted from his work as librarian of the Law School. And he came to depend to a considerable extent upon fees and prizes obtained from the acceptance for publication of stories, articles and reviews by a number of contemporary magazines. These include a novel published serially in the *American Review* for 1850. Arthur W. Machen, Jr., elder brother of Gresham, collected and was responsible for the private publication in 1917 of two substantial volumes of these materials and a number of previously unpublished items. He observed that all of this writing was done when his father was not more than 24 years old, and thus before he was graduated. This fact coupled with the further observation that the stories were published anonymously or under a *nom de plume* stresses the pains which were taken to draw a sharp line between his activity as a writer of fiction and as a lawyer. The stories themselves display ample evidence of the author's imagination and literary power, but the language and style at the present time would be considered more suitable to the essay than fiction.

Evidently the strenuous years at Cambridge had taken their toll, and the youthful graduate was not prepared at once to launch upon a career as a lawyer. For a year he worked at "Walney" to overcome ocular and dyspeptic disorders, and there was remarkable improvement in both respects. In fact, he never did have to wear glasses and he enjoyed robust health practically to the very last.

CAREER AND CHARACTER

He thus prepared to begin his legal career in the year 1853. The choice of Baltimore as the future center of his life and labors is of special interest. An opportunity of settling in New York City was appealing from the point of view of material success, and New York had been strongly recommended to his father in preference to Baltimore by Wm. H. Seward. But Arthur's preference for the South, for Southern climate and Southern people, and above all his desire to be near his family outweighed any such enticement. His brother James, on the other hand, and other Southerners advised Richmond. But Baltimore won out as preserving both the Southern advantages and the challenge of a rather large city.

Admitted to the bar of the Superior Court on June 13, 1853, Arthur Machen opened an office in association with Richard J. Gittings, an intimate friend and classmate at Harvard. The early years of practice were so unremunerative that, in order to meet his bare living expenses, he depended for a time upon assistance from his father in the amount of fifty dollars per month. After nearly three years characterized more by inactivity than legal work, he was still so poor that he wrote his father that "if that remnant of Job's poultry yard which is immortalized in the proverb were poorer than I am, I am sure the most rapacious Chaldean would never have offered to lay violent hands upon it." His clothing was so threadbare and worn that it did not permit him to seek the company of the other sex. But these discouragements did not prevent him from studying assiducusly, and sometimes he and his friends tried moot cases to keep in trim in lieu of the trial of actual cases. About 1856, however, his prospects brightened, and during the years that followed there appears to have been a rapid acceleration of success. The tide turned as he and his associate gained a reputation for conscientious and thorough devotion to the interests of their clients and skill in the conduct of their profession.

Baltimore in those days was a city of violent conflicts affecting political and civil life, days which Hamilton Owens speaks of as "the turbulent fifties" when Irish and German groups stood arrayed against each other, Know-Nothingism flourished, and riots of the Plug Ugly and other gangs were common. In the trial of two members of one of these gangs for the murder of a policeman who had testified against another member, Mr. Machen was actively associated in the prosecution with Mr. Gittings who had become State's Attorney for Baltimore County, though he himself rarely, if ever, undertook any criminal cases. His success in this case helped enhance his reputation. That same year when a vacancy occurred Machen was offered a judgeship in the Superior Court of Baltimore by the Governor of the State. Though he recognized the Court as the most considerable one in Maryland below the Court of Appeals, and the honor was unusual for one so inexperienced and still only thirty-two years old, he felt constrained to decline because of his devotion to service at the bar. Even the newspaper representing the opposite party, though criticizing the appointment because he was so young, inexperienced and comparatively unknown, characterized him as a gentleman of unimpeachable character, good capacity and untiring industry. Neither then nor later did he take the interest in political affairs and public life that his father desired.

But there was another matter concerning which his parents were even less happy at this time, namely that of his spiritual state. Disquietude had arisen already while he was in Law School. Though a regular and interested attendant upon worship services, he had not become a member of the church by profession of faith. Writing to his father in 1850, in answer to his solicitous inquiries, Arthur Machen admitted that he experienced sadness at not qualifying for full communion about the Lord's Table with Christians with whom in a previous hour he had attempted to unite in the worship of a common God. Explaining his hesitation, he asked, "What is more awfully perilous than to intrude into the wedding feasts without the wedding garment?" Apparently his was not basically an intellectual doubt concerning the truth of Christianity, for he acknowledged that he was ready to receive revealed truth. But he continued to ask whether he believed in that sense which is required by the Searcher of hearts. This was in 1850.

But now several years had gone by and he continued to remain outside of the full communion, though a pew holder and a regular attendant upon the services of the Central Presbyterian Church and an admirer of the preaching of the pastor, the Rev. Stuart Robinson. Moreover, especially on Sundays, he devoted considerable time to the reading of the Scriptures and other edifying literature, such as the works of Jeremy Taylor, Thomas Fuller, Southey's *Life of Wesley* and Philip's *Memoir of Whitefield.* On one occasion, however, in what seems hardly to have been his characteristic mood even in his early years—this was in 1857—, he spoke of his sympathy with the German spirit of free inquiry: "the release, namely, of our minds from the letters of theological forms and formulae, the inventions of a day far from the brightest in ecclesiastical history, and the consequent free access to the very Scriptures as the sole guide of our lives, and a foundation of truth needing no abutments and props of human device or building." The subject of Arthur Machen's attitude toward Christianity will be referred to again, but it may be noted at once that, in spite of the constancy of his personal commitment, he remained undecided regarding ecclesiastical affiliation until the time of his marriage in 1873 when he finally became a member in full communion of the Church. Previously, during the early part of the War, he had been a pewholder in the Christ Protestant Episcopal Church, and, when his mother and sister became members there in 1863, in the Franklin Street Presbyterian Church. It was the latter body that he joined in 1873 and with which he was to be prominently associated for the rest of his life.

The Civil War was a severe blow to the fortunes of Southerners of that day, and it fell in a peculiarly poignant fashion upon the residents of border states like Maryland. Maryland was occupied territory during the war though the sympathies of the people, at least of those of greatest influence, were largely with the South. The Machens were not extreme secessionists. Lewis H. Machen and his sons, indeed as late as 1860, were alarmed at what James Machen called "the insane disunion spirit that is so rife in a portion of the South." Arthur Machen was even appointed United States District Attorney for the District of Maryland in 1861. At first he was inclined to accept, animated as he was, as his son Arthur reported,

> by love for the Union, actuated by an innate conservatism, and believing that the election of Lincoln furnished no excuse whatever for secession. . . But when Lincoln called for troops, and made evident at least to my father's mind—for many in Maryland, including the Governor, still believed, or affected to believe, that the troops were wanted merely for defense of the national capital—that the Administration was bent upon coercion and civil war, my father reconsidered his acceptance, and declined an office which might have required him to prosecute those who adhered openly to the Southern cause.

While his brother James became a confederate soldier, Arthur made the most of the situation in Baltimore and was thankful that he escaped the draft. His contacts with men of influence were such, however, as to permit him a measure of contact with his father, mother and sister in

Virginia, and in November, 1862, he was able to secure their removal to Baltimore. Special gratification followed from the fact that along with certain household effects they were able to save the library which Lewis H. Machen had acquired. The father was by now in ill health and lived only until August 11, 1863.

Following the war the legal practice of Machen and Gittings grew rapidly and they soon acquired a measure of prosperity. Arthur Machen was to become one of the most distinguished and successful members of the Baltimore Bar. Only one or two lawyers conducted more cases than he, and his were among the most celebrated of the day. When he died in 1915, after having been an active lawyer for more than 62 years, his colleagues paid tribute to his excellencies in glowing terms. Among the tributes expressed at a memorial service of the Bar was one by D. K. Este Fisher, which included the following evaluation:

> His acumen and thoroughness were remarkable, and any adversary, no matter how high his standing at the Bar, had reason to be apprehensive when Mr. Machen was on the other side, for if anything was overlooked, he would be sure to be aware of it, and, if proper, take advantage of it. . . Thoroughness was one of his marked characteristics and this, with the natural keenness and power of his mind, had much to do with the height to which he attained in his profession, and made him ever ready to handle any kind of legal proposition or situation, and apparently gave him great confidence in legitimate litigation.
>
> Mr. Machen was a student not alone of law; and the terms in which he expressed himself attested his familiarity with general literature and the cultivation of his mind. I remember especially one occasion in this Court on which he made a short address which was a luminous model of perfect expression of thought and feeling, such as is attained only by the reading of classical literature. And his style of speaking always, as I remember it, bore the evidences of general cultivation.

And the response of Judge Soper to this and other tributes included the following impressive acknowledgement:

> His learning, his exhaustive presentation of legal doctrine in its application to particular facts, and his masterful unfolding of the merits of his cases gave him an influence and sway with the Courts, which was so great that at times the Courts seemed to desert precedent in order to follow whither the genius of Mr. Machen led.

Such a legal career, as has been noted, brought its material rewards, and it was not long after the Civil War when Arthur Machen was able to leave behind him for good the austerity of the early beginnings. Opportunities for vacations and travel at first denied because of sheer poverty now opened up. He took his first trip to Europe in 1867 and a second in 1869.

But it was the journey of another to Europe that was to spell one of the most significant and happy developments of his life. For it was in 1870 that the young lady who was to be his future wife met him in Baltimore where she was stopping over briefly at the home of her aunt, Mrs. Edgeworth Bird, before sailing for Europe. Other contacts followed and Arthur Machen and Mary Gresham became engaged in 1872 and married the following year.

THE GRESHAMS

Before continuing the narrative of developments following the marriage, we turn back to review the Gresham lineage. Gresham Machen's mother was the daughter of John Jones Gresham and Mary Baxter Gresham who, like the Machens, were descended from families of English origin which had settled in the South. The grandfather after whom he was named was the descendant of a line of Greshams which settled in Virginia about the middle of the 18th Century, and was born on a farm in Burke County, Georgia, on Jan. 21, 1818. After his academic studies were completed in 1833 at the University of Georgia (then known as Franklin College), he studied law and was admitted to the bar in November, 1834. He began the practice of law in Waynesboro but moved to Macon in February, 1836, where he carried on his profession, though not without interruption, for many years. In May, 1843, he was married to Mary E. Baxter of Athens, Georgia, whose younger sister Sarah (who had become Mrs. Edgeworth Bird) will appear prominently in the following pages. A son Thomas Gresham became a confederate soldier and after the war was associated with his father for many years before moving to Baltimore in the late eighties. Except for a son LeRoy who died in young manhood, the only other child to survive infancy was Mary who was born on June 17, 1849.

Edwin Mims, a biographer of Sidney Lanier who was born in Macon in 1842, describes the Macon of that time as "the capital of Middle Georgia, the centre of trade for sixty miles around." He proceeds:

> There was among the citizens an aggressive public spirit, which made it a rival in commercial life of the older cities, Savannah and Augusta; before the war it was a more important place than At-

> lanta. It was one of the first towns to push the building of railroads. The richer planters and merchants lived on the hills above the city—in their costly mansions with luxuriant flower gardens—while the professional men and middle classes lived in the lower part of the city . . . Social lines were not, however, so sharply drawn here as in cities like Richmond or Charleston. Middle Georgia was perhaps the most democratic section of the South. It was a democracy, it is true, working within the limitations of slavery and greatly tempered with the feudal ideas of the older States, but it was a life which gave room for the development of well-marked types.

In this community Mr. Gresham became one of the most affluent and influential citizens. He was successful in a cotton mill which he organized, apparently giving as much attention to it as to the law, was a director of two railroads, and had other commercial interests. But wealth was not to him an end in itself. As his daughter once said, "money was with him a means for gratifying the innocent desires of his loved ones, and for the achievement of noble and beneficial purposes." In contrast to his son-in-law he took an active part in public affairs. He held public office at various times; was mayor of Macon twice, judge of various courts, and member of the state legislature. He was intensely interested in public education as a leading member of the Board of Education in Macon and as president of the trustees of the University of Georgia for many years. He also was trustee and treasurer of Oglethorpe University, a Presbyterian college, and a member of the Board of Columbia Theological Seminary, where he endowed the LeRoy Gresham chair in memory of his deceased son. His interest in the Presbyterian Church naturally also came to expression in Macon where he was a ruling elder from 1847 until his death, a period of forty-four years, for forty-one of which he served as clerk of session.

He died on Oct. 16, 1891 while on a visit at the home of his daughter in Baltimore, about two years after the decease of his wife, and was buried in Macon. When the news of his sudden passing reached Macon, the *Telegraph* stated on Oct. 18:

> No man ever lived in this community, who has for so long a period enjoyed the full confidence and esteem of his fellow-citizens. His faithfulness to every trust confided to him, his generous support of all the enterprises of the city, his gratuitous services rendered in the various educational institutions of the county and State, fully entitle him to the loving remembrance and gratitude of the people of Macon, and the whole state of Georgia.

And on Oct. 20th, the day of the funeral, the same newspaper, mourning the passing of the South's golden age, said:

> He was a splendid type of that noble and chivalrous Southern manhood that has passed into history. He stood as much apart from the ordinary concerns of men of to-day as if he had been born and reared in another clime. His sympathies, white-winged and clean, never touched the sordid and the low, but went always with unerring aim to the pure and true. Born to be noble, trained in the culture of an old Southern home, as fixed as the stars in an old-fashioned and incorruptible integrity, he lived in the majesty, almost ideal now, of the grand old Southern gentleman who honored God and feared only to wrong his fellow-men. It is not surprising that there should be such a universal expression of regret at his death.

And on the following day it reported the concluding part of the message of the pastor, Mr. Jennings, as follows:

> Verily, beloved, "a prince and a great man is fallen in Israel this day." This is our deliberate estimate of his character. God's great ones of old were not faultless. Nor was he whom we bury to-day. Himself would have been the first to blush at the intimation of such a thing. But, like many of the princes of ancient Israel, his faults sprang from this very strength of his character, the intensity of his convictions, the deep abhorrence of all that was unworthy of man as made in the divine image. But with his faults, he was great, great in his sympathies, great in his purposes, great in his deeds, great in his gifts, great in his character; his was the greatness of goodness, the greatness of a life that received its inspiration and aim and strength from the indwelling Spirit of Christ.

Other estimates of his character which date from this time are worthy of mention here, not only because they serve to high-light the stock from which Gresham Machen sprang, but also because, as those who knew him well can testify, they so accurately, in almost every detail, depict the personality of the grandson. The Memorial Minute of the Board of Education, for example, dwells upon the strength of his character as follows:

> He was emphatically a strong man; strong physically and intellectually,—strong in his convictions upon all subjects, whether political, social, economic, legal, financial, or religious; strong in his prejudices; strong in his affections; strong in his attachment

> to persons and to places; strong in his adherence to any course of conduct which he may have mapped out for himself, even to the verge of obstinacy, but all those strong points of his very strong individuality, as well as his faults (for he had faults), were so toned down and controlled by his sense of right, and by his graces as a Christian, that he was known to his friends as a very tractable and attractive man.

His own daughter's estimate does not disagree substantially, though she naturally enough gave larger place to the gentler virtues. She spoke of "strength and gentleness" as being "beautifully blended in him," of his "extreme tenderness toward womankind," of his "brooding pity for the unfortunate." Defending her father's occasional impatience, she declared:

> From the very virtues of my dear father's character, sprang what some have considered faults. The faults and foibles of a truly righteous man are but surface blemishes. To one who has gone behind the veil and looked into the holy sanctuary of that soul, there was no imperfection. The indignation, the strong vehement censure, was the indignation of the good against wrong-doing and the censure by the righteous of all that is false and crooked. The impatience (how often have I marked this!) was the impatience of one who grieved because he could not bring all men to perceive the truth, crystal-clear, as he saw it, or to regulate their lives by the inflexible line which marked out his own pathway.
>
> Above all, that which pervaded and controlled every trait of my father's character was his religion. "To do justly, to love mercy, and to walk humbly with his God"—that was his life, the outward expression of his simple and earnest faith.
>
> The keynote of his religion was his belief in the Sovereignty of God...
>
> His belief in Christ as the Saviour of mankind was simple and strong...
>
> His loftiest ambition was to leave the world better for his having lived...
>
> So his memory abides with us. Strong in his will, strong in his wisdom, strong in his hatred of wrong and defence of the right, yet stronger than all was his love,—the tender abiding love which hedged us in like a mighty bulwark, the love which trained and nourished all that was good in us and lopped away even the tenderest bud of wrong or falsehood, the love which relieved our necessities before we could ourselves formulate them, the love which made doubly his own our every joy and sorrow, the love

which foresaw and if possible averted every calamity from ourselves and our children. Who can understand so well as we this type of the Divine Love, "Like as a father pitieth his children."

So, ever fulfilling his high purpose, so, living in wholesome discharge of daily duty, the few earthly imperfections were thrown off with the beloved body, and his noble spirit passed into the congenial fellowship of Apostles and Prophets and Saints of all ages.

Thus ends the glowing tribute of his daughter, a tribute which illumines her character as well as that of her father. Of Mrs. Gresham not as much has been recorded, though she was remembered at the time of her husband's death as "beautiful, refined and cultivated." And her daughter recalls that he had said to his wife in her last moments, "You have been the making of me, you have refined me and polished me and rounded off the sharp corners," and adds that "this tribute he often repeated after her death with 'a rain of tender tears.' "

Of the early life of Mary Gresham, as of the life of her mother, not many details have been published. But we do know that she came universally to be known as Minnie rather than Mary, and virtually abandoned the use of the latter, though in old age she was pleased to recall it and to indicate her desire that the name Minnie should not be perpetuated in a granddaughter named for her. And our understanding of her culture is enhanced by the knowledge of the fact that she had exceptional educational opportunities, being graduated from Wesleyan College in Macon in the class of 1865.

She was fortunate in the friends of her youth and in that the opportunity of friendly association with two of them continued long after she left her Macon home. In Macon she numbered among her dear friends Gertrude Lanier, sister of the poet Sidney, the beloved "Sissa" of his letters. Mary Day, who married Sidney Lanier in 1867, was another good friend, and was to spend a few happy years in Baltimore, where her husband won fame as a musician, poet and interpreter of literature. Another friend of those early days, and a frequent visitor in the Machen home until her death in 1921, was Clare de Graffenreid. Recommended for a position by Mr. Gresham to his warm friend L. Q. C. Lamar, Secretary of the Interior in President Cleveland's first cabinet, she resided in Washington, D. C., for most of her life, winning distinction in government service. She endeared herself greatly to the Machen household, and was referred to frequently in the correspondence between Gresham Machen and his mother. A feature article entitled, "Three Notable Georgia Women—Mary Day, Minnie Gresham, Clare de Graffenreid," appeared in *The Atlanta Journal* after their death. Written by John T. Boufeuillet who had spent his early boyhood in Macon, it recalled them as "charming and accomplished young women who adorned the social and literary life of that city."

The writer paid special tribute to Minnie Gresham as his first Sunday School teacher, whose instruction "had a refreshing influence on my life, and maturing years affect the heart with livelier gratitude to her." Though these rather meagre details permit only a rather sketchy account of her life before she made Baltimore her home in 1873, enough is known to reflect the rich religious and cultural background of her later years in Batimore.

LIFE IN BALTIMORE

After a honeymoon trip to New Orleans Mr. and Mrs. Arthur W. Machen lived at 62 W. Madison St. where Mr. Machen had made a home for his mother and sister. There Arthur W. Machen Jr. was born in 1876 and Mrs. Lewis Machen died in 1878 in her ninetieth year. The following year a home at 97 W. Monument St. (later numbered 217) was acquired. There Mr. and Mrs. Machen lived happily thirty-six years until the year of his death, and there Mrs. Machen continued to reside for the nearly sixteen years that she survived her husband. There also John Gresham Machen was born in 1881 and his younger brother Thomas in 1886.

After the war the position of Baltimore at the cross-roads of Northern and Southern life, which had caused it to suffer so acutely during the war, turned out to its advantage. It enjoyed considerably greater prosperity than most of the cities below the Mason-Dixon line. And one consequence was that members of many Southern families, from Virginia and Georgia and other States, took up residence in Baltimore. The rapid growth of Baltimore from a population of 169,054 in 1850 and 212,418 in 1860 to 267,354 in 1870 and 332,213 in 1880 is indeed not accounted for in this way, for there were immigrations in great numbers from abroad and the influx of people from other parts of the country, not to overlook the considerable increase of negro population after the war. But Baltimore's dominantly Southern social and cultural life was preserved and perhaps even intensified.

The period following the war was marked by significant cultural developments in the life of Baltimore. Through the munificence of leading citizens a number of splendid institutions were founded. The first of these was the Peabody Institute with its unique library and its conservatory of music. The library was opened in 1867. It was in 1873, the year of the establishment of the Machen household in Baltimore, that the Peabody Orchestra was organized by Asger Hamerik, with Sidney Lanier, just come to Baltimore, as first flutist. In that same year Johns Hopkins died and the provisions of his will which left seven million dollars for the establishment of a university and a hospital became operative. The following year the trustees appointed by Hopkins selected Daniel Gilman as first president of the university, and set him loose to plan and organize. After two years of study and travel Gilman was ready in 1876 to launch the university which at once was recognized as introducing a new era in American university education. Though begun with only a handful of professors, few students and no buildings, it awakened widespread enthusiasm, first of all in Baltimore, but also in the country at large. Something of that original enthusiasm was captured by Lanier's *Ode* to the University, composed in 1880, which contained the following lines:

So quick she bloomed, she seemed to bloom at birth.
As Eve from Adam, or as he from earth.
Superb o'er slow, increase of day on day,
Complete as Pallas she began her way;
Yet not from Jove's unwrinkled forehead sprung,
But long-time dreamed, and out of trouble wrung,
Foreseen, wise-planned, pure child of thought and pain,
Leapt our Minerva from a mortal brain.
And here, finer Pallas, long remain,—
Sit on these Maryland hills and fix thy reign,
And frame a fairer Athens than of yore
In these blest bounds of Baltimore,—
Here where the climates meet
That each may make the other's lack complete,—

* * *

Bring old Renown
To walk familiar citizen of the town,—
Bring Tolerance, that can kiss and disagree,—
Bring Virtue, Honor, Truth, and Loyalty,—
Bring Faith that sees with undissembling eyes,—
Bring all large Loves and heavenly Charities,—
Till man seem less a riddle unto man
And fair Utopia less Utopian,
And many people call from shore to shore,
The world has bloomed again, at Baltimore!

Soon afterward Enoch Pratt gave a large sum for the establishment of a free library, and this institution was opened in 1886.

The Machens had no direct part in the inauguration of these institutional developments, but they numbered President Gilman, Professor Gildersleeve and several other leading professors among their intimate friends from those early days onward. Moreover, their intellectual gifts and interests made their home a center of culture and brought them into contact with the leading families of the city.

Their place in the social life of the city was no doubt assured by another factor—their connection with the Bird family. As mentioned above, when Minnie Gresham first came to Baltimore it was for a brief stay at the home of her aunt, Mrs. Edgeworth Bird. Mrs. Bird, whose husband, a confederate major, had died soon after the war, had come to Baltimore with her son Edgeworth and daughter Saida in 1869. In the work *Baltimore Its History and Its People,* in connection with the biographical sketch of her son who died about a month before her own passing in 1910, we are told that her home on East Mount Vernon Place "was for more than a generation the seat of an elegant and cultured hospitality, and among her guests have been many distinguished in literature and music." "Few women," the account states,

> have known intimately so many distinguished men of the South. In her youth she was acquainted with the Southern poets, Paul Hamilton Hayne and Henry Temrod, and during her residence in Baltimore James R. Randall and Sidney Lanier were familiar guests in her home. The Southern statesman, Robert Toombs, Alexander H. Stephens and General John C. Breckinridge; the diplomat, Dr. J. D. M. Curry; the well-known humorist, Col. Richard Malcolm Johnston; the scientist, Dr. Joseph LeConte, afterward of the University of California; that distinguished divine of the old school, the Rev. Benjamin Palmer, of New Orleans —these and many others were her intimate friends . . . In her death the society of Baltimore lost a charming presence, one who had been for more than forty years its brightest ornament, and to the South was lost one of the few remaining links in the chain which connects it with the illustrious past.

These references to "Aunty" Bird, as she was affectionately known in the family, are of interest as supplementing our knowledge of Mrs. Machen's family background. Moreover, Mrs. Machen herself remained on the most intimate terms with her aunt throughout the nearly forty years from 1873 to 1910 and shared the cultural interests and outlook that gave her aunt her brilliant place in Baltimore society.

CONTACTS WITH LANIER

The writings of Sidney Lanier provide extraordinarily interesting confirmation of the truth of the observation with regard to him mentioned above, and add certain vivid details to our knowledge of the early life in Baltimore of the Bird and Machen families. Mention has been made of Mrs. Machen's contacts with Gertrude Lanier and Mary Day in Macon, and one may add that Judge Gresham, in his capacity as trustee of Oglethorpe College sought to secure Lanier's continuance as an instructor both before and after the war. The letters of Lanier contain many references to Mrs. Bird and a few to Mrs. Machen beginning directly after his arrival in Baltimore and his first concert at which Mrs. Bird had been present. Mrs. Bird extended generous hospitality to him, cared for him in his illness and in general was, as Lanier wrote his wife on Dec. 21, 1873, "my constant and true friend." On one occasion, after several years of gracious and hospitable acts, Mrs. Bird sent a basket with some hothouse grapes, and the empty basket was returned with the following verse:

> Elijah (so in Holy Writ 'tis said)
> Was in the wilderness by ravens fed:
> But my lone wastes a fairer wing supplies
> I'm pampered by a Bird-of-Paradise.

In an early letter (dated Dec. 12, 1873) having just come from Mrs. Bird's home, he tells his wife that Mrs. Machen "abideth just across the street, and, I hear, hath expected me to call ere now. I had been waiting for her husband to call on me (for, now that I am *quasi* a professional musician, I am a little sensitive) but I learn he hath been out of town ever since I came. So, I will e'en gie her a call anyhow." There were many such calls after that, one of which (on Jan. 17, 1875) he describes to his wife as follows: "Yesterday came a note from Minnie Machen inviting me to a state dinner at 5 o'clock: to which I of course duly went. The company was pleasant, the wine was good, the feast gorgeous, and the merriment uproarious, but I went through all in a longing dream of thee."

The greatest contribution which Mrs. Bird made was, however, of a different sort. Lanier had turned from music to literature and was hopeful of securing some connection with the new university. His earliest contacts with Dr. Gilman were friendly but not fruitful, and on one occasion (on Oct. 10, 1876) he expressed to his father his sorrow that the latter had spoken to Mr. Gresham in Macon in the interest of securing the friendly intercession of his relatives in Baltimore. Such intercession would only hurt his chances, he felt, since the "poor Trustees have been badgered and button-holed by the 'friends' of innumerable candidates, and so persecuted with 'letters of recommendation,' that they are utterly sickened of such processes. The president told me this . . . I would like you to understand the importance of immediately asking Mr. Gresham not to mention the matter in any way to his Baltimore kinsmen." But Mrs. Bird, without aiming at the goal, was the means of setting in motion developments which ultimately resulted in Lanier's appointment as a lecturer at the University.

Taking account of Lanier's eagerness for literary work, Mrs. Bird conceived of the idea of organizing a class of women to hear him in her home. The lectures were given between March 23 and May 11, 1878, and there was so much interest that the number invited had to be restricted to about thirty. On the basis of what Lanier wrote his wife, she in turn told his father that "Mrs. Bird's loving triumph is as irrepressible as an eager child's." Years later Mrs. Bird recalled that one day "I asked Dr. Gilman . . . to be present. He gladly came, and he too was charmed. At the close he said to me, 'I never heard a more charming lecture, and with a smile, 'I certainly hear a great many.' " These eight lectures, which Kemp Malone, the editor, calls the "Bird Lectures," formed the immediate background for the Peabody Lectures, made possible through Gilman's cooperation, which were delivered during the winter of 1878-79. These in turn led directly to Lanier's appointment as Lecturer at the University which Gilman was happy to announce on the poet's 37th birthday on Feb. 3, 1879. Thus the personal affection and literary appreciation of Mrs. Bird were ultimately responsible for the inauguration of Lanier's career as a man of letters, which was lamentably cut short by his death on Sept. 7, 1881. I possess no definite proof that Mrs. Machen was in that small group of women who met in Mrs. Bird's home, but there is moral certainty that she was present. Later she was asked by Edwin Mims to record her reminiscences of Lanier for inclusion in his biography.

In this account of the early life of the Machen family in Baltimore mention must also be made of their relations to the Franklin St. Presbyterian Church. When Mr. Machen's mother and sister took up their residence in Baltimore in 1863, they had their membership transferred to the Franklin St. Church, which was known as a church with Southern sympathies, and which after the division in the Presbyterian Church caused by the war became associated with the Southern body. Mr. Machen himself, as was observed above, was a pew holder and a regular attendant but not a member for a time, but in 1873, immediately after his marriage, he became a professing member and was to become one of its most influential members. He served as trustee after 1880 and as a ruling elder after 1893. Having twice previously declined election to the office of elder he yielded finally to the entreaty of the pastor Rev. Wm. U. Murkland, who served the church from 1870 to 1899. Mrs. Machen's cousin, Edgeworth Bird, son of "Aunty" Bird, and her brother, Thomas Gresham, were members of that church session for many years. Even before he became elder Mr. Machen served the church at large as a member of the Board of Foreign Missions and of a special committee which explored, without success, the possibility of union with the Northern Church. Mrs. Machen also found the church congenial, and was for many years President of the Benevolent Society which was especially concerned to assist in the support of the Seminary in Richmond. But for the Machens church membership was not primarily a matter of holding office and being active in special assignments. Attendance upon the regular services of worship was the primary and absorbing interest.

During those early years Mr. Machen was so devoted to his law practice that he found comparatively little time for relaxation. There had been a trip to Europe with his bride in 1873 and other holidays. However, about 1880 his health threatened to give way as the result of his concentration upon his labors which continued long after his return home from his office, and he was persuaded to spend several months in travelling through Europe. His wife and brother accompanied him. It seems, however, that only when his beloved partner, Richard J. Gittings, suddenly died in 1882 did he substantially modify his program. But he still lived a very strenuous life, judged by ordinary standards, meanwhile enjoying remarkable health and vigor to the very day of his death more than thirty years later.

When J. Gresham Machen was born in 1881 he accordingly entered a home of devout Christian faith, of a high level of culture and social standing, and of a considerable degree of prosperity. Both parents were persons of strong character and extraordinary intellectual and spiritual endowments, and our understanding of J. Gresham Machen is illumined as we observe how various qualities and interests of his ancestors were blended in generous portions in his own personality. The family was a close-knit group, though not lacking in catholic outlook and sympathies, and the intense affection and loyalty that distinguished the Machen home were to prove one of the most influential and fascinating factors in shaping the course of things to come. His contacts and relations with his parents form such a substantial part of his developing life that they will continue to receive prominent attention in the following pages.

2

GROWING UP IN BALTIMORE

The first twenty-one years of the life of J. Gresham Machen — the accepted measure of childhood and youth — now come into view. His decision to enter Princeton Seminary in 1902, one of the most decisive turning points of his life, also recommends this division. This was a period climaxed by his brilliant career as a student at Johns Hopkins, and those four years of undergraduate and graduate study will especially come under review. But fortunately for our total understanding of his intellectual and spiritual development, the earlier years as well are not veiled in obscurity.

LIFE AT HOME

In view of the devout Christian faith and life of his parents we shall be quite prepared to expect that considerable place would be given to religious instruction in the home. In mature life Machen often paid tribute to the instruction in the Bible that he received at his mother's knee. At twelve years of age his knowledge of its contents, including the names and character of all the kings of Israel and Judah, he later observed, surpassed that of the average theological student of his day. There was, moreover, careful instruction in the Westminster Shorter Catechism and a commitment to memory of questions and answers. To this he later attributed, to a significant degree, his love of the noble tradition of the Reformed Faith as expressed in its classic symbols as over against the meagre skeletal creeds of a mere "Fundamentalism."

That his memory did not deceive him is borne out by his earliest letters which had been carefully preserved by his mother. The occasion of these early letters, written when he was not yet eight years old, was a visit of his mother in Macon at the time of her mother's last illness. The following excerpts selected from the dozen or more letters of this period provide highly revealing, though not yet fully literate, evidences of the chief delights of this boy as he stayed behind in Baltimore with his father, his brother and a grown niece of Mr. Machen's.

Poply gave me two catterkiserms one little one and one bige one, just like Arlys and I study some in them every day and Carry hears me. I have leant a goodeel since you heard me last. It is verry lonsom without you and Tom.

Your loving Gresham

Arly desected a beetle, and let me see him do it, and I like it verry much. I have finished Mathu, and nearly finished Mark, and then I am going to begin at the very biginning of the whole bible. Arly said over his cattercisum, and made only one mistake. It seems to me that on sunday I can never get a nuf off my cattercisum. I like it so much and Poply always heres me on sunday, and some tims in the week.

You know that little book I told you about in my other letter, and read sum in efry morning, and I learn one of the little verses by hart, and then I find out where they are in the bible, and Carry looks them out in the revised vershun and I like it verry much and do it very often. It seems to me that sundays get nicer and nicer becous Poply reads me in pilgrime progres and hears me my cattercisum, and I like it very much. I like to play hook and lader verry much and bild up houses and play that they gech on fire and I like it verry much and do it verry much. I read in that little book so much that I forget to tar of my calnder I like it so much.

The words "I like it verry much and do it verry much" may be underscored as revealing something of his boyhood character — his intense likes and energetic participation in that upon which he set his mind and heart. Incidentally, they occasionally appeared in quotation marks in his mother's letters of later years as she observed some of the mature expressions of that philosophy. Though these letters serve to reveal the piety of his tender years, one should not suppose that young Gresham was a "goody-goody." He was hardly a placid child! Among the scattered evidences of this fact is an exchange between him and his mother in the fall of 1909, more than twenty years later. In connection with his observation of the "freshness" of certain children, he asked, "Do you believe in the method of 'prohibition' as a method in the education of children?" and indicated he was inclinded to an affirmative answer. To which his mother replied, "I do believe in 'prohibition' in the training of children until such a time in the development of the race when they may be born with full-fledged powers of discrimination. But you cured me of it rather early by asking in the most aggressive way — 'Do I *have* to?' "

Although the Bible and the Shorter Catechism occupied the regular attention of the Machen children, there was an abundance of other books. The strong love of literature which was characteristic of both father and mother naturally found early expression in their sons, and this love was stimulated by example, by reading aloud to them and by providing them with attractive reading matter. To a considerable extent Mrs. Machen supervised their reading in the home, as she did their instruction in religious matters, but here too the father made his own contribution. As his son Arthur later recalled;

> His children love to remember with what rapt attention in the days of their childhood they would listen while he told them tales from classic mythology — the story of Ulysses and Polyphemus, or of Romulus and Remus; with what never flagging delight they would hear him read aloud, with a gusto which none, at least to them, can ever equal, and with a pleasure scarcely less than their own, Southey's "How the Water Comes Down at Lodore"; and what mutual pleasure they and he would derive from his reading of tales of rahjahs and ranees and rakshas in "Old Deccan Days."

Gresham's delight in the reading of *Pilgrim's Progress* has been noted. And in a letter written to his mother on April 2, 1889, he tells of his pleasure in a history of Alexander the Great which his father had purchased for him: "I like it verry verry much and read in it verry much . . . I read anything I can get hold of."

Young Machen's formal education before he entered the university was in a private school. Though the records do not definitely identify the institution attended in his first years at school, in all probability it was the same University School for Boys, of which W. S. Marston was the principal, which he attended for at least six years before he entered the university in 1898. Though it was advertised in 1901 as "the largest and most fully equipped private day-school for boys in the South," the classes were advantageously small. Records preserved for 1892 and the following years disclose that the highest number in any of Gresham's classes was twenty-four, and the average was not much more than half that number. The regular course of study was strongly classical, Latin being included in Gresham's course as early as 1892 and Greek in 1895, both continuing throughout the rest of the course. The reports which have been preserved indicate that he was an excellent student; out of a total of 86 grades in extant reports he ranked first in class no fewer than 78 times; his marks were consistently in the high nineties and for the year 1895-6 he was given a final mark of 99 in Geometry, Algebra, Latin, Greek, Natural Science and English and 97 in French!

Outside of school hours Gresham Machen found time for various activities. He took piano lessons for a number of years, and made sufficient progress to take part in at least two recitals of the pupils of a Miss Brown. But he was not absorbed in music. Besides there were other attractions. On one occasion, in 1894, Miss Clare de Graffenreid, Mrs. Machen's friend from Macon days onward, was in charge of the household while Mr. and Mrs. Machen were in Hot Springs, North Carolina, principally in the interest of Mrs. Machen's health, and wrote to "Dearest Minnie" concerning the state of affairs at home.

> It would do your heart, as well as your mother's pride, good to see how lovely your boys are, and how "what Mother would like" is their law of action. Arthur has been studying faithfully, and having finished today his last *exam* he has put on his old clothes and gone to the circus in highest glee for a regular frolic.... Gresham is now exercised about his music lesson tomorrow, and in trying to get it put off, he shows the greatest consideration for Miss Brown. He and Tom are going with their uncle to baseball; and Tom is the happiest boy in the world at the prospect. The little fellow was too sweet about his new shirt waists; and now he doesn't wish to put on anything that has a ruffle on it, since tasting the delights of being a *real boy*.

The nineties were the era of the illustrious Baltimore Orioles: Ned Hanlon, Gleason, Kelly, Keeler, Jennings, Robinson and McGraw were stars and celebrities. Three pennants were won in succession (1894-96) and Gresham also had the baseball fever. In later years, especially following Baltimore's loss of its major league franchise, this ardor abated, but it could be aroused especially if "Uncle" (Thomas B. Gresham) or some other congenial companion proposed attendance in New York or Philadelphia. He played baseball as a boy but developed a greater fondness for and proficiency in tennis. He also learned to love to ride a bicycle or "wheel." Companions from those days included his schoolmates Latrobe Cogswell and Charlie Buchanan. But his relations with his brother Arthur, ("Arly") and his cousin LeRoy ("Loy") Gresham, though they both were several years older than he, were even more intimate and continued so throughout his life. Family affection of exceptional intensity was indeed one of the distinctive marks of the Machens and Greshams.

HOLIDAYS

The family vacations no doubt contributed strongly to this consciousness of solidarity and interdependence. But they brought other rewards as well: the development of ancestral and national loyalties, the cultivation of a profound love of nature and opportunities of fascinating recreation.

During his early youth Gresham Machen paid occasional visits to the Machen Virginian home where "Uncle James" Machen lived on the farm purchased by grandfather Lewis Machen. More frequent, however, were the journeys to Macon where until the death of her father in 1891 Mrs. Machen was wont to spend several weeks each year with her children. The memories of those idyllic days remained fresh and fragrant for years to come. Fortunately for our knowledge of the Gresham ancestral home there is extant an essay containing his own reminiscences of it, an essay prepared as an exercise in English composition for his first year's work at Johns Hopkins and dated March 21, 1899. The paper has its own significance as an example of Gresham's English style before he had turned 18. But it is set forth in full here principally because of the way in which it effectively supplements our knowledge of that Macon home where his mother was brought up and reflects his own boyhood reactions to his visits there some years before.

AN OLD HOMESTEAD

On College Street, in Macon, Georgia, stands a typical Southern mansion, almost hidden by luxuriant shrubs and tall magnolia trees. The house is built of wood in the colonial style, and is painted white. In front of the house, supporting the roof, stand four tall fluted pillars. These pillars are hollow, and were used during the war to hide the family silver from the Yankees. Behind the pillars, is enclosed a broad piazza, which is transformed by a white climbing rose into a bower of bliss.

To the left, separated from the street by an open fence, is the rose garden. Let New York millionaires spend thousands of dollars on conservatories, they can never produce such roses as here spring up almost of their own accord. Red roses, white roses, pink roses, yellow roses—roses of every conceivable shade—bloom with a glorious profusion which only a genial southern sun can give; and underneath the ground is carpeted with heartsease and violets.

Behind the house is a yard of hard, dry earth covered with berries from the China berry trees (called everywhere else Pride of India). This yard is the best playground that ever delighted a boy's heart. You can be sure that the China berry trees come in for their share of affectionate regard, for pop-guns made to shoot these berries in a hollow elder-rod are as much superior to the miserable cork-and-string affairs as a modern thirteen inch gun is to a Fort McHenry cannon.

The lower part of the yard may seem at first sight to contain nothing but weeds. But far from it. Can you not see, stranger, that those tall weeds are forests of noble pines, and that those bricks are houses in a well laid out city? And if you look a little closer you will see a noble fountain fully four inches high playing in the center of the city. And winding around the hills is a railroad with a long tunnel or two. The fun to be had in building these works of engineering is even greater than can be secured from China-berry pop-guns.

Across the yard from the house are the homes of the servants and the kitchen—all in separate buildings. Behind these is the vegetable garden, a large piece of ground laid out in squares. Back of this are the stable and the "lot," which latter is the abode of a lordly cow.

Let us go around to the front and enter the house, the center of these extensive grounds. The hall is of a breadth which is fully proportional to the generous width of the house. On the left, we may catch a glimpse of the front parlor darkened by its heavy curtains. On the right is the homelike sitting room looking out upon the shrubs of the garden. The books around the walls, the pictures, the comfortable chairs, the open fire—all these things combine to make this room a gathering place for the family.

Connecting with this room is the dining room. The cheerful appearance of this room in the evening, when the table groans with the weight of a Georgia supper, is something to do one's heart good.

Upstairs, we find a broad, bright hall with the bed rooms opening upon it. In this hall, usually are strewn toy cannons, kaleidoscopes, wooden blocks, and other such delightful things. The book-case in the hall is filled with books about Indians and cowboys and with other exciting stories. And if you ever want something new, all you have to do is to nose around in the spare (?) room a little. I wish I could spend a morning in that hall now.

Such is the outward form of the old home. But no words can tell the peculiar charm of the place. Perhaps it is the balmy southern air scented with flowers, perhaps the quiet and restfulness of the spot, perhaps the spaciousness of the old home. But more probably it is not to be found chiefly in any of these things. It lies in the "folks."

In the first place, the servants are the real, old-fashioned, kind-hearted Southern darkies. If you want proof of the fact, go into the kitchen and make investigations into the mysteries of the production of those inimitable cakes. Or go and get Charlie, the coachman, to let you watch him milk the cow. You will find that the best part of human nature does not require education to bring it out.

Of the Southern people themselves everyone knows the hospitality and the refinement. It is a beautiful sight to see the white-capped lady of the house gathering roses in the garden, or the children running daily at twelve o'clock to the cool back porch to receive lemonade made from a refreshing bucket of well water. Nowhere else can be found the peculiar air of generous hospitality which pervades the whole place.

Can we wonder that such a house as this holds a large place in a Southerner's heart? The Englishman may tell of the green hedges and well kept lawns of his father's home in old England; the New Englander may look back with affection upon his neat, plain cottage in a rocky valley; but the Southerner will never lose the affectionate remembrance of the dear old home in the midst of the waving magnolia trees and its fragrant roses.

Although the old South retained its charms, the family regularly sought relief from the humid summer heat of Baltimore in cooler regions. In 1891 they spent the summer in a cottage at South Yarmouth, Mass., which was always recalled in the family with particular satisfaction because on a certain day Mr. Machen, then 64 years old, rushed fully clad into the tidal river of Nantucket Sound to rescue a woman from drowning. During this period the vacations were usually spent in the White Mountains where an intense love of mountains and mountain climbing was developed. And they began the series of vacations at Seal Harbor along the coast of Maine which were to continue year after year, so far as Mr. and Mrs. Machen were concerned, throughout their lives except for the occasions when they travelled in Europe.

In a diary which young Machen kept over a period of about three months in the year 1893, a few of the earlier entries at Baltimore tell of assisting his mother and the gardener in planting flowers, of rides on his bicycle when "the blue line cable cars have just started running," of going down "to play at a sort of a concert in which all of Miss Brown's pupils play," of his father's reading *Evangeline* to him, of hearing Dr. Hoge preach, "and it was grand." The summer was featured, however, by a visit to the World's Fair with his father and brother Arthur and several weeks spent by the entire family in the White

Mountains, which was made memorable by ascents of Mt. Madison and Mt. Adams. A school composition, evidently written the following term, contrasts "the scene illuminated by the searchlights at the World's Fair and that lighted up by the searchlight on the rocky summit of Mt. Washington in New Hampshire." After writing at length of the fascination of the spectacles in Chicago, he comments upon the impressions created by the mountain scenes.

> Majestic mountain peaks, deep and dark ravines, and lonely cataracts are in place of the stately buildings and beautiful fountains. In the World's Fair, the hand of man is everywhere apparent, while around the cold summit of Mt. Washington, it is the hand of Nature that characterizes the scene, as the flashing search-light sends its bright stream many a lonely mile. No blazing lights, no brilliant fireworks, no eager multitudes of people here; but all is solitude.

AT JOHNS HOPKINS

Except for the significant development of the Medical Faculty, there had been remarkably little change in Johns Hopkins University between the year of its opening and the matriculation of J. Gresham Machen in 1898. Several members of the staff who had been chosen partly because of their relative youth were still active, and the promise of productive scholarship as well as inspiring teaching had been brilliantly fulfilled. Gilman remained as president, though his retirement was approaching, coinciding as it did with young Machen's attainment of his baccalaureate degree in 1901. Gildersleeve, Remsen and Rowland were others who still flourished. Nor had the general character of the institution been altered. The undergraduate department, for example, continued to be relatively very small, and the glory of the University continued to be its contribution to graduate education. This emphasis was reflected partially in the enrollment statistics. The Register for 1899-1900 lists only 159 undergraduates while, besides 34 Fellows, 149 pursued graduate courses under the philosophical faculty and 211 under the medical faculty. Consequently only about one-fourth of the students were undergraduates, a proportion somewhat smaller even than had prevailed for the first fifteen years when about one-third or even less fell in this category. Though a sharp distinction was maintained between the graduate and undergraduate departments so far as curriculum and methods were concerned, there was a single faculty and the professors who attracted brilliant students like Josiah Royce and Woodrow Wilson in the early years also bore part of the responsibility for undergraduate instruction. It was felt, moreover, that the presence of a large company of graduate scholars would tend to develop earnestness and scholarly devotion among the younger students.

The undergraduate course was of three years duration following matriculation (it was increased to four a few years later), and students matriculated and became candidates for the A. B. degree only after passing an examination in languages, mathematics, science and history, and showed that a good foundation for the undergraduate courses had been laid. Machen was thus formally enrolled on November 3, 1898. Evidently on the basis of these same examinations he was awarded a scholarship. His family was no doubt delighted at this news. Under date of Oct. 14 the following note had gone out from the President's office:

> Dear Mrs. Machen:
>
> The Board of Advisers has just awarded the Hopkins scholarships, and I am sure you will be glad to know that Gresham has the highest rank,—by several points.
>
> His adviser is particularly gratified!
>
> Yours sincerely
>
> D. C. Gilman

And on Oct. 18th his older brother, who had received his A. B. from the University in 1896, and was now studying law at Harvard, wrote:

> The glorious news (so entirely unexpected) of your getting the first scholarship requires even a man of business like myself, with four lectures today and three tomorrow, to lay aside my books and take up the pen. It will give you a big prestige with the Faculty, and will be a great thing for you. It ought to console the Machen family for Baltimore's defeat in the pennant race. . .

There is also extant a note from Dr. Gilman written on June 13, 1899 which laconically informed Mrs. Machen: "You are always welcome at our celebrations and you will not be displeased by today's undergraduate announcement." Arthur's letter of June 15th from Cambridge supplies the lacuna and again conveys hearty felicitations: "I was greatly delighted although not at all surprised to learn yesterday from Mother's telegram that you had led your class at college. It is a very fine thing to have the matter assured, even though we had little doubt of the result. Honors at the Hopkins are not cheap and a man who stands well there can well account himself the equal if not the superior of his contemporaries at Harvard or Yale or any other university. . ." The youthful scholar was elected to Phi Beta Kappa on April 15, 1901.

A Group system had been adopted at the Hopkins which combined three features. In the first place, there were studies common to all groups which guaranteed a good foundation of general education, as opposed to a free elective system. In the second place, there were studies peculiar to a group, which permitted of specialization in one of seven groups: the classics, mathematical-physical studies, chemical-biological, geological-biological, Latin-mathematical, historical-political studies, or the modern languages. Finally, there was a very limited number of purely optional studies. The University was not nearly so influential upon American education at this point as in its approach to graduate education, but it is of considerable interest in connection with the current discussion of college education to take note that it contained salutary emphases and avoided certain extremes which have been generally recognized as such only in recent years.

Machen chose the classical group which corresponded rather closely to the traditional arts course. The emphasis was laid upon Greek and Latin and considerable attention was paid to English literature and rhetoric. French and German, comparative philology as well as Economics, History and Philosophy were other required studies. The requisite mathematics having been secured before matriculation, there was no further study in this subject prescribed, but one laboratory course in science was required. The complete list added drawing and vocal and physical culture and an elective study occupying two hours weekly in the third year.

CONTACTS WITH GILDERSLEEVE

On this background one does not wonder that he was well-prepared to take advantage of the year of graduate study upon which he entered in the fall of 1901 working under Professor Gildersleeve and his able associates, C. W. E. Miller and Kirby Smith. Miller was a Hopkins A. B. 1882, Fellow, 1883-85, and Ph.D, 1886, while Smith had taken his Ph.D. at the Hopkins in 1889 after coming from undergraduate work at the University of Vermont. Both therefore had been trained directly by Gildersleeve. They were brilliant men, but Gildersleeve easily stood out as one of the real giants in American university education and second to none in the history of American classical scholarship. There was no more memorable experience in Machen's early life than that of membership in the classical seminary under Gildersleeve for that year.

A contributing factor to this enthusiastic estimate of Gildersleeve may well have been the fact that he was a Southerner, having been born in Charleston, S. C., on Oct. 23, 1831. Though taking his academic degrees in Princeton and Göttingen, Germany, he served as a professor at the University of Virginia for twenty years before he accepted Gilman's call to join him in Baltimore in 1876. Academic life was of course not normal during the Civil War, and he served for a time as a staff officer in the confederate army and was wounded. He continued to think of himself as "a man of the old South" and as identified with the Southern people "by birth, by feeling, and by fortune." In *The Creed of the Old South,"* first published in *The Atlantic Monthly* in 1892, and republished in book form in 1915, he declares: "That the cause we fought for and our brothers died for was the cause of civil liberty and not the cause of human slavery, is a thesis which we feel ourselves bound to maintain whenever our motives are challenged or misunderstood, if only for our children's sake." In his *Hellas and Hesperia,* he sums up the issue in different terms, though not contradicting the earlier formulation, when he says: "It was a point of grammatical concord that was at the bottom of the Civil War—'United States are,' said one, 'United States is,' said another." Paul Shorey, in his eloquent commemorative tribute, singles out for primary mention the fact that Gildersleeve was a "typical Southern gentleman," and mentions the following suggestive traits: "the delicate sensitiveness of honor which felt a stain like a wound; the framework of dignity and courtesy encompassing all the wit and colloquial ease of his conversation; the reticence, which was not secretiveness, about the deeper things; the unfailing and delightful gallantry which no refined woman ever misunderstood or feared."

He might have been speaking of J. Gresham Machen!

Another significant fact is that Gildersleeve was numbered among the intimate friends of the Machens and was a fellow-member at the Franklin St. Church. Southerners in Baltimore, as we have noted, were drawn closely together, especially if they shared the same religious outlook and cultural interests. Arthur Webster Machen was only four years older than Gildersleeve, and their love of books and letters and other good things made them congenial friends for nearly forty years.

Mrs. Machen and Dr. Gildersleeve, in spite of the difference in their ages, were afforded nearly fifty years of friendship due to their uncommon longevity, Gildersleeve surviving in astonishing vigor until Jan. 9, 1924, when he died in his ninety-fourth year. Himself one of the most brilliant stylists and men of letters America has seen, he was highly appreciative of Mrs. Machen's literary insight and labors. Her book, *The Bible in Browning,* published by Macmillan in 1903, was commented upon by Gildersleeve in his "Brief Mention" in *The American Journal of Philology,* which he had founded in 1880 and of which he was the editor and leading light for forty years. He also inscribed at least one sonnet to her. No wonder that after attending his funeral many years later, she wrote her son in Princeton, "I am so glad that he had at the end a 'gentle dismissal,' not being very ill until the very day he died. I feel his death very deeply. I was proud of the friendship and literary sympathy that had sprung up between him and me, and now something great has gone out of my life. . . The sight of Mrs. Gildersleeve looking so stricken and clinging to the arm of her big son recalled my own sorrow poignantly."

These relationships naturally enough increased the opportunity and delight of Gresham Machen's own contacts with this eminent man. In the years that followed graduation there were occasional contacts between them, and Gildersleeve remembered him with appreciation and affection. On Oct. 23, 1923, less than three months before his death, he wrote:

> Dear Machen:
>
> Those who have been with me longest are not always those who have understood me best. An old teacher often recalls the words of the Master to Philip. You I have always counted among my most congenial hearers.
>
> With best thanks for your kind words
>
> Yours faithfully,
>
> B. L. G.

This note was in response to one that Dr. Machen had sent in appreciation of Gildersleeve's contribution to his life's work soon after the publication of his *New Testament Greek for Beginners*. A few years before there had been a much less brief exchange between them. In a letter of Oct. 26, 1920 Mrs. Machen had written her son:

> You will be interested in my visit to Dr. Gildersleeve. I was invited to come on his 89th birthday. I dreaded it a little fearing to find him changed. But he was a fine noble figure, looking very well, as bright as a star and full of interest in everything both great and small. I went early and he gave me a most cordial welcome as I sat on the sofa by his side. He began on his sonnets immediately and recited several new ones, very well indeed with excellent emphasis and unfailing memory. One—on "The Death of an Old Confederate"—he said he thought of sending to you on account of your interest in the subject and also of a bit of *exegesis*. He thinks in the stilling of the tempest by Christ, the translation "Peace—be still" is weak. I encouraged him to send the sonnet because I knew he would like it and because I thought you would

be touched. But I am afraid now that even a pleasant incident like this which involves a note may be an interruption. I did not suggest it; it was his own motion with the "reasons annexed." He added "I think a great deal of Gresham and admire him."

Dr. Gildersleeve did write a long letter on Nov. 3, 1920, enclosing not one sonnet but two! The sonnet on "The Dying Confederate" mainly reflects upon the spirit of the confederate army, but closes with the line, "Be muzzled and stay muzzled, Jesus said," as a correction of the traditional translation, and in the letter he supports this conclusion at length. The other sonnet, entitled, "Not Yet," compares and contrasts the counsel of Pindar and that of the Beloved Disciple. The former tells of fortune which will part bestow and part withhold ("and some not yet"), and in withholding teaches him not to cherish idle hope and vain regret. But there is another voice:

Just then I heard the loved disciple's voice
It doth NOT YET appear what we shall be
O sad suspense, darkest of mysteries
Anon the words that made my heart rejoice
We know that when we see him then shall we
Be like him, when we see him as he is.

Machen wrote a warm letter of appreciation, delighting in the beauty of the sonnets, telling of his satisfaction that Gildersleeve was a true "Grecian" without being a pagan, and expressing his deep sensibility of the honor bestowed.

But these delightful contacts took place many years after young Machen entered the Gildersleeve Seminar, where no doubt it was the profound scholarship and scintillating speech of the matchless professor that impressed him most. Of him Abraham Flexner has said that he was in 1876, and remained to the end of his life, "the greatest of American Hellenists," adding:

In depth and range of scholarship, in fertility of mind, in his unique ability to create a school, in his sense of humor, he has not yet been duplicated in America. With the shift of interest and emphasis, it is less and less likely that another Gildersleeve will ever emerge. Of him it has been said: "In 1876, Gilman put him into an empty room and told him to radiate." He did. "The bare room was soon occupied by graduates of various colleges" who "year after year were confronted with a new vision, shining across wide vistas in literature and language."

And Paul Shorey regarded him as America's "foremost scholar" and recognized that during the fifty years of American classical scholarship that had just closed with his death "the figure of Gildersleeve dominated throughout." No wonder that Machen continued all his life to be filled with a kind of boyish enthusiasm at the privilege of his contacts with Gildersleeve. And how thankful the Church of Christ may be that he turned from that training in classical language and letters to the study and exposition of the Greek New Testament.

There was, however, a lighter side to Machen's life at Johns Hopkins than is suggested by his brilliant record under illustrious scholars. In view of the emphasis upon graduate study and the general tone of the university, one might have anticipated that a student of his scholarly disposition would have shown little interest in typically American college life. As a matter of fact, however, he was a representative college undergraduate who entered enthusiastically into many extracurricular activities and developed an intense loyalty to his college. In connection with the "Half-Century" drive for funds in 1926, he did not feel that he could conscientiously contribute to the general funds "because the present movement for an increased endowment seems to be intimately connected with the plea for the abolition of an undergraduate department." He did contribute, however, to the establishment of a Gildersleeve Fellowship in Greek which was initiated by Professor Miller. His protest was in part directed against the fact that the Hopkins alumni would be left in "what is, in American life, the deplorable condition of men without a college." But another consideration was that he regarded such a plan as

> distinctly a retrograde step in American education. It is a retrograde step, I think, because of the impetus which it gives to the movement away from genuine culture and toward an earlier commencement of specialization in the life of American youths. True progress would lie in exactly the opposite direction. Instead of encouraging the scantily educated sophomore to think that he is fit to enter upon a specialized course and to enjoy that complete liberty of which Dr. Flexner's article (in *The Atlantic Monthly*) speaks, what ought to be done is to tell the student that there is no royal road to learning, that short cuts lead to disaster, and that underneath all true research there lies a broad foundation of general culture.

For a partial understanding of Machen's undergraduate life at Hopkins, one may consult *The Hullabaloo,* the school annual, for 1901, of which he was the editor-in-chief. He held various other class offices, was on the Executive Council of the college Y. M. C. A., a member of the Banjo Club and president of the Chess Club. Like his older brother before him, and his younger brother later, he was a member of the Phi Kappa Psi college fraternity. He was apparently an effective debater, participating as chairman and speaker in two teams of his class, and winning both inter-class debates. In 1900 he upheld the affirmative on the question, "England's Course of Action which culminated in the present war with the Boers was unjustifiable" and in 1901 the negative on the question, "The United States should construct, own, operate and control an inter-oceanic canal by way of the Nicaragua Route." Though he did not make any of the college athletic teams, he was intensely loyal to them, and remained so throughout his life. Many years later he protested to the editors of the sports pages of metropolitan newspapers when they displayed their ignorance of college life at his alma mater to the extent of dubbing her teams "the medicos."

In the 1901 *Hullabaloo,* "A Child's Primer of the Hullabaloo Board" contains the following lines:

This is, my dear, the "Gres" Ma-chENE;
How hard it works each day!
The mass of know-ledge it doth glean
Is ve-ry great, they say,
It has no time to loaf and dream
It has no time to play
It studies hard from morn to night,
It ne-ver, ne-ver sleeps,
It "crams" its head so very tight,
And "digs" and "bones" with all its might
And all it learns—it keeps.

Though no doubt reflecting his scholarly earnestness, these verses must be taken with a few grains of salt. This is confirmed by the humorous personality sketch which shows how thoroughly accepted he was by his classmates:

> *Alias,* "GRES," *alias* MONTHLY AVERAGE.—Accused by the overwhelming majority of his class-mates who do not take the scholarships offered, of obtaining under false pretences, $150.00 annually from the Johns Hopkins University. *Hullabaloo* Bureau's agents hope to be in command of sufficient proof to convict suspected before June 15th of this year. Personality of the accused bears few of the outward marks of the scholarship-taker, besides a preoccupied manner and a pronounced bagginess of the trousers.

> Accused a leading member of the Y. M. C. A., and a victim of ginger-ale habit.

FIRST TRIP TO EUROPE

After his graduation with highest honors came the reward of Machen's first trip to Europe. He went with his brother "Arly" and cousin "Loy," who both had had the thrill of a first voyage some time before, sailing on the U. S. M. S. *St. Paul* on July 10, 1901. Regular letters written to his parents and brother at Seal Harbor, in the White Mountains, and finally at Baltimore, gave extensive reports of his fascinating experiences, shared with his two companions until they left for home at the end of August, and enjoyed alone until he arrived in America at the beginning of October. After several days in London and environs the party travelled to Switzerland where a few days were passed before going on to Milan, Venice, Florence and Pisa. Then followed the most exhilarating part of the trip—mountain climbing in Switzerland. Afterward Paris, where the others left him, and Antwerp, Ghent, Brussels, The Hague, Amsterdam and the concluding weeks in Great Britain followed. He had, he felt, "the time of his life."

It is tempting to the biographer to report the impressions made by this trip upon the twenty-year old Machen. All the new sights were charming: the fabulous cities and their peoples, the great cathedrals and art galleries, the theatre and opera in London and Paris. One would like to recall scores of his observations such as his "awe" of Leonardo da Vinci's "Last Supper" in Milan, his admiration of Fra Angelico's madonnas because of his "heartfelt spirit of reverence," and his special fondness for Rembrandt's "School of Anatomy" in the Hague and the "Night Watch" in Amsterdam. But space cannot be denied to a somewhat fuller reference to something that thrilled him to the very depths—the experience of climbing in the Alps! But even then one brief glimpse into his exhilaration, as he climbed Monte Rosa and beheld the Matterhorn from its summit, must suffice.

> Monday morning at 12:30 A. M. we were waked and then took our breakfast and started off at 1:40 for Monte Rosa . . . . Most of the climb up to the ridge of the final peak was easy snow-walking, and gave plenty of opportunity to enjoy the beautiful ice-formations, and the ever-widening views. From the "saddle" on, we climbed up the steep and narrow ridge which leads to Dufourspitze, the highest of the several peaks of Monte Rosa. . . . When at last we stood on the summit, I can assure you that it

was an exhilarating feeling to see over the summits of such mountains as the Lyskamm, and to know that at last I had reached the level of 15,217 ft. It is a fine thing to look up at the Matterhorn towering above the valley of Zermatt, but it is an even finer thing to look *down* upon its rocky summit. Mountaineers are inclined to depreciate Monte Rosa because to ascend it involves no difficult climbing, but from its great height it will always possess a peculiar charm. The view is simply wonderful, and from its vast extent gives the impression that the whole world is beneath you. The array of snow-clad peaks is so bewildering that the eye finds it difficult to fasten upon any one object. But there is one thing which I shall always remember apart from the rest. Above the confused jumble of peaks, one mountain towered up with a majesty which proclaimed it to be the king. I have never looked directly up at the snows of Mt. Blanc, but I am morally sure that if I ever do so I shall never be more impressed with its regal qualities than by that distant view above the clouds. At lower altitudes, other mountains may steal some of the homage of their king; at the summit of Monte Rosa all the other peaks are disdained as inferiors, and the monarch alone is revered.

The trip down was without important incident, and we arrived at the Riffleberg safely, after a rather fatiguing day of 19 hours, which we accomplished on a Swiss breakfast of a few eggs, and three or four sandwiches for lunch.

It was perhaps then that there was born the longing to ascend the Matterhorn, a longing which was not to be realized until more than thirty years later.

In his final letter home, sent from Wells, on Sept. 24th, he wrote his father to say how much the trip had meant in giving new appreciation of literature and art and a new interest in almost every branch of knowledge, and tells of his appreciation of his Father's "thought of it for me." Then he adds: "The trip has been almost as near perfect as anything could be in an imperfect world. It is true there is one thing necessary to complete my happiness, but that is not the fault of the trip—I mean perfect certainty as to what I ought to do next winter. But there is no use in my carrying on a one-sided conversation about it anyway, and I hope I may get into the right place."

As we have already noted, he later decided to return to the Hopkins for graduate work for the year 1901-102. But that decision by no means carried with it certainty as to his future plans or vocation. That he entered Princeton Theological Seminary in the fall of 1902 is truly an extraordinary development when one considers how exceedingly doubtful he remained as to its wisdom and propriety, not to speak of the even greater doubts with which he was perplexed as to whether he should become a candidate for the Gospel ministry.

3

THE DECISION FOR PRINCETON SEMINARY

The searchlight now turns upon Princeton Theological Seminary especially as it had developed about the turn of the century when Machen became a student there. Patton, Warfield, Armstrong and other members of the Faculty of his student years will be introduced, men who were to figure prominently in the story of the unfolding years. First of all, however, inquiry will be made into the elements and factors that entered into the decision to become a student there, reserving to the following chapter the story of his life as an undergraduate theological student, his reactions to what he found at Princeton and his other experiences of that period.

SEARCHING THE FUTURE

Concerning Machen's religious development while he was at Johns Hopkins very little can be said so far as his inmost thoughts were concerned. We know, as his mother stated several years later in reply to a query of his, that he had become a professing member of the Franklin St. Church on Jan. 4, 1896. Since he himself did not remember the date, it is not likely that this step was the consequence of a sudden or radical experience; it evidently was rather the flowering of the piety which was nurtured continuously in his profoundly Christian home. In college, as his activity in the Y.M.C.A. recalls, he was known as a Christian and was concerned to promote the cause of Christ on the campus. His interest in Christian teaching and testimony is also disclosed by the fact that he attended Y.M.C.A. conferences at Northfield on at least three occasions during summer vacations, in 1899, 1900 and 1902, and since he spoke of the pleasure and profit of the Northfield visits, certain impulses towards the ministry may have been stimulated by the speakers and the fellowship there. So everything points to the conclusion that he did not waver from his Christian profession.

But one who is seeking to live a Christian life may be far from reaching a decision to undertake the study of theology and to become a candidate for the Christian ministry. Machen was so far from it after his graduate year at Hopkins that he went to the Summer School of the University of Chicago to take courses in *banking and international law!* In a letter to his father on July 31, 1902, after describing his courses at some length, he reveals that he has been considering turning from the classics to the study of economics:

> I am afraid I am not going to feel any great enthusiasm for economics, and rather feel that my choosing it to study next year is still a remote possibility, though nothing else has come to me yet which seems better. However, light *may* come during my stay at the University, though I don't feel that way now.

A letter of August 17th shows that he is still considering the study of economics for the next year, and has been inquiring as to the relative merits of Harvard and Columbia. He is inclined to the former, and thinks of stopping off in Boston on his way to meet his parents in the White Mountains to get some specific information. But he adds:

> I am still very doubtful about studying economics. I wish that instead of thinking about these special fields, I were led to something eminently *regular*—like practicing law. The ministry *I am afraid I can't think of.*

Nevertheless, in this same letter he writes at length, in answer to an inquiry of his mother, of the strategic significance of the college Y.M.C.A. if the college community is not to be an infidel one. And commenting on another point he says that there is now "no adequate motive *to most people* to study the Bible as literature only. If we are to obtain the literary knowledge even, we must study devoutly." Even the negative reference to the ministry shows that he had been under constraint to think about that possibility.

What was said in the family councils during the two weeks or so that he spent with them in the White Mountains, and what went on in his own mind, we do not know. He must, however, have begun to give more serious consideration to the ministry. For a letter to his mother on Sept. 15, written in Baltimore but mailed from Princeton, contained momentous news. On Sunday he heard "two splendid sermons" preached by Mr. Harris E. Kirk, who had become pastor of Franklin St. Church in 1901, and later Machen sought a conference with him. Of it he wrote:

> Despite the fact that Mr. Kirk is particularly busy this week, on account of the coming meeting of the Presbytery of Rockville, I took a half hour or so of his time this morning to have a talk with him (which he seemed glad to give). He encouraged me to

> go to Princeton Seminary, and seems to think that *if* I want to leave after a year, it will do no harm. I am sorry to learn though, of the possibility that I may have to be recommended by the Presbytery etc. before admitted—or a month or so after entrance—which formality I am particularly anxious to avoid. With many serious misgivings, I have decided to go to Princeton this afternoon and look around getting information. I have almost decided to go to Princeton for the year's work, and only wish that I could go into it with more faith and more assurance that it is the right thing. Although I don't want to talk about going until I have definitely decided, I don't of course mind your telling any member of the family . . . Mr. Kirk rather supports me in thinking Princeton a better place for *me* to go (in the absence of Dr. Moore especially) than Richmond.

Soon thereafter, as his letter of Sept. 21 confirms, he is enrolled as a student, and reports: "I am very glad indeed that I am here and am coming more and more to hope that it is the true place for me." By this time no doubt his mind had been relieved to learn that even the minimal commitment to the ministry involved in being taken under care of a presbytery was not required of students at the Seminary. And so he could enter upon his studies with considerable interest and expectancy partly at least because of the very liberty he enjoyed of not being compelled, for the time being at any rate, to come to a definite decision regarding the ministry.

That he chose Princeton rather than Richmond is somewhat remarkable in view of his membership in the Southern Presbyterian Church, his mother's interests in and labors on behalf of Richmond, and his own profound consciousness of being a Southerner. Mr. Kirk approved of this choice but hardly seems to have been responsible for suggesting it. It may well be that in his state of uncertainty he felt that there would be somewhat less of commitment in attending another Seminary than one of his own Church. But taking account of the entire situation, there is certainty that the presence of Francis Landey Patton in Princeton was the magnet which drew him there. For Dr. Patton, who had been identified both with Princeton University and Princeton Seminary for many years, and who in the fall of 1902 entered upon the newly created office of president of the Seminary, was an intimate and congenial friend of the Machens and had lodged frequently in their home when he preached in Baltimore. At Princeton from the very first week onward Machen was a guest of the Pattons at dinner and on other occasions, and a cordial relationship of prior standing is assumed. In view of Machen's intense admiration of Patton as a preacher and a man, one can understand how Patton's visits to Baltimore became an important factor both in confronting him with the claims of the ministry and in drawing him northward to Princeton.

PRINCETON SEMINARY

In 1902 Princeton Seminary, within a decade of rounding out the first century of its life, enjoyed the reputation of being a gibraltar of orthodoxy and a school of eminent scholarship. As "The Theological Seminary of the Presbyterian Church in the U.S.A.," its influence through its faculty and alumni upon the life of that denomination, and far beyond its bounds, was second to none of the other Presbyterian Seminaries, though especially Union of New York and McCormick of Chicago had made at least a beginning of challenging her leadership. There might be the feeling in some quarters that the Princeton theology was old-fashioned and was bound to undergo eclipse, but there was no doubt that the Seminary had stood and was standing for the rugged, undiluted Calvinism of the Westminster Standards.

On the occasion of the centennial celebration of 1912 President Patton delivered an address on "Princeton Seminary and the Faith" in which, reminding his hearers of the commitment of its constitution to the Reformed Theology, he asserted that "the theological position of Princeton Seminary is exactly the same today that it was a hundred years ago." Though aware of and rejoicing in the progress of research and investigation, he held that none had "made necessary any modification of our belief as to the authority of Scripture or as to the dogmatic content of Scripture." He was aware that that position was being challenged as never before, and that therefore the lines of controversy were being drawn along different lines, due to the influence of non-Christian philosophical and historical perspectives upon the study of the Bible and theology. But for himself he was not ready to "leave the proud ship of Christianity, and lower the boats of philosophy."

In contrast to the speculative tendencies of the New England Theology of Hopkins, Edwards and others, observed Patton, was the conservative character of the Princeton Theology.

> Now Princeton Seminary, it should be said, never contributed anything to these modifications of the Calvinistic system. She went on defending the traditions of the Reformed Theology. You may say that she was not original: perhaps so, but then, neither was she provincial. She had no oddities of manner, no shibboleths, no pet phrases, no theological labels, no trademark. She simply taught the old Calvinistic Theology without modification: and

> she made obstinate resistance to the modifications proposed elsewhere, as being in their logical results subversive of the Reformed faith. There has been a New Haven theology and an Andover theology; but there never was a distinctively Princeton theology. Princeton's boast, if she have reason to boast at all, is her unswerving fidelity to the theology of the Reformation.

And in his closing words of response to the congratulatory addresses of the many representatives of churches and educational institutions, Dr. Patton, while rejoicing in the significant measure of agreement with other Christian points of view, gloried in the strength of the position maintained at Princeton:

> I want to say that so far as the theology of Princeton Seminary is concerned—and I admit that its peculiarities have not been brought into the foreground during this celebration—I think you will go away with the conviction that at all events, it is not actually dead. I do not think that it is even moribund, but I wish to say that, if it should die and be buried, and in the centuries to come, the theological palaeontologist should dig it up and pay attention to it, he will be constrained to say that it at least belonged to the order of vertebrates.

Patton's stress upon Princeton's constancy and conservatism, its aversion to speculation and its passion to be marked by nothing more nor less than by fidelity to the Scriptures, was in substance an echo of the dominant note at another Princeton celebration of forty years before: the semi-centennial commemoration of the professorship of Charles Hodge on April 24, 1872. It was a crowning day in the life of this man whose fifty years of association with the Seminary had included more than twenty-five years of intimate association with Archibald Alexander and Samuel Miller, the first professors. His career had been crowned by the publication in 1872 of his monumental *Systematic Theology* in three massive volumes. Recalling that Drs. Alexander and Miller were not speculative men, Dr. Hodge said on that occasion:

> They were not given to new methods or new theories. They were content with the faith once delivered to the saints. I am not afraid to say that a new idea never originated in this Seminary. Their theological method was very simple. The Bible is the word of God. That is to be assumed or proved. If granted; then it follows, that what the Bible says, God says. That ends the matter.

On the same occasion, the Rev. Dr. H. A. Boardman, speaking for the Directors of the Seminary, recalled that a censorious critic of

Hodge's *Theology* had said, "It is enough for Dr. Hodge to believe a thing to be true that he finds it in the Bible!"—to which the director's reaction was this: "We accept the token. Dr. Hodge has never got beyond the Bible. It contains every jot and tittle of his theology. And woe be to this Seminary whenever any man shall be called to fill one of its chairs, who gets his theology from any other source."

One may question whether Charles Hodge and the other representatives of Princeton orthodoxy were at every point as completely free of philosophical and speculative influences as they wanted to be and supposed they were—or as lacking in originality as they seemed to claim. But there is no doubt that their theology was basically exegetical, and that their zeal neither to go beyond nor to fall short of what stood written was derived from their cordial commitment to the infallibility of Holy Scripture. During the eighties and nineties there were within the Presbyterian Church vigorous attacks upon the position represented by Princeton Seminary, but the doctrinal consciousness of the Church was still so virile that several heresy trials were carried through to a verdict. In one of the most celebrated of these, Charles A. Briggs, professor at Union Theological Seminary in New York, was suspended from the ministry because of his views concerning Biblical inspiration. To say that the issue was whether the Princeton view of the Bible or a lower view of its inspiration and authority was true and constituted the official doctrine of the Presbyterian Church would not be a serious oversimplification. At Princeton there was therefore at the beginning of the 20th century a strong sense of continuity with the theology of Charles Hodge and his distinguished predecessors. If there was any change it was found in a new note of militancy as the issues were drawn not merely in the broad arena of the theological schools of America and Europe but also in the narrower, more intimate and sensitive life of a particular denomination.

Some account may well be taken here of the Faculty of the Seminary at the time that Machen became a student there. Of that company only Wm. M. Paxton (1824-1904), who came from distinguished pastorates in Pittsburg and New York to take charge of practical theology in 1883, had been a student in the Seminary during the careers of Archibald Alexander (1772-1851) and Samuel Miller (1769-1850), the first professors. And Paxton taught only a few courses after his formal retirement in 1902, though Machen did hear him lecture in his middle year. During his regular course work in the practical department was conducted for the most part by visiting lecturers of whom the most distinguished was Dr. D. J. Burrell, a celebrated preacher in New York.

Archibald Alexander Hodge, son of Charles Hodge, had been a member of Paxton's class but he had died in 1886 after being briefly associated with his father and then succeeding him in the chair of theology. And William Henry Green of the seminary class of 1846 had died in 1900 after more than fifty years of distinguished service to the Seminary in the field of Old Testament.

There remained strong personal ties with the older days, however, for no fewer than three of the professors, in addition to Paxton, had been trained by Charles Hodge: John De Witt (1842-1923), a student under Hodge from 1862-1864, was Professor of Church History, having served since 1892 after a career as a preacher and as a professor at Lane and McCormick. In the chair of theology as the successor of A. A. Hodge there was none other than Benjamin Breckinridge Warfield who had graduated from the seminary in 1876. The third member of this group was Patton of the class of 1865. Although all three were highly respected from the first, and came to be affectionately regarded by Machen, the influence of Patton and Warfield was the most decisive upon his life and thought, and therefore somewhat fuller attention must be given to them.

FRANCIS L. PATTON

Francis Landey Patton was born in Bermuda in 1843 and died there in his ninetieth year, never having become a citizen of the United States. His mature years, except for his period of retirement (which was frequently interrupted by return visits for lecture tours) were, however, devoted to the advancement of ecclesiastical and educational life in America.

Following his graduation from Princeton and ordination in 1865 he held pastorates in the East for seven years, and attracted attention by his little book on *The Inspiration of the Scriptures*. Published in 1869, it expounded and defended the plenary inspiration of the Bible, declaring that, in view of the direct influence of the Holy Spirit "infallibility attaches to every word." From 1872-1881 he served as professor of theology in the Presbyterian seminary in Chicago, where he immediately utilized as a text book the work of Hodge which had just appeared, and which he was later to characterize as "the greatest treatise on Systematic Theology in the English language." During this period in Chicago, Dr. Patton gained a reputation as a brilliant and militant defender of the faith because of his role as prosecutor in the celebrated heresy trial of Professor David Swing who was accused of holding to substantially Unitarian views. The trial was held in 1874 and as a consequence Dr. Swing withdrew from the Presbyterian ministry. In 1878, though he was only thirty-five years old, Patton was elected moderator of the General Assembly and was honored by the Church in many other ways in the years that followed. In 1881 came the call to go to Princeton as professor of a newly created chair, endowed by his friend R. L. Stuart of New York, known as that of "the Relations of Philosophy and Science to the Christian Religion." At the same time he became Stuart professor of Ethics in Princeton College, later adding ethics also to his teaching at the Seminary.

To the consternation of many of its supporters he was chosen as president of the college in 1888. He is said to have been widely known in 1888 "as a witty and eloquent speaker, a distinguished exponent of theism and an expert defender of Christian Ethics"; no one doubted, moreover, his "delightful personal charm, broad classical culture, extensive reading and humane sympathies." But there was widespread doubt whether this militant defender of the faith would possess the administrative qualities and educational leadership which were requisite. Nevertheless, his administration was eminently successful and he won the enthusiastic support of the alumni. At least as surprising as his appointment was his resignation in 1902, due evidently to his distaste for administrative detail, and his nomination of Woodrow Wilson as his successor. He continued as a professor at the University until his retirement in 1913, but principally served the Seminary as lecturer on theism and professor of the philosophy of religion. During these years he also, as noted above, was the president of the Seminary, the duties connected with this new office being naturally much less arduous than those at the University.

How the man and his labors were evaluated at the University is best reflected in the address of Dean Andrew West on the occasion of his presentation for the Degree of Doctor of Laws in 1913:

> Francis Landey Patton, retiring President of Princeton Theological Seminary, former President of Princeton University. His presidency there has been marked by increased gifts and large development of the faculty. His presidency here was marked by like increase in resources and professors, by the beginnings of our collegiate Gothic architecture, the assumption of our university title, the introduction of the honor system in examinations and the inception of the graduate college.
>
> There as here his full value is not measured by these outer signs. A searching critic of utilitarian, agnostic and naturalistic thinking, interpreter of the primal convictions of the human mind as to its own nature, the theistic implications of the world and the ground of moral obligation; eloquently convincing, whether in

studious mood or when flashing on the dark places of argument the sudden light of wit; an alchemist in rhetoric, transmuting the plain into brilliancy; a master-swordsman in dialectics; theologian in the school of Augustine; philosopher in the house of Anselm; vindicator of the historic Christian faith,—his kinship, in all humility of soul, is with the communion of saints intellectual and spiritual.

To Anselm, as a child in his native valley, the distant shining Alps touched Heaven, where was the Palace of God. To you, Sir, as a child in your lovely island home, the blue rim of encircling Ocean touched Heaven. From those far horizons, borne inward with "scents and murmurs of the infinite sea," there came to you surmises and surprises of thought too deep for words, and yet to take voice in words, not common or idle, elusive and not illusory, telling us of the supreme reality of the things unseen and eternal.

It is no wonder that young Machen was fascinated and enthralled by such a figure of a man and was emboldened to contemplate the question, howbeit with great trepidation, whether perhaps he might not also be called to the high office so brilliantly adorned by this illustrious man. How happy the providence that, exactly at the juncture of his wrestling with the deepest issues of his life and calling, he should have enjoyed the sympathetic interest and friendship of one whose position and prestige and influence were so great that the doubts and uncertainties of this young man did not readily jeopardize his career or threaten to ruin it!

BENJAMIN BRECKINRIDGE WARFIELD

Machen first met Warfield at Princeton Seminary, and his relationships were accordingly the ones that more normally obtain between student and professor. Nor were Warfield's talents of the scintillating kind that charmed and captivated his audiences. And devoted as he was to his research and writing, not to dwell upon his extraordinary commitment to the care of his invalid wife, he did not become a prominent public figure either as a preacher in famous city pulpits or as a leader in debating issues in the courts of the church. His was the kind of solid and comprehensive learning that only gradually would be appreciated at its true worth by those who were privileged as youthful students to enter his classroom. Moreover, as Machen frequently intimated in later years, he was not as aware as he later became of the central place and supreme importance of systematic theology in the theological curriculum. Nor did he in those early days clearly perceive the grandeur of the Reformed Theology as the system of doctrine taught in Scripture, which was to be proclaimed and defended, not as perhaps of secondary significance to a more general evangelicalism, but as Christianity come into its own. Patton's significance was the more decisive, especially in the early crucial years of decision; Warfield's was the more profound and enduring as the breadth and depth of the Christian foundations were more fully recognized.

When Archibald Alexander Hodge died in 1886, Patton declared that "the glory had departed from Princeton Seminary." No doubt a kind of turning-point had been reached in her affairs when this man who bore the name of the first professor of the Seminary as well as that of his father, and was a wonderfully gifted theologian in his own right, passed away. But it was Patton himself who, when called upon nearly forty years later to sum up the significance of B. B. Warfield, not only spoke of him as one of the three great masters of the Reformed theology of that day (the others being Abraham Kuyper and Herman Bavinck of the Netherlands) but said that he could not better describe him to Princeton men than by saying that "he combined in rare degree the widely different attainments of Charles Hodge and Addison Alexander." It is difficult to conceive of a more complimentary estimate of the qualifications and stature of a theologian.

And in the same year, on Oct. 11, 1921, on the occasion of his induction into the chair vacated by Warfield's death, Caspar Wistar Hodge, Jr., grandson of Charles Hodge and nephew of A. A. Hodge, and who had been assisting Dr. Warfield in the department for twenty years, spoke of his profound sense of unworthiness in taking up the duties of the Chair

> made famous by the illustrious men who have preceded me, and whose labors have helped to give Princeton Seminary a fame throughout the world for sound learning and true piety. We think today of Archibald Alexander, that man of God, the first Professor in the Seminary; of Charles Hodge, whose *Systematic Theology* today remains as probably the greatest exposition of the Reformed Theology in the English language; of Archibald Alexander Hodge, a man of rare popular gifts and of unusual metaphysical ability; and last, but not least, excelling them all in erudition, of Dr. Warfield, whose recent death has bereft us of our leader and one of the greatest men who has ever taught in this institution.

Like Charles Hodge and Addison Alexander, Warfield had broadened his training through the medium of European study and travel, and gave early evidence of his erudition and scholarly zeal. Following his ordination in 1876, and a brief pastoral experience in Baltimore, he was called to teach New Testament subjects in the Western Theological Seminary in Pittsburgh. During his nine years of service with that institution, he began to demonstrate his exceptional mastery of his field; and his publications on the text, canon and other aspects of New Testament study afforded proof that he was a thorough and independent scholar. His interest in Biblical criticism and exegesis continued throughout his long career as professor of theology at Princeton (1887-1920), as many of his articles demonstrate, and his expert knowledge in this field served to provide a solid exegetical basis for his more specifically theological studies. Though his admiration for Hodge's *Theology* was such that he evidently never seriously considered writing a comprehensive treatise of his own, his indefatigable labors in this and kindred fields resulted in the production of many notable books and scores of learned articles, many of which were brought together in the ten volumes of his collected writings after his death.

OTHER PROFESSORS

Most of the other members of the Faculty of 1902-05 can be referred to only briefly, though they included many eminent scholars and teachers. John D. Davis (1854-1925) had been associated with W. H. Green in the Old Testament department for about fifteen years before the latter's death in 1900 and thereupon was made principally responsible for Old Testament History and Exegesis. In the same year Robert Dick Wilson (1856-1930) came from several years of experience in Western Seminary, the earlier years as a colleague of Warfield's, to become professor of Semitic Philology and Old Testament Introduction. And Geerhardus Vos (1862-1949) was teaching in the Old Testament field as well as the New as Professor of Biblical Theology in the chair created in 1893 and which he adorned for nearly forty years. Like Davis Vos had specialized under W. H. Green and like Wilson he had taught for a number of years in another seminary, in his case, the Christian Reformed Seminary in Grand Rapids, before being called to Princeton. Since 1892 William Brenton Greene, Jr., (1854-1928) had occupied the chair created in 1881 for Dr. Patton. All these men were enjoying the full strength of mature manhood during Machen's years as an undergraduate, and were to be his colleagues to the end, or very near the end, of his career there as a member of the Faculty.

There were also a number of men on the staff who were much nearer Machen's age, and among them he was to find some of his most intimate friends for years to come. Mention has been made of Caspar Wistar Hodge (1870-1937) who had become associated with Warfield in the department of theology in 1901. Others were James O. Boyd (1874-1947) who taught as instructor and later as assistant professor in the Old Testament field, beginning in 1900 and who came to be associated for many years with the American Bible Society; Kerr Duncan MacMillan (1871-1938), who was an instructor in semitics 1897-1900 and 1903-1907 and in church history 1907-13, before he left to become president of Wells College; and Frederick W. Loetscher (1875-), instructor in church history 1903-1907, professor of homiletics 1910-13 and professor of church history 1913-45.

In this latter group of younger men, however, another stands quite apart from those mentioned because of the peculiarly intimate bonds of affection and fellowship in labor which united them. He was William Park Armstrong (1874-1944), an Alabaman who graduated from Princeton University in 1894 and from the Seminary in 1897. After two years of specialization in the New Testament in the universities of Marburg, Berlin and Erlangen, he returned to Princeton as Instructor in the New Testament. The chair of that department was occupied at the time by Dr. G. T. Purves who had succeeded Caspar Wistar Hodge, Sr., in 1892. Purves, a classmate of Warfield's in the Seminary, had remained for a year of specialization under Hodge in New Testament and Green in Old Testament, and subsequently became one of the most eloquent and scholarly preachers of his time. During his pastorate in the First Presbyterian Church of Pittsburgh, he was besieged by McCormick and Lane seminaries to undertake a professorship, and was finally prevailed upon to go to Princeton. There he proved to be an exceptionally able and influential teacher, but his love of preaching was such that he undertook regular preaching at the First Church of Princeton in 1897 and in 1899 assumed the pastorate in addition to his duties at the Seminary. His strength was soon overtaxed, however, and he resigned both positions in 1900 to accept a call to the Fifth Avenue Presbyterian Church in New York. He served at this distinguished post for only eighteen months and died on Sept. 24, 1901, three days before his forty-ninth birthday. Armstrong had been appointed as Instructor in the department in 1899 to help relieve the burdens assumed by Dr. Purves. But his success was so instantaneous that, when Purves resigned in 1900, he was placed in charge of the department, and was advanced to a full professorship in 1903 when he was only twenty-nine years old.

The fact that Armstrong was a fellow Southerner no doubt attracted Machen to him. That the young professor seemed so fully to embody the ideals of scientific investigation which Machen had learned at the feet of Gildersleeve was, however, more decisive and no doubt attracted him to undertake special studies in this field. Their personalities were quite diverse, for in contrast to Machen's natural aggressiveness and overflowing readiness to say what was in his mind and heart stood Armstrong's marked reserve and reticence which impressed some as coldness until they discovered that just beneath the surface was a deeply emotional nature. The two men complemented each other in an extraordinary way and became a strong team when in 1906 Machen became Armstrong's colleague and associate. No doubt the exceptional hospitality of the Armstrong home in the years that followed the marriage in 1904 of Mr. Armstrong to Miss Rebekah Purves, daughter of the late Dr. Purves, was an important factor in deepening their friendship and added immeasurably to the joys of Machen's bachelor existence in Princeton. From the first Armstrong seems to have been drawn to Machen and his increasing regard and sympathetic understanding proved, along with Patton's personal interest, to be a powerfully stabilizing and encouraging force in the difficult years of indecision.

4

UNDERGRADUATE IN THEOLOGY

Machen's undergraduate years will now be reviewed from the perspective of his own reactions and responses to what he encountered in the Seminary. Fortunately for our purpose we need not piece together a fragment of information here and another there. For a flood of light is cast upon this period and the years that followed by the regular letters that were exchanged, week after week, between him and his mother, with occasional contributions from his father and brothers.

There are some gaps occasioned chiefly by visits with his parents, and silences concerning other matters due to his modesty or reserve or simply because he thought they would not prove of particular interest to the members of his family. The earlier letters particularly fail fully to satisfy one's curiosity as to his specific reactions to the teaching at the Seminary and other matters of interest, though their incidental references to many things supply the reader with vivid impressions concerning his student life.

GENERAL IMPRESSIONS

The one dominant impression he gives is that he fell completely in love with life at Princeton, so much so that the only serious note of dissonance was caused by his own perplexity concerning his own future vocation. His life was so constantly absorbed with interesting work, pleasant associations with professors and students, and delightful opportunities of recreation that even the disturbing question of his calling could rather comfortably be kept in abeyance, it seems, except at the end or beginning of each academic year.

That he proved to be an excellent student cannot be doubted, though so far his letters home testify he might have been hardly more than a mediocre one. He refers in general to his studies, but never with particular satisfaction as to his own attainments. And even when he wins special awards, he is far from enthusiastic as to his efforts and attributes his success largely to the lack of serious competition. Nevertheless, mainly through the visits of Dr. Patton in their home, the parents heard from time to time of the splendid impression he was making upon the Faculty.

Of the members of the Faculty and other persons in Princeton Machen had very little to report, confining himself in the main to persons of whom his family had some knowledge. Patton accordingly is mentioned frequently, as Machen enjoyed the hospitality of the Patton home, was a member for two years of his university seminar, and delighted in the opportunities of hearing him preach. Armstrong's preaching in the Seminary Chapel proved disappointing especially since he was "a Southerner and a very bright man"; the substance was good, he reported, but the form was that of a theological lecture.

But he also remarks that "Army" seemed "radiant after his return from his wedding trip, and advised Machen to do all his work before he became engaged, as there would be little chance afterward. Machen's reply to this as reported to his mother, was simply, "I tell him I have plenty of time. The approaching exams are a more powerful incentive."

Dr. Vos received special mention, perhaps because his brother, Dr. Bert J. Vos, was a Hopkins Ph.D. and a professor of German in that university. He found the work in Biblical Theology, especially of the New Testament, of particular value, and tells of his delight in the sermon preached by Dr. Vos in his senior year:

> We had this morning one of the finest expository sermons I ever heard. It was preached by Dr. Vos, professor of Biblical Theology in the Seminary, and brother of the Hopkins Dr. Vos, and rather surprised me. He is usually rather too severely theological for Sunday morning. Today he was nothing less than inspiring. His subject was Christ's appearance to Mary after the resurrection. Dr. Vos differs from some theological professors in having a better-developed bump of reverence.

Woodrow Wilson, another Hopkins Ph.D (in 1886), was an acqaintance of the Machens. Like Lanier a decade earlier he frequently was a guest in the home of "Aunty" Bird during his student days in Baltimore. And as in the case of Lanier the contacts were promoted by associations with the Bird and Gresham families in the South. Rev. J. R. Wilson, Woodrow's father, had served as pastor of the Presbyterian Church of Augusta during Woodrow's boyhood and later became professor at the Seminary in Columbia of which Judge Gresham was a trustee. He was a frequent visitor in the Machen home in Baltimore. The Axsons—Ellen Axson became Mrs. Woodrow Wilson in 1885—were also intimate friends of the Birds and Greshams. In view of the differences of their ages, Gresham Machen had not come to know Wilson well, but he had many intimate contacts with him in Princeton. He regretted that his own acquaintance at the time of Wilson's inauguration as president of Princeton University in 1902 was so slight that he did not feel free to ask him for a ticket with a view to attending the ceremonies. But he did attend Wilson's lectures on American constitutional history and from time to time was the guest of the Wilsons in their home. Concerning a dinner at the Wilsons, he reported that the party consisted of "Dr. and Mrs. Wilson, the three daughters, 'Col' Brank of the Seminary and myself. Woodrow bristled with anecdotes in his usual entertaining way, and the company was small and informal enough not to be oppressive like a formal dinner."

There were similar social contacts with Dr. and Mrs. Henry van Dyke. Mrs. van Dyke was the former Ellen Reid of Baltimore, and was a sister of Imogene Reid Bird, the wife of Edgeworth Bird, who has been mentioned as being the son of "Aunty" Bird and a first cousin of Mrs. Machen. The Machens too were wont to speak of Dr. van Dyke as "Uncle Henry." "Cousin Edgeworth" had given Machen a letter of introduction to the van Dykes when he first went to Princeton. Though Machen conferred with Dr. van Dyke, who had begun his score of years as a professor of English literature at the University in 1900, with regard to enrollment in his seminars on English poetry, he decided against undertaking this work because of the burden of his seminary duties and of the special work under Patton and Wilson. Besides he had become engrossed in the study of philosophy under Professor A. T. ("Jerry") Ormond, which at first especially he found difficult, at one point relaying to his brother Arthur an offer of "$1,000 for a satisfactory exegesis of a single page" of Kant's *Critique of Pure Reason*.

MEMBER OF BENHAM

Among his greatest joys at Princeton were those afforded by membership in the Benham Club, ostensibly an eating club, but actually, because of the accent on the cultivation of social life and the fostering of club loyalty, possessing something of the nature of a college fraternity. His initial impressions of Benham were indeed not entirely favorable. In his very first letter written at the Seminary, he says:

> I was surprised and rather shocked to find the virulence of the club life at the Seminary. I have given my consent, after looking at the others, or most of them, to join one which is no doubt . . . "the swellest." But I am not without misgivings as the Benham Club is, to my mind, too stuck up to be spiritually minded, or to have a good influence in the Seminary. This is between you and

me, the family and the gate post. It prides itself on numbering among its former members Profs. Ormond and Baldwin etc., etc., and on being the oldest club in Princeton University or Seminary. But a fellow has to join some club, as that is the only sociable and comfortable way of feeding here. Practically everybody belongs to one or another. Still, I think I have been a little hasty, but the clubs are elective concerns, almost like fraternities, and I was tired of being taken around by fellows, who I knew were doing it for a purpose, and to whom I knew I was going to prove an unprofitable investment. I think the whole system is very unfortunate at a Seminary. Although warned by Mr. Kirk that it would be so, I have been rather shocked to find that the students here seem exactly like ordinary college fellows.

In the light of later history it appears that these misgivings were completely or largely overcome, for there is no doubt that he became an enthusiastic and loyal Benhamite. Machen had to discover sooner or later that the transition from college to seminary status does not ordinarily revolutionize human nature. And it may be that one who was gravely burdened by the implications of entering the ministry was less prepared than were students who had already made the commitment, for the shocking discovery that seminary students were quite human. There was likely a measure of truth in his evaluation of the spirit of the Benham Club. On the other hand, life in the club no doubt made an important contribution to his enjoyment of his stay in Princeton and was the means of establishing many of the most intimate friendships of that period and of later life.

Armstrong himself, especially before his marriage, continued as an active member. And there was Harold McAfee ("Bobbie") Robinson, of the class of 1904, for whom Machen developed a strong admiration and affection, whom he described many years later as "bright as a button," and who was one of his most intimate and faithful friends later on. Other members whom he mentioned with affection included Rockwell ("Col") Brank, "Jim" Brown, "Davy" Burrell, Warren R. ("Tank") Ward, Paul Axtell, "Bill" Munson, Theron Lee, Parke Richards, "Short" Mulock, and "Bup" Updegraaf. The last named was regarded as "the life of the club." Some years later Machen spoke of him as "one of the most genuinely funny fellows I ever knew," and freely admitted that his own "stunts," which were repeatedly called for on social occasions, had been learned from Updegraaf and other members of the Club in his student days.

Nearly forty years afterward the Rev. James B. Brown, D. D., the "Jim" Brown of student days (of whom Machen spoke in a letter of

Oct. 13, 1907, when he and Updegraaf were going to mission fields, as "an unusually fine fellow" and as a man "of perfect refinement") wrote a brief article relating memories of undergraduate days with Machen at Princeton. Recalling that he was then already known by the nickname "Das" (suggested by the German *Das Mädchen*), Brown records that he was known among the students for his extraordinary love of walking and railroad trains and hearty good humor rather than for his scholarship. "In the Benham Club," he says, "he was in his element and at his best. . . ."

> At the Benham Club fines were assessed for breaches of etiquette, and at the end of the year these fines were collected and the money sent to the Board of Foreign Missions as a contribution from the club. A poor throw or a bad catch (of bread or rolls), one cent; for using the word, "Mister," while at the club, ten cents; for talking shop, ten cents; for mentioning the name of a marriageable maiden, 25 cents; for refusing to give a stunt when called upon, 25 cents. There were many other fines listed in the Benham "Code" and Das seemed to enjoy nothing more than to be fined and see others fined. At the end of the year, he usually had a handsome sum to pay for the work of foreign missions. . . .

Brown also tells how the famous "Checker Club" began in Machen's room when a group, would gather informally for a social hour or two. "An abundance of food would be on hand—large, juicy oranges, apples, nuts, dates. Despite our presence he would be working on his thesis with his desk piled high with books and papers. With all the fun and confusion going on about him, he nevertheless seemed to be able to concentrate and would work awhile before entering into the fun with all his heart. He liked to have the others about him in those days, and enjoyed their fellowship just as he enjoyed the companionship of his students during his later years."

In addition to his devotion to strenuous walking Machen continued to make extensive trips—one as far as Philadelphia—on his bicycle and to engage in tennis matches with some regularity. As a holdover from his interests of earlier years, he also became an enthusiastic follower of college athletic events, especially football and lacrosse contests, of Princeton and Johns Hopkins from the spectator's point of view. The members of his family in Baltimore were frequently entreated to keep him abreast of the athletic developments involving Hopkins teams. On one occasion, for example, he wrote that he "would be willing to give a dollar a week if the Hopkins scores could be reported to me. But I hate to make requests for a postal any more insistent. . ." At Princeton he developed a particular fondness for the football games, and before long became as involved emotionally as any alumnus, and rather regularly made an annual trip to New Haven or Cambridge to witness the big games with Yale or Harvard. Speaking of one of the big games at Princeton in 1904, he wrote his mother:

> The game was a great show—a magnificent crowd of 25,000 people or more, and good football too. They say some Princeton men came all the way from California just to see the event. That enormous Princeton stand after the game was a great sight. The whole crowd were singing "Old Nassau" with as good spirit as though they had won the game, and were not all feeling about ten times as bad as we felt after the election. That was one of the most affecting things I ever saw. It almost made it worth while to lose the game.

Though, accordingly, Machen's gregarious instincts were being developed in various ways, he retained an intense love of solitude. Though Brown has been quoted as telling of Machen's ability to continue his studies with others about him, he was certainly no miracle man in this regard. His desire for privacy was bound up in part with his concern to feel completely free to concentrate upon his studies or his general reading.

LOVE OF LITERATURE

While his love of literature was not new, certain fresh impulses made themselves felt about this time. It was especially after the turn of the century that his father began to make notable additions to his splendid library, particularly fifteenth century Greek and Latin classics. On his occasional trips to New York young Machen spent a good deal of time browsing about in the second-hand book stores, and sometimes informed his father of the availability of books that would probably interest him.

On Dec. 7, 1903 his father wrote of the results of a visit to New York:

> I attended the book auction thoroughly and made a number of satisfactory purchases—principally of Aldines and Elzevirs. My less bulky purchases I brought home in my trunk, the others to follow by express. Among the latter is a 15th century edition—ed. princeps, of the Latin version of *Plotinus,* which Arthur called my attention to in the catalogue as something to be desired for the library. It is the work of a Florentine printer. Among my pur-

> chases, those already on exhibition, Arthur (and your mother too as to some) concede several to be gems, but I will spare you the tediousness of any description, as you will soon, I hope, have opportunity to enjoy them with us. The auction was a novel experience to me—so many years having elapsed since I last attended a book sale. Of course I had to put a restraint upon myself and resist much temptation to stray from my special line. Once or twice I did diverge a little, but not extravagantly. The collection sold was an unusually attractive one, and but for the crowded condition of our book shelves I might well enough have enlarged my list of purchaseables.

Nothing pleased Mr. Machen more than to share the treasures of his library with other true booklovers. A few weeks after this special purchase, for example, he wrote, on Jan. 23, 1904, of a visit of Professor Kirby Smith; "his much desired, long deferred and at the last only half-expected visit to me for the inspection of my lately purchased Aldines, Elzevirs, Stephenses etc:"

> He spent the whole evening in the library greatly to the delectation of Arthur and myself. It is so refreshing to see his hearty enjoyment of good classics and appreciation of every point about an editio princeps or other rarity including good bindings, original or moderately artistic. He expressed commendation of all my new treasures, and the intervals between the examinations were filled in with divers interesting comments and observations. Altogether it was an evening to dwell long and pleasurably in the memory.

Another event in the life of the Machen family, perhaps even more exciting and more significant, was the publication by Macmillan in the fall of 1903 of Mrs. Machen's volume on *The Bible in Browning,* a book which disclosed her masterful knowledge of the Bible as well as of Browning. It was a serious study which drew the conclusion that "no modern poet has manifested such intimate acquaintance with the Bible as Robert Browning." His writings, she found, "are thoroughly interpenetrated by its spirit, and in many of his poems a Scriptural quotation or allusion may be found on almost every page." Naturally enough, as the momentous day of publication drew near and afterwards, Machen's interest in and reading of Browning were greatly stimulated. Another poet who was read about this time was Sidney Lanier, coinciding more or less with Mrs. Machen's responses to the inquiries of Edwin Mims, who was preparing his biography of the great Southern poet. But Machen's interest in general literature did not depend on these particular stimuli, and was by no means confined to Browning and Lanier, any more than his mother's was. She read widely ranging over a broad field including the New Testament in Greek, English and French classics and even detective stories when her headaches did not permit anything heavier.

On his trips to New York Machen also often saw performances of classical and current plays when Mansfield and Jefferson, Maude Adams and Mrs. Fiske were leading actors. From time to time he also seized opportunities to see German and French plays, partly with a view to gaining experience in understanding these languages as they were spoken by good exponents. To him as to his mother occasional attendance upon the theatre was of a piece with the enjoyment of literature and of beautiful books and paintings.

CONSIDERING THE MINISTRY

Although Machen had become very fond of life at Princeton by the end of his first year, and evidently had determined to return, he had made no progress whatsoever in his search for certainty as to his future calling. He took a thrilling and invigorating bicycle trip through the Berkshires before attending the Northfield conference. Afterwards, having spent a few days in the White Mountains and having passed some time with his parents at Seal Harbor, he returned again to the University of Chicago, not now to be exploring an unfamiliar field like economics, but taking a course in Greek under Professor Paul Shorey, (1857-1934) one of the most brilliant classicists America has produced, who had been called to Chicago by William Rainey Harper when the institution was founded in 1892. The contact with Shorey was eminently rewarding and memorable. On July 31, 1903, Machen wrote his father:

> I am enjoying my work at the University very much more than last year. Pindar *is* hard, but as I have only one course, I find time to learn the metres and get real practice in reading in the Greek, without which the reading of Greek poetry always seems to me dull exercise. Professor Shorey seems to deserve the high estimate put upon him by Dr. Gildersleeve. Certainly, as a teacher, at any rate, he is inspiring, since his sympathetic knowledge of literature keeps pace with his philological learning. Of course, he is not Gildersleeve, but in one respect—that of method in teaching—he may even be held to surpass him.

> I have gotten so much interested in Greek, that to my regret I have not found much time for German. Indeed, my difficulty in finding opportunities for the latter study is my chief disappointment. However, I have made arrangements to make the journey to the Berlitz school twice a week.

That he was studying Greek and was interested also in increasing his knowledge of German seems to show that Machen was improving his opportunities of following in the general line of his work at Johns Hopkins and of preparing himself for more intensive work in the Seminary. And no doubt the ministry continued under serious consideration. A few weeks later, on Aug. 19th his father wrote:

> I wish I could believe I had improved the summer as well as you have. Pindar is an author I have had a great deal of respect for these many years, and in old Walney days I once or twice tried to make his acquaintance, but he forbade intimacy. The name Lanier too reminds me of a neglected opportunity. I admired him greatly, but did not in his life time recognize him as a poet whose verse the world was not going to let die.

The reference to Lanier was occasioned by the fact that Machen had received a copy of Lanier's *The Marsh Hymns* as a birthday gift from his mother, and there had followed a number of references to the reading of Lanier and other general literature. But the father went on in the same letter (on the background of certain comments which had appeared in one of the current church papers to the effect that in the preaching of the day there appeared to be a dangerous separation between the intellectual and the spiritual) to stress the opportunity awaiting the true preacher:

> The greatest opportunity the world has ever offered to the pulpit is with us now. Without the infusion of a spiritual vitality into really intellectual preaching, I do not know what is to become of our nation. For want of such strong utterance, here in New England at any rate, a most lamentable spread of infidelity is taking place. This generation has almost ceased to be Christian; it would not be surprising if the next generation were godless.

And somewhat earlier that same summer, on the occasion of the decision of Machen's cousin LeRoy Gresham to give up the practice of law in order to enroll at Richmond and to study for the ministry, Mrs. Machen spoke of her satisfaction in this development. Though his own father Thomas B. Gresham, grieved at the thought of his son's departure from Baltimore, Mrs. Machen, without making a direct plea to her son to follow his cousin's example, indicated that her own dominant mood would be one of profound joy at such a consummation. Referring to her brother's first reaction, she said:

> It distressed me to see his sorrow, and indeed, I feel it deeply myself. Only with me, the great desire of my heart has been to see my boys useful to the world and efficient in the Master's cause—so that my own comfort or pleasure seems small in comparison with this great object of my ambition.

Indicative of Machen's own contentment to allow the decision concerning the ministry to be postponed until a future day is the fact that his letters which followed these comments of his parents made no allusion whatsoever to the subject. And so the situation remained, judging by his letters, until near the close of his second year in the Seminary. In contrast to the caution and reserve of his father and mother was the initiative taken by Mr. Kirk, his pastor, seconded by his uncle Thomas, to urge him to come under the care of the Presbytery at its meeting on April 12, 1904. Appealing to the consideration that his cousin Le Roy Gresham and his second cousin, Andrew Reid Bird, (son of Mr. and Mrs. Edgeworth Bird, grandson of "Aunty" Bird, and a classmate at Hopkins) were definitely planning to take this step, his uncle begged him to come:

> It would be such a lovely thing to have you three boys to take this step together, and it would be a lovely thing to look back on in years to come. I know it would do me good, and I am sure that it would be a precious thing for your Father and Mother. The ordeal will not be a severe one, and I do hope that you will decide to come. God bless you, my dear boy.
>
> Affectionately,
> Uncle

But Machen was not to be persuaded by such considerations. Almost at once he wrote his mother:

> Uncle and Mr. Kirk have both written me very kind letters about the meeting of Presbytery and the action which Loy and Andrew are going to take. I appreciate very much their thought of me, but if anything, I believe I appreciate even more your not saying anything about it—if indeed, as you must have done, *you* have heard about the matter yourselves. I am *sure* it is better for me not to make the final decision this year—even if it costs me a

> year of work, But, as you can well imagine, this necessity of waiting is anything but an agreeable subject to me. . . .
>
> Of course I realize what an unprofitable servant I must seem to be—two years at Seminary, and still undecided whether I ought to go into the work. But at least it isn't mere trifling that leads me to shrink back, for I venture to say that it gives no one more pain than it gives me myself.
>
> I love you just the way I always did, and it is a great comfort to have you tell me that you are just the same to me . . . I write this letter to Father as much as to you—especially the part about the meeting of Presbytery.

The day following, on April 4th, his father understandingly concurred in his decision:

> Your letter to your mother, which arrived this morning, she gave me to read. I think you are right in wishing to be settled in your own mind before acting upon the important question referred to in it. Neither she nor I would wish to have your decision swayed by any persuasion of ourselves. The ministry is the noblest of callings. I think you are well fitted for it, and are qualified to do good service in this greatest of causes, if your own inclination leads you to undertake it. But the choice is for you to make, and you should be left perfectly free in the matter; not depriving yourself, however, of the aid of judicious and sympathetic counsel from any whom you may think qualified to speak and may desire so to consult upon points involved in the decision.

And two days later his mother wrote with equal sympathy and tenderness:

> About your coming before Presbytery, I did not speak of it because I knew you would have to decide for yourself. And you must not worry about taking time for the decision. You are not the first to whom it has been a struggle. Indeed the choice of a life-work is hard for any man even if he is not contemplating a sacred calling.
>
> You may always rest assured that you will have my sympathy and support whatever you do. You have to work out your own individuality but I am always here with my love and sympathy when you need me.

A MOMENTOUS CONFERENCE

About this very time Dr. Patton held a momentous conference with Machen, which, however, was not even mentioned in his letters home.

Though ordinarily far from reticent especially so far as his parents were concerned, he evidently kept silent because the development would have suggested self-congratulation and commitment on his own part. It was Patton himself who told of it on one of his frequent brief visits in the Machen home, and it was Mr. Machen who preserved the memory of it. On April 19, 1904 he wrote:

> We greatly enjoyed the visit Dr. Patton has just given us. Although his stay was no less brief than on other occasions we somehow had him more to ourselves, and the scraps of conversation were delightful.
>
> He told me of the proposition he had made to you to direct your mind towards a future Seminary professorship of New Testament Greek and cognate subjects, which he evidently regards as a great field and of large promise of distinction and usefulness. It is exceedingly gratifying to know that so competent a judge both of character and scholarly attainments looks upon you as apparently qualified to occupy such a position after the requisite special preparation. If the idea of such an *alternative* to the more beaten, but not less noble and inspiring work of a pastoral preacher of the Gospel, is capable of relieving your mind of the burden of deciding just now what the course of your life's work should be and so giving you a restful period, I am glad of the fact that Dr. Patton has made the suggestion. I suppose it could only be beneficial to you, no matter what your ultimate choice may be, to direct your studies somewhat especially in this direction during the coming last year of your Seminary course. If so, there will be no loss of time incurred should you ultimately, in view of the various circumstances surrounding the question, determine not to devote yourself to a professional line of work. Certainly, I gather that nothing in the suggestion held out is to have the effect of limiting your freedom of final choice in any degree. Altogether Dr. P. is most considerate as well as kind.

There is no more revealing letter from this period because of its unique disclosure of the general course of events. But it is even more illuminating in pointing up the positive, yet discerning and sympathetic, manner in which Dr. Patton was seeking to guide Machen into a channel of study and labor that demanded the minimum of commitment, so far as the ministry was concerned, and yet was calculated to provide the maximum assurance that he would enter upon distinctly Christian work. And once again Machen's delightful reserve is shown in that in his following letter home the only account he took of the contents of his father's letter was to remark that "Dr. Patton was as enthusiastic about his visit to Baltimore as you were." Finally, this letter also underscores the unfailingly sympathetic understanding with which his father and mother took account of his scruples and disquietude as well as their respect for the independence of his judgment.

That Machen had become particularly interested in the field of the New Testament within the course of his second year at the Seminary is borne out by the consideration that he won the first Middler Prize in New Testament Exegesis for 1903-04. The prize of $100.00 was awarded for the best paper on the exegesis of John 1:1-18. The work was carried on between February 1st and April 1st, and was referred to in his letters home only as some "special work" that he was engaged upon. After the award was announced, he referred to his work in a rather belittling fashion, but it may well have served to intensify his interest in New Testament studies and to confirm the high opinion which Professor Armstrong and other members of the Faculty were forming of his scholarly ability and promise.

THE FINAL YEAR

The next significant step was his visit to Germany during the summer of 1904 principally for the purpose of improving upon his command of the German language. At the close of term his plans for the summer were still up in the air, and he spoke vaguely of the hope that he might find an opportunity of teaching Greek or Latin. Exactly when the decision was reached to spend several weeks in Germany is not certain, but it is known that, after some time at the Berlitz School in Baltimore he sailed for Bremen on the steamer *Cassel,* arriving about June 21st.

Armed with letters of introduction and reference, including one from Dr. Gildersleeve, he next sought out an area where he could expect to make the greatest progress in learning German. Berlin was left behind after a few days as being hopeless from that point of view. Other contacts were with persons in Hildesheim, Göttingen and Sondershausen, and he soon decided on the last of these. Having found Berlin not as good a place to learn German as the steamer, he swung over, as he said, to the opposite extreme to try a town "where they may not speak good German, but where they *will* speak German, and, I hope German only." Sondershausen was the capitol of the tiny state of Schwarzburg-Sondershausen in Thüringen, situated between Brunswick and Erfurt, and claiming then about 7,000 inhabitants.

Later he moved to Göttingen, and enjoyed his introduction to certain aspects of life at the University where he was later to spend a term. His contact with the students became sufficiently intimate to lead to an invitation to attend a duel between members of student societies. The scars on the faces of the alumni generally he described as making them "picturesque rather than handsome" and his general reaction was expressed in the sentences, "Altogether the custom seems to me to give the maximum of discomfort with the minimum of fun. Indeed, I have come to the conclusion that the two institutions which Germany most needs are (1) The Sabbath; and (2) American football, with the idea of real sport which it brings with it." As the result of the use of Gildersleeve's letter a number of contacts with professors and students of philology developed, and these served to advance his knowledge of German as well as to afford a taste of German university life.

After lectures were concluded at Göttingen, he took a journey by bicycle of 450 miles to Hildesheim, with stops at Eisenach to see the Wartburg and at Cassel to see the picture gallery. At Hildesheim he met "Bobby" Robinson who had just arrived in Germany for his fellowship year, and these warm friends spent a number of days together, at first for a week in a private home in Braunschweig to concentrate on German and then sightseeing in Magdeburg and Leipzig. While Robinson stayed on in Leipzig, Machen again undertook travels principally by bicycle to Dresden, Mainz, Wiesbaden, Frankfurt and finally down the Rhine. He sailed from Antwerp on September 3 on the Red Star liner S. S. *Finland,* convinced that he had spent one of the most enjoyable summers of his life. No doubt he had advanced his main purpose of making real progress in understanding and expressing himself in German, though he was wont to minimize his actual attainments.

His final year at the Seminary began with considerable zest and with the determination to concentrate upon the work there rather than to have his attention diverted to any great extent by studies at the University. His concentration upon Greek and German during the preceeding summers had added significantly to his equipment to do scholarly work. From the academic point of view the most significant development was his occupation in such time as was available with the preparation of a thesis, "A Critical Discussion of the New Testament Account of the Virgin Birth of Jesus," which had been announced as the subject for the fellowship competition in the New Testament. It is thus interesting that the subject of the Virgin Birth of Christ which was to fascinate him throughout his career, and which resulted in the production of his *opus magnum,* was not of his own choosing. That he found the topic assigned a congenial one cannot, on the other hand, be doubted, if one considers how moved he was in Dresden by the sight of the Sistine Madonna and Correggio's Holy Night. His success in this undertaking was such that he not only was awarded the New Testament fellowship but also the rare, in not unparalleled, distinction of having his thesis published in succeeding issues of the *Princeton Theological Review* in Oct. 1905 and Jan. 1906.

One of the principal benefits of the fellowship award was that it strongly affected his plans for the following year. On March 26, 1905 he was still at sea as to his future and wrote of his hope of being able to discuss it with his parents on a projected visit home early in April. Plans for the summer, he wrote, "do not exist at present—much to my sorrow. I wish that I could have gotten into some business or profession which I could be sure of not doing wrong to enter." For a time he thought of returning to Princeton in the fall, but evidently the award of the fellowship encouraged him to undertake the congenial task of returning to Germany and to carry forward his specialization in the New Testament field.

The die was cast when the commencement season arrived, and he was in a somewhat gloomy state of mind as he contemplated the apparent end of his joyous student days there:

> The fellows are in my room now on the last Sunday night, smoking the cigars and eating the oranges which it has been the greatest delight I ever had to provide whenever possible. My idea of delight is a Princeton room full of fellows smoking. When I think what a wonderful aid tobacco is to friendship and Christian patience I have sometimes regretted that I never began to smoke. To think that in a few days old 39 will be empty and the old 39 crowd scattered to the four winds almost makes me wonder whether life is worth living.

His sadness at his departure from his friends at Princeton could not be his dominant mood for long. Memories of the successful outcome of his studies and of friendships that gave promise of enduring no doubt thronged him. Moreover, he was kept too busy in the ensuing weeks to permit much time for melancholy. His thesis had to be prepared for publication in the *Review*. There was the inevitable packing of his books and the clearing of his room in Alexander Hall. Then came the opportunity of several happy days with his family in Baltimore before his parents left for Seal Harbor. He was reading German novels assiduously and making his final preparations for his departure for Europe.

That he looked forward with no little eagerness to the enjoyment of his fellowship year abroad is unquestionable. The award served to justify in his mind, as in the mind of others concerned, his expenditure of a further year in study. And meanwhile he could feel relieved of the necessity of forcing himself to decide for or against the ministry at the conclusion of the regular course. The decision postponed so often was apparently no nearer than when he had entered the Seminary nearly three years before. Accompanying his feeling of relief, however, there remained a profound sense of the inevitability of having to answer sooner or later a question to which it seemed presumptuous to say "yes" but was perhaps base disloyalty and desertion of duty to say "no."

5

NEW HORIZONS IN EUROPE

As Machen was about to sail for Europe the third time, he was aware that much more was at stake than in his previous journeys. He could indeed look forward to delightful opportunities of travel, and to gaining more solid pleasures from seizing them than before because of his past experience. There would moreover be substantial benefits accruing from his participation in the academic life of German universities of which he had enjoyed an appetizing morsel the preceding year. But now he had completed a course of study designed to prepare men for the ministry, he was about to enter his twenty-fifth year, and it was devoutly hoped, both by his loved ones who would remain behind and by esteemed men to whom he was greatly indebted, that the year abroad would serve to remove every obstacle which might prevent his early entrance upon a fruitful ministry of teaching the New Testament. He himself anticipated great profit from his studies with the advantages of "a fresh atmosphere, time to read and incentive to do so, and *no* exams." Without question he prayed fervently that he might once for all pass through the mists that had enveloped him into a sea that would be aglow with light as far as eye could see. He could not know that there lay ahead storms more tempestuous than any he had ever experienced and that he would not reach firm ground until many years later, and yet that he would be emboldened to undertake his life's work at the end of the year.

Within a few days of his departure from Baltimore he received fresh assurance of the profound sympathy and support of those whose affection was his most constant source of comfort and strength. His mother's farewell letter was a brief note of affectionate parting which concluded as follows:

> This is only to bid you "God speed." My prayers and loving thoughts go with you every step of your way. Do not forget to love your mother and remember that there is one heart on this side the Atlantic that can never fail you or misunderstand you. God be with you my dear boy and good-bye from
>
> Your own faithful Mother
>
> M.G.M.

His father's letter written on the same day, though also replete with tender regard, reflected at some length upon his hopes regarding his son:

My thoughts will follow you on your voyage and afterwards. Earnest prayers for your welfare, sure progress and happiness will go up night and morning during your absence, and I have faith to believe will be fulfilled. I depend upon you, as upon Arthur and Tom, to perform that good work in the world which will make it worth while for me to have lived in my own generation. I have labored in a way, but as I look back at the top of seventy years and more I am saddened by the reflection that I have accomplished so little for mankind, have fallen so short of the service I owe as a follower of Christ. A father may hope that his sons will more than fill his place, and God has so blessed me in this respect, as in many others, that I have just ground to believe that notwithstanding my personal short-comings I will not have lived in vain when I leave *my* children here.

I shall be glad to hear from you constantly and kept informed of everything which interests you. It will all greatly interest me. I feel confident you are in the right path and will come back strengthened and prepared to perform a notable work in the world.

Machen's own letter of farewell, written July 13, 1905, and dispatched by pilot from Cape Charles whence he sailed on the steamer *Cassel* was addressed to his mother and was to bring tears to her eyes as she read his loving words:

Here I am at last, with my back turned to dear old Baltimore. When I return the old town will be unrecognizable—no more burnt district, everything up to date. But my own little corner at 217 will be just the same—I certainly hope so, for, in essentials, it could not be improved. Where else could be found a father and mother capable of writing two such letters as those which bade me farewell?

Nothing else could have so lightened my heart as the assurance that you are all fairly well, and cheered with the prospect of a happy summer at Seal Harbor. Despite it all, I can hardly keep from feeling unreasoningly selfish in leaving you all behind again. Of course, I will know with what good will and love, you and Father have been willing to send me off to partake of so much more than my share of the joys of life. Still, three trips to Europe does seem like dissipation for a fellow of 24, when so many must spend a lifetime in hopeless longing. The only cure would be for me to learn something, and I am going to try. But probably the result will by no means come up to what could reasonably be expected....

P.S. Don't talk about forgetting to love Mother. I am just as likely to forget to breathe.

SUMMER TRAVELS

Although our interest in this year abroad lies chiefly in Machen's experiences as a student at Marburg and Göttingen, there were other happenings falling especially in the long interval between his arrival at Bremen on July 24th and his enrollment at Marburg early in October which add substantially to our knowledge of the more general aspects of his life. The temptation to quote at length from his descriptions of earlier travels has been largely resisted in the foregoing chapters, but some of his letters from the present period are so fascinating that fairly liberal quotation seems mandatory if their contribution to one's understanding of his life is to come to its rights.

Passing over his descriptions of Hamburg and Lübeck, we speed southward with him as he rode his bicycle first to Soltau, on a second day to Brunswick where he had spent a week the previous year, and on to Goslar at the foot of the Harz Mountains.

> Thus the little city adds beauty of situation to its other charms, the view from Steinberg, a neighboring height, being entrancing. I enjoyed that view at sunset on Friday night, and felt more than repaid for the hot walk. You overlook the old town with its towers, spires and queer-shaped roofs and have as a background the dark, soft-colored pine woods of the mountains.
>
> The lion of Goslar itself is the Kaiserhaus, a large palace, dating from a very ancient time; but now restored, so that its age is no longer very apparent. On the whole, I found other things in Goslar more interesting—especially the peculiarly quaint and ancient appearance of the town. Such a richness in old private houses is scarcely offered even by Hildesheim or Brunswick, though Hildesheim can certainly point to more striking single specimens....

Leaving Goslar, in a single day he rode some seventy miles over the Harz to Mühlhausen to find himself on August 6th again in the haunts of the previous year—

> the pretty hills and dales of Thüringen. This country between the Harz and the Thüringerwald, surpasses for quiet loveliness almost anything I have ever seen. Somehow the church spires seem to take on more picturesque forms than elsewhere, the villages to nestle more cosily in the valleys and on the hillsides, the valleys to be more beautifully rounded, the colors of the richly cultivated fields to be more harmoniously blended. It is a country from which angles seem to have been eliminated, until nature and art unite in one universal curve.

Next followed the delights of Nürnberg and Rothenburg in Bavaria, though mention should be made of his exhilaration with the ride over the Thüringerwald and his pleasure in taking in the old fortress at Coburg because of its having lodged Luther at the time of the formulation of the Augsburg Confession in 1530. In arriving at Nürnberg he had completed a bicycle trip of some 375 miles from Hamburg. Writing from Rothenburg on August 13th, he announces:

> We have met Nuremberg and it is ours. And it is certainly worth capturing. On the whole I am afraid my cities of North Germany—Hildesheim, Brunswick, and Goslar—must give the palm to a place which everybody goes to see. Hildesheim has perhaps more picturesque houses, but she lacks the ancient walls, which with their towers and battlements lend to Nuremberg so much of her charm. But one thing I can affirm—those North German cities are no mere reprints of Nuremberg . . . The characteristic old house in Hildesheim and Brunswick and Goslar is the house with the wooden beams and wood carving, with the upper stories projecting far beyond the lower end—and this incomparably picturesque type is only scantily represented in Nuremberg. On the other hand, the way the tall, irregularly placed buildings in Nuremberg pile themselves up until they are surmounted by the wall-towers and by the castle is also peculiar. On the whole, I think the most repaying thing that one can do in Nuremberg is to walk all around the walls on the outside and over the various bridges . . . .
>
> But within fifty miles of Nuremberg, there is something yet more curious, which the public only within the last few years has discovered to be one of the most remarkable things in the world. I refer to Rothenburg, a town of former importance, which the march of modern progress has left behind with a population of 8,000, living in the same old houses, on top of the same old hill and within the same old walls. Is it my duty to attempt a de-

scription of Rothenburg? I hope not... there is nothing left but for you to come see Rothenburg for yourself.

The little river Tauber, in its course northwestwards to the Main, has hereabouts cut for itself a deep channel, which to you and Mother might perhaps be described as a mild form of canyon, but with green though steep sides. On one side of the stream, along the high crest of the hill thus formed, stretches the little town, entirely enclosed in its walls. The walls of Rothenburg differ from the walls of (for example) Nuremberg in that they still form really the limit of the city. In Nuremberg you have a set of walls stretching aimlessly about somewhere in the centre of a good-sized modern city, and enclosing a portion of the modern town something like the 'City' in London. But in Rothenburg it is different. On the side next the stream, you find no houses at all outside the wall until you get to the bottom of the valley; on the other side, the town has burst its ancient bounds only in a few places. Rothenburg is still crowded together within its walls, and is therefore a walled town in a far more visible way than anything I have seen before.

Of course the details are not so fine as they are in Nuremberg; there are by no means so many or so beautiful examples of ancient city residences and business houses. Everything is on a much more modest scale. But what Rothenburg lacks in magnificence of the individual buildings, it makes up in the harmony of the whole. After all, people have a right to live and to attain wealth and comfort. So we cannot blame the people of Nuremberg because here and there they have sacrificed sentiment and historical interest to the demands of modern life—it is only remarkable how little this sacrifice has been made in the case of a town of such remarkable commercial importance. Rothenburg has no commercial importance—hence its uniqueness. Hence there are no trolley cars on the streets, hence the narrow and crooked lanes still prove adequate to the traffic; hence there are no large modern buildings to put to shame the little old red-roofed houses, which huddle together as if for common protection, as if afraid to stand alone. The whole thing is cut out of one piece. There is practically nothing in the appearance of the place to jolt us about from one century to another. We can still live undisturbed for a little while in the time of the great burgomaster Topler of 1400. (If we lived there too long, we should be only too glad to get back to 1905, for poor old Topler had a hard enough time of it himself and met his end finally in the dungeon under the Rathaus).

It must not be thought, however, that the town is entirely composed of mean or ordinary houses. On the contrary, the houses in the neighborhood of the Market Place are, some of them, quite large and handsome, and the Rathaus really attains to magnificence. The main Church is also lofty and imposing, and forms the centre in any view of the town. Inside are to be found some fine works of art—stained glass and wood carving.

Both yesterday and today I walked in the evening across the river and up to the top of the hills on the opposite side. The view from there is not to be described and hardly to be believed, as existing A.D. 1905. Nor is it quaint and curious merely; it is also of the most entrancing beauty. Before you are the broad fields sloping down until they fall off suddenly into the abyss of the Tauber valley; beyond--the middle ages. The walls visible on both sides of the town, the towers, the gables, the red roofs piled up on the other until they culminate in the great commanding form of the church, and the whole bathed in the light of the sinking sun and set off against the broad rolling fields and the distant wooded ridges—it is all too wonderful to be true. It reminds me of the fine illustrations of Howard Pyle—but for me to be seeing the reality, that seems impossible.

A little walking on top of the hills discloses the greatest variety of loveliness—different aspects of the town and different glimpses down into the valley. The latter, with its perfect picture of peace—the quiet little stream, the picturesque farm houses, the distant village steeple—forms a delightful contrast to towers and battlements above. Well, it's a lovely spot—that is about all I can hope you will get out of these vain words and phrases.

IN THE EASTERN ALPS

After several days in these fascinating cities, he proceeded in a southwesterly direction by way of Nördlingen to Ulm on the Danube and its great church, and then on along the foot of the Alps as far as Innsbruck, Austria, having now completely traversed Germany from north to south, about 630 miles by bicycle. Innsbruck became the starting point for several days of delightful mountain climbing, in which accompanied by an expert guide he made the ascent of the *Wilder Turm, Wildes Hinterbergl, Ferner Kogel* and other peaks. September had come on when he left Innsbruck and proceeded on his wheel directly south over the Brenner Pass, taking only a little more than a day to make the more than a hundred miles to Lienz in the Tyrol. Having bought and packed a Rücksack at the Lienz he proceeded, first on his wheel, and later on foot, to the village of Kals which lay at the foot of the Grossglockner. At Kals, he relates,

> I procured as guide a man by the name of Johann Kerer, who it seems is quite famous. He has been twice to the Caucasus and once to the Himalayas, and knows the Alps from end to end, having just this summer been in Zermatt and in the Oberland. Altogether, I was very lucky, not only to get hold of a first-class guide but also because of what was to be learned from conversing with a man whose activities as mountain guide have carried him into so many different countries...
>
> On Wednesday afternoon we ascended from Kals to the Stüdhütte (a hut on the Grossglockner at a height of about 9,330 ft.), the most lofty place I ever spent a night. On the way we passed through the Rödnitz Valley, a picture of which I am sending you today on a postal card. In the course of the afternoon, the clouds kept gathering more and more, and during the night it rained brick-bats, which caused my heart to sink into my boots. After two glorious days in the valleys, was bad weather to set in the minute I got up on the heights? In the morning, the question was very soon settled in the negative, for when we started out about four o'clock with the lantern, the stars were shining with that peculiar brilliancy which you remember from clear nights at the Madison Hut. The ordinary way up the Grossglockner leads past the Erzherzog Johann Hut, which the enterprise of the Austrian Alpine Club maintains as a little hotel at the height of 11,500 ft. From there you go over steep snow and rocks to the top of the Kleinglockner, and from there over a narrow ridge ... to the summit of the Grossglockner (about 12,600 ft), the highest peak of the group and one of the highest of the Eastern Alps. The ascent is made perfectly easy by wire ropes, which are stretched in all places which otherwise might to the unpractised be a little bit ticklish—notably on the ridge between the lower and higher peak. We reached the top at about 7 A.M., and I spent a half hour or so in enjoying the wonderful view which stretches as far as the great Ortler Group to the southwest. When the air is more perfectly clear, you can see the Adriatic Sea. Nor is it the great extent alone which makes the view from the Glockner so particularly grand; for few things could be finer than the view over the almost boundless snow-fields and glaciers to the

pointed Wiessbachhorn, at the other end of the group. Such things cannot be described and I shall not attempt the impossible.

Returning to the upper hut, I partook of some solid food and instead of returning directly to Kals, decided to take a 2½ days' trip planned by the guide. For this plan, I am profoundly grateful to him, for I do not see how in any other way I could have obtained such a variety of beauty and grandeur. The same scene was never thrown on the screen a second time, but instead a continual succession. One minute, the vast circle of snow and rock to be seen from the summit; the next minute, the no less overpowering grandeur of the middle altitudes. Perhaps from the strictly aesthetic point of view, the latter scenes are the finer, for from the middle heights, perhaps more than anywhere else do you fully appreciate the enormous bulk of the mountains. And then from the peaks, there is so *much* to be seen, that the individuality of each view can hardly impress itself on the mind. The picture lacks the artistic unity of, for example, that view of the Glockner from the Rödnitz Valley. But I am not an artist, and to me the sense of boundless height and freedom which one can obtain only on such mountains as the Glockner or Monte Rosa can never be replaced by anything else. However, one kind of view rivals the view from the top—namely, the view of a fine mountain, *which you have already ascended.* At any rate, whatever kind of mountain view is the finest—you can be sure that it was represented on our three days' route. The trip amounted, in brief, to ascending the Glockner and then going entirely around it. I thus was enabled to enjoy the principal beauties of the four chief valleys that cut into the Glockner group; the valleys of Kals and Heiligenblut on the south, and Ferleiten and Moserboden on the north. Those beauties and ten thousand others!

The letter continues for seven more closely-written pages in equally gripping fashion, telling of the thrills of the descent, the ascent of the Wiessbachhorn (11,900 ft.) and his return to Lienz to spend Sunday. Summing up the benefits of his mountain climbing he declared that physically he felt in much better shape than at the beginning of the summer. His German had not suffered because he had not seen a single English or American tourist on the mountain trips. His admiration of the clean quarters and excellent provisions of the huts maintained by the German and Austrian Clubs knew no bounds, but he felt that these clubs suffered in comparison with the Swiss because of their tendency to introduce an artificial element by putting up wire ropes and building paths.

Nor was Machen quite content to call it a day so far as his first-hand contacts with the Eastern Alps were concerned, for with the Dolomites so near at hand, he could not resist coming to grips with a few samples of that strange and bizarre region, which impressed him as "savage" and yet possessed of a beauty of a peculiarly fascinating kind. But after climbing the Grosse and the Kleine Zinne, the time was running out, and he wanted to see Vienna, Budapest and Salzburg before returning to Germany and settling at one of the universities for the winter term. Vienna offered many attractive features: the general beauty of the city itself with its magnificent modern buildings in the midst of gardens, the museums, and the theatres. Budapest was found to be more grandly situated along the banks of the Danube, but its life and language more exotic than Vienna's, and his stay there was rather brief, though long enough to arouse his sympathy with the liberty-seeking Hungarians. After a brief, though satisfying visit to Salzburg and vicinity, he returned to Munich, now again on his wheel after some discouraging experiences with the crowded and crawling trains of that area. October had now come, and it was time to hurry on to Marburg. He looked back upon the fascinating experiences of the summer with delight and gratitude, but duty was now calling him to devote his energies largely to academic labors.

AT MARBURG UNIVERSITY

The decision to spend the winter term at Marburg had been reached in Vienna on the basis of published announcements of the courses to be offered in the several universities and of the professors who would be lecturing at that time. The announcement concerning Marburg indicated that Adolph Jülicher, the principal attraction, was to offer several courses, and besides Johannes Weiss and two younger men were to conduct work in the New Testament, thus assuring him of ample and varied instruction in his field. Jülicher, who had gained fame as a brilliant scholar and teacher, was known most widely for his *Introduction to the New Testament* and *The Parables of Jesus.* Although Weiss had at 42 written a number of important books he had not yet come into the prominence that he was to achieve in the nine years that remained before his untimely death in 1914.

Marburg is situated on the Lahn River in Hesse-Nassau, a province of Prussia. It is an old town, and the university, its principal claim to distinction, was founded in 1527. At the turn of the century its population was about 20,000, about half the size of Göttingen, but Machen found it "primitive and village like." It had its charm, however, as its designation "the pearl of Hesse" discloses, and from the first the town and its surroundings captured Machen's admiration. "All around," he wrote, "are high wooded hills (upon one of which towers the ancient palace), and the old part of the town is built actually upon the slope, and from a distance as well as from near at hand presents a highly picturesque appearance, with its irregular houses. The most beautiful thing in Marburg is the Elisabethkirche—not a very large church, but of a kind to impress you more and more . . . The style is Gothic; but exceedingly massive and simple, and entirely unlike the Gothic, for example, of the French churches I have seen. Thus the Elisabethkirche seems like anything but a reduced copy of the great cathedrals."

Acting on the friendly advice offered by Professor Weiss, he was able rather soon to fulfill his desire of coming into intimate contact with German-speaking families in town, and arranged to take his meals with Frau Prof. Link, the widow of a theological professor, and to lodge with Frau Kuemmel. Both he found to be jolly, sociable people, and he became much attached to them and the members of their households, though for a time a great strain was put upon him by the fact that the young children of a missionary's family who had rooms above his frequently were so noisy that he was distracted from his efforts to study.

During the first months in Marburg Machen felt rather lonely and perhaps even homesick for at first he found it difficult to cultivate friendships among the students. However cordial Frau Prof. Link and Frau Kuemmel might be, they could not satisfy his craving for the kind of fellowship that had warmed his heart at Princeton and that he had left behind so reluctantly. Even his first letter, written before the lectures got under way, was so "blue" that his mother wrote of her "sympathy and pain" at receiving it. Reflecting on this he wrote his father that "Mother must not take my fits of blue too seriously—either that or I must try to keep my letters from reflecting so clearly the feelings of the moment," and proceeded to dwell on the brighter side of things. But his mother countered with the plea: "You must never veil your mood in writing to us for fear of distressing me. I should never know a comfortable moment if I thought you would hide anything disagreeable; for I should always be trying to read between the lines. So pour out every phase of your life, knowing that I shall be eager to hear all."

How he missed also the exhilaration of the football games that had given him so much pleasure at Princeton! In urgently requesting that scores be relayed to him, he indicates that they at least might make slight compensation for the lost opportunity of witnessing the games:

> When I see a vacant field on one of these autumn days, my mind is filled with wonder at this benighted people which does not seem to hear the voice of nature when she commands every human being to play football or watch it being played. I have a positive longing to see a football game, and not being able to see one, the next best thing is scores.

LETTERS FROM HOME

Some scores were sent in response to this moving entreaty. But unquestionably the greatest cheer came in the frequent letters that he received from the members of his family. The October number of *The Princeton Theological Review* with the first installment of his article on the Virgin Birth of Christ had appeared and congratulations were the order of the day. Most amusing of these was the evaluation of Prof. H. E. Greene, professor of collegiate English at Johns Hopkins, as reported by his brother Arthur:

> The other day, I saw Herbert Eveleth Greene at the University Club. Fortunately Tom had warned me that he had shaved off his whiskers, for otherwise I never should have known him. He at once broached the subject of your article which he had read with great interest. "There," said he, "is a scholar! And I know, for I have made a special study of the same topic. It is fine work, fine work! If he keeps that up, in ten years he will be heard from. But," said he, continuing, with a grieved expression, "e'en the great orb of day is flecked with wandering isles of night." Here his eyes watered, and I thought he was going to weep and make a scene in the club-house. But he recovered himself and proceeded. "Alas, he has used the expression, a kind of a." Horror-struck at the thought, I could scarcely speak. He continued: "And he has written 'proven'—a scotticism. A pity 'tis that these —the *only* two faults in the article—should give occasion to the unbeliever to scoff. When you get the opportunity, remind him of my instruction upon these two points." I said I would mention them in my next letter. "On no account should you do so," he replied, "for that would be giving my criticisms too much prominence. But," he continued dreamily, "without these blemishes, the article would be as faultless as one of Andrea del Sarto's

paintings." I have disobeyed his injunction, and give you a report of the conversation.

In all seriousness, however, I am deriving real profit from what you have written. The style is clear, and the reasoning sound; and the whole argument is as safe and sane as Parker's Democracy.

Machen's father wrote exceptionally long letters relating to his business and pleasure, which are reported at some length because of their unusual testimony to his life as a lawyer and book-lover. As well they display his talent as a writer, which is the more noteworthy if one keeps in view the fact that he was in his seventy-ninth year. Although his father's letters through the years were marked by almost total silence with regard to business affairs, he now responded at some length to his son's request for news of this sort. In a letter begun on Nov. 26, 1905 and concluded the next day late at night, he introduces an account of legal work in which he was associated with his eldest son following Baltimore's disastrous fire of February, 1904:

> He and I latterly have been very much occupied by the Patterson Dock cases, in which we have been compelled to make the unequal fight against the City, whose strength is tyrannously used against property-owners who do not knuckle under to the dictates of the Burnt District Commission...
>
> Nov. 27... It now wants less than 10 minutes of midnight, and I have been hard at work all the evening compiling a lot of bills of exceptions, the necessary foundation for an appeal to the Supreme Court of the United States from an unsatisfactory decision in one of the Paterson Dock condemnation cases. And there is more of such work to follow.
>
> The Mayor has thought proper to send me a note suggesting, or rather inviting a visit "to talk over" the matter of the controversy between our clients and the City. I have not much hope of anything coming of it, so delusive—not to say treacherous, have been all proper colloquies with City-officers, looking ostensibly to a fair adjustment. However, I thought it my duty to accept the tender of the olive branch, and called in response, at the Mayor's office, but being occupied at the time in other official business, he made an appointment for an interview next Wednesday morning...

A later letter told of gratifying success in this litigation.

In the Patterson Dock fighting, we have come out on top. In vain did the newspaper scribblers in the service of the Burnt District Commission vituperate and abuse such persons as "Machen and Machen" who presumed to stand up for the rights of their clients against the artificially swollen tide of Public Opinion—vainly did weak and biased juries give verdicts for less than the worth of the properties condemned—vainly did judges, unconsciously swayed by the popular current, make rulings on points of law against us, we pursued the even tenor of our way, and availed of the right the Law gave us to appeal to the Supreme Court of the United States. Finally, the city authorities have been convinced of the expediency of settling with us upon the reasonable basis which was all we ever insisted upon . . . My judgment was vindicated, when the last jury trial was had. It then distinctly appeared that we were determined and able to take every case to the United States Supreme Court with a *possibility* of a decision holding the whole condemnation scheme void as far as we were concerned, and a strong *probability* of at least getting new jury trials, with more beneficial rulings upon questions of evidence. Then we were assailed publicly and privately with the cry, what, will you, by your appeals, put an obstruction in the way of a great public improvement until the gamut of judicial controversy has been run through? For my part I bore all this talk with great serenity. My clients were entitled to fair and adequate compensation and until they received it I was not going to abandon any lawful resource. The City authorities, not I, had insisted on the regular course of the law, and by the law must abide, unless a reasonable and fair amicable settlement were made. Such a settlement has been agreed upon. I demanded the same sum which, in the way of compromise, I had offered to take in October (i.e., after the rejection of my proposal of arbitration and before the expenses of any jury trials had been incurred)—*plus* those expenses. I named a round sum upon this basis; and this the controlling City authorities (to the disgust of the Burnt District Commission, who were incensed with us for our presumptuous opposition, and showed all along a strong disposition to crush us if they could) have accepted. The formal agreement is to be signed in the course of a few days, and before a fortnight is over the chancery proceedings requisite to convey title will have been completed, the money paid and the whole affair become an old and nearly forgotten story. I should have thought this a tedious and uselessly wearisome tale for the telling in a letter, but for the interest you have expressed.

The father no doubt took greater delight in recounting, in his letter of Dec. 20, 1905, the pleasures afforded by a memorable dinner:

Last evening was signalized by the meeting at our house of the club of book lovers named by Dr. Osler—taking up a sort of suggestion of mine—"The Ship of Fools." I gave them (with the valuable directing aid of your mother) a very good dinner topped out with some of my old Madeira, which all seemed to enjoy...

A family council, composed of your mother, Arthur and myself held a day or two before *the* day, determined that something in the way of originality in the dinner-cards must be devised. I invited help from the other two, but none seemed to be forthcoming; the time—three days only—afforded little space for cogitation or research; and I was compelled, like the driver of the classic stalled ox-wagon, to put my own shoulder to the wheel as vigorously as I might. Mr. Buckler—at that first dinner of his—had felicitously made it a Charles Lamb affair—a roast pig for piece de resistance and apt sentences from Elia adapted severally to the guests and written upon pieces of antique paper. I felt so imperfectly acquainted with the peculiarities and idiosyncracies of most of my fellow members that I despaired of finding appropriate individual mottoes suitable for the occasion. Happily, in this strait it occured to me to look for a motto fitting the club *collectively* as passengers in the Ship of Fools. This plan had the advantage of putting us all together in the category of fools; whereas it would have been rather a delicate matter for me, the host of the evening, to assume to fit a special cap to the head of each guest. I bethought me of the great storehouse of quaint conceits—Burton's *Anatomy*. In a few moment's I lighted in the first book upon the passage, a copy of which I enclose, which seems to me to describe aptly enough our assembly—typified in the curious cuts in the Brant-Locker edition of the *Multifera Nouvis* printed by J. Bergman de Olpe in 1497, my copy of which you have seen. I had this handsomely engrossed (though not in the more antique style I should have aimed to have effected if there had been more time) upon pieces of parchment; with names of the eleven diners inscribed respectively at the bottom.

As soon as we could dispatch the dinner, which included in the courses terrapins, capon and canvas back ducks and could not be slighted *too much*, we adjourned to the library upstairs, where, with the accompaniment of cigars etc., the inspection of the choicer books, incunabula, Aldines, Elzevirs, Stephenses, Baskervilles, etc. proceeded. Altogether we had a very fine time—at any rate, Arthur and I thought so. Kirby Smith has invited us all to meet at his house on the day in January which upon consultation with our Washington friends seemed to be practically available—I believe it is the 17th, and as it is announced that Dr. Osler is on the ocean now in expectation of spending three or four weeks in Baltimore, it is expected to receive him also. This is a long rigamarole story, isn't it? But you see, in order to be consistently one of the crew of the Stultifera, I am bound to afford a specimen of my folly.

STUDENT LIFE

The reception of such letters, and of many others which, though perhaps not as amusing or informative as the above, were replete with affection, went a long way in cheering him up those first months in Marburg. After about two months, however, an entirely new face was put on his life as a student when the barrier of the reserve of the students was broken through and he became associated with one of the student clubs, the *Franconia* Verbindung. Although not invited to become a full-fledged member, he was given the status of *Hospitant* or guest, and as such not only saw German student life at close range but made several acquaintances. This new happy change in his life in Marburg was reported at some length in a letter of Dec. 12, 1905:

> It has recently occurred to me that if I am to write a letter which shall stand even the slightest chance of arriving in time to be really a Christmas message, I must be at it at once. Although the 25th is still some time off, yet my thoughts have long ago begun to turn *specially* towards home, when I reflect that the family is soon to celebrate the first Christmas at which I am not one of the circle. Although I am not to be present in person, yet I hope this poor little line will at least accomplish the purpose of letting you know that my thoughts are up in the library, enjoying the presents, and the love which gives them their real meaning and which I am as sure of this year as though I were at home. The assurance of the continued affection of you all deprives the foreign Christmas of any dolefulness or loneliness which it might otherwise well possess. I hope that you feel as sure of my love, as I do of yours—if you do not this letter has not accomplished its purpose.

There has been a big change for the better in my circumstances at Marburg, for I have been accepted for the rest of the year as "Hospitant" by the Verbindung Franconia. I find I made a mistake in supposing I was "Conkneipant," which involves the right to wear the colors and is a closer bond than that of a mere guest. However, I could not be better satisfied, for my present relation to the society gives me a good deal more freedom than I should possess if it were possible for me to become a regular member. It would be very pleasant to be formally initiated and to be addressed as "du," but by no means so pleasant to comply with the complicated rules and regulations. For example, when wearing the colors, a member is not allowed to enter any stores except certain highly respectable book-stores, etc., he is not allowed to carry a package, he must attend all meetings (which are frequent), etc., etc. It is necessary to give a regular course of instruction to the freshmen.

As it is I have been received with most extraordinary hospitality and kindness, and find it awfully pleasant to have somebody to chat with between classes, as well as at the Kneipe. On Monday and Tuesday evenings from about ten o'clock on ad infinitum, those of the fellows who happen to have time sit together in a certain restaurant. Yesterday I went and found it delightfully informal. You come when you please and go when you please, but you are sure of company at any hour.

Franconia is, as you may judge, a Verbindung with rather different principles from those of the regular duel-fighting societies —drinking is not compulsory (though to say the least usual), a comparative moderation is observed, etc.—but the whole thing is nevertheless characteristically German.

Though Machen found some features of student life rather odd, such as the exaggerated forms of politeness observed between the men, he entered rather fully into it, and was happy at being in the swim. "If you are not in with the crowd," he wrote his father, "you see very little of one side of a German university, if for no other reason because you are usually in bed before things get really started. From 12 o'clock at night on, the streets are alive with students, and only students—so that Marburg appears in its true character as a real university town . . . " On one occasion he even joined in a *Nachtbummel,* an all night excursion on foot, to a village about twenty miles away. One result was that "that eight o'clock class—where recently I have a number of times been the only student present—had somehow to get along without me, but I managed to get in for Herrmann at eleven."

Christmas Eve fell on a Sunday in 1905, and since there seemed to be something incongruous between certain celebrations of Christmas and the proper observance of Sunday, he wondered at first whether he should not simply go away quietly by himself. But upon further reflection, he thought it would be "a violation of the spirit of the fourth commandment not to join in a simple, little Christmas celebration of the Links . . . " Describing the celebration afterward, he wrote that

> after the one servant had joined the party, a few Christmas songs were sung, and Frau Link read a passage from Luke; and then we all went into the next room where the lovely Christmas tree was resplendent with lights. The delight at the numerous presents—the German women spend a good part of the year in their "Weihnachtsarbeit"—was just as great as it is with us, and nobody could help falling in with the spirit of the occasion. Nor was I myself forgotten, for I received a lot of things to eat, and one or two other little presents, which kept me from feeling in the slightest degree out in the cold . . . The spirit of Christmas, where it is really celebrated in a family, is a good deal the same all over the world, and I was deeply touched at being so cordially received.

On the 25th he left for Berlin, and enjoyed the size and grandeur of that great city as a welcome change from primitive Marburg with its "sloughs and puddles." Goethe's "Götz von Berlichingen," Schiller's "Jungfrau von Orleans," and Shakespeare's "Othello" were among the chief attractions at the Berlin theatres. And he took some lessons in Italian at the Berlitz School. And so, in spite of interludes of depression and heart-searching, there were aspects of life in Germany, and especially at the university, which filled him with satisfaction.

THE MARBURG PROFESSORS

One would be quite unfair to Machen if the conclusion were drawn from the foregoing that he did not put in a great deal of hard study at Marburg. He was not one to enlarge upon such matters in his letters home, as his earlier letters from Princeton also show, and if he dwelt at times upon extra-curricular activities, that was due to his judgment that these, rather than the humdrum routine of lectures and reading, would prove most interesting to those at home. Nevertheless, the real story told by his letters is that of his intellectual and spiritual reaction to the teaching in the university rather than of such aspects of his life as have come under review. While immensely grateful for the emancipation from rules requiring attendance upon the classes, he was evidently very faithful in this regard, as even his allusion to his single absence from the eight o'clock lecture confirms. Moreover, he undertook a much larger program of reading than his tight Princeton schedule had allowed, concentrating on books dealing with subject matter under discussion in the class room, including naturally books written by the leading professors. Thus he took full advantage of the instruction offered, and his estimate of his professors and his response to their teaching are of extraordinary interest.

Jülicher fully lived up to the expectations based upon his reputation, and indeed Machen came to admire his work more and more as time went on. On Nov. 2 he wrote that "Jülicher even grows on me, though my first impression was very favorable. He is simply bubbling over with enthusiasm, and being gifted with lots of common sense and the power of terse expression, he is able to transmit his enthusiasm to the class." Ten days later he spoke again of his common sense "which enables him to cut short a lot of worthless over-exegesis with which the New Testament has been obscured for hundreds of years; and with a lively imagination which enables him to make the situation and the consequent emotion of the writer really alive to the class. Jülicher's learning is beyond question, hence that does not need to be mentioned. But these other gifts are not so common. That nine o'clock hour is certainly great." Machen was aware, of course, of Jülicher's very different estimate of the message of the New Testament from that taught at Princeton, but his basic Liberalism did not prevent his lectures on Galatians from being very stimulating. Moreover, the breadth of his learning was exceptional and his scholarly disposition temperate, in spite of his rejection of the supernatural, so that he could single out for special praise a work like that of Lightfoot's.

Johannes Weiss was a man whom Machen was to feel later he had done gross injustice, and this convinced him, like his later boundless admiration of Warfield, that callow students are not likely to be the best judges of the lasting worth of their instruction. He contrasted Weiss unfavorably with Jülicher, even stating that he could not think of him "to be at all a scholar of the first rank" and declaring that "perhaps his claim to renown lies chiefly in the fact that he is the son of Bernhard Weiss of Berlin." Weiss' later exceedingly learned and influential works on *I Corinthians* and *Primitive Christianity* compelled him to admit that his perception had been lamentably superficial.

The younger men lecturing in the New Testament field were Rudolf Knopf and Walter Bauer, other men who did not then seem outstanding, but who later were to gain considerable distinction. The former's lectures on New Testament Introduction and the latter's on John's Gospel were followed faithfully. Bauer lectured at 8 A.M. on four days a week, and due to his youth and the unattractiveness of the hour the enrollment was limited to two Germans, one Englishman and Machen. On Nov. 12th he reported that "the two Germans are irregular in their attendance, and on several occasions the lecture has been begun for the benefit of my unworthy self alone." Later, as noted, when he joined more fully in the student life at the university, even Machen failed to show up one morning. Since Bauer was later to publish a radical commentary on John, it is of interest that Machen noted that he then had a poor opinion of its historical worth, and had not yet shown much real understanding of its religious greatness.

CAPTIVATION BY HERRMANN

Though Machen was principally occupied with New Testament studies, he was apparently affected, for the time at least, far more deeply by his contact with another department. In fact, it is hardly an overstatement to say that Wilhelm Herrmann, professor of theology, was responsible for one of the most overwhelming intellectual and religious experiences of his life, an experience which, though not the instrument of initiating indecision and doubt, seems to have been chiefly responsible for prolonging and intensifying his religious struggle and thereby causing him to be even more sceptical than before as to the possibility of entering the ministry. Herrmann's teaching accomplished what the other instruction apparently could not do alone, but in the accomplishment of it affected more or less strongly the impact made by the other exponents of liberal views. In short Herrmann made Liberalism wonderfully attractive and heart-gripping. This he did not so much by the plausibility of intellectual argument as by the magnetic and overpowering force of his fervent religious spirit.

Herrmann's position and influence as an eloquent spokesman for the Ritschlian or Liberal Theology has often been expounded and appraised, and it would take us beyond the scope of this volume to enter upon even a summary statement of its tenets. His theological and religious views have received succinct and vivid expression in his *Communion of the Christian with God* and his *Systematic Theology.* Many years later Machen was to have basically this point of view in mind when he drew a sharp line between Liberalism and Christianity. For the present, however, when we are seeking to illumine especially his personal history, it seems best to dwell upon his thoughts and feelings of those days as he expressed them without reserve or calculation to loved ones at home who could be counted upon for the utmost sympathy and understanding.

The first reference to Herrmann occurs in a letter to his mother on Oct. 24, when he said:

> The most important thing that has happened in my three days since Sunday was my first lecture from Prof. Herrmann. If my first impression is any guide, I should say that the first time that I heard Herrmann may almost be described as an epoch in my life. Such an overpowering personality I think I almost never before encountered—overpowering in the sincerity of religious devotion. Herrmann may be illogical and one-sided, but I tell you he is alive. When Browning wrote his description of the German lecture room, he had never listened to Prof. Herrmann of Marburg.
>
> I am now engaged in the perusal of Herrmann's book, "Der Verkehr des Christen mit Gott," and postpone further estimates of the author until I have gotten a little deeper insight into what he is trying to say. Unfortunately the course of lectures is a continuation of the one of last summer; but he is helping out the new student by giving a brief resumé of what has gone before.

Four days later, in writing to his father, he said that Herrmann must be put in a different category from all the other professors:

> I can't criticize him, as my chief feeling with reference to him is already one of the deepest reverence. Since I have been listening to him, my other studies have for a time lost interest to me; for Herrmann refuses to allow the student to look at religion from a distance as a thing to be *studied* merely. He speaks right to the heart; and I have been thrown all into confusion by what he says—so much deeper is his devotion to Christ than anything I have known in myself during the past few years. I don't know at all what to say as yet, for Herrmann's views are so revolutionary. But certain I am that he has found Christ; and I believe that he can show how others may find Him—though, perhaps afterwards, in details, he may not be a safe guide. In fact, I am rather sorry I have said even so much in a letter; for I don't know at all yet what to think.

Although he confesses his lack of readiness to analyze Herrmann's position with anything like finality, he still cannot escape the feeling that he was a genuine follower of Christ when he wrote his brother "Arly" on Nov. 2nd:

> Herrmann, in his religious earnestness and moral power, has been a revelation to me. Not only has he given me a new sympathy for the prevailing German religious thought; but also I hope I may leave his classroom better morally and in every way than when I entered it. Herrmann affirms very little of that which I have been accustomed to regard as essential to Christianity; yet there is no doubt in my mind but that he is a Christian, and a Christian of a peculiarly earnest type. He is a Christian not because he follows Christ as a moral teacher; but because his trust in Christ is (practically, if anything even more truly than theoretically) unbounded. It is inspiring to see a man so completely centered in Christ, even though some people might wonder how he reaches this result and still holds the views that he does about the accounts of Christ in the New Testament.

Ten days later he expresses himself somewhat more soberly to his father: "Of course, it is not all quite like those glorious first two or three lectures, for details are never quite as inspiring as general principles—yet Hermann is never stupid or anything like it. He is a wonderful man." But on Dec. 10 he is prepared to express a somewhat more mature judgment, and it is still enthusiastic:

> Herrmann is professor of Dogmatics, and represents the dominant Ritschlian school of whose principles I have very hazy notions. At any rate, Herrmann has shown me something of the *religious* power which lies back of this great movement, which is now making a fight even for the control of the Northern Presbyterian Church in America. In New England those who do not believe in the bodily Resurrection of Jesus are, generally speaking, religiously dead; in Germany, Herrmann has taught me that that is by no means the case. He believes that Jesus is the one thing in all the world that inspires *absolute* confidence, and an *absolute* joyful subjection; that through Jesus we come into communion with the living God and are made free from the world. It is the faith that is a real experience, a real revelation of God that saves us, not the faith that consists in accepting as true a lot of dogmas on the basis merely of what others have said. Every Christian is conscious of having experienced a miracle, but it is a miracle in his own inner life. We are absolutely dependent upon the grace of God who saves us without our cooperation.

There is no use in my trying to give a resumé of Herrmann—I repent already of what I have written; for it can only make you wonder what I find so inspiring about him. But you would no longer wonder if you could hear him speak and could read what he has written. In my opinion, "Der Verkehr des Christen mit Gott," is one of the greatest religious books I ever read. Perhaps Herrmann does not give the whole truth—I certainly hope he does not—at any rate he has gotten hold of something that has been sadly neglected in the church and in the orthodox theology. Perhaps he is something like the devout mystics of the middle ages—they were one-sided enough, but they raised a mighty protest against the coldness and deadness of the church and were forerunners of the Reformation.

Later Machen was to see that the "Christ" to whom Herrmann was fervently devoted never really existed and that religious experience is not as such self-validating. Evidently to a significant extent he became aware even while he heard and read Herrmann of basic weaknesses and inadequacies. He certainly never came to the point of substituting Herrmann's views for those of orthodox Christianity. Nevertheless, he was profoundly unsettled and even overwhelmed by his encounter with this man whose fervor and moral earnestness put many Christians to shame. And even when he came to reject this theology without qualification he remained affected by the experience at least to the extent of being concerned to deal in dead earnest with the views of his opponents and of being tenderly sympathetic with those who might be passing through similar struggles of doubt.

TWO REVEALING LETTERS

Two remarkable letters of Professor Armstrong's from this period reflect the considerable change of outlook that had taken place within a month of his coming to Marburg. The first was in answer to a letter from Vienna which contained the startling message that Machen was determined not to accept the Fellowship award. It read as follows:

Princeton Oct. 11-05

Dear Das :

Your letter from Vienna dated Sept. 26th reached me on Oct. 9th. The same day Mr. Anderson forwarded me the letter you had written him saying that he had written you that the matter had been referred to me.

I have been pondering just what to write you. First of all let me say that I deeply appreciate your kind words with reference to myself. Whatever I have been able to do for you, if it has been a help rather than a hindrance, will always be a source of pleasure and gratification to me. I only wish I could impress upon you the warmth of my regard for you and the high esteem in which I hold your work. I have frequently felt that you did not do yourself justice in your own thought of yourself. The whole Faculty is quite at one with me in this judgment—having and expressing a confidence in you and your work which in my experience with them is unusual.

In regard to the Fellowship money—I do not know just what the circumstances are to which you refer as having led you to the decision expressed in your letter. I cannot therefore reason with you about your decision. I feel however that I ought to state the facts relative to the Fellowship as I understand them and leave it open to you to reconsider the whole matter and withdraw or reaffirm your decision. The Fellowship is essentially in the nature of a prize. You won it in open competition having fulfilled all the requirements connected with its bestowal. The appointment was consequently made by the Faculty and the Directors. The conditions of acceptance are quite simple involving no other obligation than study in New Testament work for one year under the direction of our Faculty. Further than this you are in no way obligated. When you have completed a year's work you will have discharged every obligation involved in accepting the Fellowship. This you apparently expect to do. I fear you have been allowing yourself to think that the receipt of the money would in some way obligate you in the future after the year of study is finished. I do not think that this is the case. So think the matter over again before reaching your final decision.

Should you then abide by your decision not to receive the money I am quite sure that the Faculty would be willing to have you remain in the position of the New Testament Fellow—and you know that in any event not only for the year you spend in Germany but so long as you may wish it any service that I can render you will be most gladly performed.

I think your decision to go to Marburg a good one. You will find Jülicher very stimulating. Herrmann also you might hear occasionally in Dogmatics if for no other reason than to come into contact with his vigorous, earnest and devout spirit. J. Weiss will tell you about as many exciting (?) things as any one. Then you might be interested in A. Thumb's work in Hellenistic Greek. It will be a pleasure to me to think of you in the surroundings in which I made my first acquaintance with German and the Ritschlian Theology.

The first part of your article is now out in the Oct. number of the Review. I think it is in pretty good shape and with Warfield's gives character to the number . . .

Now Das, don't let the Fellowship matter bother you. Do as you think best and the decision whatever it be will be satisfactory to me and I am sure to the Faculty. They all have full confidence in you.

With every good wish and the assurance of my warm regard,

Sincerely your friend,

W. P. Armstrong

The second letter discloses that Machen had remained adamant so far as the Fellowship was concerned, but reflects further upon his profoundly disturbed state of mind:

Princeton N. J. Nov. 12/05

Dear Das:

Your letter of Oct. 29th reached me on the 10th. I have read it over several times and I must confess that I am somewhat at a loss to tell you just what feeling it has called forth in me. It is easier to tell you of the decision I reached after considering the contents of your letter and of the action that I have taken—although I am confident that you are fully entitled to the Fellowship money I do not consider the reception and use of it a condition of holding the Fellowship. It is evidently intended as a means to aid the Fellow in accomplishing the work expected of him. It therefore lies within the Fellow's right to dispense with the money if he thinks best and still remain the N. T. Fellow by fulfilling the appointed work. I did not think however that I ought to act in this matter without the approval of the Faculty. At the meeting of the Faculty yesterday I stated to those present that you did not wish to receive the income of the Fellowship endowment to which you were entitled but that you were willing to do the work expected of the N. T. Fellow should they wish to continue your appointment. The Faculty were of the opinion that the money was rightfully yours but that you need not receive it if you did not desire to do so. They were also quite willing to have you remain the N. T. Fellow. They instructed me to inform Mr. Anderson that the Fellowship money was to be held subject to your order so that it might be used by you should you change your decision—as Warfield expressed it. There was no need to burn your bridges behind you before you had completed the journey. The idea of the Faculty seemed to be that the money should be held for you until you had completed your work as Fellow and then should you wish you could write me stating that you did not intend to draw it but would like to have it added to the endowment of the Fellowship.

I am very much gratified to know that you are enjoying your work at Marburg. I knew you would like Herrmann. When I heard him he reminded me more of Dr. Purves than any man in Germany whom I was privileged to hear. And now Das in regard to yourself. What you have written me has only deepened my respect for you and convinced me that my confidence in you has not been misplaced. I know perfectly well that you will do honest work—whatever may have been the trials through which you have passed—and I judge from your letter that they have been severe. I feel perfectly confident that you will come through them safely, chastened perhaps by your experience but not the less fit for the service of our common Saviour. I can not tell you how my heart goes to you in sympathy: for you have suffered. Your suffering has been in that sphere where each of us stands face to face with God. It is in this sphere that relief will come even as the desire for relief comes from God himself. I know your faith will give you the victory and with victory the joy and peace that comes from the quiet confidence in all God's providence and gracious leading of a child of His for whom Christ died. Don't let pretence, false appearance, deceit of self or others worry you inasmuch as we know well that there is no deceit of God who looks in the heart and judges of the motive. If our relation to Him be right—and it can be made right in Christ—then we need not trouble ourselves about the world. How thankful we ought to be that there is one person who knows our life even better than we do ourselves, and that knowing it in all its darkness he has yet made it possible for us to live in the light and blessings of His love.

You will think that I have taken upon myself to give the advice of a "father-confessor" without having had such advice asked of me. And I must confess that what I have written is something like advice. If it has assumed this form however let the form go and take what I have said simply as an indication and symbol or what you will, of my intense sympathy and abiding confidence in you and your work.

With warm regard,

Sincerely your friend,

W. P. Armstrong

Machen did not change his mind with regard to the fellowship award. And to some extent we can understand why. If already before his encounter with Herrmann he determined, in his unsettled state, to relieve his mind of an inescapable feeling that its acceptance involved at least a measure of commitment to carry through a definite program of preparation for the future, how could he, when deeper perplexities and doubts assailed him, abandon that somewhat greater sense of liberty to follow only where conviction might lead?

6

DEEPENING CONFLICT

A somewhat new stage in the movement away from the prospect of becoming a minister was reached in the early months of 1906. Prior to that time the extraordinarily unsettling impact especially of Herrmann had been disclosed, but now he is under compulsion to speak forth quite openly to his loved ones at home.

AN UPSETTING EXPERIENCE

His first specific intimation was in a letter written soon after the first of the year addressed to Arthur but evidently intended for the entire family. Regrettably this letter has been lost, but other references are so frequent and detailed that one need not grieve over the loss over much. Arthur's response on Jan. 21st discloses that his brother had been passing through a profoundly disturbing experience, occasioned not only by his doubts, but also by a deep sense of personal unworthiness to be a minister of Christ. The elder brother did not feel that he should urge him to enter the ministry, but warned him against losing perspective with regard to his faults: "while it is *possible* that you may not exaggerate your own defects, it is *certain* that you underestimate those of others—that is, of others who occupy, and properly occupy, high positions in the Church or in the world."

His mother's first commentary, written the same day, speaks for itself:

> My dear boy, Arthur let me read your last letter to him in which you speak of the impossibility of your entering the ministry. It would have been bad not to let me read the letter, as I would have imagined something dreadful, but he did not show it to the others. I want to assure you that, whatever you decide upon, I shall acquiesce in and do my best to help you in. You think that we would lose faith in you if we knew you perfectly. But one thing I can assure you of—that *nothing* that you could do could keep me from loving you—*nothing*. It is easy enough to grieve

me. Perhaps I worry too much. But my love for my boy is absolutely indestructible. Rely on that whatever comes. And I have faith in you too and believe that the strength will come to you for your work whatever it may be, and that the way will be opened. In the mean time, get all the good and all the fun too out of your present circumstances. And may God bless and be with you! I am glad you went to Berlin and had a good time...

On Jan. 14th he had written to his father, though perhaps not in quite the same terms as to his brother, of his new frame of mind. In reply he received an admonition, dated Jan. 26, begging him not to be hasty in entering upon new plans:

You know that I have always recognised your right not to feel precluded by anything in or connected with your past or present course of study from the final choice of a different profession, if you ever think it advisable—you yourself being the judge—to do so. None of the years of study you have had can ever be properly considered as "wasted" no matter what field of work you may ultimately enter upon. You have had a mental training and have had laid in store knowledge which are invaluable possessions. If the ministry be not felt to be your vocation, there is a whole realm of service of the most valuable sort, leaving that out of view. If you believe that to fit you for the higher walks in non-clerical learning, you would be better off for a year or more (beyond this year) in any special department—Greek in general—for instance, or some kindred study, you are quite young enough to pursue it, and prepared better by maturity of thought and a solid substructure than you would otherwise have been now to pursue it. The pecuniary question you need not bother about. I can assure you on that point.

Life's work for a man is a great affair, and no amount of earnest preparation can be out of place at your age and in your circumstances. Nowadays no student can well assume, like Bacon or Milton, to take all knowledge for his province. But breadth of vision is still a good thing, and freedom to study (when there is so much to learn, and so many steps in the ascent have been cut out by the labors of zealous predecessors for the help of the modern student) is so gloriously exhilarating that you may well permit yourself to continue a student until you are ready to go to work to instruct and benefit mankind in the most effective way given to you.

Meanwhile, in a letter of Jan 21st to his mother, he raised the question as to what he should do in March between terms, and indicated that he had been thinking of a trip to Rome. The alternative was to stay close to Marburg to do some reading. But, then, reflecting that it was very difficult to pursue his studies without relating them to his future activity, he added:

> If I were only convinced that it would ever be of any practical use to me, with what enthusiasm could I enter into the study of New Testament criticism! But how it can ever be of *direct* use to me, I do not see; though it is only right to say that the benefit I have so far received from my half-year in Europe for myself, is almost boundless.

Ten days later he expressed himself in similar terms to his brother Arthur, though somewhat more bluntly, stating that he felt "very much like a dilettante" carrying on his studies without relationship to worthy labor. He also reproached himself for having "made a failure of things so far," and concluded: "But anything is better than the old hypocrisy, which even such an un-hysterical person as yourself would fully admit as such if you knew the facts. For me to speak of the Christian ministry in one breath with myself is hyprocrisy."

The following day, in a letter to his mother, he reminds her that his seemingly rather abrupt negative decision concerning the ministry was not without a background in earlier attitudes:

> Your sweet letter of Jan. 21 arrived last night, and I hasten to drop a line in reply, though I haven't time to say much. I was grieved that Arly did not show my letter (in which I spoke of the impossibility of entering the ministry) to Father, for I should have written it directly to him; and had him half in mind when I wrote. The truth was that when I sat down to write, I did not have much idea of what I was going to say.
>
> You probably think my decision or my present feeling about the matter is something new, but as a matter of fact, it is many years old. Only my blindness, and the distance in the future of the decision have obscured things to me. I can't say I feel particularly different about it now—only that I see more clearly than before what a blessing it would be if I could get into some line of work where I could be certain I was doing right.

His hesitation in entering Princeton Seminary, of which note has been taken above, confirms the basic correctness of this observation. And yet Machen probably did not mean to deny that, to a significant degree, his seemingly final decision had come with almost explosive suddeness. Though the same conclusion might have been reached in America if he had similarly been moved by the feeling that the hour of decision could no longer be postponed, one cannot doubt that the impact made by Liberalism especially in the person of Herrmann had precipitated it.

FURTHER REFLECTIONS

Three days later, on Feb. 4th, regretful that he had not been careful to give his father the first intimation of his decision, he provides him with a more measured statement of his position. Having thanked him for the trouble he had taken in giving an account of the outcome of the Burnt District case to satisfy his own curiosity, he wrote:

> As I have indicated more or less plainly in several of my letters, it has seemed to me almost impossible even to think about going into the ministry; so that I am seriously considering what other possibilities may open themselves, as I now feel more and more keenly that the time has gone by when I can waste months and years in idleness or in aimless work. It is true that I cannot possibly look back upon the past year as wasted—as it has been a time perhaps of something more like progress than I have experienced at any other period in my life. Not that I underrate in the slightest the value of my home-training; for without what I got from you and Mother I should long since have given up all thoughts of religion or of a moral life. And it is that training alone, and the principles which have been instilled into me that enable me even now to employ my opportunities here in such a way as to make them real opportunities instead of pitfalls.
>
> Yet on the other hand there is no doubt that, through my own fault, I had so poisoned my surroundings during the past few years, had gotten into such a rut that there seemed to be no chance of escape. I had so long kept up the form of piety, and even engaged in active church work, when the whole thing was hypocrisy, that the things that are intended for moral and spiritual enlightenment had for me lost all their power. Perhaps not all, either, for I always at least had before me the ideal of a Christian life, and the wish (weak though I was) to lead one. It is this ideal which now seems to stand me in good stead—the ideal of a real Christian faith and resulting Christian life.
>
> But you have no idea what a relief it was to me to be able, in a certain sense, to start out fresh, where my external relations

had not been so connected with the habit of a false life. Don't misunderstand me by thinking I mean to say that I have now overcome the difficulties or that I am now leading anything like what a Christian life ought to be—or even what an ordinary man regards as the ordinary morals of the world. But to say that this is not better than my life for example at the Hopkins is ungrateful. At least, it is not so full of hypocrisy—at least I can begin, with something more like honesty, at the beginning. But for me to think about going into the ministry now would be simply to fall back into the old rut—and it is the partial escape from that that makes me so intensely grateful to you for making it possible for me to come to Europe. Yet the only thing that enables me to get any benefit out of my opportunities here is the continual presence with me in spirit of you and Mother and the Christian teaching which you have given me.

There follows a word of caution that his letters are not to be taken with absolute literalness, a caution—if felt necessary in the case of the members of his family who would have had every advantage in detecting hyperbole or understatement as the case might be—that is doubly pertinent for interpreters who knew the man far less intimately or not at all:

My experience, when I write a letter about anything except commonplaces, is usually that I regret either the whole or at least parts after I have put the letter in the box. All I can do, therefore, is to beg you not to take everything that I say too exactly. I am very much afraid of being misunderstood and of making a bad matter worse. Perhaps it would really be better to say nothing, as after all I only can understand the circumstances. But in view of my future plans, it has become simply a necessity to let you know something of what has been passing in my mind. Don't think that all this is anything particularly new—for in my own more honest moments I have felt for years that it is practically impossible for me to enter the ministry. My idea now is to go on and finish my year of study without thinking too much about the future (though that is mighty hard when I reflect that I am now 25 years old), unless (what would be the best thing of all) I can get directly into some line of work where I at least know that I am doing no harm.

The difficulty is more deep-seated than you can ever understand—and I can only beg of you not to think you can understand

> it by drawing upon your own experience or that of the ordinary man. Such a procedure, little as you think it, could have only the effect of making me feel more keenly my isolation.

He proceeds to tell of his reading in the New Testament field, and observes that the courses announced for the summer term at Marburg are so attractive that he is considering staying right there rather than going on to another university. Though a visit to Rome would be "glorious," he thinks that he will probably remain in Marburg and work. And having mentioned "a pleasant letter from Armstrong," he closes as follows:

> Give my love to all. Above all, don't think I am glad to break off from home. If I didn't have the remembrance of that home and of you all, and if I could not think of you all as still there and of my return—then indeed would I feel myself really in a foreign land. You can be sure that my affection for you all is rather increased than otherwise by my enforced absence. I only meant that I have been able better to put into practice what I learned, despite my faults, from you and Mother and our Christian family.

His mother on Feb. 2nd, Arthur on the 4th, and his father on the 12th urged him to take advantage by all means of the opportunity of going to Rome. His mother's letter also told of a note received from Armstrong in which, having expressed his deep interest and strong affection for her son, he declared: "I have the fullest confidence in the ultimate issue of his studies. In whatever field he may choose to labor I feel sure that his work will be not only useful but brilliant." And Arthur reported that Dr. White of the Biblical Seminary of New York had been so impressed by Machen's articles on the Virgin Birth that he had told Mr. Kirk that he wanted to get him for his staff, but that Patton had said that "you are wanted at Princeton—that indeed you are the one man they want." His father's letter may advantageously be quoted at greater length:

> I think your Easter vacation would be well applied to an excursion to Rome. A visit to Rome is part of a liberal education, and no opportunity of making it should be neglected. Unless therefore you feel very strongly drawn in some different direction I should certainly go if I were you.
>
> Your letter to your mother—your late one—has been received. Arthur's letter was *not* kept from me; as you may already have gathered from the tenor of my last to you. I have entire confidence that you will ultimately settle into some walk of life which will

> satisfy both your taste and your conscience, and whatever choice of profession you do make I shall believe it to be the best one for you. Meanwhile do not feel obliged to hurry your choice—either the choice or the *entering* upon the field chosen.

In other paragraphs he sought to persuade his son to abandon his deprecatory attitude toward his *Review* articles on the Virgin Birth and speaks of his critical interest in Jülicher:

> Your *article,* you may depend on it, whatever criticism you may yourself be disposed to indulge in, is a good one—strong, and in every sense good, and bound to *do* good. It is sure to command respect, even in quarters not predisposed in favor of the argument. You make a great mistake in undervaluing it. You had to deal with a difficult and complex problem, and have handed it fairly to all sides, and most clearly and convincingly.
>
> I have been reading your Prof. Jülicher's Introduction to the New Testament, in the English translation of Mrs. (or Miss) Janet Penrose Ward, with great interest. There is so much that is attractive in manner and spirit—so much acute and just criticism, that I feel rewarded, notwithstanding the strange departures from sound reasoning manifested in many places. I suppose what is at the bottom of the error of the school of philosophy to which he, like so many more of the modern higher critics, belongs, is the assumption that the miraculous is impossible, even if accompanying a divine revelation, and therefore per se incredible. A kindred fallacy is the dogma that a solid theory of a future life can be envolved from the phenomena discernible by the senses and cognizable by human science—alone.

In several further letters from home during the month of February, he continued to be warmly urged to avail himself of the opportunity of visiting Rome. And one might have predicted that such hearty commendation of his expressed desire to see Rome would have served to overcome his hesitation, especially since he might well have argued that such a "glorious" adventure, with a complete change of scene, would perhaps relieve his mind of its present turmoil. That he did not undertake this journey provides, therefore, another evidence that, however overwhelmed he was at times by the problems that beset him in Germany, he was of sturdier fibre than to adopt the tempting solution of escape from his environment. As he states in a letter of Feb. 18th, he had gotten "a little bit settled down to do some earnest reading."

Moreover, about this time or a little later he made a definite decision to follow up his work at Marburg with a term at Göttingen.

The interval between terms did indeed permit brief interludes of travel and relaxation. One journey of about a week included stops in Frankfurt, Darmstadt, Worms, Speyer, Mannheim, Heidelberg, Strassburg and Freiberg. Heidelberg particularly he found entrancing. Writing to his mother on March 25th, after his return to Marburg, he dwells on a memorable view of the town:

> After sunset, on the terrace near the castle, I spent the hour which was worth almost as much as all the rest of the trip put together. Like the Rhine and unlike the high mountains, the charm of Heidelberg does not force itself upon you, but is only to be caught at the proper time and place. But that evening hour was one which I shall never forget—the gathering gloom seemed to hide from view everything prosaic and commonplace, while the distance above the town made all sounds indistinguishable except a dull murmur of life and the rushing of the river just before it lost itself in a blaze of gold in the boundless plain. It seemed as though the town were the last stopping-place at the boundary of another world, where travellers bid a last farewell to human life just before entering upon the plains whose glories are too mysterious for earthly eyes.

Later there was a hurried trip to Göttingen to secure lodging for the coming term, and later still just before settling in Göttingen on April 19th, a few days featured by a little relaxation in Wernigerode and a delightful walk in the Harz Mountains from the vicinity of Quedlinburg. During a very large part of this period, however, he remained in Marburg largely occupied with study of the New Testament.

That it was not a time of serenity, free from the necessity of struggling with the pressing question of his future work, is, however, plain. Perhaps indeed he was not much perplexed by an invitation which reached him in February to consider the possibility of joining the staff of Dr. White's Bible School in New York. Though he felt complimented by the offer which, as reported above, had as its immediate background Dr. White's admiration of Machen's articles in the *Princeton Review,* he felt that, if he were to engage in religious work at all, he would be much better suited for the type of post that Armstrong and Patton had had in view. Work on the university level was his real ideal, and the devotional atmosphere of the Seminary was more congenial. Hence he declined the offer apparently without delay.

APPROACH ON BEHALF OF PRINCETON

But only a few weeks later he was compelled to face the question whether that which appeared preferable was really practicable. For on March 11th, Professor Armstrong wrote the following:

> And now, Das, what do you think about coming to Princeton in the fall? I should be greatly gratified if I could present your name to the Board of Directors at their meeting on May 7th and have them appoint you Instructor in the New Testament Department. If however you do not feel ready to decide the question now, I can and will gladly wait until you come back and we can talk the matter over. The appointment could of course be made at the fall meeting of the Directors on Oct. 9th in time for you to take up the work of the year.
>
> Should you be inclined after consideration to think favorably of coming, and I hope you will, you need have no hesitancy for fear of binding yourself for more than the one year and for this there would be no necessity of ordination.

The very terms of the letter show that this offer was not regarded as essentially new. Moreover, Dr. Armstrong suggests that he was not overly hopeful of securing an affirmative reply, though he seeks to overcome so far as possible Machen's scruples. Strangely, one looks in vain in the letters of the following period for mention of Armstrong's letter, though from later developments we learn that, while he was still in Marburg, he had written that he was not prepared to accept the invitation. How far he was from reaching solid ground is indicated, however, by the following comment to his father on March 30th:

> How I envy every humble clerk, who at least has some employment in which he can engage with enthusiasm and without doubts and qualms of conscience! If there were the slightest chance of my getting anything of a start in business life, even at this late day, it would be like a ray of hope, so do I dread the three or four years of preparation required now to fit me for anything else—even supposing I had any particular bent towards one of the learned professions. Just now my enthusiasm is waning even for the historical study of the New Testament. And without enthusiasm and a broad, free way of looking at things it is worse than useless to approach that study of all others.

His brother Arthur, whose frequent letters disclose his loving concern to overcome every difficulty, at one point argued that, though he might not feel able to undertake the peculiar demands made upon the preacher, he might more readily enter upon the work of a teacher of the New Testament, for which the "one qualification *par excellence* is sane scholarship." Evidently in reply to this effort to preserve his brother's interest in distinctly Christian work, the younger brother replied on the eve of taking up his work at Göttingen:

> In the field of the N. T., there is no place for the weakling. Decisiveness, moral and intellectual, is absolutely required. Any other kind of work is not merely useless (it might even be humbly useful in other fields), but is even perhaps harmful.

As things turned out Machen was to be influenced eventually by the consideration that his going to Princeton would not necessarily involve a positive decision to become an ordained minister. Nevertheless, his negative answer to Armstrong and his strong words to his brother concerning the qualifications of a Seminary teacher are remarkably revealing. For they show that Machen was not weakly grasping for a way out of his apparent impasse, and that he was profoundly aware that a dualism between the intellectual and spiritual was untenable. Theoretically it might be possible to contemplate an instructorship in the Seminary in isolation from decisions as to the more ultimate questions of faith and calling, but practically he realized that such a solution was at best a brief postponement of the inevitable.

AT GOTTINGEN

When Machen entered upon his life at Göttingen toward the end of April, 1906, he was not enjoying his first contact with this ancient town or its university established in 1737. For, as will be recalled, he had gone there in 1904, armed with a letter of introduction from Gildersleeve, the Göttingen alumnus of half a century, and had spent a number of enjoyable days there. His contacts had been with the philologians rather than with professors or students of theology, and so academically his life and work there in 1906 constituted a fresh experience. His choice of Göttingen had not been easily reached, partly because he was reluctant to wrench himself loose from the congenial Kümmels and Links in Marburg. On the whole, however, it seemed wise to come into contact with other scholars in his field. And Göttingen like Marburg, and in distinction from others like Berlin and Halle, did not have the disadvantages of a big city, and yet was a great centre of New Testament investigation as of learning in general.

The variety of courses that were open to him is indicated by an early letter in which he reports:

> I have been listening to Schürer on Exegesis of Matthew, Bousset on Galatians, Bonwetsch on "Apostolic Age," and last but not least Heitmüller on the Gospel of John. Also I shall be a listener at Schürer's Seminar on the Pastoral Epistles, shall hear Bousset once a week on "Jesus und Paulus"... And then I shall probably hear Kattenbusch on the History of Protestant Theology since the Aufklärung . . . . I heard the famous Wellhausen . . . once on "The Ancient Arabs and Islam," but shall probably not take the course. It probably would be mighty interesting but I haven't time for things that lie far afield.

Though none of these men possessed the personal magnetism of Herrmann, and perhaps not of Jülicher, they were all of distinguished ability and either had gained a high reputation because of their scholarly productions or were soon to do so. Schürer, the head of the New Testament Department, was known especially for his monumental and massive work on *The History of the Jewish People in the Time of Jesus Christ,* a work which remains today an outstanding contribution to the history of the beginnings of the Christian era. Machen's reactions to his teaching, formulated somewhat over a month after the beginning of the term, were as follows:

> Though his method of lecturing is somewhat dry, and is not of a sort to inspire anyone who has not already an interest for the subject, yet I am learning a good deal from his careful exegesis of Matthew, which he carries on five times a week. Indeed, even his manner of speaking, after you get used to it, has an excellence of its own, for it seems to reflect the peculiar solidity and minuteness of his learning. His conduct of the Seminar (on the Pastoral Epistles) pleases me less, since he has no conversational faculty and no power of starting an interesting discussion among the members of the class. The papers read in the Seminar are also of a very much lower order than would be expected at the Hopkins (for example), but this is perhaps chiefly due to the fact that only a week is allowed each student for the preparation, and to the inadequate library facilities. As to his critical views about the New Testament, I do not believe Schürer differs in essentials from the type that you have learned to know in Jülicher.

Wilhelm Bousset, who was then about forty, was a subordinate in the department, but possessed far greater popular gifts and was remembered as a brilliant lecturer. In 1892 he had published a little book on *The Preaching of Jesus* which was rather typically Liberal, but about 1900 he became an exponent, along with Herrmann Gunkel in the Old Tesstament field, of the *religionsgeschichtliche Methode,* which for want of more felicitous rendering may perhaps best be called the "History of Religions Method." Bousset's important volume on *Judaism* (1903), his commentary on *Revelation* (1906) and other works including especially his brilliant and sensational *Kyrios Christos* (1913) are significant exhibitions of the development of an approach which, while somewhat weakening the hold of the older Liberalism, spelled the dawn of a more radical era in the history of New Testament criticism. To expound and to evaluate this new method would take us beyond the scope of this biography, though mention may be made of Machen's estimate and criticism of Bousset in his Sprunt Lectures some fifteen years later, published as *The Origin of Paul's Religion.* Our present purpose may be served, however, if we quote from Machen's popular summary written for the benefit of his brother Arthur. Observing that "nearly all modern investigators are more or less affected" by the method, but that certain ones "have made it their special task to justify and extend" its use, he said:

> The general aim is better to understand the Christian religion, by exhibiting it (in its beginnings, as well as in its later dogmatic form) in its relations to other religions, and by pointing out the influence which other religions have had upon its origin and later history. The idea is that only when we understand the New Testament in its historical relations, shall we be able fully to appreciate it. It is admitted that the personality of Jesus, like every great personality, introduces an element which it is useless to attempt to explain; but Jesus had a place in history, and the form of his teaching and work was conditioned by that place in the evolution of humanity.
>
> The work of the scholar is to trace the lines of connection, between peoples and between religions, which gave that evolution unity. These connections are not to be sought now, chiefly by pointing out *literary* dependence or by investigating the thought of the theologians or of the learned men of ancient times. Such was the old method. The new method takes as the especial object of investigation the religion, the superstitions, the legends of the *masses of the people;* and finds that in this hidden sphere the various nations exhibit close relationships that do not so clearly appear in their philosophies, theologies, and in general in the thought of the educated. But again and again, the popular representations crop out even in the writings of the most en-

lightened—as for example in the writings of Paul, and elsewhere in the New Testament.

The tenacity with which ancient customs and legends were handed down among the common people is particularly emphasized—so that it often happens that we find the more ancient form of a myth in a *writing* which is far later than one that now contains a far more developed form of the myth. From one point of view, the *religionsgeschichtliche Methode* is a revolt against purely literary criticism.

Account was taken further of the gradual rise of the method and of its leading representatives, and then speaking more particularly of Bousset's efforts to popularize the modern theology with the aim of liberating Christianity of its "load of dead form" that the Gospel might "once more ring out with its old power," Machen commented:

The aim is a noble one, but it may well be doubted whether it is being attained. What Bousset has left after he has stripped off the form is certainly well worth keeping; but whether it is the Christian faith that has been found to overcome the world is very doubtful.

His fight against orthodoxy has made Bousset a very prominent man in German public life, and he is certainly also brilliant as an investigator, but he lacks the caution of men like Schürer or Jülicher . . .

Wilhelm Heitmüller was a young man who had only recently become associated with the University staff, and was only a Privat Dozent, but had already gained a considerable reputation as a scholar and author. His general position was similar to Bousset's, but Machen found him superior to Bousset in some respects:

He strikes me as being less passionate and less of a party-man than Bousset, and hence perhaps more cautious as a scholar; though I do not know that his critical results are less radical in the main points. At any rate his exegesis of the Fourth Gospel is probably the best course I have, as he displays a great appreciation for the religious worth of the book and tact and good sense in the exegesis. Of course his opinion of the direct historical value of the gospel is very low.

Bonwetsch he described as "conservative," but added that "the conservative view of the New Testament is not so well represented at Göttingen as by Armstrong at Princeton." And apropos of the fact that his brother had expressed wonder that, in view of his orthodoxy or conservatism, Zahn had apparently not been recommended as one under whom he should study, Machen, while recognizing the prodigious learning of Zahn, made the point that "it is a mistake, I think, to suppose that any of the Princeton faculty would be inclined to advise a student in my circumstances to seek out a conservative university just because it is conservative; for Princeton Seminary differs from some other conservative institutions in that it does not hide from itself the real state of affairs in Biblical study at the present day, and makes an honest effort to come to an understanding with the ruling tendency." Summing up, while warning that his generalizations concerning the professors at Göttingen should not be taken too seriously, he spoke of the inspiration of residing at one of the greatest centres of learning in the world and declared that "a stay at a place like this is enough to make a man humble at any rate; and I see plainly that there is a lot to be done before I could accomplish anything in academic life."

MEMBER OF THE GERMANIA

Though accordingly the academic work at Göttingen, while satisfying in many respects, lacked the luster of his studies at Marburg, there was another aspect of university life that proved far more exhilarating. For to his great delight Machen became an associate member of one of the student societies, not merely a *Hospitant* as at Marburg but a *Conkneipant.* The society was the Burschenschaft *Germania.* The name *Burschenschaft,* as distinguished from *Verbindung,* was usually reserved for the regulation duel fighting clubs, but this society, like the *Franconia* Verbindung, was more moderate than most in this and other respects. Nevertheless Machen once stated that "the temperance principle seems to be essentially that nobody is compelled to drink more beer than he chooses—a quite different principle from that prevailing in the regular Corps and Burschenschaften." The Burschenschaften, as also the motto of the *Germania*: 'Gott, Freiheit, Vaterland,' suggests, had a patriotic motif, and they on occasion had been of no little political significance, but under ordinary circumstances they had an exclusively social function. His new life as one of the *Germanen,* with the privilege of wearing the cap with the sacred "couleur," gave Machen a sense of "belonging"—which was impossible for one who was treated as a guest, with the formality and politeness customary between host and guest. Now he was addressed as "du," and had the right and duty so to address all other members. The change from "Sie" to "du," he explained, was incomprehensible unless there was a feeling for the German language and German life; actually it meant a change in the entire atmosphere of one's life, signifying a sudden change from distant acquaintanceship to at least incipient friendship. Likewise wearing the couleur, and fulfilling the meticulous rules of conduct and manners, would seem artificial and even ridiculous to an American, but "here on its historical ground, indissolubly connected with German student life," Machen wrote home, "it does not impress me at all that way, indeed I am as proud as a dog with two tails." The gymnastics and fencing indulged in by the students were rather beyond him, though he took a few lessons in the latter. But when it came to tennis, it was a great relief to be regarded as an expert at the game.

Though Machen entered rather fully into the social life of the society, membership was not without producing its own questions of conscience. The German Sunday being what it was, there were excursions in which he did not take part. This posed no special discomfort, since he had taken pains to indicate to the society before being accepted that his views concerning it were not their own. A more serious problem seemed to arise, however, in connection with his attendance upon services in a Baptist church. On July 9th, he wrote his mother:

> Things have been going by no means as smoothly with me during the past week as they did formerly. It seems that there is a disposition on the part of the 'Germania' to think that the Baptist Congregation, in which I want to come into contact with some real live religion in order to supplement the comparative deadness of the regular Lutheran Church is "uncouleurfähig," i.e., cannot be visited in couleur. I believe in adapting myself to the customs of the country as far as possible, but I must say it makes me shaky to be obliged to go as it were in disguise when I want to engage in worship with real disciples of Christ. It makes me feel as though I were a traitor to a more sacred 'couleur' than that of the Germania, and that if the two come into conflict the latter ought to give place. However, I have heard no real decision about the thing and in any case shall go slow about anything I do. But my pleasure has for the present been destroyed.
>
> The Germans are very tolerant about little questions like the person of Christ, but when it comes to the outward form of religion, they are more intolerant than the most bigoted of the orthodox.

A week later, however, he said that his gloomy remarks should not be taken too seriously, and that the troubles that he had thought confronted him did not seem to be showing up. Perhaps merely isolated comments had been made, and these had subsided. Soon thereafter he seemed to be enjoying the social life immensely, and spoke of the Germania as "a second Benham." And he even read a paper prepared in German on "The Universities of the United States" which was later published in the national organ of the Burschenschaft, a paper which he described as "a caution to cats." But it also afforded "more self-respect now that I at least have made an attempt to write some German."

New doubts arose, however, as to whether he could justify indefinite continuance of his membership in the society because he began to feel that in practice they appeared to take a position against the orthodox or conservative party. In his uncertainty as to where things actually stood he was determined to ask Dr. Heitmüller, an active alumnus, for an explanation. In this connection he writes, however, that he does not believe "in combatting religious errors by any outward means such as trying to prevent the propagation of such ideas." And then, in a rare disclosure of actual doubt and in what may well have been the mood of the moment rather than expressive of his most basic convictions, he adds:

> Nor am I by any means certain where the truth lies—probably it is something that none of us at present sees. But that Bousset and Heitmüller have gotten hold of it is something that I should be sorry to think.

The talk with Heitmüller materialized within a few days, and he was rather reassured as to his right to remain in the society, for he was told that "even now, despite the tendency of recent years, the number of alumni of the Germania who favor my way of thinking is greater than those who agree with him; so that," Machen concluded, "there can hardly be anything in the constitution of the Germania that would prevent its being subscribed even by so orthodox a person as your humble servant."

The conference was also memorable because it was not confined to the narrower question of membership in the *Germania.* It concerned also "the religious importance of the difference between the so-called 'modern theology' and the orthodox theology, Machen taking the position against Heitmüller that the difference affected the very essence of Christianity. He added, however, in reporting the matter to his mother, that "the earnest religious life of those who do not hold our view of the Person of Christ in Germany, and their earnest desire not to break with the Christian Church are at least grounds for the utmost caution in our manner of opposing them."

It appears again, therefore, in spite of the intense and painful struggle through which he went, and though there were times of agonizing doubt, that when an issue affecting the Christian faith and life arose he stood for rather than against orthodox Christianity. Much time was to pass before the issue between Christianity and Modernism was to be fully crystallized in his mind and his hesitation as to where the truth lay had completely disappeared. But as one who had gone through a severe and long-continued struggle, he never minimized the reality and the deadly seriousness of the battle in which others were engaged. And as one who finally found victory and tranquility of spirit because of the profound and constant sympathy of others, he was, as all who really knew him discovered, a man of extraordinary compassion towards those who were passing through difficulties such as he, from experience, knew only too well.

7

AN ASTONISHING DECISION

The concluding developments which issued in the momentous step of Machen's going to Princeton as Instructor in the New Testament must now be reviewed. Embracing happenings in Europe and America, especially in Göttingen and Princeton, from late Spring to early Fall, they are in some respects even more astonishing than those which have previously been related. There is at least one surprising turn of events that helped give direction to his course. Though one may trace actual development in his thinking, one remains unprepared until the last for the affirmative decision. And the decision itself, though it was to prove decisive for his future life, remained in his own thinking only temporary and tentative. And most amazing of all is the consideration that in reaching his decision he engaged in a passionate controversy with his mother which proved to be largely based on misunderstanding but nevertheless is perhaps unparalleled in its disclosure of his character and personality.

Armstrong's invitation of March 11th had been declined, as noted above. Several weeks were allowed to pass by, and then Armstrong, though careful not to put pressure upon him, indicated that the way was still open for him to take up work at Princeton. Writing on May 16, 1906, he said:

> I was disappointed—selfishly of course—in the decision communicated in your last letter from Marburg, and I have been pondering just what to write you. I want so much to have you come to Princeton and try this work of teaching for a year at least that my natural inclination would lead me to urge you to give the matter further and if possible favorable consideration. Yet my conscience tells me that I ought not to urge you to take a step for which you do not feel prepared. So I am going to leave the matter entirely in your hands. You know how I feel and should you decide to come there will be a warm welcome for you and plenty of work . . .

BOYHOOD
PORTRAIT

MEMBER OF
"GERMANIA," 1906

IN HIS Y.M.C.A.
UNIFORM
France, 1918

J. GRESHAM MACHEN
As he appeared at about fifty-four years of age

But I am glad that you are at Göttingen and are enjoying it. I think you were wise in deciding to leave Marburg, though I should have been perfectly satisfied had you remained there. Schürer is certainly a man of marvelous learning and I know you will benefit by studying under him. Heitmüller must be stimulating to judge from the way he writes. And Bousset—well he is brilliant but in my judgment somewhat erratic. He reminds me a good deal of Harnack.

I should like to see you at the Germania Kneipe. Without my experience in the Wingraf Verbindung at Erlangen I think my stay there would have been unendurable.

Well, Das, good luck to you at Göttingen . . . The little lady of our family sends her greetings and hopes to see you in September.

With warm regard, as ever

Army

INVITATION FROM LAFAYETTE

The next important development was an invitation to become an instructor in Lafayette College, an invitation extended by the president Ethelbert D. Warfield, who was a brother of B. B. Warfield of the Seminary Faculty. The terms of the offer, dated June 13, 1906, remain of unusual interest. Dr. Warfield wrote:

We are looking for a man to take an instructorship in Greek and German for the coming year, with excellent prospects of promotion at an early date to a professorship in Greek. I have at times talked to my brother with regard to you and would have written to you sooner had I not known that Prof. Armstrong had been thinking of you as his assistant in New Testament Greek. I now understand that it is not likely that you will accept that position and I write to ask you if you would care to consider a position here. The salary for the first year will be only $800 with the right to occupy a room in one of the College buildings. Our full professors only receive $1,600 and a house, so that is the limit of promotion. You doubtless know something of the College and its standing. Professors Bright and Craig at Johns Hopkins graduated here, and you have no doubt heard something of Lafayette from your classmates who have received their college education here. The work for the first year would probably be Freshman Greek with an elective in one of the upper classes and Freshman and Sophomore German with the Classical students.

It is very important that I should hear from you at the very earliest possible moment.

Very truly yours,

E. D. Warfield

If Dr. Warfield had not written that last urgent sentence, how differently things might have turned out! In the last analysis, of course, everything did not hang upon a single sentence. There was nothing abnormal or unfitting about it. It is significant only because its urgency was expressed on the background of Armstrong's extraordinary, one might even say astonishing patience, understanding and tact.

From the point of view of the interests of Lafayette College it is ironical that this very invitation, attractive though it was in important respects, evidently was the means of impelling him towards Princeton! For on June 27th, only two days after the reception of the Lafayette offer, he informed his father that the apparently decisive reason for declining had been Warfield's insistence upon an immediate answer. There were indeed contributory reasons. "Had I been in the state of mind that I was in at Marburg," Machen states, "I should have been very slow to relinquish the chance; but I am now getting so much benefit out of a continuation of my life as a student that I am not quite so eager to break it off as before." Moreover, he doubted whether he was well qualified to take up philological work. But he declined the proposition "with hesitation and regret" because

> an immediate answer was requested, and I can't make up my mind to bind myself till I am *absolutely* sure that I can't go into the work at Princeton, for which I am mentally so very much better prepared. However, that seems so far off, that I am almost beginning to regret that I have sent a negative reply to Lafayette...
>
> I have written to Army asking if I could see him in August at his summer resort in Ontario. A few minutes conversation with him would be of great service to me in clearing things up. If I go to America, it would be my idea to run as quickly as possible up to Army in Orillia, Ontario (as I could have no peace of mind until I had seen him and decided whether I am to make definite preparation for work at Princeton) and then to hustle to Seal Harbor for some days with you all. If I decide to go to Princeton, I shall be terribly rushed; for there will be an immense amount to do before Sept. 15. I do not yet understand how it will be possible for me to take up the work as I have not yet even come under care of presbytery; but have written to Army for information.

But all this is very much "in the air."

Armstrong did not delay his reply, for on July 14th, he responded with new hope and undertook a preliminary reply to some of Machen's questions:

Orillia, Ont., Canada
July 14/06

Dear Das:

I expect to be here until the first week in Sept. and we shall all be delighted to see you...

As I wrote you, the position of Instructor is open and waiting for you. If Dr. Ethelbert Warfield drives you into it I shall be grateful to him—as president of the Board of Directors of the Seminary he will be doing us a great service. I had almost given up hope of getting you for Princeton when Dr. B. B. Warfield told me that his brother had asked him for your address but he had said to his brother that Lafayette could not have you because I was going to take you for the Seminary. I then sent Dr. Ethelbert Warfield your address.

When you come to see me we can talk over the various questions that very naturally arise in your mind. In regard to the matters touched upon in your letter—you will not have to take any examination. You do not have to be licensed, ordained or even come under the care of a presbytery. You can start upon the work just as you are. And in regard to your theological opinions you do not have to make any pledge. You are not expected to have reached final conclusions on all matters in this field. Only in your teaching you will be expected to stand on the broad principles of the Reformed Theology and in particular on the authority of the Scriptures in religious matters—not that your teaching should be different from your personal convictions—but simply that in matters not finally settled you would await decision before departing from the position occupied by the Seminary. The whole matter reduces itself to simple good faith. Should you find after trying it that you could not teach in the Seminary because you had reached conclusions in your study which made it impossible for you to uphold its position you would simply say so. I am repeating in my own language the view taken by Dr. Purves when he talked with me about taking up this same work. I shall never forget the interview nor his great kindness and consideration. I had the same hesitation and more.... I told him that I had not settled everything—which made him smile. I knew it was a (?) undertaking but I was encouraged to try it because my responsibility to the Board of Directors was mediated by a man to whom I could talk fully and freely on any subject.

In regard to the work I would give you one hour with the Junior Class in Exegesis of some Epistle of Paul. You could offer an extra-curricular course on any subject you might choose. I would want you to work up a course on General Introduction—leaving the Canon to me. If you wanted a little time at the opening of the term I would lecture on the language of the New Testament and you could take the work in Textual Criticism. But we could adjust that. I might give the lectures and have you conduct one recitation on my lectures and a text book. Then I would expect you to help me with the other classes from time to time. You would have the instruction in Elementary Greek and could help me in my work as co-editor of the Review. Then of course you could contribute as much as you wished in the way of articles and book notices to the great Yellow Journal as Gimel calls it.

I am going to give the opening address of the Seminary this year and you will hear the principal part of the work I did on the origin of the Jerusalem Church.

Bobbie writes that he is going to take a fellowship in the University of Chicago and study the philosophy of religion. I think he is wise for he was fretting at Milroy away from books.

With every good wish

As ever

Army

As may be imagined, Machen was most grateful for this letter, and himself found new hope that it might prove feasible for him to undertake the work at Princeton. He still hardly dared to think of a favorable decision, and would have thought very seriously of returning for another year in Germany were it not for the fact that he did not think he could fairly ask Armstrong to put off the decision as to an assistant for another year. And so he made plans to sail for home with the intent of reaching a final decision on the basis of a conference.

No reference has been made in the survey of developments in Germany to the consideration that there were frequent exchanges of letters between Machen and his most intimate friends of Princeton days. They as well as his parents and Professor Armstrong indicated their confidence in him and his future, and encouraged him both to enter the ministry and to undertake the work at Princeton. Of these the most intimate and wittiest was Bobby Robinson. In spite of the length which this account has already reached, it would seem ungracious not to share at least a small sample or two of these comments with the readers of this work. At the beginning of the year when Machen's letters dwelt upon his growing conviction that he could not justify entrance into the ministry, Robinson felt that his "more serious animadversions on life in general seemed to me undigested, bearing the marks of mental dyspepsia, and I would suggest pepsin for your intellectual saliva." But at the time that Machen was considering the Princeton offer, Robinson was ready to offer advice. "I had a letter from Army," he wrote. "Don't be a goat. Try your hand at helping him. Wish to goodness I was worth a chance like that. You young tightwad, Prince of all Tightwads, it won't hurt you to try it." Though Machen loved Bobby and his humor, he was in dead earnest concerning the problems that faced him, and however refreshed he might be momentarily by such messages, they could not take away his doubts or constrain him to follow a course which seemed to be beckoning him and yet was of doubtful propriety.

When Machen arrived in America about August 21st, he immediately set out for Seal Harbor to spend about a week with his father and mother. The plan to visit Armstrong in Canada had not proved expedient, and an appointment was made to hold the conference in Princeton early in September. Exactly what developed at Seal Harbor and at Princeton cannot be reported. The decision reached at Princeton to undertake the work for one year is indeed plain, but let no one imagine that his mind was set at rest. Immediately before the conference took place he wrote that "I am afraid there is mighty little chance of going to Princeton." And afterward it appears that he was able to reconcile himself to acceptance of the post only on the understanding that it would be clearly understood that his service would definitely terminate at the end of the year, and that he would then probably return to Germany for a longer or shorter period in the expectation of preparing himself for a career as a teacher of the classics.

AN UNPARALLELED CONTROVERSY

From this September period, in fact, there has been preserved some of the most surprising letters of his life, letters that because of their impassioned outburst of feeling of distress at what his mother had written stand in sharp relief from the hundreds upon hundreds which were pervaded with admiration and confidence and can best be characterized as love letters. No man perhaps ever loved his mother more completely or showed his devotion more constantly, as the totality of these pages reflects. But at this juncture he was deeply hurt and there seemed to be a gulf between them. Unfortunately for our purposes, a number of the crucial letters written by his mother have not been preserved, and one might well draw a curtain over this episode for fear of doing her injustice. Since, however, a strong letter written in her own defense may be quoted, a letter which discloses that he had failed fully to understand her, this difficulty is overcome. And the extant letters are so significant, not so much because of their bearing upon our understanding of the relationship between the mother and her son, as for what they set forth in burning words concerning his deepest convictions, that one may be thankful for them.

The situation is more or less clearly reflected in a letter from his father dated Sept. 6:

> Dear Gresham,
>
> Have no doubt: the battle will be won.
>
> Whatever course you may adopt I will support you in. The great objection to a further three years in Germany is the distress the prospect of so long a separation from you would cause your mother. Law is open and would suit you admirably. Don't imagine your past studies would be lost in any event. You have had valuable intellectual training which will serve a good purpose whatever field of life's work may be assigned to you, beside the positive acquisitions. You are abundantly young enough for any fresh start. I don't give any vote *against* the German Ph.D. plan, but only give the ideas that float up. *I wish I could talk with you.*
>
> On the whole, my impression is that for the present, acceptance of the offered field at Princeton for a year would be advisable giving time for consideration and a final decision later. *Time* is not the important factor—I mean lapse of time—that it seems to you now. There is plenty of work awaiting you, and there is no occasion for hurry or anxiety on account of the supposed encroachment upon the years of preparation which may be required for the pursuit of the final choice. Fortunately there is no pecuniary difficulty in the way.
>
> Your affectionate father
>
> Arthur W. Machen

This letter had been followed by one from Mrs. Machen in which she dwelt upon the distress that his plan of returning to Germany gave her, and it brought forth the following response:

> Father's letter was very kind, also yours, which I have just received. I am distressed that you feel that way about my going to

Germany . . . If you knew what tremendous good my stay in Germany had done me, you would get down on your knees and beg me to go back . . . I have not quite given up Princeton, but my better judgment is against it . . . You have no idea of the desperate character of the situation. Your attitude makes me despair of your ever understanding it—so trivial does your objection to Germany seem, in comparison to the benefits that would come from it. Of course it is not trivial that you should be sorry to have me so far off—but you seem to put it on other grounds. What is your real reason? I needed every bit of courage I could get in order to take up life afresh—instead of being discouraged at the start. But I know you did what you thought best for me.

He expressed his position more fully in a letter of September 11th:

I simply wanted to prepare you for next year. I am looking forward to going to Germany then, and looking forward to it in a pretty definite way. It is not an easy course of action—but one of the hardest things I could possibly do. It takes every bit of courage I could muster.

Of course, it is not your being sorry to give me up that I object to—if I thought I could do you any good I should stay. But until I make a man of myself I can do nothing for you but harm. I am so eager to repay you for all the love and all the labor you have expended upon me. But as far as I can see I can do that only in the way I have indicated. My life over there would simply enable me to reap the fruit of the Christian training you have given me—I should owe it all to you just the same. As it is now, there are obstacles which prevent me from reaping that fruit.

I don't expect you to understand—but I do hope that you will come really with the whole heart and mind to *believe* me, and be convinced that I am doing right. Mere acquiescence from you whom I love so deeply and for whose judgment I have such a deep respect is not enough. It would be enough if you did not stand so near me, and if I did not therefore so want to feel unhampered by the fact of disagreement with you.

It was not your letter which induced me to come here, so you have no responsibility in the matter. Nobody ever started a work with more misgivings—indeed with anything nearer despair of being able to carry the work through. But I did so long to try to *give* something even though very little, after I have been merely *receiving* for so long. Before I get through I must go to Germany again—but perhaps the quiet year of study here will not be useless in enabling me to attain moral, religious and intellectual clearness of vision. Of course, intellectually I shall be living even to a greater extent in Germany than I was last year.

No words can tell what I owe to Father for sending me on my trip of last year. It gave me a little glimpse of the life God wants me to lead—and though in the storms of the past days I have lost this vision again, yet I have hopes that I may somehow or other come to fill a useful place in the world. But do you know what has given me this hope? It is the thought of that plan I outlined to you the other day. If my sole reliance were the career which would be opened to me at the Seminary, I should be in despair. My ambition is to be a student of the classics—who from the point of vantage of a broader philological knowledge than he would under other conditions have, and *in perfect freedom,* tries to contribute something to our knowledge of the New Testament. That is my real secret reliance (*of course don't say anything about it to the outside world*). That it is that gives me the courage to go on with my work here. I feel that I have something to fall back on—otherwise I could not have a peaceful moment.

Don't congratulate me too heartily on my decision. I am half convinced that it was a wrong one, but I had to decide one way or the other and am now trying hard to stifle vain regrets. It cost me a hard struggle to give up the thought of coming to the Seminary, as that seemed to be such a pleasant opening for me. But after I did for a time give it up, thus inwardly submitting to the will of God, I felt stronger in making my decisions. Going to Germany was not an easy course, as you think perhaps was the case—to submit to the idea of it cost me a hard struggle.

Don't think me unloving or ungrateful. It is because I love you so that I so long for you to *understand* my position and not merely reluctantly to acquiesce. This is going to be one of the most trying years of my life—my whole nervous system seems to be a-tingle at a thousand points of irritation, so that I have little peaceful time to face the problems in the calm way necessary. How I long for that peace and calmness that I had for a time last year. Perhaps that will come as I get into the details of the work. Last year, for the first time in my life, I was able for a while to stop thinking about myself and live in the natural way. The medicine was not continued long enough to give me full strength, but I am going to try to attain the same result in another way, and tide myself over till perhaps I can get to Gottingen again... It was because my friends at Göttingen were so fresh and interesting to me that I was enabled to get my thoughts off myself and thus to get a glimpse at a fresh, open life, where I could put into practice the principles that I have received from you and Father...

P. S. The position to which I expect to be formally appointed in a few weeks is that of Instructor in the New Testament Department at the Seminary. It lasts for one year. I am *not* a minister, or anything more than a mere layman.

AN IMPASSIONED OUTBURST

Another letter from his mother, in response to his request for "the real reason," is regrettably lost, but it no doubt suggested to her son that she feared the loss of his Christian faith if he carried out his plan of returning to Germany, for his letter of September 14th contained the following impassioned outburst:

Your whole position is of course a grief to me, as it makes me fear to confide in you. You make the same old fatal mistake in supposing that *intellectual* movements can be stopped by artificial means, either in general by suppressing the propaganda or in particular by preventing the propaganda from reaching a particular individual. Try to look at the matter from my point of view. Here is what seems to be purely an *intellectual* question, a question of fact, before me for settlement. The persons on one side say that all they demand is a perfectly free, impartial examination. The persons on the other side, as represented by you, tell me that I must be careful to investigate only one side, and not let myself get too much under the influence of the other side. On the basis merely of these attitudes of the contending parties there could be but one decision—namely that the party that favored a fair investigation is in the right. So such efforts as yours are in reality the greatest possible arguments *against* the side of the question that they are trying to support. And I venture to think that it is not infrequently such an attitude on the part of parents—such an obvious attempt to shut off full investigation—that leads many a young man to throw off the faith to which he might otherwise hold. Of course your present mistake has no such effect. In the first place, you displayed no such tendencies during the impressionable age when they would have had the worst effect in arousing the jealousy that every man has of his intellectual liberty, of his inalienable right to search after truth by all means in his power. And in the second place, I have now had such an opportunity of examining the question on its *merits,* that such arguments from the false attitude of one of the contending parties no longer have their full weight. And in the third place, I can fully understand your action from your point of view.

Try to repay me by looking at the thing from *my* point of view. What an impossible position you apparently expect me to hold! You expect me to say in effect, "I hold this thing to be true, but I know that if I investigated the arguments against it I should be convinced that it were not true." That is a position in which no one but a Jesuit could ever rest—it is absolutely impossible to every rational being. There is just exactly one thing for a man that feels himself getting into such a position to do—namely to go forward honestly and find out exactly how things stand (remember it is an intellectual question not a moral one that is to be decided). Only when he has done that can he attain anything like certainty. He must investigate the other side till he feels that he has gotten to the bottom of the business—whether that takes him one year in Germany or three years or ten years. As long as he feels that he has not *fully* learned to appreciate the arguments on both sides (and particularly the side to which he is inclined to be opposed)—just so long must he continue to be a doubter. Or else he must decide on the basis of the superficial knowledge that he already has. And of course there is no doubt in the present case which way that artificial consideration tends —on account of the example of the best minds of the day, it tends towards the modern views about the New Testament. The only way in which the thinker can hold to the old belief is by piercing below the surface and thus finding that on the merits of the question the old view has the facts on its side. And it is possible to satisfy oneself that one has thus gotten below the surface and has a right to decide on the merits of the question only by investigating every nook and cranny of both sides of the question. Thus when you try to induce me to give up going to Germany on the ground you mention, you are simply fighting against your own cause.

Doubly impossible is such a course of action in my case. You seem to have absolutely no appreciation of what this work is in which I am soon to be engaged. It is primarily historical work, which requires absolute honesty. The other side is honest—it asks for nothing but fair investigation. Would you have us reply that that claim is false, that we claim something more than fairness—namely a bias on our side? Don't you see, that however right your action is from your point of view—however loyal and admirable even—if I should follow you I should be guilty of simple old-fashioned intellectual dishonesty? And that, as I said to Father, is a greater sin than unbelief. If you feel about me as you do, then you have done very wrong in not advising me against this place. For this work calls not for children but for men—and you would make me still worse than a child. If I thought another three years of theological study in Germany might lead me to give up my present view of things, I should feel that it was my bounden duty to take that three years in Germany before beginning my present work. In the first place, simple honesty to myself would require it, and in the second place, *truth* is never in the long run harmful. And truth is subserved by looking at both sides of the question.

Of course, I must not let you force me to look at things at all in this light. "Safe" and 'dangerous" are words that must be banished absolutely from the vocabulary of the student. He must seek simply for truth. If I yielded to you, I should be in an attitude which would not only unfit me for my work here, but would prevent me from ever attaining the settled belief to which I hope to come. Calmness, and a desire to *learn* from all quarters, are absolutely necessary. If I should adopt your point of view I should be in a continual fever of anxiety.

Don't think me entirely lacking in the necessary qualities. I have picked them up in various ways—from you up to your present departure from your previous broad-minded course, and from my years as a student in various circumstances. The broader an experience a man has, just so much better fitted he is for dealing with these problems in a cautious, philosophical way. I have had my special difficulties—one of them has perhaps been the necessity of forcing myself, because of wanting to take up this position—but still I have probably accomplished something.

Don't think that I object to your trying to influence me about religious matters. Your own religious experience itself, and the consequent clear way in which you see many grounds of the old faith, are legitimate arguments (and by the way arguments of the very strongest kind). I only object to your trying artificially (i.e., by other means than refutation) to stifle other arguments, or to prevent my natural intellectual development.

Of course, as a matter of fact you took the thing much too tragically. I shall be more under the German influence in theology, perhaps, here than in studying classics in Germany. One reason indeed why I wanted to make the change was that I might in a certain sense rest from the feverish attempt to settle all kinds of religious problems in a hurry, and live for a while on what religion I had. After such a respite, I might have a clearer, sounder mind to settle the problems of New Testament study. Not a bad idea either, though I have given it up for the present.

Also, you take the whole thing perhaps too tragically—except as to the importance of the practical question whether to remain here or to start fresh. I have considerably more sense than you think I have.

It is needless for me to say again how I appreciate your love and sympathy, and the great help you have always given me. Forgive me if I have expressed myself inadvisedly. I am not quite clear on all that I have said, but I do know that if I look on the proposition about going to Germany with the kind of fears with which you look on it, then I am in an intolerable position—logically and morally. I hope you will see this. I tried my best to explain that it was not your desire not to give me up that I considered trivial, but only your *other* objection to my plan...

On the same day he expressed himself much more briefly to his father. He reiterated his distress at his mother's attitude towards his plan of returning to Germany, asserting that the implied lack of confidence in his judgment tended to make him believe that he was not in in the right place at Princeton. He declared also that "there is just *one* way for me to attain a strong Christian faith—namely by patient, *absolutely* free investigation of all contending views in a large-minded, reverent way."

Another letter written to his mother the following day, Sept. 15th, the last before the return of his parents from Seal Harbor to Baltimore, refers only briefly to the matters raised in the previous weeks. He does tell however of his great enjoyment of a day the previous Sunday with his brother Arthur in Baltimore, how "Arly's intelligent sympathy did as much as anything could have done towards making me take heart," and he expresses the hope that "I may have that kind of help next year when it will be necessary for me to begin preparing myself, so late in life, for an entirely new profession. Nobody who has tried it knows how discouraging that is. Yet it is before me just about as certainly as if I were to start in tomorrow—and the hopelessness of this year's work impresses itself more distinctly upon me after the first relief which came from having made some kind of a decision begins to wear off. I am very much afraid I made the wrong decision, but am trying not to open up the question again."

One may be grateful for the record of Machen's extraordinarily outspoken disclosure of his outlook at the time upon the Christian faith and his life as a whole, even though it was achieved at the cost of tortured feeling of being forsaken in a time of crisis and though it led him to speak to and of his mother in a manner totally unlike the boundless admiration, confidence and affection that distinguish the thousand or more letters that have been preserved.

MRS. MACHEN'S REPLY

The issues raised in these September letters were painfully real and continued to be so for a long time, but the disagreement with his mother had the transience of a sudden thunder storm. And this proved to be the case, not so much because they could simply forgive and forget, but because her own position had not been fully understood. This appears from her strong letter of rebuttal written on Sept. 17th:

> My dear Son,
>
> I understand you far better than ever before. But I am almost hopeless of making you understand me; for I must have failed utterly in expressing myself. I do not wish to trouble you at this time with my personal opinions and emotions. But I cannot rest under the unmerited charges of your letter.
>
> My son, my whole life has been a protest against the very position which you suppose me to take. When I was sixteen I rebelled against the trammelling of the intellect. I *could* not have a blind faith. This required some boldness and some independence. For I was little more than a child, and I have lived in an environment that discouraged freedom of thought. All my life long I have held that free investigation is the only way to climb to the mountain-top of an intelligent faith. You seem to have some memory of this in my past life. I do not need you to tell me, my boy, to "banish that false way of looking at things" from my mind. I do not and never have looked at free probing for truth as anything to be afraid of. I am an apostle of the opposite position. Certainly if a man is to be a scholar and a teacher he cannot investigate too much.
>
> Moreover, I have never opposed your going back to Germany for three years or any time. My first letter to you was purely emotional, though I hardly hope to make you understand it. My weak mother's heart cried out against it. Then when you thought me "trivial," I met your appeal for perfect frankness by showing you that I had felt just at first an emotional drawing back, and

I tried to show you that that was over entirely. It was past, and I reverted to it only to prove that my letter was not trivial.

I have a faith, as I tried to tell you, which, though not contrary to reason, does transcend reason. I have gotten this by life, with all its pains and trials and the light that has shone through them all. It is the fruit of living. As Dr. Patton said in talking of this, it is valuable but you cannot communicate it to others. That faith *of course* I long to share with my sons. The fear that I expressed, *in answer to your earnest solicitation for perfect candor,* was simply a clinging to that faith for myself and for you. This also was emotional, and I tried to show you that the fear was absolutely past, after the first wriggling of my heart was over.

If you do not believe me now, I do not know what to say more, except to reiterate that I do not, never did and never can oppose free investigation. That is as true as anything I ever said in my life.

One thing comforts me. Your distrust and disapproval of me have led you to express yourself more freely than you have ever done. I understand you better. I have always had faith in you when you did not believe in yourself.

God bless you, my dear son.

Your loving mother,

M.G.M.

Machen was "exceedingly grateful" for this letter, and it evidently served to restore equanimity so far as his family relations were concerned. Nevertheless, as he was on the eve of his career at Princeton, he was far from hopeful regarding the future and could hardly have entered upon his duties with zest and exhilaration.

8

LIFE AT PRINCETON, 1906-1914

That Machen once having begun his work at Princeton would continue as a member of the teaching staff, not for just one year or two, but for twenty-three years was farthest from his thoughts. Nor in view of his firm expectation of leaving at the end of a year to prepare for another profession, and the generally unsettled state of his mind, could one regard the beginnings of his labors as auspicious. The struggle with the problems that had erupted with white heat during the preceding year did not spend its force for a considerable period. Although its volcanic eruptions subsided fairly soon, the rumblings continued for a number of years.

It was not until the fall of 1913 that he attained to such assurance and calm that he could undertake the first step looking toward ordination, that of being taken under care of presbytery, and could confidently and joyfully look forward to ordination. Coincident with, and to a certain extent bound up with this last step, was that of his election to and the commencement of his service as a voting member of the Faculty. For the assumption of this office required that he should be a minister in the Presbyterian Church and as well that he should take the solemn vows incumbent upon all professors in the Seminary. The year 1914 therefore rather accurately marks a meaningful turning point in his life, and the period from 1906 to that year may well be considered as a unit.

Letters and other source materials cast an abundance of light upon this period, and one may trace with considerable confidence the development of Machen's life and thought during those years. Nevertheless, one cannot be as certain with regard to details as was true in dealing with the year 1905-06 for now he was in constant or frequent personal contact with the persons with whom his life was most intimately interwoven. Armstrong he saw nearly every day and he enjoyed many opportunities of exchanging confidences with his parents face to face.

HAPPY ASSOCIATIONS

That Machen enjoyed his life and teaching at Princeton far beyond his first expectations is plain. Nor is it difficult to assign reasons for this attachment. Princeton itself was no less charming than when he had fallen in love with it as an undergraduate in the Seminary and a partial student in the University. Life in Alexander Hall and in the Benham Club, which had been left behind so reluctantly when he graduated, could be resumed. Some of the old friends were still about or made more or less frequent visits to the campus, and there were delightful opportunities of establishing new friendships with the students who were not far from his own age.

More important still, perhaps, was the consideration that the Faculty was much the same as it had been during his student years, the only significant change at the beginning being the addition of Charles R. Erdman as Professor of Practical Theology in the very year that his own work as instructor began. It seemed strange, to be sure, to be attending faculty meetings now, and no doubt the professors seemed different in such intimate relationships. But he apparently found them all congenial and kind. Above all there were Patton and Armstrong, whose unfailing patience and wise counsel had been the means of keeping him on a straighter course than he knew he was following, and who now came to stand in even more intimate and helpful relations to him. And surely not far behind was Warfield who likewise sized up Machen's true worth and who, as his own stature was more and more recognized, wielded a steadying and stabilizing influence upon his life and thought. And there were the younger men on the staff who, like "Army," were congenial companions and delightful friends as well as colleagues: "Wis" Hodge second only to Armstrong, but also "Gimel" MacMillan, "Jim" Boyd and others.

Special mention must be made of the incalculable help afforded by his father and mother and older brother during those difficult years before he reached solid ground. They constantly took intelligent and sympathetic interest in every phase of his life and supported and encouraged him at every turn. His mother particularly could be counted upon to write regularly and to respond with refreshing discrimination and discernment to his own messages. She was reassuring and wrote, "My own dear boy, if you only knew how I love you, and how I long to help you in every way and never to hinder." Or sympathetic and said, "I am sorry you are discouraged with your work, but I suppose nobody ever was satisfied with intellectual work, especially if done under pressure." Or amusing in reporting that Mrs. van Dyke had said, in explaining that they would not return to Seal Harbor because the social duties were too onerous, that "you know Dr. van Dyke cannot be hidden." Or simply informative in telling of evenings at the Gilmans and the Remsens or more homely details of everyday life. Or bearing good report, yet with restraint, in telling that Dr. Patton, being a visitor, "speaks affectionately of you and says they are pleased with your work. God bless you, my beloved son, and show you what to do. *Whatever* that may be you shall have the loving support of your mother ever with you." Or overflowing with motherly gratitude and pride in writing, "I enjoyed your visit to the very depths of my heart. You were so loving to your mother that it did her good, and I couldn't help being proud of your looking so handsome."

Though Machen was frequently discouraged with reference to his qualifications as a teacher, on one occasion during the first year he concedes that there is another side of the picture, and in this connection raises anew the problem of his future course:

> In many respects, my work is very enjoyable, for I seem to get on pretty well with the fellows and enjoy the work of instruction as well as my own studies. But the thought of what I am afraid are insurmountable obstacles ahead of me, lames my effort to some extent by depriving me of that joy and enthusiasm which is necessary for the best work. However, I hope the year is not entirely wasted as it is not entirely without its pleasures. My association with Army is perhaps my greatest delight.

Several weeks later, on March 3, 1907, he reports that "Dr. Patton was enthusiastic about the good time he had in Baltimore, and I have no doubt that his experience is being repeated today. Certainly, I wish him all joy, for he is proving a mighty good friend to me in a time of difficulty and perplexity." And three weeks later, after speaking of his distress at her suffering with headache—"that terrible trial in bearing which you have been such an example of Christian patience to us all," he comments upon the outlook for the following year:

> Though the matter is not fully decided yet, it rather looks as though I should stay here another year on just the same conditions as this year. As far as I can see I am really little nearer anything like a decision to enter the ministry than I was last fall, nor does Dr. Patton, for instance, advise it for the present; but I am learning a good deal here and think I shall stay if the position is definitely offered me, as seems probable. I am of course a little restless; it does seem to be high time to start about the preparation for some line of work that I can be engaged in permanently;

> but perhaps my time here will not be entirely wasted no matter what I do afterwards. Sooner or later I shall perhaps have to carry out my plan of studying for a Ph.D., in Germany, but since I am very old for that purpose anyway, perhaps one more year will not make so much difference. Army says he has no one else in view just now, so he is willing to take me for another year, temporarily as before. He and Dr. Patton are certainly both of them proving mighty good friends to me.
>
> The spring and summer I expect to spend here in Princeton working. It is absolutely necessary that I should be here nearly all of the time, nor is the prospect altogether an unpleasant one. N. Y. is near, with lots of friends, and Army is going to stay in Princeton this summer so that I shall not lack company. Of course, I shall see our family off and on.

Though he warned in a postscript that the plans were not definite, and that he might still follow a different course, it hardly needs to be added that, though no further reference to the subject appears in his letters, evidently the offer became definite and was accepted.

The situation had not altered substantially the following year. On March 22, 1908 he wrote his mother: "Dr. Patton will be away from Princeton from about April 1 to about April 19, delivering lectures in Milwaukee and other places. His absence will be a source of great regret to me, for I shall need his advice sorely. Whether I shall return next year is exceedingly doubtful." But only a week later the situation had changed, perhaps because he had been able to see Dr. Patton before his departure. In his second letter of the day, he says:

> In my letter of this morning I forgot to tell you what I suppose was the chief piece of news that I had—namely that I am now leaning very strongly to the idea of returning here next year. I have not decided it absolutely, but I have almost done so. During next year I shall be here under the same conditions as this year—whether I shall ever enter the ministry seems to me just about as doubtful as a year ago. But I am learning something here and I hope accomplishing some work. And in any case, even if I switch around now, I shall be off the regular track in any other department—so belated any way that one more year will not make such a great difference.

Later he stated merely that the Board, at Armstrong's suggestion, had raised his salary from $1,000 to $1,250, and that he was anticipating a pleasant summer in Princeton with Army and Wistar Hodge.

In the letters written during—and after—the following academic year, on the other hand, there are no such references to a possible departure from Princeton. It may be somewhat bold to argue with finality from this silence that he could never have expressed himself in the old terms. One receives the impression from other observations, however, that by the spring of 1909 he had identified himself so closely with the work at Princeton that he could not be thinking very seriously of another field, though unquestionably he was still some years away from solving the greater question as to his possible call to the ministry.

THE "REBELLION" OF 1909

That he had identified his life with that of Princeton Seminary and his colleagues on the Faculty is borne out, for instance, by the stand he took when the much publicized "student rebellion" erupted in February, 1909. Petitions signed by considerable numbers of the members of the Middler and Junior classes complained to the Board of Directors regarding the curriculum and the teaching in the Seminary, singling out the courses of Patton, Davis and Armstrong for special attack. Without conferring with the professors mentioned, or petitioning the Faculty, appeal was taken directly to the Board which however referred the matter to the Faculty. Not satisfied with the attitude taken by the Faculty, a second petition was presented to the Board. The matter was widely publicized in the New York, Philadelphia and Baltimore newspapers, and the Seminary was pictured as being sadly behind the times. For example, an anonymous article by a "minister," whose initials were given as "A.C.D.," appeared in the Baltimore *News* of March 6th with a two-column heading, PRINCETON THEOLOGUES PROTEST AGAINST SOME COURSES AND DEMAND OTHERS IN SEMINARY, and included the following:

> Something extraordinary has happened. In the Princeton Theological Seminary, where Calvinism in its pristine state is inculcated, the students have entered into revolt against the curriculum, and threaten divers reprisals if their granting their demands for a reconstruction of the studies is not forthcoming.
>
> In the news dispatches, which are meager and not explicit, it is asserted that the candidates for the ministry complain that some of the familiar divinity school courses are not "intelligible," and that such studies as sociology are necessary in the preparation of men who will be called to minister to the flesh and blood of an immensely complex, social time.

Without presuming too much, an inside view of the situation will probably reveal the fact that in the minds of the theologues the seminary needs a modern and more scientific and practical course of instruction. This conclusion is the more emphasized when it is recalled that the sister Presbyterian institution, only a few miles away—Union, in New York—is among the foremost in all departments, representing as it does the broader spirit of the Presbyterian Church . . .

The Princeton "revolt," as it is called, is a serious thing. The head of the institution, the venerable and learned Dr. Patton who has been the leading thinker of a certain wing of the Church, comes in for the severest criticism in the news. He has evidently been charged with responsibility for the alleged shortcomings of the seminary. That he is not in sympathy with the modern ideas of ministerial preparation has frequently been charged against him.

The old order has changed. In a word, ministers of a former generation were drilled in doctrines which compelled life to be fashioned after the pattern of doctrines. The present generation pays its tribute to life and insists that all doctrines shall be fashioned according to the nature and the spirit and the laws of life . . .

Two days later the same newspaper carried a news story with the heading, "PRINCETON BREACH RAPIDLY WIDENING—Protesting Theological Students May Be Expelled From Seminary—PATTON INTERVIEW AROUSES ANGER—Grievance Committee Declares The President Is Trying to Throw Blame On Student Body."

Machen's own first reference to the matter in a letter home was on Feb. 21st, when he wrote:

The students are exhibiting a spirit of dissatisfaction with the instruction that is offered them. What they want is apparently a little course in the English Bible, about on a level with White's Bible School. They want to be pumped full of material, which without any real assimilation or any intellectual work of any kind they can pump out again upon their unfortunate congregations. I sometimes feel that we are like a monastery in the Middle Ages. We are able to do little for our own generation, and can only hope to conserve a spark of learning for some future awakening in the Church's intellectual life. Other seminaries have yielded to the incessant clamor for the "practical," and we are being assailed both from within and from without. I only hope the authorities will have the courage to keep our standard high, not bother

> about losses of students, and wait for better times. It is the only course of action that can be successful in the long run.

On March 7th he sent home a clipping of a "fairly good story" that had appeared in the New York *Sun* and referred to "a mean little knock" on orthodox theology in general which had appeared in the New York *Evening Post*. His fear was that "the matter will do the Seminary harm, and it makes me very angry when I think of some of the leaders of the trouble," referring to one prominent student as "a bright fellow who has loafed and treated the Seminary course as a joke." A week later, commenting on the stories in the Baltimore *News*, he declared that

> it is rather a revolt against modern university methods than against theological conservatism; but pure "cussedness" describes it better still... At present the matter has quieted down, and I hope that the students will come to see with increasing clearness what an ungentlemanly thing they have done. The University men are wondering why the man whom they regard as about the only gleam of light in the general darkness of the Seminary—namely Army—should have been one of those singled out for attack. My only comfort is that things have gotten so dreadfully bad as to the intellectual preparation of candidates for the ministry that a reaction is bound to set in before long. But meanwhile our task is a discouraging one.

About a month later the "revolt" was again featured in the newspapers, but now Machen felt that the difficulties had largely subsided. On April 11th, he wrote that what his mother had been reading was "merely a newspaper revival of an older trouble" and that the second student petition to the Directors had been kept out of the papers until recently. He then added:

> One curious feature about the whole thing is that there is less outward disturbance about the matter in Princeton than there is apparently everywhere else. Everything seems to be peaceful in the extreme . . . Many of the students are opposed to the course that has been pursued, but they are dominated by some clever politicians . . . Bad as the situation is it has been ridiculously exaggerated in the sensational accounts that have appeared in the papers. As for students leaving the Seminary on account of the trouble, I think it would in some cases be a consummation devoutly to be wished, but I do not think it is likely. Some of the men could hardly be driven away with a shot-gun—it is too much fun to be

> important and make trouble. And as for the good men, I do not think they are going to leave either.
>
> But whether the students go or stay, it is perfectly evident that they cannot regard themselves as one of the governing bodies of the institution. And that is what they really want to do. Meanwhile, a great deal of Christian patience is required . . .

The Board took action at a meeting in April, and entrusted the announcement of it to the students. This was done by notices on the bulletin boards. In this action the Board reminded the students that the immediate government of the Seminary lay in the hands of the Faculty, expressed confidence in their wisdom and regret "that the students have presented their communication in such form and manner." It also entertained "the hope that the students will express their regrets to the President for their mistakes," and informed them that their communication would be taken into consideration by a committee on curriculum of the Directors which would confer with the Faculty, gather information and report to the Board. A happy aftermath, so far as Machen was concerned, was that, as he was able to write home, "Army was rather encouraged by the papers that he received and some of the men who formerly 'knocked' on his Gospel History course began to appreciate it after they had put in some of the real hard licks of work that such a course requires."

Without question Machen was deeply disturbed by this entire episode in part because of the attack made upon Patton and Armstrong whom he regarded as among the most brilliant men on the Faculty and who had put him greatly in their debt by their exceedingly wise and patient dealing with him and his problems. His loyalty to and regard for Patton and Armstrong were such that the attack upon them was felt as a personal wound. For Armstrong particularly the blow must have been severe, for by nature he was reserved and even shy, whereas Patton had been toughened by years of public conflict. Patton's own reaction was amusingly told the present writer, about 1926, by Armstrong himself, though without specific reference to the "revolt." Armstrong had said to Patton that he understood that the students were complaining about his teaching, and maintaining that they had difficulty hearing him, and that the little they could hear they could not understand. And to this Patton replied, "The trouble with the students is that they sit too far back—*intellectually speaking!*"

Though the personal factor entered into Machen's judgment, it would be quite unfair to suppose that this was basically determinative of it. For there is cumulative evidence, covering some time prior to this incident and many years afterward, which shows that he was deeply disturbed by such steps as were taken, and by the general tendency to substitute courses in English Bible and other "practical" courses for hours traditionally assigned to theology and the study of the Scriptures on the basis of a knowledge of the original languages. Though the students were not vindicated, the issue of the nature of the curriculum remained one of great moment, and Machen lamented the gradual increase of "practical" studies as marking a downgrade course in the life of the Seminary. On the surface the issue might have appeared rather superficial, but ultimately it was bound up with one's total view of the nature and purpose of a Seminary. Machen's own position was no doubt in large measure identical with that expressed editorially in *The Presbyterian* of May 12, 1909. The difference of opinion, it stated, "arises out of the deeper difference as to the purpose of a theological seminary. If its primary purpose is to give young men a clear and systematized understanding of the truth of God revealed in His Word, and the history and life of His Church, one course of study will be readily outlined. If the purpose is, in some haste, to prepare young men to study the varying thought and attempt the regulation of the social order of the present time, a very different method of instruction will be necessary."

CHRISTIAN CHARACTER AND ACTION

Let no one, however, conclude from the above that Machen was out of touch with life, disinterested in the practice of Christianity, or without compassion upon men in their suffering and temptations. The evidence to the contrary is overwhelming. The record is one of countless acts of humble service and of devoted ministry to the needy and distressed, which were never publicized and in most cases were known only by those immediately involved and in a measure by those at home.

One is not surprised to observe that he did very little preaching during the years prior to his ordination. The first year at the Seminary he was not required to preach at the Seminary Chapel because the list of older faculty members and of invited guest preachers was so long that no Sunday was open. But on March 29, 1908, an hour or so before the service he is "writing letters vigorously in order to keep my courage up," remarking that this is "the first time I have attempted anything of the kind." When his mother pressed him later on for details, he said that the sermon had been a working over of a senior class sermon on Gal. 3:21a, and added: "I don't believe I could write a new one to save my life. The comments of my friends of the faculty and of the student body were very kind, but I suppose their friendship warped their judgment." However, at least one friend of the Faculty was so moved that he did not trust himself to speak after the service, for this letter was found in the files:

Dear Das:

I didn't speak to you this morning just because I really couldn't trust myself to speak. What a glorious gospel it is! When you preach it, you may be sure from the testimony of this poor man, at least, it "finds" men. Personal friendship may have contributed something to the effect of your words on me. But whatever different elements entered into it, the effect was profound. The simplicity and sincerity of your words and manner, the clearness of your line of thought, the touches of restrained feeling, the depth and breadth and central character of your theme, made this sermon one of the great Christian sermons of my experience as a churchgoer. I am confident that I shall never forget it, but shall always associate that great text and idea with you. It never pays to be afraid to preach—before anybody—when we have a message like that.

Your friend Jim Boyd

In the years that followed he preached regularly once a year at the Seminary Chapel when his turn came round, but in spite of the encouragement of Jim Boyd and others, he did not feel free to welcome preaching opportunities. On very rare occasions, beginning in August, 1909, he undertook to preach when no one else was available to fulfill an urgent request. One must wait until the fall of 1913 before hearing him tell of his "love of preaching."

Prior to this, however, he had been for a number of years a faithful worker in the Sunday School of the First Church of Princeton. He began to teach there only when he was pressed into it as a substitute for an absent teacher by the superintendent Professor "Billie" Magie, whom he was wont to see often on Sunday afternoons at the home of his brother-in-law "Wis" Hodge. Beginning about 1910 he taught regularly, and when his colleague MacMillan, who had succeeded Magie as superintendent, left Princeton in 1913, Machen acted in this capacity for a considerable period, resigning only when the pressure of other work and opportunities overwhelmed him. He took great personal interest in the boys in his class, and no doubt the entire experience was a fruitful one. On one occasion he later attributed his love of the Old Testament, and his frequent use of texts therefrom in his preaching, to the fact that as a teacher he had been compelled to give far more minute attention to its contents than he as a teacher of New

Testament might otherwise have done. Growing out his service in this Sunday School, and also motivated by the concern to serve the Church at large in a practical way, was the arduous task of the preparation of Sunday School lessons for the Board of Christian Education which was undertaken in 1914 and later years.

No one who knew Machen in these years could doubt that he had an unusual capacity for friendship and that he experienced extraordinary delight when his cordial overtures were reciprocated. By nature he was not exactly gregarious and he continued all his life to enjoy the liberty and relaxation of privacy and solitude. But as he grew to maturity he entered with greater and greater joy into the privileges of comradeship and friendship with others. Thus his participation in the life of his college fraternity, the Benham Club and the German student societies may be understood. There was indeed a certain exclusiveness about these organizations, but it was not this feature which accounted for their particular appeal. The choice before Machen was not membership in such a society or fellowship with a more comprehensive circle of friends, but rather the former or almost no friends at all. It will be recalled that when he entered Princeton his first reaction to the Benham Club was that it was "too stuck up"; but he accepted membership and became an enthusiastic member because this was the way in which in the concrete situation real friends could be found. Similarly in Germany he accepted the exclusiveness of the student society life because this was the only way in which he could break through the reserve and formality of student relations in general.

On his return to Princeton the Benham Club again came to his aid, providing not only a place to board but also healing medicine for his hours of loneliness. The Checker Club at which he played host in his room was soon revived after his return, and it is significant that what had at first been a gathering of Benhamites soon lost its exclusiveness and students were cordially invited without regard to club membership. The words of invitation that were to become the paradoxical synonym for the heartiest possible extension of hospitality, "Don't be a tightwad!" were never to be forgotten by hundreds upon hundreds of Seminary students. An aristocrat in the best sense, and always a gentleman, Machen was never stuffy or affected. One soon came to feel that he was utterly genuine and without guile.

MAN OF COMPASSION

But there was another quality which was more remarkable in revealing the true depths of Machen's Christian character, though it may not have been observed as widely as his warmhearted hospitality and comradeship. Perhaps this quality is not to be sharply distinguished from his friendliness, if we think of it as raised to the highest power and confronted with human need of one sort or another. To call it generosity is to be feeble, though he was generous without calculation and almost to the point of prodigality, and could hardly turn away any one who came to borrow, though that which was lent usually turned out to be a gift. It is pernaps best described as a strong and tender compassion for the weak and suffering and erring that expressed itself in untold, almost inexhaustible acts of mercy, and could be compared—though he would have indignantly rejected the comparison—with that which had provided the supreme example of such compassion while its even greater meaning lay in its being the redemptive source of power to live after that example.

One who reads his intimate letters to his mother and father begins to sense the measure of this quality. This provides only a beginning however, for his expansive files, which were allowed to preserve, oftentimes without evident purpose, apparently all the letters that came his way, contain intimation after intimation of acts of benevolence known only to Machen and those who became the objects of his compassion. Two cases stand out, however, as of special interest because they both involved almost constant activity over periods of many years duration, though neither of these was unknown to his parents. One concerned a relative who was a man of culture and achievement; the other a ne'er-do-well, illiterate drunkard.

The former was Edgeworth B. Baxter, a cousin of Machen's mother, being the son of a brother of her own mother, and thus a nephew of "Aunty" Bird who has figured prominently in our first chapter. His early life was spent in Augusta, Georgia, but he took his college work at Princeton where he graduated as a member of the class of 1890. At Princeton he took prizes in literature, philosophy, debating and oratory; and his classmates, in a memorial resolution passed at a dinner in New York after his death, recalled that they had "marvelled at the brilliancy of his intellect and gloried in the brightness of the future that lay before him." For a time he practised law in Augusta but had to abandon it following a nervous breakdown. In 1907, however, he returned to Princeton with a view to launching a new career, engaged in two years of graduate study, and thereafter served as instructor in jurisprudence and in philosophy until his untimely death in 1916.

Though Machen met Baxter for the first time in 1907 at Princeton, they at once became good friends and remained so throughout the nine years that followed. There were hours of pleasant association, and Machen was charmed by his brilliant cousin. To a large extent, however, Baxter's life was a tormenting struggle with wretched health until the time of his death in a hospital in Trenton, and this fact added severe burdens to every aspect of his life. In this unhappy situation Machen was not merely sympathetic and helpful in a general way, but gave unstintingly of his time and energy (not to dwell on monetary aid) as emergency after emergency arose. The correspondence from 1907 to 1916 abounds with so many references to Baxter's welfare, amounting usually to misfortune, that one or two concrete items must serve to make our point regarding Machen's character.

Shortly after Baxter's arrival in Princeton and even before the more critical problems developed, he had occasion to comment upon his first impressions regarding Gresham Machen. Writing on Nov. 29, 1907, he was thanking his "dear cousin Minnie" for the gift of her book on Browning, welcoming it, like all such efforts, "to arrest the pragmatic spirit of our times and direct it back to the deeper, truer, formative forces which issue from genuine culture," and was anticipating "more than pleasure in learning how the largest and richest spiritual influence of all time has wrought itself into the fibre of one of England's best creative minds." But he could not find it in his heart, he said,

> to close this letter until I have confessed to you how great an attachment I have formed for Gresham. Indeed, Cousin Minnie, I think your boy is quite altogether admirable. I suspect that I am not wholly unbiased in my estimate of him; for his unfailing kindness to me—his never-ceasing, unselfish efforts to serve me in all ways which friendship, kinship, and inborn courtesy could suggest, have already made me set too high a value on him to see aught but good in him. Yet, our closest contact with truth is gained through the higher immediacy of *feeling*. And I do not doubt my estimate of Gresham. His obviously innate love of culture; the fullness of his mind; the unusual maturity and sanity of his judgment; the excellent poise of his nature; his fine manliness—these are quickly seen. But there is more than these—for
>
> *Kind hearts* are more than coronets,
> And *simple faith* than Norman blood!

One wonders what language Baxter would have employed in later years after his younger cousin's "unfailing kindness" was demonstrated under more exhausting and painful circumstances!

A BATTLE AGAINST RATS

A rather amusing story of a battle to exterminate some rats which were robbing Baxter of hours of sleep night after night is illustrative of Machen's persistent solicitude. During the year 1908-09 Baxter was occupying a room above the Benham Club. The rat episode began to unfold early in the year 1909 when "they made such an unconscionable racket right at the head of the bed between the partitions and all around the ceiling" that Baxter was unable to get to sleep until about half-past two. Measures taken by members of the club all failed. "The rats refused flatly either to go into the trap or eat rat-biscuit. Finally," said Machen, "I went in search of ferets, and by going from one place to another making inquiries finally discovered a man that used to have ferrets until he let them in once where rat-poison had been placed, and all four died. But he turns out to be a kind of rat expert—and we had him come up to look over the ground. He seems to appreciate the spirit of the chase anyway, and we have hopes."

The following week's letter is largely taken up with the battle to eliminate the rats, but no progress had been made. New traps were set in holes opened up in the floor, sulphur was burned in the attic, more poison was placed about from garret to cellar. Expert rat-catchers did not seem to know much, no ferret could be secured in Princeton or in Trenton. Another week followed, and still no success. Now it could be reported that "ferrets have at last been discovered in Princeton, but the man who owns them wants ten dollars for running the rats out of the house, and besides wants us to guarantee his ferrets against the poison that Edge rashly scattered around soon after Christmas. We hope to buy a ferret ourselves from Matawan, N. J., unless the Princeton ferret man comes down from off his high horse." Later, in spite of their expense, the Princeton ferrets were hired, but they gave relief only so long as they remained about, and had to be brought back again and again. On one occasion a ferret got into an encounter with the club dog Toby, and got the worst of it. At this point Machen gives away the fact that all along he himself was mainly bearing the brunt of the battle, for he says, "This business of getting rid of rats is about the biggest job I ever struck." The following fall Baxter moved into a house, and Machen helped him get settled in his quarters. His cousin, he said, was glad to get away from the rats which were still running around in his room when he had stopped in a few days before, and as for himself Machen was glad "to be freed of the responsibility of combatting them."

A touching little sequel to this valiant but futile struggle with the rats at the Benham Club suddenly finds expression nearly a year later, for in a letter to his father on August 28, 1910, he says:

> During the summer I have been having the cat in the garret of the Benham house regularly fed, the milk wagon stopping every other day. It seems like a good deal of trouble to take just for a cat, but I didn't like to let the poor thing shift for itself. Considering that the cat was successful where ferrets and every other rat-destroyer known to modern science failed miserably, I think the cat deserves its keep. I should think the poor thing would be a bit lonesome, but the woman who feeds it says its spirits are good.

Baxter's difficulties were not overcome by settling in more congenial rooms, for it appears that he was rarely well and often miserably sick with severe headaches and nausea. On one occasion in December of 1909 Machen stayed with him for three nights straight in order to minister to his needs. And so through the years that followed Machen was ever at hand to give succor and encouragement until toward the end, when hospitalization was required, he was nearly overwhelmed with the burden. When Baxter died, Machen arranged for the sending of the body to Georgia and himself made the trip there for the funeral. But his labors were not at an end, for his cousin's effects had to be disposed of and his papers sifted, and many an hour was taken up. Though there is evidence that he assumed far larger financial responsibility in connection with medical and other expenses, perhaps the most revealing item is that of a letter written on Jan. 7, 1917, to a Princeton address with the following content: "I have found a bill for 88 cents among the papers of Mr. E. B. Baxter, deceased. Please inform me whether the bill is still unpaid. If it is, I will pay it upon receiving the information." The letter was returned with the note that it had not been paid, and it contained the further notation in Machen's hand, "Paid $1.00."

In the nature of the case there is no record of the more spiritual ministry of Christian counsel and comfort of those years. But something of it shines through a letter referring to a note that his mother had written Baxter. Writing on Jan. 16, 1910, and reporting that "Edge has had another dreadful attack, and after getting over it is much pressed by work piling up on him," he said:

> If you could have witnessed Edge's pleasure in your note, you would have been fully repaid for the trouble of writing. I have seldom seen him so deeply affected by anything, and after he had let me read the note, I could fully understand his feeling. It has been a great help and encouragement to me as well as to him. In the midst of a kind of learning, which in the mass of historical details loses the simplicity of the gospel, and on the other hand,

in the midst of cant phrases or at any rate a somewhat vociferous expression of Christian experience, I do not know anything more strengthening and encouraging than the strong faith of a true and refined character. Especially when that character happens to be such a mother as mine. I feel exalted by the admiration and affection which Edge feels for you.

THE STORY OF R. H.

Having brought the curtain down upon this largely tragic story, one has the feeling that Machen's own compassionate role has been set forth with understatement. It may, however be discounted by some because, after all, Baxter was of the same flesh and blood and a man of unusual refinement. But there is another story which gives all the proof that any one could ever dare to demand that his compassion was exercised without respect of persons, the story of a man who will be referred to here only by his initials R. H. There are a fairly large number of references to this man in Machen's letters to his mother, and one is able from them to piece the story together more or less clearly. But the extent of his ministrations on behalf of R. H. come to view only when one takes account of the scores and scores of letters written by R. H. himself in answer to Machen's regular pastoral letters, which were filed over a period of more than twenty years. There are also a fairly large number of letters from a number of pastors of churches in communities where R. H. lived and who, in addition to their spiritual ministrations, served as stewards of funds which Machen provided to meet his needs.

The first reference to R. H., found in a letter Machen wrote his mother on May 22, 1910, discloses that his first contacts with the man were through the Rev. Sylvester W. Beach, pastor of the First Church of Princeton:

> I have taken up with an old fellow by the name of H., who has been a drunkard most of his life, but was converted a year or so ago (before I knew him) and came into the First Presbyterian Church. He has a hard time with his old failing, but is trying to do better. For the last few weeks he has spent a considerable part of the time in my room reading Pilgrim's Progress. He has read both parts over twice with avidity, and displays a taste for other equally improving reading. Though he has been just a laborer most of his life, he is by no means devoid of intelligence. His father was an architect in Richmond before the war, and the four years of the war he spent in Richmond as a boy. He is pretty well broken down

> in health and we are having some difficulty getting the right kind of light work. We are especially anxious to get him away from Princeton, where he will be more out of the way of temptation. About a month ago he had a terrible lapse, when two nice suits of clothes that I gave him were sold to get money for drink. That was discouraging, and has made me very cautious about helping him in a pecuniary way, but we are paying for his board and lodging till he gets regular work. Just now he is well on his feet again.

The situation was kept fairly well in hand until early in 1912 when R. H.'s drunken sprees became more frequent, and things became "dreadfully unsatisfactory." One morning after he had come in drunk the night before, Machen got up at 4:30 A. M. to keep him from sneaking off. It became imperative to find a lodging place at some distance from his old companions, and Machen went off to Vineland, N. J., to look up a favorable place for him. No immediate solution was found, but eventually in the course of the year arrangements were made, and R. H. lived there and later in Millville until his death in August, 1933, at the age of 84. The move to Vineland seems to have been a good one for his moral and spiritual progress. He even undertook a limited amount of labor for a while, but due to his poor health and advancing infirmity, he was almost completely dependent upon charity for his support. This support was undertaken by Machen almost single-handedly, for this score of years, and finally his funeral expenses and of the small cemetery lot were also paid by him. The total outlay no doubt ran into hundreds and even thousands of dollars, and provides an outstanding example of a benevolence that was known—except in part to his mother—only to those whose services were indispensable to its fulfillment. Since, however, it might be held that Machen could easily afford such charity, no special emphasis upon it would be placed here were it not for the fact that it was motivated by an extraordinary concern for R. H.'s spiritual welfare, and was also accomplished by a spiritual ministry of exceptional devotion. Though few examples of them have been preserved, Machen wrote regular pastoral letters, often every week. An example of a brief one from near the end of his life may well be quoted:

> I am so glad to get your good letter of yesterday. God has indeed been good to you, and I rejoice in your love for Him. You do me good by being so brave and full of faith in the midst of all the suffering through which you have passed. Just now I cannot write you a very long letter, but I just want to say how happy your letter made me, because it shows me so clearly that you are

> relying upon your Saviour and have no fear of anything that may come to you, in sickness or in health, because you are safe in the love of God.
>
> It is good news that you are feeling better, and I am certainly glad to hear you speak as you do about Mr. B. He is certainly a good friend of yours.
>
> May the rich blessing of God continue to be with you.
>
> Cordially yours,
>
> J. Gresham Machen

Though the latter years of this man were on the whole characterized by soberness and godliness, they were not without crises which made demands upon Machen far beyond the pecuniary and epistolary ministrations to which reference has been made. There were many friendly visits to the south Jersey towns where H. lived, but some were occasioned by the development of circumstances beyond the control of the local pastor. For example, during the summer of 1916, he had to make an urgent journey to Vineland. As he wrote just before undertaking the trip,

> Bad news has arrived from Mr. H. He has become very much discontented, and this together with increasing untidiness has made him unbearable to the people with whom he has stayed for several years. They have requested me to take him away. If you knew the extreme difficulty that we have always found in getting a proper place for H. to live you would sympathize with me, especially since Dr. Beach is away on his vacation and good Dr. King who has befriended H. in Vineland is becoming much broken by growing old age. I am going to Vineland this afternoon to try to straighten things out, but the prospect is by no means pleasant. The people with whom H. has been boarding think that there has been moral deterioration in H., but I am by no means sure of the truth of their suspicions. Certainly there has been absolutely no alcoholic breakdown of that complete kind that was so common at Princeton.

Two days later he reported sadly concerning his journey:

> My trip to Vineland to investigate H. was very wearisome and very discouraging. It is extremely difficult to get at the truth, since he flatly denies the charges of misconduct that are made against him but it does look as though he had been carrying on a system of deceitfulness for a year or so at least. For one thing he seems to be dishonest about using the money which is given

him for small incidental expenses for his own purposes—lying about the matter the while. But what am I to do? I am too far away to be able to *prove* things against him in any stringent way. One thing is clear, he has gotten rid of his habit of drinking in a most surprising way. Instead of going to pieces every little while as he did at Princeton, he keeps the things that are given him and looks fairly well. But if he is a systematic liar, it does rather look as though the years of labor that have been spent upon him are in vain.

Our immediate problem is to get him a place to live, since his present landlord very naturally refuses to keep him longer, H. being unbearably suspicious and discontented. If we put him in any kind of a "home," he would probably run off at the first opportunity as he did once before. The natural thing would be to send him to Millville, a neighboring town, where he has been very fond of going to church; but there are certain puzzling charges about his conduct in that town. Good old Dr. King is investigating, but I shall have to go down again in a few days.

A few days later he reported that another trip to Millville and Vineland had passed off with much less annoyance, that measures were being taken to secure another boarding place for Mr. H., and that he himself seemed to be in pretty good condition. And his mother encouraged him not to feel that his labor had been lost. "I have felt the greatest sympathy for you about Mr. H.," she wrote on August 5th. "As to the deceptions of which you suspect him, you must remember that lying is not as terrible a sin to some people as it would be to you and me, trained as we have been to hate untruth as we do the Devil. You know the Catholics rank it among the venial sins as distinguished from the deadly. I do not mean to condone it at all; but only to encourage you not to think all your work for the man wasted because he might, under temptation, deceive you. Poor struggling old man—he has much to contend with. And I believe he is in the main sincere even if he does do little bad things. I suppose he is a bit afraid of you, and that may tempt him to deceive or prevaricate." The move to Millville was arranged for, but in September, 1917, a new boarding place had to be found, and arrangements entered into with a layman to look after H. when the pastor of the church took a six months' war leave. And when at the end of the year Machen himself was about to go abroad for war service, one of the most perplexing matters was to make satisfactory arrangements for H.'s supervision and counselling. Evidently things went well with H., for about a year later, Machen received a very encouraging letter from Dr. Beach dated Dec. 5, 1918 and addressed to him c/o the American Y.M.C.A. in Paris. It is incidentally the most informative among all that refer to Machen's relationship to H. since Dr. Beach ordinarily had been able to see Machen regularly in Princeton. After dealing with certain financial aspects of the case, and noting that the sum of $450 deposited in the special H. account was now depleted, Dr. Beach said:

> I am hoping soon to have a letter from you concerning your future plans in respect to H. I want you to know that I consider R.H. as one of the most marvellous monuments of grace I have ever known. He is living a consistent Christian life after more than fifty years of dissipation. He cares for nothing so much as the church and the services of it. His whole thought is of the various meetings for religious worship. He is also bent on doing good as he has opportunity. His letters to soldiers have done much good I have no doubt. The only drawback to that particular service has been the cost in stamps. You would hardly believe it possible were I to tell you the amount I have paid out for postage for him. But this is his mission he believes, and I have not liked to put the money side of it in the way.
>
> What R. is, under God, we owe to you. The expense of time, thought, labor and money has been large, but I do not believe an investment ever yielded greater dividends to the glory of God. You have saved a man, and one redeemed life is worth more than the whole world, our Lord Himself has declared.
>
> We have been looking forward to the time when you will be home again. Princeton is missing you more than in your modesty you are ready to admit. For myself I can say that it seems to me that a great spiritual force always in exercise in our midst has been withdrawn by your absence. We shall indeed welcome your home-coming.
>
> Praying God's richest blessing on the work you are so well doing for the men who need just what you can give them, and with affectionate kind wishes, I remain
>
> Cordially and faithfully yours,
>
> Sylvester W. Beach

One wishes that it might be possible to record that H. had backslid for the last time in 1917, and that there were only encouraging responses to Machen's ministrations. But such was not the case. Soon after his return from France, he had to hurry down to Millville to look for H. who had disappeared after selling several articles of clothing that had been given him, but H. avoided him, apparently getting wind of Machen's presence in town. Inquiries were also made in Philadelphia at the Salvation Army Industrial Home, and by letter to the Keswick Colony, to see whether "they have room for our man." No wonder that Machen lamented: "A good many people might think H. is not worth working for—there is deceitfulness in him as well as his recurrent weakness—but in the providence of God I have been given absolute responsibility (so far as any one has it) for the welfare of a human soul, and I cannot put the matter out of my mind. Meanwhile, my academic work has absolutely gone by the board." A week later Machen finally saw H. and was not able to dissuade him from his announced course of taking up life on a farm near Princeton where he hoped to get light work, and felt that he was compelled to let him shift for himself for a while and try to earn his own living. He could hardly bear to think of H.'s return to his old Princeton haunts; and said: "I am afraid it means beginning the old misery for all concerned. Really I am not yet reconciled to assuming the terrible burden again. Nobody knows what I went through when H. was around here before." For some time nothing was heard of H. but in July the pastor of the church at Millville wrote that H., who had been working at the glass works, had been laid off and that the situation was well in hand. Correspondence between Machen and H. was now resumed, and so far as the evidence goes there was no further episode that marred the relations between them, and H. progressed in sanctification through the years that followed until his death.

When accordingly Machen later on in *Christianity and Liberalism* illustrated his teaching concerning the folly of trusting in the golden rule to solve the problems of society by appeal to the life of a drunkard, he was not simply theorizing.

> Help a drunkard get rid of his evil habit, and you will soon come to distrust the modern interpretation of the Golden Rule. The trouble is that the drunkard's companions apply the rule only too well; they do unto him exactly what they would have him do unto them—by buying him a drink . . . Strange indeed is the complacency with which modern men can say that the Golden Rule and the high ethical principles of Jesus are all that they need.

Machen's experience with R.H. had provided an overwhelming confirmation of the Christian message of salvation by grace. Can any one doubt that he had him in mind when he was writing these lines?

Coincident with the favorable report from Millville, to which reference has just been made, another act of benevolence was mentioned to his mother which brought back memories both of Edgeworth Baxter and R.H. It may well be noted here in rounding off this account of these disclosures of his persevering compassion. As a detail in his account of a summer day in Princeton, he wrote.

> In the early part of the afternoon I went to the Mercer Hospital in Trenton to see Charlie Wykoff, the colored janitor of Alexander Hall, who has undergone an operation for cataract. I am financing the operation and standing for the modest hospital charges. Charlie has been here for some thirty years at the Seminary and he and I are old friends. We get along very finely together. I hope the operation may be successful, since it would be sad for poor old Charlie to get blind. Visiting people at the Mercer Hospital seemed like old times. I really hated to get back in the old groove, where Edge Baxter and Mr. H. used to take me so often.

The stories of Baxter and R.H. have taken us far beyond the proposed limits of this chapter, but they refused to stay nicely within the framework of the early years of Machen's professional work at the Seminary. Who can deny, however, that they add significantly to our knowledge of Machen's character and personality during those first years?

OTHER ATTITUDES AND INTERESTS

Machen was indeed not of a placid or easygoing temperament. He carried with him into an atmosphere dominated by distinctly Northern political views his own passionately-held Southern perspectives and sympathies. At times therefore he reacted strongly against aspects of his environment. His view of the race question, for example, was distinctly Southern. He could also be irritated by annoyances which to other persons, who perhaps had other pet abominations, would have seemed trifling. Noises overhead, noises of steam radiators, noises of typewriters, and other noises could readily upset his calm. He reflects on this "weakness," for example, in a letter to his mother on Jan. 21, 1912:

> A big valve connected with the heating plant seems to be out of order in the cellar of Alexander Hall and creates a little thumping which bothers me a good deal. I should rather have a brass band under me than some little piddling noise like that. The engineer was not altogether encouraging about the prospects of fixing it. To my intense disgust the student under me has got

> the use of a typewriter. But after the first enthusiasm died away, he has been less constant in the use of his machine. Typewriting is an awesome noise, when the floors are thin. Being bothered by these things is a weakness, I know, and I am going to try to get over it.

To this his mother replied: "I told you that you and I are alike in little peculiarities. Another case is in the extreme annoyance suffered from noises like the crackling of a heater. A loud-ticking clock during the stillness of the night is worse than the tramping of a regiment."

Faults of character there no doubt were, but they were largely the faults of a strong man such as his mother attributed to her father. His integrity and sincerity of purpose were unassailable. A man of intense loyalties, he marked the line between the highest and lower loyalties and possessed the will to give each its proper claims. Overflowing with warmth to his friends, he was ever ready to confide in them and quick to praise them. He could be hurt or stunned by their reticence but was eager to excuse and defend them and to resume his guileless, openminded and outspoken relationship with them. In the face of what he felt to be wrong his indignation became white-hot; confronted with human misery his heart melted with a tender sympathy which constrained him to assume any burden designed to meet that need. Nor are signs lacking that through the years there was genuine growth in character both as regards the petty and the profound elements. As his mother observed early in the year 1908, following his visit at home during the holidays,

> Your loving letter was a great comfort for it seems to me I never hated to give you up so much. The pleasure of your visit is not past for I love to remember all your loving words and little helpful acts. You do not like praise very much, but I must tell you one thing. The way that you have overcome everyday faults of your character is a lesson to your elders. I cannot look into your heart except as it shines through your face, but I mean the outward faults that make or mar our working-day world. I have been trying to improve this part of myself for lo, these many years, and I have not made the impression that you have upon the frailties of the flesh.

But besides the progress in overcoming the faults that peculiarly come to expression in the midst of family life, there was undoubtedly a profounder growth in character that manifested itself during those early years at Princeton. The intense intellectual and spiritual struggle of that period as well as the increasing practical involvement of his life with that of people about him enlarged his sympathies, deepened his compassion and tempered his judgments. And thus with growth of conviction and clarification of vision he became a more vigorously Christian man.

There was a much lighter side to the life at Princeton than has been suggested by the foregoing. His pleasant association with his colleagues has been mentioned, but one might add that he became more and more fond of the Armstrongs and their growing family and enjoyed their hospitality to the full. The Sunday dinners with them were a constant delight, though they constituted only a small part of his contact with them. Nearly as frequent were the late Sunday afternoon suppers at the Hodges with the family of "Wis" Hodge, including his mother and sister Madeline and usually the "Billy" Magies. On rare occasions he would take "a girl to a concert" but engagements of this sort evidently did not greatly appeal to him, however much he might enjoy the presence of female company in a larger circle.

Football continued to fascinate him and when a cousin's wedding was set for a Saturday afternoon, he complained that "if I were going to get married I should certainly choose some other time than Saturday afternoon in the middle of the football season." Tennis, walking and riding his wheel were his chief means of securing exercise, though one summer he performed an immense amount of manual labor in his efforts to put the tennis court at the Seminary into fair condition. Golf he tried for a while, with momentary bursts of enthusiasm, but with a rather early conclusion that the sport was not for him. During the summer months he occasionally took in baseball games in New York or Philadelphia, accompanying his Uncle Thomas B. Gresham who had encouraged his interest in the game in the nineties, or Wistar Hodge who was reported as knowing, in 1909, "all the players in the National League the way I used to in the great days of baseball in Baltimore." But he never became a dyed-in-the-wool baseball fan, for his interest in the game had to be aroused by the enthusiasm of others. Still he did think that "Ty" Cobb and later "Babe" Ruth were worth going to see.

During his teaching career at Princeton his contacts with the University were naturally not as intimate as in his student years when he took courses with Patton, Wilson and Ormond. But he remained intensely interested in the academic life there as well as in its football. The administration of Woodrow Wilson was a topic of frequent discussion, especially as the big fight between Wilson and Dean Andrew West developed, and Wilson, the loser, was catapulted into national politics. Though Machen's most intimate friends were strongly opposed to Wilson, and he admitted that Wilson had shown great faults as a man and an administrator, he sided with him rather than with West and was delighted both with Wilson's election as Governor of New Jersey and as President of the United States two years later, though the bitter battle that centered about his person served to blunt slightly Machen's "youthful enthusiasm for Wilson." John G. Hibben, Wilson's successor at the University, was known as a "West man," but due to the difference in Hibben's personality, a more intimate and friendly relationship developed between the University and the Seminary, and between the University President and Machen, than had been true during Wilson's stay in Princeton. On a number of occasions Machen was invited to lead the chapel exercises at the University. On the whole however, there was a considerable coolness between the two institutions, and Machen regretted deeply that the doctrinal stand of the Seminary prevented the men at the Seminary from having the recognition there that they were accorded in other parts of the country and abroad.

In general then Machen was fascinated with life in Princeton. In fact he spent a very large part of his long summer vacations in the town rather than travelling or even joining his parents at Seal Harbor for more than very brief visits. In 1910 and 1911 indeed he spent several weeks abroad with his parents, and he unquestionably enjoyed these opportunities of travel, relaxation and fellowship with his father and mother. But he accompanied them for only a portion of their time abroad and remained as long as possible in Princeton. He undertook these journeys rather reluctantly, considering his own personal interests. He did so readily, however, because of a sense of obligation to relieve his brothers from assuming the full burden of conducting the party, a task which had now become necessary because of the advancing infirmities of Mr. and Mrs. Machen. The varied pleasures of life at Princeton may explain its attractions beyond those of the school year, but there was a more serious reason. For Machen had become thoroughly devoted to the study of the New Testament and consistently rose at an early hour to give several hours to it. To his development as a scholar, teacher and writer closer attention must now be given, with special emphasis upon events in the years immediately preceding his ordination and installation.

9

EARLY TEACHING AND WRITING

In view of the brilliance of Machen's later labors as a teacher, as attested by scores of students who still enthusiastically recall his instruction, and his eminence as an author whose books continue to be widely read, the student of his life is understandably interested in the earlier phases of his work as professor and writer. The earlier activity serves to illumine the later since it substantially prepared the way for it. There was greater continuity than Machen evidently realized. Nevertheless, the record is hardly that of instant success and of settled convictions as to the methods that were most conducive to a successful impact upon his audiences.

Throughout his years at Princeton Machen's teaching schedule remained fairly uniform. His part in the conduct of the required work was largely confined to the Junior introductory courses in exegesis and in the language and text of the New Testament. For a time, however, he taught the Senior course in Apostolic History. He was regularly responsible for instruction in New Testament Greek which came to form an important part of the seminary course for a large percentage of the students in spite of its technical classification as a propaedeutic study. Nevertheless, the opportunity of contact with graduate students and upper classmen was afforded through the offering of graduate or elective courses. And so it was possible to range over the broader reaches of the New Testament field and to retain a fresh interest in aspects of New Testament study that otherwise might easily have been lost.

TEACHING GALATIANS

The Epistle to the Galatians was traditionally chosen as the portion of the New Testament with which the seminary students grappled in the required course in Exegesis. Though Machen had heard Armstrong, Jülicher and Bousset lecture on the Epistle, he never seemed to be passing on a rehash of the opinions of others. He engaged indeed in a thorough study of the literature, and his analysis of exegetical problems and questions, which he came to prepare for the students, exhibits his insistence upon the most painstaking evaluation of the text in its minutest details. Nevertheless, Machen possessed an unusual gift of bringing into bold relief the larger questions, and thus giving a vision of the forest as well as the trees.

The Epistle to the Galatians, moreover, was admirably suited to the purpose of exegetical study as well as to bring to expression Machen's special gifts as a teacher. Historical questions currently in hot dispute and doctrinal issues bearing upon the very nature of the gospel confronted the student in forceful and fascinating fashion and stimulated him to engage his best powers of analysis and decision. The message of Galatians may take on an extraordinary freshness and contemporaneity, especially in an age when the gospel of the grace of God in Christ is undergoing eclipse, as Luther had discovered. And in the hands of Machen it became alive and relevant to the present situation, though his devotion to his task of expounding the text was such that he did not yield to the temptation of making direct applications to the ecclesiastical scene of his own day. At least when the present writer was in his classroom, it was felt not merely that Luther had been reborn, but that Paul himself had become alive, and was teaching and proclaiming as a fresh message the evangel that stands in irreconcilable opposition to "another gospel which is not another."

Perhaps one's impressions were influenced by the knowledge that Machen had come forward in the twenties into the arena of public ecclesiastical life as the champion of that gospel of liberty in Christ Jesus. One must allow also for development in thought and presentation. And yet, in spite of early qualms and perplexities, there was a large measure of continuity in his teaching due to the basic constancy of his character and personality. In one matter there is specific evidence of a modification of his method of teaching, for he happened once to tell his mother that he was abandoning his earlier method of a fairly slavish use of a manuscript in favor of a semi-extemporaneous manner of presentation. His exceptional facility in extemporaneous speech, which was precise, lucid and attractive as regards diction and style without any suggestion of verbosity or meretriciousness, was to later generations of students, at any rate, a constant occasion for wonder. Because of such qualities he was regarded, in the late twenties at least, as the most interesting and successful teacher in the Seminary.

His earlier letters indicate that he was often discouraged with regard to his success as a teacher, and one would be guilty of inexcusable idealization to discount such estimates entirely. Nevertheless, they will be taken with a grain of salt by those who have become aware of the modest and often unduly deprecatory attitude that he took toward his own work. And there is extant at least one commendatory estimate of his powers as a teacher from the early period which is chiefly in view in this chapter. For a man who entered Princeton in the year 1909, and later became the president of a western college, found occasion in a letter written in 1928 (in which he was largely concerned to indicate his radical difference from Machen concerning the doctrinal and ecclesiastical issues of the day) to add: "But I always look back with pleasure and inspiration to the associations with you, and I remember you as the most inspiring teacher I ever had."

That Machen was so highly regarded as a teacher is the more remarkable because he was known as a very strict marker. His files contained carbon copies of scores of letters politely informing students that they had failed to pass. A fairly typical sample is the following:

> Dear Mr. W.... :
>
> I am very sympathetic with you about your difficulties with New Testament Exegesis, as evidenced in the recent examination; since, inasmuch as you are a senior, it will be troublesome for you to be burdened further with this subject. At the same time, I am obliged to say that your papers in the double test that we have just held are below the passing mark. I made allowance for your creditable showing in the previous test in January, and yet, despite that, I cannot conscientiously say that you have passed the course. An opportunity will, I think, be given you to take an examination on Wednesday, April 27th, the same day as that which is assigned to the examination in the New Testament Canon. Will you please confer with me about the matter?
>
> If I can be of any assistance to you in your further preparation, please let me know.
>
> Cordially yours,
>
> J. Gresham Machen

There is, moreover, a memorandum of a faculty study of the marks given in a certain year by the several professors in the regular courses, a study chiefly designed to discover whether groups 1 and 2, denominated as "honors groups," were actually being maintained as such. If liberal marking were a criterion of popularity, Machen would have been indicated as far from a favorite. For he gave far fewer "1's" and "2's" than any other professor, only 32 per cent. of the total, the next lowest 52 per cent., and the others in an ascending scale that included several 80's and 90's in terms of percentage. Yet at this period he was at the height of his success as a teacher.

INSTRUCTION IN GREEK

As a result of the initiative of Professor Armstrong, and through the vigorous cooperation of Machen, a preliminary test in Greek was required of all entering students with a view to assessing their qualifications for exegesis and other required studies in the department. Only such students as acknowledged their lack of adequate preparation were excused from this test, and on the basis of these disclosures students were excused entirely from further special work in Greek, were required to take a rapid review or a thorough review course, or were subjected to the necessity of taking an elementary beginner's course. It was distressing indeed to Armstrong and Machen that the standards of preparation for work in the Seminary had fallen so low that they had to adopt this procedure, but it is a tribute to them and their conception of what study in their department involved that they insisted upon it and were willing to perform the wearisome burden of labor that it involved. On one occasion at least questions were raised as to the propriety of giving so much attention to courses in Greek, and Machen wrote a fairly elaborate exposition and defense of it, which included the following illuminating paragraphs.

> You will observe that the basis of the whole administration of the New Testament department is provided by the "Preliminary Test in Greek." Without that test, in my judgment, the course in New Testament Exegesis would be farcical, and the exegetical foundation of all the other courses would be altogether lacking. I am convinced that the test has fully accomplished its purpose; it has enabled our students to use their time in the New Testament department to the best advantage, by preventing them from attempting the regular courses until they are really able to accomplish them.
>
> In order to pass the Preliminary Test it is not necessary to have a large vocabulary, or a systematic memory of the forms. All that is required is the ability to make, not necessarily a successful, but at least a reasonably intelligent effort at translating very simple Greek prose. No student who fails in this test would be able to make a correct translation of easy Greek prose, or in particular of the Greek New Testament, even with the free use of a vocabulary.

In the conduct of the three Greek courses Machen employed for a considerable period the best text that seemed to be available, Huddlestone's *Essentials of New Testament Greek.* But he found it "so wretchedly poor and meagre" that he began, as early as 1909, to supplement it with some extra exercises of his own. One might regard this as the beginning of a labor which eventually, in 1923, was to see the publication of a work of his own, *New Testament Greek for Beginners,* a splendid text that has continued to be widely used until the present day. No textbook was perhaps a greater joy to the instructors in the elements of a language. Though it overcame the extreme brevity of Huddlestone, and is marked by the lucidity of its formulations and the abundance of translation exercises to put the student's grammatical knowledge to the test, its most conspicuous merit perhaps lies in a different direction. This is its studied restraint in the presentation of technical materials which permits concentration upon the acquisition of a reading knowledge of the language. This point is underscored here because it reflects Machen's own talent as a teacher whose one concern was to make a successful impact upon the student rather than to impress him with his philological learning or scholarship in general.

Though his high standards of achievement did not permit him to become a sentimentalist in his relation to his students, he was a most sympathetic and attractive teacher in classes that otherwise might have been considered dry. Though never letting things get out of hand, he was delightfully informal in the Greek classes, and his propensity to humorous little gestures and expressions was given free play. He regarded the Greek classes as so distinctive from the other regular courses in the curriculum that in the interest of maintaining their informality it was not his custom to commence the hour with prayer. On one occasion he was taken to task by a student for this, and his reply expands upon his indicated outlook upon the matter:

December 29, 1927

My dear Mr. G.... :

I have your note of December 20th, with an inquiry regarding the offering of prayer in connection with the class in Greek.

It is perfectly clear that Christian people ought to engage constantly in prayer to God, and that they should lay before God not only unusual and special things but also the daily duties and cares of their lives. But the question just exactly what set times of public prayer should be observed is not to be determined by hard and fast rules. Too frequent an observance of such set times may tend to produce formalism and coldness in prayer. I have had rather the feeling that that might be the case if the somewhat informal classes in Greek were opened regularly with public prayer. And so it has never been my custom to open those classes with prayer, as I do in connection with the other classes in the New Testament Department.

> The authors of the Plan of the Seminary, with their customary wisdom and their customary knowledge of the devotional needs of the Christian man, have expressly left the decision on this matter to the discretion of the professors.
>
> I do trust that the blessing of God may be with you and with the other students both in their studies in Greek and in everything else that they do.

That the informality of the classes in Greek was due to his desire to relieve the tension of the students, rather than to any lack of serious purpose so far as their attainments were concerned, is also borne out by the special measures which he took from time to time with students who appeared to be threatened with failure or seemed to be making mediocre progress. At times he divided his classes into separate sections so as to be able to deal more satisfactorily with the weaker men, at times he himself undertook private tutoring of them, and finally when he was overwhelmed with a multiplicity of duties, he was accustomed to employ and pay out of his own pocket the more accomplished students to tutor the weaker ones.

During the early years Machen developed a number of graduate, or elective, courses, most of which were devoted to the exposition of particular books of the New Testament including the Gospel according to John and several of the Pauline Epistles. As early as the year 1907-08 he announced a course on the Birth Narratives, for which his fellowship thesis had provided the initiative and background, and which was to be offered year after year as one of his most celebrated and successful courses. His opus magnum, *The Virgin Birth of Christ,* published in 1930 was thus the fruit of a quarter of century of study and reflection. The other comparable course, "Paul and His Environment," was not developed until about the time of his delivery of the Sprunt Lectures in 1921, published the same year as *The Origin of Paul's Religion.* Though this may come as a surprise to the students who crowded his classrooms in the twenties and later, the number of students who elected Machen's graduate courses during the earlier years was quite small. At times this was a source of considerable discouragement to him, and contributed to his doubts as to his own qualifications as a teacher. A more reasonable explanation, however, is that, as a very young man whose reputation as a distinguished scholar had not yet been established, he could not be expected to compete in this regard with Warfield and other older men of renown.

LITERARY ACTIVITY

Machen's literary adventures in his field were rather limited during the first five years of his instructorship. Following his articles on the birth of Christ, which were published during his year abroad, no article from his pen appears in *The Princeton Theological Review* until 1912. There were, however, several carefully written reviews of books, a number of which concerned the narratives of the birth of Christ, and others a variety of subjects rather closely related to his courses of instruction. Mention may also be made of his translation from German into English of an article by August Lang of Halle on "The Reformation and Natural Law," for the April, 1909, number of the *Review,* an article which with others by Doumergue, Bavinck and Warfield was published the same year in book form under the title, *Calvin and the Reformation.* Such labor on Machen's part, though arduous and exacting, was not especially rewarding. Machen was greatly cheered, however, by several kind notes sent by Gildersleeve in connection with it. Acknowledging Machen's gift of the published volume, for example, Gildersleeve wrote on Oct. 9, 1909: "The stately volume in which your translation of Lang's study is incorporated has just reached me and I beg to renew my thanks for remembering me. You may always count on my special interest in all the words and work of one of the most sympathetic students I have ever had in my classroom."

The year 1909 was celebrated far and wide as marking the four hundredth anniversary of the birth of John Calvin, and Princeton sought in a number of ways to pay tribute to, and stimulate interest in, the Genevan Reformer. The articles in the *Review* for the entire year were largely devoted to Calvin and Calvinism, and on May 4th a special Calvin Celebration was held at the Seminary. It would have been strange indeed if Machen's interest in and commitment to Calvinism had not been stimulated by his participation in these events, even in the modest role of translator, as well as by the impact of the celebration of the event. Certain it is that Warfield's contribution impressed him greatly. His address on "The Theology of John Calvin," Machen told his mother, was "the feature" of the Calvin Celebration. "Not only did it exhibit Dr. Warfield's well-known mastery of the subject," he wrote, "but also it was really eloquent—certainly the finest thing of the kind that I have ever heard from Dr. Warfield." In the address Warfield had defined the formative principle of Calvinism as lying

> in a profound apprehension of God in his majesty, with the poignant realization, which inevitably accompanies this apprehension, of the relation sustained to God by the creature as such and par-

> ticularly by the sinful creature. The Calvinist is the man who has seen God, and who, having seen God in his glory, is filled on the one hand with a sense of his unworthiness to stand in God's sight, as a creature, and much more as a sinner, and on the other with adoring wonder that nevertheless this God is a God who receives sinners. He who believes in God without reserve, and is determined that God shall be God to him, in all his thinking, feeling, willing,—in the entire compass of his life-activities, intellectual, moral, spiritual,—throughout all his individual, social, religious relations,—is, by force of that strictest of all logic which presides over the outworking of principles into thought and life, by the very necessity of the case, a Calvinist.

Warfield had insisted in the lecture that it was gravely misleading to identify the formative principle of Calvinism with the prominent points of difference from Lutheranism, "its sister type of Protestantism," or from Arminianism, "its own rebellious daughter." And speaking of Calvinism and Lutheranism, he said that "they have vastly more in common than in distinction." On the other hand, he was zealous to guard against the view that Calvinism might be regarded as simply a variety of Christian thought, experience and faith along side of other varieties. Calvinism in its fundamental idea, he said, involves three things:

> In it, objectively speaking, theism comes to its rights; subjectively speaking, the religious relation attains its purity; soteriologically speaking, evangelical religion finds at length its full expression and its secure stability...
>
> I think it is important to insist that Calvinism is not a specific variety of theistic thought, religious experience, evangelical faith, but just the perfect manifestation of these things. The difference between it and other forms of theism, religion, evangelicalism is a difference not of kind but of degree. There are not many kinds of theism, religion, evangelicalism, each with its own special characteristics, among which men are at liberty to choose, as may suit their individual tastes. There is but one kind of theism, religion, evangelicalism; and if there are special constructions laying claim to these names they differ from one another not as correlative species of a more inclusive genus, but only as more or less good or bad specimens of the same thing differ from one another. Calvinism comes forward simply as pure theism, religion, evangelicalism, as over against less pure theism, religion, evangelicalism. It does not take its position then by the side of other types of

> these things; it takes its place over all else that claims to be these things, as embodying all that they ought to be.

There is little wonder that such incisive and lucid analysis and expression, developed on the background of encyclopedic scholarship and penetrating thinking, appealed to Machen. There was a breadth of vision in his point of view which removed him far from all taint of sectarianism and yet was combined with a stedfast commitment to and love of the truth which gave no quarter to a vapid doctrinal indifference and latitudinarianism. As a student and evidently in his early years as an instructor Machen had not come under the full impact of Warfield's approach, and had supposed that a minimizing apologetic for a broad Biblical Christianity would best meet the needs of the day. But as his letters and other testimony establish he came more and more to see that Warfield's position was the only strong position, and that Calvinism, or the Reformed Faith, had the advantage, not only of being the Biblical view of Christianity, but also of constituting the faith which was incomparably the easiest to defend.

THE VIRGIN BIRTH

The year 1912 was a memorable one in Machen's literary career. In the course of it no fewer than three major articles, all dealing with the subject of the birth of Christ, were published in the *Review.* Two were closely related studies on "The Hymns of the First Chapter of Luke" and "The Origin of the First Two Chapters of Luke," the third a distinctive essay on "The Virgin Birth in the Second Century." In addition a significant paper on an entirely different theme, "Jesus and Paul," appeared in the Princeton centennial volume of *Biblical and Theological Studies.* Though these substantial contributions to Biblical scholarship marked something of a turning point, one should not suppose that they represent the results of a sudden outburst of energy after a period of comparative quiet. The articles on the birth of Christ in particular had been in the making for some time, and the Pauline study constituted a fruit of a number of years of reflection on the life and message of the apostle to the Gentiles.

For a considerable time prior to 1912 Machen had been contemplating the publication of a major book on the Virgin Birth of Christ, and had been working diligently on various aspects of the subject. As early as August 28, 1910 he observes that since his return to Princeton from Europe he has been working on the subject of the Virgin Birth and is rather discouraged as to his progress. "At any rate," he adds, "it is difficult to say how long it will be before my magnum opus will appear." It appears that his brother Arthur was the first to suggest the possibility of such a major work, though on one occasion he credits Harris Kirk, the pastor of the Franklin St. Church, with the first suggestion. At any rate the members of his family continued through the years to encourage him in the undertaking. On the particular occasion of his discouragement in 1910 it was his father who, writing from London on Sept. 6th, counseled patience and expressed confidence as to the realization of his ideal. "I sympathize with you," he said, "in regard to the hindrances daily duty interjects in the way of your work upon your book, but at your age time (as well as art) is long, and you need not fear that the opportunities you will have of writing *con amore* will suffice for the accomplishment of your purpose and enable you to make a good book while taking pleasure in the making."

In connection with the articles on the opening chapters of Luke it is of interest that Professor Adolph Harnack of Berlin, one of the most distinguished and perhaps the most influential New Testament scholar of that time, figured in a prominent and unexpected way. In Machen's article published in Jan., 1906, some notice had been taken of Harnack's view, first published in 1900, that the hymns of Luke 1 were the free compositions of the evangelist, rather than genuine tradition going back to the persons who are described as uttering them. But when in 1906 and the following years Harnack published a series of studies in which, despite his rejection of the historicity of their supernatural content, he came to adopt the tradition of Lucan authorship and assigned Luke and Acts to the early sixties, no little astonishment was created and a new era in the evaluation of Luke and Acts was ushered in. If even Machen's father in 1907, in his eightieth year, was taking discriminating notice of Harnack's surprising change of viewpoint, the son would not be behind him in his careful examination of the details of Harnacks argument. There was much that met approval, but it was noticed that Harnack reiterated his argument that the style of the Magnificat and the Benedictus betrayed Lucan authorship. Machen decided to subject this theory to a painstaking analysis. He was able to demonstrate that virtually every detail that Harnack had characterized as Lucan could be paralleled in the Greek version of the Old Testament known as the Septuagint, and that therefore Harnack's theory as to the origin of the hymns was without support. But now comes the unexpected development. When Machen's masterful studies were brought to Harnack's attention, he did them the honor of reviewing them at some length in the *Theologische Literaturzeitung* of Jan. 4, 1913. Although Harnack did not approve of Machen's main argument, he praised it for its thoroughness and declared that his "admirable study was deserving of every attention."

Machen himself was greatly encouraged by this notice, for it was most unusual for articles, as distinguished from books, to be reviewed in this leading journal, not least because Harnack was the author of it, and also because "the general tone of the review is generous, and avoids that kind of sarcasm and imputation of dishonest defense of tradition which sometimes appears when liberal theologians are discussing anything that ventures to defend supernatural Christianity." Here was the first important public recognition of the work that he had undertaken. It served to give standing to one who was still thirty at the time of their publication. Moreover, it stimulated his work in the field and provided assurance that he was at a post in which he was qualified to do good work.

JESUS AND PAUL

The article on "Jesus and Paul" was in certain respects even more important than the studies praised by Harnack. Though not comparable as an exhibit of minute and thorough investigation, it excelled them in that it grappled with a problem of far more embracive import and struck a strong blow in support of supernatural Christianity. Whereas in the studies on the Virgin Birth, the broader questions of the historicity of the supernatural event of the birth of Christ were not strictly under consideration, and it was more or less necessary to read between the lines to observe the author's Christian point of view, the article on "Jesus and Paul" approached being, in certain respects, a confession of faith. Though he modestly designated it as "merely a sketch" and as raising "many questions which it does not answer," it contains the kernel of his great book on Paul written nearly a decade later. A refutation of the view that Paul was "the second founder of Christianity" is presented. And the view that Paul might still be regarded as religiously a disciple of Jesus while his theology was abandoned was denounced both because it made a "thoroughly vicious" distinction between religion and theology and because it is contradicted by Paul himself. It is in the great *theological* passages of the epistles, Machen said that "the current of Paul's religious experience becomes overpowering, so that even after the lapse of centuries, even through the dull medium of the printed page, it sweeps the heart of the sympathetic reader on with it in a mighty flood . . . In these passages, the religious experience and the theology of Paul are blended in a union which no critical analysis can dissolve."

And he is even more revealing of his own faith when he undertakes positive summaries of his understanding of Paul:

> When Paulinism is understood as fellowship with the risen Christ, then the disproportionate emphasis which Paul places upon the death and resurrection of Christ becomes intelligible. For these are the acts by which fellowship has been established. To the modern man, they seem unnecessary. By the modern man fellowship with God is taken as a matter of course. But only because of an imperfect conception of God. If God is all love and kindness, then of course nothing is required in order to bring us into his presence. But Paul would never have been satisfied with such a God. His was the awful, holy God of the Old Testament prophets—and of Jesus. But for Paul the holiness of God was also the holiness of Christ. Communion of sinful man with the holy Christ is a tremendous paradox, a supreme mystery. But the mystery has been illumined. It has been illumined by the cross. Christ forgives sin not because he is complacent towards sin, but because of his own free grace he has paid the dreadful penalty of it. And he has not stopped with that. After the cross came the resurrection. Christ rose from the dead into a life of glory and power. Into that glory and into that power he invites the believer. In Christ we receive not only pardon, but new and glorious life.

Though written as a paper to be published in the centennial volume, and not as an address, a distinctly personal note is heard. Even the language and style, as observed in these crisp, brief sentences, seem more at home in a sermon than in a scientific essay. A similar impression is made at a later point:

> Paul was a disciple of Jesus, if Jesus was a supernatural person; he was not a disciple of Jesus, if Jesus was a mere man. If Jesus was simply a human teacher, then Paulinism defies explanation. Yet it is powerful and beneficent beyond compare. Judged simply by its effects, the religious experience of Paul is the most tremendous phenomenon in the history of the human spirit. It has transformed the world from darkness into light. But it need be judged not merely by its effects. It lies open before us. In the presence of it, the sympathetic observer is aghast. It is a new world that is opened before him. Freedom, goodness, communion with God, sought by philosophers of all ages, attained at last!

One must not read into that final sentence more of personal confession than it properly bears. For, in spite of times of doubt, his entire life was largely characterized by affirmations of Christian faith. Nevertheless one is not far wrong in observing here a sign of an emergence from his period of questioning into one of profound certainty. The day that he would commit himself definitely to ordination to the ministry did not lie far ahead.

Among the congratulatory messages was one in the hand of Dr. John De Witt, who was about to retire from active service in the Faculty. Writing on April 29th, 1912, he said:

> I must please myself by writing to say how greatly I have enjoyed reading your paper on Paul's relation to Jesus. I do not see how the subject could have been discussed more thoroughly or presented in a more interesting, indeed I may say, fascinating way.
>
> I particularly admire your loyalty to your great subject. One is tempted in treating a question raised by another on a great subject to leave the impression that he is thinking more of his opponent than of his great subject; in this instance to make more of Wrede than of the relations of Paul to Jesus. It would have been a great mistake. Either you escaped or you successfully resisted the temptation; and have written a noble, positive and constructive paper which will be fresh and valuable when Wrede's conjectures shall have given away to others just as temporary as themselves.

THE PRINCETON CENTENNIAL

To enter upon a detailed description of the other aspects of the centennial celebration would take us too far afield. If one were to do justice to it, it would be necessary at the very least to survey the contents of the massive but beautifully edited *Princeton Seminary Centennial* volume as well as the other splendid contributions, besides Machen's, to the volume of *Biblical and Theological Studies*. Since, however, it was a memorable event, and Machen's own interest in its various aspects had been sharpened by the fact that his intimate friend "Bobby" Robinson had been serving as administrative secretary in active charge of arrangements of all sorts, his account of some of his impressions written for family consumption is given here.

His parents had just fulfilled the promise of a visit to Princeton, but had had to leave after a week's stay on the day following the baccalaureate sermon. The experience of being with their son in the setting of his Princeton life had been a great treat, and his mother had written: "The memory of my week in Princeton will abide with me as one of the happiest I have known for years. Everything combined to make it delightful. Nature did her best for me, one of her truest lovers; we were so comfortable; physical disabilities did not interfere with my simple pleasures as is so often the case; I liked your friends so very much; you were so good to us; and Dr. Patton's praise of you was 'like apples of gold in pictures of silver.' We got off comfortably. I was sorry to go when I saw some of the dignitaries arrive and don their fine gowns."

At the conclusion of the celebration Machen wrote:

The Seminary Centennial was very successful indeed, and for its success Bobby deserves great credit. The successful housing of the hundreds of alumni and guests—which was accomplished without the sligliest confusion—was a feat of good management. There were about eight hundred men at the dinner on Monday and at the luncheon on Tuesday, but the arrangements were admirably made, and despite the crowded condition of the hall the excellent meals were well served. But you will be more interested in other aspects of the celebration.

The academic processions on Monday and Tuesday mornings were exceedingly brilliant. The Scotch moderators were a show. They had knee trousers, buckles on their shoes, lace cuffs, three cornered hats, and I forget what kind of colored gowns . . .

Tuesday was the big day, Alexander Hall at the University was filled with a magnificent assemblage. The stage and the central part of the lower floor were brilliant with many-colored gowns, and the rest of the hall was occupied by ordinary folk. The singing of the first hymn, "Ein' Feste Burg," was one of the most inspiring things in the whole celebration. I never heard any hymn-singing like that. The speeches were by Dr. Stewart, moderator of the Church of Scotland, Dr. James Wells, moderator of the United Free Church of Scotland, and Dr. Macmillan, moderator of the Presbyterian Church of Ireland. Dr. Stewart was very poor. He seems to believe very little, and what he does believe, he is unable to express. Dr. Macmillan had only half a chance on account of the lateness of the hour. But James Wells was glorious. He believes in the Gospel and doesn't mind saying so. I don't know when I have seen such a combination of deep religious feeling and perfect dignity as was exhibited by his address. And his cordiality and respect towards Princeton

Seminary was evidently unfeigned. His speech and Dr. Patton's were the great things of the celebration.

The speeches at the Alumni luncheon on Tuesday afternoon were fine. Perhaps the best, besides Dr. Patton's, were the speeches of Bishop Greer (Episcopal) and Mullins of the Southern Baptist Seminary at Louisville. The latter was brilliant. Although Dr. Patton was very hoarse, his five-minute closing speech was one of the most eloquent things that I have ever heard from him.

A great deal was said during the celebration about Princeton's Calvinism. But comparatively few of the speakers—whether friend or foe—seemed to recognize clearly the real thing for which Princeton is fighting, namely *supernatural* Christianity. Dr. Patton was almost alone in isolating the big issue clearly from all the others and putting it squarely in the foreground. What opportunities the speakers missed! How few big men there are in the Church and in the world!

This paragraph constrains one to draw a breath before proceeding with the description of the celebration. It is at once illuminating and somewhat puzzling. On the one hand, it discloses that Machen had already come to believe that the issues at stake in the world and involved in the perpetuation of Princeton Seminary were new and modern rather than merely a revival of controversies that had divided classic Protestantism. He saw the issue as a profound and world-shaking one in which the very existence of Christianity—fairly deserving the name—was under debate. On the other hand, there is a somewhat diconcerting element in the apparent disjunction drawn between Christianity and Calvinism, since it is doubtful that Machen at this stage of his development really disagreed with Warfield in judging that Calvinism was simply Christianity "come into its own." It may be that he was not as self-conscious on this point in 1912 as he was later on. One should take care, however, not to overburden words not intended for publication and that might have been somewhat revised if they had been read even twice. At any rate, there is another evidence that by 1912 he was aware of a deep gulf separating historic and merely nominal Christianity and that he had made a profound commitment to the former.

Machen's graphic description now continues:

A pleasant feature of the celebration was the presence of President Hibben at all the exercises, and his cordial words at the Luncheon. In marked contrast was the attitude of Woodrow

Wilson. Though appointed a delegate by the General Assembly, and though he was in town during the celebration, and even addressed a political club at the University at the time of our Monday-night dinner, he never showed his face at any of the Seminary meetings. I am not quite sure that the University need regret the change from Wilson to Hibben. A little less brilliancy and a little more courtesy may not be such a misfortune after all.

I was glad to see Mrs. Wilson at the exercises on Tuesday.

Yesterday was the University's big day. We of the Seminary faculty were invited to march in the procession along with the faculty of the University and had the best of everything. The perfect weather contributed to the success of the out-of-door exercises. The inauguration ceremony in front of Nassau Hall was certainly a brilliant scene, and the procession beforehand was great sport. Clad in all colors of the rainbow the hundreds of guests and members of the faculty lined up around the cannon while President Taft, Chief Justice White, Dr. Patton, Dr. Hibben and a few other notables marched past, and then we all fell in behind and marched to the other side of Nassau Hall. Chief Justice White's speech after he had received the LL.D. degree was magnificent. It was only a few words in length, but it ought to have made T.R. and other anarchists feel pretty small.

About 1,600 people sat down to the luncheon in the University Gymnasium. The first three speeches were by Taft, White and Dr. Patton, and then followed Presidents Lowell of Harvard, Hadley of Yale, Butler of Columbia, Schurman of Cornell. Taft made a good speech, White and the college presidents were pretty fair. But the great speech was Dr. Patton's. It makes no difference how many presidents, jurists and educators you may assemble—you might assemble all the crowned heads of Europe, but give President Patton of Princeton Seminary a chance to speak, and he is always supreme.

After the luncheon, the crowd, including President Taft and the Chief Justice, witnessed the Princeton-Cornell baseball game. Princeton's defeat was the one discordant note in the harmony of the day. After the ball game there was a reception at the President's mansion. I went in too late to shake hands with President Taft. I was glad when the day was over. A little of this kind of thing goes a long way. President Taft in his speech spoke about the quiet of these academic shades. Probably they are quiet—comparatively. Certainly Taft seemed to enjoy himself. I thought he would burst at one humorous point in Dr. Patton's speech. Dr. Patton sat next to him at the luncheon. I am anxious to get his impressions...

A number of people have expressed their deep regret that they could not get around to see you at the Inn. Among them are Wistar Hodge, who was ill on Sunday when he had intended to visit you, and Mrs. Armstrong who had Centennial guests who prevented her from coming. The Pattons were extremely regretful that they could not see more of you. But I told everybody that you understood perfectly the busy time that was going on. Dr. Patton seemed greatly pleased at your admiration of his sermon. About the sermon, there was only one opinion on the part of all who heard it.

CHRISTIANITY AND CULTURE

The year 1912 was therefore a memorable one. It was a year of celebration, commemoration and expectation. Great strides forward as a scholar of reputation had been taken. A foundation had been laid for fruitful labor in the future. Moreover, there was increasing evidence that his Christian faith was rooted and grounded in sturdy fashion. Opportunities to preach were accepted with greater readiness. An invitation to address the Philadelphia Ministers Association was accepted as affording "the biggest opportunity that has come to me." And he delivered for the first time the address on the occasion of the opening of the Seminary in September, though he undertook this appointment with diffidence and was far from enthusiastic about his discourse especially when it appeared in print in the January, 1913, issue of the *Review,* under the title "Christianity and Culture."

As a contribution to the *Review* this article stands indeed on a quite different plane from those published in 1912, but this does not detract from its merit. It was not conceived as a scholarly contribution, but as an address that was designed to speak a word that would take account of student attitudes and perplexities as they entered upon their theological studies and would inspire them to engage with zeal and understanding in their labors as students for the ministry. Judged in that light it is a gem, and the forty years that have passed have hardly dimmed its relevancy.

In his six years as instructor he had become painfully aware of a tendency among students, as well as in the Church as a whole, to set up a sharp disjunction between knowledge and its pursuit, on the one hand, and piety and its cultivation, on the other. The scientific or academic tendency expressed itself in men "who devoted themselves chiefly to the task of forming right conceptions as to Christianity and its foundations"; the practical in the rejoinder: "While we are discussing the exact location of the churches of Galatia, men are perishing under the curse of the law; while we are setting the date of Jesus' birth, the world is doing without its Christmas message." Since it was intolerable to leave these tendencies irreconciled, the question of the proper relation between knowledge and piety was an urgent one.

Rejecting as unthinkable the proposed solutions which would destroy Christianity by subordinating it to culture or would destroy culture in the interest of giving religion a clear field, Machen defined the true relation in terms of "consecration" and said:

> Instead of stifling the pleasures afforded by the acquisition of knowledge or by the appreciation of what is beautiful, let us accept these pleasures as the gifts of a heavenly Father. Instead of obliterating the distinction between the Kingdom and the world, or on the other hand withdrawing from the world into a sort of modernized intellectual monasticism, let us go forth joyfully, enthusiastically to make the world subject to God.

Commending this solution he stressed the point that the work of evangelism could not ignore the state of mind of those to whom the gospel was preached.

> We may preach with all the fervor of a reformer and yet succeed only in winning a straggler here and there, if we permit the whole collective thought of the nation or of the world to be controlled by ideas which, by the resistless force of logic, prevent Christianity from being regarded as anything more than a harmless delusion. Under such circumstances what God desires us to do is to destroy the obstacle at its root. Many would have the seminaries combat error by attacking it as it is taught in its popular exponents. Instead of that they confuse their students with a lot of German names unknown outside the walls of the universities. That method of procedure is based simply upon a profound belief in the pervasiveness of ideas. What is today a matter of academic speculation begins tomorrow to move armies and pull down empires.

To engage in labor in this world of ideas, Machen insisted, comes as a special challenge to the regenerated man. Whatever useful work other men might do in detail, "they are not accomplishing the great task, they are not assimilating modern thought to Christianity, because they are without that experience of God's power in the soul which is of the essence of Christianity." Modern culture is a tremendous force either subservient to the gospel or else it is the deadliest enemy of the gospel. For making it subservient, religious emotion is not enough, intellectual labor is also necessary. And that labor is being neglected. The Church has turned to easier tasks. And now she is reaping the fruits of her indolence. Now she must battle for her life.

The situation is desperate. It might discourage us. But not if we are truly Christians. Not if we are living in vital communion with the risen Lord. If we are really convinced of the truth of our message, then we can proclaim it before a world of enemies, then the very difficulty of our task, the very scarcity of our allies becomes an inspiration, then we can even rejoice that God did not place us in an easy age, but in a time of doubt and perplexity and battle. Then, too, we shall not be afraid to call forth other soldiers into the conflict. Instead of making our theological seminaries merely centres of religious emotion, we shall make them battle-grounds of the faith where, helped a little by the experience of Christian teachers, men are taught to fight their own battle, where they come to appreciate the real strength of the adversary and in the hard school of intellectual struggle learn to substitute for the unthinking faith of childhood the profound convictions of full-grown men ... The twentieth century, in theory, is agreed on social betterment. But sin, and death, and salvation, life, and God—about these things there is debate. You can avoid the debate if you choose. You need only drift with the current. Preach every Sunday during your Seminary course, devote the fag ends of your time to study and thought, study about as you studied in college—and these questions will probably never trouble you. The great questions may easily be avoided. Many preachers are avoiding them. And many preachers are preaching to the air. The Church is waiting for men of another type. Men to fight her battles and solve her problems. The hope of finding them is the one great inspiration of a Seminary's life.

Thus in simple, yet eloquent and ringing words Machen voiced his plea that the students of the Seminary should catch a vision of a ministry that would be thoroughly Christian in its evaluation of knowledge and vigorously intellectual in the interest of Christian piety. At the same time the address was an *apologia* for the kind of theological education identified, in his mind, with Princeton Seminary, and was the more timely because voices near at hand were clamoring for change in its emphasis. And it may not be overlooked that pervading the discourse was a note of certainty concerning what the Christian faith is and his own wholehearted commitment to it.

One does not wonder that Mr. and Mrs. Machen, staunch and devout Christians as they were, and whose love of culture was as free and natural as breathing itself, should have greeted this address with delight. His mother said,

> I cannot half express to you my pride and profound joy in your work. You have handled in a very able manner the most important problem of the age, and you have given voice to my own sentiments far better than I could myself. I feel as if I made the mistake of my life in not hurrying to Princeton last September in time to hear you.

And his father wrote:

> That is a grand article . . . It is a strong presentation of a great thesis, and pitched upon exactly the right key . . . I cannot wait to tell you how delighted I am with this splendid work of yours and my firm belief that it must do good and is impregnable as an argument, setting forth the real truth upon a subject so greatly befogged in these days.

10

ORDINATION AND INSTALLATION

The decisive step of coming under care of presbytery with a view to ordination to the Christian ministry was finally taken by Machen in November, 1913, when he was thirty-two years old. His licensure the following April, his election as Assistant Professor of New Testament at the May, 1914, meeting of the Board of Directors, his ordination in June, and his installation to his professorship in May, 1915, all received more publicity. But none was more memorable or marked more of a turning point in his life than his initial appearance before the presbytery. Having made the great decision that he was at last ready to seek ordination, the other developments ensued more or less as a matter of course. This series of events will chiefly concern us in this chapter.

Back of that first big step stood years of indecision and perplexity and even times of torturing doubt, as this narrative has taken some pains to show. Though his course at times seemed to be as much backward as forward, there was undoubtedly, especially in the latter years, a rather gradual movement towards the consummation. Not every stage is explicitly marked but there appears to be a growth of commitment to the Christian faith, to Princeton Seminary as a cause representing a great principle, and to the Christian ministry as his calling. Exactly when the great decision was made one cannot say, but he evidently had determined not later than the early summer of 1913 to appear before presbytery in the fall. Even then, however, there was still a degree of hesitation. But this was rather decisively removed during the summer as the result of a rewarding sojourn among the Eastern and Southern Alps. About a year later Machen spoke of that holiday as "just the breath of life to me," and as having had "a very large place in enabling me to go forward and be ordained." Accordingly, it seems appropriate to dwell briefly upon it.

A JOURNEY FOR HEALTH'S SAKE

This sixth stay in Europe recalled earlier trips and none more than his journey in 1905 since he spent most of it in the same general

Alpine regions on the borders of Austria where he had passed many exhilarating days in 1905. In respect of its occasion, however, the 1913 journey was entirely distinctive. Now his principal concern was not simply to see Europe, or to enjoy a holiday, or to master a language, or to pursue an academic course, or to act as companion for his parents, but *to improve his health.*

The fact is that Machen had been feeling rather unwell for a considerable period. Prior to his thirtieth year he seems generally to have enjoyed robust health. There were brief indispositions but in most cases they disappeared quickly when he took time to secure relaxation from his usual labors. A long hike or regular tennis usually was all that was required to restore his accustomed vigor. During his student days at Princeton he had once spent a number of days in the Mc Cosh Infirmary with tonsilitis and he seems afterward to have had recurrent attacks of sore throat in later years. Finally, in the summer of 1912 he underwent a tonsilectomy with a measure of improvement resulting, but before long there came the disillusionment of his hopes that the operation would guarantee him against the recurrence of severe colds. The most distressing development of the year and more that followed, however, was the onset of violent attacks of indigestion, which failed to respond to the remedy of Morrison's Pills, by which his father had sworn for several decades, or any ordinary prescription. Following the close of the academic year in 1913, he felt so discouraged that he became convinced that he had to take some extraordinary measure in the hope of regaining his usual physical well-being and buoyancy. What could do as well as exercise in the mountains, "the all-sufficient medicine," and what mountains offered more inviting and challenging summons to engage all his powers than those in the Tyrol, the Alpine crownland of western Austria?

Leaving about the middle of June on the steamer, *Kaiser Wilhelm der Grosse,* he proceeded, upon arrival in Bremen, to Munich, and after a brief stay in that charming city, he hurried on over the Brenner Pass into Tyrol. Eight years before he had traveled leisurely on his bicycle; now he went by rail in order to reach the mountain country as soon as possible. The six weeks that lay ahead were precious and had to be fully utilized for his special purpose. Whereas on the earlier occasion Innsbruck and Lienz had been the centres of operation, now Bozen, St. Ulrich and Cortina were chosen. Working out from Bozen he managed to cover considerable portions of the four valleys extending eastward and made several ascents including the Grasleitenspitze, Kesselkogel and Schlern. St. Ulrich, in the Grödner Valley, made several groups of the Dolomite peaks accessible. And Cortina, "the Zermatt of the Dolomite region," was the starting point for thrilling experiences in climbing Italian Alps including Campanile di Val Montanaia, Monte Cristallo and Monte Pelino. The final climb was that of the Kleine Zinne, which had also been ascended on his previous visit to this region. Now he was able to compare his present skill with his former aptitude; and he confessed that the "impression of terrific and almost insurmountable difficulty is gone." While still cautious in making the steep ascents, he set speed records in traversing the slopes that amazed the guides. And at one point he boasts that "knocking spots out of the guidebook time is the best remedy that I have yet secured for indigestion."

In spite of such minor and major successes, in one respect at least the stay in that area was disappointing. The weather so it seemed was constantly conspiring against him. Frequent torrential rains, or freshly fallen snow, or spells of warm weather interfered with his plans on several occasions. Once he spoke of the considerable delay occasioned by his observance of Sunday: "The trouble with Sunday in the mountains is that it involves a wait not of one but of two days. Had today not been Sunday I should have gone to a hut yesterday afternoon and made a climb today. As it is, I must wait till Monday afternoon to go to the hut, so that the climb cannot be made till Tuesday. But I am thankful for Sunday rest and do not regret my principles." In spite of much bad weather, and the failure to make as much progress with his special problem of indigestion as he had anticipated, he came to the close of his use of the "mountain medicine" with the assurance of that it had done him a world of good:

> My summer, I think, has done me just lots of good and I am very grateful to Father who so whole-heartedly entered into the plan. The mental benefit of it has been as great as the physical. If there is any sphere of work where an occasional complete relaxation is beneficial it is theology. Now, were it not for that worry about coming before presbytery, which fills me with dread, I should really look forward to taking up the year's work again at Princeton.
>
> My digestion, I regret to say, is still not quite perfect. But I think I have got over all acute trouble, and with a return to food to which I am more accustomed I hope to be all right.

Perhaps, however, the mental and spiritual benefits were far greater than the physical. Though the complete change of scene, the fresh air and exercise toned up his system as a whole, he was not able to free himself entirely from his susceptibility to colds and indigestion.

And most distressing of all it was not long after he resumed life at the Seminary in the fall that fierce attacks of indigestion again made his life miserable.

Fearful that his work at the Seminary would be seriously impaired, or that it might even have to be suspended, he sought out a New York specialist for diagnosis and treatment. Acting on his advice he spent virtually the whole of the Christmas vacation and a week beyond at his private hospital, a step taken the more reluctantly because he had been counting strongly on being an attendant at his younger brother Tom's wedding late in December. The final diagnosis was chronic appendicitis and intestinal catarrh. Surgery it was judged could be avoided or at least postponed. But a program of medication and highly restricted diet was entered upon, and this was continued for more than a year until gradually he was able to resume a more normal existence and appeared to be permanently cured. Though he later on had his share of the everyday miseries of mankind, perhaps more than he allowed any one to realize, he evidently never again was called upon to pass through experiences comparable to those of his early thirties. Until the final week of his life, though one often had cause to wonder that he did not collapse under the overwhelming burdens that he carried, his health was on the whole exceptionally good and his energy, both physical and mental, was so prodigious that far younger men despaired of keeping pace with him.

LICENSURE AND ORDINATION

The extent of Machen's attachment to the church of his fathers, the Southern Presbyterian Church, is observed from the fact that he remained associated with it until shortly before his ordination. Since his field of labor was to be in the Northern Presbyterian Church his ordination appropriately took place under its presbyterial auspices. But he had continued as a member of the Franklin St. Church of Baltimore, where he had been baptized and where he had made public profession of faith, throughout the years of his instructorship at Princeton. Moreover, the preliminary steps looking towards ordination were taken in the presbytery of jurisdiction over his home church, the Presbytery of the Potomac. The date appointed for coming under care was Nov. 3, 1913, and thus he placed himself on record as desiring to seek the sacred office. Following the traditional Presbyterian requirements he then gave satisfaction as to "experimental religion" and his motives for seeking the ministry, and the Presbytery in turn assumed supervision of his further preparation. At this stage the required examination and pledge were quite simple, though the experience was a most solemn one since he had now undertaken a commitment which had first been proposed more than a decade earlier.

During the nearly six months that followed before the time appointed for licensure, Machen was called upon to prepare the written "parts of trial," including a Latin thesis, a critical exegesis, a lecture and a sermon. Since he was permitted to choose his own topics, none of these involved an immense amount of labor. His Latin thesis, for example, was on the subject of the birth of Christ. Nevertheless, it was not an exercise to be dashed off in an odd moment or two. As he wrote in the midst of preparations, "Of course the Latin thesis has gotten to be more or less of a form, but still I should feel mortified to have mine too thickly peppered with atrocious solecisms." Finally these exercises were completed but the real ordeal was the appearance before the presbytery which convened in Alexandria, Va., on April 22, 1914. He was thankful especially that the meeting was not to be held in his native city:

> My only comfort about Presbytery has been that the meeting is to be *not* in Baltimore. So of course I hope that none of my friends will go over to Alexandria. I should be glad to have them hear me preach, if I should preach—which is unlikely—but very sorry to have them hear me examined. Of course, I should not mind you, but it would at best not be worth your while . . . I should not mind Uncle if he should be sent to presbytery.

Looking back upon the experience afterward, however, he was lighthearted and relieved that no severe demands had been made upon him.

> My experience with Presbytery was on the whole good fun. It was a good Christian body of men, and with a cordial spirit which sometimes is lacking in this part of the world.
>
> Arriving at Alexandria about nine o'clock on Wednesday morning we found them engaged in devotional exercises. After the exercises were over, all of my examinations except experimental religion, church government and theology were referred to committees. The committees were to meet during the recess. They were, however, conspicuous by their absence, or rather they took a gratifyingly lenient view of their functions. The upshot of the matter was that the only examinations which I had to stand were those which came before open presbytery after lunch. My examination in church government was not passed very brilliantly, but when I could not answer the questions the

examiner answered them for me. In this way embarrassment was avoided. The examination in theology was conducted by Dr. Kirk. The object of the examiner was to ask the candidate only those things which he would be most likely to know. Despite this fact the answers were by no means what they might have been. The "aetiological argument" came in handy. I had looked it up in the syllabus of Dr. Patton's lectures in theism. Though I did not know much about what it is, yet I think the casual mention of it was rather impressive ...

At about four o'clock I decided to go into Washington for gastronomic reasons. The excellent lunch provided for presbytery contained nothing which was not strictly forbidden on my diet list, and consequently I had had practically nothing to eat since six o'clock in the morning. I was feeling a little rocky, but a good orthodox dinner at the Willard at about five o'clock helped me to get through the rest of the day.

In preaching in the evening I was for some reason not at my best, but my efforts seemed to be cordially received. I was sorry to rush off so hurriedly, but wanted to take the first car in order to be with Uncle ...

Of course I was sorry that it did not seem proper for me to be ordained; for now the whole bother will have to be gone over with before the dreadful New Brunswick presbytery. But it is quite clear that the procedure which was adopted was the only correct one. I hope to present my letter at the June meeting of New Brunswick Presbytery. Perhaps Uncle will stir the clerk up—whoever he may be—to send the letter along.

Evidently, however, not every one agreed with Machen's own perhaps half serious, half facetious estimate of the demands made of him. A short time later his mother wrote of Dr. Kirk's appraisal:

Dr. Kirk came to see us after the service and talked about you in a way that made my heart burn within me. He says that when you gain a little more experience and let yourself go, you will make a *great* preacher, that your sermon was remarkable in its depth of thought, your introduction was a masterful account of the steps by which a thoughtful soul struggles up to faith. You had given him a new idea. He talked very quietly and calmly and said if I had been present he was sure I would have been profoundly and humbly grateful. He spoke of the great satisfaction he felt in asking you questions on Theology and meeting such perfect understanding and ready response.

Another, not less sympathetic report was given Mrs. Machen by her brother, Thomas B. Gresham, who had been a delegate to presbytery. And "Uncle" himself wrote on April 23rd:

> I was sorry not to meet you again last night, for I had hoped for an opportunity for expressing my joy and intense satisfaction with the way you came through your trial with the Presbytery. As I told your mother this morning, it was a triumphal march and I never saw a body of men so impressed as was this presbytery. Your sermon too was simply great and a fitting climax to the examination. I am delighted to hear that you have consented to preach for Dr. Kirk in June, and we all look forward to it. I am sorry we couldn't keep you in our Presbytery, but I am sure the right thing was done in transferring you . . .

And his brother Arthur's letter of congratulation contained the following:

> The news of the flattering impression you made at the meeting of the Presbytery was exceedingly pleasant to all of us, and to nobody more pleasing than to me—always excepting Mother, whose interest in each of us surpasses everything. It ought to be encouraging to you, beyond words, to know how highly you are esteemed, and how much good you are capable of accomplishing, and are accomplishing. According to all accounts, it must have been a triumphal acclamation rather than an examination.

Cousin Lewis H. Machen, who was practising law in Alexandria was present at the evening service, and wrote his aunt that "it would have done your heart good to hear the venerable chairman of the examining committee say publicly in the church tonight that he had never known such a brilliant Latin exegesis as Gresham's. He said the committee felt they had some marvellous sort of a leader in thought among them. Naturally, my family pride was keenly stirred. Gresham's sermon was the best I had ever heard from a young man. I was glad of this, for it had been rumored during the day that it was I who was going to preach!"

The chairman referred to was Dr. Parke P. Flournoy, whose evaulation was perhaps more detached and objective than that of Machen's relatives and pastor. A month after the examination he wrote Machen urging him to publish his exegesis paper in the Union Seminary Magazine. Though complimented by this action, and admitting to his mother that the paper embodied "the results of my experience in teaching for the past ten years," he felt it was premature to publish it. It was this same Dr. Flournoy who had occasion more than a decade later to recall the examination to Dr. Albert Sidney Johnson of Charlotte, stating that, as the one to whom had been assigned the duty of examining and reporting on the Latin Thesis and the Greek Exegesis, he had reported both as "the best of all that had been examined by me in the long course of such duties."

In none of the reports of contemporary witnesses is there any mention of the act of licensure itself, though the taking of the constitutionally prescribed vows was actually the most meaningful event of the day. That Machen did exceptionally well in the examinations is not particularly surprising considering his academic training and experience. But assenting to the questions for licensure was a different matter. That he did so after so many years of postponement was noteworthy. That he did so at all considering his former conviction that he would probably do wrong to seek ordination and that at times he had been shaken by profound doubts as to the truth of Christianity was memorable. That he did so at last is proof that, through the grace of God, manifesting itself in his own valiant struggle for truth and certainty, and utilizing the marvellous sympathy and patience of loved ones at home and senior colleagues at Princeton, he had emerged with steady and firm tread out of the morass that had threatened to hold him captive. Now at last he was ready to affirm solemnly that he believed "the Scriptures of the Old and New Testaments to be the Word of God, the only infallible rule of faith and practice," and to receive and adopt the Westminster Confession of Faith and Catechisms "as containing the system of doctrine taught in the Holy Scriptures." Having arrived at such convictions through fierce struggle, and having counted the cost of such commitment, he could be expected to stand by them through thick and thin, regardless of the opposition that he might encounter by doing so.

The ordination service took place about two months later, on June 23, 1914, at Plainsboro, N. J., just outside of Princeton. Though he had characterized the examination of the New Brunswick Presbytery as "dreadful"—no doubt with something of a twinkle in his eye—apparently it was not necessary to repeat the licensure examinations to any considerable extent, and his admission seems to have been regarded as little more than a formality after his credentials had been received from the Southern Presbyterian Church. The total time set apart for the examination and Machen's sermon was just one hour and a half. Few details have been recorded.

REJOICE WITH TREMBLING

Incidentally one discovers that the sermon was on the text, "Rejoice with trembling," taken from Ps. 2:11, and a manuscript of that sermon is still extant. In it he began with the observation that rejoicing is power, that joy is the prime requisite for high achievement, that religion without enthusiasm is a dead thing. The religious life is indeed not a mere matter of inclination.

> It must be diligently and consciously fostered—by attendance upon religious exercises, even when they are a weariness to the flesh, by maintaining the form of prayer even when the spirit of it seems gone for the time without recall, by reading the Bible even when you are far more interested in something else. Duty is therefore necessary to religion. But religion that is only duty is but a dead thing. If the world is to be conquered for Christ, duty must be supplemented by mighty enthusiasm.

Modern religion, with its emphasis upon good citizenship and social well-being, he went on to observe, is not really joyful. The happiness of the world is superficial and at best precarious. The thought of the real underlying problems of life cannot always be avoided. Browning's *Bishop Blougram's Apology* was quoted to make this point.

> *Just when we are safest, there's a sunset-touch,*
> *A fancy from a flower-bell, some one's death,*
> *A chorus-ending from Euripides*
> *And that's enough for fifty hopes and fears*
> *As old and new at once as nature's self,*
> *To rap and knock and enter in our soul,*
> *Take hands and dance there, a fantastic ring,*
> *Round the ancient idol, on his base again,*
> *The grand Perhaps!*

The question was then raised, "May we find in religion something deeper than the pleasures of this world, some peculiar, basal joy, which will substantiate all the rest? There is the problem. How is religion to be made a joyful thing?"

The answer, he averred, is not to be found merely by cheering up religion. "Noble churches, good music, brilliant preaching—these things, in themselves, are none the less worldly because enjoyed within consecrated walls. Sometimes they are not religion, but a diversion from religion." If it is recalled that religion is communion with God, men are ready with the answer that joy may be found by emphasizing the comforting attributes of God. But this approach, when examined, breaks down. In view of the reality of sin, men refuse to break forth into ecstacies of joy when they hear such a message. Moreover, such a message is shown to be false whether one appeals to nature or to the Bible as a whole or to Jesus only. How then may true joy be found?

> The text gives the answer. "Rejoice with trembling." That looks like a paradox. Joy and fear are opposite. At any rate, surely the trembling must limit the joy. Rejoice although you have to tremble. Or, rejoice, but in your joy do not forget to tremble. Or, is the trembling positively necessary to the joy, intimately connected with it? Is the trembling the key to the joy? If we learn to tremble, will the way be open to the joy that we have sought so long in vain. Rejoice, says the modern preacher—but sadness somehow does not flee; Rejoice with trembling, says the psalmist—and the Lord put gladness in his heart.

Men no longer tremble before God because they have lost their sense of mystery and their sense of sin, Machen now argued at length. Their minds should faint before the overwhelming mystery of the creator as they contemplate the vastness of nature. If they kept close to the living stream of revelation in apostles and prophets, they would realize that they are dealing with unspeakable mysteries, and would not be too exact in charting the course of the Almighty, or too ready to say, Because God does this, therefore He must do that. Others attack the transcendence of God claiming that God does not exist apart from the world. Thus mystery has been eliminated from religion.

> But at what a cost! Inconvenient interference by the ruler of the universe is no longer to be expected. But no more is help in time of trouble. God has no more thunderbolts, but neither has He gifts... He is no longer to be feared but neither is He worth seeking. Mystery is gone. But its place has been taken by despair.

The sense of guilt also produced the fear of God, he went on, but that too has been lost. Sin is now viewed as a necessary stage in the development of humanity and inevitably as necessary in the life of God too. The old view that sin is rebellion against the Creator's will is called morbid or even over-wrought, but that settles nothing. Paul too was thought to be mad. Give up such madness and you sink to the level of the beasts. With it comes a terrible revelation of the righteous God. The search for joy in religion has seemed to end in disaster. God enveloped in impenetrable mystery and in awful righteousness. Man confined in the prison of the world, trying to make the best of the situation, beautifying the prison with tinsel, yet secretly dissatisfied with his bondage. No hope; God separate from sinners. No room for joy. Only a certain fearful looking for of judgment and fiery indignation.

> Yet such a God has at least one advantage over the comforting God of modern preaching. He is alive. He is sovereign. He is not bound by His creation or by His creatures. He can perform wonders. Could He even save us if He would? He *has* saved us. It could not have been foretold; still less could the manner of it have been foretold. "That Birth, that Life, that Death!"—why was it done just thus and then and there? It all seems so local, so very particular, so very unphilosophical, very unlike what might have been expected. "Are not Abana and Pharpar, rivers of Damascus, better than all the waters of Israel?" Yet, what if it were true? So, the All-Great were the All-Loving too.
>
> God's own Son delivered up for us all. Freedom from the world, sought by philosophers of all the ages offered now to every simple soul. Things hidden from the wise and prudent revealed unto babes. The long striving over. The impossible accomplished. Sin conquered by mysterious grace. Communion at length with the holy God. Our Father which art in heaven!
>
> Surely this and this alone is joy. But a joy that is akin to fear. It is a fearful thing to fall into the hands of the living God. Were it not safer with a God of our own devising? Love and only love? A father and nothing else? One before whom we could stand in our own merit without fear? Let him who will be satisfied with such a God. But we, God help us, sinful as we are, we would see Jehovah. Despairing, hoping, trembling, half-doubting, half-believing, staking all upon Jesus, we venture into the presence of the very God. And in His presence live.

Thus concludes this sermon that even stylistically bears the marks of its early origin. Later Machen came to feel, on the background of criticism of loved ones, that he had been extreme in his use of brief and incomplete sentences. The sermon also no doubt expressed much of the religious temper of his mind and heart just at that time. What text could serve as well—as it had served Christian in *Pilgrim's Progress*—to voice his restrained and trembling sense of exultation? Yet the sermon theme was one that continued to appeal to Machen, for he often dwelt upon the majesty and transcendence of God, and continued to preach on this particular text for many years.

Among those who were present at the services were Machen's father and mother. Mrs. Machen was to rejoice in that event for years to come, and wrote as follows concerning it:

> The memory of the ordination services abides in my memory and that day of days will cast its radiance over many less favored ones. I wouldn't have had it different in any respect. The simplicity of it all—the little church in its setting of greenery with flowers blooming about the door, the crowd of ministers in their everyday clothes, the absence of all form and yet the strict following out of the Scriptural idea, your own great sermon—all made it so deeply spiritual. Take away the inner meaning and nothing was left. One felt that there was a great transaction and God was taking part. I really feel that I can make a new surrender of my life to God and that I can trust Him for others too. One thing you said in your sermon has been of material help to your mother—about the *mystery* and *transcendence* of God. I have been resting in that. You made me feel the comfort of those awe-inspiring conceptions.

Among those who took part in the service were Dr. Kirk and Bobby Robinson. The latter wrote later that the whole ordination service had been "a memorable experience" and that he felt that "we did not bear witness alone to the realities of the faith." And Dr. Kirk expressed himself as follows:

> Baltimore, June 25th, 1914
>
> My dear Gresham,
>
> I am very grateful to you for allowing me to have a share in your ordination. You realize how fully we all feel our prayers were answered, and I never from the beginning had any doubt but that God would direct you to a favorable conclusion in the matter.
>
> It fills me with great encouragement to see a man of such rare powers devoting himself to the noble but difficult task of preaching in these days and with your absolute loyalty to the living Lord, your keen appreciation of historical Christianity, and your strong inclination towards scholarship I feel confident that you will do a vast service to the church. I am proud indeed to have numbered you among my friends, and church members, and shall count your friendship and sympathy in our common work among my highest blessings.
>
> With warmest affection believe me always,
>
> Yours sincerely,
>
> Harris E. Kirk

NOMINATION AS ASSISTANT PROFESSOR

Acting on the background of Machen's licensure, the Faculty of the Seminary was not slow to recommend his election as Assistant Professor of New Testament in its report to the Board of Directors at its meeting during the first week of May, 1914. Dr. Warfield, who had been president since Patton's retirement the previous year, reported that the recommendation had been adopted without opposition. His salary as an instructor had been eventually increased to $2,000.00 and it might now have been increased $500 more had Machen not made it clear to Warfield in advance that "such a change would not increase but diminish my pleasure in my improved status." The reason for this feeling was, as he expressed it in a letter to his mother, that he would "have felt like a dog" in endangering a salary increase for another member of the staff, an increase "imperatively required on account of his approaching marriage." His brother Arthur, who had himself just at this time been honored by an appointment as Special Assistant to Attorney General McReynolds, commented on this point in the course of his congratulatory message:

> I want to congratulate you cordially upon your advancement to professorial rank. The honor is small recompense, I know, for your years of work; but it is satisfactory to find it given so promptly and willingly. That it is not accompanied by an increase in stipend is, I judge, due to your own modesty. My own feeling in such matters is that, however free one may be from mercenary motives, yet some adequacy in the pecuniary reward is desirable, because it *does* add a stimulus to one's zeal. It is very hard to render the very best service when you know that the service is not appraised at its real worth by those to whom it is rendered. But of course in your case these considerations are not applicable—certainly not applicable to their full extent. I mention them merely in order that you may not hereafter be led to err by excess of unselfishness . . .
>
> It is a great pity that you should be so harassed with work, especially at this season of the year. You really must try next year to lighten your labors, that is to say, your routine labors, so as to leave you free to seize the opportunities for the highest usefulness when they present themselves.

SUNDAY SCHOOL LESSONS

The work which was particularly harassing just at this time, and which constrained him to postpone his installation for nearly a year, was an exceedingly onerous burden of writing which had been undertaken some months previously. His labors in the local Sunday School were beginning to restrict his liberty of accepting preaching opportunities, and more than two years were to ensue before he would be able to secure release from his responsibility there. But these duties were child's play compared with the program of grueling work that he entered upon in response to an invitation of an editorial secretary of the Board of Christian Education to prepare the Senior Course of Sunday School lessons for a year. He did not undertake the work without misgivings. To mention one unattractive consideration, he felt that the outline of the course provided by the "International Lessons" seemed, in a certain bias against historical facts, to be proceeding from a bad pedagogy and perhaps even a bad view of the Christian religion. But if he did not accept the invitation, would the work perhaps be undertaken by a liberal in theology? It is not so easy, he wrote his mother,

> for conservatives to get a really free hearing. I am afraid, in order to get our views before the Church, we shall have to adapt ourselves to circumstances... The course is in the apostolic age. It attracts me keenly. This is the kind of work that Princeton men ought to be doing. Of course, I should much rather write a book of my own on Paul, which would give me more scope for any power of expression which I may have. But the question is whether I could ever get my book published. The task that has been offered me is a humble one, and in it I shall be sadly hampered. But it is the thing that has come my way and if I can I want to take it.
>
> Beginning about three weeks from today, I shall be required (if I am approved) to hand in one lesson a week (for both teachers' and pupils' book) without fail, and the grind would go on for a year. Of course if I want holidays, I can work ahead. But I must not get behind. The compensation offered is $1,000, which I was informed will prove to be not overly much in view of the work involved. And I can well believe it. It is evident that my work is going to be blue-pencilled very freely, and some lessons I shall probably have to rewrite.

This letter was written early in February, the agreement was entered into about two weeks later, and the work begun early in March. Though he had foreseen some of the difficulties, it is doubtful that he would have undertaken it had he been aware of all the toil and distress that were awaiting him. Just because his own standards were very high, even the obligation to write a more or less elementary course of lessons, with the deadlines coming up week after week for fifty-two weeks, became a hard taskmaster. Harassed by interruptions that were difficult to avoid at Princeton, he several times sought the tranquility and solitude afforded by a hotel room in one of the near-by large cities. The Vanderbilt Hotel in New York became a special favorite, and he often returned there when it became imperative to get some pressing work out of the way.

During the summer of 1914 on one occasion he stayed there for about two weeks, and wrote at some length of its various advantages over Princeton.

> Aside from the delightful comfort of this hotel—the freedom from dust and dirt, the bed that is every bit as high in the middle as it is at the ends, the bully clean bath tub that empties or fills in two seconds—New York is always a great diversion to me. Trips to Europe, under peaceful conditions, may be fine, but it is hard for me to see how they can be much more delightful than two weeks at the Vanderbilt . . .

Then commenting on his delight in taking walks of several miles in New York, and observing that they were very beneficial to his health, he said:

> I suppose I am a born sightseer. With me it does not take the form of minute interest in museums or collections or of antiquarian interest in historic associations—these things are to me too much like work—but I just love to walk and walk and walk and get the general lay of the land and see how the people live. For these purposes Greater New York offers a never-ending variety of interest . . . .

The ease with which he could get just the things that he was allowed to eat at the time was another advantage. And there was the enjoyment of other diversions that appealed to him. But now he comes to the consideration which is responsible for the quotation of this letter in the present connection:

> This account of the pleasures of summer life in New York may perhaps create the impression that I have been having a big loaf. But such an impression would be far from correct. On the contrary after rising rather early I have gotten in pretty long mornings of work, which has also been continued often during other parts of the day. Progress has been dreadfully slow, but the total

> volume of work has not been inconsiderable. Indeed the fear of interruption is one of the things that keeps me from pulling up stakes. I do want to get a little ahead before I move again. This is such a satisfactory place to work.

Besides the mountain of labor involved, however, there was another distressing aspect to the task of turning out the course of lessons. Editorial blue-pencilling had been foreseen as a possibility, but the actuality of it was sometimes gall and wormwood to his soul. At times the editor silently changed the substance of what Machen had written; and the style was rather pervasively modified. Privately—which means in his communications with members of his family and with sympathetic friends at Princeton—he sometimes exploded. But it appears that in his correspondence as well as in conferences with the editor he was restrained, and won recognition and praise not only for his thorough and scholarly work but also for his "helpful and gracious attitude." The necessity which Machen felt of taking up the numerous points, and of ironing out the differences of judgment, entailed an immense amount of additional labor. But the total result at any rate won praise not only from the editor but also from colleagues and dear friends. Bobby Robinson found it "admirable" and encouraged him to continue to do "what needs most to be done." Dr. L. B. Crane of Elizabeth, a Seminary Director of unusual scholarship, said that he did not believe that "any such work has ever been done for Sunday Schools." Dr. Warfield read the instalments as they appeared—"greedily at once," he said—and declared that Machen had done "a very difficult piece of work admirably and we are all proud to have these lesson-helps emanate from Princeton." And Machen himself confessed as the work reached a conclusion that he had not always been entirely just to the editorial authorities of the Church. "I am sorry about the spoiling of the Teachers' Book on the Gospels, but on the other hand probably my style of writing was very faulty at first. In one way or another I have got benefit from the experience of the year."

HISTORY AND FAITH

However rewarding the year of hard work on the lessons had been, it was a relief to be able to enter upon a time of greater liberty to engage in a variety of challenging tasks. His installation lay just ahead, and it was necessary to prepare an address for the occasion. The day appointed for the service was May 3rd, 1915, and therefore the time available was not at all too long if he were to do justice to its demands.

For the inaugural address Machen chose the theme, "History and Faith." The subject was as profound as any that he had ever treated in a public address, concerned as it was with a question that sharply divided the orthodox Christianity represented by Princeton from opposing viewpoints at home and abroad. The view that faith might be valid regardless of one's conclusions concerning the history of Jesus Christ had been presented in a fascinating and captivating manner by Herrmann and it had appeared increasingly that this or a similar viewpoint stood at the basis of a growing opposition or indifference to the gospel in ecclesiastical life in America. Hence this utterance was most timely.

Though it constituted a significant contribution to the subject under discussion, it was not weighted down with obscure allusions to critical discussions or with heavy technical apparatus. Machen did not indeed minimize the importance of debate with the critics, and as his 1912 articles on the birth narratives had shown he could present minute and technical details if it suited his theme and purpose. But one temptation to which he seemed never to yield, either now or later, was that of aiming to establish in the minds of his hearers or readers a reputation for scholarship. A distinguishing feature of Machen as a teacher and writer and preacher, which was really rooted in his character, was that he spoke or wrote with a view to the edification of his audience rather than to center attention upon himself. This was, in my judgment, the real secret of the lucidity of expression which was a marked characteristic of his utterances. At his installation accordingly one feels that he was concerned to sound forth a clear note for the gospel rather than to prove, for example, that the Directors had made no mistake in judging that he possessed the requisite scholarship for his new position. Incidentally, of course, the address disclosed to the discerning ample evidence of scholarly equipment and discrimination.

The address contains certain echoes of his ordination sermon and reflects some of the emphases developed in his work on the history of Christianity in his Sunday School course. But in the main it was freshly concerned with its peculiar theme. Taking account of the modern view that "religion has been made independent, as is thought, of the uncertainties of historical research," he characterized the separation of Christianity from history as "an inspiring attempt" but as actually "a failure."

> Give up history, and you can retain some things. You can retain belief in God. But philosophical theism has never been a

powerful force in the world. You can retain a lofty ethical ideal. But be perfectly clear about one point—you can never retain a gospel. For gospel means "good news," tidings, information about something that has happened. In other words, it means history. A gospel independent of history is simply a contradiction in terms.

Considering the modern reconstruction of Jesus in the perspective of the Pauline Epistles and the Gospels, he showed why it must be considered a failure. In the first place, the natural and the supernatural in the Gospel narrative are inextricably intertwined. If the supernatural is rejected, the whole must go. In the second place, even if one could reconstruct the historical Jesus by such a process of separation, that Jesus would be an impossible figure because of a tremendous contradiction that would remain at the very centre of his being. For this teacher or prophet who is not allowed to be thought of as more than a humble worshipper of God supposed that He was the Messiah, "a heavenly being who was to come on the clouds of heaven and be the instrument in judging the earth." In the third place, supposing that the critical sifting could be accomplished and that the resulting picture of Jesus were not self-contradictory, there would remain the insoluble problem as to how the Christian faith with its belief in a superhuman Jesus could have come into being. "The modern substitute for the Jesus of the Bible," he concluded, has been tried and found wanting. The liberal Jesus—what a world of lofty thinking, what a wealth of noble sentiments was put into his construction! But now there are some indications that he is about to fall. He is beginning to give place to a radical scepticism. Such scepticism is absurd; Jesus lived, if any history is true. Jesus lived, but what Jesus? Not the Jesus of modern naturalism! But the Jesus of the Bible! In the wonders of the Gospel story, in the character of Jesus, in His mysterious self-consciousness, in the very origin of the Christian Church, we discover a problem, which defies the best efforts of the naturalistic historian, which pushes us relentlessly off the safe ground of the phenomenal world toward the intellectual abyss of supernaturalism, which forces us, despite the resistance of the modern mind, to recognize a very act of God, which substitutes for the silent God of philosophy the God and Father of our Lord Jesus Christ, who, having spoken at sundry times and in divers manners unto the fathers by the prophets, hath in these last days spoken unto us by His Son.

The reference to the Bible attracts special attention on this occasion when vows spoken at the time of ordination were repeated. If this reference and others that follow in the concluding words of the address were taken as expounding Machen's total view of the Bible, they would seem rather inadequate. But it would be a mistake to insist that he was required by his theme or the occasion to deal systematically with this subject. His aim was the much more limited one of indicating the apologetic significance of the faithfulness of the Biblical portrait of Jesus for the truth of the Bible as a whole. But he is not sympathetic with those who judge that the Bible is expendable. The Bible has been viewed as a ladder "to scale the dizzy height of Christian experience," which may be kicked down when one is once safely on top. But this figure, Machen felt, was misleading.

> The Bible is not a ladder; it is a foundation. It is buttressed, indeed, by experience; if you have the present Christ, then you know that the Bible account is true. But if the Bible *were* false, your faith would go. You cannot, therefore, be indifferent to Bible criticism. Let us not deceive ourselves. The Bible is at the foundation of the Church. Undermine that foundation, and the Church will fall.
>
> Two conceptions of Christianity are struggling for the ascendency; the question that we have been discussing is part of a still larger problem. The Bible against the modern preacher . . . The Church is in perplexity. She is trying to compromise. God grant that she may choose aright. God grant she may decide for the Bible!

PERSONAL TRIBUTES

This address was published in the *Princeton Review,* and copies were run off on orders of the Board of Directors for distribution to the 3000 alumni of the Seminary. The published form, however, did not contain all that Machen said on the occasion. For his files preserved a page of prefatory remarks which, because of their intimate and personal character, he decided, or was persuaded, not to include in the copy sent to the printers. He began by remarking that "the position to which I have been called by the Board of Directors involves for me precious personal associations as well as an inspiring task," and then he spoke particularly of his obligations to and esteem for Professor Armstrong.

> The professor in charge of the department in which I am to labor has made of me an intimate personal friend, and bestowed upon me a thousand kindnesses. My impression of his scholar-

> ship was formed during the very first hour that I spent in his classroom, and has been immeasurably deepened since that time. The assistance that he has given me in the establishment of my Christian faith has been simply incalculable. I shall never be able to acquire one tenth part of his learning, but to his constant guidance and example I shall owe at least whatever breadth of outlook and loyalty to the truth I may ever be able to attain. My dependence upon him has become only more and more apparent, and to me more and more welcome, with successive years.

How Machen must have rejoiced in this opportunity of saying publicly just how great a man his beloved "Army" really was! His letters home gave him repeated occasions to do so, and they glow with admiration and affection when they mention him. When Armstrong had been attacked by certain students in 1909, Machen could hardly speak publicly in his defense. He could only mourn in the deepest sympathy. But now he could speak forth with complete propriety. And the biographer, as one who, though from a greater distance, came many years later to share something of that admiration and affection for Armstrong, takes special delight in the fact that this work may be the means of publishing Machen's tribute.

But there was one other who was singled out for special mention on the occasion of Machen's installation. It was Dr. Patton who had consented to giving the charge to the newly installed professor. Of him he said:

> The distinguished preacher who has done me the honor of delivering the charge on the present occasion has been to me, since I came to Princeton, my spiritual father; for him I cherish every bit of gratitude and affection of which I am capable. No one else in the wide world could possibly have filled the place that he has filled in my life; without his sympathy and help you may be very sure that I should not be standing before you today.

Finally he referred more generally to the rest of the faculty as known and honored for many years. He recalled that he had sat under most of them in the classroom, and declared that "they are all, today at least, my teachers." And then he introduced his theme as follows:

> Personal associations such as these afford immeasurable encouragement for the work in which, by the grace of God, I hope to be engaged. The general purpose of that work may perhaps be outlined—in a sadly inadequate and elementary way I am

afraid—in what you are now permitting me to say with regard to "History and Faith."

That Machen did feel that the address was not up to his best possibilities was expressed later on in a letter to his father:

> I should have originally preferred not to print the address at all—which is exceedingly "light" and lends itself to spoken discourse rather than to the printed page—but have gotten somewhat into the notion of the thing now. I should not like to have the few experts into whose hands it may come take it as a fair sample of what I can do. A similarly wide distribution of my "Jesus and Paul" would have given me much more pleasure, for I am bold enough to think that in that article I said something in a way which (right or wrong) is at any rate somewhat distinctive. This time I have simply given a sketch of well-worn arguments.

To this his father, who with his mother had been present at the service of installation, responded with the encouragement that could still be counted upon in his eighty-eighth year.

> I have read "History and Faith" all through very carefully, and the impression I received at the delivery has been *fully* confirmed. You need not doubt that the wide circulation given it by the Seminary Trustees was well justified. It will hold its own, whenever and wherever read. This you may feel assured of. True, it does not occupy the same ground as "Jesus and Paul," nor does "Jesus and Paul" crowd out the critical article which extorted the commendation of Harnack: each piece of work has its own place, and I am rejoiced that you have been able to accomplish them all. Your work for the Sunday School lessons is admirable too, and has given us a great deal of pleasure and profit to read, as I must not omit to say in connection with this comparative discussion.
>
> We are all feeling pretty well. For myself I have a lot of jobs, professional and other, which I am desiring to dispose of, in preparation for the long vacation. So I am kept right busy—the right road to happiness in life after all.
>
> Your affectionate father,
>
> Arthur W. Machen

Another faithful supporter was Dr. John De Witt, now in retirement, who wrote: "I read with even greater pleasure than the pleasure I had in hearing it your Inaugural Discourse. Terse, strong, and clear, and every way most admirable." He added, however, the comment that Machen might have given "more words than you did to the internal arguments by which the Bible authenticates itself, and above all to the *Testimonium Spiritus Sancti.*" Among others who offered their congratulations was President Hibben of the University and Jesse Benedict Carter, Director of the American Academy in Rome. The latter had inadvertently opened a copy of the address intended for another whose forwarding address was unknown, and said that he had received so much pleasure from reading it that he was "selfishly unwilling to return your article to you on general principles," and that "I have seldom read anything which has pleased me more, and when I noticed the footnote that you are to be professor of New Testament Literature and Exegesis I was more pleased still, for that is the sort of spirit in which it seems to me New Testament literature should be treated."

Thus Machen was formally inducted into the office which he was to hold for the rest of his stay at Princeton, a period of fourteen years. But already the previous year, following upon his election, he had been accorded the right of voting privileges in the Faculty, and thus was qualified to take a direct part in the government of the Seminary so far as the authority of the Faculty was concerned. It was just at that time that momentous developments affecting the Seminary's future were taking place. And it is therefore necessary to retrace some of our steps so as to look beyond the horizon of Machen's personal history to the larger circle of the life of the Seminary as a whole.

11

AT THE CROSS ROADS

It is an ironic coincidence that the very year that marked the resolution of Machen's profound personal conflict was to usher in an era of grave tension in the life of the Seminary. This was the tension that was ultimately to issue in the convulsive struggle that led to the radical reorganization of 1929. Machen himself had come to peace of mind and heart at the very time that issues in a controversy embracing the very life of the Seminary were being drawn. Had the tensions of the years subsequent to his ordination been present beforehand to any considerable degree, it is most doubtful that he would have attained the courage to seek ordination. Certainly he would not have been able to identify his life with that of the Seminary as committed to a principle in theological education that won his enthusiastic allegiance. Because of the very struggle through which he had gone to win his certitude and commitment, however, he was prepared to be steadfast and unmoveable in the broader conflict that was taking shape.

CHOOSING PATTON'S SUCCESSOR

The year 1914 marks the dividing line in the history of the Seminary principally because of the election and installation of J. Ross Stevenson as president in that year. In singling out Dr. Stevenson in this manner, there is a danger of over-simplification which ought to be avoided if at all possible. There were no doubt other significant factors that were to emerge later on. Moreover, one may observe prior to 1914 the very forces at work which were responsible for the election of Stevenson as the successor of Patton. He did not elect himself to this office; that was the responsibility of the Board of Directors, and they ultimately must be held accountable, for good or ill, for this decision. Nevertheless, the Stevenson administration was more than a product of earlier decisions and circumstances. Stevenson himself, seemingly more and more self-consciously, became active spokesman and agent for a point of view which was ultimately destined to revolutionize the Seminary.

There is another estimate of Stevenson's place in that struggle, which however in its own way confirms the correctness of the position expressed above. His successor, Dr. John A. Mackay, once said that in that conflict the Princeton tradition "was worthily incarnated in the person and attitude of President Stevenson." In this same article, which speaks of Stevenson's two master passions as "foreign missions and the unity of the Church of Christ," special attention is centered upon his prominence in the modern ecumenical movement. He was a leading member of the Edinburgh Missionary Conference of 1910 "which inaugurated the modern ecumenical movement." And it is recalled that the World Council of Churches was launched by the Archbishop of York in the livingroom of "Springdale," the presidential residence at Princeton, with the full sympathy and support of Dr. Stevenson. "It is fitting," Dr. Mackay writes, "that Dr. Stevenson should be the chief representative of American Christianity in the city of Utrecht where the Council became a reality in 1938." These statements are of special interest because of the light they cast upon Stevenson's dominating interests and because in 1920 the issue of church union served to bring Machen into open conflict with him.

That story still remains before us. Here one must reflect on the earlier aspects of the situation. Considering the fact that Stevenson was not a graduate of Princeton, it is at least somewhat remarkable that he came to be chosen president. How did this come about? Joseph Ross Stevenson was born in 1866, the son of a Presbyterian pastor in a small country community in western Pennsylvania. Concluding his arts course at Washington and Jefferson College in 1886, he entered McCormick Seminary in Chicago, where he graduated three years later. Following a year of study in Berlin, he was ordained and served as a pastor for four years in Sedalia, Missouri. Thereafter he was professor of church history at McCormick for eight years, resigning to become pastor of the Fifth Avenue Presbyterian Church as the successor to Dr. Purves. Not long afterward he was elected as a Director of Princeton Seminary, and continued in this capacity during the seven years of his New York pastorate and the five that followed in Baltimore where he had gone to serve the Brown Memorial Church. Thus back of his service as president commencing in 1914 there was a decade of active participation in the government of the Seminary.

During those years the directors were confronted with pressing questions relating to the practical aspects of instruction. Following Paxton's retirement the chair of homiletics remained vacant for several years, and the teaching in this field was conducted by special visiting lecturers or members of other departments. Dr. Erdman's inauguration as professor of practical theology in 1906 relieved the situation somewhat, but the perplexing problem of homiletics remained. As Machen's letters also reflect, one person after another was considered for the chair. A number of men including Harris Kirk of Baltimore and Maitland Alexander of Pittsburgh were elected but declined to serve. Dr. Loetscher did serve from 1910 to 1913 but then returned to his first love, church history.

It is lamentable that these difficulties occurred just at the time when there was something of a hue and a cry for more practical instruction and a more practical emphasis in the instruction. The account of the "student rebellion" has recalled an acute manifestation of this tendency. And though the Directors did not regard it as wise to support the student approach, they did undertake further study and ultimate revision of the curriculum so as to expand the place given to practical studies. Evidently among the Directors there was a considerable body of sentiment sympathetic to the modification of the curriculum in this direction, and there is little doubt that Dr. Stevenson lent his support to this movement.

The problems facing the Directors were accentuated by the fact that Dr. Patton reached the age of retirement in 1913. At the time it appears to have been widely held that this would not necessarily complicate the situation. If only the problem of the presidency and of homiletics would permit of a single solution! Machen himself indicates that for a time the man who was thought of as the solution to this double problem was Dr. Wm. L. McEwan of Pittsburgh.

Following Patton's retirement, at a meeting of the Directors held in June 1913, a step was taken which Machen felt offered new hope of a happy decision. That was the election of Dr. Loetscher to the chair of church history. Moreover, he remarked in a letter of June 15th, "if he does accept, then his present chair (that of homiletics) will be left vacant for the man who I hope will be elected president. A number of steps remain to be taken before the consummation can be reached. But at least no step has yet been taken in the opposite direction." What he had in mind appears more explicitly in a letter of July 11th written from Bozen in the Tyrol on the background of a letter from Armstrong:

> A letter from Army brings the satisfactory news that Loetscher has consented to take the chair of Church History, instead of his present chair of Homiletics. That is satisfactory news, for it leaves open the Chair of Homiletics for a president. But there will be anxious months before McEwan of Pittsburgh is elected.

We can only hope. He is unquestionably the man for the place—a splendid man personally, a great power in the Church at large, and with sound ideas with regard to scholarship. Were he elected, we should feel that there was opportunity for genuine progress at Princeton. But certain other men who have been mentioned for the place would be, if elected, a constant hindrance in the way of any enthusiastic work in the defence of the faith, and to me personally a sad blow. Of course McEwan is not a candidiate. Whether he would accept the chair if it were offered him is exceedingly doubtful—especially in view of the great importance of the work which he is now performing with signal success. So you see my hopes are based on ifs and ifs. But still they are hopes which are not impossible of fulfillment.

Apparently McEwan eliminated himself from consideration. At any rate no one was elected to the presidency or the chair of homiletics at the fall meeting of the Board, and the entire matter remained under discussion until June, 1914. Evidently a number of men were under consideration during that period with Dr. Erdman mentioned most prominently for the post.

Charles Rosenbury Erdman was born in 1866, a few months later than J. Ross Stevenson. Graduating from Princeton Seminary in 1891, he served as pastor of churches for fifteen years, first in Overbrook and later in Germantown, both in outlying areas of Philadephia. As has been noted, he began his service as professor of practical theology in Princeton in 1906, the very year that saw the commencement of Machen's service as instructor. And he concluded it thirty years later on his retirement. During this entire period and beyond it he was prominently associated with the Board of Foreign Missions, as a member 1906-42 and as president 1926-1941. He had been present at the World's Missionary Conference in Edinburgh in 1910. Thus he shared certain special interests with J. Ross Stevenson and the two men were intimate friends of long standing.

Though Machen did not number Erdman among his intimate friends at Princeton, it appears that their relations were cordial until well beyond the present period. One of his first impressions of Erdman, as reported on Sept. 23, 1906, was that he, as well as Armstrong, was "the right stuff." And it was Erdman who in 1914 recommended Machen to the editorial staff of the Board of Christian Education for the literary work which he undertook that year. Nevertheless, as Machen's letters home during the academic year 1913-14 frequently show, he was alarmed at the prospect that Erdman might be chosen president, and it is rather clear that in this regard his concern was shared by several other members of the Faculty. His opposition to Erdman was clearly not personal. Nor was it based on any lack of appreciation of his work in his own chair. But it centered in his judgment that he lacked the special qualities requisite in a president. As late as May 10, 1914, shortly after Machen had received his advancement to professorial standing, Erdman was still being prominently mentioned for the office, for on that date Machen indicated his objections at some length in a letter to his brother Arthur. He felt that Erdman possessed attractive personal qualities, but that he lacked the solid appreciation of genuine scholarship which would prove essential in one who would be a spokesman for the Faculty in the meetings of the Board and before the Church and the world. Still more serious was a certain lack of discrimination with regard to issues which seemed to close his eyes to real differences between himself and others. "I should rejoice in Erdman's good qualities," he wrote, "if he were not sinned against by being proposed for what he is not fitted for."

THE ELECTION OF STEVENSON

A few weeks later, shortly before the Board was scheduled to convene on June 11, 1914, the complexion of affairs had taken a new turn. Suddenly the name of J. Ross Stevenson came to the fore. On May 31st Machen wrote his mother: "Ross Stevenson is rumored as the prominent presidential candidate. Erdman is said to be boosting him hard. Do you wonder that we become discouraged? Think of Ross Stevenson as president of this institution! I really believe Erdman would be better. Stevenson's notions about theological education are ruinous—they are especially bad with regard to New Testament work—and then of course you know what an extremely weak man Stevenson is." His mother replied on June 4th that she hoped his fears were groundless (about the possibility of Ross Stevenson for president) and remarked what a tragic pity it was that Patton could not have held on to the office until some really suitable successor appeared. But the unexpected did develop, and Stevenson was elected president to the dismay of Machen and other faculty members. The opposition to Stevenson no more than that to Erdman was based on personal considerations. There was a fervor and frankness about him that Machen distinctly liked. And there is considerable evidence that Machen, however regrettable he found Stevenson's election, not only made the best of the resulting situation but also positively sought to maintain cordial relations and to cooperate with the new administration. But his basic objections to Stevenson were essentially the same as to Erdman. And the dangers in the situation were aggravated by the fact that Stevenson, not being a Princeton man, could hardly be expected to possess and maintain a profound commitment and devotion to the historic Princeton position, especially in a time of crisis affecting the Church as a whole. In a time when a drift away from the historic moorings was much in evidence, and Princeton was seeking to resist the current, the position of the faculty as a whole would naturally appear to be partisan whereas Stevenson's outlook would likely be controlled by broader churchly and ecumenical perspectives.

The election of Stevenson underscores a grave weakness in the government of the Seminary in that day. The president of the Seminary, or its acting president, sat in the meetings of the Board in an advisory capacity. But it appears that the Faculty itself had little or no direct voice in the determination of matters affecting the life of the institution in the most crucial manner. Evidently there was, for example, no consultation with the faculty with regard to the acceptability of Stevenson as president. And thus the Board, either because of an unfortunate conception of the exercise of its operations or because of lack of vision, was responsible for creating a situation in which the seeds of deep division within the faculty were sown.

At the same meeting another action was taken that was regarded as far more salutary. This was the election to the chair of Homiletics of J. Ritchie Smith, who for many years had enjoyed a reputation as one of the most scholarly and attractive preachers in the Church. Born in 1852, and graduating from the Seminary in 1876, his work in the pastorate included a ministry of twenty-two years in Peekskill, N. Y. and one of fourteen years in Harrisburg. During his latter ministry in 1903 he had published a substantial volume on *The Teaching of the Gospel of John,* which was respectfully, though not uncritically, reviewed by Dr. Warfield in the *Princeton Review.* He hailed it as an "excellent study" and as overcoming the evil that "the scientific exegesis and the practical exposition of Scripture fall commonly into different hands." He recognized moreover, that although the ordinary run of sermons would profit greatly "if a little more scientific exegesis lay at their foundation," the attitude of mind which belongs to the practical expounder of religion "is essential to the assimilation of the message of the Word, we do not say merely in its fulness, but even in its general color and chief relations." Warfield therefore, no less than the other members of the Princeton Faculty who were mainly concerned with scientific studies, was alive to the claims of the practical life of the Church. And the delight at Dr. Smith's acceptance is not surprising. Though the new professor had already celebrated his sixty-second birthday when he commenced his labors in the fall, he was not to lay down the responsibility until fifteen years later, and he lived on until 1936.

Machen had long been an intense admirer of Smith's preaching, and following his election had written to urge him to accept. The result was that the first word that reached the campus of his acceptance was received by Machen in a note dated June 27, 1914. In it Dr. Smith stated that he "was profoundly sensible alike of the honor and the opportunity and I shall esteem it a high privilege to be associated with you and the other brethren whom I have long held in honor for their character and their works." A few days later Machen wrote his mother that Dr. Smith's "presence is going to be a fine thing for the Seminary, and the personal association is going to be a delight to us all."

Though therefore the Directors made a gratifying decision with regard to homiletics, there was an incidental aspect of it that was less happy. There had been the hope that the man chosen for homiletics would also serve as president. But the choice of Stevenson as well as Smith meant that a third full professorship in the field of practical theology had been created. The task of administration was not considered a full-time job, and so Stevenson was given courses in the history of religion, missions and homiletics. The total effect therefore was a further step downward in the scholarly emphasis of the Seminary since additions of courses in the practical department inevitably encroached upon the time allotted to theology, exegesis and similar studies.

INTRA-FACULTY RELATIONS

At the beginning of the new academic year, the new additions to the staff were on hand. Dr. Stevenson was of course most conspicuous in his various capacities. And Machen acknowledged that his conference talk on "Prayer" had deeply impressed him: "the apparent genuineness of the man and the reality of his faith carried me along with him." On the other hand, his trepidation concerning the effects of his leadership remained. "In his wisdom as a Seminary head I have no confidence, as you know, and the violent intrusion of some extra 'cinch courses' into the Seminary curriculum for the benefit of the President is most unfortunate. If we only could have had a somewhat broader man!... Dr. Ritchie Smith has been conducting his classes during the past week... There is a man worth having. There is something really distinguished about even the most insignificant things that he does and says. Moreover he is very friendly and cordial in his manner."

The year that followed was, however, far from a peaceful one for the Faculty. The Directors had requested the Faculty to give further consideration to the curriculum, and with the active support of the new president, this matter was pushed forward to a decision. A committee of the Faculty prepared a report calling for certain further revisions, but it met with vigorous opposition. At one point it failed of adoption as the result of a six to six tie. A week later, however, it was adopted by a narrow margin when Armstrong and Machen became reconciled to it, not as really a good thing, but on the ground that "the scheme is as good as we can expect to get from the Board."

It is remarkable that at this point Machen deserted the leadership of Warfield, and chose the way of moderation and compromise. This was an exceedingly hard decision to make for a number of reasons. He was greatly indebted to Warfield who had been extremely kind to him in connection with problems that arose out of his difficulties with the Sunday School lessons and in general had been generous in offering encouragement and advice. Moreover, Machen felt that Warfield was "incomparably the biggest man at Princeton Seminary—indeed one of the very biggest men that I ever knew." He had come more and more to see the gigantic stature of Warfield and he was in enthusiastic agreement with him as to the great things for which the Seminary stood. Nevertheless, he came to feel that Warfield was unnecessarily "uncompromising about some little things."

Machen himself had put up a big fight to insure the preservation of the necessary courses in Greek as a foundation for the work of the New Testament department, and had won his point. Taking stock of the attitude of the Directors, he felt that it was wise to make certain sacrifices in the hope of conserving a great deal of good. Still, when Warfield ceased attendance at the faculty meetings in disgust at the course developments were taking, Machen could not but be sympathetic with and sorry for him. At times Machen shared something of Warfield's pessimism as to the future of the Seminary. He even considered the possibility of departing, and might have done so if he had not been constrained by his devotion to Armstrong. Moreover, the psychology of an old man nearing the end of his career and that of a young man virtually at the beginning of his are likely to differ. Both might agree basically as to their analysis of the crisis confronting the Seminary, but one might recognize that the battle had been lost and retire from the front ranks whereas the other might possess the youthful determination to fight on to the end.

These developments indicate that Machen, though a man of intense loyalties, did not slavishly follow any man, not even Warfield. Nor was he blind to the faults of those who he thought were dead right on the big issues. On the other hand, he was quick to recognize virtues in those who, as he became persuaded or as he feared, were taking a wrong stand.

Machen's regard for Warfield did not diminish in the years that followed. This appears, for example, in his lengthy report to his mother of the death, in 1915, of Mrs. Warfield who for many years had been a bed-ridden invalid and of the likely consequences for Dr. Warfield:

> I have faint recollections of her walking up and down in front of the house in the early years of my Princeton life, but even that diversion has long been denied her. I never spoke to her. Her trouble has been partly nervous, and she has seen hardly anyone except Dr. Warfield. But she remained, they say, until the end a very brilliant woman. Dr. Warfield used to read to her during certain definite hours every day. For many, many years he has never been away from her more than about two hours at a time; it has been some ten years since he left Princeton (on the occasion of the experiment of taking her away in the summer). Despite the care of the thing Dr. Warfield has done about as much work as ten ordinary men. What the effect of her death upon him will be I do not know; I think, however, that he will feel dreadfully lost without her.
>
> As Mrs. Armstrong said, he has had only two interests in life—his work, and Mrs. Warfield, and now that she is gone there may be danger of his using himself up rather quickly. If so, I do not know who is to take his place. I am more and more impressed with him; he is certainly one of the very biggest men in the Church either in this country or in any other.

Nor did he have occasion to change substantially his opinion of Dr. Stevenson, though it is noteworthy that for all of his sense of alarm he did not become bitter. Writing on Feb. 24, 1916, for example, he tells of a speech he heard Stevenson deliver at an alumni luncheon in Philadelphia. The speech, he wrote,

> was perhaps more discouraging than anything that I have yet heard from him. He emphasized the "intensely practical," and advocated the choosing of professors from among the active pastors. My only hope is that although he falls in with the current

> cant, he may not act so badly as he talks. But it will be an anxious time when the first of the major chairs falls vacant; for it may be filled with some pious liberal before we know it, or else with some "intensely practical" incompetent, such as other Seminaries are getting. Fortunately, I *like* Dr. Stevenson much better than I did at first.

Meanwhile the situation in the Presbyterian Church was giving him increased concern, and he could not but wonder as to the future of the Seminary which was indissolubly bound up with its life. The 1915 General Assembly, the first to follow his ordination, was disappointing since nothing was done to relieve the intolerable situation in New York and Brooklyn presbyteries, where year after year "virtual unbelievers are received into the ministry." "The Church," he held, "is still fundamentally evangelical—but sadly indifferent to the big questions. I fear that Stevenson, the moderator, rather shares the general attitude, though I have not altogether given him up." The following year he is even more discouraged, and reflects upon the situation at some length.

> Dreadful things seem to be going on at the General Assembly, the "liberal" candidate for moderator having been elected by a large majority. Of course a good many brethren did not know how bad he is. He posed as a "moderate conservative." But I fear the Union Seminary men, with their deceitful phrases, and their contempt for the Christian faith, will go quite unmolested. I trust the Southern Church will keep quite separate. If things get much worse in the North, I should hardly like to continue making contributions to the foreign missions fund, for example, of the Northern Church. Our Southern Board may continue to provide for the preaching of the gospel, and it will be well for those who believe in the gospel to have some faithful administrators of their funds. The mass of the Church here is still conservative—but conservative in an ignorant, non-polemic, sweetness-and-light kind of way which is just meat for the wolves. I do not mean to use harsh phrases in a harsh way, and my language must be understood to be Biblical. But men like McGiffert and William Adams Brown at Union Seminary are perfectly clear about the enormous gulf that separates their religion from orthodox Protestantism—just about as clear about it as Dr. Warfield is. Why then do they try to deceive simple-minded people in the Church? There is the real ground of my quarrel with them. As for their difficulties with the Christian faith, I

have profound sympathy for them, but not with their contemptuous treatment of the conscientious men who believe that a creed solemnly subscribed to is more than a scrap of paper.

BILLY SUNDAY

Though the lines of future conflict were being drawn not only in the Church but also in the Seminary, there remained a large measure of agreement. This is disclosed in the attitude taken by the Faculty towards William A. ("Billy") Sunday who had become a sensationally successful evangelist after a career as a major league baseball player. And since we are to recall this incident in terms of Machen's own personal observations and reactions, a fascinating light is cast upon his own personal views.

One learns first of his original impressions of the Sunday meetings in Philadelphia. Writing to his mother on Jan. 24, 1915, he relates:

> On Wednesday afternoon I went to Philadelphia to get some type-written copy, and seized the opportunity of staying over night and hearing Billy Sunday. Two meetings are held daily except Monday and three on Sunday. The attendance at every meeting is about 20,000. Since I had not had time to get a ticket entitling me to a seat with the ministers, I was advised to go at about five o'clock in order to get a seat for the half-past seven meeting. At five o'clock there were great crowds of people standing around the doors of the Tabernacle. After standing about an hour in the rain I learned from a policeman that the public was to be admitted only if, at a quarter past seven, places were left over after certain delegations had been accomodated. Fortunately the night was terrifically rainy, so that when I returned after seven I was able to get into the building. I stood up at one of the back corners, at such a vast distance from the platform that I could scarcely make out the features of the speaker. Most of the sermon, however, I could hear, though I missed the "asides," and was too much out of things to get any proper impression of the meeting. After the main meeting was over I pushed my way up towards the center of the building, and listened to the enormous choir and afterwards to the discussion of methods before the hundreds of workers on the platform. This last part impressed me as much as anything else. Those people are in dead earnest — it is a great movement for the highest possible end. As I say, I had no proper opportunity to judge Billy Sunday himself—

standing as I was in a sort of passage way, and looking through a lattice work, I felt so detached from the crowd as to be a spectator rather than a participant. The text of the sermon was Rom. 12:1, and the treatment was thoroughly textual. I was impressed as I have seldom been with the permanent power of great words. In an environment so intensely modern, the words of Paul seem to be as up-to-date as they ever were. There was one good thing about the sermon, too. It was of a kind to engrave that great text upon the memory of all the listeners. At the time it did not seem to me to be anything extraordinary—unobjectionable, but rather common-place. But I was in no position to judge. And the big argument for Billy Sunday is the result of his preaching. "By their fruits ye shall know them."

An audience of 20,000 people or more under the same roof is simply overpowering. I have seen such a crowd at least once before—at the Democratic Convention in Baltimore—but when you consider that in the Sunday meetings it is a matter of daily occurrence for two months—and indeed two or three times daily—the thought is even more overpowering. Think of an audience about eight or ten times as large as the seating capacity of our Baltimore Music Hall assembling twice or three times a day for two months!

Machen's letter home a week later tells of attendance at another Billy Sunday meeting in which he had the opportunity of making more satisfactory observations and judgments:

I took another look at Billy Sunday last Friday night, utilizing a trip to the Board of Publication in this incidental way. This time, on Bobby's advice, I applied for a ticket and had a far better place to hear and see than in my first visit. I was very greatly impressed—far more so than on the other occasion. The text was II Sam. 12:13: "And David said unto Nathan, I have sinned against the Lord. And Nathan said unto David, The Lord hath also put away thy sin." The sermon was old-fashioned evangelism of the most powerful and elemental kind. Much of it, I confess, left me cold—I "took" some of the touches of humor and did not "think that they were mine." But the total impact of the sermon was great. At the climax, the preacher got up on his chair—and if he had used a step-ladder, nobody could have thought the thing excessive, so dead in earnest were both speaker and audience! The climax was the boundlessness of God's mercy; and so truly had the sinfulness of sin been presented, that everybody present with any heart at all ought to have felt mighty glad that God's mercy *is* boundless. In the last five or ten minutes of that sermon, I got a new realization of the power of the gospel.

The surprising thing is that the gospel which is having this unprecedented effect in Philadelphia is so aggressively and uncompromisingly old-fashioned. The magazines are expressing wonder at it. This wretched, immoral conception of the atonement! This absurd view of the authority of the Bible! And not a thing about the "social gospel," which everybody knows is the really powerful thing today! Instead of it just the old notion of the individual soul in the presence of God! Even the opponents have to admit that the thing is bringing results. Of course, the Church is going to reap an evil harvest from all this error, from all this obscurantism, from all this realistic way of conceiving of heaven and hell! But meanwhile it must be admitted that the results are partly at least mighty good. That is very much the tone of an article I read last night in the "Independent."

The Unitarians in Philadelphia are carrying on an active fight against the Billy Sunday movement. Bobby told me the other day that he had attended one of their meetings and was having the time of his life composing a sermon suggested by what he had heard. Every morning, on the page of the paper devoted to Billy Sunday, a Unitarian statement appears in opposition. I like Billy Sunday for the enemies he has.

Machen was indeed not uncritical of the evangelistic methods often employed, and he was both fearful and distressed with regard to a series of meetings being held in the First Presbyterian Church of Princeton early in February, 1915, with a Dr. Mimhall as the evangelist. At an afternoon service especially for young people eighty-two young persons made profession of faith, and Dr. Beach reported that it had been a dignified meeting. Machen had decided to stay away, however. He did not want to seem to oppose the evangelistic movement, but he was afraid that, as superintendent of the Sunday School —a position from which he was not able to secure release until about a year later—, he "might be called upon to adopt methods which would be of doubtful wisdom in our school." He determined, however, as soon as he could get a list of the young people who professed conversion, to do what he could to follow up at least any that had been in his own class at one time or another. On Sunday night he attended the regular evangelistic services, but was not much impressed. The sermon, he said, "had upon me a rather depressing effect. An extreme literalism of Bible interpretation, coupled with vulgarity in the preacher, and a certain false pretense of learning, sometimes makes it a little hard to accept even a message that in itself is true and good."

His mother's response to this disclosed her characteristic agreement with his outlook. The professed conversion of eighty young people at once was impressive, but not "the tinge of vulgarity and pedantry" in a preacher of the gospel we believe in. "I have forgotten," she added, "which one of the great novelists it was who said, 'There is nothing more trying than to hear our own cherished faith proclaimed by a pedant or a charlatan.' Still St. Paul was glad to have Christ preached 'whether in pretense or in truth'—and so we may rejoice also. Your Uncle was thrilled by Billy Sunday's work. He wrote a long letter about it to Loy which seems to have been very vivid judging from Loy's joy in it."

About this same time the Faculty of the Seminary decided to invite Billy Sunday to speak in Princeton, and this precipitated a furor which comprehended the university and the town in its scope. The use of Alexander Hall at the University, the only large auditorium in town, was sought for this purpose. But President Hibben refused. Machen thought this was unjust, especially since the building was "constantly opened to most any Tom, Dick and Harry of a lecturer" and liberal preachers were often invited to speak there. A general evangelistic meeting accordingly seemed impossible, since the address would have to be given in the much smaller auditorium of the First Church, and admission would have to be by ticket. But the Faculty went ahead with its plans to hold the meeting on March 7th.

Now the fires of resentment really blazed up as the opponents of Sunday became more outspoken and made it an occasion for attacking the Seminary. On Feb. 28th, Machen wrote:

> Princeton is in a tremendous tempest over Billy Sunday. The action of the Seminary in inviting him to speak in Princeton has been sadly misrepresented in the "Daily Princetonian," the University paper, and the "Princeton Press," the town paper. The Princetonian particularly is violently opposed to evangelical Christianity. In one editorial it said, "The Seminary authorities have seen fit to endorse, partially, the peculiar Sunday theology by inviting him to speak in the town under their auspices. His coming will serve one good purpose—has served it already in fact: It will emphasize a fact that needs to be thoroughly advertised, that Princeton University and the Princeton Seminary are in

no way connected with one another." Of course "the peculiar Sunday theology" is really just a circumlocution for the old word "Christianity."

Dean West has published in the "Princetonian" a most unfair collection of horrible expressions from Billy Sunday, which collection West is charged with having cribbed from an anti-Christian article. Yet he pretends to be conservative (and no doubt is) in his view of the Bible, though he has always been a bitter opponent of such defenders of the Bible as are to be found at the Seminary. To my mind his article is immeasurably more vulgar than anything that Billy Sunday ever did at his worst. Hibben is very weak—tries to be decent and square, but is subject to evil influences. It made me sad to read his contribution in the "Princetonian" to a series of articles on religion. There are Christian men in the University, but none of them is making much of a public confession of his faith. The active opposition of a militant materialist like Dr. Paton, who in a Princetonian article takes the position that the emotional reaction from a revival will endanger the neutrality of the United States at the present crisis (!), is to me far less distressing than the total failure of men who call themselves Christians to see what Chrisianity is.

As for the abuse of the Seminary, I do not think that will do us any harm. What I regret more is the misrepresentation or concealment of the facts, of which newspapers are always guilty. The Seminary has been entirely courteous throughout the whole matter—a tentative engagement was made with Mr. Sunday before the discussion at the University ever arose, and our last move was made only after a conference between Dr. Erdman and President Hibben in which Hibben said he had absolutely no objection to what we are doing. The result of the whole thing is to make me more and more enthusiastic for the work that Billy Sunday is doing. His methods are as different as could possibly be imagined from ours, but we support him to a man simply because, in an age of general defection, he is preaching *the gospel.* We are not ashamed of his "antiquated theology"; it is nothing in the world but the message of the cross, long neglected, which is manifesting its old power.

The great mass of the students of the University are very anxious to hear Billy Sunday; the Seminary committee is simply being overwhelmed with requests for tickets. The situation is delicate; despite Hibben's private assurances we do not want to appear as though we were engaging the University students in something to which the authorities are opposed. Despite all the trouble, however, I am glad that the Seminary in this public way is giving the right hand of fellowship to a man who is doing the Lord's work. There ought to be the closest kind of cooperation between real evangelism and the type of theology that we represent—indeed the two things are absolutely necessary to each other.

And writing on March 7th, Machen said:

Tomorrow is the fateful day of Billy Sunday's coming to Princeton. Pretty nearly everybody in town wants to attend the services, one of which is to be at the inconvenient hour of 1:30 P. M. Of course we had to turn down many applications for tickets, since even with extreme over-crowding only about 1000 people or so can get beneath the roof of the First Church. We had two long faculty meetings on Monday and Tuesday evenings. The former of these lasted from eight until twelve o'clock, and absolutely nothing was done. The decision about the courteous thing to do towards the University was very difficult, but finally the difficulty was largely removed by a conference which President Stevenson and Dr. Ritchie Smith had with President Hibben, and by a note which Dr. Hibben then wrote to the former of these two gentlemen. Naturally we could not call the meeting off or refuse University students admission without a very nasty situation; and the former alternative, of course, would have meant a serious betrayal of our principles. We have come in for a great deal of abuse—Dean West of the Graduate College (Woodrow Wilson's great enemy) being particularly ungentlemanly and unfair in his violent attacks upon the guest of the Seminary. The town paper, the "Princeton Press," as well as "The Princetonian," is bitterly hostile. Despite all the criticisms, however, we are absolutely right, and, for once, absolutely and unanimously agreed. I do not think the criticism will do us harm; Billy Sunday's work is too splendid a thing to be stopped by a hundred Dean Wests. As Bobby Robinson said when Army sent him a copy of West's attack, the fact remains that the city of Philadelphia has been deeply stirred.

I was asked this week, on exceedingly short notice, to lead the Seminary prayer-meeting on Wednesday evening. The whole meeting lasts only about twenty-five minutes, but it offers rather a good opportunity of addressing the students in an informal way. I talked about Billy Sunday evangelism and Princeton theology and the relation between them—which I think is a very close relation. There is going to be an increasing need for pastors who are really able to teach the people; in Philadelphia for example the ground has been broken in a wonderful way, and the question is whether the seed is to be planted. My trip to Pittsburgh last year gave me a vivid impression of the intellectual interests which are awakened—though of course not satisfied—by the Sunday campaigns.

Having carried the fascinating story so far, one must confess to a certain feeling of frustration at not being able to report Machen's assessment of the actual meetings in Princeton. But the simple fact is that no such report is available. Either the customary weekly letter following the meeting was lost or it was omitted because of a visit home. In the last analysis, however, the loss is not tragic since the comments of which note has been taken disclose in a vivid and extensive way a remarkable episode in the life at Princeton and Machen's own personal estimate of evangelism of the Sunday type.

PREACHING AND PREACHERS

In rounding out this chapter, and taking account of developments before the entry of the United States into World War I, one must record certain evidences of Machen's own increasing activity beyond the call of duty at the Seminary. And one or two other distinctly personal matters may not be passed over in silence.

Coincident with the emergence of clarity of vision and purpose in the year 1913, Machen's attitude toward preaching underwent a decided change. In place of his earlier reluctant attitude there was henceforth an eagerness to undertake invitations which came to him. He spoke now of his love of preaching though he was not constantly assured that he made a success of it. Depending at first very largely upon a prepared manuscript, he developed more and more freedom as time went on. During the fall of 1913 on an occasion when he was preaching for his friend Bobby Robinson in Germantown he used to practical advantage some advice given by his colleague "Gimel" MacMillan: "when you forget the thread of your discourse, it is advisable to roar." At times he was dissapointed that more opportunities did not open up though the time was to come when he would be overwhelmed with invitations. After MacMillan went to Wells College as president in 1913, he could count on preaching there and in the college town, Aurora, N. Y., year after year. And other interesting and challenging opportunities came to him with considerable frequency. One reason that he felt that he had to secure release from his activity as teacher and superintendent in the Sunday School at Princeton was that he did not enjoy the liberty of absenting himself with easy conscience so long as a successor could not be found. He could not but judge that he might perform a greater service to the Church by accepting the invitations to preach which were coming to him in increasing numbers.

Due to various circumstances, including in later years the delay of his ordination and his devotion to the Sunday School of the First Church, he enjoyed an exceptionally large number of opportunities of hearing other preachers. There was, first of all, the venerable Mr. Murkland, his pastor during his youth at Franklin St., Baltimore. Occasionally visiting preachers were heard, and his fragmentary diary for 1893 records under date of July 9th the entry, "I went to hear Dr. Hoge today and it was grand." Later in Northfield and Chicago and other summer vacation scenes he heard many preachers of greater or lesser renown. At Princeton variety was afforded not only by the services at the churches but also at the Seminary and University Chapels, and a few comments upon the preaching that he heard have been presented in earlier pages. When opportunity came, however, he also liked to hear some of the celebrated preachers in New York City.

A few of his early impressions of such preaching follow. On Nov. 14, 1914, for example, he wrote:

> Last Sunday I had a very interesting time in New York. In the morning I went to hear Dr. Parkhurst on Madison Square. The interior of the church building, like the outside, is characterized by a certain rich and magnificent simplicity, and the music seemed to me the finest church music that I have ever heard. The whole service was possessed of perfect unity—there was a splendid cadence about it which was never broken. The sermon was exceedingly stimulating. There was not a touch of Christianity in it; but its periphery bristled with sermons that a man who believes in the gospel might preach in supplement to it. Do not suppose, because of Dr. Parkhurst's newspaper notoriety of a few years ago, that there is anything cheap or vulgar about him. On the contrary his preaching is the perfection of art; he reminds me strikingly of Sparhawk Jones. He is evidently a powerful man.
>
> In the evening, I went to hear Henry Sloane Coffin on Madison Avenue, pursuing my policy of searching out a kind of preaching that I should not be likely to hear in the Seminary Chapel. The congregation impressed me. It filled the church to the doors. It was composed chiefly of young men and women. Evidently

there was a genuine congregational life. Evidently, too, the congregation was devoted to the preacher; the people fairly hung on his words. To me, I must say, he seemed rather commonplace—a contrast to the powerful man that I had heard in the morning, and more like the current type of liberalism of the day. He had a splendid idea for a sermon, but it was not well worked out. I am coming, by the way, to prefer sermons that are read; ex tempore speaking, on the whole, is more likely to put me to sleep; it is apt to involve floundering.

One thing in connection with the church provoked me. While a half-hour series of selections from the Stabat Mater was being rendered by the choir, I examined the hymn book, which was compiled by Dr. Coffin himself, with the cooperation of Ambrose Vernon, a wild fellow in New England. Though the preface said that the effort was to select only hymns that were specifically Christian, I was surprised to see the name of Felix Adler among the list of authors. Naturally enough his hymn was anything but specifically Christian. What, in Coffin's mind, *is* Christianity?

A letter of March 14, 1916 tells of an exceedingly varied diet that he had followed the preceding Sunday. Special interest attaches to these observations because Dr. Fosdick like Dr. Coffin was to figure prominently in the controversies in the Presbyterian Church of later years. Moreover, his criticism of a Roman Catholic service is noteworthy because he sometimes annoyed his friends by his "tolerant" attitude toward the Romish faith.

In the morning I went to hear Jowett, and was most favorably impressed. A great deal is to be learned from Jowett about the art of sermonizing—especially the art of making a little go a long way. I do not say this by way of criticism—quite the reverse. I am coming more and more to see that if sermons are to be effective with the mass of the people the points that may be made must be few; and variety in expression and in illustration must be relied upon to maintain the interest. But what pleased me far more than the good homiletics of Jowett's work was the true evangelical ring in what he says. Jowett on upper Fifth Avenue is like an oasis amid desert sands.

In the afternoon, by way of contrast, I heard Harry Emerson Fosdick, of Montclair, who was supplying Dr. Merle-Smith's church on Madison Ave. Fosdick has a great vogue—especially, I believe, among college men. And he is dreadful! Just the pitiful modern stuff about an undogmatic Christianity. I can listen to liberals like Dr. Parkhurst—powerful, earnest seekers after God—without becoming impatient. But this kind of stuff does make me somewhat tired—though I may do the man an injustice. Dr. Griffen of Hopkins, for example, used to be, if I remember right, deeply impressed with Fosdick. Certainly I am not. I should hate to think that Christianity were reduced to such insignificant dimensions.

In the evening I attended one of a series of "doctrinal lectures," given by the Roman Catholic Church for the explanation of Catholic doctrine to non-Catholics. The title of the lecture caught my eye, when I saw it advertised — "Creedless Christianity." Good, I thought, that's the thing I should like to see get a good hard knockout blow. I had been having "creedless Christianity" in the afternoon—fully enough of it to last me indefinitely. It would be refreshing to see it demolished. But I was on the whole somewhat disappointed. The lecture was held in the Church of the Paulist Fathers, on the corner of Sixtieth St. and Columbus Ave. I had often noticed that church, as I passed on the Elevated, and had thought that the interior must be imposing because of the great height of the building. I was right. The vast proportions of the edifice, which seems to my untrained eye to represent a sort of mixture of Romanesque and Gothic architecture, with an immensely high nave and lower side aisles without a transept, and the rich ornamentation, made me think I must be in some European church. The church is as big as five or six large Protestant churches put together, and was packed with an immense audience. I suppose five thousand or so people must have been there. When I entered I was asked whether I was Catholic or non-Catholic, and when I answered that I was non-Catholic, I was shown to an excellent seat. The lecture was by a certain Father Conway of the Paulist Order. It was, I really regret to say, a poor lecture. With a good deal of it I could agree perfectly, for example with its insistence upon the necessity of authority in religion; as long as the Protestant churches go on giving up that great idea they will open themselves up to Roman Catholic attack. But on the whole the lecture was confused and weak. If the Catholics would only make use of the rich heritage of their creed! But there is just the trouble. They don't seem to feel that the individual must see any importance in the incarnation and in the atonement; these things must be accepted simply because the Church commands it; any other doctrines would do just as well if submission were exhibited by acceptance of them. Nevertheless I was intensely interested in the whole proceeding.

EARLY LECTURES

During these years one encounters also the beginnings of Machen's activity as a lecturer at educational institutions and Bible conferences, a type of service which later on was to make large demands upon him. One of the earliest of these was undertaken in response to an invitation from a student society of the Seminary of the Christian Reformed Church in Grand Rapids, and developed on the background of the fact that the more energetic students of that institution often supplemented their regular course with a year or more of graduate study at Princeton. Two lectures on "The Authority of the Bible" and "The Virgin Birth" were delivered on Dec. 10 and 11, 1914.

During the summer of 1915 he filled his first major Bible Conference engagement at Winona, an event which was the forerunner of many that followed in later years there, at Grove City, Stony Brook and other places. Among the speakers that year was Dr. A. T. Robertson of Louisville, whose books and letters had not filled Machen with enthusiasm, but who proved to be an entertaining lecturer and who improved "greatly on personal acquaintance." Another speaker was Dr. Matt Hughes, a Methodist from California, who had "the humor and the power of illustration and the personal magnetism which are necessary to get hold of the crowd, and yet what he said had also the rare advantage of being true." Such gifts Machen greatly admired, and felt that in contrast his own manner of public address was far from being an outstanding success. Still he felt that the effort to be popular, especially as it expressed itself in some of the other speakers, was overdone, and he expressed his criticism rather picturesquely to his mother:

> My criticism of Winona is that the "rough house" element is overdone. I do not object to a little of it, or even a good deal of it, but it does seem to me to be a pity that it should almost crowd everything else out. Practically every lecture, on whatever subject, was begun by the singing of some of the popular jingles, often accompanied by the blowing of enormous horns or other weird instruments of music. And the lectures themselves, if they were to be successful, had to be a good deal after the manner of stump speeches. Mind you, I do not despise that kind of thing. For myself I confess that to save my life I cannot make my sermons funny, but I do not despise the element of humor even in speaking

that deals with serious subjects. On the contrary, I believe that every really great speaker, like Dr. Patton, can play on the whole scale and not only on a part; there must be power of adaptation if results are to be obtained. I learned something about public speaking by contrasting the success of Matt Hughes (who really had big thoughts and yet got them into the mind of the rank and file) with my own failure. The only question is whether I can put what I learned into practice.

Machen's success, as a matter of fact, was without doubt far greater than the above quotations might suggest. He himself goes on to say that after his last lecture "one gentleman said that I had had paid me during the lecture the best compliment that had been paid to any speaker during the conference—there had been no applause whatever while I had been speaking. This may seem to be a rather back-handed compliment, but I am bold enough to take it altogether as such. The man who spoke to me meant it very earnestly as a compliment, and I was well pleased by it. There may be a few—though a very few—people even at Winona who are content to consider a serious subject in a serious way." But there is confirmatory testimony of the favorable impression Machen had made. One minister, the Rev. W. C. Logan of Plymouth, Ind., wrote Machen afterward that he had advised the *Biblical World* and the *American Journal of Theology* to secure him as a contributor, particularly after Logan had been told by their editors that it was difficult to get writers on the conservative side who had sufficient scholarship. And the Secretary and General Manager of the conference, Sol C. Dickey, wrote in appreciation that "I heard good things of your lectures and a number of ministers have told me that they received more help from you than from other speakers." That he returned frequently to Winona and later to other conferences is perhaps the best evidence of his success. As the years went on, he increased in power of effective utterance, and yet he never could be anything but a straightforward, dignified and earnest speaker who was deeply concerned that he should be understood but never made use of cheap tricks in order to be popular.

INVITATIONS FROM RICHMOND

Far and away the most significant recognition that Machen received during this period, not counting his advancement to professorial standing at Princeton, came in the form of two invitations from Union Theological Seminary of Richmond. In view of the fact that Mr. and Mrs. Machen were active supporters of this Seminary of the Southern

Church, and were friends of Dr. W. W. Moore, the president, there was a certain background of acquaintance and interest which may well have commended consideration of the son of these good friends. Nevertheless, the character and the standing of Dr. Moore and the Seminary at Richmond, and the nature of the invitations, were such that personal factors cannot have been of decisive weight. The first invitation took the form of an approach which Dr. Moore made about the end of March, 1915, with the hope that Machen might be willing to leave Princeton for Richmond to become professor of New Testament. The chair had recently become vacant through the sudden death of Dr. English, and what Dr. Moore wished, as he later wrote to Mrs. Machen, was, if possible, "an assurance from him that he was in a position to consider it before a formal election should be made by the Board." At the same time he indicated that, so far as he was concerned, the matter had not been a private or confidential one. The matter, he wrote, "was fully known to our large and widely scattered Board of Trustees, to our faculty, and to many in our Seminary community . . . There is no doubt that he would have been unanimously elected if he could have seen his way to let the Board proceed."

Machen had, however, pledged his mother to secrecy because he felt that his position in his own church in Baltimore would be distressing when, as he felt that he would probably do, he declined the offer. On the other hand, he felt compelled to give the invitation serious consideration. A call to serve his ancestral church made a strong appeal to him. And, as we have observed, there were dark clouds on the horizon at Princeton that made him uneasy about the future there. He wrote at once that he was bound to take the approach made by Dr. Moore under serious advisement, but within a week sent a definite statement of declination. He was virtually on the eve of his installation at Princeton and he had developed a profound sense of commitment to Princeton and to Dr. Armstrong. But the main reason he gave for declining concerned the apologetic character of his work. Writing to his father on April 9, 1915, he said:

> It would be impossible in a brief letter to detail my reasons for sticking to Princeton, as I set them forth in my letter to Dr. Moore. Before long I hope to see you—perhaps in Baltimore, certainly in Princeton—and shall then seize the opportunity of talking the thing over.
>
> My fundamental reason for my decision—aside from the quite exceptional opportunities and facilities which Princeton offers me—was that Richmond hardly needs at present that *apologetic* treatment of the problems of the New Testament which for the

> past twelve years has been my chief concern. Of course I feel most deeply distressed at rejecting any proposal — even of a merely preliminary and personal and private character like Dr. Moore's — which comes to me from the Southern Church.

This summary is in agreement with Dr. Moore's report to Mrs. Machen. But he also tells her that her son's letters on the subject "were perfect, and I hold him in higher respect and admiration now than I did before, though it was a sharp disappointment to me that we could not secure him, and that I could not have the pleasure of association with him in our great work here."

Though the Richmond Seminary could not have Machen as a member of its staff, it was determined to gain the advantage of his instruction and to honor him by inviting him to give a course of lectures in the James Sprunt series, which had been established in 1911. The purpose of the richly endowed lectureship was to "enable the institution to secure from time to time the services of distinguished ministers and authoritative scholars, outside the regular Faculty, as special lecturers on subjects connected with various departments of Christian thought and Christian work." Machen informed his mother on Oct. 24, 1915 of the invitation to deliver the lecture in 1920 or 1921. Machen welcomed the opportunity partly because it would stimulate him to get out at least one book in the intervening time, which then seemed far away. An immense amount of painstaking labor was required, however, before he was prepared early in the year 1921 to deliver the lectures and somewhat later that year to publish his brilliant book, *The Origin of Paul's Religion.*

Though he did not publish very much for some time after the spring of 1915, he was busily engaged in writing up a new course in Apostolic History which he gave for a time beginning in the fall. He was also working with a view to the preparation of the Sprunt lectures. One gets a somewhat new impression of his method of composition, as well of his continued love of walking, from a letter written from the Vanderbilt Hotel in New York on June 9, 1915:

> For me these are days of rest and refreshment in my favorite spot. On Monday and Tuesday afternoons I saw Baltimore play Brooklyn in the Federal League. After the Tuesday game I footed it all the way back to the Vanderbilt—first a mile or so through Brooklyn, then a most delightful walk across the new Manhattan Bridge (with a most astounding view of the Brooklyn Bridge and lower Manhattan in the evening light), then up through the Bowery and Fourth Ave. The total distance was

about six miles—and the scenery was certainly varied. Including incidental walking in the morning I suppose I made about ten miles that day. This afternoon I took the train to Tarrytown, my previous pedestrian "farthest north" on the Hudson, and from there took a most delightful seven or eight mile walk to Ossining, whence home by train. This gives me a pedestrian knowledge of Broadway all the way from the Battery to Ossining, about thirty-five miles from there. The glimpses out through the trees and over magnificent lawns on today's walk were lovely, though most of the way the road runs away from the river. If there is a more beautiful small town than Tarrytown, N. Y., I don't believe I happen to remember it just now.

On Monday night I went to "the Pirates of Penzanse." This is the bulliest opera ever put on the stage except Iolanthe. Some of the rest of Gilbert and Sullivan's I do not like quite so much, though the poorest of theirs is better than the best of anybody else's.

Dear me, how I linger in this restful, health-giving and soul-restoring spot! But I must go back to Princeton tomorrow or next day on Sunday School business. In the mornings I have been doing some writing on my new course, and in the afternoons as I walk I try to outline what I shall say. I also have to get up a sermon for a week from Sunday. Fortunately the outline of it took shape in my mind during one of my walks. But it is very poor.

THE PASSING OF MR. MACHEN

Thus there were some recreation and relaxation in the midst of severe trials and toil. But the year 1915 was to bring one unspeakably sad development. That was the disruption of the family circle by the death of Machen's father on Dec. 19th. Though he lived five months beyond the eighty-eighth anniversary of his birth, he remained until the end in full possession of his extraordinary mental vigor and with little abatement of his physical powers. He had become somewhat deaf, and a few days before his death felt slightly indisposed. But on the day before his passing Mrs. Machen had closed her letter with the words, "I am better—your father well." He walked to church as usual on Sunday morning, listened with close attention to a sermon by Dr. Kirk on John 1:14, walked home, but sank into a chair at the door and passed away almost immediately. As his son Arthur recalled in his biographical sketch,

Here, quietly without a word or groan, surrounded by his family, and with the great words of the text yet ringing in his ears, his strong, self-reliant spirit, securely trusting in his Saviour, left his outworn body.

Sad, indeed, and broken, was the household which remained. The vacant place in every heart was such as no one else could fill, and each survivor knew that throughout life the sorrow, changing indeed in character with the passage of time, would yet always be present. Nevertheless, in the midst of grief, none—not even the one upon whom the blow fell with most annihilating force—failed to rejoice in the memories and associations over which, even in this world, death has no power.

In estimating the character and achievements of Arthur Webster Machen, we had occasion in the first chapter to take note of certain resolutions that were adopted at the time of his death, and limits of space do not permit any considerable notice of the numerous letters of sympathy which followed. But extracts from two or three letters from persons who knew him intimately for many years may serve to round out our picture of this man of rare Christian character and culture. Dr. Patton's long letter of sympathy to Machen, written from Bermuda on Jan. 6, 1916, contained the following words: "How much you have to be thankful for in the loving memory of one who in his home was such a model of what we love to see in the relations of domestic life. I count it one of the rare privileges of my life to have known Mr. Machen and to be counted among his friends. I read with great interest the extracts from the Baltimore papers which you sent me, and as I read I felt that the beauty and ripeness, the patience and contented enjoyment of old age was never more beautifully illustrated than in your dear father's life."

And Dr. Gildersleeve wrote the following charming note to Mrs. Machen:

Dec. 21, 1915

Dear Mrs. Machen:

My own sense of loss gives me some right to share in the bereavement that has come to you and yours. My grief at the death of Mr. Machen is deeper than some of his intimates might suppose. We were fellow-travellers over a stretch of time that few are destined to reach and that of itself made for companionship. What gaps in the ranks of our friends and acquaintances since the death of Richard Gittings, his partner and my classmate, who first brought us together! We often met on our several ways, going home, going to work, and I shall miss his pleasant greeting, his half-humorous smile for in this busy Baltimore he was one of the few that understood my like of work for my work was his pastime and his smile was that of one who shared a weakness for nowadays a love of the ancient classics is a weakness.

A beautiful life and what a fair end! His mind filled with the image of our Elder Brother evoked by text and sermon and then the translation to an unseen that had no terrors for him. It is such an end that an old man like myself might pray for day and night. I dare not offer words of comfort to one who is so familiar with the higher ranges of thought and knows so well the higher sources of consolation. I can bring you only this expression of human sympathy in which my wife begs to join.

Yours sincerely,

Basil L. Gildersleeve

And Miss Clare de Graffenreid, the intimate friend of Mrs. Machen from Macon days and of the family from the beginnings of its life in Baltimore, wrote to Machen on Dec. 30th:

As the days go by, the great bereavement of Mr. Machen's leaving us weighs more and more upon me, the first excitement having passed. I do not know how any of us is to face life without him, so much a part of us he has always been, friend, counselor, model to look up to, companion rarely gifted to enjoy. Where else is there a man of such character and tastes?

Except his own sons I know few men now who combine the highest standards of living with high culture. Specialists are having their day. Therefore your father's life and character shine more brightly, and will continue to be a blessed and cherished memory.

You, dear Gresham, have a bereavement and a mission now—the mission to be like him, and to comfort your mother. She leans on you as on no other person in some ways. She delights in you without an arrière pensée, except for your uncertain health of late. I trust this is re-established, and that you are able to go on with the work you love to the honor of us all, and serving the higher aims you live for.

That Machen was to comfort his mother in word and deed for the rest of her years is one of the remarkable features of the story of his life. Always strongly devoted to her, his affection and concern for her seem now to have been intensified. He could not take the place of his father but more than any one else he stepped into the breach, and there was perhaps never a more tender and dutiful son. Particularly during the long summer holidays, when it was Mrs. Machen's continued custom to stay at Seal Harbor, he spent as much time with her as his duties allowed. He often declined attractive engagements at home and abroad that would have interfered with his fulfillment of what he considered his obligation to her. Unquestionably the inner development as well as the outer course of his life was influenced by his mother. Nevertheless, however rare and strong the love between them, it never became an enervating force so far as his commitment to the demands of Christian discipleship was concerned. It was the love, not of weak and selfish sentimentalists, but of two powerful personalities, whose exceptional strength of character was energized by their whole-hearted acknowledgement of the exclusive rights of Him whom they worshipped as God and Saviour.

Although his father did not live to share the years of struggle that lay ahead, one may rejoice in the providence of God which permitted him to live to see the day when his son was firmly established in his Christian faith, ordained to the gospel ministry, and installed as a professor in a distinguished theological seminary. Considering that he was fifty-four years old when this son was born, and that more than a decade was to elapse after his son entered the Seminary before these happy events were to take place, it is truly remarkable that he lived to see that consummation. He had never lost faith in the ultimate issue. And it was now as if, having lived to see that day, he could be dismissed in peace.

12

THE ROAD TO WORLD WAR

A singular period in Machen's life opens up with the entry of the United States into World War I. He at once began to set in motion inquiries which were to result several months later in his commencement of more than a year's service abroad as a Y.M.C.A secretary. The story of that service is told at some length because on the dark and sombre background of the war some of the facets of Machen's character light up with exceptional brilliance. The service in the main was indeed quite unspectacular; for the most part it was drab and monotonous. One might even question whether, considering the high spiritual purpose which motivated him in seeking such activity and taking account of his peculiar gifts as a teacher of the New Testament, the undertaking was not to a considerable extent a failure. Machen himself had reason to regret certain developments and the lack of others. Nevertheless, there is no serious question but that he was profoundly grateful that he volunteered for this wartime service. And in some respects his Christian character appears not less conspicuously when his activity seems least specifically Christian than when he is engaged in a preaching mission.

ATTITUDE TOWARD GERMANY

The fact that Machen set about energetically, when war broke out on April 6, 1917, to enlist in some form of active war service is in itself somewhat surprising when one takes account of his previous general estimate of the issues involved. Though not militantly partisan he was decidedly not pro-British in his sympathies and was not at all impressed by arguments as to the necessity of maintaining Anglo-American solidarity. To say, on the other hand, that he was pro-German would be to overstate the matter, though he clearly had a far greater appreciation of things German and of the German outlook than most Americans. In fact this was one of the few points on which he differed rather vigorously with members of his family whose generally Anglophile attitude was shared by most influential Americans.

That Machen had acquired an unusual fondness for Germany and Germans, and an admiration of their culture, especially as a result of his stay at Marburg and Göttingen, was to be expected. Nor did the more unhappy aspects of his life and struggle in Germany affect substantially his judgment as to the unique benefits of graduate work in German universities. Advice which he had occasion to offer in later years—some twenty years after his own year in Germany—bears out this conclusion. When, for example, a promising Southerner, who had spent a year of graduate study at Princeton, indicated that he was probably going to Harvard for a degree since Princeton did not offer a doctor's degree, but indicated that he would be interested in "any better plan" that Machen might offer, he strongly urged him to go to Germany as "incomparably the most valuable thing that he could do" and lamented "the very foolish degree hunting craze!"

About a year later, another young scholar contemplating graduate work in Oxford and Berlin was urged to spend the entire year of study in Germany.

> It would be a mistake, I think, for you to devote six months of the year to Oxford. You have already come into contact with the British point of view in Edinburgh, to say nothing of the fact that that point of view is easily accessible to an American even without actual study in Great Britain. But a year is not too long a time for you to become familiar with the German language (supposing that you are not already master of it) and with the German atmosphere. Such an acquisition has a wonderfully broadening effect. It will put you into possession of intellectual tools which will be of enormous value to you all through the rest of your life.
>
> I am in full sympathy, of course, with your desire to become acquainted at first hand with the other side in the debate that is going on at the present day. And that you can do best of all in Germany... In Germany, at most of the universities, you will be living in a highly stimulating intellectual atmosphere that will be entirely foreign to Christianity. It is not altogether an easy experience for a Christian man; but at least, when it is over, you will have the satisfaction of having come into first-hand contact with those forces which underlie all the doctrinal indifferentism in Great Britain and in this country which really presents the serious danger of the life of our Church. There will be much, of course, which you will heartily admire, despite your disagreement with it; and you will learn to distinguish what is really important from what is superficial. After the experience is over, you will, I hope, come to see that the world without Christ is a

> very dismal thing; and at least you will know that there is a tremendous issue in the religious world at the present day, and that the optimistic talk of some men, themselves evangelical, who decry doctrinal controversy is absurd. You will come to see, I think, that we are facing today a clash of really titanic spiritual forces; and that those who are contending for the gospel of Christ must seek a power that is greater than that of men, and must, if they seek to be faithful, devote all the talents that God has given them to their great work.

In order to understand Machen's position it is necessary, however, to guard against the supposition that graduate work in Germany was recommended regardless of the previous preparation of the student. This appears strikingly from a reply to a minister who inquired on behalf of a graduate of another seminary than Princeton who was contemplating graduate work either in a British university or an American university, both of a liberal stamp. Though commending study in Germany, above that in the universities mentioned, he prefaced this advice with the following paragraphs:

> Your inquiry of April 21st reminds me of an incident which occurred in Dr. De Witt's class when I was a student at the seminary. Dr. De Witt asked the students whether they would prefer to have an examination on one day or on another day. One of the students piped up and said that they would prefer not to have it at all. Dr. De Witt then uttered the following parable:
>
> "Said the butcher to the ox, 'Would you prefer to be knocked on the head or to have your throat cut?' Said the ox to the butcher, 'I should prefer not to be killed at all.' Said the butcher to the ox, 'You are wandering from the question.' "
>
> Like the ox in this parable, I am tempted to wander from the question which you put to me, because I think that by far the best thing for the young man you mention to do is . . . to come to Princeton Seminary and obtain that grounding in the Reformed Faith which he can hardly have at present. I do rejoice greatly when men hear everything that can be said against the conservative position to which I myself hold, but I do maintain that it is only fair to give that evangelical faith a hearing at least before one relinquishes it. And the only way to give it a hearing is to come into contact with those who believe it consistently and with their whole hearts. If the reorganization of Princeton goes through, of course Princeton will no longer supply this need. But until that is done, I am convinced that a graduate year at

Princeton would be the thing most needed by the man to whom you refer.

Machen's admiration of Germany and its universities was therefore not unqualified in spite of his general enthusiasm. But as a person who never recalled his stay in Germany without deep gratitude, and who continued for many years to cultivate friendship with persons with whom he had become acquainted in Germany, the outbreak of the great war was a distressing event. As Paul Shorey said in speaking of Gildersleeve:

> To Gildersleeve the scholarship and the life of that older Germany were a revelation and an inspiration of which he always treasured the grateful memory—about which he overflowed in anecdote and reminiscence to congenial auditors. The division of the records of the mind brought by the great war was to him, as to many other American scholars, an irreparable tragedy that in his less cheerful moods darkened his later years. He could not agree with his German friends, and he could not vilipend the culture to which he owed so much.

EVALUATIONS PRIOR TO 1917

The approaching conflict was already envisaged to some extent in 1906 when Machen was at Marburg. He was much impressed with what he observed of the German soldiers whose drills he often saw as he walked from his lodgings to the University. "My advice to poor old France," he wrote on Jan. 28, 1906, "is not to monkey with the band wagon; but in the expected war with England, I do not see how this magnificent army will do much good unless somebody invents a submarine boat that will really work and that will make England's channel squadron useless." A few days later he reflected at considerable length upon German politics, and indicated that he had come to have more sympathy for the ideals and efforts of the German Empire than he had had before. "My chief mistake, before coming over here," he wrote, "was that I looked upon the Empire as a finished product, which was using its power with the single aim of crushing out anything like the beginnings of democracy. I have now, however, learned that the German nation is laboring under difficulties which threaten its very existence, and which do much to excuse a good deal of what seems to us like ruthless tyranny." Though he found the measures taken to repress the Socialists thoroughly repulsive, he could not have "unlimited sympathy with a political party whose principles are 'international' in the sense that it discourages the old fashioned love of country without which the soul is dead."

The summer of 1914 brought such questions again to the fore, and though the isolation and isolationism of America made them seem rather academic to many, they could not but be living issues to one with Machen's background and outlook. One of his first comments upon the developing situation is found in a letter to his mother dated Sept. 17, 1914:

> When the Germans were in front of Paris, I was wild against them; but now I have withdrawn my support from the allies! No doubt the Germans placed themselves technically in the wrong in this war; but the more I reflect the more I see their side. They are military; but probably all of us would be military if we had the countless barbarian hordes of Russia within easy striking distance of us. The alliance of Great Britain with Russia and Japan seems to me still an unholy thing—an unscrupulous effort to crush the life out of a progressive commercial rival. Gradually a coalition had to be gotten together against Germany, and the purpose of it was only too plain. An alleged war in the interest of democracy the chief result of which will be to place a splendid people at the mercy of Russia does not appeal to me. On the whole, while a few weeks ago I confess that I joined Arly in wishing for a few months of Napoleon, now my wish is for about seven years of Frederick the Great!
>
> This talk about British democracy arouses my ire as much as anything. Great Britain seems to me the least democratic of all the civilized nations of the world—with a land-system that makes great masses of the people practically serfs, and a miserable social system that is more tyrannical in the really important, emotional side of life than all the political oppression that ever was practised. And then if there is such a thing as British democracy it has no place for any rival on the face of the earth. The British attitude towards Germany's just effort at a place in ocean trade seems to me one of the great underlying causes of the war. And unless that spirit can be overcome, there never will be permanent peace. I am afraid that I have become rather a confirmed partisan of the underdog in the present struggle. For France, I must say, I have full sympathy.

The difference of viewpoint from that of members of his family came to expression in the months that followed. One of his Christmas gifts for the year 1914 was an openly pro-English book by J. A. Cramb on *Germany and England*. His reaction was not long in forthcoming, for on Jan. 11th he wrote as follows:

> I have finished reading with great interest the book of Cramb on "Germany and England." Every one seems to be reading it, so that it was a very timely and acceptable present indeed. I am bound to say, however, that the book seems to me as shallow and vicious and cynical a thing as I have read for some time. It is a glorification of imperialism. "To give all men within its bounds an English mind—that has been the purpose of our empire in the past." A very immoral purpose indeed! If these fine Dutch fellows that we have here in the Seminary from South Africa are given English minds, the world will be the loser. That is quite aside from the question whether English minds are better than Dutch minds; for why not have both? The true ideal is mutual influence of two nations for the betterment of both. Imperialism, to my mind, is satanic, whether it is German or English. The author glorifies war and ridicules efforts at the production of mutual respect and confidence among *equal* nations. Such cynicism seems to me to be unwarranted despite recent events. The ideal actually has been realized in smaller spheres many times in the history of the world, and more than ever perhaps in recent years. Why not work to make it universal? True, it will never be realized if men like Cramb are allowed to mould public opinion. As Bobby says, Cramb is just an *English* Bernhardi; "might makes right," scarcely disguised, is the motto of his book; a nation loses its rights so soon as it ceases to be strong. Therefore up, Englishmen, and arm!
>
> In its account of German aims and ambitions the book, unless I am greatly mistaken, is a ridiculous caricature. Does any sane man believe, for example, that the religious ideal which the author apparently attributes to Germany, is really that of the German people? The whole thing can only be characterized as sophomoric.
>
> Yet so many people suppose that this kind of writing is leading us to truth. There is the interest of the book. It was a mighty good present. I may some time get a sermon out of it. It makes me feel anew the need of Christianity. When men like Cramb are looked up to as prophets, what a need for the gospel! The gospel has a big fight in this world—that is the conclusion I draw from such a book and from its popularity. And despite all ridicule of peace movements I cherish the hope that the gospel is going to win.

You see, I am interested in the book; that appears from my opposition more clearly than from perfunctory words of thanks.

The discussion concerning Cramb's book and the war in general went on for some time, and Machen was pleased that the disagreement was not as complete as had first appeared. As over against his mother, however, he was not impressed with the argument that the allies were unprepared, and cited the Boer war as an evidence of England's imperialism. But he did not want to be understood as excusing Germany for everything she was doing. As he wrote on Jan. 24th, "I am opposed to *all imperial ambitions,* wherever they may be cherished and with whatever veneer of benevolent assimilation they may be disguised." A month later he wrote sadly of reports which were reaching him from Germany (through the German student paper published by the Verbindung with which he had become associated in Göttingen) of the death of a person with whom he had been intimately associated in Germany. "The enormous lists of casualties," he wrote, "impresses me, as nothing else has, with the destructiveness of the war." His mother was duly sympathetic, and said, "I have none of the vindictiveness that is now so common. I have to wish them defeated, because that seems best for the world and for ourselves. But I do not hate them, and when I think of the kindly folk we used to meet greeting us with 'Tag,' and the women and children who watched our motor fly past, and all your friends who offered to come to the train and sing for me at Göttingen—why my heart aches for them as it does for everybody in distress of 'mind, body, or estate.'"

EVE OF AMERICA'S ENTRY

In later stages of the war before the entry of the United States, Machen's attitude apparently underwent very little change. It was galling to him that, for the sake of commercial profits, we were timidly allowing our ships at sea to be searched. Writing from Boston on August 23, 1916, and under the impact of recollections aroused by walks in that area, he said: "Alas, the spirit of '76 seems to be dead at last, now in this time when America is tamely submitting to the curtailment of the liberty of the seas for which in better ages she bravely stood, but submitting when not war but merely a threat of trade reprisals would conserve the great principles at stake. The trouble is, the sacrifice of principle is being well paid for by an unheard of prosperity, and dollars are preferred to everything else. It is a far cry from the Boston tea-party!"

And President Wilson's efforts to maintain neutrality and to achieve a peace that would rest on a surer foundation than partisan politics were greeted with delight. His famous Senate speech in which he pleaded for "peace without victory" was exactly what Machen had been hoping and praying for. "I do not think that there will be any permanent peace," he wrote on January 26, 1917, "so long as two wrongs are regarded as making a right. It is an eternal see-saw. But it may be the fate of the world for many years to come. I am not saying that Wilson's ideal can now be realized."

Wilson's attitude and policies were, however, to change drastically in the weeks that immediately preceded the declaration of war as the Germans announced unrestricted warfare. Various measures were considered in order to increase our military preparedness. Machen's own thinking did not, however, wholly keep pace with Wilson's—whether to his credit rather than Wilson's I shall not now attempt to judge. As late as March 25th, he wrote:

> The country seems to be rushing into the two things to which I am more strongly opposed than anything else in the world—a permanent alliance with Great Britain, which will inevitably mean a continuance of the present vassalage, and a permanent policy of compulsory military service with all the brutal interference of the state in individual and family life which that entails, and which has caused the misery of Germany and France. Princeton is a hot-bed of patriotic enthusiasm and military ardor, which makes me feel like a man without a country.

And on April 2nd, on the very day of Wilson's war message to Congress, and only four days before war was declared, he wrote to members of Congress from New Jersey urging that in contemplating various measures with a view to greater preparedness, the United States should at all costs avoid the danger of militarism. The entire letter is quoted because it effectively sums up his outlook at the time:

> In urging the defeat of measures involving a permanent policy of compulsory military service, I am not writing in the interests of "pacificism," or even of any one method of raising an army for the present war, though I am opposed to conscription of men for that purpose. I am only pleading for the separation of permanent policy from the measures necessary in the present emergency. The adoption of a permanent plan for compulsory military training cannot further, and indeed may even hinder, our preparation for the business now in hand. Certainly, therefore, the adoption of such a permanent policy should not be rushed through under the unavoidable excitement of a moment like the present. Once established, a policy of conscription would for various reasons be

almost incapable of being abandoned. The mutual distrust which would be set up between this country and Canada would combine with certain even more obvious developments to make the step irrevocable. Hence the desire shown by the advocates of universal military training to press for a decision now, instead of really waiting to ascertain the judgment of the American people.

After a residence in Europe I came to cherish America all the more as a refuge from the servitude of conscription. That servitude prevails whether the enforced service be required by a vote of the majority or by an absolute government. Compulsory military service does not merely bring a danger of militarism; it is militarism. To adopt it in this country would mean that no matter how this war results we are conquered already; the hope of peace and a better day would no longer be present to sustain us in the present struggle, but there would be only the miserable prospect of the continuance of the evils of war even into peace times.

I do not deny that compulsory military service is sometimes necessary. Even that brutal interference of the state with the life of the individual and of the family is sometimes necessary. But it is assuredly not necessary in the case of the United States. That it is not necessary is shown by the example of Great Britain, where a voluntary system was sufficient not merely for defence, but also actually to build up the greatest of foreign empires, and where that system allowed ample time for the adoption of emergency measures in the hour of need.

In short Americanism is in danger—American liberty and the whole American ideal of life. Is it to be abandoned without consideration, under the unnatural stress of an emergency with which the proposed change in policy has absolutely nothing to do? Just when other nations are hoping that the present war will result in the diminution of armaments and the broadening of liberty, is America to be the first to take a radical step in exactly the opposite direction?

I am not arguing against preparedness. I believe, in particular, that we should have a much more adequate navy. What I am arguing against is *compulsion,* which I believe to be brutal and un-American in itself, and productive of a host of subsidiary evils.

Respectfully yours,
J. Gresham Machen

This background of opinion prior to April 6th, 1917, has been presented at some length for a number of reasons. It is significant, first of all, because of its revelation of Machen's broad political philosophy with its accent upon justice and liberty. Avoiding jingoism and other manifestations of narrow nationalism he yet stood for a stout-hearted patriotism which was the stronger because vigilance was a pronounced ingredient. Machen's general temper was also admirable because, in a time of giddy excitement, he displayed unusual restraint and objectivity concerning the underlying issues. Even if one were in disagreement with his analysis of the facts, and attributed his rather exceptional sympathy for the German point of view to prejudices derived from his sojourns in the country of its origin, one would still have to pay respect to his remarkable independence of judgment and the force of his convictions.

Finally, the disclosures of Machen's views are of particular interest because they seem to prepare so meagerly for what was to follow. Although, as the letter to Washington discloses at least between the lines, Machen seemed finally to reconcile himself to the inevitability of war with Germany, his general attitude had been one of opposition to involvement in accordance with the hue and cry of the times. In the midst of all the criticism of current points of view, however, one fact stands out which does after all point the way to his future course. He might not share the popular estimate of Germany's nationalism. He might not regard the plea to join the British to save the world for democracy as based on a sober estimate of the situation. But of his profound love of his country there never was occasion to doubt for even a moment. That his patriotism was of a particularly robust and unselfish character is demonstrated beyond all cavil by the single-mindedness with which he sought, following the dawn of a state of war, to serve his country, remaining nevertheless true to his calling as a minister of the gospel.

FACING DECISION

Although the declaration of war did not modify Machen's basic outlook on the world situation, it did constrain him to give immediate thought to the possibility of taking some direct part in the war effort. On April 7th, in a long letter to his mother, he reflected upon his state of mind following the actual declaration of war the previous day. And referring to his letter on conscription to members of Congress, he said:

> I feel a little encouraged at Wilson's explanation in the paper this morning that his plan for conscription is for the purposes of the present emergency alone, although it is also capable of being the first step in a permanent policy. Even temporary conscrip-

tion goes against the grain with me, unless it is resorted to to repel actual invasion, but my fundamental objection is directed against compulsory service in time of peace...

Naturally I feel somewhat restless. If I were engaged in the work of a pastor I could continue with perfect satisfaction in the even tenor of my way, but as it is I feel as though I ought to have some immediate part in the manifold work that is going forward. Perhaps I may find some useful work to do. I believe I should be terribly footless as a chaplain, but if the demand became very great I might try. As to my health, I am a little afraid lest I should prove unfitted for a very strenuous life, though undoubtedly there has been general improvement in the last year or so.

Though forthrightly opposed to conscription and fearful of a developing tyranny of the majority, Machen bent every effort in the ensuing months to volunteer for such service as suited his capacities and was open to him. For months he was intensely occupied with the question whether he should become a chaplain, a Y.M.C.A. secretary, or a member of the ambulance corps. One reason for the delay in reaching a decision was that there were a number of important speaking engagements ahead for the summer; another of greater influence was the very difficulty of arriving at the wisest course of action since it was very difficult to secure definite information as to the responsibilities involved in the various types of service. Very serious consideration was given to work under the American Ambulance Field Service, but he was discouraged at one point by the declaration of one of its officers that there would be no guarantee that volunteers for that service would not be switched to munitions transport. The chaplaincy was made the object of earnest inquiry, but apparently no vacancies opened up during the period of indecision. Moreover, he came to feel on the basis of observations at a military camp that as a chaplain, with officer's standing, he would not be able to be nearly as much of an "enlisted man's friend" as would be true if he were a Y.M.C.A. worker. And reports reached him that many commanding officers were extremely critical of chaplains.

Gradually he came to the conclusion that the Y.M.C.A. offered the better opportunities of Christian service. President J. Ross Stevenson had come to have charge of religious work at the camps under the auspices of the International Y.M.C.A. and late in August introduced him at the New York office to the leader of a conference of men who were about to go into Y.M.C.A. work abroad. His impressions were rather favorable though not without a mixture of concern. As a result of what he observed, he wrote on August 25th, that he was inclined to think that this was the work that he would try to get into.

> The Y.M.C.A. workers at the front are right with the men, and some of the work that they do seems to be fine. On general principles I feel very cool toward the Y.M.C.A., but in the war it does seem to offer better opportunities than the severely official position of the chaplains. My chief fear is lest I should have objections of principle to some of the things that might be required of me as a Y.M.C.A. worker—such as desecration of the Sabbath in the name of Christianity and the like. Disregard of the Sabbath in the name of military necessity is a very different thing. But the work of the Y.M.C.A. as presented by the principal speaker at the conference is evangelical and Christian. On the whole I feel less hopeless about getting a real job in connection with the present need. That I ought to do something abroad seems to me to be clear, and the Y.M.C.A. seems to offer better opportunities than the things I had been thinking of. Of course it is another question whether they will want me, but I think they will.

His first opportunities of observing the work of the Y.M.C.A. in the camps came in connection with a preaching engagement in Washington, D.C., and his impressions were not particularly favorable. In fact, after talking to the workers and being on the ground of its operations, he concluded that

> the work seems to be just the kind of work I *dislike* the most, but that is no insuperable objection to my going into it. It consists largely of selling postage stamps and "mixing." The opportunities for true Christian service are undoubtedly enormous for one who can really get the confidence of the men. The work is carried on by conversation with individuals, and very little by set religious services. You have to make the work for yourself—otherwise you are pretty useless. There seem to be very few set tasks, except of course being present in the tent or "hut." Conditions abroad are no doubt different, and it is of course abroad that I am eager to work.

Considerable impetus was given to a decision in favor of the Y.M.C.A. when, about the middle of September, he suddenly was offered the opportunity of speaking under its auspices at various military camps. Bobby Robinson had written on Machen's behalf to Ned ("Dusty") Russell, a Princeton alumnus, who had direct charge of arranging for speakers at the army and navy encampments. This brought immediate action, and on an hour's notice he was sent off to speak three times on the following day at Newport, R. I. Arriving at Newport on Saturday evening, he wrote on Sept. 19th,

> I put up at the Army and Navy Y.M.C.A. building in the centre of the town. The place was packed with bluejackets all the time, and a hundred or so slept in the gymnasium, which was right next to the physical director's office where I was assigned a cot. They love to get away from the camps whenever they have leave. The Y.M.C.A. is performing an absolutely necessary service, availed of apparently by all, in providing food, lodging, entertainment, etc. On Sunday morning I spoke at the "Naval Reserve" camp, where some hundreds of men—mostly college men—are stationed. There was scarcely anybody at the service—perhaps a dozen of the men—and those who were present were so far as I could see entirely uninterested. In the afternoon I spoke at the "Naval Training Station," where there are some 8,000 men. There is a compulsory chaplain's service in the morning—or rather two, one Protestant and one Catholic. I spoke at a Y.M.C.A. building that has been built by the men themselves. It is called "The House that Jack Built." Several hundred men were there, the building being well filled. Only, they were not there to attend the service, but to play games and write letters. So it was hard to make them realize that we were trying to start something, and since only one previous service had been held in the afternoon, the two young Y.M.C.A. workers were about as much up in the air as I was. There was nobody to play the piano, but after one of the Y.M.C.A. men made a sorry attempt to lead the singing, I did attempt to play myself.
>
> It was a feeble effort, but occasionally I would strike the right note, and "Onward Christian Soldiers" went fairly well. Then after I was introduced I got up on a table and tried to get the attention of the crowd. It was a new kind of experience for me, but I think it went fairly well. I saw it was quite hopeless to get them to listen to the reading of anything, even the reading of the Bible, and so I told the story of the Bible passage informally as part of my address. Most of the crowd listened, though some did continue their letter writing instead. One or two spoke to me afterward—one in particular in a way that made me feel the profound need of this work. This young boy seemed simply appalled at the foulness of life that prevails, and seemed mighty glad of a little Christian encouragement. In the evening I spoke at Fort Wetherell, on a big island a half hour's trip from New-

port. It is a coast defence post, the quarters being right back of the big guns. About three hundred Rhode Island former national guardsmen are stationed there. Small lots of them are being drafted to go to France from time to time. About ten men attended the meeting, and they were uninterested. It was about the toughest proposition I ever was up against. I don't mean that as many as ten attended the meeting for the purpose of attending it; on the contrary they attended it only because they happened, for other purposes, to be in the tent. The tent was cold as Greenland. It's going to be a pretty rough life as winter comes on. The Y.M.C.A. men work tremendously hard—about sixteen hours a day—some of them...

I saw Army in Princeton the other day. He is content to have me start the year at Princeton (along with the Y.M.C.A. work), and then leave whenever I get a permanent position. If the chaplaincy does not pan out I think I shall volunteer for overseas Y.M.C.A. work.

In the weeks and months that followed, there was engagement after engagement on Sundays and many weekdays—at Mineola, Portsmouth, N. H., Little Silver, N. J., Fort Hamilton, Bedloe's Island, Fort Totten, Camp Mills, Camp Dix, Plattsburg, Camp Upton and other places. The experience was often strenuous and fatiguing; frequently he found no time to eat his evening meal until ten or eleven at night after the conclusion of a service. At times the response was so negligible that he was disheartened; at others there was greater encouragement that a wonderful opportunity for the preaching of the gospel was being offered and that some real Christian work was going forward. But he confessed that "after I get through with a Sunday of this work I feel as though nothing but prayer is in place."

APPOINTMENT AND FAREWELL

Early in November there were conferences with Y.M.C.A. leaders in New York concerning the possibility of his undertaking service overseas, and it began to appear that if he could pass the physical examination no insuperable obstacles to appointment would remain. He was warned that it would be mandatory "to go through a period of routine work, as all are required to do in order to bring them into close touch with the men, but there is a high degree of probability that I shall soon find my way into the work for which I prove myself best fitted." Explaining his desire to go overseas, he added:

I am afraid that Y.M.C.A. work does not, in the usual forms at least, mean that I really play a man's part in the dangers of war, but it does perhaps seem to be the most useful thing that I can do. Naturally it is hard to think of deserting you in all the troubles you have. But I do not think you ought to get an exaggerated idea of what it means to go to France in the way I am going. Men with dependent families can do the home work that I am now doing, but cannot do the Y.M.C.A. work in France, far from home, and with salary insufficient for the support of dependents. Hence I think that instead of continuing to board here at hotels I ought to go abroad. That is my calling in a nutshell. I am glad to believe that you will agree with me. Certainly it is a sense of duty that impels me; for the life that I have been leading in this country for the last eight weeks is just the life I love—the life that I have been longing for for ten years. It is not easy for me to leave it, to say nothing of the temporary separation from you at home. Of course, I do not know whether I shall go. But the negotiations have progressed so far now that I ought not to turn back without good reason. I have said that I could not go till Dec. 1 at the earliest. They are anxious for me to go as soon as possible if I go at all.

The following day the physical examination was conducted by a doctor in Trenton, one whom he had known and liked when he had been trying to help his cousin Edgeworth Baxter. To his delight his health had improved sufficiently so that the examination proved satisfactory. A formal application for service overseas was filed at the same time. In the same letter he gave fresh expression to the basic motive of duty to his country which stood back of his efforts since April to enlist in some form of war service. "Those fellows *in my situation,*" he said, "who do not get to the front in this war are going to count their manhood cheap afterwards. I do not know what the Y.M.C.A. involves, of course, but lots of the work is not particularly heroic. At any rate I believe I am doing about the best I can. I hope I shall be blessed of God in my decision, if I really do decide for the Y.M.C.A."

Not long afterward the definite appointment came through, and with a sailing date early in January in view, there were a thousand things to do before he could push off—uniforms, innoculations, arranging for the supervision of R. H. who figured prominently in an earlier chapter, revisions of his course of Sunday School lessons for an elective course edition, visits to the Berlitz School during the final days to brush up on his French, the packing and shipping home of civilian clothes, and numerous other tasks. And special mention must be made of the fact that on Dec. 1st he served as best man to his brother Arthur who was married that day to Miss Helen Chase Woods of Baltimore, for he not only was delighted for his brother's sake, but also came to regard his new sister with extraordinary affection and admiration.

Soon after the first of January he said farewell to loved ones in Baltimore and set off for New York to await definite sailing instructions. There was time, however, for a few days in Princeton, and he was scheduled to preach in the Seminary Chapel. "Preaching came off fairly well, I thought," he wrote to his mother on January 6th. But the next day there was to be a more enthusiastic report in a letter written by Mrs. Armstrong to Mrs. Machen:

Dear Mrs. Machen:

My thoughts have gone out to you so often during these last few days that I am prompted to let you know how deeply we share at least in part the great anxiety and sorrow you must bear in having Gresham go over to France.

We are feeling very much depressed over the good-by that had to be said tonight. We shall miss Gresham more than I can tell you, not only in the Seminary but also in our own household where I think you know the place he holds with us.

If we did not know the tremendous good he will be able to do in places where a life and faith such as his are so sorely needed, it would be even harder to see him go. I wish you could have been with us on Sunday and heard him preach in the Chapel. It was an impressive service, the Chapel was filled, and Gresham's power as a preacher was never more evident, but what impressed me especially was the earnestness and beauty of his prayers. The congregation was moved in a way I have seldom seen. Such gifts as his will surely be used by God to carry conviction and healing to men in trouble.

Our thoughts and prayers will be with him and with you, that his journey may be safe and that the clouds may lift, so that he may not be kept long away from his place here. We realize more than ever before what a large place it is, and how much we need him.

Always sincerely,

Rebekah Purves Armstrong

And thus he went off for New York while dear friends at Princeton already were longing for the day of his return. In the ten days or so that followed before he actually sailed, he continued to keep in close touch with his mother and the others at home—there were no fewer than ten letters home during this period—but finally the day of departure came on the 15th. His dominant mood was summed up in one of his last letters as follows: "I feel happy in the great privilege that is mine. The chief thing that mars my happiness is that I am afraid the work is hardly going to be giving me anything like my just share of the dangers or hardships of the war. But I hope I can be useful, even though it is in some non-adventurous and prosaic way." And he was as usual overflowing with affection for and praise of his mother. Her fervent love he counted the greatest possession and help in his work. At the very last he was grieved to learn that she had had to take to her bed because of illness, a frequent development in her life, but one that her son never could treat casually. And this time he added to his expression of sorrow the words: "but I feel profoundly thankful in the assurance that it is only the flesh that is weak. You are so brave and good, my dearest Mother, that it would really be not the slightest credit to me if with such a Mother I should ever come to be the same."

13

AT THE FRONT

When the French liner on which Machen sailed docked at Bordeaux on January 26th, 1918, after a trip that was without alarms, the party of forty workers proceeded at once to Paris to report to the Y.M.C.A. headquarters at 12 Rue d'Agnesseau. The decision as to the particular kind of work that Machen was to undertake was still to be reached. General conferences concerning the history and principles of the Y.M.C.A. and its methods of work abroad had been undertaken aboard ship and were continued at headquarters, and provided a background for reaching a decision. At a private interview with two of the leaders in Paris, Machen had the opportunity of indicating his own state of mind. This he summed up as follows:

> (1) I have some start in French, and as far as my own personal preference goes would greatly prefer to go into the French work. Just think of what an interesting experience that would be, and what a broadening effect it would have on all the rest of my life! But I was afraid it was selfish. For (2) all my training is for Bible teaching and the like which is not done by the Y.M.C.A. in the slightest among the French troops, and indeed for certain reasons must be carefully excluded.

In the end the decision was reached quite independently of his own will; he was now under orders. And a directive was issued assigning him temporarily to the French work, with the possibility of a change later on. In this capacity his functions would be humble ones, he realized. But he did not think his mother should take a gloomy view of what seemed to be turning aside from his life-work. "A preacher who is preaching *all the time,*" he remarked, "is apt to run dry. There are many kinds of preparation that I need; and the kind of thing that I am going into now, just because of the academic life that I have been leading, is perhaps a thing that I need most of all. That does not mean that it is to be looked upon as mere preparation for something in the future! On the contrary it is a most glorious opportunity to render service where service is most deserved. I only hope I can make good. I feel inadequate enough in various ways."

Machen's admission that he had "some start in French" was a characteristic understatement. Actually his facility in speaking French, not to dwell on his reading knowledge, was really extraordinary. French had been read and spoken in the Machen household since he was a boy, and he had seized upon numerous opportunities of improving himself in this regard. But being a modest perfectionist he disparaged his attainments and eagerly sought out ways of making further progress. In the fortnight that preceded his assignment to his first post of duty, he did this in two main ways. In the first place, he discovered an elderly French woman, the widow of a Protestant pastor, who desired to take boarders, and made arrangements to take his lunch and dinner at her home. He arranged to take a lesson a day with her, but explained that the lesson was "just to salve my conscience for getting a free lesson the best part of the day." And the second means that he employed was to attend performances at the leading French theatres, where plays by Victor Hugo, Moliere, de Musset and others could be seen. He found that practically all of the plays accorded "with those standards of taste to which we are accustomed on our English-speaking stage. Indeed they are vastly superior morally to many of our plays." As these references suggest, life seemed remarkably normal in Paris, though many women were in mourning, the military hospitals were crowded, and there was an occasional air alert.

CANTEEN SERVICE AT ST. MARD

Soon, however, the life of beautiful Paris was left behind for the hard realities of life at his first post. He was assigned first to duty at the *Foyer du Soldat* in the village of St. Mard not far from Soissons, which though cruelly bombed remained inhabited and continued as the Y.M.C.A. headquarters for the district until three weeks of bombardment some time later dictated removal to another city. St. Mard itself was a scene of desolation. Scarcely a house had escaped bombardment; many had been smashed to bits. In many quarters it was a city of the dead; such population as it had was almost altogether military. The front was six or seven miles away, but once this town had been the center of battle. The *Foyer* was set up in a house whose roof had been almost entirely blown off, but the ceiling of the first story remained and so there was some shelter for the large room which was to serve as the canteen as well as for living quarters for Machen and his French colleague. Under these circumstances the quarters were constantly damp from the frequent rain and were more congenial to the rats which thrived in the ruins than to men. But Machen was irked more by the fact that his French associate, probably because of "an excess of kindness" or perhaps because he simply found it easier to do most of the things that had to be done than to confer about them with his foreign colleague who had been "suddenly dropped" upon him, left him largely in idleness. Before the canteen was actually in operation, Machen sought to organize some games for the soldiers but not with great success. Later there were trips to neighboring towns to get supplies and an immense amount of time was spent in preparing hot chocolate and selling it to the soldiers.

To an astonishing extent, in fact, his activity for months seemed to consist largely in manufacturing and selling chocolate for twenty centimes per "quart" or one fourth of a liter. The daily task of preparing the chocolate was a singular one for any ordained professor and doubly so for Machen. The process was quite involved. First large bars of sweet chocolate had to be shaved up; a fixed quantity of water was boiled, the chocolate mixed in, a larger quantity of water added, the whole brought again to a boil, condensed milk added and the process concluded with a final boiling. Since the French liked this drink "which cheers and warms but does not inebriate" especially in the early morning, Machen opened the canteen at 7 A.M. and postponed his own breakfast until after 9 A.M. Of course this meant that he had to rise long before 7 to have the chocolate ready for consumption at that hour. Though he longed for somewhat greater responsibility, and hoped eventually to get into distinctively religious work, he rather surprisingly was happy at the opportunity of performing such menial tasks.

The thoroughly secular character of his situation was often trying, especially since he was a conscientious observer of the Christian sabbath. Nevertheless, he found it possible to adjust himself to the extraordinary circumstances of life at the front. "You may be somewhat surprised," he wrote his mother on Feb. 18th, "when I tell you that I organized a game of quoits on Sunday afternoon—my first efforts as athletic director. There is no Sunday at the front. My idea is that this is war, and also it is France. I just have to do the best I can in my own life, and not altogether destroy my usefulness in the place where God has put me. Of one thing you can be dead sure—this experience will never destroy my own devotedness to the Christian Sabbath. On the contrary it will make me feel all the more profoundly the inestimable blessing of it." A week later he reflects on the same subject in acknowledging a letter from his mother:

My dearest Mother:

Your letter of January 27 (No. 3) has just come to hand. To say that it was welcome would not express my feelings about it at all. It is a brave and splendid letter. I treasure your quotation from the Psalms all the more because of the non-religious atmosphere in which I am living. Never before have I felt quite so keenly, I think, the value of the Christian Sabbath. Here every day is exactly like every other day. In the monotony of the schedule one feels oppressed almost to suffocation. I wish I could hear the church bells ring. As for your choice of a quotation, it is a striking coincidence that in my last letter I spoke of the peculiar fittingness of the Psalms here amid the desolation of war.

In that previous letter he had mentioned his delight in reading the Psalms in the French Bible, and said that they were "the best reading imaginable for army life. They seem just to fit the needs of the soul. In reply his mother, writing on March 28, 1918, said in part:

I was gratified that my quotation from a favorite passage in the Psalms gave you comfort when needed and inspiration. Such is often the case with a familiar word from the Bible. It comforts me too to know that thought can flash between you and me though we are so far apart. I do sympathize with you, with perfect understanding, in your longing for privacy. I do find it so essential myself and besides I know how you have cared for it even in childhood. The text that I think will help you is, "My life is hid with Christ in God." I always think of "my life" as flowing underground, a serene current, hidden from all the surface troubles and strife of tongues. But I know how hard it is to realize such an ideal—nobody knows better than I.

The noise and destruction and sordidness of war he found repulsive. Occasionally he had to take shelter during bombardment and the firing of guns was heard rather constantly overhead. Once he said:

At times I feel a longing for a land of peace and for home. I feel as though it would be a relief to the eyes to see a window-pane once more, and a relief to the ears *not* to hear at intervals the noise of the guns and distant shells. There is one little baby in our village. In the midst of the military surroundings it is refreshing to see its little face. I wonder what its first impression of life will be in the midst of all this ruin.

On a later occasion he spoke of his great loneliness in that atmosphere and of his intense hatred of war:

> Somehow your being able to answer my letter, even though the letter is a long way back, makes me feel less absolutely lonely in my European experience. I never felt so lonely in my life. As you will remember, loneliness on a foreign visit is not at all one of my failings. But here in this desolate environment things are different... And even here, on the bare edge of war, I feel an intense longing for peace. Last night after supper I had an experience unique during the time after my arrival at this post—namely an hour of quiet. It was a beautiful starlit night, absolutely without wind. For a considerable time there was not a shot or the buzz of an airplane. What an inestimable blessing! The great blessings of life are those that we often appreciate least. And one of the greatest blessings of all is quiet. It did not last long here. At nine o'clock or so the anti-aircraft guns were making night hideous again, reinforced by the sinister buzz of the German planes on their way to some work of destruction, I suppose, in the cities of France.
>
> If this war is ever concluded in a really satisfactory way, I am going to be an active worker for peace. And the kind of work that I believe might be really effective is the work of moral education in all the languages of the world. War is righteous when it is conducted as in France for the delivery of women and children and the repelling of an invader. But how any human being can have the heart or the utter absence of heart to continue this war for one moment merely for conquest reveals to my mind as nothing else in the world the abyss of sin. After this war is over, providing it is over in the right way, I do believe that there is going to be a spiritual rebellion of the common people throughout the world which if taken at the flood may sweep away the folly of war. I only hope that other things of a different character may not be swept away at the same time.

There was not much occasion for amusement in these circumstances, but he did find a bit of humor when a copy of *The Presbyterian* for Feb. 7th arrived with its inclusion of his article on "The Minister and his Greek Testament." The article contained in substance a message that he had given the preceding summer at a conference for ministers at Northfield to which he had been invited by Will Moody, son of the great evangelist D. L. Moody. One may note in the article certain echoes of "Christianity and Culture" and "History and Faith," but there is a distinctive plea to ministers to take full advantage of a knowledge of the Greek New Testament and, if that knowledge is inadequate, still to acquire such familiarity by reading it aloud every day. The humorous feature of the *Presbyterian* was of course not to be found in this message. It was rather in an editorial note which stated that the "Rev. Professor John Gresham Machen has the distinction of being the youngest professor in Princeton Seminary, and we think the youngest professor in any Presbyterian Seminary." Apropos this statement Machen wrote his mother, who had expressed her admiration of the article, that "the editor's emphasis upon the extremé youth of the author may possibly be an answer to an impression which I understand prevails in one of our Presbyterian colleges to the effect that none of the professors in Princeton Seminary is under seventy years of age." At the time Machen was in his thirty-seventh year.

A NEW POST

Having indicated to his superiors that he did not believe there was sufficient work for two men at St. Mard, he was transferred after about a month to a new post in the same sector at Missy-sur-Aisne. about half way between St. Mard and Soissons. This village was even more completely demolished than St. Mard and there was no civilian population whatsoever, but there was far greater activity because it was located on a principal military highway.

Machen's functions remained much the same as at his earlier post. There were, however, two distinct advantages in the new situation. The principal change was that he was now alone in charge of the hut and such associates as he had were soldiers appointed to assist when the work proved unbearable for one man. Consequently he felt a new liberty to devote himself with all his energies to the work. His sleeping quarters also took a turn for the better, for now he was able to sleep in a dry cellar of a church of which little more than a portal of the upper structure remained. For some reason the rats as well as dampness were absent, though they swarmed the hut after dark and got into the supplies regardless of the measures taken to prevent their depradations. The number of rats in the ruined villages and trenches was so enormous that he became convinced that after the strife was over "the entire human race" would have to unite in a war upon the army of rodents. Fortunately the extermination of rats was not his main problem as it had been when they had been disturbing the slumbers of his cousin Edgeworth Baxter in Princeton some years before! Fortunately too his sleep was more healthful and less disturbed when he could find time for it.

There was a good deal of work to do in managing the canteen. Frequently there were threatened shortages of supplies, and trips had to be made to headquarters to insure sufficient quantities. The sale of chocolate, confections, tobacco, candles and letter paper continued through most of the twelve or more hours that the canteen was kept open. The preparation and sale of the chocolate became the chief burden as the number of cups sold per day gradually increased from a mere fifty or so per day at first until new records were being set week after week—200 cups per day was a great attainment, but this record was left far behind when the number reached 378, later 399 and finally a high water mark of 510 cups in a single day! The average for the month of April was 358 cups per day. These statistics were more than tabulations kept to satisfy curiosity, for records of supplies and finances had to be kept day by day. So Machen was a bookkeeper as well as a cook and salesman. And then he was constantly seizing upon opportunities of talking to the men.

Though Machen continued to hope that he might eventually be transferred to specifically religious work, he got a deep satisfaction out of the work in which he was engaged. For one thing his health improved in spite of the strain of bombardment and other abnormal features of his life. As he wrote on April 2nd, "I sleep well, and enjoy the best digestion that has been mine for some time. For digestive trouble let me recommend the battle-front of France! The food is good, and the habit of eating and sitting around after meals adds to the wholesomeness of the regime." But there was a deeper satisfaction in the assurance that he was carrying on a useful work. "For the first time, since I arrived in France," he wrote his brother Arthur on March 28th, "I really feel as though I were now performing a service, small and humble though it be. The only trouble is I have enough chocolate for only about two or three days more. Then what? It will not be a pleasant business turning away the crowds." Two weeks later, on April 12th he expressed his estimate of his work in greater detail:

> I have worn one uniform ever since leaving Paris. And it is now all spotted up with hot chocolate. The washing that I have had done here has served to leave the clothes rather wet, but not very clean. My effort to secure a regular bath has not yet been crowned with success, but I still have hopes. I am not sure whether the baths that I took at my last post were much in the interest of cleanliness. Clean water is rather a scarce commodity in these ruined villages.

> As yet I have not been as successful as I should like to be in getting really acquainted with individuals among the men. I have conversed with one user of our library who admires Poe very greatly . . . Also I have helped out another man in his English studies and incidentally talked to him a little on serious subjects. But for the most part I am a cook and nothing more. And I like it for a change. More, perhaps, than for years, I feel a desire for New Testament study. I certainly did need a change. The hand of a good Providence may perhaps even now be detected in the decision of the Paris authorities. If God will I may return to the preaching of the gospel with new appreciation of the privileges just because for a time I have been engaged in a totally different kind of work.

March had brought on a period of great anxiety in France and throughout the allied world as the Germans took to the offensive, and the great armies were locked in a life and death struggle. Machen shared the tension of the time, though censorship did not permit him to be specific in his letters. If he had had doubts as to the justice of the allied cause, they were now dissipated. During a time of fierce overhead bombardment, he wrote:

> The concussion of the air is terriffic. To call that hideous sensation a "noise" is not to do it justice. It is rather a brutal violation of the two elements, earth and air. I hate it, as I hate the whole business of the war. But I am convinced that in the interests of peace the allies have simply got to win. And I pray that they may be given their righteous victory.

A PERILOUS EXPERIENCE

The German drive seemed to gain momentum, however, and suddenly about the end of May there was a powerful breakthrough which enveloped the entire area and placed Machen's own life in great jeopardy. A long and vivid letter of this experience is extant, a letter which members of his family at home furnished to the Baltimore *Sun* for publication in the issue of June 19, 1918. When Machen heard of its publication, he expressed his regret. Such publication should really have been cleared with the Y.M.C.A. authorities, and therefore might be a source of embarrassment to him. Moreover, he felt modestly that his own actions were rather inadequate to the emergency. The letter itself is the best refutation of the latter, and the former fear proved to be of no particular consequence, especially as the turning of the tide had come. Hence the letter is given nearly in its entirety as an interesting account of an exciting incident in Machen's life and as a further disclosure of his life and character. On May 29th he wrote as follows to his mother from Paris:

My dearest Mother:

The impressions of the last few days have followed one another in such rapid succession that I despair of being able to produce anything like an adequate narrative.

On Sunday afternoon all was peaceful at our little post. In the slack time at the Foyer I even took a little stroll with the "planton" that I like so much, leaving another assistant, who helps me on Sundays, temporarily in sole charge. Little did we anticipate the convulsion that was to follow. At five o'clock there was "alerte"—that is, the order was given that everything should be packed up and the wagons made ready to depart at a moment's notice. Sometimes such an "alerte" proves to be a precautionary measure merely, as it was on one occasion some time ago. Consequently I was not greatly disturbed. My planton being unable to come to the Foyer because of military orders, I was particularly busy during the evening serving chocolate and receiving the library books that were hastily returned. This was one thing that prevented me from making my own preparations for departure more carefully. How glad I should be now if I had packed a little bag of necessities that could have been carried on my shoulder! Instead I depended on a suitcase that would have to be put on a wagon. Also I expected to be able to carry my small army-locker.

In the evening I descended into my "abri," [shelter] and got an hour or so of sleep. At one o'clock a violent bombardment began; a number of non-commissioned officers crowded the abri; and I sat up the rest of the night. The bombardment far surpassed anything that we had experienced before. Shells hit right in the village as well as in the environs. One which struck a point a couple of hundred yards from our Foyer killed a man, who however was not one of the men of the cantonment but a soldier who was passing along the road. At the beginning of the bombardment there was some gas—fortunately of the "lachrymozene" variety instead of one of the deadlier kind. I thought I merely had a slight attack of "snuffles" until those who came from the outside reported that things were worse there. We stopped up chinks in our door and put on our masks, at least for a moment or two. One of the non-commissioned officers was kind enough to bring me a better mask than the little one which I keep always with me. Fortunately the gas was not continued, and the little that I experienced of it could scarcely be dignified even by the name of discomfort.

Early in the morning we were ordered to vacate our cellar in order that wounded men might be put in it if necessary, but another abri near by was assigned to us. A non-commissioned officer took me to inspect a pleasanter cellar some distance off, but profundity and proximity appealed more to me. The noise of the bombardment was terriffic; though shells were not falling actually in the center of the village. While I was standing at the door of my abri near the center of the village, they brought in a man who had been killed near by.

Still I rather expected that we were to stay. Meanwhile I did not know exactly what to do. The Foyer evidently could not be kept open in the ordinary way. Perhaps I might have been there to receive library books, but for all I knew that might be accomplished at a more propitious time later on. Certainly I might also have gone to get my suit case. But I anticipated time to do that and other necessary things after the order to depart should be actually given.

At about nine o'clock the troops began moving to the bridge. One of the men that I had known well at the Foyer called out to me something about the Boches being two kilometers away. This, if I understood it aright, was a great exaggeration. But everything began to move, and move quick. So in order not to miss the chance of putting away my suit-case in a wagon I rushed to the Foyer and got it. The non-commissioned officer in charge of the wagons told me, since I was unattached, to get across the river at once and let the suitcase follow. I was glad to do so. The bridge was only a few hundred yards away, but, to adapt a remark of Mark Twain, the time required to get across it was one of the longest weeks that I ever spent. A solid train of wagons and men was moving across the bridge and along the road. A teriffic cannonade was going on, and fresh shellholes could be seen along the road, but for some reason the Germans did not seem to be trying particularly just then to cut that bridge. Thus I got away from a place to which I had really become attached. I saved nothing, not even a clean shirt or a tooth-brush or a clean handkerchief. And I did hate to leave my Foyer. Perhaps I might have stayed a little longer. But you see I was on the wrong side of the river—the bridge might be cut at any minute—and I did not want to make hot chocolate for the Boches.

After getting across the bridge I decided not to wait for my suit-case, but to beat it at once to a place where I could get in touch with the authorities of the Foyer. A soldier informed me that the town where the Direction régionale had been was under particularly heavy bombardment. He advised me to get away from the main roads. This I did, particularly since it enabled me to pass by a neighboring Foyer where I might get instructions. The village of that Foyer had been bombarded, and the place had a very empty appearance. The Foyer was closed, but fortunately I met the directors. The French director is a man of years, has had military experience and possesses the *Croix de Guerre.* Thus he was a man whose advice was worth having. His advice was that we spend the rest of the day and the following night in the neighboring "carrière" [quarry] and await developments. So we took a little chocolate, a can or so of sardines, some bread and some blankets about half a mile to our abri. The carrière in question extended underground for a hundred feet or so, but rather too close to the surface for perfect safety. It served our purpose very well, especially since a few steps from the entrance there was a fine view of the valley and the heights beyond where great things might be expected. There were three [?] of us, the French director of the Foyer, the American director, the French director of a neighboring annex and myself. The afternoon was full of interest. Huge clouds of smoke could be seen ascending here and there where buildings or materials were on fire. My Foyer, which I could plainly discern, still seemed to be untouched. The German air-planes added to the interest; they came close to the ground in order to mow down the troops on the roads with their machine guns. One German plane, I believe was brought down by a French machine close to the entrance of our carrière. But I did not witness the event. The rattle of machine-gun, close at hand, is not an encouragement to staying out in the open.

About five or six o'clock the American director and I went down to get something to eat at his Foyer. I appreciated the dinner very much, since I had had almost nothing to eat all day, but I did not see the use of lingering after dinner merely for the sake of lingering. As it turned out there was an opportunity of serving coffee to some men who had returned from the thick of the fight, so that my colleague may congratulate himself. But this was not anticipated, and at the time the thing was put on the ground of the additional comfort of his own room. In general the gentleman in question was inclined to take an optimistic view of the situation, which was not based on knowledge. Deliver me from a Christian Scientist at such times—entirely too cranky for me.

The ground in the carriere was hard and the night was cold. I had no overcoat, but the two blankets that my comrades were able to lend me from the stock of the Foyer enabled me to snatch a few minutes of sleep. During the night a medical officer dropped in and said that he might need the part of the carriere where we were sleeping for the wounded, and also if there were many of them he might need our help. Needless to say we placed ourselves at his disposal; but no wounded men arrived. I forgot to say that during a part of the afternoon and early evening the carrière was occupied by some five hundred men of passing troops; and also by the men of a "saucisse" [sausage] which was raised immediately over the carrière. But towards morning all had gone. I cannot say that the night was pleasant—much too chilly to suit my taste.

You can imagine the interest with which at early dawn I took my first look at the valley. The surprising thing was that the appearance of the scene was so little changed. There were the puffs of arriving shells here and there and the smoke of what I took to be more of the fires observed the evening before. As a matter of fact, in accordance with the communiques that I read later on, the Boches must have been at or across the river at the point within plain view. So far as I can make out they were only two or three miles away from us at the time when we left the carrière for the rear. But I had no idea at the time that they had advanced so far. However, I did not take the optimistic view of my Christian Science friend, who returned to his *Foyer* for breakfast. The bombardment became exceedingly intense, and we finally decided that there was no chance of our being able to return to our respective posts and that our duty was to get into touch with the Foyer authorities.

The first mile and a half we walked. When we got up in the plateau back of our carriere the appearance of things was not encouraging. Great clouds of smoke were rising here and there in the rear, and all the reports that we could get indicated that the Boches had advanced in such a way as to risk cutting us off. Loaded down with the blankets and the hand-bags of my companions, we were glad when we reached the headquarters of the "Dames Anglaises" who run a concern somewhat like a *Foyer du Soldat* in a neighboring village. There through the extreme kindness of the commandant who was attending to the moving of the Dames Anglaises we were able to load our belongings on a wagon—at least the belongings of my comrades, since I had none. On the road the rattle of the German aviators' machine guns was not pleasant; passing troops on a road are pretty much at the mercy of an airplane. But after something like a four or five mile trip we got to a little town [later identified as Chairise] where there was a railroad station of a branch line. We just caught the last train that was to be run. It was filled with women and children leaving their homes and trying to carry some of their personal effects. Mighty pathetic that train was, I can tell you. But you from personal experience know what such scenes are like. After a trip of ten or fifteen miles we reached a station on a main line [Outchy]. Since we had all afternoon, or rather most of the whole day, to wait for the Paris train, I seized the opportunity of inquiring at the Foyer du Soldat of the town about the Direction regionale. I was informed that it was established at a small city [Meaux] not very far from Paris. So instead of going at once to Paris I decided to get off at the city in question and report to the regional directors. Arriving at nearly midnight I was fortunate enough to get a room at a hôtel. You may well imagine that after two such nights as I had just spent, a bed looked mightly good to me.

The next morning the French regional director told me to go to Paris, report to the Direction centrale, and wait until it was to be decided what should be done. So here I am at Paris, as the paper upon which I am continuing my letter will show. Life has to be begun over again. I have my skin, and the very dirty clothes with which it is covered. But that is all. My letters, my thousand little cherished knick-knacks, and my equipment are all gone. If I can locate that suit-case, I shall recover some things of importance. As for what I left at the Foyer I suppose that is lost even if the Boches are not actually in possession. And from my interpretation of the official communications, I should judge that they are. It is interesting to read that the Boches were attacking the heights upon which our carriere was situated in the course of the very day when we left.

May 30

Good-by to all my things. The Boches have swept over my post [at St. Mard]. One of the Foyer directors of the region is rumored to be a prisoner; others had a very much harder time escaping than I had. My former post was the scene of hard fighting.

I have been directed to wait here in Paris till tomorrow when instructions may be given me. Naturally clothes are almost my first concern. The prices are something terrific—for instance I paid 185 francs plus a war tax for a pair of high boots. But I should not mind if I could only get the things that I desire. French underwear is cut in the queerest way imaginable, and the American variety cannot be found. But this morning I am at least fairly clean. I even had a bath! Still I am just about the toughest looking person in Paris. How other Foyer directors manage to look as though they had just come out of a bandbox when in reality they have been sleeping in a carrière is beyond my comprehension. I must think quick about my purchases, since of course tomorrow I may get the order to leave town at once. Without doubt I shall forget just the most important things; I think, however, that I shall be here some days.

Let me say that nothing that the papers say about the "sang-froid" of the Parisians is exaggerated a bit. The town is being bombarded again, but everything goes on just as unconcernedly as before. The city presents just the same busy, bright, normal appearance as at the time of my last visit, before the "grosse Bertha" had begun its deadly work. Of course, the risk to an individual is almost infinitesimal. Paris is big, and there could be an explosion somewhere in its great area even every few minutes for a long, long time without getting around to you or me. Also the bombardment is only occasional. In general it is far less terrifying than I had anticipated. As for the much more dangerous air-raids, an admirable system for the opening of cellars to the public has been devised. There are placards, "Abri," where the cellars are good. Still, the bravery of the people of Paris is admirable. The Germans are never going to win the war by trying to play upon their feelings . . .

I hate to think of the Germans enjoying our stock of chocolate. And still less do I like to think of them fussing in my trunk.

The above letter I know is very inadequate. The scenes that I have witnessed can never be forgotten, but it is not so easy to make anyone else realize what they were like. The refugees, I think, constituted the saddest part of all. The roads for miles and miles were crowded with the wagons containing household effects piled on in direst confusion. On the train by which I arrived at Paris there was a middle-aged woman with an aged man

—utterly infirm—who she told me was her grandfather! I helped with the bundles, and got an employee at the station to look out for the party. On arrival, it must be said, the government authorities are doing everything in the world for the unfortunate people. But it is terribly sad.

Those days had been filled with anxiety for the loved ones at home. Mrs. Machen gave expression to her mingled disquiet and faith in a letter of May 31st:

> I must send you a letter although I feel so uncertain about its reaching you. This last German drive, as reported by all the papers, must have taken the village in which you were first stationed and swept over the Foyer in which you were working so hard. We long to know how you fared amid all the horror of battle and what you were able to do. I am thankful for what you said in your book—that no harm can come to the Christian.
>
> The imprecatory Psalms do seem most expressive and appropriate. But I am such a two-sided person that I find myself sorry for "the wicked" who have somehow gotten wrong and who have not the blessed consolations of faith in God.

On June 7th her heart was well-nigh bursting with joy:

> Arthur came into my room yesterday about five o'clock with a radiant face, exclaiming "Good news! Good news from Gresham!" Then he gave me your cable with the assurance "Safe and well." I cannot tell you the relief. We knew approximately where you were from the postmarks, and it was quite evident that the tides of war had swept over your little hut and wiped out the flowers and the nightingale and made the rats scurry. "And what happened to my boy?"—that was the query of my anxious heart. So, you were good to send me the cable and thoughtful to let Arthur have it first to spare me the fright. All our friends have been so kind in rejoicing over the cable.

TRANSFER TO AMERICAN AUSPICES

The ill wind that blew Machen out of Missy-sur-Aisne, and carried most of his personal effects beyond recall, also opened the door to a welcome change in his career as a war worker. The decision to transfer him from the French to American work was not long in forthcoming, and was accepted gratefully because now the prospect of doing religious work might find fulfillment. At this stage, however, such hopes were realized to a very limited extent. His first preaching opportunity was that of addressing colored troops from Virginia in a camp near the Swiss border, and several others came in quick succession in various camps. Unfortunately, however, from the viewpoint of his interest in the preaching, a shortage of secretaries to manage canteens had developed because of the arrival of great numbers of troops. About the middle of June he was ordered to take charge of a Y.M.C.A. hut, and this type of service was not concluded until after the Armistice. He served at various posts, first in the Lorraine and then in the Argonne sector, and in the closing weeks of the war had moved forward well into Belgium with the troops.

In many respects his activities throughout this period were not unlike that of the period when he had been working among the French. To a large extent he was occupied with the management of canteens, and he once observed that a Y.M.C.A. secretary "is a grocery clerk and nothing else." In some respects the situation had even deteriorated because more services to the soldiers were being demanded—including, for example, the preparation of a steady flow of money orders—and there were fewer men to perform them. Often he found time for only three or four hours' sleep. There were frequent gas alarms, the noise of aerial combat, and sheer back-breaking toil. It was a nerve-wracking experience. The fact that due to the demands of the changing situation, mail service was even more undependable than before and he was often without a word from home for weeks at a time, added greatly to the burdens that had to be borne.

For at least one distinctive aspect of the new situation he however had occasion to be grateful. Under the American auspices a definitely religious program could be integrated with the other activities, though the severe strain of the routine tasks and the general indifference of the men prevented the religious work from being as successful as he had hoped. The difficulties with which he struggled are reflected, for example, in a letter of June 29, 1918 when he was the only Y.M.C.A. worker in a large camp at Baccaret in the Lorraine sector. Incidentally the letter indicates why the Y.M.C.A., without being necessarily blameworthy, became unpopular with many soldiers and was the subject of considerable criticism for its conduct of war work.

> The demand for things to eat and smoke is insatiable. Pretty much every day I have had to go (often on foot) to a town about four miles or so away to stir up the Y.M.C.A. supply department. The worst of it is that supplies cannot be sent direct to camp in Y.M.C.A. trucks, because of bad roads, but can only be sent to the nearest point in the main road. Thence they have to be brought in by army wagon. The process is long and difficult.

It involves numberless pedestrian trips to two separate and distinct villages. The other evening I did succeed in obtaining 1,000 packages of cookies, which we sell for a franc apiece. Limiting each man to one package, we sold the whole thousand in about three hours, in addition to many boxes of cigars and other merchandise. Yesterday our sales amounted to about 1,900 francs. There was a line extending out from our canteen that looked like the line at the ticket-window of a world series game. Of course, we could sell perhaps ten times this amount a day if we could only get the goods. I do not think the Y.M.C.A. divisional headquarters realizes the relative importance of this post. Other canteens serving one-fourth the number of men are well stocked, whereas I am left in the cold. However the difficulties are great and the Y.M.C.A. is undermanned. I am able to get along here only because of the help of a sergeant and one or two of the men who have done the work of the counter as much or more than I. But we need a force of about three or four secretaries.

A big part of the routine work is the job of making out money orders for America. Their name is legion, and some of them are for substantial sums. In addition, I have been sending many money orders to Italy. This is a particularly troublesome job. For the American money orders there is a regular Y.M.C.A. form, and the thing is done by Y.M.C.A. machinery, but in the case of the Italian orders I have simply to take the men's money, give a purely personal receipt, and then put the orders in my own name at the French post office on my next visit to a neighboring town. But I am glad to do the work. The sending of money to relatives seems to me to be one of the most important routine services that the Y.M.C.A. is rendering.

The letter was continued on Sunday, June 30, and he went on to tell of the continued difficulty of supply, of the inadequacy of the hut because it was used by the military authorities at the time as a guard house for prisoners, of being kept awake at night by the arrival of new prisoners and their conversation as well as by gas alarms and the noise of the war in general. There had been a good Roman Catholic service, but his own efforts were beset by special difficulties.

This morning the chaplain of the regiment, who is a catholic, has just held a general service and is now celebrating mass as I write. The general service was frankly supernatural—the loaves and fishes—and satisfactory. The reading of the Gospels was urged, and the moral exhortations were good. As hymns we had "Onward Christian Soldiers" and "Lead, Kindly Light." I was pleased with the service. It was far, far better than what we get from the Protestant liberals.

One night during the week I held a little service, but had very few men in attendance (They nearly always had a roll-call or the like just at the hour of my service, was Machen's later annotation in the margin). This morning before service I had a little Bible study with about a half dozen men. The chaplain's service, I am exceedingly glad to say, was well attended.

He continued to conduct Bible classes and organized religious services whenever possible, even playing the piano for the singing when there was no alternative. At one point he tells of his decision to close down the canteen during the three brief services that he was conducting during each week, even though this gave some dissatisfaction to men who were in the canteen at the time. "If I stay here long enough," he wrote, "I hope the men will see that it is not mere neglect or stubbornness which leads me to take this stand. Meanwhile, it is very discouraging to see so desparately little interest in the deeper things of life. But the condition is the same over the whole world today."

Nevertheless, he was happy to be of such use as he could be, and the prodigious amount of labor he performed would seem to constitute some evidence that the work was regarded as beneficial. At the end of August he reported that during the month he had turned over some 46,000 francs to the Y.M.C.A. headquarters of which more than half was canteen receipts and the rest money to be sent to America. "Pretty big business I call it," he remarked. "It is a lot of work, but I am awfully glad to be doing it." In the midst of his loneliness and strenuous life there were consolations of a spiritual nature and the contentment born of devotion to duty. At the middle of September he was saying:

You don't know how I long for home these days. Home things acquire a new value. For many years, for example, I have read very little in my English New Testament, the Greek having taken the place of the English. But very often in the evening during the past weeks, my Greek Testament having been left at the Y.M.C.A., I have been reduced to the little pocket English Testament that Loy gave me. And the grandeur of our old English Bible has appealed to me as never before. The grandeur and the comfort too of the old familiar words, which had become almost unfamiliar through an over-dose of erudition.

Orders are for Y.M.C.A. men to continue at their work despite the raising of the draft age, until some definite notice comes to the contrary. As long as I am as busy and (I think I can say) as useful as I have been during the past seven weeks, I am not impatient for any change in my status.

MOVING FORWARD

Later as he moved forward with the troops of the 37th Division in the Argonne, the service took on a somewhat distinctive character. Conditions did not permit the ordinary canteen service, but chocolate, cookies and cigarettes were distributed to the wounded at a dressing station.

One thing that made the thing more satisfactory to me was that I found myself again associated with the same ambulance men that I had known at my last post. They are certainly a splendid lot of men. And how finely those medical officers did work day and night with practically no sleep at all. Sometimes I had a night shift at the dressing station and sometimes a day shift. Our hot chocolate was especially appreciated—not only by the patients but also in a professional way by the doctors, who constantly called for it when badly wounded men were brought in. One German fellow said when I gave him the chocolate that it was "wie bei der Mutter." It would have taken a harder heart than mine to keep from being a bit touched by that. By the way along with the hatred and bitterness incidental to the war, there are some examples of the other thing which like fair lilies in swampy ground are all the more beautiful because of the contrast with the unlikely soil in which they grow. Thus at one of the dressing stations near the front, I saw an American wounded soldier deliberately take off his overcoat and give it to a wounded German who was suffering a lot worse than he. When one reflects what that little act meant—the long cold hours of rain and damp on the long way to the rear and the interminable waits—it becomes clear that magnanimity has not altogether perished from the earth.

The walk from my dug-out to the dressing station seemed almost interminable. Hard rains made of the road a sea of mud and water which surpassed anything that I could have believed to be possible. Progress at times, even for a pedestrian, was almost impossible, the road being so crowded with wagons, automobiles and horses that you could barely squeeze along beside them. At times one was tempted to take to the ruins on one side or the other of the road, but progress there would soon be blocked by caved-in cellars. My shoes gave out completely under the strain . . .

On one day I walked out with some other secretaries toward the front. On the way we passed what had recently been no-man's land and the German lines beyond it. Right here all attempt at description would be vain. It was a scene of desolation so abominable, so unlike anything that could have been expected on our fair earth, that neither words nor even photographs could bring any realization of it. For miles the front had been reduced to a few straggling stumps. I have seen burnt and ruined forests before. But the effects of shell fire are different. There was something indescribably sinister about that scene of ruin. Everywhere there were enormous craters caused by the big shells —at places running into one another. Along the road in one or two places the unburied dead were lying, enough to indicate the horrors which were probably concealed by that ghastly desert on either side.

At last we came to another dressing station, where the wounded were lying in considerable numbers—of course unsheltered along the road. We distributed some of the chocolate and cigarettes that we were carrying on our back and pushed on. Our objective was a recently captured town on a high cliff. The fighting was going on perhaps a mile or so beyond. At last we reached the town [later identified as Montfaucon], which had been a famous German position during the Verdun fighting, and had been thought impregnable. But we were soon driven out. The Germans seemed to have our range, and after a shell-burst a few feet from us, we beat a retreat, seeking the comparative shelter of ditches and shell-holes on our way . . .

At last, with the withdrawal of the troops to which we are attached, it became time for us to go. About a day was spent at the ruined village of which I first spoke [Recicourt]—selling goods to our men and living in a mighty crowded and uncomfortable way.

It is unbelievable that I have not written for two weeks. But what was the use of writing when there seemed to be absolutely no chance to get a letter censored and mailed? I have just sent a "safe and well" telegram to Arly. That ought to relieve the anxiety which you might have felt on account of the long gap in my letters.

After similar experiences at or near the front for a number of days, Machen along with other secretaries was relieved for a while, and ordered back to Paris to await further orders. Victory was now in the air, and Paris was more delightful than ever after the hardships that he had been enduring. At the end of October he was on his way to the front again. He had heard indirectly that an order had been issued some time previously that he should report to Paris in order to enter into specifically religious work. If such an order was ever issued, it failed to reach him. But now at any rate he received official assurance that he would soon have an opportunity of doing that kind of work in the near future. For the present, however, his duty appeared to be near the front. Calais, Dunkerque, Thielt, Eyne on the Scheldt were among the principal stopping points on the journey back, and until after the armistice he carried on in the same general area in Belgium where he had previously been.

EVE OF THE ARMISTICE

His final letter before the close of the war reflected at length upon his experiences and impressions during those exciting and hectic days, and it serves well to conclude this chapter.

Thursday, Nov. 7, 1918.
Address: Care of American Y.M.C.A.
12 Rue d'Agnesseau, Paris.

My dearest Mother:

Life has been so full during the past few days that I am quite at a loss as to how I am ever going to reduce to anything like a semblance of order the bewildering wealth of my impressions. The first part of the time since my last letter, it is true, was not particularly exciting, but Monday and Tuesday of this week, as I look back upon them, seem as though they must have been each about a month long.

The journey from Paris was as usual rather troublesome. There was one pleasant day of waiting in a fairly large town, then we started out again on the search for our troops. There was about a day in another large town, where I think I wrote you a letter. Then it looked as though I were side-tracked. Most of the men had succeeded in getting on, but I secured no transportation. Finally an officer's car took another secretary and myself on to a small place where two of our other men had succeeded in getting one carload of canteen stock, which they had started to sell. It soon became apparent, however, that we were not near enough to the front to render real service to the men of our division, and transportation consequently became the pressing problem. There were no freight-cars, and no American army trucks, but the French authorities as usual treated me fine and placed three large trucks at our disposal. With these we moved our merchandise and ourselves (three secretaries) to a good-sized town which seemed likely to be our Y.M.C.A. distributing point. By conference with the "town-mayor" or "mayor de cantonnement," I secured a provisional ware house, where we dumped our stuff and began selling it to the American soldiers. Five secretaries of our division were all that were in the region: I was therefore this time in an advance guard. It was determined that two of us were to push on toward the front, leaving two to watch for freight that might come in and run the canteen. One was already at the front. I was one of the two additional men chosen to push on. Our transportation was secured in ambulances, since we intended to work in the dressing-stations, as we had done several times before. The ambulances of course go back to the front often nearly empty after having discharged the wounded men at the rear.

The first night was spent at a hospital some five miles from the front. It was not a pleasant night for me. Wounded children make a pitiful noise, and the noise of German air-craft bombs and shells, some of them rather close, was more disturbing still. I confess that I slept hardly at all.

The next day two of us rode on an ambulance, with our little stock of powdered chocolate and cookies, to a dressing-station about one mile from the front line. There we proceeded to make our hot chocolate and distribute it to the wounded men. To my great delight I found myself again associated with the admirable ambulance company that I had been with several times before. But no amount of pleasant comradeship can conceal the fact that the twenty-four hours which I spent in that dressing-station was a strenuous time.

The small cellar of the house which we occupied was packed with some fifty civilians, mostly women and children, who had not been able to get away from the front after the Germans had left. The rest of us therefore stayed in three rooms of the ground floor, one of which was used for the wounded also. No one displayed a great enthusiasm for the upper floor; certainly it was much too far from the cellar to suit me. The house, though not large, was solid; its walls afforded considerable protection against the fragments of exploding shells. And shells in the immediate vicinity were not lacking, though while I was there only one came close enough to permeate the house with the odor of the high explosive. Fortunately there was work to do. We had two little stoves to make our hot chocolate on, in two separate rooms, and although my colleague was the leader in cookery I spelled him during a good part of the night. A little rest on some straw, with perhaps a snatch of sleep, was the extent of my repose. In the early part of the night I had my first experience in stretcher-bearing; a shell had struck a house some hundred yards or so away with disastrous results. My services were accepted, though as it turned out there would have been enough to do the work without me. I made two trips to that house with men of the ambulance company; and I confess I was glad when the job was over, though nothing hit very close to us.

What in the world was to be done with the fifty civilians, including some twenty children and infants, and a number of pitifully aged and infirm men and women? It seemed cruel to make them try to walk away in the midst of the shell-fire, but on the other hand there was no room for them where they were, and they were in danger all the time. Finally, the lieutenant in charge determined to send away a crowd of the most needy in an ambulance. In view of my linguistic qualifications it fell to my part to choose the ones who were to go. Can you imagine a more pathetic task? It was like the last boat-load leaving the Titanic. Finally with the help of one young fellow of superior intelligence among the civilians I got a good number of the smallest children with their parents aboard. We had to shove in one or two people ruthlessly when they wanted to get some bundles of clothes. It was *some* wagon-load, I can tell you. I am afraid they were not taken very far, since of course it is not possible to use ambulances ordinarily for such a purpose, but at least we got them started. Unfortunately the thing could not be repeated.

Before and after this departure I distributed our hot chocolate in that cellar. It was astonishing how they were cheered up by the nourishing drink, and also by a few kindly words from someone in uniform. It was somewhat out of the line of the Y.M.C.A., but I must confess that no bit of service that I have been privileged to render since I have been in Europe has begun to give me the joy that I derived from ministering to those sweet little children in that hour of deepest distress.

Certainly it was a night that I am not likely to forget. Outside the whistle and roar of the arriving shells, and from the cellar the monotonous prayers of the frenzied women. In the morning the sight in the road outside was the most pathetic that I have ever seen. Nothing that I witnessed in the great retreat can compare with it. Tiny children and aged men and women, some of them loaded on wheelbarrows along with the pathetic fragments of household effects, were all madly endeavoring to escape over the shell-menaced roads. I hope never to see another such sight; yet I think I shall always have a tenderer and better heart on account of what I saw. Somehow I feel more certain that there must be a Father somewhere who cares for those little ones.

During the forenoon a medical major gave me the opportunity of going to a still more advanced dressing-station, located in a sort of convent about three hundred feet from the front line. I did not want to go one bit, but duty seemed to call. Part of the way I went in an ambulance; then a detail of two men was given me to help carry my powdered chocolate, my sugar, my condensed milk, and my little biscuits. We paused a number of times on the way in shells of houses, and finally arrived at our destination without untoward incident.

The dressing-station was in a large house occupied by some sisters of charity. Now I am a Protestant of the most uncompromising sort, and I do not believe a bit in nunnery; but I want to testify that those ladies were admirable. You should have seen the way in which they cared for the American wounded and doctors and ambulance men, as well as for the crowd of children that had fallen to their care. In fact it looked as though I were going to be rather useless. The sisters were far better cooks than I. But several people suggested that I might serve the soldiers in the line. This I did, on the day after the day in which I arrived. But on that previous day I had excitement enough. Just after I had been taken out by a captain to be shown the way to the lines, as I was returning a shell hit the street just at the door where I was to go in, and there were several direct hits in the house where I was to stay. The captain and I threw ourselves on the ground in the orthodox way, and after repeating the gesture when the second shell arrived got safely into a little cellar. Fortunately no one was hurt in the house where I was staying or in the house where I took temporary refuge—at least not hurt that time.

The next day I went twice out to the line carrying kettles of hot chocolate with the assistance of a fine young fellow among the enlisted men, who volunteered to help and guide me. There was a couple of hundred feet where one had to walk across a field in view of the enemy and be prepared to duck if machine-guns opened up. But nothing happened. It must not be supposed that the trip was specially dangerous; it was only the kind of thing that is done many times a day by the men in the army. To me it was most exciting, being my first experience in what may be called the front line. The service that I rendered was certainly most trifling, but it is a satisfaction to have made an effort at any rate.

That evening we were relieved. The night before I had spent in the cellar and had gotten some good sleep despite crowded conditions. The relief itself was satisfactory in its results, but rather nerve-wracking in the process of execution. Burning farms lit up the country side for miles, and why the Boche planes which could be heard buzzing above us did not catch sight of us I do not know. But by the mercy of God they did not. On the way I looked in for my colleague at the other dressing-station, but the place was empty. It had finally been smashed by the shells. My Y.M.C.A. colleague escaped injury.

My blanket and other belongings were badly arranged for carrying and when I arrived at the stopping-place at about ten o'clock or so at night I was as dead tired out, I think, as I have ever been in my life. I imagine the feelings of the men when told that the place was crowded to overflowing and that there were no billets except, I believe, one little room for the officers and runners. I was invited into that room, but to avoid the congestion found a cellar next door for a captain and myself. Practically no roofs were on the houses in that village, since severe fighting had taken place there some week or so before.

The next day, I "hiked" back well to the rear, securing several welcome lifts. Just now I am in a town at the rear, enjoying the comparative peace and quiet, though there has been work enough to do. When I arrived from the front dead tired out I did hope for a rest, but long lines of men were waiting outside the Y.M.C.A. canteen, and I just had to step in and help out as a salesman. Instead of sleeping somewhere on the floor crowded together with the Y.M.C.A. secretaries, I went to the French town mayor's office and got a sergeant in charge to find me a room, which he did in the most obliging possible way. So for two nights I have had the luxury of a room, a bed, and a quiet time. You can therefore, without worry, simply share my thankfulness for being brought safely through dangers now past. God has been very good to me. That is the one great fact that stands out amid the confusion of the past days.

My landlady does not want to charge me anything for my room. She says that having had to house Germans for so long she is only too glad to house Americans on equally good terms. Of course I have taken pains to explain that I have no right to requisition a room, and of course I shall pay her a good rent; but at any rate her good will is significant and typical.

Your most welcome letter of Oct. 6 has arrived since I began the above. I am sorry to hear of Dr. Kirk's illness, but the good news about yourself, about Nena, and about Arly has cheered me beyond measure. You write about the socks just after I had sent you the label. I hope it may arrive in time; but if it does not don't worry. The prayers that accompany the making of those socks will do me good in any case. I am thankful to-night for two great blessings—for the preservation of my life and for the possession of such a Mother.

Your loving son,
Gresham

14

FINAL MONTHS IN FRANCE

The armistice came at last! To one who detested war as thoroughly as Machen did the prospect of peace and of leaving the business of war was calculated to provide a thrilling state of exhilaration. And how eagerly he must have embraced the prospect of reunion with his mother and the others at home with whom he had been even more firmly knit in the bonds of affection because of the critical and anxious days of separation! The armistice did not however spell a quick journey home. There were responsibilities toward the troops that remained, and they could not be shirked, least of all by one as conscientious and self-denying as he was. And the coming of peace became the occasion for the opening of opportunities to engage in specifically Christian activity of the kind that had been his first love throughout the many months in which he had uncomplainingly undertaken the most menial and humdrum tasks.

ARMISTICE MOOD

His mood as the armistice was announced is vividly set forth in a letter written three days later:

Care of American Y. M. C. A.
12 Rue d'Agnesseau,
Paris, France.
Nov. 14, 1918.

My dearest Mother:

The Lord's name be praised! Hardly before have I known what true thanksgiving is. Nothing but the exuberance of the psalms of David accompanied with the psaltery and an instrument of ten strings could begin to do justice to the joy of this hour. "Bless the Lord, O my soul." It seems as though the hills must break forth into singing. Peace at last, and praise to God!

On the evening of the tenth of November I was again at the front. Little news had been coming through about the progress of negotiations. Without a doubt you were far better and far more promptly informed in Baltimore. There were rumors, but they could not be definitely confirmed; other rumors have often disappointed us. Was there hope of an immediate peace? We did not know.

I was to spend the night in a little house near a dressing-station where we hoped to serve the wounded with hot chocolate. We were in the midst of our own artillery, which made the most infernal noise that I ever listened to. There was absolutely no cellar or dug-out in which to take refuge, and I thought the German reply would blow us to pieces. Shells had been landing in the environs during the day; in the early part of the evening a man was slightly wounded just at the door of the house where I was staying. But although the whistle of the German shells could be heard from time to time, in general things became quieter as the night wore on. I got some sleep on the floor of our little hovel. Then rumors began to come in. The armistice was said to have been agreed on at 2:10 A.M. Desultory firing continued, but this was said to be usual even after an armistice is signed. At four o'clock the French could be heard singing in their quarters. When I poked my head in they said that the news was not official. But somehow there was a new atmosphere of hope. With the morning light the news was confirmed. Firing was to cease at 11 A.M. Meanwhile there was quiet. A strange peacefulness pervaded the air. The walk to the Y.M.C.A. canteen, which the night before had been hideous with the flash and roar of the guns and with the menace of arriving shells was now safe as though we were at home. I shall never forget that morning. Perhaps one might regret not having been (say) at Paris when the stupendous news came in. But I do not think I regret it. We heard, indeed, no clamor of joyful bells, no joyful shouts, no singing of the Marseillaise. But we heard something greater by far—in contrast with the familiar roar of war—namely the *silence* of that misty morning. I think I can venture upon the paradox. That was a silence that could really be heard. I suppose it was the most eloquent, the most significant silence in the history of the world.

About noon I took a walk out through the village to what had recently been the German position. Instead of the sinister appearance of a front-line town, with streets deserted or occupied only by men walking warily close to the walls, the place had almost taken on a holiday appearance. Of course the great gaping holes in the houses were still there, the pedestrian's feet would still crunch into the broken glass scattered by recent shells: but people were walking freely about as though life had begun. But lest joy should be careless or exuberant, the dead were being brought in just as I passed, and along the road an occasional poor fellow was lying who would never hear the news of peace. It seemed almost impossible. On that exuberant joyful morning when the whole world was shouting, what possible place was there for death and sorrow? God knows and He alone. Meanwhile I felt more humble but not less thankful.

Across the river an American soldier showed me the German machine-gun emplacements which he had been trying to "get" with his own gun a few hours before. The cartridges were still strewn around.

But I must go back and bring my little narrative up to date, to explain how I happened to be near the front again, after the relief of a few days before. After the two exciting days which I spent at the front about a week or so ago, there was a period of about four days in a considerable town in the rear, where I had work at the Y. M. C. A. canteen, but also considerable rest in a real bed. I had rather expected that our division would be given a long rest, and was not overjoyed, I confess, when it became evident that we were to go to the front again. However, I was encouraged by a little word of praise that was handed on to me by one of the Y.M.C.A. secretaries from the colonel of the regiment for which I labored that day in the line. The colonel wanted me to know that he would be glad to help me in any way, and that he appreciated what I had done for his men. Such words of cheer have not been so numerous in my experience as a Y.M.C.A. secretary but that I could enjoy this one considerably. As a matter of fact I really just drifted along into the service in question, indeed was almost forced into it (others deserving what credit there was), but still I could not help being pleased by the message.

The first night after leaving our Y.M.C.A. warehouse base was spent in a town about half-way to the front, where we had a busy time selling things to the men. Peace rumors had been coming in, and the guns were phenomenally quiet. I confess I thought the war was over. The impression was reversed when we got out near the front the next day. Shells were dropping around quite frequently enough to suit me. A Y.M.C.A. canteen had already been located in a village perhaps about a mile and a half from the Germans. I worked a while selling goods there and then was sent to a dressing-station perhaps a half-mile further to the rear. About what happened there I have already told you. The opportunities of service were so slight that after making our chocolate and having it kept on the fire during the night, my companion and I returned in the morning to the Y.M.C.A. canteen, where there was at first a good deal of work to be done. Soon, however, our stock was exhausted, and the next day was really a day of idleness. So yesterday I came back to the Y.M.C.A. base, where I am now established in my old room.

I came to an important decision, which I hope may prove to be a wise one—the decision namely to ask for my movement order to Paris in order to report to the "religious work" department. You will remember that according to Mr. Gardiner of Princeton I was actually ordered to Paris, to engage in the work of that department, some weeks ago, though the order did not reach me. President King, head of the department, seemed to be able to find no record of such an order. But as soon as he found out who I was he received me cordially and told me very definitely that he would have useful work for me and that he thought my place was elsewhere than in a canteen. My movement papers away from Paris had, however, then already been made out, and besides I was not at all sure that I could feel justified in leaving my division as long as the fighting was going on. So President King agreed that I could go on with the division while at the same (time) leaving the way open to enter his department at the first convenient opportunity. That opportunity, I think, has certainly now arrived. For the present, there is no question of shirking the danger of war, that danger having been removed by the armistice. I could therefore work in Paris or anywhere in Europe with as good a conscience as with a moving division; and the opportunities for my kind of work would be enormously greater where life is a bit more stable. In general, the present situation offers an unparalleled opportunity both for religious and for educational work. If the truce is of long duration there will be millions of men over here relieved from the stress of war whose minds will be open.

Perhaps the safer procedure would have been for me to write to President King telling him that I would welcome a repetition of the order to report to Paris. But it would have taken weeks, probably, to get the reply, and meanwhile I am eager to get at my own work. It must be confessed that I feel a little like Esther in the presence of the king. If the golden sceptre is not held out to me I shall be in a very embarrassing situation. But although

I have only oral assurances, I think that if either Mr. Gardiner or President King is in Paris I shall be well received. And the heads of our division Y. M. C. A. appreciate my position. No one can say that I have shirked the simple, homely service of the canteen; for I have had some nine months of it. But I am not a business man. Others can do that important work as well or better than I. I am impatient now for my own work. I am going for it with all my might, even though I am compelled to blow my own horn just a tiny little bit.

Meanwhile I am thankful to God for the preservation of my own life. Or rather, that does not just express what I mean, and I am not quite sure whether I can express it. I mean rather that I am thankful that God has not put upon me more than I could bear. It is obvious that other men are far braver and cooler than I am. I lose sleep when they seem to think nothing at all of the dangers that hover in the air. But out in that dressing-station, when the shells were falling close around, I somehow gained the conviction that I was in God's care and that He would not try me beyond my strength; that courage would keep pace with danger, or rather that danger (for I confess it turned out rather that way) would keep within the limits of courage.

In short, I believe I understand the eighth chapter of Romans better than I did two weeks ago.

Oh, what a relief to enjoy once more the glory of a crisp autumn day or the beauty of a moon-lit night. I confess that during the last nine months I have longed for clouds and rain. There has scarcely ever been a time when I could stand under a clear sky without keeping one ear open for the nerve-wracking sound of a German motor. Cloudy nights have sometimes brought me my only chance to sleep. No doubt such an attitude is very mean and wrong. Perhaps I ought to have been glad when it was clear, for if it gave the Germans a chance to bomb us, look what a splendid chance it also gave us to bomb them! But although reason might feel thus, feeling, I may as well confess, never did.

And, oh, the joyful silence that we are enjoying now. Pray God it may not be interrupted again.

The best of love to all.

Your own loving son,

Gresham

From J. Gresham Machen
care of American Y.M.C.A.
12 Rue d'Agnesseau,
Paris, France.

The armistice letter was supplemented later by a more specific recital of the final course of events, which dealt especially in geographical terms. After a number of days at the Y. M. C. A. headquarters at Thielt, he went with certain associates to East Deyuze on the Lys, a tributary of the Scheldt, then proceeded to Synghem, several miles north of Eyne. The last day before the armistice was spent in a little house perhaps three quarters of a mile west of Synghem. "The next morning," he related in Jan. 5, 1919, "to the piping tunes of peace I walked out across the Escant. Then I went back to Thielt and after a day or so secured my movement order to Paris. Luckily securing a ride in an auto I went in fine style to Dunkerque—passing the ancient no man's land at Dixmunde. Thence train to Calais, and thence sleeping-car to Paris."

DECISION TO REMAIN ON

At long last, after about nine months of the routine of canteen work—which had been assigned as simply preliminary to the definitely religious work—the way was opened for the activity for which he had felt himself best fitted. Except for brief holidays in Paris between engagements, he was busy until well into February, a period of nearly three months, in carrying out speaking assignments at a great number of military camps. His mother's armistice letter had closed with the words, "Oh, I wonder—will you come home, home! Or will you think it your duty to stay over and help a little longer! I was so pleased by your helping the old soldier. I want you to take care of *this* old veteran in the battle of life. Your own loving mother, M.G.M." To this Machen answered:

> In explanation of my hesitation about joining the crowd of secretaries who are besieging the authorities for permission to go home, let me say right off that it is not due to any lukewarmness of desire to see the home folks and especially my dearest Mother. What wouldn't I give to be with you this moment! But the opportunities for my kind of "Y" work are vastly greater now than when the war was going on. The men's minds are freer; they are bound to have more leisure; the need for the proclamation of the gospel is unparalleled. I don't suppose there ever was such a need or vast an opportunity. As far as the Seminary

is concerned, I don't see a tremendous amount of use in landing in the middle of the term. Of course I ought to work on my Sprunt Lectures, and I don't suppose I shall be able to get down to that over here. But under the circumstances, especially since I do not know whether I could secure my release even if I wanted to, I think that I ought to stick to my work here for the present. Of course any day may bring a fundamental change in the situation, which may hasten my homecoming. Meanwhile I am eager for a chance at something other than the canteen service in which I have been engaged most of the time.

I feel sure, my dearest Mother, that you will appreciate the opportunities of preaching the gospel when there are so few to do this work. You know how well some of the sacrifice you have made has turned out. And of course nothing permanent is determined on. I shall be guided, I hope rightly, by circumstances.

I am signed up for the period of the war. The "Y" therefore can hold me. It would be a *favor* to release me. And I believe that the reasons for my going home at once are not quite so imperative as those that prevail in the cases of the vast majority of the secretaries. For example the vast majority are married and have children; the vast majority have work that can be taken up equally well at any time of the year; many are pastors—and you know the special danger of the protracted absence of a pastor. Furthermore, I do not know that any secretaries—except those who were engaged only for a definite period—are being sent home as yet. So a little patience is needed.

Have you engaged your passage for this summer? This, I am afraid, is a joke. I fear it will be difficult to secure passports for European travel this summer. There are too many millions of soldiers to be moved. But before very long Europe will have need of the tourist industry again. What times we shall have!

Sometimes a longing for the mountains comes over me that is almost like a passion. I hate to see the best mountaineering years of my life slipping by unused. The passion grows on me, instead of diminishing, as physical vigor declines. Sometimes I imagine that I am just starting up for some great peak on one of those frosty Alpine mornings. I tremble with delight at the thought of the joys alone. But the subsequent plunge into the humdrum of mere lowland life is cruel deception. The air of the heights is to me more intoxicating than wine.

> Home and the mountains—on account of early training the two will always be associated in my heart. I shall never stand on a great height without thinking of the times when we followed the shadow of the Castles or of Mount Madison up across the great ravines of the White Mountains. The love of the mountains in me comes from same source where I have derived everything else worth while--namely from Mother.

There were to be no further trips to Europe with his mother, and many years were to pass, nearly a decade, before he himself would find opportunity of returning to Europe. As his mother became more infirm and his own duties more pressing, these delights had to be denied. And indeed his devotion to his mother was such that he was loath to leave her, especially during the long summer vacations, unless the most urgent summons came to him. And thus at the end of the war only a strong sense of duty kept him in Europe for a time; if he had consulted only his personal inclinations, he would have rushed home by the fastest mode of travel.

Machen had kept in close touch with Armstrong as to his possible responsibility to return to Princeton as soon as possible, at the same time setting forth the considerations which commended his remaining for a time in France. To this letter Armstrong replied on Dec. 18, 1918, as follows:

> Your letter begun on the 8th of Nov. and completed on the 12th came a day or two ago. I wrote you recently but I'll send this along to tell you about the situation here.
>
> So far as the Seminary and myself are concerned you need give yourself no anxiety. As I wrote you, I shall be glad beyond expression when you are back again and we can take up our work together, and that for many reasons which I shall not stop to retail.
>
> But the point is this. I can get along and the classes can get along for the remainder of the year. If new men should come in after the holidays it might be necessary to organize and conduct courses for them through the second term; but at most that would mean only two additional hours and I can manage that...
>
> This however is intended simply to relieve your mind of an anxiety so that you may feel, so far as the situation here is concerned, quite free to remain and carry on your work should it seem wise to you to do so. But if for any reason you should determine to return, your place is here for you and a warm welcome and opportunity for work. And I must confess that, selfish though

it is, I like to contemplate the latter course as a possibility. What it would mean to the Seminary you would appreciate better if you could see the need. What it would mean to me—well, if anything as good as that happened, I might in the enthusiasm of the experience shake off the lethargy which has held me now for the whole long year.

So take this note instead of a friendly chat and don't postpone too long that for which it is but a poor substitute.

We are all well and send love.

As ever,
Army

Machen's own comment on this letter, in one to his mother on Jan. 25, 1919, was that "a most satisfactory letter has just arrived from Army—expressing just that mixture of willingness to have me stay over here and warm desire to have me in Princeton which puts me most at my ease. If there is or ever was on this earth a better fellow than Army I have yet to hear of him."

Life at the Seminary was as a matter of fact rather abnormal during that period. The enrollment was reduced by the engagement of men in war service of one kind or another. The Senior class held its own fairly well with 44 students; the middlers numbered only 24, and there was a mere handful of juniors—ten to be exact. In the course of the year, when Dr. Stevenson went abroad under the auspices of the Y.M.C.A., Dr. Warfield again became the leader of the Faculty and according to reports which reached Machen was enjoying the responsibility. Meanwhile, however, Machen met Dr. Stevenson in Paris, and found him most cordial and eager to use his influence to advance the program of preaching upon which Machen had embarked.

ITINERANT PREACHING

Concerning this itinerant preaching activity not much detail need be set forth. It is an understatement to observe that the opportunity was most welcome, and that it was seized with enthusiasm. Although the response was not always what Machen hoped for, frequently he had a sense of engaging in the work with marked evidences of divine blessing. Vigorous activity was carried on in the camps from various centres including Tours, Saumur, Angers, Le Mans and Chaumont. In a letter written on Dec. 28, 1918, he told of one exceptionally encouraging service near Le Mans:

The large room was full; there seemed to be no eagerness for mere amusement. I preached on Rom. 8:31. After the meeting

I talked a long time to one fellow in particular who has been going through agony of soul in his effort to find peace with God. It made me think of Pilgrim's Progress. Well, I never before knew what the preaching of the gospel is. The Y.M.C.A. men who assisted me in the service thought I had missed a great opportunity in not calling for some kind of expression on the part of those who were touched by the gospel message. But when I was talking I did not know that it was anything more than an ordinary meeting, though I did get unusually good attention from the boys. There was certainly very little of mine in the sermon. But the grace of God still finds an answer in the human heart.

At a later stage he gives a picture of his activity in more general terms.

At Bussières I had occasion to go to see the village Curé in order to ask him to let the Protestant chaplain have some of his wafers for the Sunday communion service. When I went in he was engaged in teaching Greek and Latin to two little boys —the village school not providing the instruction in those languages necessary for the lycee or the college. It was like a picture out of countless French biographies and novels. The curé was very gracious about the wafers, but asked me how I interpreted "Hoc est corpus meum," and also why the clause, "He descended into hell" is omitted from the Apostles' Creed in a little book of devotion intended for the use of the American soldiers. About the latter point, I could assure him that I disapproved as much as he did of the mutilation of the creed.

But it is time to speak of my work. Beginning with Monday night I have spoken every evening during the week so far, and the series of services is to be continued through Sunday. The services are under the care of the chaplain, Chaplain Whyman, a Methodist minister, with whom I get along fine. Like Chaplain Williams, with whom I was associated last week, Chaplain Whyman believes in dignity in connection with religious services, and an avoidance of too much calling for a show of hands and the like. So far the services have been fairly well attended, but we have not succeeded very well in reaching the non-Church members. This latter circumstance is of course a bit discouraging, but the chaplain agrees with me in exalting the function of conserving the spiritual life of the Christian men as the best preparation for future evangelization. He seems to think that I have been able to give the boys some of the solid instruction that they want and need. In addition to the evening service, we have started a little Bible class which meets in my room in the afternoon.

Our "singer" is inclined to want to be a speaker on his own hook, and contributes a little more fun and "pepe" than at times we might desire; but perhaps, rightly guided, it is all for the best.

Breakfast is at 6:15 A.M. That is the most military breakfast hour that I have yet encountered.

Don't imagine us as holding the services in a finely equipped Y.M.C.A. hut such as you will find in the camps at home. On the contrary we count ourselves unusually fortunate in having a shack with dirt floor, dimly lighted with candles and with just the edge taken off the chill by wood stoves. Life in the American army in these little villages is undoubtedly rough for the men in the ranks. But the boys are hardened to it.

My barrel contains only six talks. Yet here I have to speak seven times to the same crowd. Poor old Dassy!

CULTURAL PURSUITS

One should not suppose, however, that during the period following the armistice and prior to his departure for America on March 2nd, 1919, there was time for nothing save his evangelistic and educational activity. In connection with his travels there were opportunities for seeing fascinating parts of France that he had not visited previously. And since his specific assignments at the most required several hours a day in contrast with the grueling program during the war, he could again find time for reading. Moreover, between assignments there were often intervals in Paris where he could avail himself of the cultural advantages of the city. As a matter of course he sought out the lecture halls where the leading Biblical scholars of France were being heard. But above all he became absorbed with the study of France, its history, literature, art and architecture, regretting that he had not done so in earlier life, and determined, now that he was in the midst of it, not to allow this opportune time to be lost. After he had been at Tours and had "unfeignedly" admired the cathedral there, and had begun to steep himself in French history and literature, he wrote on Dec. 5, 1918:

It is a sense of profound regret to me that my appreciation of the beautiful things of Europe and my interest in history have been awakened so late in life—after so many of the opportunities for enjoyment and enlightenment are past. This is the sixth time that I have been in Europe. Before this time I engaged in considerable sightseeing, which I enjoyed and the memory of which will always be with me. But not till this time did the enjoyment of a Gothic church become a passion, and never before did I feel that life was too short to read what I am eager to read. Along with a certain lamentable decline in "pep," and hopeful ambition, and the desire to *do* things, has come a new desire to *receive*—to receive an intellectual equipment which will never be of any immediate use. A perverse desire has come over me to steep myself in the history of the renaissance of the "grand siècle" instead of preparing my Sprunt lectures. But I am entirely ignorant, and in need of the most elementary instruction. I am just finishing the perusal of an "Esquisse d'une histoire de France" by Cavaignac, recommended by the intelligent matron who runs the leading bookstore of the town. Dear me, before I read that book I hardly knew the difference between Saint Louis and Louis-Philippe! Today I came away from the bookstore with "Le Siècle de Louis XIV" by Voltaire and a volume of Brunetiere's "Histoire de la Littérature francaise" under my arm. I have not the slightest idea whether these are the food I need . . .

At the beginning of Voltaire's history, in exalting the age of Louis XIV the author says that when Louis XIII came to the throne there were not yet four beautiful buildings in Paris, and as for the other cities of the realm they resembled those towns which are to be seen across the Loire. In short there was nothing but "grossièrteté gothique." Considering that France has passed through an age so sure of its inerrancy of taste the only wonder is that there are now any remnants of mediaeval splendor. The older things have been preserved almost by accident—like the château at Blois where the fortunate death of Gaston d'Orleans is commemorated by the ragged edge where his destruction was left off.

One afternoon I went to Marmontier across the river, with its memories of St. Gatieu and Martin of Tours, and its remnants of the great monastery. Another day I visited Le Plessis-les-Tours, but the château and grounds are now used as a vaccine institute and strictly forbidden to all except physicians. I wanted to make the acquaintance of old Lous XI, as Scott introduces him at the beginning of Quentin Durward, which always seemed to me one of the most interesting scenes in all the range of the Waverly novels.

As for reading, the question is where to begin. Shall I investigate Jeanne d'Arc, as she had her banner made here at Tours, of shall I assist in the murder of the duc de Guise in the chateau, at Blois, or shall I sink myself in the "grand siecle" as I was anxious to do after reading "Le bourgeoise gentilhomme"?

Among the French works which he read were not only this play by Moliere but many others of a classical character. And then as the opportunity presented itself he saw the plays enacted. The play mentioned he found delightful, and, in the telling of it, he made a remark which will prove of special interest to those who had the privilege of hearing him give his elocution stunt: "The scene where the 'maître de philosophie' sets forth the principles of elocution reminds me vividly of that London elocutionist who taught us to pop our p's. But if I started calling attention to the things that made me chuckle particularly in that play there would be no time to give you further news." Another play of Moliere's which was to please him greatly some time later was "Le Misanthrope." With regard to it he wrote that he had to confess that "in order to attain the full comprehension of the play I needed the magnificent rendition of it on the stage. But now it has become a possession for life. It is different from such plays as 'Le Bourgeois Gentilhomme,' 'Tartuffe' and 'L'Avare' where a character is held up for pure ridicule or execration. Here you smile at the dear old 'misanthrope,' but before the play is over you love him too."

Other dramatic works that proved of interest included *Esther* and *Les Plaideurs* by Racine, *L'Arlesienne* by Daudet; *Le Mariage de Figaro* by Beaumarchais; and *Horace* by Corneille. On one occasion he comments upon his delight in the last-named writer. He became interested in Corneille when reading the large history of classical French literature. And having been constrained to buy a volume of his works, he declared: "It is great. I love to sit up in my room and spout it all to myself. When nobody is near to embarrass me by criticism it really seems to *me* that my rendition of heroic verse is fully as good as that of the best artists of the Comèdie francaise! At any rate I take as much pleasure in it."

He was also reading Pascal and Bossuet and other writers, and was spending some time in the libraries reading theological literature. What a feast he was enjoying! There was a boyish enthusiasm about it all as well as good taste and discriminating criticism. He knew life and beauty as God's gift and was profoundly thankful for them, and was a more effective servant of God because of it.

RELIGIOUS LIFE IN PARIS

One may also appropriately take note of a few impressions which Machen received of the religious and theological life of Paris. His own speaking engagements on Sunday prevented him from frequent attendance upon the services in the churches. Soon after his arrival in France, he had gone to hear one of the celebrated preachers of the day, M. Alfred Monod, at the Oratoire. His text was, "Give us this day our daily bread," but the sermon was concerned principally with a loyal use of the bread rationing system. Machen was disappointed because while "all perfectly good in its way," it was not at all "the bread of life."

Later he was to hear a good sermon at the Temple du Saint-Esprit —"very different from the Monod variety." It was a sermon on the New Jerusalem, and the central thought was that it "comes from heaven—it is not a product of human civilization, but a gift of the grace of God. The sermon was more than good—in places it was really eloquent. And it was very timely in these days." Two weeks later he went back to the Oratoire to hear Monod, and heard another sermon on a text from the Book of Revelation. It proved to be in marked contrast with the sermon on the New Jerusalem. The crowd to his regret was, however, at the Oratoire. At this time he also remarked upon the service in general: "How dreadfully poor the French Reformed liturgy is! Unlike the liturgy of the English Episcopal Church it seems studiously to avoid the great verities of the faith, notably the atoning death of our Saviour!"

He was also seeking out opportunities of hearing the leading New Testament scholars of France. On Jan. 12, 1919, he wrote:

> One day I went to the French Protestant Faculty, and attended two classes of Goguel, the New Testament professor. He is very wrong in his views, I regret to say. Among the students were two fellows from Strassburg, where they had been students at the University before the German professors were deported... What wouldn't I give for a few hours' pillage in the theological bookstores of Strassburg? Absolutely no German theological works since the war are obtainable here, and we received in America only the books up to the early part of 1916. My Sprunt lectures will be out of date if I write them before I can get access to the current literature.
>
> Yesterday morning I attended a lecture by the famous Loisy at the Collège de France. He is now no longer the Abbe Loisy, his connection with the Catholic Church having been terminated.

And no wonder it has been terminated! It was rather interesting to see a man who has been so much in the public eye, and a man whose books are exceedingly important even though they are not true. He is a little weazened old bit of a man, with a funny little stuttering voice. To get his permission to attend the lecture (which by the way proved unnecessary, the lectures at the College de France being public) I went up to his apartment in the Rue des Ecoles, where I was pleasantly received. The subject of the course was just what is most interesting to me at the present time, L'Apotre Paul et le Christianisme judaisant. I have just been studying Loisy's recent book on Galatians, which I had not seen in America. Also I attended a lecture at the Sorbonne (on a less interesting subject) just to see what it was like. I have a ticket for the Bibliotheque Nationale, but have unfortunately had little time to make use of it, the library being open only during the few hours of daylight. I wish I could get to work on my Sprunt lectures.

A week later he told of hearing Guignebert at the Sorbonne and finding him "very shallow and rather flippant." Another radical was Dujardin who, in dealing with the origin of the Eucharist, "seemed to have some wild idea about a pre-Christian 'Jesus-cult,' after the manner of Drews or W. B. Smith." In addition to such lectures in the field of religion he heard a variety of lectures on such subjects as Alsace and Lorraine, de Musset and German socialism.

On the eve of his departure for home his suit-case finally turned up! But it proved a bitter disappointment after all, because it contained almost nothing of the things that he had thought he had put in it. His most prized personal possessions of the earlier days of his war experience were gone for good. But he had little time to linger sadly over such losses as he prepared for the journey home. The prospect of reunion with his mother and other loved ones at home afforded an almost ecstatic joy. And there was the sterner note of the summons to return to his post at Princeton and to face the challenging demands that were to be his as a minister in the Presbyterian Church.

15

IN POST-WAR AMERICA

Upon his return from France Machen entered with new enthusiasm and energy upon the tasks which awaited him. Matured and broadened by his experiences, he had gained poise and assurance to meet the varied situations that were to challenge him to enter upon a position of leadership in the Seminary and in the Church. He was still very young compared with most of his colleagues in the Seminary —not yet thirty-eight—and was inconspicuous and largely unknown so far as the life of the Church as a whole was concerned. And when one considers his modesty and restraint, which were the more remarkable because of the strength of his own convictions, it is clear that Machen could not have foreseen the prominent role which he was to fill in the march of things to come. He did not ambitiously grasp after a place of special honor. But he was as it were caught up in the crucible of history and assigned a greater and greater prominence as he responded conscientiously and diligently to the demands that were made upon him.

THE WAR IN RETROSPECT

Though overjoyed at his return home the aftermath of the war could not bring repose to one who had been so profoundly and poignantly involved and concerned with its issues. That the peace for which he had longed ardently and greeted with ecstasy would evidently not usher in a new era of justice for all filled him with grief. This is reflected, for example, in one of the first letters his mother wrote after his return to Princeton, a letter dated May 1, 1919, which included the following touching observation:

> Dear son, you must not be disappointed in me if I do not agonize over all the struggling nations in Europe or even all that goes amiss in our own government. I try to take a tolerably intelligent interest in the making of history now going on so vigorously. But my own life is so filled with small endurances, sacrifices, anxieties, self-abnegations that surely it is not wrong for me to leave in God's hands the "groanings and travailings to-

gether" of the great world. I wish I could exercise more of the same spirit in regard to my own private affairs. But my heart is so sensitive and my body so insufficient for these things, that I sometimes miss the peace that was Christ's parting benediction to His disciples.

Machen's following letter reveals his attitudes more specifically. He was alarmed at the "vindictiveness and unfairness" toward the Germans that was coming to expression in America, and which he had noted, for example, in an address by an American naval officer at the Nassau Club. And the peace treaty was far worse than his fears with regard to it: "The war for humanity, so far as its result is concerned, looks distressingly like an old-fashioned land-grab. It is very unfair to the men who laid down their lives for the founding of a better society."

Several days later his mother wrote to explain her own position more precisely. "I do agree with you," she wrote, "in many things, and I am most emphatically a sort of political agnostic in others. I agree with you in thinking the terms for Germany too hard—they overreach themselves for one thing. Also, it looks to me like a horrible muddle which may never be straightened out without more struggle and strife. And I who will not live to see the end of it and who have no influence—I cannot and must not agonize over it all." There the matter rested so far as their written exchanges were concerned for some time. But at a later stage of developments, when the action of the Reparation Commission became known, he had new occasion to express his dismay at the turn of events. He felt that this action "removes all hope of a real settlement in Europe. Any indemnity, however large, would have left a door of hope; but a practical confiscation of Germany's exports for 42 years will make it impossible for Germany to get to work at all. The settlement is the result of the devilish French policy of obtaining security by keeping the rest of Europe in starvation. It is a dangerous game."

Several years later Machen took occasion to protest publicly against one development that grew out of the provisions of the Versailles Treaty with regard to a minority racial group. Italy which had been assigned control over South Tyrol under the treaty instituted a policy discontinuing instruction in German and forbidding the operation of German language schools in certain areas. The German government had made certain protests, and the New York *Herald Tribune* editorially had stated apropos these complaints that Italy was within her rights "in Italianizing school instruction in south Tyrol." Quite apart from the strictly legal aspects of the matter, Machen, whose knowledge of the region had been enlarged by his visits to Tyrol, was aroused because of the tyranny involved. His letter of Feb. 10, 1926, which was published in the *Herald Tribune,* concluded with the following paragraph:

> You are incensed by the protest that has been made in behalf of the Tyrol by Germany. But what has the attitude of Germany or what have the past sins of Germany to do with the real question now at issue? The oppression of the Tyrol does, indeed, concern the kinsfolk of those oppressed people north of the Alps; but it also concerns the people of the whole world. It concerns the people of the whole world because a policy like the one which Italy has followed in the Tyrol since the Treaty of Versailles constitutes an attack upon international and interracial peace. So long as such things are condoned or commended war will follow upon war in a wearisome succession; when they are condemned by a truly universal public sentiment which even dictators shall be obliged to respect, not merely in the countries immediately interested but in all the countries of the world, then, and then only, shall we have peace.

Machen thus displays again his strong sense of justice, his aversion to tyranny in every realm, his zeal to protect the rights of the weak and oppressed. His hatred of war was intense, and he was far from taking the position that it was inevitable or that it ought to be asquiesced in. But to his mind even worse than war itself, and the awful carnage of it, was the loss of liberty it involved or carried in its wake. Though he had come to regard the cause of the allies in the great war as just, he mourned the lack of vision and of zeal for justice in places of leadership that were manifested afterward. And nothing distressed him as much as the evidence at home and abroad of a readiness to sacrifice liberty for the sake of material prosperity.

THE CHURCH IN THE WAR

As Machen envisaged the situation after the war, however, his deepest concern was with the Church's approach to the problems of life rather than with political or social agencies. An exceptionally gratifying opportunity to disclose what was on his mind and heart in this regard was given when he was invited to be one of the speakers at the alumni luncheon held in connection with the Princeton Seminary commencement on May 6, 1919. Although his address was only about ten minutes long, the manner in which it was received encouraged him as nothing had in a long time. "Evidently," he wrote his mother, "there are some people left who still believe in the grace of God in Christ." It warmed his heart also "to be with a body of men who can unite with me in their prayers." He was impressed with Princeton as he had never been before, and he expressed the hope that the younger graduates would continue to preach the same gospel.

The address was published a few weeks later in *The Presbyterian* under the title "The Church in the War," and proved to be a timely and ringing affirmation and defense of the gospel of divine grace. Since the war it had been widely alleged that the church had failed the men in the armed forces and was failing the post-war generation. Much of this criticism Machen found extreme and unjust. But he could not overlook the many evidences of failure. Fortunately, however, said Machen,

> if the church has failed, it is at least perfectly clear why she has failed. She has failed because men have been unwilling to receive and the church has been unwilling to preach the gospel of Christ crucified. Men have trusted for their own salvation and for the hope of the world in the merit of their own self-sacrifice rather than in the one act of sacrifice which was accomplished some nineteen hundred years ago by Jesus Christ. That does not mean that men are opposed to Jesus. On the contrary, they are perfectly ready to admit him into the noble company of those who have sacrificed themselves in a righteous cause. But such condescension is as far removed as possible from the Christian attitude. People used to say, "There was no other good enough to pay the price of sin." They say so no longer. On the contrary, any man, if only he goes bravely over the top, is now regarded as plenty good enough to pay the price of sin.
>
> Obviously this modern attitude is possible only because men have lost sight of the majesty of Jesus' person. It is because they regard him as a being altogether like themselves that they can compare their sacrifice with his. It never seems to dawn upon them that this was no sinful man, but the Lord of glory who died on Calvary. If it did dawn upon them, they would gladly confess, as men used to confess, that one drop of the precious blood of Jesus is worth more, as a ground for the hope of the world, than all the rivers of blood which have flowed upon the battlefields of France.

This Christian conception of the majesty of Jesus' person was to be regained, Machen continued, only as there is a conviction of sin, only as men, like Peter and the dying thief and Paul, contrast the holiness of Jesus with their own sinfulness. The leading characteristic of the present age, however, is "a profound satisfaction with human goodness." The war had advanced this spirit because in their indignation against the sins of the enemy men have been in the moral danger of losing sight of their own sinfulness. Moreover, the sense of a great achievement in winning the war served to blunt the sense of sin. But the deepest roots of this modern spirit of self-satisfaction lay in something deeper,—in nothing less than "the substitution of paganism for Christianity as the dominant principle of life." Whereas paganism "finds its ideal simply in a healthy and harmonious and joyous development of existing human faculties," Christianity is "the religion of the broken heart." Christianity is not merely that. For the Christian "the guilt has been removed once for all by God," and he may now proceed "without fear to develop every faculty which God has given him." Christianity therefore does not end with the broken heart but it does begin with it.

It may be very attractive to preach to men, and say, "You men are very good and very self-sacrificing, and we take pleasure in revealing your goodness to you. Now, since you are so good, you will probably be interested in Christianity, especially in the life of Jesus, which we believe is good enough even for you." But that preaching is useless; it is useless to call the righteous to repentance. But there is another kind of preaching, and with this Machen concluded his message:

> But it is hard for men to give up their pride. How shall we find the courage to require it of them? How shall we preachers find courage to say, for example, to the returning soldiers, rightly conscious as they are of a magnificent achievement: "You are sinners like all other men, and like all other men you need a Saviour." It looks to the world like a colossal piece of impertinence. Certainly we cannot find the courage in any superior goodness of our own. But we can find the courage in the goodness and in the greatness of Christ.
>
> Certainly the gospel puts a tremendous strain upon Jesus of Nazareth. The gospel means that instead of seeking the hope of the world in the added deeds of millions of the human race throughout the centuries, we seek it in one act of one Man of long ago. Such a message has always seemed foolish to the wise men of this world. But there is no real reason to be ashamed of it. We may feel quite safe in relinquishing every prop of human goodness in order to trust ourselves simply and solely to Christ. The achievements of men are very imposing. But not in comparison with the Lord of glory.

When I survey the wondrous cross
On which the Prince of glory died,
My richest gain I count but loss,
And pour contempt on all my pride.

Machen's appearance before the Princeton alumni and the publication of his address in *The Presbyterian* served to bring to the attention of wide areas of the Presbyterian Church the fact that there was a young professor at Princeton who was to be reckoned with. He knew what he believed, believed the gospel with all his heart, and was singularly effective in its public proclamation. It is not surprising therefore that he was much more in demand as a preacher and popular lecturer than had been true in the earlier stages of his career following his licensure. By the year 1920 he was frequently invited to supply the pulpits of large and influential churches especially in the Northern Presbyterian Church. And the number of his speaking engagements of other sorts was growing apace. He was thankful for such opportunities and filled his engagements with enthusiasm.

As the foregoing has shown, however, his enthusiasm was tempered by a sober and even anxious estimate of the state of the church as a whole. When therefore he was elected as a commissioner to the General Assembly of 1920 at the Spring meeting of the Presbytery of New Brunswick, he was not animated by a spirit of self-congratulation or elation. It was a distinction, but he felt that there was less interest than usual in the outcome of the elections since the choice involved a trip merely to nearby Philadelphia rather than, as often, the opportunity of travel to a distant and more novel locale. Moreover, though this was to be his first Assembly, he did not relish the prospect of the busy routine of meetings that membership in the Assembly involved. But his basic mood was one of profound disquietude as to the state of the Presbyterian Church. He had come to recognize, as his address before the alumni also underscored, that there had been a drift away from the moorings of the gospel in the Protestant churches, and that various evils attendant upon the war had accelerated this movement. There had been a marked growth in recent years of outspoken and blatant denials of the truths of Christianity and, what was even more alarming, a widespread indifference on the part of men of evangelical profession to this debilitating trend. It was in this latitudinarian atmosphere that vague movements for church union and cooperation flourished rather than sturdy commitment to the historic creeds. In the period preceding the Assembly the Inter-Church World Movement was in the foreground of attention, and gave expression to this tendency. And the fact that it gained considerable vogue in the

Presbyterian Church, and even made an appeal for a time to such a solid person as Machen's intimate friend "Bobby" Robinson, was evidence to Machen of the acute danger that was confronting the distinctive testimony of the Church to its Calvinistic confession and even to historic Christianity in general.

The distress at such tendencies in the Church was aggravated by the spirit of the times as it manifested itself in the life of the nation. Centralization and bureaucracy were growing rapidly, and there was a feverish outbreak of "100% Americanism." Machen confessed that at times he was "world weary" as he contemplated the situation. "When I turn for refuge to the Church of Christ," he wrote his mother on Jan. 28, 1920,

> I find there exactly the same evils that are rampant in the world —centralized education programs, the subservience of the church to the state, contempt for the rights of minorities, standardization of everything, suppression of intellectual adventure. At least it destroys my confidence in any human aid. I see more clearly than ever before that unless the gospel is true and there is another world, our souls are in prison. The gospel of Christ is a blessed relief from that sinful state of affairs commonly known as hundred per-cent Americanism. And fortunately some of us were able to learn of the gospel in a freer, more spiritual time, before the state had begun to lay its grip upon the education of the young.

To this his mother replied: "I don't believe you are more tired of hundred per-cent Americanism and the subservience of the church to the state than I am! And I am truly thankful that you hold on to the gospel of Christ, of which I am not ashamed. You are a son after my own heart in that."

THE 1920 PLAN OF UNION

The opening of the Assembly did nothing to allay Machen's fears. At a preliminary meeting on evangelism the impression received was that there was a greater emphasis upon Americanization than upon salvation in the modern missions program. And the main emphasis of the retiring moderator's address was upon "pseudo-patriotism." But the big issue of the Assembly was that of church union, and the action taken with regard to it was so distressing that everything else seemed in comparison with it to be a mere trifle. The opportunity of association with old friends had been delightful; the routine business had been tolerable; but as he wrote his mother:

> The great disaster and disgrace of the Assembly was the adoption of the plan of organic union with about twenty other church bodies. This action now goes down to the presbyteries to be ratified by them in order finally to become law. The Preamble of the Plan of Union sets forth the things in which all the constituent churches are to be agreed. Everything else is regarded as of secondary importance. The Preamble is studiously vague; a man could subscribe to the creed contained in it without believing in the essentials of the Christian faith. The action, if ratified, simply means that the Presbyterian Church, so far as its corporate action is concerned, will have given up its testimony to the truth . . .

To add to Machen's dismay the majority report of the committee on the church union proposal was presented by President J. Ross Stevenson of the Seminary! And there was a sense of outrage that a matter of such far reaching consequences had been allotted a total of only one hour for presentation and debate. In the ten minutes which the opposition managed to secure, a minority report opposing the plan was presented but to no avail.

Machen did not sleep much the night following the adoption of the report. "The defeat of the proposed Plan of Union in the presbyteries," he averred, "is the most important object now before the Church. I wish I could devote myself exclusively to that for a year." During the succeeding months he did indeed give himself unstintingly to this cause. No fewer than three articles from his pen on the subject appeared in *The Presbyterian*. He also engaged in public debate on a number of occasions. In view of its far-reaching implications for our understanding of later developments affecting Princeton Seminary and the Presbyterian Church, the story of this battle must be set forth in some detail.

The Plan of Union called for the erection of an organization to be known as "The United Churches of Christ in America." It did not contemplate actual union of the churches, for they were to retain their autonomy. A supervisory council, however, was to deal with questions that arose between the constituent denominations, and the ultimate goal was clearly that of church union. This movement was therefore a phase of the modern ecumenical movement.

The much-discussed Preamble to the Plan was as follows:

> Whereas we desire to share, as a common heritage, the faith of the evangelical Church which has from time to time found expression in great historic statements, and

> Whereas we all share belief in God the Father, in Jesus Christ His only Son, our Saviour; in the Holy Spirit, our guide and comforter; in the holy Catholic Church, through which God's eternal purpose of salvation is to be proclaimed and the kingdom of God realized in earth; in the Scriptures of the Old and New Testaments as containing God's revealed will; and in life eternal; and
>
> Whereas having the same spirit and owning the same Lord, we none the less recognize diversity of gifts and ministrations for whose exercise due freedom must always be offered in forms of worship and in modes of operation.

Machen's first published attack upon the Plan appeared as early as June 10, 1920, being a revision for publication of an analysis that had been prepared before the Assembly met. The action of the Assembly, if concurred in by the presbyteries, involved, he contended, "the substitution of vague generalities for our historic standards, as the expression of what we are to regard as fundamental in our faith." Examining the Preamble in detail, he observed that sharing the great historic statements of the faith "as a common heritage" is by no means equivalent to accepting them as true. The language of the second paragraph, he noted, was "studiously vague and colorless: there was, for example, no clear statement of the deity of our Lord or of the deity or personality of the Holy Spirit. And the declaration regarding the Scriptures, in using the word "containing," allowed for subscription by one "who accepts as the revealed will of God only a single sentence of the entire Bible." Summing up he noted that the statement omitted "not some, but practically all, of the great essentials of the Christian faith—all those things which are dearest to the heart of the man who has been redeemed by the blood of Christ."

Most disquieting of all he found the final paragraph of the Preamble, the paragraph concerned with "Autonomy in purely denominational affairs."

> For among the purely denominational affairs are placed the "creedal statements" of each constituent church. Is the Westminster Confession a purely denominational affair? It is a purely denominational affair to those who believe that it is merely one expression of the progressive Christian consciousness. That is the point of view of the "Plan of Union." It is not a purely denominational affair to those who believe it to be true. Those who believe it to be true will never be satisfied until it has been accepted by the whole world, and will never consent to be limited

> in the propagation of it by any church or union of churches whatsoever . . .
>
> Co-operation is certainly possible even with Christians who are in very serious error with regard to many important matters. But co-operation under the present plan involves unfaithfulness to our Lord. It means simply that the campaign of witnessing which in Acts 1:8 is put as the main business of the church has, so far as the corporate action of our Presbyterian Church is concerned, been abandoned.

Though developments at the Assembly, in view of Dr. Stevenson's intimate and conspicuous association with the Plan of Union, pointed up the presence of a deep cleavage within the Faculty of Princeton Seminary, Machen did not have to wait long before he received assurance of hearty agreement with his viewpoint from several colleagues. On the very day that his article was published in *The Presbyterian,* Dr. Warfield sent the following note: "I have read your article in today's Presbyterian on the Union proposals with great comfort. I do not want to let it pass without explicitly expressing my thanks to you for writing it, and for what you have written in it." And on July 26th, Dr. W. Brenton Greene, Jr., writing from Newport, said:

> My dear Dr. Machen,
>
> I regret that I have been so slow in writing you how delighted I was with your criticism in the Presbyterian of the Basis of Union. I do not see how it could have been clearer, more timely or more to the point. To me it seems to leave nothing to be added or strengthened. To some of us, at least, such a union as that proposed would appear inconceivable, had it not been conceived. It is unspeakably sad to me that a church of Christ could ignore a doctrine so essential and distinctive as the resurrection of the body.
>
> With many thanks, I am
>
> Cordially yours,
> W. Brenton Greene, Jr.

Nor was the support of Dr. Machen's opposition to the Plan of Union restricted to private communications. For in the course of the next year *The Presbyterian* published articles from the pens of Professors Warfield, Greene, Hodge, and Allis, all condemning the proposed plan on doctrinal grounds. Warfield pointed out that there was nothing at all evangelical in the creedal statement. Allis stressed the fact that it omitted all reference to the cross of Christ.

FOR CHRIST OR AGAINST HIM

Another effective blow was struck by Machen in an article which appeared in *The Presbyterian* on Jan. 20, 1921, under the title, "For Christ or Against Him." Its effectiveness was due to the fact that he was able to lay bare the specifically modernist background of the vague doctrinal statement of the Plan. This was done by setting forth at some length the doctrinal position of Dr. George W. Richards, a minister in the Reformed Church in the U. S., who was chairman of the Committee on Deputations of the American Council on Organic Union, and who was recognized as largely responsible for drawing up the proposed plan. Machen brought out the fact that in an article entitled, "The Necessity of Reconstruction," that had appeared in 1914, Dr. Richards had disclosed basic agreement with the modern theological viewpoints of Schleiermacher and Ritschl. Richards not only openly repudiated the doctrine that the Bible is "God's Book, because he was its author," but also disclosed his thoroughgoing hostility or indifference to the orthodox doctrines of God, Christ and salvation. The pervasively anti-doctrinal, modernist character of this viewpoint was summed up in the characterization of Christianity as a life. To this evaluation Machen replied, in concluding this article, as follows:

> If that be true, then God help us! We are then still in our sins. If Christianity is a life, if we have to appeal for our standing before God to our lives, then we are of all men most miserable. For our lives are sinful. But, thank God, Christianity is not a life, but a life founded upon a message, an account of the blessed act of God by which the Lord Jesus Christ took our place and died for our sins once for all on the cross. If so, the Book of Acts is correct; the business of the church is a campaign of witnessing. And the witnessing, if the church is faithful, must be true witnessing. But if the organized church accepts the programme of the new plan of union, under the lead of Dr. Richards, it is engaging in an anti-Christian propaganda; wherever its missions may extend it is giving men a false answer to the question, "What must I do to be saved?"

Following the publication of his second article on the union issue, Machen was again encouraged by the warm support of his respected senior colleagues. He had gotten it out under great pressure as he was in the throes of getting off to Richmond for the delivery of his Sprunt lectures, and it was heartening to be assured of their agreement. On Jan. 30th, ten days after the article appeared, he wrote his mother that "it is splendid to see the way my Princeton fathers and brethren have stood by me. Dr. Warfield wrote me a note about the article from his sick room, and Dr. Greene also wrote me a note. Army was right with me in the fight—also Wistar."

The battle had now developed in the presbyteries, and at first the tide had seemed to run in favor of the union plan. The issue in his own presbytery was naturally most crucial to Machen. He had been appointed as a member of a preliminary committee to prepare recommendations for the January meeting to consider, and met with other members—only three attended—in Trenton early in December. At the meeting Machen made, as he declared, "a speech as though I were addressing a town-meeting." The committee agreed unanimously to make an adverse report on the overture. This was encouraging, but was not necessarily indicative of the final result. However, ultimately there was a decisive victory for the viewpoint Machen had been vigorously advancing, as he reported in a letter of Jan. 30, 1921:

> My dearest Mother:
>
> The big fight in New Brunswick Presbytery is over. It occurred last Tuesday. I opened the debate against the overture on "Organic Union." A layman who had been at the Assembly spoke against me. Then the battle proceeded. The two chief speakers against us were Dr. Frank Palmer and Dr. Dixon, former secretary of the Home Board. Wistar Hodge made a most eloquent speech on our side, and also Dr. Davis. I had been a little afraid about Dr. Davis, but he came out magnificently for the Christian faith. In general I was deeply stirred by the utterances of the members of Presbytery. The debate made me feel anew the depth and reality of true Christian conviction. There are some Christian men left in the ministry, though the anti-Christian propagandists at times seem to be having everything their own way. The vote was 38 to 8 against the overture.

THE DEATH OF WARFIELD

In the midst of elation over the victory in his presbytery there came a crushing blow in the passing of Dr. B. B. Warfield on Feb. 16, 1921. The following day Machen recorded his profound sorrow:

> My dearest Mother:
>
> I am writing to tell you of the great loss which we have just sustained in the death of Dr. Warfield. Princeton will seem to be a very insipid place without him. He was really a great man. There is no one living in the Church capable of occupying one quarter of his place. To me, he was an incalculable help and

> support in a hundred different ways. This is a sorrowful day for us all.
>
> Dr. Warfield had been in poor health since Christmas, having suffered from shortness of breath ever since his attack. But yesterday he took one of his classes for the first time since his illness. He seemed to suffer no ill effects. But at eleven o'clock at night—after about twenty minutes of acute distress—he died.

Three days later he wrote of Warfield's funeral and recalled an extraordinary conversation that he had had with him a short time before his death:

> Dr. Warfield's funeral took place yesterday afternoon at the First Church of Princeton . . . It seemed to me that the old Princeton—a great institution it was—died when Dr. Warfield was carried out.
>
> I am thankful for one last conversation I had with Dr. Warfield some weeks ago. He was quite himself that afternoon. And somehow I cannot believe that the faith which he represented will ever really die. In the course of the conversation I expressed my hope that to end the present intolerable condition there might be a great split in the Church, in order to separate the Christians from the anti-Christian propagandists. "No," he said, "you can't split rotten wood." His expectation seemed to be that the organized Church, dominated by naturalism, would become so cold and dead, that people would come to see that spiritual life could be found only outside of it, and that thus there might be a new beginning.
>
> Nearly everything that I have done has been done with the inspiring hope that Dr. Warfield would think well of it. The thought that he at least would read my book has been with me all the time. I feel very blank without him. With all his glaring faults he was the greatest man I have known.

These words are illuminating in more than one respect. They confirm emphatically earlier impressions that in the course of time Warfield's influence upon Machen was even greater than Patton's had been. Each man made an extraordinary impact upon him. Without Patton's more spectacular gifts, his gracious hospitality reciprocating that shown him in the Machen home in Baltimore, and his unfailing sympathy with Machen in his early struggles—without these his perseverance at Princeton and his entrance upon the gospel ministry are inconceivable. But on the background of such influences the more profound impact upon Machen's life and thought was made by Warfield.

In breadth and depth of his scholarship and in clarity of vision with regard to the doctrinal and ecclesiastical issues of the day Warfield excelled Patton, and in these respects Machen's life and work marked him as a disciple of the former rather than the latter.

In one respect at least, however, Machen excelled Warfield. Though Warfield possessed a keen awareness of the issues of the day, he was a man of the study rather than of the ecclesiastical arena. Even before Warfield died, it began to appear that Machen, though also loving the quiet of study and library, was singularly effective as a man of action who was under a powerful sense of compulsion to fulfill his vows as a minister. No one could fail to observe that here was a man, if there was one anywhere, who was "zealous and faithful in maintaining the truths of the gospel, and the purity and peace of the church whatever persecution or opposition might arise unto him on that account." There was a void left by Warfield's death that no one could fill, but the mantle of his leadership before long appeared to have largely fallen upon Machen. There was no formal or deliberate choice of any man, and in the situation there was a strong sense of solidarity and co-operation. Machen least of all would have thought of himself as "the leader." But he undoubtedly came to occupy a position of leadership due simply to the incisiveness and the power of the blows that he struck for the cause of the Christian faith.

THE BROADER ARENA

Though the battle had been won in his own presbytery, Machen's activity in the cause had not come to an end. On February 14th he engaged in a public debate on the issue in Philadelphia, Dr. Matthew J. Hyndman, a member of the Presbytery of Philadelphia, being the spokesman for the organic union overture.

Another aspect of the controversy, however, was in certain respects even more significant than that which related directly to the decision in the presbyteries. That had to do with the emergence of a profound doctrinal difference within the faculty of the Seminary. The fact that Dr. Stevenson, the president of the Seminary, had presented the report of the committee in favor of the plan at the General Assembly in Philadelphia has been noted. Due to his absence in Europe at the end of the war, indeed, he had not been present at certain important meetings of the Committee. But he had agreed to present the report and was recognized in the ensuing struggle as one of its most influential supporters. And to add to the dismay at this revelation of a radical difference of viewpoint on an important matter of principle, in the course of time Dr. Erdman also came out in favor of the Plan.

It was on the eve of Dr. Warfield's burial that he made known his position in an address to the students of the Seminary. Machen was invited by the students to present the other side, and did so the following week. The drawing of lines of profound differences of viewpoint between Stevenson and Erdman on the one side and all or nearly all the rest on the other side was prophetic of things to come. For in the course of that decade, in 1929, the Seminary was reorganized as the result of the influence of Stevenson and Erdman in the Church at large, and this was to occasion the resignation of Machen and other colleagues from the faculty. The struggle of the early twenties is illuminating, among other ways, in that it displays so plainly that the underlying difference was a profoundly doctrinal one rather than one of personalities. Machen sought to persuade Erdman of the error of his position but without success.

Evidently the Committee on Deputations of the American Council on Organic Union came to realize that a powerful and somewhat successful attack had been made upon its position. Following up Dr. Richard's statement, which had been answered by Machen in his January article in the *Presbyterian,* a "Second Declaration" of the Ad Interim Committee was issued. When this was reported in the *Presbyterian,* Machen immediately telegraphed Dr. Kennedy, the editor, requesting him to send a copy of the Declaration. Upon receipt of it he at once set to work to prepare the article which appeared on March 17th. He showed that the new Declaration afforded no real assurance as to the Christian character of the union plan and movement. In view of the criticism that had been directed against its doctrinal platform, only a ringing declaration of such facts and doctrines as the vicarious atonement, the virgin birth and his bodily resurrection would have served to allay fear. But in the entire document of fourteen pages there was an avoidance of such affirmations. The Declaration did state that the Committee had given expression to some of "the great Christian truths held by all Christian believers." But taking fresh account of the Preamble, Dr. Machen observed that the "great Christian truths" are

> nothing but the well-known tenets of modern anti-Christian liberalism. The committee, it is said, gave expression to "some" of the great Christian truths. But why were just these truths chosen and others left out? Here again the answer is only too plain. Those truths are left out—the transcendence and omnipotence of God, the deity of Christ, the virgin birth, the resurrection, the atoning death—which could not be accepted by modern naturalism. Just those things which are under fire, then, are

> the things which are left out. To leave them out means capitulation to the deadliest enemy of Christianity and treason to the Lord who gave his life for us.

The Declaration had sought to defend the plan against the charge of minimizing the historic creeds of the church and the significance of acceptance of them by its declaration that the creeds were shared as a common heritage. This defence took the form of admitting that the declaration at this point was a concession to prevalent points of view. "A large body of Christians to be affected by the union," it declared, "do not believe in creedal statements as such, although they have sincere convictions as to the great Christian truths held by all Christian believers." The fact that those who did not believe in creeds were asked in the Plan to accept the historic creeds as a part of our common Christian heritage was stated further to be a mile-stone in the progress or development of the plan. Machen's answer was that it was indeed a mile-stone—a mile-stone on the way to complete skepticism, as had been previously indicated in the radical indifference to the question of the truth of the historic creeds, which found expression in the Preamble of the Plan.

In opposing the Plan and its defence as bluntly and vigorously as he did, Machen indicated that he was not denying that his opponents were deeply religious men, men of complete sincerity of conviction. And on the background of his own struggle for his faith, he gave expression to a certain "fellow-feeling for those who are constrained to adopt that naturalism which is characteristic of modern religious thought."

> But no good end is achieved by obscuring the issue. Modern naturalistic liberalism and Christianity are two distinct religions; they are not only different religions, but religions that belong to two entirely different categories . . . A man who decides for one decides against the other . . . The great controversy between the two ways of thinking will be carried on by spiritual weapons, it should be carried on in love, and the truth finally will prevail. But what is thoroughly evil, what leads to strife, bitterness, hypocrisy, and every evil thing, is a unity of organization which covers radical diversity of aim. Every man, whatever his way of thinking, should speak his mind fully and plainly, and should associate himself, not in a forced union, but with those with whom he is really and heartily agreed.

As a consequence of the effective campaign against the Plan of Union, it was defeated in the presbyteries. When the General Assembly met in May, 1921, it was reported that only 100 presbyteries had voted approval while 150 had declared themselves opposed. Thus the immediate battle was won but the same issue was to arise in one form or another during the coming years. The final vote in 1921 on the union issue was especially illuminating in pointing up a profound disunity not only within the life of the Presbyterian Church as a whole but also within the very body of men who constituted the Faculty of Princeton Theological Seminary. The developments within the Seminary and the Church in the ensuing years may be viewed as the crystallization of the drawing of lines that came into view in the union conflict of 1920-1921.

ARTHUR W. MACHEN
At about 75 years of age

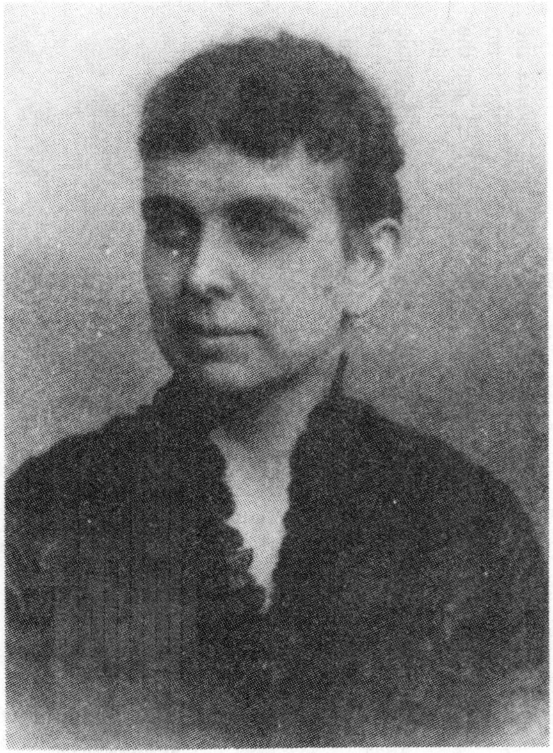

MRS. ARTHUR W. MACHEN
In her late fifties

after the forme
brilliant
Though

Macaulay
as an exam
more
mental

Howe
Volume and
work, perha
tion. As
tures delivered
mond, to
to service
return, and
well be post
was placed
His own
a revealing

If only
rice, he might

16

FIRST MAJOR BOOK

A climactic event in Machen's earlier career — occurring not long after the fortieth anniversary of his birth—was the publication of his brilliant book on *The Origin of Paul's Religion* in the year 1921. Though the designation *opus magnum* has to be reserved for *The Virgin Birth of Christ* published in 1930, the book on Paul, in the judgment of the biographer, excels in some respects even that volume whose preparation was a principal concern for about twenty-five years. It is considerably smaller than the later book, is less demonstrative of Machen's massive scholarship, and perhaps is somewhat less masterful as an example of fine scholarly writing. But it was dealing with a more comprehensive and more difficult theme—really with the fundamental question of the origin of Christianity. And the acute manner in which this question was analyzed, the clarity and vigor in which his discussion and argument were carried through from beginning to end, and the persuasiveness of his reasoning contribute to the verdict that it is a book of rare excellence.

Though we shall be concerned here with the publication of this volume and the reception accorded it in the Church and the scholarly world, perhaps even more interest attaches to the story of its preparation. As has been observed the book consisted substantially of lectures delivered on the Sprunt Foundation at Union Seminary of Richmond, to which Machen had been invited already in 1915. The call to service in the war had prevented any sustained activity until his return, and when it appeared that the date for their delivery could not well be postponed beyond the early weeks of the year 1921, Machen was placed under extraordinary pressure to do justice to the occasion. His own comments on various phases of this preparatory labor form a revealing and fascinating story in themselves.

EXACTING DEMANDS

If only Machen had not had anything else to do during this period, he might have been much more at ease. Our preceding pages have shown, however, that he was practically overwhelmed with a multiplicity of duties. Following his return home from the war he was under a severe burden in seeking to provide the pastoral care required by R.H., the former drunkard, and several exhausting trips had to be taken to deal with emergencies which arose. And the preceding chapter has indicated how absorbing and demanding of time and energy the church union battle had been for a period of somewhat over a year. He was preaching nearly every Sunday and oftentimes during the week. Of course there were also the constant demands made by his teaching schedule.

It was during this period also that his peace of mind was somewhat disturbed by invitations which, if accepted, would have taken him away from Princeton. One of these was from Dubuque and the other from Louisville. The former approach was undertaken by a friend from student days at Princeton onward, David Burrell, who was on the Faculty at Dubuque, and it was made on the authorization of Dr. Steffens, president of the institution. Evidently Machen did not require prolonged reflection to reach the decision that he could not see his way clear to accept this call.

Rather serious consideration was given for a time, however, to the approach made on behalf of Louisville (The Presbyterian Theological Seminary of Kentucky) by the president of the institution, Dr. C. R. Hemphill. As a student and faculty member at Columbia Seminary Hemphill had become acquainted with and had esteemed Machen's grandfather, Judge John J. Gresham, a director of that Seminary. On June 20, 1919, Hemphill wrote Machen that he had long had "a covetous eye" on him. It appears also that Harris Kirk was in touch with Dr. Hemphill, and was encouraging him in his desire to secure Machen's services for this Seminary which was partially under the supervision of certain synods of the Southern Church. In his reply Machen did not offer much encouragement, but he did add that he would not "like the impression to be fixed among my friends that I am determined to remain all my life at Princeton Seminary without careful consideration of opportunities of usefulness which may be offered to me elsewhere." Some time went by before this was followed up very definitely, but early in the year 1920 Dr. Hemphill wrote at length concerning Louisville and the opportunities it offered, and expressed the desire to see him. By this time, however, Machen felt more firmly bound to Princeton, its opportunities and its problems, and, as he informed his mother on Feb. 3, 1920, he asked Dr. Hemphill to drop consideration of his name. One factor influencing this decision may have been the fact that commencing with the fall of 1919

Machen had entered upon a period of greater satisfaction with the response to his teaching, which was partially indicated by the fact that considerably larger numbers of students than in the years prior to the war were enrolling in his elective courses. Moreover, he was just then engaged with the herculean task of preparing his Sprunt lectures, and he feared that if he changed the scene of his labors he would not be able to fulfill that appointment, supremely important to him, with the prospect of the publication of a solid book. One cannot doubt, furthermore, that his sense of commitment to the cause represented by Princeton in the great Christian conflict of the day was so profound that he could not have conceived of leaving Princeton without suffering a severe wrench. And one may not overlook the deep bonds of affection that united him with Armstrong, Hodge and other colleagues at Princeton.

ROMANCE

The unity of this chapter may not appear to be too seriously disturbed if, in addition to the matters mentioned above, space is given here to a reference to Machen's romantic life. The isolated mention of young women in his earlier letters does not, it must be confessed, provide a very firm basis for judging why he remained a bachelor. Nothing is clearer than that he was not a misogynist and that women found him attractive. His affection for and devotion to his mother was one of the most memorable characteristics of his life. But neither her attitude toward him nor his toward her was marked by a possessiveness which would have left little room for affection for other women. He was clearly very fond of many such members and friends of the family, and of the Armstrong and Hodge households. That he felt at ease in such company is also plain. Occasionally as a young man at Princeton he went out with girls, usually in company with male companions, on a picnic or to a concert. The prevailing impression, however, is that his romantic interests were not highly developed, and that for the most part he preferred the company of men and the opportunity of engaging in the various aspects of his life without incumbrances often attendant upon marriage. The example of his father and his older brother, moreover, may have influenced his attitude. Or the fact that they waited until they were forty or beyond to marry may disclose a distinctively Machen approach to the subject. One must most seriously allow for the possibility, however, that the real reason that Machen did not seriously pursue romance is that he did not, at least for many years, meet any available young woman who fascinated him.

On one occasion, in May, 1917, in connection with a visit to his cousin, the Rev. LeRoy Gresham, in Salem, Va., he preached at nearby Hollins College and was charmed by several members of the Senior Class to whom he was introduced. Somewhat facetiously he observed to his mother: "They are the only pretty girls—except that one cousin of mine in Sparta and one girl at Princeton now long married—whom I had seen for fifteen years. Had I enjoyed such advantages before I got too old, my life might have been different! It was really lots of fun. I wish I could preach to that same Senior class every Sunday, and join the class-meeting afterwards."

After the war the subject of marriage was mentioned somewhat more seriously on a few occasions in the exchange of letters between his mother and himself. In January, 1920, in connection with one of his preaching trips in New York State, he paid a call on a "Y.M.C.A. steamer acquaintance" with whom he had had some correspondence. He spoke at length of the enjoyable visit he had had, and of the lady as being vivacious and having lots of sense. But he seemed to think it necessary to warn his mother not to draw premature conclusions. For he added, "Do not, however, detect any possibility of an incipient romance!" His mother was quick to answer that she was glad that he had not dropped the friendship, and said, "I will not construct an 'incipient romance' out of it since you tell me not to, but, from your account of the girl and the family, it would not seem to be such a bad thing!"

There was however one real romance in his life, though unhappily it was not destined to blossom into marriage. One would never have learned of it from the files of his personal letters since it seems that he did not trust himself to write on the subject, extraordinary though that may seem when one considers how fully he confided in his mother. He did tell his brother Arthur about it, and in a conference concerning the projected biography in March, 1944, the elder brother told me that the story to be complete would have to include a reference to Gresham's one love affair. He identified the lady by name, as a resident of Boston, and as "intelligent, beautiful, exquisite." He further stated that apparently they were utterly devoted to each other for a time, but that the devotion never developed into an engagement to be married *because she was a Unitarian.* Miss S., as she may be designated, made a real effort to believe, but could not bring her mind and heart to the point where she could share his faith. On the other hand, as Arthur Machen hardly needed to add, Gresham Machen could not possibly think of uniting his life with one who could not come to basic agreement with him with regard to the Christian faith.

With the key provided by this conversation a number of items in Machen's correspondence receive a significance that they otherwise would not have had. She was known to his mother, apparently because she was wont with members of her family to take vacations at Seal Harbor. It is likely that Machen met her there, and this was certainly not later than the summer of 1920. On this background, Machen could refer to Miss S. in his letters to his mother without divulging his deeper thoughts and feelings. The first reference to her is in a letter of Oct. 31, 1920, in which he speaks of his expectation of taking Miss S. to see the Princeton-Harvard game in Cambridge after luncheon at the S. home. A week later he spoke of his enjoyment of the occasion, but nothing more. A number of similar, quite casual references, appear in later letters.

Meanwhile, his mother continued to occupy her supreme and unique place in his affections. On March 6, 1921, for example, he began a letter as follows:

> My dearest Mother,
>
> My own dear Mother, what could I ever do without you? Who else would cheer me up by some good letter just when I need cheering the most? Who else would treasure up all the good things that were ever said about me, and pass them on to me? What other letters could break in upon the dull monotony of life like your letters, and bring the only little touch of warmth and love?

Her own response was at once indicative of her profound enjoyment of such affection and of her unselfish concern for his lasting happiness. Her letter of March 10th began:

> My beloved Son,
>
> Since my letters to you give you such real satisfaction, I ought not to let my day slip by, as I did yesterday. It is certainly a joy to be first still in one heart, but a little pathetic for you, so that I find myself wishing that you could have a good wife, to understand you and share your work.

That Machen's mother knew far more than he or any one else suspected is shown incidentally by a remark in a letter of the following summer. Writing after he had left Seal Harbor she closed a letter with the following statement and observation:

> Miss S. paid me an evening visit and we talked a little about Bible-study and kindred topics, but I don't think I helped her much.

I know more about your perplexities than you expect, and everything that troubles you is redoubled in my heart.

Your own loving faithful mother,

M.G.M.

In addition to these data Machen's files bring to light perhaps two scores of letters from Miss S., several from the fall and winter of 1920-21, and others at infrequent intervals through the years that followed. None is exactly a love letter: they contain no particular expressions of affection and are always signed with a simple "Always sincerely." But they serve to confirm and to enlarge the impressions gained from the other sources. They reflect from the beginning the fact that Machen had been advising her with respect to study of the Bible. He must have counseled her to read the Gospels through consecutively. He had a copy of his course of Bible study prepared for the Board of Christian education especially bound for her. He sent her copies of his books as they appeared. He had copies of Dr. Erdman's little commentaries and other books sent to her. On her part she indicated an interest in these things, but evidently it was stimulated more by the desire to please Machen than by an earnest agitation of spirit. At any rate her mind was set awhirl as she read some of the books and she was forced to come to the conclusion that, judged by his views as set forth for example in *Christianity and Liberalism,* published in 1923, if she was a Christian at all, she was a pretty feeble one. How tragic an ending to Machen's one real romance or approach to it! It does serve to underscore once again, however, how utterly devoted he was to his Lord. He could be counted upon in the public and conspicuous arenas of conflict but also in the utterly private relations of life to be true to his dearly-bought convictions.

LOVE OF CHILDREN

Brief mention may be made here of the happy consideration that, though he was not to enjoy the bliss of marriage and fatherhood, the circle of loved ones at home was being enlarged. There had been the children of his younger brother to charm, and later his older brother's children came to captivate him. First there had been Mary Gresham Machen, named for her grandmother, whose name was really Mary, and did not wish to have "Minnie" perpetuated. Later when a third Arthur Webster Machen was born, he said: "Probably Arly is glad it is a boy, but for my part I don't think anything could be lovelier than little Mary. Now that her parents have another baby, and so presumably have no further use for her, I think I shall just take her along with me to Princeton." To this his mother replied that the baby's parents were very happy about their little son, "but you will not get Mary Gresham!" This is but one bit of evidence of the deeply affectionate nature of Machen. He was a man of the tenderest compassion and sympathy, as all who really knew him delighted to testify. He loved children and was able easily to enter into their world, and they on their part responded to his attentions with adoration and rapturous delight. In this respect, as in others, he reminds us of another illustrious bachelor in the history of Princeton Seminary, the genial Joseph Addison Alexander.

The six Armstrong children were his chief source of joy at Princeton and held almost the place in his heart that he accorded his own nieces and nephews. Since he spent so much of his time in Princeton he did not see nearly as much of the latter as he desired, though the letters from Baltimore kept him well-informed of their welfare. Christmas was the great opportunity of seeing them and sharing in their joys. He contributed to their happiness by giving considerable time and thought to the selection of gifts that would please, but his rare ability to enter with simplicity of manner and warmth of feeling into their experiences was remembered when the gifts were forgotten.

Machen's attitude toward children was basically a fruit of his extraordinary humility. As his prayers constantly disclosed, if ever a man received the kingdom as a little child, it was he. This characteristic is also reflected in a story of a Christmas celebration of some years later than this period after a third child, Betsy, had become a member of the Arthur Machen household. Betsy, while playing with a mechano toy, had become naughty, and was told by her mother to pack it up and place it in another room. Evidently upset, she dropped the container on her way out with the result that the parts scattered far and wide. Instantly her Uncle Gresham was on his knees to help her pick them up, when the little girl's mother forbade him on the ground that the child was clearly at fault and the punishment was just. "But," answered Machen, "that is exactly why I sympathize with her and want to help her; so frequently in my own life the troubles that have overcome me have been my own fault."

TOILING ON PAUL

The recital of events in this and the preceding chapters has indicated that many duties and cares were resting upon him during the period when he was faced with the preparation of his Richmond lectures and the labors connected with the publication of his book on Paul. Considering his years of interest in Paul, as reflected in his earlier teaching and writing, one might suppose that the composition of the book would have been a relatively easy task. But such an evaluation would display little knowledge of the toil involved in writing a book, least of all a Machen book.

Some of his comments on the subject are most revealing. When the date for the lectures was definitely settled for the winter of 1920-21, he was rather overwhelmed at the burden that had come upon him. "The only question is," he wrote on Dec. 2, 1919, "Can I get ready for next year? Work, work, work must be the rule." Work, indeed, was the master day after day—at Princeton, on holiday at Seal Harbor, and wherever he happened to be.

It is fascinating how much was done in hotel rooms where he could feel free from the eventuality of interruption. July 15, 1920 finds him in the Hotel Lenox in Boston, and he writes:

> My dearest Mother:
>
> I am still at this charming spot. It is the best place to work in that I have found for a long time. My room is on the top floor; there are no nuisances, and everything is fine and dandy. The last two mornings have been devoted without interruption to writing on my book. It has been as painful as pulling teeth. I suffered intensely; I paced the floor in agony; I dawdled because nothing would come to me. But I was quite uninterrupted, and I did get something done. The product, I am afraid, is miserably poor, and I do not see how even the skilled Mrs. Donehower is going to read my handwriting when she tackles the typewriting job. Furthermore I have been working only on the introduction, which had long been in my mind and which had even taken shape to a considerable extent in informal lectures. But at least I have made a beginning. I wish I could stay right here.
>
> In the afternoon I have been going out to work at the Harvard Library. Then I have taken long walks and a good bath.

Later he was working intensely at the Vanderbilt Hotel in New York, and he must have produced a fairly large portion of the work before the Seminary opened in the fall of 1920. However, there was still considerable ground to cover at the time, and he had to insure uninterrupted quiet away from Princeton in order to bring the work to completion. As it happened he had preaching engagements for several Sundays at the First and Central Church in Wilmington in November and December, and by staying on in his room at the Hotel Dupont he was able to utilize the Mondays to great advantage. On Nov. 15

(he was now at a hotel in New York) he wrote of the progress made the preceding Monday:

> On Monday morning at the DuPont Hotel I got in the best work on my Sprunt Lectures that I have been able to accomplish for some time. I composed or wrote from 8:30 A.M. till after 3 P.M. without stopping for lunch. Charlie Candee wants me to stay with him on my next visit. But I must get out of it. I simply must have another of those precious mornings of work. You may remember that I cannot write at any time except in the mornings, and I cannot write in the mornings if I have to talk to anybody before I get started.
>
> Fortunately my classes at Princeton this year do not begin (except Thursday) till 10:30 A.M. I usually get started on Sprunt at about 8:10 and work hard till 10:30. During this past week I wrote about ten pages a day (one hundred words to a page). Just now I am at the portion of my lectures about which I am best prepared. A sticky stage will come soon. Yesterday I preached at Stamford, Conn. In order to get that all-important, uninterrupted Monday morning I came to New York Sunday night, Stamford being only thirty-five miles from here. Unfortunately I lost sleep both Saturday night and Sunday night, so that the results of this morning's work were disappointing. I worked hard from about eight o'clock 'till about half past one. But a large part of the time was spent in the throes of unsuccessful efforts at composing. I got only about eighteen pages written, and a considerable part, I am afraid, will have to be torn up.

He began to fear that he might have to cut short his precious days with his mother at the Christmas season, and asked for her understanding. She was of course most generous in her response, and writing on Nov. 25th said:

> My beloved Son:
>
> I take the first opportunity of writing in answer to your letter to assure you, as far as words can, that I do thoroughly understand the pressure you are under about the work on the Sprunt lectures. I know also that the present labor is not by any means a pleasurable recreation to you but involves the intellectual effort and moral strain that come from the carrying out of a difficult undertaking. To me it is the most important thing in life; and for me to be perfectly willing for you to use your holidays or such part of them as necessary is not unselfish because the work ranks far above any lesser consideration. I *sympathize,* and I

> *understand.* If I cannot make you see this, it is because language is inadequate. Here is where faith in a *person* comes in. You love me very dearly and admire me in some ways more than I deserve. But somehow, somewhere, I have failed to inspire you with faith. I could not do otherwise than understand you, my own beloved son. I would not be *myself* if I did not! It would be a comfort if you could rest in my perfect love a little more securely. The Divine Love is infinitely greater but it cannot be more true.
>
> I do not "take too seriously" what you say about your lack of preparation. I believe you are now in the throes of a great work. But I sympathize too with your evident discouragement and shed some tears over it. Because I cannot bear to see you suffer.

In his reply of Nov. 29th he said that he "felt repentant" for having caused her to shed tears about his lack of preparation for his lectures. He was now back at the DuPont in Wilmington, and on that Monday had gotten in some very fruitful work. "There is something about the eleventh floor of the Hotel DuPont which stimulates literary activity," he wrote, but he was more encouraged about the quantity than the quality. He stayed over two more Sundays at that "delightful spot," and the following Friday went to New York and was able to put in a good forenoon of work, regretful however that his conscience with regard to sabbath observance did not permit him to continue when his mind had gone into "high-gear." He had now written "enough for four or five courses of lectures" and would have to give thought to preparation with a view to their delivery. How he longed for at least two months longer to give to the lectures! The labor was finally brought to a conclusion without the sacrifice of his stay at home over the holidays, and early in January he went to Richmond to deliver the lectures.

The stay in Richmond proved most delightful. He was the guest of President Moore, whom his mother described as "one of the finest and best men I have ever known" and with whom, as has been recalled, Machen had previously had pleasant contacts. There were also delightful associations with the professors of the Seminary and he enjoyed the experience of hearing several of them teach their classes. To add to the pleasure of the occasion, his cousin Lewis H. Machen and his wife Aldine resided in Richmond, and it was always a joy to renew fellowship with these affectionate and appreciative relatives.

Eight lectures were scheduled in all, and Machen chose to deliver them, except for part of the first, completely without benefit of notes. Though he was characteristically deprecatory in his estimate of the impact which he had made, his cousin reported to his mother that he had made a "hit" and that Dr. Moore had told him that the lecturer "had made a splendid impression and helped the students greatly." And Dr. Moore himself, though evidently restrained in his remarks to Machen had been quick to apprise his mother of the unqualified success of the lectures. His letter was as follows:

Richmond, Va.,
January 15, 1921

Mrs. Minnie G. Machen,
217 West Monument Street,
Baltimore, Md.

My dear Mrs. Machen:

This is a congested week with us, but I must snatch a moment to tell you how greatly delighted our professors, students and people are with Gresham's James Sprunt Lectures. He is giving us one of the most instructive series we have ever had and they are delivered with remarkable ease and effectiveness. There was a suggestion of nervousness at the beginning of the first lecture, which, however, soon passed away, and since that time they have proceeded in a full, golden stream. I wish very much it had been possible for you to hear them.

In addition to the benefit of the lectures, we have had great pleasure in the personal association with him which we have enjoyed. He came right into the current of the life of the seminary and community in a way that no preceding lecturer on this foundation has done, and he is taking in the various activities of the seminary every day he has opportunity, and so his days have been full and busy, and he has seemed to enjoy the fellowship of the campus, which has always been one of the attractive features of the institution.

This is not merely a conventional note. I knew that you would be deeply interested in the success of his lectures here, which are to constitute his first book, and I have given you the facts without adornment. His lectures have been an unqualified success.

Cordially yours,
W. W. Moore

THE BOOK

The press of duties at Princeton did not even permit Machen to stop off at Baltimore on the way back from Richmond. He was determined not to rest until his manuscript was ready for publication, and, with all the other matters that were pressing upon him at the time, including the church union issue in its crucial stages, he had to "strain every nerve" to complete it by March 26th.

"The Origin of Paul's Religion" had come by this time, at the suggestion of Dr. Moore, to be adopted as the title instead of the more prosaic, "Paul and His Environment"—not because Machen liked the title very much, for he disliked the word "religion" especially because of unsavory associations. But he became reconciled to it, declaring that "after all in the book I am trying to meet the modern historian on his own ground and take the religious life of Paul first of all as a phenomenon of history that requires explanation. I worked hard to get some better title, but could find nothing. Army at first disliked 'The Origin of Paul's Religion,' but later came to favor it. My own development was somewhat similar."

Meanwhile Dr. Moore and Dr. Kirk had interested themselves in the publication of the work, and an approach was made to Macmillan which resulted in an expression of interest. The manuscript was sent off to New York on March 26th, but this was only the beginning of drawn-out negotiations. Two chief obstacles to publication developed. It seemed to Macmillan that the manuscript—running to 560 typewritten pages—was so long that the sales price would have to be at an inadvisedly high level, and they insisted that it would have to be reduced by about one-third. That was distressing and involved considerable labor as well. Moreover, since Machen was virtually unknown in the world of book sales, they stipulated that he should purchase 500 copies—the number was finally reduced to 400—at half of the retail price of $3.00. Though taken aback by this condition, and wondering whether there might not be prejudice against his theological viewpoint as a representative of Princeton, he was not unduly alarmed at the demand for subsidy. He had been paid liberally under the terms of the Sprunt Lectureship—the honorarium was $1400.00—and he was hopeful of disposing of the copies especially among the students of the Seminary. In the course of the next fifteen years no doubt he gave many, many times the 400 away to students in seminaries and colleges! The contract was finally signed about June 1, 1921.

Even then his difficulties were not at an end. There was of course the routine work of proof reading both in galleys and pages, and this had to be done meticulously. But there was an unexpected development in connection with the proposed publicizing of the book. Machen had been asked to prepare a statement giving the scope and viewpoint of the book, but when it was returned for his approval, he discovered that it had been revised in such a way that it was closer to expressing a liberal point of view than his own. He naturally had to insist on correction of this inadvertent misrepresentation but no further difficulties arose. The book was finally published on October 9, 1921.

When Machen received his first copies, his immediate concern was to send one to his mother. At the same time he wrote her a lengthy letter giving his first impressions of the book and expressing his general satisfaction with its appearance. The book had been dedicated to "William Park Armstrong—My Guide in the Study of the New Testament and in All Good Things," and Machen wanted to explain this to his mother.

> Army was not expecting me to dedicate the book to him. You know the reasons that impelled me to do so. In my own heart, the book is really dedicated—despite my profound gratitude to Army—to the one who has never failed me either in joy or in disappointment and sorrow. That person is my own dearest Mother.
>
> My debt to Army, so far as the contents of the book are concerned, is enormous. I felt that the least I could do was to make public acknowledgement of the debt. Of course I do not mean that my gratitude to Army is not of the heart. On the contrary he has meant to me far more than I can possibly say. He never made life miserable for me with the drudgery which is otherwise universally placed upon assistants. And he led me always in the right path by example and by counsel. How many times he straightened me out when I was in a tangle about the Sunday School lessons! Yet he never gets the slightest public credit for what he does. Hence I felt impelled to pay him at least the slight tribute of dedicating my book to him. I wanted to say to the alumni of the Seminary and others that whatever I do in the sphere of the New Testament study is due to Army's help.
>
> But in my heart it is to my dearest Mother that the book and everything else that I do is dedicated.

Can any one take account of this letter and fail to acknowledge that if ever there was a man of nobility, magnanimity, gentility and tender considerateness Machen was that man?

But one can never forget that these qualities were not original with him. One is reminded of that again in reading his mother's response upon receiving his letter and a copy of the book over which she had agonized with her son:

> Hurrah for The Book. I have been full of excitement all day trying to steal a moment for writing. Now The Book has arrived, and I can tell you what a thrill it gave me to hold It in my hands. To me it seems a very successful presentation—dignified in aspect,

readable and convenient in size, the print and paper good. I know I would think it appetizing even if I did not know the author. But I am not such a good critic, though I do believe I know a nice book when I see one. The main satisfaction is that you are even tolerably satisfied yourself, after all the hard work and the many apprehensions and vexations of last summer. I feel as if I had been through the throes of creation with you. I am so glad the much tortured passages came out correct at last and that the mistakes are clearly printers' errors, and altogether I am happy about it.

Now my prayers will follow it—for the accomplishment of good to the cause of Christ. That makes my life count for something. I love it all, including the dedication which is just the right thing. If it belonged to me first, how glad I am to give it to dear "Army" who has been our guide and friend. I can have the Virgin Birth and that will be an especially appropriate book to dedicate to a mother. All the beautiful things you say in your letter fill my heart with overflowing joy, and I do not need the public dedication. Of course, I haven't read it, for I have this moment taken it out of the box . . .

GENERAL ESTIMATE

It is beyond the scope of this biography to present a detailed analysis or a critical evaluation of this volume or of the other important Machen books. My primary purpose is not to estimate his significance as a theologian and New Testament scholar, though a study of that kind that was really well done would be eminently worth while. But even in a narrative stressing the more personal and intimate aspects of his life it would be inexcusable to say nothing concerning the contents of a volume that meant as much to Machen as *The Origin of Paul's Religion*. And some attention must be given to the reception which the book received in the press of the day in order to disclose the standing which it gave him as a thinker and scholar.

The message of the book is that the religion of Paul, as reflected in the teaching of his Epistles, is at its heart a religion of faith in Jesus Christ as the divine redeemer, and that the only satisfying explanation of the origin of that religious faith is to be found in the trusting acknowledgement, with Paul, of that Jesus as the person who, as the divine Redeemer, had lived and died in Palestine. Machen's exposition of this theme was at the same time a refutation of various alternative views which had been prominently held. His book is, first of all, a powerful critique of the view of modern Liberalism. Paul's position was not based on the merely human "historical Jesus"; if Jesus was only what he is represented by modern naturalistic historians as being, then what is really distinctive of Jesus was not derived from Jesus. In connection with the refutation of the Liberal view Machen effectively appealed to the testimony of Wrede and Bousset. Wrede had convincingly argued that the religion and theology of Paul were inseparable, and therefore one could not save Paul as a disciple of Jesus if one's theological estimate of Jesus' person and work were given up. And Bousset stressed the conclusion that according to Paul the Lordship of Jesus involved an acknowledgement of him as a divine person; he was the object of faith and worship.

Then Machen turns to examine the answers of Wrede and Bousset as to the origin of Pauline Christianity and finds them wanting. It was not derived, he showed, from the pre-Christian apocalyptic notions of the Messiah, as Wrede held; for the apocalyptic Messiah was neither an object of worship nor a living person to be loved. Nor was it derived from pagan religion, in accordance with the hypothesis of Bousset; for pagan influence is excluded by the self-testimony of Paul and the pagan parallels utterly break down. But even if the parallels were ten times closer than they are, the heart of the problem would not even be touched. The heart of the problem, Machen contended, is to be found in the Pauline relation to Christ, and in accordance with this thought he closes his book in the following eloquent and glowing words:

> That relation cannot be described by mere enumeration of details; it cannot be reduced to lower terms; it is an absolutely simple and indivisible thing. The relation of Paul to Christ is a relation of love; and love exists only between persons. It is not a group of ideas that is to be explained, if Paulinism is to be accounted for, but the love of Paul for his Saviour. And that love is rooted, not in what Christ had said, but in what Christ had done. He "loved me and gave himself for me." There lies the basis of the religion of Paul; there lies the basis of all of Christianity. That basis is confirmed by the account of Jesus which is given in the Gospels, and given, indeed, in all the sources. It is opposed only by modern reconstructions. And those reconstructions are all breaking down. The religion of Paul was not founded upon a complex of ideas derived from Judaism or from paganism. It was founded upon the historical Jesus. But the historical Jesus upon whom it was founded was not the Jesus of modern reconstruction, but the Jesus of the whole New Testament and of Christian faith; not a teacher who survived only in the memory of

his disciples, but the Saviour who after His redeeming work was done still lived and could still be loved.

RECEPTION IN THE PRESS

The reception given the volume was on the whole most gratifying. Among conservative Presbyterians it was hailed as a splendid example of orthodox scholarship and telling argument and as offering evidence of the emergence of a new eloquent spokesman for the truth. Thus only a month after the publication of the book *The Presbyterian* in its leading editorial expressed itself as follows:

> Within the last year, the Christian church in general and the Evangelical church in particular, suffered a great loss in the death of the three outstanding scholars of the Reformed Theology, namely Abraham Kuyper, Benjamin B. Warfield and Herman Bavinck. Such a great loss within so short a period, and in these days of such vigorous contention against insistent rationalism, would be depressing if it were not for the appearance of a stalwart company of younger men who are now coming to the front to maintain the standard of the Christian faith against its opponents. Prominent among this company of virulent [corrected to "virile" in the next issue and explained as due to "some demon influence of the press"] young scholars may be named the Rev. J. Gresham Machen, assistant professor of New Testament Literature and Exegesis in Princeton Theological Seminary.

The editorial, in connection with its general characterization of the book, also said: "We certainly congratulate the students of Princeton on their opportunity to sit under a teacher of such power, scholarship, logical faculty and wholesome and attractive personality."

A few weeks later *The Presbyterian* carried a lengthy review article under the title "A Powerful Apologetic for Christianity" from the pen of Dr. Samuel G. Craig. He spoke of it as dealing with its theme "in so masterly and convincing a manner as not only to greatly enhance Professor Machen's reputation as a New Testament scholar, but as to entitle him to the gratitude of every lover of Christianity." And in summing up he spoke of "its exact and discriminating scholarship, its kindly tone, its lucidity, its many-sidedness, the depth and vigor of the Christian faith by which it is inspired." He also observed that

> while Dr. Machen sticks to his main theme throughout, yet in the course of his discussion he tells us more about the real nature of Christ, the real nature of the Gospel, the real nature of Chris-

> tianity, than many books that are devoted exclusively to these subjects. His book constitutes a powerful apologetic for Christianity—and one fitted to appeal powerfully to an age in which the conflict between naturalism and supernaturalism has concentrated itself in the field of history—by one who has a correct conception of Christianity.

Within a few months the book was being reviewed in magazines and newspapers throughout the country and indeed in many other countries around the globe. Benjamin W. Bacon treated it in the *Literary Review* of the New York *Evening Post.* Lyman Abbott devoted a leading article to it in *The Outlook.* Henry J. Cadbury reviewed it as "An Outstanding New Book" in *The Congregationalist.* James Moffat commented upon it in *The British Weekly* and followed this up with a review in the *Hibbert Journal.* Adolph Jülicher, one of his former teachers at Marburg, evaluated it for *Die Christliche Welt.* It was also reviewed in other leading periodicals of England and Germany as well as France, Italy and other countries.

Not all the comment was favorable in every particular though it was consistently respectful. Even scholars whose viewpoints were to a greater or lesser extent under criticism in the book expressed their admiration. The volume of B. W. Bacon on *Jesus and Paul* had been subjected to particular criticism, but Bacon praised it as "worthy of a high place among the products of American biblical scholarship." He said that it presented "a bold challenge to those who offer a 'naturalistic' answer to the problem of the origin of Paul's religion" and characterized it as a book which in spite of "minor defects . . . commands respect." His review also stated:

> Professor Machen grapples with the most vital problem in the history of Christianity, the question of the worship of Jesus as a superhuman being, arising as it did very shortly after his ignominious death, and dominating the religious life of such a man as the author of the Pauline Epistles . . . Professor Machen's solution is not new. It is a strong defence of old-fashioned supernaturalism . . . But this by no means implies an unscholarly book or one of negligible value. On the contrary it is entitled to a wide and careful reading and will doubtless receive it.
>
> Professor Machen may expect his warmest welcome and widest circulation among readers to whom attempts to explain the origin of Paul's religion by inquiry into contemporary Jewish theology or contemporary Hellenistic religions of personal redemption are obnoxious as tending to undermine or obscure its real source in

> direct divine revelation. Such readers have learned to look to Princeton Seminary as the headquarters of apologetic and polemic theology, and in seeking here a strong, clear, and logical defence of the traditional supernaturalistic viewpoint they will not be dissappointed. Professor Machen upholds the best standards of his school. He does not profess to write without bias; but he has read thoroughly, presents clearly and fairly his opponent's view, and answers it logically. The work is a good example of sound American scholarship in the field of apologetics.
>
> But its chief value to scholarship lies elsewhere. So long as Christianity endures men will seek the explanation which supernaturalism pronounces a hopeless quest. It is well for such efforts to be subjected to the keenest criticism that partial and inadequate explanations may not pass unchallenged. Professor Machen performs this service well....

James Moffat in the issue of *The British Weekly* for Jan. 12, 1922 stated that the "eight chapters are a sustained, trenchant argument that the religious interpretation of Christianity in Paul's epistles requires an estimate of the historical Jesus which must be richer in supernatural content than the 'liberal' school of critics is prepared to admit . . ." We have here

> a strong conservative pronouncement. It is significant for its insistence upon the need of a genetic connection between Jesus and Paul, and for its exhibition of the loose statements which are still being made about the mystery cults in the first century. Dr. Machen is nothing if he is not acute.

In his later review in the *Hibbert Journal,* while praising highly Machen's work, Moffat charged that in his eagerness to demolish the interpretations of his opponents, he had not put anything satisfactory in its place. In particular Bacon felt that some psychological account of the "faith-mysticism" of Paul was missing. Cadbury also criticized Machen for not being more positive in his exposition and establishment of the "supernatural view" which he presented as the true explanation of the origin of Paul's religion.

> He assumes that the reader knows it as the established view of Christians for many past generations. He defends it, principally, by refutation, that is by refuting three alternative views of more recent origin . . .
>
> It is doubtful whether, on its positive side, this is a wholly convincing method of proof—but by attacking vulnerable alterna-

> tives the author certainly carried his readers with him and gives the impression of having proved his thesis. And the theories he attacks, especially the last two, are very vulnerable.

And Jülicher, while praising the book for its thoroughness and objectivity and literary qualities, and characterizing it as an excellent defense of supernaturalism, criticized it as oversimplifying history and historical problems due to a tendency to stress the logical consequences of a position.

Certain criticisms of detailed points were no doubt well taken. Machen would have been the last to claim complete invulnerability for himself. But the more general criticisms he could harldy have accepted as valid. He did not charge critics personally with holding to the logical consequences of their positions, but he did maintain that there was a certain logic in their positions as in Christianity itself, and that it was the business of persons dealing seriously with these views to analyze them with their implications as sharply and clearly as possible. The criticism that he largely assumed his position rather than proved it was not without an element of truth. But it is asking a great deal to expect a representative of supernaturalistic Christianity, every time he expresses himself on particular questions connected with the Bible, to expound and to substantiate his Christian presuppositions. Machen was entirely self-conscious in realizing the great gulf that was fixed between his basic philosophy of reality and history and that of the representatives of various "naturalistic" positions. But conscious as he was that his basic outlook was that of historic Christianity, he could understandably regard the refutation of various critical theories as confirmations of the truth of his Christian position. He often seemed indeed to be meeting the critics on their own ground rather than on his own as he engaged in an exposé of the inconsistencies of their positions as they appealed to the data of the New Testament. In the final analysis, however, his apologetic was neither mediating nor minimizing. Everywhere, he was convinced, the data were intelligible only as it was recognized that they taught and implied the uncompromising supernaturalism of the revelation and redemption contained and taught in the Bible. Thus both the total estimate of the nature and message of the Bible and particular exegesis in individual passages involved and confirmed the supernatural view of the origin of Paul's Christian faith.

Considering the intrinsic worth of the book and the gratifying response which it received in the press, it comes as no surprise that the book, though it virtually was introducing a new author, had a good sale. Judging from records supplied Machen by the publishers, about 2000 copies were sold in a little more than a year, and it continued to be in good demand year after year. Arrangements were made by Macmillan for a second printing at a reduced price as early as January, 1923, and there were several other printings later on. Finally in 1946 publication rights were secured by the Wm. B. Eerdmans Publishing Company and still another printing was made.

17

CHRISTIANITY AND LIBERALISM

Although the churches participating in the movement for union refused to adopt the plan proposed by their committee, the forces committed to theological orthodoxy could hardly feel secure as a result of this victory. As a matter of fact this movement, like no previous ecclesiastical development, had served to concentrate attention upon a profounder disunity within Christendom than that which had perpetuated traditional denominationalism. For the disunity which came into sharpest focus at this time was not that of external ecclesiastical divisions but of basic disagreement as to the very nature of the Christian religion. Thus Presbyterians were disclosed as never before to be divided against Presbyterians, Baptists against Baptists, Methodists against Methodists. The defeat of the union proposals, accordingly, rather than heralding an era of peace, proved to be merely the end of a skirmish in a war that was soon to engulf every phase of the life of the churches. The final tabulation of votes in 1921 had hardly been registered before the Presbyterian and other large denominations were engaged in the flaming controversies of the twenties which have generally come to be known as the fundamentalist-modernist controversy.

In these developments J. Gresham Machen came to occupy a conspicuous role as one of the most effective spokesmen for the conservative side. His little book *Christianity and Liberalism,* published early in 1923, remains the best evidence of this fact, and so merits the considerable attention devoted to it in this chapter. Defining the issue of the day more incisively than any other publication, it made a profound impression on all sections of the religious world. Thousands of copies were sold within a year. While the book on Paul established Machen's reputation as a scholarly defender of historic Christianity, this smaller volume catapulted him into the center of the arena of ecclesiastical and religious life where the broader controversy between Christianity and modernism was being fought. The development and outcome of this controversy were to have far-reaching consequences for the Presbyterian Church and Princeton Seminary and so also for Machen himself.

In order to place his activity in its proper perspective some account must be taken of fundamentalism in general and of Machen's relation to it.

FUNDAMENTALISM

The definition of fundamentalism is beset with difficulty because of certain broader and narrower connotations which persist until the present time. The term appears to have been derived from the publication about 1910 of a series of small volumes called *The Fundamentals* which dealt with higher criticism and the Bible, the inspiration of the Scriptures, the deity of Christ, the Virgin Birth of Christ, Sin and Salvation, evolution and "isms," evangelism and missions, and related subjects. The treatises were written for the general public, and several were prepared by pastors and evangelists. Renowned scholars like Professors B. B. Warfield and James Orr, however, also contributed to the series. "Fundamentalists" thus was the designation that came to be given to those who, singling out certain great facts and doctrines that had come under particular attack, were concerned to emphasize their truth and to defend them.

To the extent that fundamentalists were stressing the doctrines of the sovereignty of God as Creator and Ruler of the universe, the infallibility of the Scriptures, the deity of Christ and the reality of his incarnation, the supernaturalism of salvation, and the certainty of the coming consummation, they were simply defending historic Christianity. In this sense the fundamentalist-modernist controversy was but a phase of an age-long struggle. It was rooted in the antithesis between Christianity and the efforts toward synthesis with pagan thought which may be traced back to the first and second centuries of the Christian era. A more proximate background is found in the conflict between the God-centered thought of the Reformation and the man-centered evaluation of life and history which came to conspicuous expression in the so-called Enlightenment of the 18th century. But the full impact upon the churches, at least so far as America was concerned, was not felt until the latter part of the 19th century. In the Presbyterian Church the union of the Old and New Schools, the Swing Trial (with Patton as prosecutor), the developments at Union Seminary which led to the break with the General Assembly, the movement for revision of the Confession of Faith, and finally the movement for church union may be recalled as conspicuous features. Meanwhile, as similar indications of conflict and division in other denominations appeared, there developed a growing sense of oneness in faith which crossed denominational lines, and co-operative efforts in the defense of the faith once for all delivered unto the saints were undertaken.

On the other hand, though many modern critics are blameworthy for failing to distinguish within fundamentalism between the solid core of Biblical Christianity and certain excrescences, fundamentalists have often contributed to the judgment that it is essentially a religious novelty. The emergence of new emphases and the lack of others, the presence at times of zeal not according to knowledge and the frequent absence of historical perspective and appreciation of scholarship, have influenced this evaluation. The substitution of brief, skeletal creeds for the historic confessions tends to shatter the organism of revealed truth into isolated and meagre fragments and to promote lack of concern with precise formulation of Christian doctrine. Oftentimes pietistic and perfectionist vagaries have come to be accepted as the hallmark of fundamentalism. And a one-sided other-worldliness, often associated with a dogmatic commitment to a futuristic chiliasm, has come to be widely regarded as essential to fundamentalist orthodoxy.

In estimating Machen's place within the fundamentalist-modernist controversy, one must take account of the fact that, judged by various criteria adopted by friend and foe, he was not a fundamentalist at all. His standards of scholarship, his distaste for brief creeds, his rejection of chiliasm, the absence of pietism from his makeup, and in brief his sense of commitment to the historic Calvinism of the Westminster Confession of Faith disqualified him from being classified precisely as a fundamentalist. And he never spoke of himself as a fundamentalist; indeed he disliked the term. He often expressed himself in such terms as the following:

> The term fundamentalism is distasteful to the present writer and to many persons who hold views similar to his. It seems to suggest that we are adherents of some strange new sect, whereas in point of fact we are conscious simply of maintaining the historic Christian faith and of moving in the great central current of Christian life.

At the same time, conscious as he was of taking sides in the great debate as to the nature of the Christian religion, in which he came to insist that modern liberalism in its depreciation of doctrine and its denial of central doctrines had no real right to the name Christian, he did not think it worthwhile to quibble about the term. As he said on one occasion, in 1926,

> Do you suppose, gentlemen, that I do not detect faults in many popular defenders of supernatural Christianity? Do you suppose that I do not regret my being called, by a term that I greatly dislike, a "Fundamentalist"? Most certainly I do. But in the

> presence of a great common foe, I have little time to be attacking my brethren who stand with me in defense of the Word of God. I must continue to support an unpopular cause.

In spite of significant differences in outlook and emphasis which distinguished him from many fundamentalists, he was convinced that what he shared with them was more basic than what distinguished him from them.

Hazards and penalties were entailed in walking this road. There was the risk of being judged in terms of all the characteristics that came to be associated with the name fundamentalism. There was also the difficulty of bringing into sufficiently clear relief the positive features of his viewpoint and thus of adequately preparing his readers and hearers for an appreciation and awareness of the limitations imposed by his convictions upon co-operation in certain forms. At times he appears not to have fully realized how severe these handicaps were. It is, however, a tribute to his sense of the catholic character of Christianity, and a demonstration of his sense of the crisis which had overtaken Christianity because of the attack of modernism, that he forthrightly and energetically took sides in the great battle.

In this controversy Machen came to be charged with bitterness, intolerance and bigotry. It is perhaps inevitable that such charges should be leveled against any one so valiant and uncompromising in his defense of the faith and exposure of current error. His opponents in the main had moved so far away from the evaluation of Christianity in terms of commitment to the truth once delivered that any such viewpoint as Machen's would be roundly condemned as bigotry. Those who really knew Machen, however, were aware of his unusual understanding of and sympathy with his modernist antagonists. He never could forget the attraction which Liberalism had come to possess for him in the person and thought of men like Wilhelm Herrmann. But this understanding and sympathy did not settle the matter in his mind. Liberalism he indeed regarded as another gospel, not really a gospel at all. But if its advocates had merely associated themselves in organizations committed to their own liberal views, he would not have been so profoundly disturbed. It was, however, their presence in churches constitutionally committed to the very historic Christianity which they were repudiating which compelled Machen to conclude that a most fundamental issue of the controversy was that of honesty. Church officers who took solemn vows affirming their belief in the Scriptures as the Word of God, the only infallible rule of faith and practice, and their reception and adoption of the Confession of Faith as containing the system of doctrine taught in the Holy Scriptures, and then proceeded to demand liberty to propagate views at variance with these positions, were judged to have forfeited their right to positions of responsibility. A distressing aspect of the entire controversy is that the charges of intolerance and bigotry were often made by men who simply by-passed the issue of honesty.

By the early twenties Christians in many communions had been aroused by the inroads of modernism both at home and abroad. In China in the year 1922 a Bible Union had been formed to arrest the advance of modernism in the mission field, and more than a thousand missionaries became members within a brief period. Such a development had significant repercussions at home as doubts were raised as to the soundness of the church's program. Meanwhile the modernists themselves became restive as it appeared that a serious challenge to their position was making itself felt. Evidently they decided to meet the challenge head on. The most publicized and illuminating features of their campaign were their defense of the preaching of Harry Emerson Fosdick in the First Presbyterian Church of New York City and their publication of the Auburn *Affirmation.* Though they lost battles, including their fight to retain Fosdick in his Presbyterian post, they won the war in achieving their principal goal of guaranteeing liberty of unbelief with regard to "the fundamentals." Eventually, in the interest of consolidating this victory on behalf of inclusivism, the Presbyterian Church felt compelled to suppress those who could not make peace with its broad church policies. In that conflict the old Princeton and Machen himself, as the exponents of specific and militant orthodoxy, were regarded as expendable.

ORIGIN OF THE BOOK

Machen's prominence in the church union decision, his fame as the author of *The Origin of Paul's Religion,* and his great effectiveness as a public speaker combined to make his services in great demand as the lines were being drawn in the Presbyterian Church. Records of his activities prepared for publication in the Seminary *Bulletin* disclose that during the academic year 1921, and in the years that followed, he preached nearly every Sunday, oftentimes in prominent pulpits in New York and Philadelphia, and frequently preached and lectured during the week. He was ever afterward compelled to decline many such invitations simply because there were not enough days in the week.

Among these engagements an address before the Chester Presbytery Elders' Association on November 3, 1921, proved to be the most consequential. For it was soon to develop into his immensely popular and influential book *Christianity and Liberalism.* Within ten days of its delivery Machen was writing his mother of the interest of the Association in its publication, and of the labor that would be involved because he had not written it out, even to the extent of an outline. He began work at once, however, on an article on "The Fundamentals" (as he himself at first characterized it) which was published in the January, 1922 issue of *The Princeton Theological Review* under the title, "Liberalism or Christianity."

Towards the end of January his mother was discouraging a plan under consideration to distribute reprints of the article:

> I should think you would be sorry to distribute it too widely because the paper embodies parts of your best sermons which you *must* go on preaching . . . *Please* do not give up preaching those sermons. Indeed you ought not to give up your sermons because they are old; for they seem to ripen and grow by the repetition. I want you to revive the first sermon I ever heard from you from Matt. 4:23; Matt. 28:20. Oh how I love it! And, in all these sermons, I can hear my dear Boy's fine voice ringing out the truth of God. It always makes my life seem worth while.

Machen's reply spoke at length of the article and plans for distributing it at least to the alumni of the Seminary.

> You are correct in supposing that my article on "Liberalism or Christianity" embodies parts of previous sermons, but some of that material is already in print, in "The Presbyterian," and I have become quite shameless in continuing to use orally material which I have already printed. I am rather expecting to distribute my article to all of our 2,700 alumni. It will be a rather heavy expense, but I believe the time has come for vigorous propaganda in the Presbyterian Church.

His concluding comment was that "the alternative to the distribution plan would be to expand the article into a small book, but I do not feel competent to do that." This was a plan which his mother encouraged: "I do wish it were feasible for you to 'expand that article into a little book'; it is worthy of that and would be read much more than in a pamphlet form. But I would not like your attention diverted from the Virgin Birth." Other encouragements of the idea of a book were not slow in coming, and by the end of February he was projecting not one book but two—an elementary New Testament Greek Grammar in addition to the one on Liberalism.

At first the publication of the Grammar seemed more feasible, and he concentrated upon it with the hope that it might be ready for use in his classes in the fall. By May 12th he was working on that book "morning, noon and night," an intensity of activity that was exceptional even for Machen who usually found that he could undertake constructive writing only in the morning hours. This work was completed and sent to Macmillan about the middle of June. But well over six months were to elapse before it was published—as things turned out, about six weeks *after* the publication of *Christianity and Liberalism.*

In view of previous comments on Machen's instruction in Greek and upon this book, attention is called here only to its extraordinary success. It has continued in strong demand throughout the more than a quarter of a century since its publication. During the author's lifetime its sale averaged 800 copies annually. Even more impressive is the rare distinction of its wide demand year after year ever since. In recent years indeed annual sales have skyrocketed to astonishing totals of more than 4500 copies. The work is now in its twenty-fourth printing.

Having sent the *Grammar* manuscript off to the publisher, Machen concentrated on *Christianity and Liberalism* especially during the summer months when he was somewhat free from routine appointments at the Seminary. It was not completed, however, until about the first of November. Macmillan accepted it early in December, evidently influenced by the attention that had been drawn to the Fosdick and Grant controversies, and the strength of the movement in reaffirmation of the fundamentals. The processes of manufacture were accelerated so that it was published about the middle of February, 1923. That Macmillan had no reason to regret this action is demonstrated by the phenomenal sale of the book. During the rest of the year apparently somewhat less than a thousand copies were sold, but in 1924, as the book caught on and the controversy became even more intense, the total was nearly five thousand copies. The book has continued in steady and at times in strong demand ever since.

Following its publication and his reception of his first copies his first act, as he wrote,

> of course was to send a copy to my dearest Mother, who contributed so very much by her love and sympathy to the making of this book as well as to the making of whatever Christian convictions the author may have. You were very sweet and dear to me in the midst of all my contrariness when I was trying to get the book written. And what in the world could I do without the one person in whose loving interest I can always count?

The book was dedicated to his mother, and her response was warmly appreciative:

> The book is to me a sort of spiritual grandchild; and it is doubly mine with my name upon it—given to me, an offering of love and tribute of praise by the noble son who created it. I would have expected it (from what you said about "Paul") had I not thought that perhaps you were saving the "Virgin Birth" for me. But I might not be here to enjoy the tribute when that comes out. (I hope I may be at your side then as now). And so there was a little element of surprise when I saw first thing—"To My Mother." Your precious words at the beginning of your letter add a deeper meaning to the dedication...
>
> You have written a very able arraignment of "Liberalism" and defense of our Faith. I find myself pausing now and again for prayer. God grant that you may be the chosen instrument for great good to the Church! I well know you are in for a fight and that you will make enemies. But many will be encouraged to stand by their faith and the unwary will be warned of hidden dangers. I should think the prospect for good sales would be most promising. My whole heart and soul are with you and with *It — my Book!* I feel that "life with all it has of joy and pain" is well worth while to have a son who is a Defender of the Faith!

THE BOOK'S MESSAGE

Machen's own estimate of contents and aim of the book was succinctly expressed in a statement prepared for an advertizing circular at the request of the publisher:

> What is the difference between modern "liberal" religion and historic Christianity? An answer to this question is attempted in the present book. The author is convinced that liberalism on the one hand and the religion of the historic church on the other are not two varieties of the same religion, but two distinct religions proceeding from altogether separate roots. This conviction is supported by a brief setting forth of the teachings of historic Christianity and of the modern liberalism with regard to God and man, the Bible, Christ, salvation, the Church and Christian service. If Christianity, in its historic acceptation, is really to be abandoned, it is at least advisable that men should know what they are giving up and what they are putting in its place.

Thus Machen regarded the volume as concerned with a positive exposition of Christian doctrine as well as a defense of Christianity against Liberalism. It was perhaps inevitable that greater attention should be drawn to the latter feature since it was a tract for the times, directed very specifically to the controversial situation of the day. Machen himself regretted, however, that the early reviews failed, as he wrote his mother on April 13, 1923, "to get the 'Christianity' side of Christianity and Liberalism—they have failed to see that the book purports to be a summary of Christian Doctrine, in the light of modern attacks, it is true, but still with a positive purpose." Machen could not regret the fact, however, that it was widely recognized that he had made a most impressive and persuasive case for his thesis that modern liberalism is essentially different from historic Christianity all along the line. His only later regret was that he had not used the term "modernism" rather than "liberalism." The latter designation seemed to him to give greater credit to this religious phenomenon than it deserved; the former served at least to suggest that it lacked the support of the charter of Christianity and had emerged from modern thought as an innovation.

One can easily understand that fundamentalists in many denominations cordially welcomed the book because of the powerful support which it lent their cause. In its drawing of lines with regard to the doctrines of the Bible, Christ and salvation, it might be regarded as basically a fundamentalist book. Yet it transcended ordinary fundamentalist productions in more ways than one. Though written simply and plainly the book handled its theme as only a scholar could do. Moreover, there is in the book a penetration to the deeper issues at stake that takes it considerably beyond the range of ordinary fundamentalist thinking and writing. This appears, for example, in the consistent supernaturalism of the Christian doctrine of salvation. It comes to expression distinctively in the recognition that the issue is basically one concerning God and not merely certain more or less isolated doctrines of the Bible. Machen emphasized the fundamental character of the "awful transcendence of God."

> From beginning to end the Bible is concerned to set forth the awful gulf that separates the creature from the Creator. It is true, indeed, that according to the Bible God is immanent in the world. Not a sparrow falls to the ground without him. But he is immanent in the world not because He is identified with the world, but because He is the free Creator and Upholder of it. Between the creature and the Creator a great gulf is fixed.

Back of the disagreement concerning particular doctrines, including even the doctrine of God, Machen discerned other issues of profound significance. These had to do with one's estimate of the place of history and of doctrine itself within Christianity. Machen's study of modern theology had made him aware, as few fundamentalists were, that one of the most crucial issues concerned the place of history in the Christian gospel. For modern thought generally has found the *history* of Christ, regarded as central and essential to the gospel, a great stumblingblock. Here there has been at play the assumption that the gospel as an eternal or universally valid message cannot be indissolubly connected with supposedly contingent and relative developments on the plane of history. It is beyond our present purpose to show how such an evaluation of history is bound up with an essentially non-Biblical conception of the world and life to which the teaching of divine creation and providence are foreign. But the unwearied and effective manner in which Machen brought into sharp focus the centrality of the Christian view of history and its decisive significance for the understanding of the gospel must be noted. In *Christianity and Liberalism* he expresses this thought as follows:

> All the ideas of Christianity might be discovered in some other religion, yet there would be in that other religion no Christianity. For Christianity depends, not upon a complex of ideas, but upon the narration of an event. Without that event, the world, in the Christian view, is altogether dark, and humanity is lost under the guilt of sin. There can be no salvation by the discovery of eternal truth, for eternal truth brings naught but despair, because of sin. But a new face has been put upon life by the blessed thing that God did when he offered up His only begotten Son.

Machen was also beyond fundamentalism in recognizing that perhaps the most basic issue of all concerned the significance one attached to *belief* of the Christian message, in short, one's attitude toward the truth itself. He held that a man might accept all the articles in the creed, including the virgin birth and resurrection of Christ, but that, if in the end he asserted that it didn't really matter whether one believed or not, and that unbelief was as tolerable as belief, he had far more emphatically denied Christianity than the person who merely denied certain isolated doctrines. In accordance with this evaluation, Machen introduced his work, following the introductory chapter, with an entire chapter on "Doctrine." Here he shows that the message of Christianity, and of Christ himself, was doctrinal through and through from the very beginning. If one is to have a non-doctrinal religion, or one founded merely on general truth, one must be prepared to give up not only Paul, not only the primitive Christian church, but also Jesus himself. Skepticism or indifference with regard to the history of Christ, therefore, constituted in his judgment the most profound heresy of all.

Machen's approach was also somewhat distinctive in the particularity of its application to the ecclesiastical situation of his day, and especially the one with which he was most immediately concerned. It will be recalled that the address which was to develop into the book was delivered before an elders' association. On that occasion he had taken pains to admonish the elders to discharge their own responsibilities in all faithfulness. They were, first of all, to encourage those who were in the forefront of the battle for the Christian faith. In the presbyteries, also, they were to be faithful, and in the crisis of the day there was need of insistence that only men who were wholly loyal to the faith should be admitted to the ministry. In their local congregations they also were to take their stand for the faith; they were, for example, to demand that in the calling of a pastor primary consideration should be given to the candidate's beliefs.

This practical emphasis finds expression especially in the final chapter of *Christianity and Liberalism* which is devoted to "The Church." It contains a powerful indictment of the inclusivism which allowed great companies of persons who had never made any adequate confession of faith, not only into the membership, but even into the ministry and other places of influence. There could be no peace within the church so long as this condition persisted. "A separation between the two parties in the Church is the crying need of the hour." There could moreover be no program for unity in the church which disregarded the doctrinal issue on the assumption that the doctrinal differences were trivial. Moreover, he pointed out, it would be dishonest to "sink doctrinal differences and unite the Church on a program of Christian service" in view of the solemn commitment of ministers and other officers of the church to maintain the doctrines of the church. The path of honesty is the path trod by the Unitarians who frankly and honestly desired a church without an authoritative Bible, without doctrinal requirements, and without a creed.

In speaking of the deadly weakness with which the present situation was fraught, Machen, though not referring explicitly to the boards and agencies of his own denomination, in effect included them under his general indictment.

> The proclamation of the gospel is clearly the joy as well as the duty of every Christian man. But how shall the gospel be propagated? The natural answer is that it shall be propagated through

> the agencies of the Church—boards of missions and the like. An obvious duty, therefore, rests upon the Christian man of contributing to the agencies of the Church. But at this point perplexity arises. The Christian man discovers to his consternation that the agencies of the church are propagating not only the gospel as found in the Bible and in the historic creeds, but also a type of religious teaching which is at every conceivable point the diametrical opposite of the gospel.

Machen went on to speak of the difficulty of contributing financial support under such circumstances and the unsatisfactory character of the alternative of designating gifts for particular missionaries. Nevertheless he was so sure that the true missionaries should not be allowed to be in want that he was asking whether it would not be better that "the gospel should be both preached and combated by the same agencies than that it should not be preached at all." Thus the essential elements of the problem with which Machen was to be faced in the thirties following the publication of *Rethinking Missions* were already present in the early twenties; indeed there are some evidences that this issue had previously been present in his mind for at least another earlier decade.

PUBLIC RECEPTION

Soon after its appearance his colleagues gave expression to their appreciation of his book, and this was duly reported to his mother. Of special interest in connection with Machen's references to the ecclesiastical situation is the fact that Stevenson and Erdman, with whom he had differed profoundly on the church union issue, were critical of these utterances. Writing on March 3rd, he says:

> Next to Army Charlie Erdman seems to have been the first man in Princeton to read my book through. He wrote me a very nice note — but expressing regret that I had not made an exception of Presbyterian missionaries on p. 171. Dr. Erdman really seems to think that Presbyterian missionaries are all O. K.

And the following week he said:

> Dr. Stevenson wrote me a long letter with praise of the book, but expressing the view that we should not stir up trouble by cutting the liberals out of the Church, but should let them remain in the Church and try to win them!

Though cordially received by the conservative religious press both within his denomination and without, the book was roundly criticized by the liberals. One facet of criticism, represented by *The Presbyterian Advance* and *The Continent,* was that Liberalism as depicted by Machen was unknown in the Presbyterian Church. Machen indeed had not declared that all the Liberals held to Liberalism as he expounded it. While maintaining that Liberalism represented "no mere divergence at isolated points from Christian teaching," and that it constituted "in essentials a unitary system of its own," he said:

> That does not mean that all liberals hold all parts of the system, or that Christians who have been affected by liberal teaching at one point have been affected at all points. There is sometimes a salutary logic which prevents the whole of a man's faith being destroyed when he has given up a part. But the true way in which to examine a spiritual movement is in its logical relations; logic is the great dynamic, and the logical implications of any way of thinking are sooner or later certain to be worked out.

On the other hand, Dr. John A. MacCallum, an outspoken modernist minister of the Presbyterian Church, reviewing the book in the Philadelphia *Public Ledger* for April 28, 1923, admitted that Dr. Machen's position was that of "traditional Presbyterianism." He insisted, however, that Liberalism, viewed as an attitude and atmosphere that had moved away from the ancient constitutions, had every right to remain in the Church. The Liberals he held are men who "have accepted the enlarged view of the universe which has been established by modern astronomy, geology and biology. Instead of blindly denying scientific facts as the obscurantists have always done, they have adjusted themselves to them, and in so doing have increased their faith and urbanity and consequently extended their influence, particularly with the educated classes . . . Liberalism is an atmosphere rather than a series of formulas." It is noteworthy that Dr. MacCallum did not face the issue involved in the fact that all Presbyterian ministers were called upon to subscribe in the most solemn terms to the constitutional formulas of doctrine.

The Unitarians were more sensitive on this point, as a review in the *Pacific Unitarian* (June-July, 1923) discloses:

> What interests us is that from the point of view of a certain type of theology, Dr. Machen's arguments are irrefutable. His logic, it seems to us is impeccable. The issue does exist and does confront us. For the first time he has done us the great service of putting it in a clear-cut and definite form. You must be either a believer or an unbeliever, an evangelical or a liberal, you cannot be both at the same time. Our judgment is that Dr. Machen puts

the liberal party within the evangelical church where it has not a sound leg to stand on.

The extent to which *Christianity and Liberalism* came to be read, as account was taken of the struggle in the churches, is indicated by the diverse comments of Walter Lippmann and Lewis Browne. The latter. in *The Nation* for June 27, 1923, takes delight in the "godly mischief" which he discovers in the current situation as men like Percy Stickney Grant were "throwing off the cumbersome baggage" that has kept the church lagging far in the rear. And Browne characterizes Machen's book as follows: "If any imagine that the work of godly mischief, of ridding Christianity of its doctrinal barnacles, is unopposed in theological circles, they should read this precious volume. It is a broad and inclusive condemnation of any and every attempt to let light into the attic of theology." In contrast to this vitriolic and superficial estimate stands that of Lippmann who, in 1929, stated in *A Preface to Morals*:

> It is an admirable book. For its acumen, for its saliency, and for its wit, this cool and stringent defense of orthodox Protestantism is, I think, the best popular argument produced by either side in the controversy. We shall do well to listen to Dr. Machen. The Liberals have yet to answer him.

COMMENT ABROAD

Indicative of the wider repercussions of the fundamentalist-modernist controversy, and of the recognition of Machen's leading role in it, is the attention given to *Christianity and Liberalism* in the summer of 1924 in the influential and brilliantly edited *British Weekly*. In a series of leading articles on "Fundamentalism, False and True" an effort was made to indicate the limits which should properly be placed upon fundamentalism in the light of modern science while at the same time showing what was to be retained. Machen's book and argument were given prominent and respectful mention in the first article in the series, but issue was taken with his view of Scripture. It was maintained that men could and should retain the fundamental faith, but should not burden it with bondage to a doctrine "which honest study of the Bible has itself for us discredited."

Machen undertook an extended reply which was published in full in the *Weekly* on September 11, 1924. In the course of his declaration he showed that the doctrine of Scripture which he had expounded in his book was not "a comparatively late doctrine," as had been asserted, but actually was the teaching of Jesus, of the apostolic church and of the great ecumenical creeds and the confessions of the Reformation. He allowed nevertheless that men like Bishop Gore might deny the infallibility of Scripture and yet would not be classed as "modernists" be-caused their position was basically not one of scepticism but of genuine faith in God. But Machen was mainly concerned in his letter to call attention to the deeper issue, that of the relation of doctrine and experience.

> Apparently you assume . . . that doctrine springs from experience, dogmas being divided into grades according to the degree of directness with which they come from the religious experience of the community. If that be correct, then, of course, the whole debate is over—what is primary in that case is a mystic experience which clothes itself in new intellectual forms in every generation, no one of those intellectual forms being of permanent validity. And that means simply that a thoroughly sceptical mysticism has been substituted for the Christian religion.

Machen went on to show that from the beginning Christianity

> was certainly not a way of life as distinguished from a doctrine, or a way of life expressing itself in a doctrine, but it was a way of life founded upon a doctrine. It was founded more especially upon a proclamation of something that happened. The primitive Church proclaimed the happening after the first great act in it had occurred; Jesus proclaimed it by way of prophecy, but the primitive Church and Jesus were alike in proclaiming an event.

In the same issue of the *Weekly* the leading editorial article on page 1 took account of Machen's comments under the heading "Doctrine and Experience." The writer sought to establish the priority of experience, though not as isolated from something given in the early Church. Something was however given in experience, it was maintained, and the dogmas of the Church are largely that experience crystallized. And in order to get a fresh view of what is fundamental we must come as closely as possible to "the original normative experience."

There was no further comment on Machen's part, but from his known point of view it is plain what his reaction must have been. He had shown that the experience of men was not the foundational fact of the Christian gospel but what God had accomplished once for all in Christ, and that Christian experience is essentially the response which men through the Holy Spirit make to the proclamation of these glad tidings. He also must have challenged the right, in terms of the New Testament, to speak of the original *normative* experience. What would justify the evaluation of the original Christian experience as normative for others unless it could be demonstrative to be the only legitimate response to divinely authoritative disclosures in word and deed? The position of *The British Weekly* was therefore somewhat mediating, but it could hardly serve as a golden mean between the more forthright positions of orthodoxy as represented by Machen on the one hand and modernism for which Dr. Fosdick was an eloquent spokesman on the other.

18

EXPLOSIVE DEVELOPMENTS

Though Machen's analysis of the doctrinal issue of the day as an antithesis between Christianity and Liberalism envisaged the struggle in world-wide terms, and thus as affecting all denominations, he was, in view of his personal and official commitments, most deeply concerned with the struggle as it affected the denomination in which he was a minister. There it developed in a distinctive manner due to a number of considerations. That the Presbyterian Church was a constitutional church with specific formulas of subscription binding officers to the Bible and the Confession of Faith was highly significant, as appeared both in the Fosdick case and in the publication of the Auburn *Affirmation*. Another distinctive factor was the consideration that many Presbyterians still vigorously maintained the traditional Calvinism of the Westminster standards, and that effective instruction and leadership were being provided by Princeton Seminary, the largest and oldest of the Presbyterian theological schools. As the lines were more sharply drawn, however, it came to appear that the Church had largely drifted away from a strict interpretation of its constitution, and that the modernists would gain support for their cry for tolerance from large numbers of ministers and members who were wont to reckon themselves conservatives in theology. The ultimate result accordingly was that distinctive Presbyterianism was largely given up in favor of a broad ecumenism.

THE FOSDICK CASE

One intense phase of the Presbyterian conflict developed in connection with the preaching of Harry Emerson Fosdick in the First Presbyterian Church in New York City. At the time he had not yet attained the fame he was to receive as a radio preacher on a national hookup and as minister of Riverside Church in New York. But his labors as a Baptist minister since his ordination in 1903, membership in the Faculty of Union Theological Seminary, and publication of several popular religious books had made him widely known. In the controversy that had developed about modernism on the mission fields in the

Orient, Dr. Fosdick, who had visited the fields, took quite the opposite position from that of various evangelicals. He was reported as having criticized the more conservative missionaries as being often unintelligent, backward-looking, obscurantist and standing for a type of Christianity that was not worthy of being transplanted at all. His ministry as stated supply at the First Presbyterian Church began to attract the special notice of Presbyterians when from time to time his pulpit utterances were publicized. But it took a particular sermon preached on May 22, 1922 to bring matters into open conflict, a sermon circulated widely under the provocative title, "Shall the Fundamentalists Win?"

The sermon probably had in view fully as much the situation that had developed among American Baptists as in the Presbyterian Church. And if it had been preached from a Baptist pulpit its consequences, at least for our narrative, would have been far less significant. Even if the same sermon had been preached by a Presbyterian, it is probable that it would have stirred up less excitement. But the fact that a minister not even subject to the authority of Presbytery and General Assembly should have used a Presbyterian pulpit to make what was widely regarded as an attack upon the constitution disclosed a situation bordering on lawlessness.

The sermon in the main took the form of entering a plea for tolerance of the position of the Liberals. At the same time it excoriated the "intolerance" of the fundamentalists. Its attack upon orthodox doctrines was later played down by the argument that the sermon did not involve commitment on Fosdick's part to the position of Liberalism. In view of the fact, however, that Fosdick admitted that he was speaking "from the viewpoint of liberal opinions," this effort to minimize its liberalism was rather astonishing. But even apart from this admission, the very plea for tolerance as expressed in the sermon constituted an even more radical attack upon various doctrines than their outright denial would have been. For the underlying philosophy, as Machen's later discussion of the issues also stressed, was that it was a matter of ultimate indifference exactly what one believed and whether or not one believed the doctrines of historic orthodoxy at all. By implication at least Fosdick was giving expression to a point of view, which was to come to more explicit formulation later on, that the essence of Christianity consists of certain abiding experiences. On this approach the doctrinal formulations of the Christian religion as found in the Bible are viewed as merely temporary mental categories in which those experiences came to expression. Accordingly quite new doctrinal formulations might, and should, from time to time emerge to enshrine those experiences.

Thus, the sermon contended, there are those who hold to the Virgin Birth as an historical fact. In the evangelical churches other "equally loyal and reverent people," however, look upon the Virgin Birth simply as an explanation of great personality and one of the ways in which the ancient world was accustomed to account for unusual superiority. The doctrine thus serves to express the conviction that Jesus came especially from God and the consequent adoration of Jesus "in terms of a biological miracle that our modern minds cannot use." Some Christians, it was declared, hold that Christ is literally coming on the clouds of heaven, but others when they say "Christ is coming" express the "exhilarating insight which these recent generations have given to us, that development is God's way of working out his will . . . that, slowly it may be but surely, his will and principles will be worked out by God's grace in human life and institutions, until 'he shall see of the travail of his soul and shall be satisfied.' "

The man who now came forward to spearhead the opposition to the preaching of Dr. Fosdick was not Machen but Clarence E. Macartney, a classmate of Machen's at Princeton. His eloquent and vigorous preaching at the Arch St. Presbyterian Church of Philadelphia, where he had become minister in 1914, had come to attract considerable attention. Machen himself, though previously not more than an acquaintance of Macartney's, came to share the general admiration of his preaching, and later became an intimate friend and associate in the struggle of the years that followed. Writing to his mother on March 27, 1922, he gave his impressions of an evening service at Arch Street: "It was a rainy night, yet the huge church was so filled that it was difficult to get a seat. Macartney is the preacher of the day in America, so far as my observation and judgment go." A later characterization, written to another Seminary classmate on April 30, 1923, indicates his growing appreciation of the man:

> Our classmate Macartney has turned out to be a great man. I use the term advisedly—really I do think he is a great man, or as great as any man can be pronounced to be by his contemporaries. Despite the calumnies of the "Liberals" Macartney is animated solely by love of Christ and of the truth. When he preaches I know that I am in the presence of a man of God. It does not seem like an ordinary sermon at all.

Macartney undertook a reply to Fosdick's sermon in the columns of *The Presbyterian* for July 13 and 20, 1922. Under the title, "Shall Unbelief Win?", among other things, he said:

> Those who agree with the position held by Dr. Fosdick will hail it with delight as a sort of declaration of principles . . . But there are not a few others who do not think of themselves as either "Fundamentalists" or "Moderns" but as Christians, and are striving amid the dust and the confused clamor of this life to hold on to the Christian faith and follow the Lord Jesus Christ, who will read the sermon with sorrow and pain. The Presbyterians who read it will deeply regret that such an utterance, so hopelessly irreconcilable with the standard of belief required by the Reformed churches, could be made by the stated occupant of a Presbyterian pulpit, and apparently either without any protest or wonder on the part of the session of the church or the presbytery to which the church belongs.

Macartney was not content with the utterance of this protest, but, suiting action to the word, prepared an overture for presentation to the Presbytery of Philadelphia at its fall meeting. In connection with the preparation of the overture he corresponded with Fosdick to check whether the printed form was accurate. Fosdick affirmed its substantial accuracy, though he did claim that the discourse was essentially "a plea for tolerance," contrasting extreme conservative and extreme liberal positions in the interest of saying that even when people are as far apart as these positions, one must still strive to keep them within the fellowship of the family of Christ. He also affirmed belief in the deity of Christ, adding however the significant interpretation, "He is the place where I find God and He finds me."

The Philadelphia overture was adopted at the October, 1922, meeting. It drew direct attention to the preaching at the First Presbyterian Church of New York and the widespread distribution of sermons preached there, including especially the sermon of May 22nd. It also recalled the deliverance of the General Assembly of 1916 affirming the five fundamental doctrines as essential on the background of dissatisfaction with the Presbytery of New York. And it petitioned the Assembly to direct the body to take whatever steps might be necessary to see that the preaching in that Church should conform to the Confession of Faith.

When the Assembly of 1923 convened at Indianapolis, it appeared to be rather evenly divided between liberals and conservatives. The former gained a great advantage, however, when their candidate for moderator, Dr. C. F. Wishart, won by a majority of 24 votes over William Jennings Bryan. Their advantage appeared even greater when the influential Committee on Bills and Overtures recommended by a majority of 21 to 1 to reject the Philadelphia overture and to allow the Presbytery of New York to conduct its own investigation in the Fosdick matter. But the minority report of one, presented by Dr. A. Gordon Mac Lennan of Philadelphia, nevertheless won the day by a majority of 80 votes in a total of about 900. Besides directing the Presbytery to require that the preaching and teaching at the New York Church should conform to the Bible and the Confession of Faith, the Assembly, in adopting the minority report, again affirmed as essential the infallibility of the Scriptures, the virgin birth of Christ, his substitutionary atonement, his bodily resurrection, and the miracles of Christ.

The Presbytery of New York largely ignored the mandate of the Assembly. It minimized the liberalism of the Presbytery, and even proceeded to license Henry P. Van Dusen and another candidate for the ministry who refused to affirm belief in the virgin birth of Christ. Thus the victory at the Assembly proved a hollow one.

GROWING ALARM

Such developments, however, stirred up the evangelicals to concerted action. Dr. Walter D. Buchanan, conservative pastor of the Broadway Presbyterian Church, was host at a dinner in New York City in October, 1923, which led to the formation of a group, later to be organized as a League of Faith, which sought to hold the line for historic Presbyterianism. Among the speakers on that first occasion were Macartney and Machen who were to be among the most influential members of the group. Concerning Machen's presence at that meeting a contemporary report said:

> No man today is contributing more to the cause of evangelical religion than Dr. Machen. His trenchant utterances rouse the loyalists to great enthusiasm and are the despair of those who would like to see the Presbyterian Church turned into a Total Toleration Society. For inexorable logic, mastery of the Scriptures, and fervent appeal Dr. Machen has few equals. His tireless efforts deserve the prayers of the whole church. In him, Princeton again speaks with a mighty voice.

Mass meetings were held in a number of cities, including one in Philadelphia, largely sponsored by Macartney, which received unexpected publicity when Dr. Henry van Dyke, even before the meeting was held, released to the daily press a letter written to Macartney, in which he gave vigorous expression to his unwillingness to support the objectives of the rally. In part he said:

> How can a man claim to approve the spirit of "this meeting" unless he knows what that spirit is to be? If it is to be divisive and ex-

clusive, a beginning of theological word-battles and heresy trials; if it is to set up new tests of orthodoxy unknown to our standards and the Bible, and attempt their rigid enforcement by expulsion or the ecclesiastical boycott; why, then, I should be in hearty discord with such a spirit as highly injurious to our branch of the Christian church.

It was about this time too that *The Presbyterian* girded on fresh armor as the urgency of the situation in the Church became more and more apparent. In its first issue of 1924 it stated: "We are facing a great crisis in the history of the church in America, and with the loyal support and cooperation of its friends, *The Presbyterian* intends to do its full share in maintaining and strengthening the faith and in resisting those tendencies which imperil the very life of the Church of Christ." At the same time it announced that henceforth Dr. David S. Kennedy as Editor-in-Chief would enjoy as associates on the staff of the paper several of the most influential conservatives of the Church: Wm. L. McEwan, Maitland Alexander, Samuel G. Craig, Clarence E. Macartney, and J. Gresham Machen. The result was that Machen, though no more than the other associates responsible for the contents of the paper, made even more frequent contributions to its pages than in previous years.

Though intensely concerned with the broader ecclesiastical developments in the Presbyterian Church, Machen was largely absorbed with his duties at Princeton. In truth he had no other choice during the period of his service as stated supply preacher at the First Presbyterian Church of Princeton beginning in October, 1923. As he wrote his mother the previous June 5th, he had accepted the invitation of the session "with great trepidation." The opportunity afforded was "immense," but the preparation of sermons would be very demanding and his liberty of movement gone. Little did he realize how much attention would be drawn to his labors in proclaiming and defending the gospel in what had promised to be a far more isolated and quiet post than the First Presbyterian Church of New York!

THE VAN DYKE INCIDENT

Among those who were wont to attend the services at old First Church of Princeton were some persons of distinctly liberal outlook, and they understandably were not pleased with Machen's uncompromising messages. Before long he began to receive indirect reports that Dr. Henry van Dyke, one of this group, had been openly critical of his preaching. He was entirely unprepared, however, for the scorching outburst which van Dyke sent to the session on December 31st, and forthwith released to the newspapers:

> Having had another Sabbath spoiled by the bitter, schismatic and unscriptural preaching of the stated supply of the First Presbyterian Church of Princeton (directly contrary to the spirit of his beautiful text) I desire to give up my pew in the church. The few Sabbaths that I am free from evangelical work to spend with my family are too precious to be wasted in listening to such a dismal, bilious travesty of the gospel. We want to hear about Christ, the Son of God and the Son of Man, not about Fundamentalists and Modernists, the only subject on which your stated supply seems to have anything to say, and what he says is untrue and malicious. Until he is done, count me out, and give up my pew in the church. We want to worship Christ, our Saviour.

No wonder, considering the prominence of the persons concerned, and the explosiveness of the language employed, that the newspapers gave the incident conspicuous publicity. It was reported throughout the country. In such Eastern papers as the Trenton *Evening Times* and the Philadelphia *Public Ledger* the story was featured on the front page.

When one recalls the family ties dating back to Baltimore days and the pleasant contacts of Machen's early years at Princeton, the violence of van Dyke's attack is rather overwhelming. These considerations only serve to point up, however, the thoroughness of van Dyke's opposition to Machen's point of view as well as certain facets of his own character. He suggests indeed in his letter to the Session that he is quite evangelical in his beliefs. But actually van Dyke had been for several decades in the very forefront of the Liberal forces in the Presybterian Church, as the biography by his son Tertius van Dyke affords ample proof. As preacher of the Brick Presbyterian Church of New York he had been an intimate friend and supporter of Professors Briggs and McGiffert. He had been openly and vigorously opposed to the specific Calvinism of the Confession of Faith and had been one of the leading advocates of revision. He also had supported the policy of the Presbytery of New York in allowing various young men to be licensed in spite of their unwillingness to affirm the five points insisted upon by the General Assembly of 1910 and later years. When the Auburn *Affirmation* was published, he became a signer. His record as disclosed at these points and many others was that of a pronounced Liberal.

One might be misled by the attack to suppose that there was some particularly offensive feature in Dr. Machen's sermon on "The Present Issue in the Church" which was preached on that final Sunday morning in the year 1923. The sermon was published in the Trenton *Evening Times,* in *The Presbyterian* and in pamphlet form for all the world to read what had actually been said. An unbiased reader of this sermon and others preached during the preceding weeks will be astonished that they could have provoked this bitter and uncharitable attack. On the other hand, the sermon contained a telling exposure of the sophistry of many modernists and this may have struck home. "Formerly," said Machen, "when men had brought to their attention perfectly plain documents like the Apostles' Creed or the Westminster Confession or the New Testament, they either accepted them or else denied them. Now they no longer deny, but merely 'interpret.' Every generation, it is said, must interpret the Bible or the Creed in its own way. But I sometimes wonder just how far this business of interpretation will go." He illustrated his point from mathematics, and history, and finally from the resurrection.

> And then finally the examination turns (though still in the sphere of history) to the department of history that concerns the Christian religion. "What do you think happened," I am asked, "after Jesus was laid in that tomb near Jerusalem about nineteen hundred years ago?" To that question also I have a very definite answer. "I will tell you what I think happened," I say, "He was laid in the tomb and then, the third day he rose again from the dead." At this point the surprise of my modern friend reaches its height. The idea of a professor in a theological seminary actually believing that the body of a dead man actually emerged from the grave! "Everyone," he tells me, "has abandoned that answer to the question long ago." "But," I say, "my friend, this is very serious; that answer stands in the Apostles' Creed as well as at the center of the New Testament; do you not accept the Apostles' Creed?" "Oh, yes," says my modern friend, "of course I accept the Apostles' Creed; do we not say it every Sunday in Church?—or if we do not say it, we sing it—of course I accept the Apostles' Creed. But then, do you not see, every generation has the right to interpret the Creed in its own way. And so now of course we accept the proposition that "the third day He arose again from the dead," but we interpret that to mean, "The third day He did not rise again from the dead."

Machen retained an admirable calm and decided that he would make no comment whatever upon the published attack. But many were quick to rise up to his defense. The Newark *Evening News* on Jan. 5 editorialized on "Dr. van Dyke's Original Way of Seeking Peace." Dr.

John Fox of Easton was quoted in The New York *Times* for Jan. 4 as saying that, though Dr. van Dyke says he hates heresy-hunts, "the tone and language of his attack upon Dr. Machen sounds to me like heresy-hunting at its worst." Dr. Macartney, in an interview published in the Philadelphia *Public Ledger* for Jan 5, praised Machen as "one of the chief ornaments of the Presbyterian Church in its witness to the truth of divine revelation," and reflecting on the liberal views of van Dyke, stated that "no higher tribute could be paid to a true minister of Jesus Christ than that which Dr. van Dyke has paid Dr. Machen by withdrawing from the First Church of Princeton." *The Presbyterian*'s editorial included the following:

> We think Dr. van Dyke has done the right thing. If we held a pew in a church where the minister was preaching according to the requirements of the church, and at the same time contrary to what we sacredly believed, we should quietly give up the pew and seek fellowship elsewhere . . . But Dr. van Dyke ought to go further . . . Dr. van Dyke's opposition is not only against the preacher, but against the whole Presbyterian and Protestant Church. He ought therefore to move on across the line into some body like the Unitarian, and then he will no longer be troubled with the doctrine of the inerrancy of Scripture or the doctrine of the blood atonement.

Machen received a flood of letters, mostly from persons who sympathized with him in the obloquy cast upon him and desired to encourage him to continue his forthright stand for the Gospel. The love and sympathy of members of his family were as unbounded and timely as usual. His mother was very upset at the attack and spoke of Dr. van Dyke's reputation for conceit:

> Dr. v. D. plays for public notice as always. Of course, if he really cared for the peace of the Church, he would have quietly absented himself until the "stated supply" was no longer preaching.
>
> This is no comfort except that I must assure you before I go to bed that we are all with you. I hope you can keep out of a controversy with that man—personal, I mean. If he chooses to leave in a fit of temper and advertise the fact in the public press—why let him do so and just go quietly on preaching the Gospel.

On Jan. 4th he had written his mother:

> No doubt the Baltimore papers along with all other papers have published Dr. van Dyke's attack on me. I am enclosing a clipping or two. Yesterday was a busy day. Reporters in the vicinity of

Dassy were as thick as flies. I gave the sermon in full to several of them, but it has not yet been printed in full.

I am not worrying at all. Dr. van Dyke has very obviously made a fool of himself. He has clearly done harm to his own cause. Of course it is unpleasant, but I do not mind unpleasant things when they are not my own fault.

What a joy the holidays were! My mother is more precious to me all the time.

I must proceed now to the multitudinous letters of the day.

His brother Arthur wrote as follows on the 5th:

"Uncle Henry's" splenetic outburst will, no doubt, be a splendid thing for your propaganda, and I hasten to tell you so. Some of the publicity experts, on either side of the question, would deliberately have provoked such a situation for the sake of advertising value. Of course, you have not done this, but you can derive comfort from the reflection that what you were too much of a gentleman to do for yourself, van Dyke has done for you.

I am glad too that you have not allowed yourself to be drawn into a newspaper quarrel, but have maintained a dignified silence.

In reply Machen said:

Your letter of today has given me a world of encouragement. It warms my heart to have your support against the attack which Dr. van Dyke launched against me. As to the particular way in which the attack was made I do not see how even "Modernists" could feel anything but reprobation.

Yesterday from morn till night I was talking to reporters—either to those that the New York and Philadelphia papers sent to cover the case or else to the offices over long distance phone. I had nothing to say about Dr. van Dyke's letter itself, but saying that one has nothing to say sometimes seems to take hours. My voice was nearly gone when the day was over.

I sent to Mother the complete sermon, which was excellently printed in the Trenton *Times*. Unfortunately none of the big papers seems to have done this fair and satisfactory thing.

MESSAGES OF APPRECIATION

Among the other messages was one from Professor Frederick N. Willson of the University Faculty, who wired: "Regret prevented by absence from hearing you Sunday. Approve your line of goods heartily." A fellow minister (J. M. Corum, Jr., of Norristown) said merely,

"Dear Das: Stick to your guns. With much love, Co." Another minister (H. M. McQuilkin of Orange, N. J.) wrote: "Just a word to commend you for courageously proclaiming the truth. . . . God bless you, my dear brother. I love you for your loyalty." Another minister (Parke Richards) remarked that the action of van Dyke

> appears to me to be ill-advised, but it may have resulted in some good by bringing about a "broadcasting" of your thotful sermon and causing it to reach a far wider audience than it otherwise would have done. The manner in which you dealt with "interpretation" and with the importance of a truly exalted conception of the Person of Jesus was, in the first instance, an exposure of the sophistry of the Modernists and, in the second, a joy to humble followers of our Lord.
>
> I am writing this not because of any feeling that you need moral support, but only to assure you that my sympathy is with you in this bit of publicity which has come to you, not because it has been courted, but because of your faithful proclamation of the truth.

One of the most encouraging tributes that came to Machen during this period was sent by one of his colleagues concerning his son's reactions to Machen's preaching as a whole:

> I want to express to you my own but especially also L.'s deep appreciation of your preaching in the First Church. Of course, I have not been able to hear you often, but L. . . . goes almost every Sunday morning and evening, and I want to do what I told him to do but what he hesitates to do because he expects soon to be a member of your seminary classes—tell you how much you have helped him with your clear-cut and persuasive presentation of fundamental evangelicalism. A summer or two ago he was at Silver Bay and was much impressed by Drs. Fosdick and Coffin, and he was evidently, judging from his arguments with me, quite ready to endorse their views. But he had little satisfaction in his Christian faith and hope. He has now come to see things in a different light. I always felt he would in due time, but it is only the truth to say that it has been your preaching that has given him what he is now sure is really the gospel, and he has great peace and joy in believing it and a great desire to make it known to others. He feels much indebted to you, and of course his parents are greatly pleased with the help you have given him. He admires your courage and fidelity to conviction, and his remarks about your ministrations are so fragrant and so commendatory that I felt I ought, in view of some of the trying features of your task in the First Church, to give

you this word of assurance and encouragement. I wish there were more college boys who might be led to see things as L. . . . now does, and as you have enabled him to do.

In due course Machen also heard from Dr. Patton after he had had the opportunity of reading the sermon. Writing from his Bermuda home on July 22, 1924, he said that he was sorry that Dr. van Dyke had taken the attitude he did—"there was no good reason for it. With your position I am in hearty sympathy." But Machen was to receive another heartwarming tribute from Patton which was not less appreciated because it was not occassioned by the van Dyke attack. On Christmas Day, 1923, Machen had been in Patton's thoughts and he had composed the following poem which reached Machen right after the first of the year.

TO J. GRESHAM MACHEN

"This is the month and this is the happy morn
Wherein the Son of Heaven's eternal King
Of Wedded maid and Virgin mother born,
Our great redemption from above did bring."

To you who have so well defended
The faith which Milton sings
Whose thought has far transcended
The look of "earthly things,"
I send these lines
Which are the signs
And tokens of my love
(Confusions wild
Of trochee and iambic
Which have beguiled
An hour with my alembic)
I pray that coming from above
Strength may be yours to fight
For truth, until life's night
Has curtained you in rest;
Till taught by you
To seek the true
Men find the Highest and the Best.
And those who doubt and those who scorn
With those to false views leaning

Shall learn the joyous meaning
Of this bright Christmas morn.
Bermuda Affectionately
25 Dec. 1923 Francis L. Patton

Machen continued his ministry at the First Church through the Spring of 1924, and then, as the Seminary year drew to a close, he asked to be relieved of this responsibility. He had enjoyed the experience immensely, but it had been a strain to prepare two sermons every week especially since his "barrel" had never been packed by the demands of a pastoral charge. And he missed the opportunities afforded by the many invitations that came to him to preach in other churches.

When his resignation became known, it was inevitable that it should be represented by some in an unfavorable light. *Time* magazine flatly stated that "he was relieved of his position," and then equivocally went on to say:

> It was not announced whether or not Dr. Machen's withdrawal was an aftermath of the flurry that occurred when Dr. Henry van Dyke, genial Princeton patriarch, protested against "the bitter, schismatic and unscriptural preaching of the stated supply" . . . In connection with the release, however, the session of the First Presbyterian Church published a tribute to Dr. Machen in *The Presbyterian.*

The facts are however perfectly clear. They show that Machen himself took the initiative in this matter, and that there was a cordial relation between him and the session. The letter of this body accepting his resignation was as follows:

> In releasing Dr. J. Gresham Machen, at his own request, from his relationship of Stated Supply of the First Presbyterian Church of Princeton, N. J., the Session wishes to express to him its appreciation of his faithful ministrations over many months, and its recognition of the force of his reasons for the severance of the connection, as its continuance could not, as he states, be otherwise than at such further considerable sacrifice of his primary work in the Princeton Theological Seminary as the preparation of two new sermons per week involves, while preventing such responses as he should be freer to make to demands on his time outside of Princeton.
>
> The Session would pay an especial tribute to his able and logical defense of the doctrines with which the "Old First" has always

been identified, and wishes to assure him, that as he has led the congregation in the Apostles' Creed they have said it with and like him—without mental reservations.

His more intimate relationship of Moderator of the Session has been sustained with dignity and most helpfully, while his versatility and adaptability to the exercises of special occasions should not fail of mention in this, our parting, word.

It is with highest respect and personal regard that we release him from the position of Stated Supply.

The Session of the First Presbyterian Church of Princeton, N. J.

(signed) H. E. Hale, Jr., Clerk

THE AUBURN AFFIRMATION

In the midst of Machen's year as preacher at First Church in Princeton there emerged a new development of overwhelming proportions and scope. This was the publication on the 9th of January, 1924 of a statement of 150 Presbyterian clergymen entitled, "An Affirmation Designed to Safeguard the Unity and Liberty of the Presbyterian Church in the U. S. A." Because of its origin at Auburn Seminary it came generally to be known as the Auburn Affirmation. It seems, however, to have been publicized chiefly from Union Seminary in New York City, and eventually nearly 1300 ministers subscribed. The Affirmation was in the first place a protest against the deliverances of the Assembly of 1923 in connection with the Fosdick case, and thus it was not an isolated development. Indeed, because of the breadth of its support, and the ultimate victory achieved for its point of view, the defense of Fosdick and the van Dyke attack upon Machen may be best understood as warning swells of a tidal wave of inclusivism that was about to sweep over the Presbyterian Church.

The radical significance of the Affirmation is not immediately apparent for it states at the outset that the signers are loyal to their ordination vows and the doctrines of evangelical Christianity. Moreover, it takes the form, to a large extent, of pleading for the maintenance of constitutional liberties in the face of "persistent attempts to divide the Church and to abridge its freedom." In support of its plea it enjoyed a measure of plausibility from the fact that, besides finding allowance for diverse interpretations in the terms of the formula of subscription, it centered attention upon the inclusivism manifested in the reunion of 1870 and the Cumberland Union of 1906.

Further analysis discloses, however, that the Affirmation contains a bold and thoroughgoing attack upon the doctrines of the Confession.

It was most forthright in opposing the doctrine of the inerrancy of the Scriptures: "The doctrine of inerrancy, intended to enhance the authority of the Scriptures, in fact impairs their supreme authority for faith and life, and weakens the testimony of the church to the power of God unto salvation through Jesus Christ." The word "inerrancy" is indeed not found in the Confession, but what is connoted by it, namely, the complete truthfulness and trustworthiness of the Scriptures, certainly is. And the ordination vows also use the word "infallible" which historically has the same connotation.

The attack upon the other doctrines of the 1923 deliverance was somewhat more subtle. It took the form of declaring that the doctrines were really "theories." The action of the Assembly, it stated,

> attempts to commit our church to certain theories concerning the inspiration of the Bible, and the incarnation, the Atonement, the Resurrection, and the Continuing Life and Supernatural Power of our Lord Jesus Christ. We hold most earnestly to these great facts and doctrines; we all believe from our hearts that the writers of the Bible were inspired of God; that Jesus Christ was God manifest in the flesh; that God was in Christ, reconciling the world unto Himself, and through Him we have our redemption; that having died for our sins He rose from the dead and is our ever-living Saviour; that in His earthly ministry He wrought many mighty works, and by His vicarious death and unfailing presence He is able to save to the uttermost. Some of us regard the particular theories contained in the deliverance of the General Assembly of 1923 as satisfactory explanations of these facts and doctrines. But we are united in believing that these are not the only theories allowed by the Scriptures and our standards as explanations of these facts and doctrines of our religion, and that all who hold to these facts and doctrines, whatever theories they may employ to explain them, are worthy of all confidence and fellowship.

Thus, the Virgin Birth of Christ, for example, is viewed as a theory of the Incarnation and the bodily resurrection of Christ as a theory of the Resurrection. And liberty is claimed for other theories.

On the very day that the Affirmation was published, Machen sent a communication to the New York *Times* which appeared in its columns the following day. He felt that the document was "a deplorable attempt to obscure the issue" of the day and it might mislead plain people who regard as basal facts what the signers regard as theories. Those familiar with the present religious situation, no matter what their own religious views may be, he went on to say, "will understand perfectly well that many of the signers of this declaration agree with Dr. Fosdick in being opposed not only to the creed of the Presbyterian Church, but to everything that is really distinctive of historic Christianity... The plain fact is that two mutually exclusive religions are being proclaimed in the pulpits of the Presbyterian Church."

That Machen was right in asserting that conservatives were not the only persons who recognized the profundity of the current religious issue appears from a contemporaneous utterance in *The Christian Century*, the acknowledged voice of religious liberalism. Perhaps it was reflecting on the Affirmation for it had been privately circulated for some time before its official publication on January 9th. At any rate, in its issue of January 3, 1924, the *Century* stated:

> The differences between Fundamentalism and modernism are not mere surface differences which can be amiably waved aside or disregarded, but they are foundation differences, structural differences, amounting in their radical dissimilarity almost to the differences between two distinct religions... Two world-views, two moral ideals, two sets of personal attitudes, have clashed, and it is a case of ostrich-like intelligence blindly to deny and evade the searching and serious character of the issue. Christianity, according to fundamentalism, is one religion. Christianity, according to Modernism, is another religion... Christianity is hardly likely to last much longer half-fundamentalist and half-modernist. It is not merely the aggressiveness of fundamentalism that is forcing a choice, it is the inherent nature of the issue itself.

Thus Machen's thesis, enunciated in *Christianity and Liberalism*, as applied to the Affirmation won support from an unexpected quarter. About the same time a group of Unitarians headed by Charles Eliot, former president of Harvard, issued what amounted to a severe indictment of modernists in the evangelical churches, and of the Presbyterian signers of the Affirmation in particular:

> With all courtesy and consideration, let us make it plain that religious teachers who play with words in the most solemn relations of life, who make their creeds mean what they were not originally intended to mean, or mentally reject a formula of belief while outwardly repeating it, cannot expect to retain the allegiance of men who are accustomed to straight thinking and square dealing.

For a time after the publication of the Affirmation, consideration was given to the possibility of circulating a counter-affirmation. After conference with Macartney and others it was decided that conservatives would be on stronger ground in not making any formal and signed reply, but Machen's tentative draft remains as a masterful analysis. It reads as follows:

A Counter-Affirmation designed to Safeguard the Corporate Witness of the Presbyterian Church to the Gospel of Jesus Christ.

We the undersigned, ministers of the Presbyterian Church in the United States of America, having been made cognizant of an Affirmation signed by one hundred and fifty ministers in protest against the action of the General Assembly of 1923, and being convinced that the Affirmation will have an effect detrimental to the unity and to the corporate witness of the Church, desire to make the following answer:

I. The constitution of the Church, though it does not claim infallibility for itself, clearly does claim it (in the pledge required of all officers) for the Scriptures. This fact is ignored and in effect denied in the Affirmation.

II. The right of interpretation of the Scriptures and of the system of doctrine contained in the Confession does not mean that any officer of the Church may interpret the Scriptures or the system of doctrine described in the Confession as he pleases. Every interpretation must conform to the meaning of the Scriptures and of the system of doctrine contained in the Confession where the meaning is clear. The interpretations for which tolerance is asked in section IV of the Affirmation, on the contrary, reverses the plain meaning. Thus the Affirmation really advocates the destruction of the confessional witness of the Church. To allow interpretations which reverse the meaning of a confession is exactly the same thing as to have no confession at all.

III. In Section IV of the Affirmation, the five points covered in the pronouncement of the General Assembly of 1923 are declared to be "theories" which some of the signers of the Affirmation regard as satisfactory but which all of the signers unite in believing not to be the only theories allowed by the Scriptures. This means that the Scriptures allow the Virgin Birth, for example, and the bodily resurrection of our Lord to be regarded both as facts and not as facts. We protest against any such opinion. The redemptive events mentioned in the pronouncement of the Assembly are not theories but facts upon which Christianity is based. and without which Christianity would fall.

IV. We believe that the unity of the Presbyterian Church in the United States of America can be safeguarded, not by a liberty of interpretation on the part of the officers of the Church which allows a complete reversal of perfectly plain documents, but only by maintenance of the corporate witness of the Church. The Church is founded not upon agnosticism but upon a common adherence to the truth of the gospel as set forth in the confession of faith on the basis of the Scriptures.

THE ASSEMBLY OF 1924

It was clear to all, following the publication of the Affirmation as a protest against the decisions of the Assembly of 1923, that the Assembly of 1924 would be a critical one. During those tense months before the Assembly was to convene in Grand Rapids, Machen contributed no fewer than three articles to *The Presbyterian,* one being a two-part article on "The Parting of the Ways" which appeared in April. In this article he analyzed at length the situation with which the Church was confronted as the result of the revelations of the unwillingness of large elements of the Church to submit to the last Assembly's decision. "The Presbyterian Church in the United States of America," he declared, "has apparently come to the parting of the ways. It may stand for Christ, or it may stand against him, but it can hardly halt between two opinions." In the course of the article he also corrected certain misapprehensions as to the aims of the conservatives. "We do not wish to split the church; on the contrary we are working for the unity of the church with all our might. But in order that there should be unity within the church, it is necessary above all that there should be sharp separation of the church from the world. The carrying out of that separation is a prime duty of the hour."

The choice of a moderator was obviously a matter of prime importance, and the Presbytery of Philadelphia heartily endorsed Macartney for the position. When this became known Machen was delighted for he felt that nothing would serve so well to draw the lines clearly, and he had a special responsibility since he was a delegate of his own Presbytery. In view of his considered judgment as to the urgency of the situation confronting the Church, it is understandable that he favored Macartney above his own Seminary colleague, Dr. Charles E. Erdman, who won the support of the modernist and mediating elements in the Church. Macartney was elected moderator and this was one of the most encouraging developments in a long time.

After the Assembly was over, and its total work was more soberly assessed, however, Machen was far from joyful. Indeed, he was convinced that a decision taken with regard to Fosdick near the end of the

Assembly more than outweighed the advantages which the conservatives had gained. This developed in connection with action upon a complaint sent up to the Assembly by certain New York conservatives led by Dr. Buchanan because of the failure of their presbytery to comply with the directives of the 1923 Assembly. On recommendation of its Permanent Judicial Commission the Assembly took the astonishing position that the Fosdick issue was really administrative rather than doctrinal. It merely required of the New York church that it take up with Dr. Fosdick the question whether it was his pleasure to enter the Presbyterian Church and thus to be in regular relationship with that Church as one of its pastors. Hence, though there were minor victories, slight changes for the better in the personnel of the Boards were made and pious resolutions relating to the theological seminaries and foreign missions were passed, Machen was clear that the doctrinal issue of the day had been largely by-passed. In analyzing the Assembly on June 10, 1924 Machen said in a letter to Dr. Maitland Alexander:

> I do not think that we ought to agree quite with the New York men when they maintain that Dr. Fosdick's teachings have been examined and approved, and on the basis of the examination he is graciously invited to become a minister in our Church. Yet we did suffer a great defeat at the end of the Assembly; and I think that if we represent it as a victory, or if we give the impression that we regard the battle as over, we are traitors to our cause...
>
> Army greeted me as though I were a defeated soldier returning from the field of battle. But I am informed that his delight at Macartney's election was most refreshing. That was what made the Fosdick matter hard; we were suddenly plunged from joy to grief.
>
> However, a number of glorious victories were won at the Assembly, and I think that we can continue to fight with renewed hopefulness. *The Continent, The Presbyterian Advance* and other papers are representing the Assembly very much as though they had altogether their way; but the editors of those papers know perfectly well that that was not the case.
>
> Did you see Craig's article in *The Presbyterian* on "A Monstrous Proposal"? It was fine.

Expressing his amazement that the Fosdick issue was regarded as merely a question of his ministerial membership, Dr. Craig had written, on June 5, 1924, that the Assembly's proposal to the Presbytery of New York quite overlooked the fact that the disturbance arose from the belief that Dr. Fosdick's teachings "not only openly deny the essential doctrines of the Presbyterian Church but they are subversive of the truth of Christianity as received, confessed, held and defended by the Christian church of all ages."

To Dr. Fosdick's lasting credit he did not respond favorably to the invitation of the Presbytery of New York regarding his ministerial membership, stating in outright fashion that he was unwilling to subscribe to any confession of faith on the ground that it would violate his conscience. He also indicated his intention of resigning his post as associate minister. With the encouragement of the session, however, he continued to occupy the pulpit until March 1, 1925.

During the earlier phases of the struggle over Fosdick's preaching, Machen had remained largely in the background except for his stirring article on "The Parting of the Ways" referred to above. Later, however, in October, 1924, when Fosdick's letter of resignation was published, a page of comment was contributed to *The Presbyterian* in which he laid bare the scepticism involved in Fosdick's expressed attitude toward Christian creeds. And taking note of Fosdick's declaration that his opinions coincided with those of thousands of Presbyterian ministers, Machen called upon the Church to face the duty of purifying itself so that creedal subscription would "cease to be the miserable farce which in many quarters it has now become." Shortly thereafter, upon invitation of the editor of *The Christian Work,* he engaged in a debate as to the real nature of Fosdick's views. And he also undertook a searching analysis of Fosdick's new book on *The Modern Use of the Bible.*

19

VALLEY OF HUMILIATION

As the ecclesiastical conflict became more intense, it was inevitable that Princeton Seminary as the largest and most influential Seminary of the Presbyterian Church should become increasingly involved. Had the Faculty and Boards of control been solidly united in doctrinal and practical outlook, the Seminary might well have continued for many years to maintain its historic position. Perhaps even considerable reformation of the Church might have been achieved. As we have observed, however, such unity had been lacking for many years. And since the disunity to a considerable degree related to different appraisals of the state of the Church and the proper course to pursue in ecclesiastical matters, the deepening of the larger conflict was bound to have serious repercussions within the Seminary. The student of the earlier phases of difficulty at Princeton might have forecast such an outcome, but he would hardly have been prepared for the volcanic suddenness with which a radical reorganization was effected. Some of these astonishing features of the development involved Machen in a personal and poignant way, and in turn his own personal fortunes had some significant consequences for the broader story.

To persons who analyze history in terms of persons rather than principles, the Princeton conflict seemed to be largely a matter of personalities—the personalties of Erdman or Stevenson on the one hand and that of Machen on the other. Such elements were no doubt involved but they were actually subsidiary and superficial aspects of the struggle. The issue turned about the larger questions of the nature of Christianity and the meaning of the modern religious situation. And so far as Princeton was concerned, it is plain that the defense of orthodoxy was far from being identified simply with Machen's activity. Throughout most of the struggle, if not all of it, the traditional orthodox position was supported vigorously by the overwhelming majority both of the Board of Directors and of the Faculty. So far as Machen's own desires were concerned, he had no zeal for leadership. Frequently even against better judgment he held back when older men in the Directors seemed to be taking the reigns of leadership. In the last analysis, however, he was as prominent as he was because he was the most effective spokesman for this position and was willing to labor in season and out of season regardless of personal cost. He was bound therefore to be identified prominently with that cause, and to be attacked by those who were attacking it. But there were also several times when be became the victim of false charges and rumors that were widely circulated, and so his good name was besmirched. Dr. Macartney once characterized the abusive letters which he and other valiant defenders of the faith received as "the liturgy of execration." But the letters themselves could easily be destroyed. It was not so easy to destroy the evil effects of slander and false rumor.

As Dr. Frank H. Stevenson was to say:

> Dr. Machen has received his share of personal abuse. He accepts it calmly. He is not contending for an immediate verdict. In London this summer he is reported to have said: "Defenders of the Bible are called extreme and bitter men; their opponents usually are called kind and tolerant. I am reminded of an article I saw in an American magazine, *The Saturday Evening Post,* in which an intelligent American Indian humorously characterized descriptions in histories of the wars between white men and the men of his race. 'When you won,' said the Indian, 'it was, according to your histories, a battle. When we won, it was a massacre.' So much for transient verdicts. We will do well to rest our case with the more mature judgment of time, and with the permanent judgment of God.

MACHEN AND ERDMAN

The history of Machen's differences with Dr. Erdman requires close attention because it lays bare the real nature of the controversy and casts a penetrating light upon Machen's own personal character. In spite of the differences of principle with regard to the 1920 plan of union, no personal unpleasantness resulted. Such was not to be the case, however, in the ensuing developments. As has been observed briefly in the preceding chapter, Machen supported Macartney rather than Erdman for the moderatorship of the 1924 General Assembly. The thinking back of this decision must now be set forth somewhat more fully.

For many years Machen had been convinced that the Church was in deadly peril and that it was in imminent danger of being controlled by that indifference to the gospel which had already enervated the larger Protestant churches of the continent of Europe. To him therefore the question of questions in the ecclesiastical sphere was whether the undermining process would go on unchecked, or whether the Presbyterian Church would be aroused to its peril before it was too late.

It was Macartney, as Machen was to say later on, who had spoken out a strong, true word in defense of the witness-bearing of the Church. He thus appeared to be the man of the hour. Perhaps his stand presaged the dawning of a new day for the Church. Machen's whole heart went out to the man who had spoken so bravely, and he felt a loyalty to him in every fiber of his being since what was involved was his own loyalty to the Lord Jesus Christ. In his judgment, moreover, Macartney was "a man of gravity and moderation, scrupulously fair to opponents, singularly free from unworthy personal motives, opposed to extreme unconstitutional methods, and yet full of a holy zeal for the Word of God."

Yet in this situation, to Machen's distress, Dr. Erdman allowed his own name to be forwarded as a candidate for the moderatorship. It was not that Machen was unwilling to think of Erdman as a candidate for the moderatorship under any circumstances. If, for example, in spite of the differences which had emerged in 1920, Dr. Erdman had come to take a stand like that of Macartney, he would gladly have supported him. But the decisive fact was that precisely in this hour of peril Erdman had come to be identified with a policy of inclusivism. He had taken no part in the Fosdick issue except to say, if men are not loyal, "let the law act" — as if the law could act unless the officers of the church discharged their responsibility for its enforcement. According to the Philadelphia *Public Ledger,* moreover, Erdman had declared on the eve of the 1924 Assembly, that he wanted the constructive work of the Presbyterian Church to go on without interruption on account of any doctrinal controversy. To Machen this added up to doctrinal indifferentism. For in his judgment the great question facing the Church was whether the Gospel was being, or was to be preached, at all. And when Erdman was nominated he was commended as "standing" for a united front rather than the encouragement of controversy.

Machen's opposition to Erdman's election was based therefore wholly on principle. Believing that the Church was in peril of losing its evangelical witness, and that if the peril should continue to be ignored the Church would be destroyed, he felt bound to support Macartney rather than Erdman. But at least so far as Machen was concerned this did not have to result in personal bitterness. He carefully avoided any public reflection on the situation which might suggest personal estrangement. It was Dr. Erdman however who gave expression to his resentment at developments at the 1924 Assembly. For in a statement published in the Trenton *Times* on Oct. 15, 1924, he charged that Macartney had been elected as the result of "political maneuvering" on the part of a clique or party headed by William Jennings Bryan. But this charge might have been overlooked were it not for a statement which involved Machen in a most personal way.

This significant development took place early in the year 1925 as an aftermath of the van Dyke incident. The fact that Dr. Erdman had now become the stated supply of the First Church of Princeton was in itself of no special moment in this connection. At this juncture, however, Dr. van Dyke chose to return to the First Church, and this was given wide publicity especially in the liberal papers.

A PROVOCATIVE EDITORIAL

The Presbyterian also chose to comment on it, and in view of the van Dyke attack of the preceding year understandably raised the question whether it did not point to an alignment between modernists like Dr. van Dyke and evangelicals like Erdman. This might perhaps have been expressed in carefully guarded language. But *The Presbyterian* was hardly restrained in some of the questions it raised:

> Does the return of such a pronounced and avowed modernist as Dr. van Dyke to the old church, under the new pastor, mean that he is anticipating more liberal preaching under the new regime? But Dr. Machen and Dr. Erdman are both professors in the same seminary, and both have been regarded as loyal to the position of the seminary and the Standards of the Presbyterian Church to which it belongs. Does this action of Dr. van Dyke signify that two parties are developing in the faculty of Princeton Seminary, or does it simply show a confusion outside? In a recent notice of the installation of Dr. Erdman, the inquiry was raised as to the significance of attempting to unite the rationalism of the university, represented by Drs. van Dyke and Hibben, with the evangelicalism of the seminary represented by Dr. Erdman. Does this action of Dr. van Dyke signify that the rationalists have gained an important advantage from the combination?

The publication of this editorial was, to say the least, a *faux pas*. Somewhat later, in a letter to Macartney, Machen referred to it as "a great blunder, undermining my standing in the community of Princeton and in the Church at large." That it was embarrassing to Machen is entirely understandable. As associate editor he did not see the editorials before publication and he had no responsibility for their contents. On the other hand he agreed cordially with the general policy of the paper against modernism and indifferentism, and would not have been human if he had not appreciated its defense of his name. Machen himself would not have written in this fashion. Though the editorial was mainly a criticism of Dr. van Dyke, and spoke of Erdman as an evangelical, it did suggest that perhaps Dr. van Dyke anticipated more liberal preaching at the First Church. One can appreciate the fact that Dr. Erdman should have been greatly upset when it appeared. But it is particularly unfortunate that he was so aroused that he lost his temper, and wrote a reply which, rather than laying such blame as existed at the feet of the editor of the paper, embraced others in his charges and used language which was bound to be understood as having Machen chiefly in view.

Erdman's letter was in the main a blistering repudiation of the implication, as he understood it, that his ministry was strengthening the forces of rationalism. But it also contained a paragraph in which he reflected on the situation in the Seminary, and stated that "the only division I have observed is as to spirit, methods or policies. This division would be of no consequence were it not for the unkindness, suspicion, bitterness and intolerance of those members of the faculty who are also editors of The Presbyterian." There had been nothing like this charge in all the years that had preceded; the charge was not confined to a difference in principle, but involved a sharp personal attack. *Dr. Machen was the only member of the faculty who was an editor of The Presbyterian, and thus it seemed to center upon him!*

Due to the severity of its language the editor of *The Presbyterian* delayed publication hoping to confer with Erdman about it, but Erdman had chosen to send a copy to *The Presbyterian Advance,* an organ of the liberal party, whose editors published it on Jan. 22, 1925. Wide publicity was given in the daily papers to this letter, with particular prominence to his charges against his colleagues in the Seminary Faculty. And when interviewed by the Trenton *Evening Times,* Erdman became even more explicit in attacking Machen by stating that Dr. van Dyke had left the church "because of the spirit embodied in the preaching of the Rev. Dr. J. Gresham Machen."

It was only then that Machen undertook a reply to Erdman's attack. Even then, however, Machen refrained from answering in terms of personal abuse. Neither he nor any other colleague in the faculty, he pointed out, had any responsibility whatever for the reference to Erdman in *The Presbyterian.* He did not feel that he could restrict his reply to this matter, however, for the intimations of differences at Princeton made it imperative to say plainly what, in his judgment, the issue really was. It was not a matter of personal animosity at all but one solely of principle, he declared. His letter to *The Presbyterian* included the following:

> In the first place, I regret the personal tone in which the letter is couched. If I have ever said anything, in controversy either with Dr. Erdman or with others, to justify such a characterization of me, it has not yet been brought to my attention. I differ from Dr. Erdman profoundly, but I have tried never to allow our differences to prevent me from holding him in high personal esteem.

Having reviewed the differences that emerged chiefly in the Church Union and Fosdick controversies, he spoke of the difference in principle as follows:

> Dr. Erdman does not indeed reject the doctrinal system of our church, but he is perfectly willing to make common cause with those who reject it, and he is perfectly willing on many occasions to keep it in the background. I, on the other hand, can never consent to keep it in the background. Christian doctrine, I hold, is not merely connected with the gospel, but it is identical with the gospel, and if I did not preach it at all times, and especially in those places where it subjects me to personal abuse, I should regard myself as guilty of sheer unfaithfulness to Christ. It is, I hold, only as He is offered to us in the gospel—that is in the "doctrine" which the world despises—that Christ saves sinful men; and never will I create the impression that there can be Christian prayer or Christian service except on the basis of those redeeming facts which are now called in question by a large party in our church . . .

One of the most astonishing features of the situation was that Dr. Erdman never acknowledged, at least not in print, that Machen had been unfairly attacked. An editorial note, accompanying Machen's reply in *The Presbyterian Advance* for Feb. 12, 1925, says that Erdman sought to change the plural reference to "editors" to the singular, but that this correction arrived too late. As a matter of fact this change would have made the apparent allusion to Machen even more specific! Meanwhile Erdman again became an active candidate for the moderatorship, and benefited from the widespread charges that he had been abusively attacked by Machen. Nothing was done publicly to correct this impression. Strangely, however, when the Seminary was under investigation more than a year later and he was interrogated concerning the matter, he stated that he had had Dr. Allis rather than Machen in mind! Meanwhile, Machen had suffered the injustice and indignity of being refused confirmation in a new professorship principally because of his supposed faults of character.

THE LEAGUE OF EVANGELICAL STUDENTS

Still another incident affecting the reputations of Erdman and Machen occurred in the spring of 1925 in connection with the failure of Dr. Erdman to be re-elected as faculty adviser to the students. If it had not been widely publicized and misrepresented as being part of a campaign to undermine confidence in Dr. Erdman, it would not in itself be worthy of mention. For it was a purely intramural development concerned properly with certain aspects of student life at Princeton. And Machen should never have received special mention in view of the fact that he came to be involved only incidentally as a member of the Faculty. But this incident likewise was used to support charges being given widespread circulation in the Church and before the general public that Machen was engaging in a personal campaign against Erdman.

This incident developed out of the formation of a student organization called the League of Evangelical Students, which grew out of dissatisfaction with developments within an interseminary movement as they came to sharp focus at a conference held at Drew Seminary in October, 1924. The Princeton Seminary student delegates soon found themselves sharply at odds with the large majority of students present concerning the doctrinal position and program of the organization. The majority favored the admission of a Unitarian seminary to membership. And when consideration was given to the doctrinal platform to be presupposed in recruiting men for the ministry, it was disclosed that there was not agreement even as to John 3:16 in its reference to the only begotten Son.

When the students made their first informal reports at Princeton, there was apparently unanimous agreement that such association with modernist students was intolerable. At first both President Stevenson and Dr. Erdman advised withdrawal and the formation of a new organization in accordance with the recommendation of the student delegates. Machen, however, was for a time very hesitant as to the wisdom and practicability of such an organization. The entire matter was aired at a meeting of the students held on Oct. 21st, and as a consequence definite steps were taken to form a new organization. From that day forward the business of preparing for the organization of the League became the chief concern of the Princeton student association, and letters were sent out to many institutions stating the case for it.

Members of the Faculty took no active part in the forming of these plans, but as it happened Dr. Erdman's name was listed on the letterhead of the association as student adviser along with the names of the student officers. Suddenly a new face was put on the situation when the president of McCormick Seminary, who had been apprised of the development by students of his own seminary, inquired of Dr. Erdman whether he was in agreement with the position of the students. This appeared to embarrass Dr. Erdman, and in conference with the student officers at Princeton he requested that the institutions be informed that he had had no particular responsibility for the letter. The students concerned drew the obvious conclusion that Dr. Erdman had modified his attitude toward the League or at least did not want to be associated with its promotion. Thus Erdman himself disclosed that he was at odds with them in what seemed to the great majority of the students to be the greatest challenge with which they had been confronted.

Plans for the formation of the League went forward with the general support and advice of the Faculty, and it was officially organized at Pittsburgh in the spring of 1925. Throughout this period Dr. Erdman had continued as student adviser, but when the new officers of the student association and a new student cabinet—of which the present writer was a member—were installed that spring, this situation was reviewed. It appeared to the student cabinet that it was incongruous to perpetuate the status quo. Since it was doubtful that the students themselves had the power to terminate Dr. Erdman's services, and such action in any case would have been of doubtful propriety, it was determined to refer the matter to the Faculty and to request them to elect a faculty adviser. Being cognizant of these developments, and sympathizing with the students in promoting the League, the Faculty elected Dr. R. D. Wilson.

It is incontrovertible that Machen had not taken any initiative in this entire matter, though he had come to believe that the organization of the League was salutary. Nevertheless, before long it was charged that Erdman had been ousted from his position, and Machen was singled out as having inspired the action! Who was responsible for this publicity is unknown, but there were special dispatches published in such papers as the New York *Times,* the New York *Herald Tribune* and the Philadelphia *Public Ledger* for April 6, 1925 which represented it as a significant aspect of the ecclesiastical struggle rather than as a purely academic affair. The *Herald Tribune,* while otherwise not more sensational than the other papers, contained the statement that "it is understood that Dr. J. Gresham Machen is the faculty member who inspired the action." Indicative of the attention given the episode are the headlines and opening paragraph of the long account in the *Times*:

> Dr. Erdman Deposed by Fundamentalists—Princeton Theological Seminary Professor Removed as Student Adviser—Opposed by Dr. Macartney—His Enemies Win by a Close Vote Following a Faculty Contest—Dr. Wilson Succeeds Him.
>
> (*Special to the New York Times*)
>
> Princeton, N. J., April 5.—The Faculty of the Princeton Theological Seminary has removed Dr. Charles R. Erdman, Professor of Practical Theology, long the object of bitter attacks by the extreme Fundamentalists in the Presbyterian Church, from the position of Student Adviser, which he has held for the last eighteen years. He retains his position in the Faculty.

More than a year later, when the Seminary was under investigation, Dr. Machen's private comment on this development included the following:

> When the Faculty finally appointed an Adviser to the students it would obviously have been most unwise to appoint one who was opposed to the policy which was favored by the majority both of the students and of the Faculty. I regret therefore that Dr. Erdman has not discouraged the public agitation which has followed the exercise by the Faculty of a perfectly plain right. Every member of a body, I think, ought to acquiesce freely in the principle of majority rule. The lack of such acquiescence has given rise to whatever unpleasantness there may have been in the Faculty in recent years.

Another evidence of the manner in which the evangelical cause was subjected to misrepresentation at this time, and Dr. Erdman was publicized as a martyr, is found in the part played by Dr. Herbert Adams Gibbons, the well-known lecturer and writer. Gibbons was an intimate friend of Dr. van Dyke, and like him was a graduate of the Seminary who had been ordained and retained his ministerial standing though engaged in other work than that of the ministry. He was also a signer of the Auburn *Affirmation.* At the time of the discussion in the public press concerning *The Presbyterian's* editorial regarding van Dyke and Erdman's preaching in the First Church, Dr. Gibbons, in an interview published in the Trenton *Times* for Feb. 7, 1925, had singled out Machen for special attack. Some weeks later, on April 27th, in connection with efforts to boom Dr. Erdman for the moderatorship, a statement in the Trenton *Times* attributed to Dr. Gibbons gravely misrepresented the situation at Princeton. Roundly asserting that Dr. Machen "had urged the Faculty to dismiss Dr. Erdman" from his post as student adviser, it interpreted certain recent developments on the campus as a vindication of Dr. Erdman.

> A signal victory seems to have been won by the friends of Dr. Charles R. Erdman in Princeton Seminary itself. In the faculty itself, Dr. Machen won a victory. But the Presbytery of New Brunswick passed a resolution endorsing Dr. Erdman's policy in spite of Dr. Machen's opposition to the measure on the floor of the Presbytery. And now it has just come out that the students of Princeton Seminary themselves have repudiated the Machen policy by refusing to enter the new association, thus giving full endorsement to the position of Dr. Erdman.

As a result of this statement, the undergraduate Friars Club at the Seminary undertook a public rebuke and correction even though Dr. Gibbons was president of the Alumni Friars, an organization closely allied with the undergraduate organization. Its statement, as published in the Trenton *Times* for April 29, charged him with "gross misrepresentations" in the following particulars:

> First, the vote in favor of the new League of Seminaries was 140 for, as opposed to 70 against.
>
> Second, this vote did not directly concern Dr. Erdman.
>
> Third, although there was not the three-fourths vote necessary for entrance into the new league, an overwhelming majority of students in the Seminary voted for it.
>
> Fourth, if Dr. Gibbons' statement is correct, that Dr. Erdman opposed entrance into the new league, this vote in no way can be taken as a "signal victory" for him.
>
> Fifth, as Dr. Erdman's position was not an issue in the vote, the vote cannot possibly be interpreted to be a "full endorsement of the position of Dr. Erdman."

Dr. Gibbons, as reported in the *Times* for April 30, 1925, retaliated by calling the action of the club unfair and typical of the un-American methods of the extreme fundamentalist faction. He further claimed that he had not given the interview, and that he was being condemned without a hearing.

POLITICS IN NEW BRUNSWICK

About this time, as the 1925 General Assembly was approaching, and as Erdman's candidacy for the moderatorship was being widely discussed, the Presbytery of New Brunswick was engaged in the important matter of electing delegates to the General Assembly. This meeting, held on April 14th, was also significant because of the consideration of a resolution commending Dr. Erdman for the moderatorship and criticizing those who were alleged to have misrepresented him. This resolution carried by the close roll call vote of 43-39. The Presbytery determined that, when the result was given to the press, the vote should also be given. Despite this provision of the Presbytery, the Stated Clerk, the Rev. George H. Ingram, undertook the widest possible circulation of the resolution by mailing it to all the ministers in the Church on his official letterhead but without giving the figures of the roll call vote. Thus the ministers might have gained the impression that the vote was unanimous; they certainly failed to learn that the vote had been extremely close. (The closeness of the division in the Presbytery was also evident in that five of eight commissioners elected to the General Assembly were men who stood against Dr. Erdman's policy.) Hence, in order to rectify the impression given by the official letter, the minority of 39 felt compelled to issue a statement indicating their dissent. Among the ministers in this group there were, besides Dr. Machen, Professors Armstrong, Greene, Hodge and Vos of the Seminary and the Librarian Joseph H. Dulles.

Machen asked Ingram to explain several features of the publicizing of the resolution: the authorization for it; the directive regarding the figures of the roll-call vote; the funds used in distributing it. In reply Mr. Ingram said that the resolution on its very surface gave evidence of being intended for the whole church, and so no special authorization was necessary; that he had literally carried out the directive regarding figures in publicity for the press, but could not, without special action, be expected to do so in the case of the distribution to ministers; and that the funds were supplied by a committee of alumni of Princeton "whose aid in so promptly carrying out the will of the Presbytery is, I am sure, appreciated by us all." Thus it appears that the Stated Clerk, as a supporter of Dr. Erdman, made political capital out of the resolution, justifying his partisan handling of the matter in a way which gives further disclosure of the dubious methods that were being used to advance the Erdman boom.

By such means as these the sparks of hostility to the Faculty in general and to Machen in particular were fanned into a flame. It came to be widely believed that Erdman was being persecuted in spite of his theological conservatism and only because of his zeal for constitutional methods.

THE ASSEMBLY OF 1925

The election of Dr. Erdman as moderator of the Assembly of 1925 afforded further confirmation of the trend of events within the Presbyterian Church. Although the issues before the Church were not finally settled, it had become rather clear that there was little hope of the inauguration of a program of reformation and purification.

At this Assembly indeed a Commission of Fifteen was appointed "to study the present spiritual condition of our Church and the causes making for unrest, and to report to the next General Assembly, to the end that the purity, peace, unity and progress of the Church may be assured." But its constituency was generally regarded by the militant conservatives as offering little hope of a report that would support their basic analysis of the situation. The Committee did seek to gather evidence and opinions from various quarters, and Machen was among those invited to make a statement. His carefully prepared analysis, submitted to the Committee on Dec. 2, 1925, took the position that the causes of unrest were all reducible to one great underlying cause — "the widespread and in many quarters dominant position in the ministry of the Church as well as among its lay members of a type of thought and experience, commonly called Modernism, which is diametrically opposed to the Constitution of our Church and to the Christian religion." In support of this thesis he reviewed five principal indications: the disclosures in connection with the 1920 Plan of Union, the defense of Fosdick, the Auburn *Affirmation,* the defiance of the constitution and Assembly on the part of the Presbytery and Synod of New York, and the failure of the boards and agencies to sound a clear evangelical note in a time of crisis.

When the Report of the Committee was finally published, it was far from sharing Machen's analysis of the state of the church! It disputed the view that there was evidence of any substantial departure from orthodoxy and even appealed to the terms of its creation as evidence that "the Assembly believed in its own evangelical unity and in the evangelical unity of the Church at large." Its recommendations included nothing in the way of rebuke of doctrinal error, but did warn against "hasty or harsh judgments of the motives of brethren whose hearts are fully known only to God." And thus the report, while not taking sides in any forthright way, was generally viewed by the liberals with delight and by the conservatives with sorrow. In approving this report the Assembly of 1926 therefore gave further evidence of the drift toward latitudinarianism.

Meanwhile, the situation at the Seminary did not improve. Efforts made among the Directors to adjust the differences which had emerged in the Faculty bore no fruit, and the Faculty became divided more sharply into two groups, the majority group of which Machen was a member, and the minority group led by President Stevenson and Erdman. A widespread feeling developed among the Directors and the majority group in the Faculty that Stevenson should resign as president, but no definite steps were taken to bring that about. And though a very substantial majority of the Directors (who were in authority in the realm of administration and instruction) favored the majority of the Faculty, it had become evident that the Board of Trustees (who officially held and administered the property and funds of the institution) were largely sympathetic with the minority of the Faculty. Full advantage was taken of this extraordinary situation by the supporters of Stevenson and Erdman as the 1926 Assembly approached when the Trustees and a minority of the Directors appealed to the Assembly to appoint a committee to make a special investigation of the Seminary. The acceptance of this proposal was one of the major decisions of that year and was a decisive step toward the reorganization of the Seminary which was consummated in 1929.

ELECTION TO APOLOGETICS

Another development within the Board of Directors affected Machen even more immediately and poignantly. This was his election at the May meeting of the Board of Directors as professor of Apologetics. Although the Assembly possessed the prerogative of a veto in such matters, it had apparently never exercised it, at least in the history of Princeton, and so Machen's election was widely regarded as a strong reinforcement of the conservative cause at Princeton. But coincident with its appointment of a committee of investigation, the Assembly at Baltimore took the unprecedented step of postponing action on Machen's appointment! And so what at first appeared as a major victory for the cause with which Machen was associated turned out to be a stunning and crushing defeat. This story must be set forth in some detail.

William Brenton Greene (1854-1928) had served since 1892 in the Stuart chair first occupied by Patton, which in 1903 became known as the professorship of Apologetics and Christian Ethics. As he approached the normal age for retirement, and his health failed, efforts were put forth in various directions to secure a successor. Several names were considered: Harold McAfee Robinson, Wm. Hallock Johnson, and others. Finally, at its fall meeting in 1925, the Board elected Macartney to the professorship. When Macartney delayed acceptance and appeared to be unwilling to undertake the post, Machen urged upon him vigorously that he should accept. The question whether Princeton would be preserved as an institution set for the defense of the faith seemed to be hanging in the balance. Hence, from Machen's point of view, the question whether Macartney then possessed all the qualifications desirable for this field was secondary. Moreover, his evaluation of Macartney's ability was such that he could not doubt that he would prove to be a very successful teacher, and if a vacancy occurred in the department of homiletics, for example, he might be transferred to it if that seemed wise. But Macartney gave his official declination at the May, 1926, meeting of the Board. And the Board proceeded at that same meeting, by the decisive majority of 19-9, to elect Machen to the post.

This development was not as abrupt as it perhaps appears. From time to time in previous years certain Directors, including Dr. Ethelbert Warfield, the influential director who many years before had sought Machen for the faculty of Lafayette College, suggested that Machen should be given a professorship in the department of systematic theology. Machen never gave any encouragement to such suggestions; in fact he was accustomed to stress his devotion to the New Testament field. There is evidence, however, that at least as early as the year 1924, he had discussed with Armstrong, though evidently in quite informal fashion, the question whether he should give some thought to a transfer to the field of Apologetics. And as Machen's interest in Apologetics and brilliance as a Christian apologist became increasingly evident from his published works, the idea of appointing him to Greene's chair must have occurred to several directors of the Seminary. Though this is not precisely documented there is little doubt that Machen must have been under consideration well in advance of the spring meeting of the Board, especially when the report was circulated that Macartney was almost certain to decline.

Machen himself had rather mixed emotions concerning his own appointment. Particularly disappointing was the consideration that the faculty had not been reinforced by the addition of Macartney, though there remained hope that he might be elected to the chair of homiletics perhaps within a year. Moreover, Machen would have preferred to give careful reflection to all the implications of this considerable change in his status and functions. It was only a few days before the meeting that certain directors, including Dr. Beach and Dr. Crane, approached Machen with regard to an appointment in Apologetics, expressing their zeal for it. Machen was quite hesitant therefore with regard to the appointment especially when he reflected upon the situation as a whole.

As he wrote to his Mother on May 12th, the day following his election, however,

> Seven or eight of the Directors had a session with me Monday night and were very insistent as to the great importance of my announcing my decision at once. The situation was very different from what I had anticipated. I had been spoken to on the subject of the chair of apologetics only informally. Dr. Beach had been enthusiastic about my election to that chair, and had reported to me that the movement for it in the Board was strong. But I told Burt Crane, who also spoke to me casually a few days before the election, that what I particularly thought ought to be avoided was my election to the chair of apologetics coupled with Macartney's non-election to the chair of homiletics, since that would mean the sacrifice of Dr. Greene's vote in the Faculty and would bring no new vote to take its place. This undesirable thing was exactly what happened. I fully expected that I would make my decision at my leisure. But I could see how those Directors felt. It had been unfortunate for the cause that Macartney had delayed so long and then declined; and if another call were announced with a delay in the acceptance it would seem as though the invitations of the Board to conservative men were being treated with contumely, and confusion would result in the minds of the evangelical party in the Church.
>
> Early Tuesday morning I went to see Dr. Greene—the retiring professor of apologetics—and of course found him cordial. Then I went over to the Seminary Treasurer's office to look up the terms of the deed of gift of the "Stuart Professorship of Apologetics and Christian Ethics," which I was invited to occupy. Then I communicated my decision to Burt Crane, chairman of the Board's committee appointed to notify me of my election; and the announcement of my election and acceptance was made at the commencement that immediately followed.

It appears therefore that Machen's attitude toward the appointment was determined largely by his judgment as to what would be likely to save Princeton Seminary for the faith rather than by concern for his own personal advancement. In undertaking the new field he would to some extent be venturing out upon an unknown course. He could not doubt that he had been successful as a teacher of the New Testament. But could he be as sure that he would succeed in the new field in accordance with his own high standards? The same letter contains certain comments on this point:

> Wistar Hodge evidently thinks I have made a mistake; others are non-committal; and others think that I have done well. I do not know what Army thinks, since he would never want to stand in the way of what is obviously (in a formal sense at least) an advancement for me . . . Obviously I am making a great venture. I love the teaching of elementary Greek, and I hope that I do that fairly well. Also, I love the advanced work in the New Testament. It is true that recently I have a zest for reading on subjects related to my new department. Is that merely a passing taste for an avocation? Or is it something that I can build my main work upon? That is the big question, the answer to which can only be afforded by time.

He had little doubt that his decision would be determinative of the matter, for he also stated:

> My election has to be confirmed by the General Assembly; but hated though I am, I hardly think that the unprecedented step will be taken of contesting the confirmation of a professor's election by a Seminary Board of Directors.

When news of Machen's election to his new post became known, he received many congratulatory messages. His mother and other members of his family in Baltimore were elated, and wrote to say that they were sure he had done the right thing in accepting. Fairly representative of the reaction of alumni was the message of the Rev. Weaver K. Eubank that "I know of no other man on the face of the earth better fitted or qualified for this eminent place than you. I certainly am thrilled through and through and I know all of the Princeton men are equally happy." But his colleague Wistar Hodge's rather distinctive reaction was expressed as follows:

> I want to express to you my feelings over your election further than the casual congratulations I gave you.
>
> First I want to say that I think you will make a great professor of Apologetics and fill the place better than any one I know. Also I rejoice in your advancement in status.
>
> I would not be honest, however, if I did not tell you of the sadness in my heart as I see you leave what I regard as the most important department in the Seminary. I have followed you with affection and your career with admiration. I looked forward with joy to further scientific books from you in the sphere of N. T. criticism and exegesis. Much as I admire your two latest books, I took greater delight in "The Origin of Paul's Religion."

To "open the Scripture," to expound its truths, I consider the highest of all tasks, and even of greater "apologetic" value in the long run than its "defense."

I think you will disagree with me but I know you will not misunderstand me. I do *not* agree with any of the *three* types of thought which are at present depressing the value of Apologetics; I give it the highest importance; I am glad we are to have a man like you in the chair. But personally I cannot but feel sad also when I think of what you are leaving. My feelings are torn two ways in this matter.

As ever your friend,
C. W. Hodge

THE BALTIMORE ASSEMBLY

How determined and ruthless the opposition to Machen was he, as noted above, did not foresee. Indicative of the atmosphere that prevailed is the consideration that, taking advantage of the fanatical prohibitionist temper of the times, his enemies advertized and distorted a matter which had no proper bearing upon the issue of his confirmation. The facts in the case are simply these. At a meeting of the Presbytery of New Brunswick on April 13, 1926, when Machen was one of a handful of perhaps eight members who had not left for home, a resolution was introduced endorsing the 18th amendment and the Volstead Act. When the vote was put, Machen voted "No," though he had not spoken to the motion. Nor did he ask that his vote be recorded. Nevertheless, in a highly irregular and audacious way, the moderator, the Rev. Peter K. Emmons, turned to him and asked whether he wanted his negative vote recorded. Machen indicated that he did not. As he explained later (in a letter to Macartney on May 24th),

> I had no intention of concealing my vote, but neither had I any intention of obtruding it, and thus introducing a new issue when other issues are engaging my full attention and should, I think, engage the full attention of the Church.
>
> It is a misrepresentation to say that by this vote I expressed my opinion on the merits of the Eighteenth Amendment or the Volstead Act—and still less on the general question of prohibition. On the contrary, my vote was directed against a policy which places the Church in a corporate capacity, as distinguished from the activity of its members, on record with regard to such political questions. And I was particularly offended by the presumption with which a small group of men undertook to express the public atti-

> tude of a court of the Church with regard to such an important question.

Nevertheless, the widest publicity was given to Machen's vote, and it was interpreted as indicating that he had a loose and evil attitude toward temperance and even drunkenness itself. That this matter should have been dragged in by Machen's enemies demonstrates that the case against him as a man and professor was woefully weak even from their own point of view. But thus the Christian public and especially the delegates as they gathered at Baltimore were inflamed and predjudiced. As unimpeachable private testimony bears out, many of his opponents were in high glee as they met on the eve of the Assembly; they felt that at last they had an issue on which they could hang him.

Machen's own supporters at the Assembly, as they observed the inroads this evil propaganda was making, became alarmed and informed him at his Princeton address of the situation. Machen himself was greatly distressed, not for himself, but for the Seminary's future, when he became aware that the opposition to his person might be made the occasion for an investigation of the Seminary. He was ready to sacrifice his own advancement and even his own membership in the faculty if it would prevent an investigation which might well bring the institution in greater jeopardy. In this connection he gave expression to the following appraisal:

> No doubt I have been at fault in many ways in the manner in which I have tried to maintain what I believe to be right; but I earnestly hope that my faults may not be allowed to bring harm upon the institution that I love—an institution which is performing today, to a degree attained perhaps never before in its history, a worldwide service in the defence of the Reformed or Calvinistic Faith. The appointment of an investigating committee, whatever its ultimate findings, would be a serious blow to the prestige of the institution; and in comparison with the injury the loss of whatever trifling services I have been able to render as a teacher would not be at all worthy of consideration.

That the offer of partial or complete withdrawal—submitted in a telegram to his intimate supporters in Baltimore—was not made officially to the Assembly was due solely to the consideration that, as it seemed on more reflection, it might appear that the conservatives at Princeton were fearful of what an investigation might disclose.

When the Assembly's advisory committee brought its report to the floor, it was discovered that only a minority favored confirmation of Machen's election. The majority report recommended the appointment of a committee of five to make a sympathetic study of conditions affecting the welfare of Princeton Seminary and to co-operate responsively with seminary leaders in striving to adjust and harmonize differences and to report to the next Assembly. It recommended further that meanwhile no action, either of approval or disapproval, should be taken on Machen's election. In commending the Report it was stated that its terms did not reflect particularly upon Machen since the entire institution was to be made the subject of investigation. Nevertheless the proposed action as it concerned Machen was so unprecedented and radical that, when it became the action of the Assembly, it was regarded on all sides as extremely humiliating.

This interpretation of the significance of the majority report is also confirmed by the nature of the arguments advanced in support of it. The debate, which was reported at length in the New York, Baltimore and other leading newspapers, was featured by attacks upon the character and personality of Machen. No reference was made on the platform to the prohibition issue, but it was generally regarded as having undermined confidence in him. But Stevenson and Erdman astonished even Machen's friends with their attack upon Machen's fitness to serve in this post. He was charged with "temperamental idiosyncrasies," though no particulars were given. President Stevenson, in spite of Machen's well-earned reputation as a brilliant apologist and the decisiveness of the vote of the Directors, gave the impression, which is contradicted by a mass of evidence, that Dr. Maitland Alexander, a leading conservative Director, thought of Machen as a man of "serious limitations." Stevenson also effectively capitalized on the prevailing sentiment of the day when he declared that the object of his leadership was to have Princeton represent the whole Presbyterian Church and the spirit of the report of the Commission of Fifteen—in short an inclusivist position. And, as reported in the New York *Times* on June 3, Dr. Erdman said that "what is questioned is whether Dr. Machen's temper and methods of defense are such as to qualify him for a chair in which his whole time will be devoted to defending the faith. There must be a serious question as to the wisdom of his confirmation when we debate it for an hour or more."

Machen was of course not without his supporters in the Assembly. Dr. John B. Laird, vice-president of the Princeton Board of Directors, said that it had never occurred to the Board that "a man who had served the Seminary with acceptability for twenty years, who had won distinction beyond that of most scholars, would find such opposition in changing from one chair to another." The charge of temperamental idiosyncrasy, he stated further, was inconsequential; if there was anything to it at all it was the idiosyncrasy of genius, and he thanked God for it.

Dr. O. T. Allis of the Faculty, who was a commissioner, also made a strong plea for Machen, and answered the charges made by his other colleagues. In reply to Stevenson's declaration that Maitland Alexander had labored with Machen for many hours after the meeting at which the election took place, Allis made the point that he labored with him *to get him to accept.* Dr. James Palmer, another delegate, charged that Machen was being made a scapegoat and that he was singled out because he had been a leader on one side of the Church. This was no doubt the conviction of many. The issue was not fundamentally personal but doctrinal, and was a revealing aspect of the struggle between the upholders of constitutional orthodoxy and a coalition of modernists and others who above all wanted tolerance.

Following the action of the Assembly, Macartney wired Machen in the following terms:

> Dear Machen: Be of good courage. The happenings of this day will greatly increase your influence and will serve to awaken a sleeping church. The reproach of Christ is your honor and reward.

And he released a strong statement for publication:

> The complete and sweeping victory won by the coalition of modernists, indifferentists and pacifists, which reached a terrible climax in the repudiation of Dr. Machen, will prove a blessing in disguise. It will open the eyes of Presbyterians all over the world to the fact that our Church is rapidly drifting from its historic and fearless witness to the great truths of the Reformed Faith.

And Dr. Allis, writing for *The Call to the Colors* for July-August, 1926, stated that "the principal reason that Princeton is under fire is that Dr. Machen and the majority of the Faculty and the majority of the Board of Directors of the Seminary are strongly opposed to the policy of broad toleration of the liberals for the sake of peace ... The action regarding Dr. Machen is a signal illustration of the fact that this 'toleration' is meant for the liberals, not for the conservatives ..."

During the following days and weeks Machen was in receipt of scores of messages of grief, indignation and outrage because of the Assembly's action. The messages came from his immediate family and intimate friends, from ministers in the Presbyterian Church and students in the Seminary, from prominent Lutherans, Methodists and Baptists, from persons in Canada and in lands beyond the seas. On June 5th Dr. Greene wrote of his indignation and deep concern for the future of the Seminary, and later, after he had been asked to return to Princeton to conduct some of the courses in the department in which he had served, he said:

> A split in our Church will perhaps be averted—how wisely I do not know; but a split in our Seminary Faculty cannot be avoided, nor do I think that it should be . . . There remains the brutal insult inflicted on you on the floor of the highest court of our church. But it is not an insult to you alone. "In all their afflictions *he* was afflicted, and the angel of his presence saved them." Keep thinking on that, and eternity itself will not exhaust its comfort.

To persons who have had the privilege of observing the extraordinary meekness and gentleness of "Brenny" Greene, this evaluation will bring further confirmation as to the true nature of the situation. On July 22nd, Dr. Beach sent a second message from Paris in which he said: "I so often think of you, and my indignation deepens as the days pass. The action of the Assembly on your case is an outrage and the wrong must and shall be redressed. So far as any hurt has been inflicted on you, it will turn out in 'the furtherance of the gospel.' May the peace of God keep your heart and mind."

EVIL REPORTS

Such is the mischief caused by slanderous and malicious reports, and the perversity of men to believe the evil rather than the good, that throughout the rest of Machen's life, and indeed for many years afterward, credence has been widely given to outright falsehoods concerning his attitude toward intoxicating beverages. They sometimes took the form that he was a "wet" and even a drunkard. Most frequently it was stated that the Machen money was made in the brewery business and that he continued to depend on that source for his income. Such reports were in circulation in the far west in 1934, for example, and were being spread by one of the leading clergymen of the denomination as a basic reason why Machen had to be opposed. Graduates of Westminster have frequently encountered such charges, and the present writer has been told by a number of persons that, regardless of what he might say to the contrary, there was absolute proof of their veracity.

Such charges were completely without foundation in fact. It is true that Machen did not regard the 18th Amendment as wise, but this was basically due to his political philosophy with its antipathy to centralized government. And he was opposed to the church's entry into the political field, as we have observed, in accordance with the Southern Presbyterian emphasis on the limited scope of the church's functions. His family background was hardly prohibitionist, though the godly and exemplary character of the lives of his parents is beyond cavil. Nor was Machen himself committed to total abstinence *as a principle.* His view of the teaching of the Bible did not permit that. Moreover, as he once wrote his mother, he was vigorously opposed to certain efforts of William Jennings Bryan in behalf of an Assembly deliverance on the subject because he felt its net result would be to obscure the gospel. Nevertheless, so far as his actual personal conduct was concerned, he virtually practised total abstinence, at least during his career as a minister. At most he would indulge in a sip of egg nog when he was in the family home in Baltimore during the Christmas vacation. In the countless happy social occasions at which Machen was host, the memory of which his associates still cherish, the possibility of drinking alcoholic beverages was never even mentioned. Unfortunately, commitment to the Biblical principle of temperance, or moderation as distinguished from total abstinence, is identified by some persons with license, and no allowance is made for the possibility that the defender of Christian liberty may consistently refrain from the exercise of that liberty.

And as for the charges concerning the source of Machen's income, it can confidently be asserted that they were pure inventions. Though no worthwhile purpose would be served by presenting the observations in detail, the biographer, having through the courtesy of the family been given access to the wills and other documents that bear upon the subject of the Machen wealth, can testify that the inventories show that among the family assets there has never been a single share of brewery or distillery stock.

In connection with this subject it seems appropriate to add a few details concerning the sources of the Machen assets and Dr. Machen's attitude toward and his use of money. His father, as has been observed, was eminently successful in his legal career following his early poverty. The comfortable position of the Machen family in later years, however, was due principally to the fact that Mr. Machen purchased certain parcels of land in the city of Washington in the eighties, and as these were sold over a period of decades in the present century, a substantial sum of money was accrued. Mrs. Machen had inherited some assets under her father's will and, when her husband died in 1915, she became the chief beneficiary. Before his mother's estate was distributed following her death in 1931 J. Gresham Machen was far from being a wealthy man.

Nevertheless, his very meagre salary had been supplemented somewhat by other income, and he was able, as a bachelor, to live rather comfortably. Under his maternal grandfather's will he inherited $50,000 chiefly in stocks at his 21st birthday, and a similar amount in 1916 under the will of his father. The additional income allowed for some creaturely comforts but for the most part he lived very modestly. Sensitive as he was to the needs of others his benefactions were very liberal, as has been indicated to a certain extent in the preceding narrative. And he spent many thousands of dollars in his fight to save Princeton as bills for legal services had to be paid and he sought to reach the Church with the most effective and readable presentation of the cause. Later his contributions to Westminster Seminary, *Christianity Today* and other causes at times cut deeply into his assets. At the time that his own will was probated it appeared that his estate totalled some $250,000 in addition to his interest in certain remnants of the Washington lands.

Only during the last five years of his life therefore did he have access to substantial assets. Meanwhile, however, his living costs had greatly increased and particularly the Seminary frequently met its obligations only because he was ready to write out a sizeable check. Moreover his actual income was by no means large. As indicated by his income tax return for 1936, for example, his total income from interest on bank deposits and bonds, dividends and royalties and miscellaneous fees —excluding therefore only his modest Seminary salary—was only $6,661.94. His contribution to the Seminary alone for that year was $4,000. Other causes were also supported by substantial gifts. If there is anything to the advice that "the first thing to be done by a biographer in estimating character is to examine the victim's chequebooks," Machen stands the test in this respect as in others *magna cum laude*.

This brief recital has been offered as a kind of work of supererogation. The real defense of the character of the Machen family and of our particular subject has been presented in page after page of the foregoing where the devout and godly quality of their lives has been attested as they have disclosed their inmost motives and guiding principles without any thought that the world might some day listen in. What has been added in these few pages is thought advisable only because of a concern to put to silence once and for all malicious and irresponsible false witness by means of disclosure of the facts. It has indeed been a sordid piece of business that, in the name of religion, men have resorted to the spread of false rumors in order to weaken Machen's testimony and to belittle the cause for which he suffered and toiled. But he bore this trial with such self-denial and patience, and with such single-minded dedication to the cause of the truth, that the nobility of his character shone forth the more brightly because of the ignominy that was heaped upon him.

20

QUESTIONS OF FAITH AND LIFE

During the months that immediately followed the debacle at Baltimore, Machen made no public utterance concerning his evaluation of what had taken place. He indeed was passing through heavy waters. He had been unfairly attacked and humiliated, and the institution that he loved had been placed in great jeopardy. His consolation was that he could still "look to Him who is Invisible" and be assured of an ultimate judgment without respect of persons.

Since the next step would be taken by the Assembly's committee, it was advisable to relate his further activity on behalf of the Seminary to its approach. As will be observed in the sequel, the appointment of this committee in the historical situation virtually guaranteed the reorganization of the institution. Machen foresaw this as the likely result, but he was of sterner stuff than to cease his witness and action because he appeared to belong to the minority and the prospects of victory for his point of view were dim. Accordingly, significant efforts to prevent what was feared would happen remain to be set forth.

It seems appropriate, however, to seize upon the brief lull in the conflict that followed the Baltimore Assembly to survey certain other aspects of Machen's life which have been passed over because of the concentration upon the ecclesiastical struggle. Several events and activities underscore the eminent and conspicuous place which he had come to enjoy in the life of his times.

WHAT IS FAITH?

Among the unmentioned events of these years none is perhaps more important than the production of another successful book, *What is Faith?* which was published by Macmillan in November, 1925. As Machen himself described it, a central purpose was to combat the anti-intellectualism of contemporaneous modernism, with its false separation of faith and knowledge. But there was also a positive aim, namely, to expound the nature of Christian faith in terms of the teaching of the Bible, and since this demanded reflection also upon the object of faith, it constituted a summary treatment of considerable portions of Christian doctrine. In both respects the book may be thought of as a sequel to *Christianity and Liberalism,* though its theme was somewhat less comprehensive.

As in the case of *Christianity and Liberalism* the new book utilized lectures and sermons delivered in former days. The book was largely written during the summer of 1925 with a view to a course of lectures which he was scheduled to deliver at the Grove City Bible Conference, where he frequently was a featured speaker. The book indeed was not a sudden inspiration, hurriedly assembled, for it had been in process of creation especially during the previous couple of years as he had been vividly confronted with the centrality and decisiveness of the doctrinal issue involved in the religious and ecclesiastical controversies. Several of the extant manuscripts of sermons preached at the First Presbyterian Church of Princeton during his service as stated supply show that he dealt with the theme of faith and these studies were largely utilized. He also used materials from several major articles including a popular one which he had been invited to contribute to a series which appeared in *The Women's Home Companion* on the subject "My Idea of God."

Though treating a profound theme, one with significant theological and philosophical overtones and implications, the book is marked by the manner in which, in eloquent simplicity, it deals with the basic problems of men everywhere. Thus in expounding faith in Christ, he said:

> It is very natural for a child of the covenant to learn first to trust Christ as Saviour almost as soon as conscious life begins, and then, having become God's child through Him, to follow His blessed example. There is a child's hymn—a child's hymn that I think the Christian can never outgrow—which puts the matter right:
>
> O dearly, dearly has He loved,
> And we must love Him too,
> And trust in His redeeming blood,
> And try His works to do.
>
> That is the true order of Christian pedagogy—"trust in His redeeming blood" first, and then "try His works to do." Disaster will always follow when that order is reversed.

How one wishes that his famous sermon on "The Green Hill," as the biographer once heard it preached with extraordinarily moving power, had been preserved! But its message does come to effective expression in this book.

Other excerpts, chosen almost at random, serve to illustrate its qualities. Speaking of faith born of need, he writes:

> A new and more powerful proclamation of that law is perhaps the most pressing need of the hour; men would have little difficulty with the gospel if they had only learned the lesson of the law. As it is, they are turning aside from the Christian pathway; they are turning to the village of Morality, and to the house of Mr. Legality, who is reported to be very skillful in relieving men of their burdens. Mr. Legality has indeed in our day disguised himself somewhat, but he is the same deceiver as the one of whom Bunyan wrote. "Making Christ Master" in the life, putting into practice "the principles of Christ" by one's own efforts—these are the new ways of earning salvation by one's own obedience to God's commands. And they are undertaken because of a lax view of what those commands are. So it always is: a low view of law always brings legalism in religion; a high view of law makes a man a seeker after grace.

Hear Machen also as he expounds the grace of God, and emphasizes that evangelicalism in its purity is the Reformed Faith!

> To say, therefore, that our faith saves us means that we do not save ourselves even in slightest measure, but that God saves us. Very different would be the case if our salvation were said to be through love; for then salvation would depend upon a high quality of our own. And that is what the New Testament, above all else, is concerned to deny. The very center and core of the whole Bible is the doctrine of the grace of God—the grace of God which depends not one whit upon anything that is in man, but is absolutely undeserved, resistless and sovereign. The theologians of the Church can be placed in an ascending scale according as they have grasped that one great central doctrine, that doctrine that gives consistency to all the rest; and Christian experience also depends for its depth and for its power upon the way in which that blessed doctrine is cherished in the depths of the heart. The centre of the Bible, and the centre of Christianity, is found in the grace of God; and the necessary corollary of the grace of God is salvation through faith alone.

The book was very well received, and evidently had a sale of about 6,000 copies in the first couple of years counting both the American and the English editions, the latter a Hodder & Stoughton publication in 1926. And there has continued to be a steady demand also for the

Eerdmans edition of 1946. There were to be sure some unfavorable reviews. *The Christian Century* rather grudgingly said it was "not as bad as *Christianity and Liberalism.*" And *The Presbyterian Advance* charged that it represented Christianity as "a narrow, exclusive system." But by and large the reviews were enthusiastic. *The Anglican Theological Review,* for example, regarded it as "one of the five best books of 1925."

BRITISH WEEKLY DISCUSSION

The attention given to it by *The British Weekly* was most exceptional and gratifying of all. For during the spring and summer of 1926 this distinguished and widely-read journal published a series of eight articles on the book, written by as many distinguished theologians. The editor of the *Weekly* at this time was Dr. John B. Hutton, who as it happened had been present at Grove City as one of the speakers when Dr. Machen delivered the substance of the book. This contact proved to be very pleasant, as Machen's letters to his mother record, and clearly Dr. Hutton was much impressed. In introducing the series to the *Weekly's* readers on March 4, 1926, Dr. Hutton said:

> We make no apology for drawing the attention of our more serious readers to a volume by Professor Machen of Princeton, which is about to be published . . . We ourselves had the very great privilege of hearing Dr. Machen deliver, in Grove City, Penn., the lectures which form the larger portion of this volume. At the moment we were moved deeply and variously by the spoken word, delivered as it was with that firmness and passion and conviction which are the very constitution of Dr. Machen's personality. It is not possible for any one to be indifferent to what Dr. Machen has to affirm. He may agree, or he may disagree; in the latter case he will be compelled to gird up the loins of his mind. But always he will be moved. One passage the present writer recalls descriptive of our place here in the unfathomable depths of space, which, for grandeur and vastness and its almost intolerable truth as to our position as men and women—*except for faith in Christ*—seemed to be on a level with "A Dream" in Jean Paul Richter's "Flower, Fruit and Thorn Pieces," and the closing passages of John Henry Newman's "Apologia."
>
> It is a book of controversy in the highest and most honourable sense of that word. It will do us all an immense service, in the way of helping us to state to ourselves what it is we have come to mean. For these are bad days for the Church when we avoid the deepest questions, when we content ourselves with saying that there is

truth everywhere, on one side perhaps as much as on the other. As Frederick Denison Maurice long ago reminded his age: "It was not the real mother of the child who said, 'Let us divide it and give her a portion and me a portion.' "

These articles, which appeared as leading page 1 features, were written by Principal Samuel Chadwick under the title of the book; Principal W. B. Selbie, "Let Us Christianize our Theology"; the Rev. C. Rydar Smith, "The Way of the Peace-Maker"; Prof. H. R. Mac-intosh, "The Gospel of the Centre"; Prof. W. M. MacGregor, "Fundamentalism: A Friendly Admonition"; the Rev. J. T. Forbes, "Faith and Knowledge"; Prof. A. B. Macaulay, "Preacher and Controversialist"; Principal W. M. Clow, "The Puritan Gospel."

By no means all that was said in these articles was commendatory; indeed in several of them a substantial difference of point of view between Machen and his reviewers came to expression. But all the articles were eminently respectful and even laudatory. There is an amusing as well as an ironic side, therefore, to the observation that in the "Letter Box" columns of the *Weekly* for June 3, 1926 (thus at the very time when Machen had been humiliated at Baltimore), there appears a letter from an American Presbyterian minister, then at Oxford, in which "he confesses to a certain amazement at the tone of commendation which has for the most part pervaded" the articles. The writer says that "the adherents of fundamentalism are no doubt rejoicing at the unexpected approval of the views of one of their chief spokesmen," and then he advises that the book cannot be reviewed adequately "without reading between the lines," which for him means in the light of the American situation in which Dr. Machen has "attacked the leaders of constructive liberal thought in the churches—men like Dr. Fosdick, Dr. Coffin, Dr. Merrill and others, who are recognized in England as well as in America as outstanding representatives of a vital Christianity."

Among the most sympathetic discussions of the book was that of Principal Chadwick whose comments on theology and creeds included the following refreshing words:

> It is really pathetic to see the helplessness of educated people in the presence of theological thought. They have been told the task is hopeless and so they never really attempt to think. This is entirely a pose of culture. I have never heard a working man dismiss theology because it could not be understood, but I have heard a Professor inform university students that the creeds were hopeless and useless. Another went round the colleges telling students that they must get rid of all words in their religious vocabulary

that ended in "-ation"—such as Inspiration, Justification, Regeneration and Sanctification—because no one knew what they meant. They are told it is no use to think of these things. Religion is reduced to the terms of Kindergarten, symbolism and emotion. Religion cannot be separated from theology and theology does not call for great learning, but it does demand hard, honest thinking. Professor Machen contends for catechetical instruction and the objective validity of the creeds. Religion is languishing from lack of intellectual virility. The Professor comforts me, for I have been troubled at my impatience with unconventional sloppiness, and it makes me positively cross when an uncomfortable issue is shelved in a period of silent prayer. Pious cant does more harm than all the infidels. Our young people have been spoon-fed long enough.

Most critical perhaps was Principal Selbie whose article disclosed an impatience with Machen's conservative approach to theology. Appealing for a living and progressive conception of Christian faith, he said:

Perhaps our greatest need at the moment is to Christianize our theology, *i. e.,* to read God strictly in terms of Jesus Christ. When we do this, faith in God so revealed will carry us a very long way, and will render unnecessary many of those limitations and interpretations which we have put upon it. For, *pace* Dr. Machen, the thorough apprehension of God as love puts out of court at once all forensic and judicial interpretations of His relations with men. When modern theology seeks to explain the ways of God to men in ethical and personal rather than in judicial, governmental, or even metaphysical terms, it is only following the example of Jesus Christ Himself.

Professor Mackintosh began his discussion as follows:

No reader of Dr. Machen's book can fail to be grateful to him for an argument which lives and moves from first page to last. It is full of force and knowledge: above all, it is full of religion. It is a statement of the case for Christianity as set forth in the New Testament, without the deductions and reserves habitually made by idealistic naturalism, and the statement is inspired by deep and impassioned feeling. I think that Dr. Machen will find that sympathy with his aims is much more widely spread (at least in this country) than he supposes; but that at the same time many sympathizers will shrink from certain theological inferences which he asserts or assumes to be bound up with his fundamental positions.

As the development of the article discloses, Mackintosh had in mind, in differing from Machen, especially his strict doctrine of Scripture and the sharpness with which Machen distinguished in modern theology between those who were for Christ and those against him.

The manner in which, in the other articles of the *British Weekly* series and in the press the world over, the volume *What is Faith?* was received and evaluated will not be reported in detail here. There were scores and scores of reviews and editorials, some of them taking up particular points which had been raised by the British writers. And Machen himself, in the *Weekly* for September 23, 1926, was heard in a letter of "heartfelt gratitude and appreciation" of the generous attention his book had received, and in which he offered brief comments with regard to the individual contributions. In spite of such dissent as was registered at home and abroad, the response was in general most gratifying to Machen personally. And it disclosed again that in him the cause of the Gospel in general, and the Presbyterian Church and Princeton Seminary in particular, enjoyed the advantage of a spokesman of extraordinary distinction and power. However much men might differ from him in theology and in analysis of the contemporaneous situation, they observed that in respect of scholarship and learning he stood at the top level. And they recognized that because of his simple and moving eloquence, set aglow as it was by his fervent spirit and faith, he compelled attention and decision.

ARTICULATE CITIZEN

Like his grandfathers, Lewis H. Machen and J. J. Gresham, Machen was intensely concerned with the public questions of the day. He frequently addressed communications to the papers on the various burning issues. That he found and took time to do so is the more remarkable when one considers how his mounting academic and ecclesiastical activities absorbed his attention. Particularly following the publication of *Christianity and Liberalism* his correspondence grew by leaps and bounds. And being a very conscientious correspondent, even to the point of answering letters from persons who asked him not to answer, he came soon to require the services of stenographers to whom he dictated his replies. Only when he got away from civilization on an occasional mountain trip did he enjoy even brief surcease from what was to become a grievous burden. The many steel filing cabinets jammed full of letters and carbon copies and miscellaneous items disclose how tyrannical this obligation became to him. Meanwhile he could accept only a portion of the invitations which came to him to speak and to write. At times he pleaded that his obligations to his mother did not permit him to take extensive journeys to the Orient or to Europe since then he would not have been able to spend sufficient time with her in her advancing years, though she on her part was constantly urging him not to let his devotion to her stand in the way of seizing various attractive opportunities for service with which he was confronted.

If Machen had been a man of narrow interests and outlook, satisfied to be occupied wholly with his books and teaching and scholarly writing, his life would have been much simpler and he might have been spared much of the strain that characterized it throughout the twenties and the thirties until the day of his death. But the impact of his home and education was such as to stimulate his dynamic qualities to the point where he took an intelligent and spirited interest in all phases of contemporaneous life. In keeping with his high standards of scholarship, Machen expressed himself on public questions only if he had made a careful study of the issues and felt that he had a contribution to make. It would be a mistake to conclude that his fame gave him delusions of grandeur and that he supposed that he qualified as an expert on every question under the sun.

EVOLUTION AND EDUCATION

His attitude toward the issue of evolution, as that was debated about the middle twenties, serves to illustrate these qualities. The position which he had gained in the public eye as a spokesman for conservative Christianity about the year 1925 is highlighted by an invitation which he received that year to engage in a debate on the subject of evolution in the New York *Times*. The occasion was the approach of the highly publicized trial of J. T. Scopes at Dayton, Tenn. in which William Jennings Bryan and Clarence Darrow were opposing counsel. Mr. Scopes, a high school teacher, was charged with violating a law which forbade the teaching of evolution in the public schools of that state. Machen declined the request of the *Times* that he should deal specifically with evolution. But he consented to write an article on the subject, "What Fundamentalism Stands For Now," which was published on June 21, 1925 along with an article entitled, "What Evolution Stands for Now" contributed by Vernon Kellogg, Zoologist and Permanent Secretary and Chairman of the Educational Relations of the Natural Research Council. Machen's article was confined to an eloquent statement as to the nature of Christianity.

The reason why Machen declined to write on evolution at this time, declined invitations from *Current History* magazine and other journals to discuss the issue, and refused to take part in an anti-evolution convention that was sponsored by certain fundamentalists becomes clear from various letters bearing on the subject. He was by no means indifferent to the issue. And to the extent that evolution involved a philosophy of materialism, and contradicted the plain teaching of the Bible, he was quite opposed to it as a matter of course. On occasion he also indicated that similarity of structure between man and animals, even if it were far greater than was now supposed, could not eliminate the possibility and fact of divine intervention in creation or miracle. As a specialist in New Testament studies the great issue with regard to Christianity appeared to be that of the supernatural, and though not claiming to be a specialist in the Old Testament, he observed that the same issue was at stake there. But for the rest Machen was exceedingly cautious—some would say excessively so—in expressing himself on the subject of evolution. His scholarly instincts simply did not permit him to pose as an authority in such fields as biology and geology.

On matters of public interest relating to the field of education he had more pronounced views, and he gave vigorous expression to them from time to time in the public press as well as in his books when his theme permitted of such comment. Thus in a letter to the New York *Tribune,* under date of Feb. 26, 1923, he sounded an alarm with regard to a Nebraska language law which provided that no language other than English should be studied in any public or private school until the eighth grade had been passed. One of Machen's objections to this law was directed to its educational consequences: it meant, he felt, that children would be deprived of the advantage of studying a foreign language until they were too old to learn it well, and that even their English would suffer because it "can never be used with real vigor and ease without the discipline of language study at a very early period of life." His main objection, however, was one of principle.

> But the principle of the law is far worse even than its immediate results. It may be that literary education must be abandoned. It may be that we must ultimately content ourselves with the drab utilitarianism involved in the Nebraska law. It may be that "Main Street" is the highest type of life into which America can ultimately aspire. But if there are still those who desire to give their children some contact with the spiritual heritage of the race, should they not be permitted to do so? Is literary education so deadly a thing that it must be crushed out by force?

The Nebraska law was later invalidated by the Supreme Court as was a radical Oregon law which prohibited attendance of children upon any other than public schools. But the tendency toward uniformity and state control of education was very strong.

Another expression of this tendency found place in the Lusk laws of New York State which prescribed strict state control of schools including the requirements that non-public schools, institutes, classes or courses should not be conducted, maintained or operated without a special license. Eventually these laws were repealed, largely through the initiative of Governor Alfred E. Smith. But Machen, ever alert to threats to individual liberty, had been among those who had sought to influence public opinion. Writing to the *Herald Tribune* on April 12, 1923 he protested the popular support given to such legislation in the interest of checking "radicalism" in the colleges and elsewhere. Maintaining that the alarming prevalence of radicalism is an argument not in favor of repressive measures, but against them, he said:

> By such curtailments of the right of free speech we are destroying the only instrument which offers the slightest chance of combatting subversive tendencies and of preserving our institutions. That instrument is reasonable persuasion. And reasonable persuasion can thrive only in an atmosphere of liberty. It is quite useless to approach a man with both a club and an argument. He will very naturally be in no mood to appreciate our argument until we lay aside our club.

On the other hand, Machen's concern for liberty compelled him at times to oppose certain contemporary approaches to the subject of tolerance and freedom. This appears, for example, in a letter on free speech in colleges which was published in the New York *Times* on Sept. 12, 1925. At its triennial convention the National Council of the Phi Beta Kappa society, opposing "the present tendency to suppress freedom of thought and speech in our colleges," had declared it to be the sense of the convention that "no college that gives evidence of denying this freedom will be considered worthy of a chapter in Phi Beta Kappa." Protesting this action as a member of the society, Machen said in part:

> In attempting to establish a virtual boycott against colleges which do not share the views of the convention, the resolution is striking a serious blow against the very vitals of civil and religious liberty. One of the essential elements of civil liberty is the right of voluntary association—the right of persons who have come to have any view upon any subject whatsoever to associate themselves for the propagation of their view and to educate their children accordingly. This right is denied in principle by the present res-

> olution. It may be that many members of Phi Beta Kappa society are opposed, for example, to the principle of obligatory morality—to the conviction that there is a moral law that is no mere result of the experience of the race but is absolutely binding. Such members have a right to their view, and they are perfectly free to offer their services as teachers to any institution which is indifferent, as they are, to the transcendent validity of the moral law. But if they deny the right of other institutions to seek only teachers who uphold the moral law, they are interfering very seriously with that very freedom which they are claiming to defend.

In the sphere of family responsibility, as well as in that of the church, therefore, Machen was profoundly concerned to emphasize that liberty included the right of individuals, voluntarily associated together for common purposes, to exclude from their association all who might be out of harmony with the principles which brought it into being and gave it its *raison d'être*. This was the answer to the charge of intolerance both when hurled at those who were insisting that the church should be reformed and when leveled at persons who were concerned to maintain distinctively Christian institutions of learning.

Machen took an even more prominent role in an educational issue which was acutely raised in the year 1926. This concerned the effort to establish a Federal Department of Education. He not only wrote to leading newspapers on the subject but, on Jan. 12, 1926, delivered a major address on the theme, "Shall We Have a Federal Department of Education," before a meeting of the Sentinels of the Republic, of which he had become a member. The address was published in *The Woman Patriot* the following month. And on Feb. 24th Machen appeared before the joint hearings of the Senate and House committees on education to give expression to his opposition to the bills under consideration. For the record he presented substantially the argument of his address before the Sentinels, and then answered questions put by members of the committees. He was particularly concerned to oppose the principle, the establishment of which he thought would be accelerated if educational controls centered in the national government, that the children belong to the state. The aim to achieve a more uniform system of public education he also held would have disastrous results for education itself, especially in a time when a mechanistic theory of education was prevalent. Uniformity and standardization were fine in a Ford car—he had had reason to be thankful for that—but in the sphere of human personality and relationships individuality must be protected and even fostered.

Other questions of social and political significance were also constantly drawing his attention, and from time to time he gave public expression to his views. The *Survey Graphic* magazine for July, 1924, featured a debate on the question, "Does Fundamentalism Obstruct Social Progress?", in which, upon invitation, the affirmative was maintained by Professor Charles P. Fagnani of Union Theological Seminary of New York and the negative by Professor Machen. As in the case of the debate in the *N. Y. Times* the following year, referred to above, the terms of the question were not Machen's own. But understanding Fundamentalism as designating the position of supernatural Christianity over against the Modernism of the present day, he maintained that "far from being inimical to social progress, 'Fundamentalism' is the only means of checking the spiritual decadence of our age." This evaluation was based upon his analysis of the Biblical doctrine of history, of sin and salvation, and of society and the individual. The Christian welcomes the discovery of new facts with all his mind and heart, Machen insisted, but he also maintains that events of the past including the foundational events of Christian history may not be set aside in the interest of supposed progress. Christianity is not "a kind of sweet reasonableness based upon confidence in human goodness," but it "begins with the consciousness of sin, and grounds its hope only in the regenerating power of the Spirit of God." Christianity is social as well as individual; it is a caricature to represent it as offering man a selfish escape from the world and leaving society to its own fate. Nevertheless, Christianity "must place itself squarely in opposition to the soul-killing collectivism which is threatening to dominate our social life; it must provide the individual soul with a secret place of refuge from the tyranny of psychological experts; it must fight the great battle for the liberty of the children of God."

THE CHILD LABOR AMENDMENT

One of the burning questions of the day was that of the proposed Child Labor amendment to the Constitution, and Machen's vigorous opposition to the proposal stirred up considerable discussion and opposition in the newspapers, in the weekly, *The New Republic,* and in certain religious periodicals.

There were those who thought such opposition spelled pure reaction, smacking of a *laissez faire* approach to economics, and even disclosing a heartless disregard of the exploitation of children. That was, however, far from being the case. In terms of the connotation which "liberalism" has acquired in modern times, as a designation for a point of view which has sought social progress chiefly through a comprehensive program of federal governmental action, Machen would indeed be classified as a conservative or even as a reactionary in politics. Judging him, however, on the background of his historical antecedents and his own basic thinking, one would be nearer the truth to associate his viewpoint with that of Jeffersonian democracy or liberalism, though of course there were other determinative influences, including specifically his Christian principles. So in later years, in the 1932 and 1936 elections, he deserted the Democratic party because his study of the record of Franklin D. Roosevelt convinced him that his administration would signalize an enormous increase in the interference of the state in the life of its citizens. Machen's outlook is not grasped at all unless one discerns that he was passionately devoted to liberty and that this commitment was anchored profoundly in his Christian faith and outlook. In an era when the state was encroaching more and more upon the liberty of the individual, Machen was greatly exercised that men should be aroused to pay the price necessary to preserve it.

Thus his opposition to the proposed Twentieth Amendment was directed only in part to the fact that the federal constitution would be significantly modified, that thus the bill of rights itself would simply stand alongside of the new amendment, and that legislation under the amendment would involve a dangerous centralization of government. The designation "Child Labor Amendment" was really a misnomer since it falsely gave the impression that it was concerned with the protection of children who were laboring under unhealthy or oppressive conditions. As a matter of fact the proposal granted to the Congress *quite unqualified power* "to limit, regulate, and prohibit the labor of persons under eighteen years of age." As such Machen felt that it represented "the most sinister attack upon American institutions and the sanctity of the American home that has been made for half a century; it represents . . . a heartless cruelty masquerading under the guise of philanthropy." Under its unqualified terms all labor of children, even that under the direction of parents on their own farms, could be prohibited, and the activities of young persons could be regulated quite independently of parental control.

OTHER ISSUES

Other public utterances of Machen appearing during this period, chiefly in letters published in the New York *Herald Tribune,* included a criticism of alien enrollment as "a step in the already alarming bureaucratization of the United States"; of a provision in the Vestal copyright bill which would have made it virtually impossible for scholars to import books directly from abroad; and of Italy's forced "Italianizing" of the Germans of the Tyrol. Somewhat more distinctive, as reflecting his love of nature and his characterizations of the areas that were his chief vacation locales from his early years onward, are his comments on the dangers involved in the establishment of national parks. The White Mountain Reservation in New Hampshire, a national forest, had been managed with admirable wisdom.

> The region is thoroughly accessible to lovers of nature, there is cheap accommodation in hotels and camps, plenty of good forest paths and trails . . . but the mountains are not scarred by excessive road building nor are the forests ruined by landscape gardening.

In contrast, however, Machen felt that the policy adopted in the management of the Lafayette National Park on Mt. Desert Island, which had been under his observation since the beginning of the century, marred the natural beauty of nature:

> Mt. Desert Island twenty-five years ago contained a small but exceedingly beautiful wilderness of mountain and forest, lake and stream. It was not at all inaccessible. Good roads led within a few miles of every point in the region, and within the forests an excellent system of trails provided encouragement for exercise. But the charm of natural beauty was still unspoiled.
>
> Then came the Federal Government. At first its coming seemed to be a blessing: it checked the ravages of the lumbermen and prevented the region from being closed to the public through inclusion in private estates. It would be difficult to overpraise the generosity with which the land was devoted to the public good or the public spirit of the director of the park. But the sad thing is that so much generosity and so much public spirit should be productive of harm as well as good.
>
> Such unquestionably has been the case. A net work of carriage roads, completed or contemplated, is scarring almost every mountainside: at the side of the roads the forest is being ruthlessly "cleaned up" until every bit of natural charm is destroyed; no mossy glen or shady ravine is apparently to be spared. And all this is being done, not in a region which needed the hand of man to make it beautiful, but in one of the most charming lake and mountain districts in the entire East. The delicate beauty of those forests is being systematically forced into the commonplace mold of a city park. To every lover of nature it seems as though some delicate living creature were being brutally destroyed.

We are well aware that there is no disputing about tastes. There are many men about whom it can be said:

A primrose by a river's brim
A yellow primrose was to him,
And it was nothing more.

There are many men to whom a tree is a tree, whether artificially planted or not, and to whom a shady glen with its tangled foliage and moss-covered rocks means nothing at all. But there are also in this country some lovers of nature whose hearts are grieved. Are they altogether wrong?

Must the love of nature be crushed out by Government funds? Or ought it to be cherished as a sentiment without which a people is a people with a shriveled soul? Are the national parks to be used to destroy natural beauty, or are they to conserve it for the benefit of generations yet unborn?

21

A FATEFUL INVESTIGATION

Although Machen went quietly about his labors as he contemplated the investigation of Princeton Seminary, no one was so naive as to suppose that an era of peace had dawned in the Seminary and the Church at large. As a matter of fact the Seminary year began in an atmosphere of grave tension and foreboding. The developments at Baltimore were hardly calculated to quench or contain the flames of conflict within the Faculty. This appears most strikingly from the fact that, at an early meeting following the commencement of the new Seminary year, the Faculty took the unprecedented action of passing a motion of censure of President Stevenson because of his conduct at the Baltimore Assembly, maintaining that he had disregarded the proprieties involved in his position as a member of the faculty.

COMMENDATION AND DEFENSE

As the current religious periodicals disclose, the Christian public, both within and without the Presbyterian Church, was likewise not silent. Among the contemporaneous tributes, none is perhaps more pertinent, as bearing upon Machen's character and personality as well as his scholarship, than that of a Southern Methodist minister, the Rev. T. H. Lipscomb, who had heard him lecture and preach at a conference in Mississippi during the summer of 1926:

> We had expected to find him a thorough scholar and a thorough Christian, with what super-additions of genius and grace we knew not. To our delight and increasing joy we find him endowed with an intellectual clarity and felicity of expression which causes to flow forth into the minds even of unlearned hearers a sparkling stream of pure truth, quickening and convincing, out of a mass of detailed knowledge from which most scholars bring forth only negations or inconclusive theories. His mental idiosyncrasy in this regard is quite marked—hitting the nail on the head, causing the sparks to fly; and in the light of vindicated truth driving error from the field. We recall, as we think of him, Bunyan's Mr. Valiant for

Truth, and we would that the ten thousand silver trumpets might sound to do him honor—they will, some day, if not now, as he, too, crosses over into the Celestial City. Then woe to those who have said, "let not such light of truth *which also refutes and condemns error*—shine among us. We must be tolerant and considerate of error nowadays." A graduate of a Northern theological seminary myself (Drew '03), and having heard many of the ablest scholars of Europe and America, we affirm frankly and sincerely that we know of no man in any church so eminently qualified to fill a chair of "Apologetics and Christian Ethics," provided you want the chair *filled,* the Christian faith really defended, and Christian ethics elucidated and lived. For, let me add that Dr. Machen is a humble saint, as well as a rare scholar, not a "saint of the world," who stands for nothing and against nothing, but a saint of God who loves truth, seeks truth, finds truth, and upholds truth against all adversaries, however mighty. . .

Another gratifying word of defense was spoken across the waters from Bermuda, as Dr. Patton wrote glowingly of Machen's achievements and promise. His letter of Oct. 1, 1926, to another member of the Board, included the following:

In considering this matter, it must be remembered that what a man can make of himself depends largely on what God has already made him, and that Dr. Machen began life with an endowment of a very unusual nature. Besides that, he has benefitted by superior educational advantages. He is an assiduous student, has a wide range of information and a commanding style. He is learned, logical and eloquent. He is well-trained in all the departments of theological study, and is an enthusiastic defender of the Confessional system of the Reformed Churches.

The department of Apologetics covers a very wide area; and it can hardly be expected that one who is about to enter upon the duties of a chair in this department should be as completely equipped for them, as a man of equal ability may be, who has already devoted some of the best years of his life to the department. The most that can be reasonably asked is, that a candidate for the chair shall have the qualities of mind that fit him for the work, a broad foundational preparation for it, an intellectual bent that will enable him to enter upon it with enthusiasm, and that these qualifications be revealed in some creditable work already accomplished. These conditions, I do not hestitate to say, Dr. Machen satisfies in a preeminent degree. They are manifest in his books, entitled "Liberal

> Christianity" and "What is Faith?" But Dr. Machen has given still more specific proof of his eminent fitness for the vacant chair.
>
> In order to defend Christianity, one must have a definite conviction in respect to what Christianity is; and no man, I think, is better acquainted than Dr. Machen is with the current forms of minimizing theology, which, in some respects, are the most insidious foes of Christian faith, inasmuch as the gist of their teaching seems to be that the fruits of Christianity will continue to flourish after the axe has been laid at the roots of the tree that bears them.
>
> But Dr. Machen has done specific work of a very important kind in apologetic theology. Christianity exposes a large frontier to the attacks of the enemy, and its defenders are called upon to discuss the relations of science and Scripture, to say whether philosophy will give us leave to believe in the Living God, and to meet the challenge of history, when we are told that Christianity is only a developed paganism.
>
> Some of our apologetes may be better versed in science and others more widely read in philosophy, but in the department which just now challenges the special attention of the apologete, Dr. Machen is a master. The evidence of this is found in his book on "The Origin of Paul's Religion"; and I confidently say that any seminary in any part of the world might well be proud to claim that man as a member of its faculty; for whether measured in terms of learning or logic, it is unquestionably a great book.

This appraisal was most welcome as it disclosed that Patton retained through the years an unbounded confidence in Machen and a profound appreciation of his worth. Nevertheless, one must observe that the letter was disappointing to Machen in two closely related respects. In the first place, it failed to touch upon Machen's character and personality which were under fire rather than his scholarly qualifications as such. Thus Patton disclosed that he was largely out of touch with the actual situation, though he is not to be blamed when one considers that he was now beyond eighty and nearly blind. The same historical factor appears from the consideration that in the same letter, in the second place, he expressed the hope that "these difficulties may find an amicable settlement through a reasonable compromise." Although Patton admitted in the same breath that he was "ignorant of all the facts which enter into the difficulties," and Machen felt assured that Patton would have expressed himself somewhat differently had he been well informed, nevertheless Machen grieved at the fact that his enemies would be sure to make their own appeal to the letter so as to discount its central plea.

In this connection, moreover, it must be admitted that there were other utterances of Patton in his later years which disappointed Machen and seemed to point to a certain weakness. In his *Fundamental Christianity*, published in 1926 when the author was beyond eighty, and comprising substantially the brilliant lectures with which he had regaled and stimulated his audiences upon scores of occasions throughout many decades, Patton had given comfort to the latitudinarian forces by certain declarations regarding tolerance. From his correspondence with Machen it appears that his personal theological position had not changed but that he held that various historic decisions of the Church, including especially the adoption of the 1903 amendments and the resulting Cumberland Union, had in actual effect given the constitutional position of the Church a considerably broader base than the original documents themselves had in view. That Patton thus touched upon a vulnerable spot cannot be doubted. But Machen differed from him in maintaining that the specific commitment to the historic standards involved in the vows taken by church officers did not allow for substantial liberty with regard to Calvinism, although he lamented the manner in which the historic decisions of 1903 and 1906 had served to impinge somewhat upon the purity of their testimony. In spite of this difference in their appraisal of the history of the Church, it remains true, if one takes account of the basic thrust of Patton's book rather than merely of certain isolated statements, that Patton was no doubt in full agreement that the Liberalism or Modernism of their day had no rightful place within the household of the Presbyterian Church. Confirmation of this appraisal will appear in the sequel.

Another gratifying word of appreciation came from the students of the Seminary. Meeting as a Students' Association on November 16, on the eve of the first meeting of the Assembly's investigating committee, they passed without a dissenting vote a resolution which expressed "unbounded confidence in Dr. J. Gresham Machen as a scholar, as a teacher, as a gentleman, and as a Christian."

Machen was deeply grateful for this resolution, coming as it did at a time when he had been subjected to abuse on the part even of men at Princeton, and expressing the attitude of those who enjoyed the advantage of intimate fellowship in the classroom and on the campus. A minority of students indeed was sympathetic with the policies of Stevendon and Erdman, but even they, certainly almost to a man, agreed as to the injustice of most of the attacks upon Machen's person. He was immensely popular and successful as a teacher, and there was no member of the Faculty who had proved to so many students that, for all of his intense involvement in a great conflict, he could meet them on their own level and be a warmhearted and generous friend. In reply to this resolution, after due acknowledgement, Machen said:

> I do not feel worthy of the high terms in which the resolution speaks of me; on the contrary, this generous action of the Students' Association has led me only to pray with renewed earnestness that God may make me less unworthy. But you have given me profound encouragement in the trying days through which I am passing, and have strengthened yet more the ties of affection with which already I felt myself united to the students of the Seminary. I trust that God may bless us ever more richly in our association with one another and may lead us into an ever better and truer service of Him.

THE INVESTIGATION BEGINS

The Committee convened at Princeton for the first time on November 22, 1926 for three days of hearings, returned for another meeting early the following year, and published its findings and recommendations in April, 1927, only a few weeks before the Assembly met. Nearly 200 alumni were present for the first session: many were heard and communications of others were read. They proved to be divided in their sympathies.

Some who were extremely critical were extraordinarily ill-informed and biased. The claim was advanced, for example, that Machen and his associates were seeking to espouse a fanatical fundamentalism and to make Princeton the seminary of an extreme party of the Church. Some who had the most advanced liberal outlook, in criticism of Machen's election to the Chair of Apologetics and Ethics, laid major emphasis upon his vote at the spring meeting of the Presbytery of New Brunswick on the enforcement of the 18th Amendment! Others attacked his person alleging that he was "queer" and unsociable, and that as a bachelor he was not aware of the responsibilities of family life and therefore lacked sympathetic experience of the larger aspects of social life!

But there were many also who vigorously urged that the Committee should not consider recommending a basic change in the government and policies of the Seminary. Among these perhaps the most effective were Dr. Frank H. Stevenson and Dr. B. M. Gemill. The former stressed the profoundly doctrinal significance of the issue involved. And the latter showed that according to actions of several Assemblies the basic control over the Faculty was committed to the Board of Directors and that an election, if not vetoed by the next Assembly, was to be regarded as complete. On this evaluation Machen's election should have been recognized as valid and the Directors, in spite of the action of the 1926 Assembly, might have proceeded to install him in his new office.

Certain students were also heard in connection with the issue that had been raised by the formation of the League of Evangelical Students, and the eventual termination of Dr. Erdman's service as student adviser which grew out of it. At the Baltimore Assembly President Stevenson had charged Machen with responsibility for the latter development. A letter to Dr. Stevenson from the pen of J. Anderson Schofield, Jr., of the class of 1925 answered this charge (Mr. Schofield testifying as one who had participated in student affairs affecting the League that Machen had had nothing to do with initiating the student action), and was circulated in pamphlet form among alumni of the Seminary. Hence alumni as well as students, and members of the Faculty likewise, spent considerable time in reviewing this entire phase of the controversy.

Of greatest moment was the testimony of members of the Faculty. Machen presented his own testimony in a number of printed pamphlets in which, with careful documentation, he surveyed the entire issue. Since his evaluation of various developments has been reviewed in preceding chapters, it need not be set forth again.

Dr. Stevenson repeated many of his previous charges. He disagreed basically with Machen's diagnosis of the state of the church with which, however, he admitted, the majority of the Faculty agreed. Nor was he sympathetic with the reformatory measures proposed by Machen and Macartney. He indicated further his opposition to the participation of the Seminary in the League of Evangelical Students. Such participation, be maintained, disassociated Princeton from the other Seminaries of the Presbyterian Church in the U. S. A. and united it rather with institutions which in the main were associated with "secession bodies," thus representing a spirit of division, and repudiating the long established policy of the Presbyterian Church as regards cooperation and union. Union Seminary had swung off to destructive liberalism in becoming an independent Seminary, Stevenson averred, but Princeton faced the great danger that it might swing off to the extreme right wing so as to become an interdenominational Seminary for "Bible School-premillennial secession fundamentalism." This approach of Stevenson was no doubt shrewd and effective, especially when considered as an appeal to the Church at large which was moving rapidly in the direction of inclusivism. It was also revealing, however, as indicating how far his own thinking had turned away from the Reformation principle of ecclesiastical separation for conscience' sake, and how fully he embraced an essentially latitudinarian position. It is rather ironically amusing, at the same time, that he chose to dub Machen's viewpoint as premillennial, when as a matter of fact Dr. Erdman was the only premillenarian in the Faculty.

ARMSTRONG'S STATEMENT

Dr. Armstrong acted as spokesman for the Faculty in presenting its principal statement. There were, however, separate statements prepared and submitted by several members of the Faculty, as well as extensive participation on their part in discussion at the different sessions of the Committee. Armstrong also offered a significant personal statement concerning his relations with Machen in the work of the New Testament Department, in which they had been associated for twenty years, and in the more intimate sphere of personal intercourse "where friendship removes restraints and motives may be judged by knowledge of the disposition of feeling and thought from which they spring."

> During all these years my association with him has been close and our personal relations have been altogether delightful. He has been like a member of my family whose respect and affection he has won from the youngest to the oldest. We have labored together not only in the work of our Department but in the Faculty and in the Church, holding as we do similar views concerning the purpose of the Seminary and concerning the public policy of the Church. Ever sensitive to the high obligations of his calling, he has never been willing to sacrifice principle to expediency; but while devotion to principle has brought him into debate with those from whom he differs, he has been mindful always of the proprieties, as his writings will testify. Thinking clearly and of strong convictions, he has not hesitated to state issues with precision; but though his methods of presenting his opinions have seemed to some to be severe, and have been characterized as harsh, they have never descended to the level of personalities. And the dominant motive in all his activity has been no other than zeal for the Gospel as it is set forth in the Scriptures and expounded in our Confession of Faith. Moreover his zeal has been unselfish. He has never spared himself. He has not sought personal advantage or preferment, neither has he abated his response to duty by any consideration of consequences. Even in that trying time when his election was before the Committee of the General Assembly, the unselfishness of his devotion to the Seminary was manifested in the telegram which he sent to his friends in Baltimore asking that his name be withdrawn from consideration if by doing so the interests of the Institution could be served.
>
> Knowing him as I do, I feel that he has been misunderstood and misjudged, not so much among scholars who generally have recog-

nized and have expressed their respect for the ability with which he presents his point of view even when they differ from it, but rather in the ecclesiastical sphere where his attitude toward the public policy of the Church has aroused opposition. But here also I am confident that his course has been guided by principle; and where he has opposed persons, he has done so because of their relation to an issue which for him was determined not by the persons but by the principle involved.

Distressed as I was and am by the decision of the Assembly, I am grateful for the opportunity of testifying to my warm personal regard for my friend and associate, to my knowledge of the high and unselfish motive which has guided his public activity, to the eminent qualities which have distinguished his work as teacher and writer both in the scientific and in the more popular fields of theological literature, to his fine sensibility for and response to the nobler values and standards of personal intercourse, and to the devotion and consecration of his talents to the service of that cause which is cherished here and which is above every other cause.

Dr. Wistar Hodge also came to the defense of Machen's qualifications and character. After dwelling in highest terms upon Machen's abundant qualifications for the chair, he stated:

What I desire especially to speak of is Dr. Machen's exceptional personal qualifications for this Chair. I have known him intimately for some twenty years. His love and zeal for the truth of the Gospel, his high-mindedness, and his scrupulous fairness toward those holding opposing views have won my admiration. His Christian disposition, and the Christian life he has lived among us these past twenty years, has won my highest regard, and above all his personal qualities have won my love.

But perhaps above all that has called forth my admiration for Professor Machen, is his spirit of Christian patience and forbearance in the midst of the most bitter attacks and unfounded slanders—attacks—the bitterness and groundlessness of which are so far as my knowledge goes, without parallel in the history of our Church.

Referring then to Erdman's letter to *The Presbyterian,* Stevenson's and Erdman's speeches at the Assembly, and to charges of alumni at the Assembly, he went on to say that Machen

> has borne himself in the midst of these slanders with amazing Christian patience, and that while in his case this patience is a virtue, silence and patience on the part of myself and his colleagues, I would regard as ignoble . . . If the time has come when a man cannot make a bold and noble defense of the Truth without being subjected to abuse, then indeed the darkness of mediaeval intolerance threatens to overwhelm the Presbyterian Church, and to stifle its witness to the Truth of God.

Commenting upon the theological position of the Seminary, Dr. Hodge showed that what was at stake was not the preservation of a distinctive or peculiar Princeton theology as distinguished from other brands of Calvinism, but simply the Calvinism of the Confession of Faith.

> It has sometimes been mistakenly supposed that there is a "Princeton Theology." Drs. Alexander and Hodge always repudiated this idea. Princeton Seminary has always taught and upheld the theology of the Westminster Confession—the majesty and sovereignty of Almighty God, the total inability of fallen man to save himself, and that the whole of salvation is to be ascribed to the power and grace of God. This is simply the pure and consistent form of evangelicalism which says, with Paul, "by grace have ye been saved, through faith and that not of yourselves; it is God's gift."
>
> This generic Calvinism has been taught in Princeton Seminary under the specific form of the Covenant Theology, so richly developed in the Westminster Confession, and grounded in the Scripture statement, "I will be your God, and ye shall be my people."
>
> The newer modifications of Calvinism have passed away, and this pure and consistent form of Christian supernaturalism and evangelicalism alone stands as an impregnable barrier against the flood of naturalism which threatens to overwhelm all the Churches of Christendom. "Soli deo gloria" may well be called the motto of Princeton Seminary, as it is of all true theology and religion.

So Wistar Hodge eloquently set forth the issue of the day, and stressed the consideration that Princeton's answer to the naturalism and scepticism of the times was not a general fundamentalism nor a lowest common denominator evangelicalism but the pure evangelicalism of the Reformed Faith. What was at stake, therefore, was not merely the question whether Princeton would be allowed to retain its historic position but the more momentous one whether it would be preserved to teach and to defend the faith in the sovereign God as the only answer to the deepest problems and needs of men.

THE DIRECTORS' ANALYSIS

At the hearings most of the members of the Board of Trustees took the position that the interests of the institution would be advanced by the merging of the Boards. On the other hand, the majority of the Directors sought to maintain their legal and traditional authority. Their formal statement, which had been passed by an overwhelming majority, was presented by the president, Dr. Maitland Alexander. It included an enthusiastic endorsement of Dr. Machen for the Chair to which he had been elected. Mention was made of "his scholarship, his reputation here and in other countries, his ability as a teacher, his inspiring work in his classes" as supporting Dr. Hutton's evaluation that any seminary might be proud to number him among its faculty. Then the Directors' statement addressed itself to the point where Machen had been subject to special attack: his supposed deficiencies of character and personality, and at this point it was no less vigorous in his defense.

> The criticism of Dr. Machen by those who oppose him is based on his relations with those with whom he disagrees on matters of the seminary's policies and doctrinal positions. The Board contends that in any disputes which have arisen in connection with the policy and position of the seminary in which he has expressed himself that he is in agreement with the policy and position of the Directors.
>
> We hold that Dr. Machen has been sorely tried by charges that are false and misleading and we call attention to the fact that those with whom he differs in the church at large, especially in the scholarly world, emphasize his excellent spirit in controversy.

Several quotations from reviews of his books were then quoted—reviews which spoke of his "sweet reasonableness," of his "truly fine and catholic spirit," of his avoidance of vituperation in dealing with his opponents. Summing up its conclusions on this matter, the Directors said:

> The Board feels that his stimulating and helpful relations to the students of the Seminary are of tremendous value to them as may be ascertained by your committee by impartial inquiry. They feel that for the seminary not to avail itself of Dr. Machen's scholarship in the Chair of Apologetics instead of keeping him as the Assistant Professor of New Testament, which chair he now occupies, would be foolish in the extreme, hold the Seminary up to the ridicule of the scholarly world, and be a distinct loss in the tremendous

battle now being waged against the Reformed faith for which this Seminary stands.

Turning then to a review of the office of the president, the Directors observed that many of the troubles of the seminary were due to his administration, and declared that in view of the ever widening breach between him and the faculty and Directors, "his usefulness is at an end." That the Board had not acted in this matter was indicated as being due to the hope that he would voluntarily resign. As later discussion indicated, a further deterrent was the consideration that the removal of the president would have had to be confirmed by the General Assembly, and there was concern lest the Church which had moved considerably to the left of the theological position of Princeton Seminary might vindicate the inclusivist policies of the president, a fear that was later to be demonstrated as well grounded. In the report itself a plea was expressed that Princeton should be allowed to stand according to its plan as representing the conservative wing of the Church. The appeal to the plan was indeed in point and involved doctrinal and ethical principles which should have been determinative. But the plea for toleration implied an acknowledgement that Princeton was but a part of a larger ecclesiastical and theological situation which could offer little promise of its preservation. This official position was vigorously supported by individual Directors in the discussions with the Committee of Investigation.

The minority members, on the other hand, expressed their dissent and in general favored unification of the Board. One of these directors held that the trouble originated in the faculty rather than with the president, and analyzed the cleavage in these terms: on the one side, the men of the cloister, and on the other side, the men of the open road; on the one side, the men who are chiefly concerned about facts and deductions and conclusions, and on the other, men who are in touch with human needs and deeply impressed with the importance of carrying to them a gospel of reconciliation, and helping men into the right life. He added, however, that he thought that both types of men were desirable and should have supplemented one another. This analysis was also echoed within the faculty by a minority member, and serves to point up the advantage the minority possessed when once the issues were to be determined by the vote of the church at large.

THE COMMITTEE'S RECOMMENDATION AND ACTION

When the report of the Investigating Committee was published shortly before the Assembly of 1927 was to convene at San Francisco, it became evident to Machen and the conservatives generally that apart from some quite unforeseen turn of events, Princeton Seminary as it had existed for more than a hundred years, as an institution vigorously committed to the Bible and the Reformed Faith, would soon reach the end of the road.

The Report recommended what was in effect a complete capitulation to the reorganization point of view. Its principal recommendation was that the necessary steps should be taken to bring about a single Board of control. Pending the reorganization the appointment of Machen was to be deferred and all other nominations and elections were likewise to be held in abeyance. It was expected at the time that the reorganization could be completed by the 1928 Assembly, and thus that the Directors were virtually to suspend activity in managing the major concerns of the Seminary for the time being. In support of its recommendations the Committee displayed its partisan outlook, among other ways, by declaring that "under the present conditions the drift of Seminary control seems to be away from the proper service of the Church and toward an aggressive defense of the policy of a group."

The state of Machen's mind at this time is perhaps most clearly reflected in his letters to his mother. He had welcomed the election in March, 1927, of "Bobby" Robinson to the new chair of Christian Education and of Dr. O. T. Allis to Davis' chair in Old Testament as "a great strengthening of the cause of decency." But of course the recommendation of the Board also involved a postponement of their confirmation.

What dismayed him most of all was what he judged the recommendation would mean to Princeton itself. On May 16 Macartney wrote Machen a note stating that he had just seen a letter from Luccock, a member of the Investigating Committee, to McEwan, a prominent Director, suggesting that "we compromise by an agreement to confirm you and Allis, and then proceed with a reorganization of the Board." To this Machen replied the following day:

> Of course the proposal of a compromise does not in itself interest me at all. You are already aware, I think, of my view of the matter. As I have said in my public statement in the New York *Times*, the really important question is the question of control of the Seminary. If the reorganization plan is adopted, there will be no advantage either to me personally or to the Seminary in having my election confirmed; the history of Princeton Seminary as a conservative institution will in that case have come to an end. I do hope

that attention may not be diverted by any compromise proposals whatever from the really important question.

The full report of the Committee had not reached the men at Princeton until early in May, leaving precious little time to marshall the conservative forces for the battle at San Francisco. His letter of May 9th is one of the most illuminating from this period:

> My dearest Mother;
>
> I have been through so much the past three days that tonight I feel pretty limp; but I really must try to send a line to my dearest Mother, whose sympathy and love I value now as never before. Your letter of May 3 was an immense comfort. What could I possibly do without the one unfailing human source of help?
>
> Army went to Pittsburgh on one of the early days in this past week to see Mr. Dickie, our lawyer, and Dr. Alexander. It was there arranged that Mr. Dickie should come to Princeton Friday night arriving at Princeton Saturday morning and spending the day in conference with us and with some conservative directors. Meanwhile the galley proof of the Report was to be available. But no galley proof was given to us and all that was secured was the first part of the report (containing all but part of the Appendix). That did not come to hand till Friday night! On Saturday Mr. Dickie was called to a funeral. So the best he could do was to be with us all day Sunday. Never did I spend such a Sunday in my whole life; but never was there a more obvious work of necessity with the meeting of the Board of Directors coming the very next day. Stonewall Jackson's decision to fight a more ordinary battle on Sunday was nothing compared with this! . . . .
>
> The Report is almost unbelievably unfair—both in its own opinion and recommendations and in its highly partisan choice of the portions of the record for print. But I have not given up hope. . .
>
> Things are not all bad. Weakness and defection among our own men are the worst things. But I rejoice in Mr. Dickie's help.

Almost immediately after the Committee Report became available, *An Open Letter to the Commissioners of the Next Assembly Regarding the Special Report on Princeton* was prepared and signed by 17 Directors. It was published in *The Presbyterian* for May 12, 1927. This statement challenged the propriety and necessity of the proposal to merge the Boards, declared that the recommendation concerning Machen would work injustice to him personally and would be prejudicial to the best interests of the Seminary. It further maintained that the proposal not to approve other elections pending the reorganization was a most serious menace to the welfare of the Seminary, especially since no fewer than five chairs were vacant at the time. In conclusion it made this moving appeal:

> For more than a century Princeton Seminary has stood four-square for the infallibility of the Scriptures and the faith of the Church. Has it ever in its long history been charged with disobedience to the General Assembly, or disloyalty to the Christian Faith? Princeton is today our largest Seminary, justly famed in all lands for its scholarly defense of the Bible and its witness to our Lord Jesus Christ. Her ministers, teachers and missionaries have gone out throughout the earth and her words to the end of the world. Do you wish Princeton Seminary to continue its glorious witness to Jesus Christ in the everlasting Gospel? If you do, then we ask you by your prayers, your counsel, your arguments, and your vote in the General Assembly to contend earnestly against the recommendations of the Special Committee.

In an editorial in *The Presbyterian* the following week, Samuel G. Craig reported his experience as a Director and succinctly summed up the issue as he had seen it develop. When he had joined the Board two years before, he had determined to be a mediator between the conflicting groups. But as he began to inform himself as to the situation he became convinced that there would have been no serious administrative differences at Princeton except for certain major doctrinal issues. These he summed up as follows:

> The real reason why the confirmation of Dr. Machen was opposed was the fact that he was and is such a cogent expounder and defender of the seminary's policies and doctrinal positions as held by the large majority of the Board of Directors. And again, the real reason why an investigating committee was asked for by President Stevenson was, we are persuaded, the fact that President Stevenson, realizing that his position in opposition to the majority of his Board of Directors had become untenable, and that their next step would probably be the exercise of their power under the Plan to remove him, subject to the approval of the General Assembly, hoped by this means to secure a merger of the Board of Directors and the Board of Trustees in the expectation that thereby he would be able to obtain a Board of Control, the majority of whom would favor his policy, since the majority of the Board of Trustees, unlike the majority of the Board of Directors, does favor his policy.

The *New York Times* editorialized at considerable length on the Report stating that "the majority faction, headed by Prof. J. Gresham Machen, has little patience with the liberals; the minority, headed by President J. Ross Stevenson and Prof. Charles R. Erdman, while in virtual doctrinal agreement with the majority, stands for a policy of tolerance." It observed that so far as the majority was concerned the report "was in the nature of a bombshell." The minority, on the other hand, approved the plan, and Dr. Erdman rejected the implication that the issue of fundamentalism was involved in the controversy. There seems to be some danger, concluded the editor, that the term will become so firmly associated in the public mind with intolerance that the position of "fundamentalists" like him will be misunderstood unless they adopt another designation.

The Brooklyn *Daily Eagle* for May 10, 1927, on the other hand, published an editorial entitled "Who Owns Princeton Seminary?" It too noted the profound cleavage reflected in the struggle over Princeton, and suggested that an appeal might be made to the courts to determine where the ultimate control and ownership really existed. It declared that Dr. Thompson, chairman of the committee, had lined himself up with the modernists, with Dr. Erdman and Dr. Henry van Dyke. Finally, it viewed the General Assembly battle as in doubt, and declared that if the Fundamentalists should win, the modernists would have to surrender Princeton to their foes and seek a center elsewhere.

The *Eagle* was not a very good prophet, for the Report of the Special Committee was adopted by a decisive majority. A vigorous fight was made by various spokesmen for the historic Princeton. J. Roy Dickie was a wise counsellor, and especially Directors Laird and Inglis spoke eloquently. But all to no avail, except that it was conceded that an additional year would be required. An enlarged committee was set up to perfect organization plans.

Dr. Armstrong voiced his sorrow in a letter to Machen, who was on a speaking trip in England. Under date of June 2, he said:

> The Assembly proved to be against us on every issue. I am distressed for the Seminary and for you and Allis. I cannot see how good can come . . . until the wrong is righted. We shall have to be patient and continue to fight.

And Wistar Hodge gave out a statement, which was published in several newspapers including the Philadelphia *Bulletin* and the New York *Times,* declaring that the action of the Assembly constituted one of the darkest pages in the history of American Presbyterianism, and that the failure to confirm Machen and Allis in their professorships was an act of grossest injustice.

VARIOUS INVITATIONS

Following the Assembly Machen was invited to become the president of the newly launched Bryan Memorial University at Dayton, Tenn., a development significant chiefly because his declination serves to enlarge one's understanding of his commitment to the Princeton cause. This was by no means the first effort to entice Machen to leave Princeton. Many years before, as observed above, there had been insistent overtures from both Union Theological Seminary of Richmond and the Presbyterian Seminary in Louisville. Early in the year 1926, he was approached by the influential Rev. John Gibson Inkster of Knox Church, Toronto (where Machen frequently occupied the pulpit) with a view to his occupancy of the principalship of Knox College. Inkster was not easily discouraged and urged Machen to permit him to nominate him at the Assembly as the man around whom their church could be united. Machen had taken great interest in the ecclesiastical life of Canada, and had assisted great numbers of theological students of Princeton to labor in Presbyterian Churches in Canada. His reply indicated, however, that he was too deeply involved in the struggle to preserve the historic position of Princeton to consider this approach favorably.

In the fall of 1926 Machen was approached again from the South, this time as Dr. Gillespie, president of Columbia Theological Seminary, acting for the Board visited him at Princeton, and urged him to consider acceptance of the chair of New Testament. Southerner that he was in tradition and in various aspects of his outlook and spirit, and anxious as he had become for the future of the Church in which he was brought up, Machen could not but be moved by this approach. But again the urgency of the Princeton situation, and his sense of responsibility in the crisis of its life, did not allow of a favorable response. And so Dr. Gillespie, writing on Nov. 23, 1926, to thank him for his hospitality and time, said that "it is a great disappointment to our faculty and to the few representatives of the Board with whom I have had the opportunity to talk, that you could not give favorable consideration to the overtures which I made." He further expressed the hope that Machen might be fully vindicated. The relations with Columbia continued most cordial, and in the spring of 1927 Machen fulfilled an engagement to deliver the Smyth Lectures at that institution. His theme was the Virgin Birth of Christ, and the specific preparation for this course of lectures marked another milestone on the way to the completion of his great book. He had chosen to deliver the lectures in a largely extemporaneous manner, and they were received with enthusiasm by the large audiences which turned out to hear him.

The decision to invite Machen to the presidency of the Bryan Memorial University was reached while Machen was still in England in connection with his tour initiated by the Bible League of Great Britain. On the supposition that the developments at the 1927 Assembly offered substantial hope that Machen might welcome a new position, the association sponsoring the new University acted early in June. Assuming that Machen had been present at the Assembly in San Francisco, Mr. F. E. Robinson, president of the association, sent the following telegram to Malcolm Lockhart, promotional director of the university, in New York:

> Please see Dr. J. Gresham Machen, of Princeton, immediately upon his return from the General Assembly and ask him if he will consider accepting the presidency of the Bryan Memorial University, effective June, 1928. We consider Dr. Machen one of the most scholarly and conservative theologians in America.

Without waiting for Machen's return from England, Mr. Lockhart gave out the news to the newspapers, and the leading metropolitan dailies gave the story feature coverage.

Time magazine, in its issue for June 20, published Machen's picture with the sub-caption, *Bryanites told the newspapers,* and in reporting the invitation included the following interesting, if hardly accurate, comments:

> An invitation went to Dr. J. Gresham Machen of Princeton Theological Seminary last week, the sort of an invitation that could have only caused more embarrassment to an already harassed man.
>
> Dr. Machen is a great and learned theologian, a philosopher among preachers. Also he is a literalist. He interprets the Bible strictly, and that has made him vastly unhappy at Princeton, for the greater number of the authorities there have been opposed to his views. When he was named for the Chair of Apologetics, the Board of Directors fought with the Board of Trustees over the appointment. That has been the scandal of the Presbyterian Church in the U. S. A. The General Assembly a year ago would not order the appointment. Three weeks ago at San Francisco the General Assembly again snubbed Dr. Machen (*Time,* June 6).
>
> Here, decided Fundamentalists, was a man who could command attention for their religious-scientific arguments, which a world busied with crime, catastrophies and aviators has of late ignored. Forthwith President F. E. Robinson of the association promoting Bryan Memorial University at Dayton (Scopes Trial), Tenn.,

sent a 48-word telegram to his Promotional Director Malcolm Lockhart in Manhattan, ordering him to offer Dr. Machen the presidency of the proposed Bryan Memorial University. Promotor Lockhart made the offer, told the newspapers. Dr. Machen harassed, unhappy, kept silent.

To underscore only one of several incorrect details, Machen did not return to the United States until a number of days after the date of this issue of *Time!* And as his 55-page steamer letter to his Mother begun on June 16 intimates, all he knew of this development was derived from an allusion in a letter of his mother written on June 5. She had referred to his "being called to be president of the new University at Dayton." Machen said only that this was "very intriguing, since it brought me my first and only news of any such call. I wonder what in the world it is." Shortly after his arrival in the United States the formal approach was made through Mr. Lockhart, and Machen indicated his decision without delay. As early as June 25, Machen prepared his formal acknowledgement and declination, which was given to the press by the University authorities. In view of its highly significant disclosures as to Machen's views regarding the contemporaneous situation, and of his own position in relation to it, it is given in full:

June 25, 1927

F. E. Robinson, Esq.,
President of the
Bryan University Memorial Association,
Care of Malcolm Lockhart, Esq.,
840 West End Avenue,
New York City.

Dear Sir:

On my return from a lecture trip in Great Britain, Mr. Lockhart has conveyed to me the question of the Bryan University Memorial Association as to whether I could consider accepting the presidency of the University.

In reply, I desire above all to say how very great is my appreciation of the honor which has thus been conferred upon me. Particularly at the present moment, when I have just been subjected by the General Assembly of the Church to which I belong to a most extraordinary indignity, it is profoundly encouraging to me to know that there are those who do not acquiesce in such a low estimate of my services and of my character. In these days of widespread defection from the Christian faith, I rejoice with all my heart in the warmth of Christian fellowship that unites me with those who, like you, love the gospel of the Lord Jesus Christ, and are willing to bear the reproach to which a frank acceptance of the gospel subjects them in the presence of a hostile world.

At the same time, though to my very great regret, I am obliged to say that I should be unable to accept the important position to which your suggestion refers.

In the first place, I do not feel that just at the present moment I can honorably leave my present position. Princeton Theological Seminary is an institution which for a hundred years, and never more successfully than now, has been defending and propagating the gospel of Christ. It is now passing through a great crisis. If the reorganization favored by the General Assembly which has just met at San Francisco is finally adopted next year — if the proposed abrogation of the whole constitution of the Seminary and the proposed dissolution of the present Board of Directors is finally carried out, if, in other words, the control of the Seminary passes into entirely different hands—then Princeton Theological Seminary as it has been so long and so honorably known, will be dead, and we shall have at Princeton a new institution of a radically different type. But meanwhile — during this coming year — the Seminary is still genuinely and consistently evangelical. And it is by no means certain that the work of destruction will really be authorized next May. The report of the Committee that dealt with the subject this year was adopted only because of the gross misrepresentations of fact that the report contained, and it is quite possible that the true facts may still become generally known and that the sense of fair play which, we hope, is still possessed by the rank and file of our Presbyterian Church may make itself felt, so that the right of thoroughgoing conservatives in the Presbyterian Church to have at least one Seminary that clearly and unequivocally represents their view may still be recognized and Princeton may still be saved. Meanwhile — until this issue is decided — I do not think it would be right for me to desert my colleagues here or to desert the institution that I so dearly love.

In the second place, I doubt very seriously my fitness for an administrative position like that which you have done me the honor of connecting with my name. My previous efforts, to say nothing of their imperfections even in their own sphere, have been of an entirely different kind. The very importance of the position which you are seeking to fill makes me question very seriously, to say the least, whether I am at all fitted to be its occupant.

In the third place, I am somewhat loath, for the present at least, to relinquish my connection with distinctively Presbyterian work. I have the warmest sympathy, indeed, with interdenominational efforts of various kinds; I have frequently entered into such efforts on my own part; and I understand fully that the real attack is not directed against those points wherein Calvinism differs from other systems of evangelical belief, and is not directed even against those points wherein Protestantism differs from the Roman Catholic Church, but that it is directed against the points wherein the Christian religion — Protestant and Catholic — differs from a radically different type of belief and of life. That radically different type of belief and of life is found today in all the larger ecclesiastical bodies; and in the presence of such a common enemy, those who unfeignedly believe in the gospel of Jesus Christ are drawn into a new warmth of fellowship and a new zeal for common service. Nevertheless, thoroughly consistent Christianity, to my mind, is found only in the Reformed or Calvinistic Faith; and consistent Christianity, I think, is the Christianity easiest to defend. Hence I never call myself a "Fundamentalist." There is, indeed, no inherent objection to the term; and if the disjunction is between "Fundamentalism" and "Modernism," then I am willing to call myself a Fundamentalist of the most pronounced type. But after all, what I prefer to call myself is not a "Fundamentalist" but a "Calvinist"—that is, an adherent of the Reformed Faith. As such I regard myself as standing in the great central current of the Church's life — the current which flows down from the Word of God through Augustine and Calvin, and which has found noteworthy expression in America in the great tradition represented by Charles Hodge and Benjamin Breckinridge Warfield and the other representatives of the "Princeton School." I have the warmest sympathy with other evangelical churches, and a keen sense of agreement with them about those Christian convictions which are today being most insistently assailed; but, for the present at least, I think I can best serve my fellow-Christians — even those who belong to ecclesiastical bodies different from my own — by continuing to be identified, very specifically, with the Presbyterian Church.

Finally, however, let me say how warm is my sympathy with you in the noteworthy educational effort in which you are engaged. Very amazing to me is the complacency with which many persons contemplate the educational conditions that prevail at the present time. As a matter of fact, we have fallen, I think, into a most deplorable and most alarming intellectual decline. I do not, indeed, underestimate the achievements of modern science in the material realm; and the Christian man should never commit the serious error of belittling those achievements. This is God's world, and those who penetrate into its secrets are students of God's works and benefactors of their fellow-men. But such material advances have gone hand in hand with an intellectual decadence in many spheres — an intellectual decadence which is now threatening to engulf all of human life. I do not see how anyone can contemplate present-day educational conditions without seeing that something is radically wrong. And about one thing that is wrong—indeed by far the most important thing — there can be no doubt. It is found in the widespread ignorance of the Christian religion as that religion is founded upon the Word of God. If, indeed, the Christian religion were not true, I should not desire to see it continued on the earth, no matter what benefits its continuance might bring. But then as a matter of fact I hold that it *is* true; and I do not believe that there can be any truly comprehensive science that does not take account of the solid facts upon which the Christian religion is based. Hence I sympathize fully with your desire to promote an education that shall be genuinely Christian. And I pray that those who, like you, wherever they may be, cherish such a desire may not be discouraged by the opposition of the world. You represent a cause which cannot ultimately fail. And even now, despite all the forces of unbelief, despite hostile actions even of the organized church, the gospel of Jesus Christ still shines out from the Word of God and is still enshrined in Christian hearts.

Very truly yours,

J. Gresham Machen

22

FAREWELL TO PRINCETON

The rest of the Princeton story, so far as Machen was concerned, was one of herculean efforts to counteract the movement towards reorganization, of occasional moments of hope, of frequent discouragement and of ultimate bitter defeat. Others might become faint-hearted and compromise, but Machen carried on regardless of the odds and the seeming hopelessness of the struggle. He was of sturdier purpose than to trim his sails to every new wind.

Had he conceived of the issue as essentially concerned with his own vindication, he would not have had the heart or the interest to be engaged in the battle as he was. He would gladly have retired from the faculty and the entire ecclesiastical struggle if by so doing he might have saved Princeton for the Reformed Faith. His livelihood was not involved, and frequent opportunities for service in other fields, including the beloved Church of his ancestors and youth, had presented themselves. But in the providence of God his lot had been cast in Princeton and his duty appeared to be there. Out of a profound sense of commitment to a great cause, therefore, he continued his straightforward course until the very end.

Inasmuch as the action of the Assembly of 1926 centered so largely in his own advancement he adopted, as we have seen, a policy of silence. Following the decision of the Assembly of 1927, however, when the central question became that of the drastic reorganization of the Seminary, he spoke out plainly and vigorously in criticism of the plan. Thus on Sept. 29, 1927 the New York *Post* carried a statement in which Machen declared that the plan would so radically change the control of the Seminary, by putting the present minority in power, that the "well-known conservative institution . . . will be destroyed, and we shall have at Princeton a new institution of an entirely different type." He appealed to the sense of fair play of the rank and file of the Church to avert the injustice that was contemplated.

The Faculty of the Seminary also adopted a formal statement at its meeting on October 1st, strongly criticizing the Report of the Special

Committee and the action of the Assembly based upon it. Declaring that the Report "is manifestly an *ex parte* document supporting the administrative policy of the President of the Seminary against the policy of the Board of Directors and of the Faculty," it called attention to the illegal delay in the publication of the Report which deprived its opponents of the opportunity of presenting their view to the commissioners prior to the meeting of the Assembly. Several serious misrepresentations in the Report were noted. It further declared:

> Believing that the proposal to establish a single board of control for the Seminary, if made effective, would be fatal to the maintenance of the historic doctrinal position of the Seminary, the Faculty earnestly hopes that the next General Assembly will reverse this decision and will continue both the Board of Directors in its control of the educational policy of the Seminary and the Board of Trustees in its administration of the property of the Seminary. Furthermore, the Faculty hereby formally protests against the misrepresentations of the Faculty in the Report.

In conclusion, it stated that the Secretary of the Faculty, in view of the publicity given to the Report, was instructed to send the Faculty statement to the press after it had been presented to the Directors and the Chairman of the Special Committee.

A PLEA FOR FAIR PLAY

Among Machen's most strenuous and significant efforts on behalf of the Seminary cause was the preparation of a full statement which was printed in a 48-page booklet in December. Published under the title, *The Attack Upon Princeton Seminary. A Plea for Fair Play,* it was given the widest possible distribution — more than 20,000 copies — at Machen's personal expense. Disregarding the personal attack that had been made upon him, he set forth in an eloquent manner what his views regarding the situation really were. In the foreground Machen placed the stand of the Seminary for "the full truthfulness of the Bible as the Word of God and for the vigorous defence and propagation of the Reformed or Calvinistic system of doctrine, which is the system of doctrine that the Bible teaches." Involved in this was an attitude toward doctrine which ruled out inclusivism, the inclusivism that was really intolerant of those who have determined to warn the Church of its peril and to contend earnestly for the faith. If the reorganization takes place, Machen held, "the only men who will be tolerated in the Faculty will be men who hold a complacent view of the state of the Church, who conceal from themselves and from others the real state of religious opinion throughout the world, and who consent to conform to the opinions of the party dominant for the moment in the councils of the Church." The defence of the faith, he went on to show, is a task of magnitude and even of peril, but it must nevertheless be undertaken, and the utmost pains must be taken to understand the position of one's opponents. Such an approach is not negative, but positive:

> All our examination of objections to the gospel is employed only as a means to lead men to a clearer understanding of what the gospel is and to a clearer and more triumphant conviction of its truth. But the attainment of such conviction leads, for many men, through the pathway of intellectual struggle and perplexity of soul. Some of us have been through such struggle ourselves; some of us have known the blankness of doubt, the deadly discouragement, the perplexity of indecision, the vacillation between "faith diversified by doubt," and "doubt diversified by faith." If such has been our experience, we think with gratitude of the teachers who helped us in our need; and we in turn try with all our might to help those who are in the struggle now. Nothing can be done, we know, by trying to tyrannize over men's minds; all that we can do is to present the facts as we see them, to hold out a sympathizing hand to our younger brethren, and to commit them to God in prayer.

In the rest of the pamphlet Machen reviewed the history of the difficulties at Princeton, laid the basic cause of it at the door of the minority who were unwilling to follow the principle of majority rule, and showed that the one reason that Princeton had remained true to its historic position while other Seminaries had espoused other views was the faithfulness and vigilance of the Board of Directors. In the reorganization of the Seminary there was involved (in view of the distinctiveness of Princeton as it stood, and was recognized throughout the world as standing, uniquely for the Bible and the Reformed Faith) not merely the destruction of a single institution. Rather, Machen forecast, "the end of Princeton Seminary will, in some sort, mark the end of an epoch in the history of the modern Church and the beginning of a new era in which new evangelical agencies must be formed." There would be, if Princeton were lost, imperative need of a truly evangelical seminary to take its place, which would be a sound source of ministerial supply.

Pulling no punches Machen laid the blame for the threatened development squarely upon those who were hostile to the historic position of the Seminary:

It may seem at first sight strange that in a church professing to be evangelical a seminary which is just now at the height of its success — attracting a very large body of students from all over the world, holding the respect even of some who disagree most strongly with its position, looked to with almost pathetic eagerness by evangelical people in many communions and in many lands — it may seem strange that such an institution should be the one that is singled out for attack. But the truth is that Princeton is being attacked not in spite of its success, but because of it. The warm and vital type of Christianity that not only proclaims the gospel when it is popular to proclaim it, but proclaims the gospel in the face of a hostile world, the type of Christianity that resolutely refuses to make common cause, either at home or on the mission field, with the Modernism that is the deadliest enemy of the cross of Christ, the type of Christianity that responds with full abandon of the heart and life to the Saviour's redeeming love, that is willing to bear all things for Christ's sake, that has a passion for the salvation of souls, that holds the Bible to be, not partly true and partly false, but all true, the blessed, holy Word of God—this warm and vital type of Christianity, as it has found expression, for example, in the League of Evangelical Students, is disconcerting to the ecclesiastical leaders; and so Princeton Seminary, from which it emanates, must be destroyed.

The *Plea* attracted a great deal of attention in the secular and religious press, and scores of letters of comment were received. Macartney, Frank H. Stevenson and many others spoke of it as a masterpiece. But there were others who saw in it only a further expression of Machen's supposed lack of love. It was attacked, for example, by *The Presbyterian Advance* on Jan. 5, 1928. When it refused to publish Machen's reply to this attack, the only recourse was to have it published in *The Presbyterian.* In an extensive letter to the N. Y. *Herald Tribune,* on Jan. 29, Henry W. Jessup criticized Machen's appeal to the binding character of the Plan of the Seminary (as not permitting the outright abrogation of the Plan as proposed by the Thompson Committee). Jessup alleged that the Plan was an effort to establish a *modus vivendi* between the two boards, and that the Board of Trustees actually possessed the power to abolish the Directors. In a learned and trenchant reply on Feb. 12, Machen was easily able to show the invalid character of this argument. The plan and the directors existed for a dozen years before the board of trustees, and the plan was an integral part of the agreement between the Seminary and the General Assembly. Moreover, the trustees came into being only when the directors, with the approval of the Assembly, secured a charter from the State of New Jersey in 1824.

THE PRINCETON PETITION

Meanwhile the battle was being waged also by other effective spokesmen including Samuel G. Craig, who had become the editor of *The Presbyterian,* Frank H. Stevenson and others. A number of Presbyteries protested against the proposed reorganization. Perhaps most effective, however, was a brief petition to the 1928 Assembly which contemplated with alarm the possibility of any change in the Plan of the Seminary. It summed up the issue as follows:

> The noble conservatism of the institution, its valiant and trenchant blows in defense of Evangelical Christianity as understood by us and our fathers, and its steadfast adherence, in the midst of a world of doubt, skepticism and mysticism, to the full truthfulness of Holy Scripture and the simple faith through which alone men can be saved—these qualities have been due solely to the wise conservation of the Board of Directors in selecting a faculty which would not lapse into modern vagaries, but with learning and ability would defend and propagate the faith clearly expressed in our Confession.
>
> The present Faculty carries on the best traditions of the Alexanders and the Hodges, of Green, Warfield and Patton. The only offense laid to the charge either of the Faculty or of the Board of Directors is excess of zeal for the purity of the faith. Is this a time when such a change can safely be entertained by the Church? When there is rampant everywhere in the world, and even in some parts of our Presbyterian Church, denial, doubt, or disparagement of the virgin birth of our Lord, the miracles which He and His apostles wrought, the reality of His resurrection and the veracity of the Scriptures as a whole—when such things are found, is it a time for the Church to abolish the Board of Directors for strongly and earnestly believing in and defending the truth of the Bible and the gospel that the Bible contains?
>
> Shall the control of Princeton Seminary be disturbed at such a time as this? We believe that it is dangerous, and injurious to the best interests of the Church and of Evangelical Christianity.
>
> We, therefore, the signers of this Petition, earnestly pray you to reject the reorganization of the Seminary recommended to the General Assembly of 1927 by the Special Committee to visit Princeton, and thus to leave the control of this great institution where it now resides.

That this Petition had gained more than 11,000 signatures, including some 3,000 ministers, by the time the Assembly met may have influenced the decision to postpone action for another year. Likewise the doubt that was cast upon the legality of the proposals by a number of legal opinions and studies, including one by Dr. Armstrong, were not without influence.

On the other hand certain alumni sought to minimize the significance of the Petition by the claim that the overwhelming majority of the signatories were not well-informed as to the actual situation, and by appeal to the support for reorganization given by a resolution passed in New Brunswick Presbytery. Though the actual majority was not large, it was stressed that the ministers and elders in favor of the resolution represented the largest and most prosperous churches. At the same time, they circulated a statement which Dr. Erdman had given them under date of March 19, 1928, which gave the assurance that "no person is endeavoring to change the doctrinal teachings of Princeton Seminary nor are any influences working to that end." An astonishing evaluation of the state of affairs indeed! And how utterly unrealistic it would appear when the reorganization had been effected!

A far more sober estimate of the situation was expressed at this time by Dr. Patton, whose somewhat unguarded utterances in *Fundamental Christianity* had been appealed to by the liberals in the past. As the Assembly approached, on May 7, he wrote to the Editor of *The Presbyterian* that he was

> not at all in sympathy with the present attempt to disrupt the government of Princeton. . . Princeton Seminary has always stood for the unmodified Calvinism of the Westminster Confession. It has a right to remain so. . . The change proposed may indeed result in an increase of the Seminary's endowments; but no outward show of institutional prosperity could make up for Princeton's loss when the heritage of faith associated with the memory of the Alexanders and the Hodges gives place to a nerveless inclusivism however evangelical that inclusivism may be in outward profession; and when larger and later gifts have nullified the purpose of those endowments which are represented by the names of Lenox, Green, Stuart and Winthrop.

This letter was published in *The Presbyterian* of May 17 and reported, in part, in the N. Y. *Times* of May 21.

THE TULSA ASSEMBLY

When the enlarged committee of eleven reported at the Assembly of 1928 at Tulsa, a minority report in opposition to reorganization was presented by Dr. Ethelbert D. Warfield. Exactly how the vote on these reports would have gone cannot be estimated, for a motion prevailed to postpone action until the next Assembly, and requiring the Directors to seek to compose the differences in the Seminary. This decision meant that the Seminary was for the moment saved, and new hope arose that the point of view that had prevailed at the previous Assemblies would still be overcome. *The Presbyterian* editorially greeted the decision as a Christian one.

Machen himself was not optimistic concerning the eventual outcome, though not despairing altogether that the membership of the Church could be sufficiently aroused to thwart the movement for reorganization. The fact that Dr. Thompson had succeeded in securing the adoption of another motion giving notice that the proposals of his committee would be legally acted upon at the 1929 Assembly was particularly revealing. Writing to his mother on May 31, he said:

> This is an immense calamity to our cause . . . it was anything but a "sweeping" victory. Yet the knowing ones do feel that it gives us a great tactical advantage; and certain it is that Thompson was bitterly opposed to it. Bobby Robinson told me over the phone from Tulsa that although the seminary had been in deadly peril, he thought that our side had at last won a victory and that the institution could now be saved.
>
> Wistar Hodge is disgusted, and so is Dick Wilson. I trust that the more optimistic view is right. The Assembly is against us doctrinally; and if we can get them to tolerate us for the present, perhaps that is all that we can expect. For my part, however, I think the straightforward defence advocated in a certain splendid Directors' statement of which we know would have been better in the end.

The statement alluded to was one drafted by Arthur W. Machen which was printed for distribution but not released, due to indecision among the Directors.

Soon thereafter Machen decided to ask the Directors to withdraw his acceptance of the chair of apologetics, but the Board was so taken up with discussion of the general situation at its meeting of June 20th that the president did not venture to present Machen's letter. Under date of June 20, 1928 he had written to Dr. Alexander as follows:

> After careful consideration, I am venturing to ask you to present to the Board of Directors a request that I be permitted to withdraw my acceptance of the call to the Stuart Professorship of Apologetics and Christian Ethics.

> Even when that call was first tendered me, in May 1926, I was, as you know, very hesitant about accepting it. The work in Apologetics would have led me into a field which is, partly at least, very different from that in which I had hitherto labored; I was very doubtful whether I could at all adequately meet the requirements of that new field, and whether the transference of my activities would not seriously hinder whatever slight contributions I might be able to make to the exposition and defence of the Faith. But these considerations are more powerful now than they were in 1926. I am older now than I was then, and would have less time for fruitful service after the necessarily unsatisfactory period of adjustment would be over. I am strongly inclined to think, therefore, that I can serve the Seminary better by remaining in the New Testament department.
>
> Will you permit me, however, to say in presenting this request how greatly I appreciate the expression of confidence which was involved in the issuance of the call. That expression of confidence will always be to me an encouragement to more worthy service.

Machen was most happy, accordingly, when in the fall of 1928 instruction in apologetics was undertaken by Cornelius Van Til, who had majored in systematic theology in the Seminary and had recently graduated as a Doctor of Philosophy at the University. In an otherwise gloomy letter to his mother on September 25, he said:

> The best piece of news for some time is that Mr. Van Til, a recent graduate of the Seminary, has, despite Dr. Stevenson's vigorous opposition, been asked by the Directors' Curriculum Committee to teach the classes in Apologetics during this year, *and has accepted.* It is the first real forward step that has been taken in some time. Van Til is excellent material from which a professor might ultimately be made.

Van Til in fact was so extraordinarily successful in his instruction that the Board elected him to the Chair the following spring. In his letter of May 12, 1929 Machen expressed his intense gratification at this development, speaking of Van Til's special equipment for the work and his great success with the students. Van Til was a minister of the Christian Reformed Church, a denomination which Stevenson classified among the separatist sects whereas Machen had come to an intense admiration of its forthright stand for the Reformed Faith. On a number of occasions he had had contact with its life in Grand Rapids and other cities, and in letters to his mother he was wont to speak of his observations of its faith and life. So he had once, in 1925, spoken of his delight in the piety he had encountered when he was a guest in the home of Professor Samuel Volbeda—"a piety rooted deep in the great historic Reformed Faith . . . very different from the shallow emotionalism that lacks a basis in the theology of the Word of God." And speaking of the attendance upon the services of worship, he remarked:

> There is no trouble about Church attendance in the Christian Reformed Church. The reason is that the children do not go to the public schools but to the "Christian schools" of the Church, where they get a real, solid education with a sturdy Calvinism at the very centre of it. There is nothing like it elsewhere in America. I wish it could leaven the whole lump.

During the year 1928-29 the Directors were confronted with their final opportunity of saving the Seminary. In all probability, in view of the strong drift of the Church toward latitudinarianism, no measures that they might have conceived could have arrested the course of action which had been running full tide especially since the 1926 Assembly. It is distressing to report, however, that the Directors in the majority came to disagree among themselves as to the wisest policy to pursue, and several who had valiantly resisted the current seemed to reconcile themselves more or less to an eventual reorganization, and sought to adjust themselves to it. This approach took the form of advocating a union of the two Boards which would assure the present Directors and Trustees of their membership in the new Board. If there had been at least a measure of hope so long as they insisted upon their rights and the right of the institution to be preserved without substantial change, that hope went glimmering at the evidences of defection from the uncompromising stand of earlier days.

During this period, when the responsibility rested squarely on the Directors, Machen undertook no further public discussion of the issues. Though the tension and uncertainty with regard to the future hardly afforded the requisite peaceful atmosphere in which to perform scholarly labors, he did succeed to some extent in advancing toward completion his work on *The Virgin Birth of Christ* which was published the following year. There were however numerous and wearisome conferences with Directors and members of the faculty, and his letters contain many evidences of the turmoil and agony of those days.

During the course of the year another sorrowful blow came in the passing of William Brenton Greene. As he wrote his mother on Nov. 18, 1928:

I loved Dr. Greene. He was absolutely true, when so many were not. He was always at Faculty and Presbytery, no matter how feeble he was. He was one of the best Christians I have ever known.

Another painful aspect of his life during that year developed as it became increasingly inevitable that the reorganization would be effected, and he was realizing that he could not serve under the new government. This was the burden which bore heavily upon him as he thought of the severe hardships which would be involved for several of his dearest colleagues if they were faced with the necessity of resigning their professorships. Again and again his letters to his mother spoke of his distress at their peculiar predicament since they lacked the financial security which made it possible for him to think of taking a "sabbatical" year.

THE ST. PAUL ASSEMBLY

The 1929 Assembly convened at St. Paul with Machen as a commissioner. Apart from the reading of various majority and minority reports emanating from the Special Committee and the Boards of the Seminary only about twenty-five minutes altogether were allowed for debate. A motion to leave the time for the vote unsettled in advance was presented by Machen but lost by a vote of 530-309. In this situation, in spite of the gravity of the matter at issue, five minutes was as long as Machen could speak. Under compulsion to confine himself to a general appeal, he expressed himself as follows:

> Mr. Moderator:
>
> We at Princeton Seminary have been proclaiming an unpopular gospel, which runs counter to the whole current of the age; yet it is a gospel of which we are not ashamed. We have proclaimed it in great human weakness, and we are conscious of our unworthiness to be entrusted with a treasure so great. Of some charges, indeed, our hearts acquit us; many things have been said about us that are not true. Yet weak and faulty enough we are, and we confess our weakness freely in the presence of the General Assembly and of Almighty God. But who of you, my brethren, is sufficient unto these things?
>
> We have derived our authority to preach this unpopular gospel not from any wisdom of our own, but from the blessed pages of God's Word. But from this gospel that the Scriptures contain the the world has gradually been drifting away. Countless colleges and universities and theological seminaries throughout the world, for-

merly evangelical, have become hostile or indifferent to that which formerly they maintained. They have done so often with many protestations of orthodoxy, and often with true evangelical intentions too, on the part of those who were unwitting instruments in the change. So it is with Princeton Seminary. We impugn no man's motives today; many of those who are lending themselves to this reorganization movement no doubt themselves believe in the Bible and are unaware of what is really being done. But no one who has the example of other institutions in mind, who knows the trend of the times, and who knows the facts about the present movement, can doubt but that we have here only a typical example of the same old story, so often repeated, of an institution formerly evangelical that is being made to drift away by insensible degrees from the gospel that it was founded by godly donors to maintain.

I cannot show you how that is true; for I have but a few minutes to speak; but there are many throughout the world who well know that it is true. I cannot show you how unjust it is; but there are many of Christ's little ones whom the injustice of it grieves to the very heart. With these grieved and burdened souls, who are perplexed by the uncertainty of the age, and who are looking to Princeton Seminary for something to be said against modern unbelief and in favor of the full truthfulness of God's Word — with these we are united today in a blessed fellowship of sympathy and prayer. To that fellowship I believe that most of you would belong if you only knew the facts. It is hard for me to look into your faces and see many of you ready to do that ruthless thing which, if you only knew its meaning, you would be the first to deplore. I cannot reach your minds, for the time does not suffice for that; and God has granted me no gift of eloquence that I might reach your hearts. I can only hope that a greater and more mysterious persuasion may prevent you from doing unwittingly that which is so irrevocable and so wrong. One thing at least is clear — there are many Christians in many lands who will feel that if the old Princeton goes, a light will have gone out of their lives. Many are praying today that you may be kept from putting out that light. If you destroy the old Princeton today, by destroying the Board of Directors which has made it what it is, there are many, I admit, who will rejoice; for there are many who think that the old gospel and the old Book are out of date. But if there are many who will rejoice, there are also those, Mr. Moderator, who will grieve.

The Thompson Report was adopted by a decisive majority, reported as in a five to three proportion. Thereupon the doctrinal implications of the reorganization were laid bare *as two signers of the Auburn Affirmation were appointed to serve in the new Board!* Thus the radical doctrinal change, that had been forecast by many, but discounted all along by Stevenson and Erdman and their supporters, became without delay an unmistakable reality.

Another radical step was the action determining that the new board should serve as directors till the new charter changes could be secured and reported to the General Assembly, and thereafter as trustees. This procedure constituted a new amendment to the Plan of the Seminary, and since due notice of it had not been given, it could not lawfully be adopted at that Assembly except by unanimous consent. Machen's dissent as a matter of fact was recorded. And so in his judgment, and in that of many legal experts, the new Board did not have lawful authority to govern the institution. This development complicated the situation for several Faculty members and dissenting Directors who considered whether it was not their duty to make a fight in the courts for the Seminary on the basis of its historic plan and in view of the illegal procedures. It moreover placed an additional burden upon faculty members who were considering whether they could continue to serve the institution. Machen later blamed himself for not having proposed for adoption at the 1930 Assembly a resolution putting the Seminary back under the old Plan, and this on the understanding that the action taken in 1929 would inevitably result in legal chaos.

INTERLUDE OF INDECISION

His mother was as ever overflowing in affection and comfort, taking intelligent and sympathetic interest in every detail and phase of the struggle as she always had. Writing on June 3, she said

> I don't know what to wish you to do, Whatever you decide upon will be brave and steadfast—that's one comfort! Your speech in Assembly is very strong, very moving — I know there were true hearts that responded.
>
> I do hope you will not let yourself be tormented by regrets for what you call "lost opportunities" or self-reproach for supposed mistakes. You have done the very best you could — have sacrificed much — worked like a Trojan — given your life-blood. Now please do not waste energy in regrets. It isn't wise or just or right. I am very proud of you, I know that.

In his next letter to his mother, Machen told of conferences with lawyers, in which Dr. Craig and he had taken part, regarding the legal status of the new Board. But before there was any clear answer to that inquiry, he said:

> One question I have decided. I am *not* going to serve under the new Board. If they do take legal control on Friday, I am going to send in my resignation. It seems to me to be all-important that it should go to them before and not after the meeting...I should be quite untrue to the evangelical people in the Church if I consented to act as a piece of camouflage to conceal what has been done. It is a kind of comfort to have gotten that far in my decisions.
>
> Allis is all for the founding of a new Seminary at once, and so is Frank Stevenson. It is not beyond the bounds of possibility. Philadelphia will be the place if we do it. We shall have the students all right if we can get the money. Who can say? It might be the beginning of some genuine evangelical effort...A really evangelical Seminary might be the beginning of a really evangelical Presbyterian Church.

The advice on the legal matter was not unitary. And even if the legal point were granted, it was feared by many that the courts might approve the new Board as *de facto* having authority. The doctrinal issue, the most important one, at least was crystal clear, and a golden opportunity might be lost if there was delay in planning for the new Seminary. So Dr. Frank H. Stevenson and others thought, but Machen hesitated since he felt keenly the ethical implications of the legal point and was overwhelmed at the thought of the difficulties involved in commencing a new Seminary. His mother's response on June 10 began as follows:

> I waited a little that I might better know how and what to write for I knew Princeton was seething. It is good that some fight is being made against injustice. But I cannot think otherwise than you about your remaining at Princeton if the two [new?] boards take control and Stevenson is placed in autocratic control of the Faculty. Like you I see that you cannot — if the new plan is put into execution — without humiliating yourself and betraying the trust of the Conservatives in our Church remain at Princeton. I am of course very anxious about the outcome, and I pray most earnestly for guidance. If only the money were forthcoming, the real Seminary would be a wonderful solution. God be with us and make plain the pathway!

His strongest instinct, as late as June 16, was to continue the battle in the courts, but the other approach also moved him:

> It will be a terribly hard thing to me to leave the seminary. But really I am so sick of the uphill battle that I am almost willing to have it over. Perhaps it may be led ultimately into some "large place" in the sense of the Psalmist. I long for a year of change or travel, but fear that it is not to be mine. I wish that I could *live* at Princeton, say what I please, and write big, thick books. There could be worse programs. Remoteness from a good theological library would be very bad.

As the new Board convened about the middle of June, Machen's dilemma also appears in a letter addressed to Dr. Lewis S. Mudge, its convener. He spoke first of his embarrassment due to the fact that, as he had been advised by counsel, the new Board was without valid authority. In order that there might be no misunderstanding, however, he informed them that he could not serve in the Faculty under the new Board, even if its authority should be upheld. "Princeton Seminary," he said, "is committed by the most solemn trust obligations to a certain doctrinal position, with which it is perfectly evident that the new Board, in its overwhelming majority, is out of sympathy." As evidence he cited the presence of two signers of the Auburn *Affirmation* on the Board, and the indifference or hostility to the historic position on the part of others which this reflected. "While I am willing, therefore, to continue my service to the Seminary under the old Board of Directors, I cannot do so if the authority of the new Board is established."

Dr. Wm. L. McEwan, who had become chairman of the administrative committee, replied on June 18, asking him to withdraw his "resignation," reminding him that the Board as its first action declared its purpose to maintain the Seminary in its historic position and to do nothing to change or alter the teaching of its professors, and reminding him of the rule requiring any member of the Faculty who wishes to resign or retire to give six months notice to the Board. Machen on June 21 informed Dr. McEwan that he was mistaken in supposing that his letter of June 14th was a letter of resignation, and stated that the declaration of purpose passed by the Board, in view of the considerations advanced as to its constituency, only strengthened his determination not to serve under it. "By serving under the new Board," he said, "I might lead evangelical people in the Church to attribute significance to that declaration of purpose, and that I cannot conscientiously do."

At this time Machen, when interviewed by a representative of the New York *Times,* issued a statement delineating his position substantially in terms of the above correspondence. He added however that, since evangelical people could not depend on Princeton being saved by an appeal to the courts, they ought at once to appeal for funds for the founding of a truly evangelical seminary that should be ready to take the place of the one which has apparently been lost. The *Times* and other leading newspapers, beginning with the issue of June 17th and for several days following, carried lengthy treatment of Machen's statement and others that followed in reply to a defense of the Seminary's doctrinal soundness and legality on the part of Dr. Erdman and others. The newspapers seized upon the rather incidental reference to the possibility of a new Seminary and made that the main feature of their presentation. Thus a headline on June 18 read, MACHEN PROPOSES A NEW SEMINARY. That the same hesitant position reflected in Machen's letters and public statements still prevailed generally, however, is borne out by a resolution passed at an informal meeting in New York on June 17 which stated:

> Resolved, That this group will support the loyal members of the former Board of Directors of Princeton Theological Seminary in any step they may see fit to take (1) Toward preventing by legal means the misuse of the Seminary's funds; or (2) Toward the formation of a new seminary if they decide that it is necessary.

During this period of uncertainty regarding his duty with reference to Princeton Machen was trying to put his mind on his big book. Under ordinary circumstances he would have taken his Mother to Seal Harbor, and would have spent some time with her there. But if there was not already enough in the Princeton situation to require his presence there, he felt that he had to spend considerable time near large libraries if he was to make any certain headway. He was deeply distressed that his desire to join her was being hindered still further by new obstacles. Happily his mother—now eighty years old—continued to be able and willing to subordinate her personal comfort to the larger purposes that had been her guiding star and that of her son. And so she repeatedly reassured him as to her willingness to have him remain away. Thus on June 25th she wrote:

> I have something especial to say to you. This is a crisis in your life, and I want you to take all the time you need, without worrying about me. You must *take time* to do your best on your book, when allowed by all those who are privily shooting at the upright in heart. If only you can get out your book just at this

time, it will be *wonderful!* There is nothing I want more—so do not think of my being here alone. . .

My heart goes out in sympathy for you in the possible breaking up of your home in Princeton. I feel for you so deeply in that and especially in "Army's" being left in the enemy's camp. It is all so distressing. We must believe that God's large designs are to be worked out through our tribulations and trials—"His most holy, wise and powerful preserving and governing." For all the small duties and perplexities that may come to you, *take time.* Your mother gives it to you freely and gladly out of her summer.

And a little later (on July 4) she wrote:

Please *do not hurry* your coming. Take all the time you need. I cannot do much as yet except to aid Nature in restoring my battered old body. I am doing that. . . . I know the wrench of giving up will be hard, especially parting from your good students. It will be hard—I hope, by the grace of God not *too* hard.

In reply to the letter, he began his letter of July 7th as follows:

My dearest Mother:

To my great surprise I find that I have not with me, here in New York, the last letter which I received from you. But there is no fear of my forgetting it. In it you spoke in a lovely, sweet way about your willingness to have me go on with my work on my book. I think I answered the letter, but whether I did so or not I want to say how deeply grateful I am. It distresses me a great deal to protract in such a way my absence from my dearest Mother; and the only comfort I get is your cheerfulness about it and your interest in what I am trying to do. I am afraid I have not been able at all times to work as I might, since I feel dreadfully stale and restless, but I do want to get the library part of the work done if I possibly can. I wish that I could work in a more steady and efficient way.

23

THE BEGINNINGS OF WESTMINSTER

Fresh impetus towards the formation of a new Seminary—it turned out eventually to be decisive—was given when Dr. Charles Schall, pastor of the Presbyterian Church in Wayne, a suburb of Philadelphia, in conference with elders T. Edward Ross and Frederic M. Paist, became persuaded that the support of the conservative forces should be rallied behind the idea in an effort to give it concrete realization by autumn. They sponsored a small luncheon meeting of eight prominent elders in the Philadelphia area. Machen along with Drs. Wilson and Allis was also invited. That legal steps would be taken to establish the authority of the old Board of Directors at Princeton now appeared unlikely. And when the laymen indicated a readiness to back the proposed Seminary in substantial fashion and to rally others behind it, Machen began to abandon his attitude of hesitation. This is reflected in his telegram to his mother at Seal Harbor on July 10:

> AM DEEPLY GRATEFUL FOR YOUR TELEGRAM AND FOR YOUR LOVELY LETTER OF JULY FOURTH STOP THERE HAVE BEEN IMPORTANT DEVELOPMENTS SINCE I WROTE STOP MEETING OF LAYMEN IN PHILADELPHIA WAS STRONGLY IN FAVOR OF STARTING NEW SEMINARY NEXT AUTUMN STOP THERE IS TO BE A LAYMEN MEETING IN PHILADELPHIA ON JULY EIGHTEENTH AND IT IS ABSOLUTELY NECESSARY FOR ME TO BE PRESENT STOP. I AM GREATLY DISTRESSED AT NOT BEING WITH YOU SOONER BUT REJOICE IN YOUR PERFECT UNDERSTANDING OF THE MOMENTOUS ISSUES THAT ARE INVOLVED STOP THAT MEETING ON MONDAY WAS DISTINCTLY HOPEFUL SINCE MEN OF CONSIDERABLE MEANS WERE PRESENT AND SINCE THEY SEEMED TO THINK THAT THE CHURCHES WOULD RESPOND STOP IT IS TERRIBLY HOT HERE. J GRESHAM MACHEN

Mrs. Machen wrote at once to say how thrilling she found the news of the telegram, and Machen in turn was again refreshed at her understanding and support. Writing on July 14, he said

> Never did my dearest Mother show up as more completely her own self (and nothing better could be said) than in that note of July 11th, commenting on my telegram. I am so deeply troubled about leaving you alone at Seal Harbor for so long a time, as I have not done for many years, that for you to show that you are aware of the momentousness of the issues that are involved in the plans for the new seminary is just the thing to give new heart for the battle. Of course I knew that your heart would be in our project; but still your note does show such enthusiasm that I have taken courage anew after reading it.

He then went on to speak in greater detail of the meeting of July 8th. For the first time he began to regard the establishment of the seminary in the autumn as a possibility, as "a spontaneous movement outside of our little group seemed to be under way; and these men seemed to be perfectly willing to get down to brass tacks." He spoke also of his apprehensions, however, as he observed that there were large pitfalls that would have to be avoided: "only a few men have even the slightest inkling of what scholarship is." If the seminary were to be launched, moreover, he would have an immense amount of labor to perform, and the outlook of joining his mother at Seal Harbor would be even less promising. . .

> I have been endeavoring to finish my book—you can imagine with what maddening distractions.
>
> In short, I am simply *"up against it."* My greatest consolation is that you understand me heart and soul. What could I do if I had a mother who could not understand the reason why apparently (though not in heart) I am neglecting her so shamefully. . .
>
> Now, my dearest Mother, you simply must not write me long letters. I love every single word that you write, but I also have a picture of you working and working at that desk when you ought to be getting a rest. I will not add to your burden any more than I can possibly help.

THE MEETING OF JULY 18TH

July 18, 1929 may well be regarded as the natal day of Westminster Theological Seminary. For it was on that day, following the significant preliminary conference on the 8th, that conviction was crystallized into action, and specific steps were taken for the opening of the new seminary in the fall. Though the meeting was called on short notice, and in the midst of a scorching Philadelphia summer, more than seventy persons responded, including former directors, professors and students of Princeton. Machen made the opening address and Drs. Wilson and Allis also spoke. Recent graduates including Paul Woolley and Edwin H. Rian also were heard. Dr. Charles Schall of Wayne, to whose initiative in the present situation most of the credit was due, then moved the following resolution which was adopted without a dissenting vote:

> Being convinced that the action of the General Assembly of 1929, establishing a new Board of Control for Princeton Theological Seminary, will inevitably make the institution conform to the present doctrinal drift of the Church and so desert the distinctive doctrinal position which is bound by the most solemn trust obligations to maintain, we believe that immediate steps should be taken for the establishment of a new theological seminary which shall continue the policy of unswerving loyalty to the Word of God and to the Westminster Standards for which Princeton Seminary has been so long and so honorably known.

Decisions were taken to set up an organizing committee of fifteen, with Professors Wilson, Machen and Allis as advisors, to establish an organization office, make arrangements for physical facilities and proceed with the appointment of the Faculty. At the meeting more than $22,000 was subscribed toward the budget of the first year which was estimated at from $50,000 to $60,000.

Though yeoman service was done by the ministers and laymen who formed the temporary organization, in the nature of the case the advisory members found the greatest burdens and responsibilities placed upon their shoulders. And in view of Dr. Wilson's age—he was well past 70 when he might have retired on his well-earned pension—, Machen and Allis entered upon a period of labors that consumed nearly all their time and energies. The major decisions concerned personnel of the Faculty and administration, but also every other aspect of the project from curriculum to physical facilities and finances pressed upon them. In the midst of it all Machen was trying to reserve a number of mornings for the writing of the concluding chapter of his book on *The Virgin Birth of Christ.*

On July 25th at a meeting of the Committee of the Seminary there was further progress with the choice of "Westminster" as its name and Philadelphia as its site. Among the most felicitious decisions was the choice of Paul Woolley as Registrar and Secretary. Following graduation from Princeton University in 1923, he studied at the Seminary for two years and in Berlin and Cambridge, England, for two further years. Thereupon he returned to Princeton to complete his course, receiving both the Th. B. and the Th. M. degrees in 1928. Appointment to serve in China under the China Inland Mission followed, but due to unsettled conditions in the Orient the inauguration of this service was delayed. Meanwhile he had served with distinction as general secretary of the League of Evangelical Students for a year. Fortunately for the Seminary, when further delay in undertaking the missionary task developed, be became available for service to the Seminary. An office was set up in space donated by Mr. Morgan H. Thomas in his establishment on South Sixth Street, and there Woolley commenced his indefatigable and efficient services on behalf of the cause, conducting the correspondence and doing a hundred other necessary tasks.

SELECTION OF THE STAFF

The major task of the Seminary was the organization of the Faculty. With the assurance of the presence of Drs. Wilson and Allis in the Old Testament field and Machen in the New Testament, the Seminary was assured of great strength in the Biblical departments. On July 21st Machen wrote the writer of this biography inviting him to be associated with him in the New Testament department, and received an acceptance without delay. In view of Dr. Wilson's age it was thought advisable to secure some assistance for him, and somewhat later correspondence was directed to Allan A. MacRae, who had specialized under Dr. Wilson and was carrying on graduate work in Berlin. Due to the practical difficulties of the situation this arrangement was not immediately effected, but MacRae did return in time to begin work two weeks after the Seminary opened on Sept. 25th.

The filling of the Biblical posts, however, was far from guaranteeing a well-rounded Faculty. There remained the crucial work in Apologetics and Systematic Theology and in addition that of Church History and Practical Theology. Attention centered first on filling the first two chairs. It was generally assumed that the chair of Apologetics was to be filled as a matter of course by Dr. Van Til, who had given indications of his thorough agreement with the stand of Machen and his associates in the struggle at Princeton.

When attention was given to the work in Systematic Theology, which Machen regarded as the most important chair in the Seminary, they were confronted with a colossal problem. In view of his brilliant gifts as a theologian and his militant stand for the Reformed Faith, Caspar Wistar Hodge was the obvious choice. Dr. Hodge, however, though never wavering in his outspoken commitment to the position which he had espoused, decided, like Vos and Armstrong, to remain at Princeton. These decisions are not fully explicable, though Machen had grieved for months over their apparent inevitability and had sympathized with the men in the peculiar predicament in which they were placed. It is also clear that these decisions were not made with enthusiasm; rather it appears that the spirit manifested was one of sorrowful resignation. The wife of one of those concerned once told me, following the establishment of Westminster, that it was very difficult to work for one institution and pray for another.

If however Hodge had apparently to be ruled out of consideration, where was one to turn? It is an illuminating commentary on the theological competence of the ministry that Machen and his associates did not know where to turn within the Presbyterian Church in the U. S. A. to find a man for this chair of genuine scholarly attainments and of undoubted understanding of and commitment to the Reformed Faith. In this crisis it was judged that the best hope was offered in considering ministers of the Christian Reformed Church, several of whom had taken graduate work in theology and had made a lasting impression upon their teachers. Dr. Hodge was consulted as to who among these students was likely to be the best qualified, and without much hesitation he named R. B. Kuiper as the one who had made the deepest impression upon B. B. Warfield. Kuiper, a graduate of the University of Chicago (A. B., 1907) and University of Indiana (A. M., 1908) had studied systematic theology under the direction of Dr. Warfield during the academic year 1911-12, following his graduation from Calvin Theological Seminary. In the interval he had served most successfully in several pastorates. On the basis of Hodge's recommendation Kuiper was invited, and Machen undertook a journey out to Grand Rapids to endeavor to secure his acceptance. Kuiper took the invitation under serious consideration, but brought acute disappointment when he decided that he should not leave his work in the Christian Reformed Church.

This disappointment was the more unbearable since at approximately the same time the Philadelphia forces had learned to their consternation that Van Til had declined to serve. As observed above, he had enjoyed great success as a teacher and was fully in agreement with the stand that had been taken. Moreover, when he was apprised of developments at Princeton, he had no hesitation in reaching the decision not to return there. But Van Til was profoundly loyal to his own denomination. And realizing that the acceptance of the call to Philadelphia almost certainly would mean a severing of his relations with that cause, he could not bring himself to the point of venturing that step. Another aspect of his character—his humility—is highlighted by the consideration that the alternative was a continuance as pastor in a small church in Michigan, which had given him a leave of absence that he might undertake the work as lecturer at Princeton during the year 1928-29. Machen and Allis made journeys to Michigan to seek to dissuade Van Til, but without apparent success. And thus when September arrived, and the Seminary was announced as opening its doors within a few weeks, there remained these glaring gaps in the Faculty.

It appeared for a time that the new Seminary would have to be satisfied with stopgap arrangements in these departments. But early in September there was a thrilling turn of events when both Van Til and Kuiper accepted, although the latter stipulated that he could consent to serve for only one year. The story of this development is so complex, and withal involves so many personal factors, that no attempt will be made to tell it here. In brief, it is plain that these brethren finally responded favorably because of the unrelenting importunity and urgency with which the Seminary's needs and its plight, apart from their acceptance, were pressed upon them. Their own devotion to the Reformed Faith and vision of the opportunity which faced the Seminary were likewise factors indispensable to an understanding of their final action. Their joining together in the closely related fields of theology and apologetics provided the Seminary with very able instruction in other departments than the Biblical.

The teaching staff was further rounded out as Paul Woolley was appointed Instructor in Church History, a field he was to adorn with his splendid endowments and learning. For the time being no appointment was made to the chair of practical theology. Some of this important work was undertaken by Professor Kuiper, other by Dr. Frank H. Stevenson, who had been eminently successful as pastor of the Covenant Church of Cincinnati. Still others contributed part time service. Kuiper in accordance with the terms of his acceptance felt free to leave Westminster to undertake the post of president of Calvin College which came to him in 1930, but he returned to Westminster in 1933 to become the first occupant of the Chair of Practical Theology, a position he was to occupy until his retirement in 1952.

The loss which the Seminary faced in the departure of Professor Kuiper from the field of theology was happily offset when in 1930 John Murray agreed to undertake instruction in this department. Mr. Murray, a Scotsman who had taken his arts work in Edinburgh and Glasgow, graduated from Princeton Seminary in 1927. After graduate work in Edinburgh he had responded to Dr. Hodge's overtures to assist him. Murray did not find the atmosphere in the reorganized Princeton congenial (he had accepted the appointment before the reorganization took place), and it was the good fortune of Westminster that he became available just at that time. He was to become a mainstay in the Faculty as professor of systematic theology.

The Faculty was accordingly organized with five professors and three instructors. Early in the second year Dr. Wilson died, and all the Old Testament work was placed in one department under the direction of Dr. Allis. Coincident with the formal organization of the Faculty under its charter and constitution in the spring of 1930, however, the three young instructors were advanced to the status of assistant professors. Mr. Murray began as an instructor and chose to remain in that capacity for a number of years. Dr. Allis resigned in 1936, Dr. Machen died in 1937, and professor MacRae resigned the same year. But the Faculty has remained remarkably constant through the years, and due to the relative youth of most of the men at the time of their appointment, their terms of service have been of remarkable length. Thus the stability of the Seminary was fostered, and it was able to weather storms that were to encompass it later on.

POWERS OF THE FACULTY

One of the most attractive and fruitful features of Westminster's organization, as that was perfected in its Charter and Constitution (adopted in 1930), was the extraordinary participation that it afforded to the members of the Faculty in shaping policies and plans. To a remarkable degree Westminster was organized as and continues to function as a Faculty-directed institution. This is bound up significantly with the consideration that its Constitution made no provision for the office of president but only for a chairman of the Faculty elected by the Faculty. On the one hand this has meant that no person elected by the Board itself, and not necessarily representative of the Faculty's outlook and policies, would *ex officio* sit with the Trustees as the spokesman for the Faculty. To fill this gap, however, an ingenious procedure was adopted which, in the judgment of many observers, has proved to be one of the most salutary features of the Seminary organization. This is the provision whereby three members of the Faculty, elected annually by the Faculty, sit with the Trustees in an advisory capacity. Thus the Board is kept in intimate touch with the viewpoint or viewpoints of the Faculty and the Faculty in turn is assured of being fully and adequately represented in the Board.

Another significant power reserved to the Faculty is that of nomination of members to be elected to the teaching staff. Moreover, if a nominee of the Faculty does not prove acceptable to the Board, it may not proceed to elect any other person before it has sought the advice of the Faculty with regard to that person. The ultimate authority reposes therefore in the Board, but the Faculty as the body charged with instruction and the general administration of the academic life of the institution is recognized as possessing, under most circumstances, the greatest competence to insure continuity in the perpetuation of the standpoint and scholarly ideals of the Seminary. To the present time no one has been elected to the staff except by way of Faculty nomination, and there resides in the Faculty a profound sense of the greatness of the trust reposed in it in this matter.

Another corollary of the omission of the office of president is that the Faculty's business is conducted in a highly democratic manner. Even instructors, though not granted voting power, are encouraged to participate in the discussion of the varied business that comes before the body in its Saturday morning meetings. And from the first the youthful instructors and assistant professors were treated by their elders as colleagues rather than as green subordinates. This fact has been highly instrumental in perpetuating in the Faculty a sense of belonging to a great cause rather than simply holding down academic jobs.

These features receive partial explanation from the hard lessons learned at Princeton. They also spring however from the fact that Machen and Allis (and Wilson as well in the year that he served) proved themselves to be men of rare graciousness and considerateness in dealing with their younger colleagues. It is a particular delight to bear personal witness here to Machen's singular magnanimity of spirit in his relationships to his subordinate in his department over a period of more than seven years. Though men of lesser achievement and prestige might have yielded to the temptation to lord it over their inferiors, and Machen himself might well have laid various burdens upon his chosen assistant, he invariably treated him as an equal with whom he could discuss matters relating to the work of the department. And in the exceedingly rare instances when Machen asked him to perform some small service—like giving out a test to a class when he was forced to be out of town—he always made the request as if he were asking the greatest favor in the world. Never once was there a "do this" or even "I should like to have you do this." Rather his request would characteristically take the form, "Stoney, can you possibly favor me by handing out a paper for me tomorrow?" And when—as a matter of course—assent was gained, he overwhelmed one with warmhearted expressions of profound appreciation! No one who has enjoyed such a relationship with its uniquely intimate features and inevitable disclosure of basic character could be taken in by the belittling and slanderous accusations that were scattered abroad concerning his supposed pettiness and self-seeking. Like the charges of bitterness and bigotry they were expressed by those who revealed by their very utterance that they possessed little or no genuine understanding of Machen's character.

OTHER DECISIONS

The survey of the formation of the Faculty has taken us somewhat beyond those early days of organization before the Seminary actually opened its doors for the first time. It is necessary, therefore, in connection with our effort here to concentrate upon the beginnings of Westminster, to take up again the thread of its unfolding. Due to preaching engagements in Toronto and Boston Machen had been able to spend three or four days with his Mother early in August. Later he had to fulfill an engagement of long standing to lecture at Grove City. But for the most part he was busy day and night in the completion of plans for the opening of the Seminary.

Through the generosity of Dr. Allis a site at 1528 Pine Street in the center of the city was made available, and thus that major problem was settled at least for the time being. This location proved very satisfactory to Machen because he had been able to secure an apartment in the Chancellor Hall Apartments on South Thirteenth Street, where on the 22nd—the top floor—he was able to enjoy creaturely comforts which his simple rooms in Alexander Hall had never afforded. Commenting on this development, his mother wrote on August 19th:

> I hope you will have a nice little apartment with some of the conveniences of life. And it is a comfort to think that you will be a little nearer to Mother next winter. Even so, I have grieved over your breaking up your modest rooms where you have been so useful, so faithful, so undaunted. . . I have shed few tears over you, but yesterday I stood in the doorway of your little room, and wept over all you are going through. God grant it all may bring forth the "peaceable fruits of righteousness," for which all lesser gratifications would be well lost. . .

In response on the 25th he began as follows:

> Your letter of August 19th stands out even among the series of letters to your boy, and that is certainly saying a good deal. It is one of the finest letters that I ever received, and I have just received a new spiritual refreshment from re-reading it. I am certainly thankful that I have a Mother who can write a letter like that; for it reflects the wonderful qualities of the writer. In the course of these conflicts in which I have been engaged, I have come into contact with many dull and with many cranky and selfish people; and even the best people do seem to have their faults. The

more refreshing is it that my Mother does seem to be just about perfect. My Mother is so quick to get a point, so sure in her insight, and so sound in her judgments. That is certainly refreshing. And even more refreshing are her qualities of heart. I am certainly fortunate in being the son of such a Mother.

At this time, in addition to all the problems concerning the Faculty which remained unsolved, he was discouraged by a suggestion from Harpers (made on the background of a reading of his manuscript on *The Virgin Birth of Christ*) that he make the book more saleable by diminishing its technical and controversial character. Though he might have been willing to make small concessions, he felt he had to hold his ground with regard to the book as a whole. But suddenly the matter was happily settled, and he wired his mother on August 30th:

HAVE JUST RECEIVED GOOD NEWS FROM HARPERS STOP THEY ARE APPALLED BY COST OF MANUFACTURING MY BOOK WHICH WILL HAVE TO SELL AT FIVE DOLLARS STOP BUT THEY THINK THEY CAN MARKET THE BOOK DESPITE HIGH PRICE AND OFFER ME CONTRACT FOR PUBLICATION WITH TEN PER CENT ROYALTY AND WITHOUT COST TO ME STOP FACULTY OF NEW SEMINARY NOT YET SETTLED BUT THERE IS SOME PROGRESS.

As it turned out even that report of progress proved premature. Suddenly the whole situation changed, however, with the acceptances of Van Til and Kuiper a few days later, and from that time forward to the opening there were no major crises.

There were a thousand odds and ends besides the major business of promotion. Once again he had to resign himself to further separation from his mother, as he wrote on September 15:

I come now to the thing that I so dread to say that I can hardly bring myself to do so. It is that I do not see how in the world I am going to get up to Seal Harbor. I just feel cut to the heart at neglecting in such a way the one who is nearest and dearest to me; and if you need me for the getting off, you must telegraph to me to that effect. On the basis of such a call, I could leave things here, but otherwise I do not see how I can face my associates if I do so. Our affairs are in a most unsettled state: the curriculum of the new seminary has not been determined upon, and there is to be a meeting of the governing committee on Friday, September 20th. For me to run off without absolutely imperative reason would be to sacrifice the confidence of all my associates. If I did

> have such a reason, by a telegram from you, then of course the case would be different. . .
>
> Remember, in the last dismal moments at Seal Harbor, that you are going *to* your boy this time and not away from him as in other summers. I can get down to see you much more easily than I could when I was at Princeton, and I have a wild idea of showing you the apartment some time when you can get on for a visit in Philadelphia. You will like the view.

The new venture was widely publicized in such leading newspapers as the New York *Times*. The religious press generally also kept the new Seminary before its readers. *The Sunday School Times* for August 31 published a feature article from the pen of Dr. Allis on "The New Presbyterian Seminary." And *The Presbyterian,* under the editorship of Dr. Craig, constantly reported the progress of the new institution. There had been an enthusiastic meeting of Presbyterian ministers in New York City on September 16 at which Drs. Buchanan, Schall, Frank H. Stevenson, Wilson, Machen and Allis spoke, and this meeting was described at length in *The Presbyterian* for October 3rd.

BASIC PRINCIPLES

On September 25th, meanwhile, the opening exercises were held in Witherspoon Hall, with Dr. Wilson making a brief address of welcome and Dr. Machen the main address on "Westminster Theological Seminary: Its Purpose and Plan." This significant utterance has been republished in *What is Christianity?* and still serves to capture something of the spirit of that historic occasion as well as to sum up the basic position of the Seminary. The address began with the following arresting words:

> Westminster Theological Seminary, which opens its doors today, will hardly be attended by those who seek the plaudits of the world or the plaudits of a worldly church. It can offer for the present no magnificent buildings, no long established standing in the ecclesiastical or academic world. Why, then, does it open its doors; why does it appeal to the support of Christian men?
>
> The answer is plain. Our new institution is devoted to an unpopular cause; it is devoted to the service of One who is despised and rejected by the world and increasingly belittled by the visible church, the majestic Lord and Saviour who is presented to us in the Word of God . . . No Christ of our own imaginings can ever take his place for us, no mystic Christ whom we seek merely in the hidden depths of our own souls. From all such we turn away

> ever anew to the blessed written Word and say to the Christ there set forth, the Christ with whom then we have living communion: "Lord, to whom shall we go? Thou hast the words of eternal life."

Machen went on to speak of the Bible as being therefore the centre and core of that with which Westminster Seminary would have to do and set forth the chief elements of the curriculum on that background. In stressing the central importance of systematic theology, he spoke of the unqualified commitment of the new institution to the Reformed Faith:

> That system of theology, that body of truth, which we find in the Bible, is the Reformed Faith, the Faith commonly called Calvinistic, which is set forth gloriously in the Confession and Catechisms of the Presbyterian Church. It is sometimes referred to as a "man-made creed." But we do not regard it as such. We regard it, in accordance with our ordination pledge as ministers in the Presbyterian Church, as the creed which God has taught us in his Word. If it is contrary to the Bible, it is false. But we hold that it is not contrary to the Bible, but in accordance with the Bible, and true. We rejoice in the approximations to that body of truth which other systems of theology contain; we rejoice in our Christian fellowship with other evangelical churches; we hope that members of other churches, despite our Calvinism, may be willing to enter into Westminster Seminary as students and to listen to what we may have to say. But we cannot consent to impoverish our message by setting forth less than what we find the Scriptures to contain; and we believe that we shall best serve our fellow-Christians, from whatever church they may come, if we set forth not some vague greatest common measure among various creeds, but that great historic Faith that has come through Augustine and Calvin to our own Presbyterian Church. Glorious is the heritage of the Reformed Faith. God grant that it may go forth to new triumphs even in the present time of unbelief!

Dwelling briefly on the situation that had brought the new Seminary into existence, Machen reflected upon the fresh evidence that Princeton was lost to the evangelical cause. For the authorities had commended the new Board to the confidence of the church in spite of the presence on it of two signers of the Auburn *Affirmation*. The calamity at Princeton was to make unprecedented demands for sacrifice on the part of all associated with Westminster, but perhaps the pathway of sacrifice would prove to be the pathway of power. And then Machen concluded on this solemn note:

> No, my friends, though Princeton Seminary is dead, the noble tradition of Princeton Seminary is alive. Westminster Seminary will endeavor by God's grace to continue that tradition unimpaired; it will endeavor, not on a foundation of equivocation and compromise, but on an honest foundation of devotion to God's Word, to maintain the same principles that the old Princeton maintained. We believe, first, that the Christian religion, as it is set forth in the Confession of Faith of the Presbyterian Church, is true; we believe, second, that the Christian religion welcomes and is capable of scholarly defense; and we believe, third, that the Christian religion should be proclaimed without fear or favor, and in clear opposition to whatever opposes it, whether within or without the church, as the only way of salvation for lost mankind. On that platform, brethren, we stand. Pray that we may be enabled by God's Spirit to stand firm. Pray that the students who go forth from Westminster Seminary may know Christ as their own Saviour and may proclaim to others the gospel of his love.

This wholehearted commitment to the Bible and the Reformed Faith therefore was given the greatest possible emphasis. The same emphasis was found in its promotional literature, as the first leaflet entitled "For the Bible and the Reformed Faith," confirms. Unfortunately, however, the full impact of this commitment was not adequately grasped during the early years. The opposition to modernism rather than a positive understanding of the Reformed Faith had come to characterize the evangelicalism of the Presbyterianism Church, and in this context the difference between the Reformed Faith and current fundamentalism frequently failed to come to full disclosure and understanding. Accordingly in the course of years some supporters who had stood by the Seminary because of its opposition to modernism withdrew when they became more fully aware of the significance of the commitment to historic Calvinism.

An element of great strength in Westminster's position—though at times it proved to be an occasion of stumbling—was therefore its complete loyalty to the Scriptures together with its sense of historical perspective ultimately rooted in the former. It enjoyed accordingly a vantage point from which it evaluated the present and sought to effect reformation. Thus it was guarded from the tendency to elevate current fundamentalism to a point of simple identification with historic Christianity, however appreciative it was of certain emphases in fundamentalism. It could not adopt as its standpoint any current or recent manifestation of Presbyterianism as a standard by which to evaluate the contemporaneous scene. Moreover, in this standpoint of principle there was present a dynamic for future progress in the scholarly and practical spheres. The profound concern to draw the line sharply between Scripture and tradition, and to give Scripture its full rights, guaranteed that its teaching would not become a mere repetition of a tradition in stereotyped form. The goal was that fresh light might be discerned breaking forth from the Word and that more and more self-consciously the implications of the Biblical world and life view would be understood and applied to every sphere of life.

A FREE INSTITUTION

Although Westminster was resolved to perpetuate the Princeton tradition so far as scholarship and militant commitment to the Reformed Faith were concerned, there was no slavish bondage to details in organization, curriculum or methods of instruction. One of the most conspicuous differences between Princeton and Westminster was that Westminster chose to remain free from ecclesiastical control. Indeed, as the history of recent events had demonstrated in tragic fashion, ecclesiastical control was no guarantee of the preservation of the Reformed Faith in the academic sphere. Moreover, in the situation the only assurance of liberty to do so was provided through an organization of individuals united by their common loyalties to the Word of God and the Reformed Faith. As Dr. Macartney observed at Westminster's first commencement, while men had felt it necessary in the interest of maintaining a liberal theology at Union Theological Seminary of New York to break away from General Assembly control in the nineties, it had now become necessary to establish an independent seminary in the interest of maintaining the historic faith of the Church.

Certain critics of Westminster charged inconsistency and duplicity when it became apparent that the new Seminary would have only one Board of control. But this was to miss the point at issue in the Princeton struggle over two boards or one. The question at issue had never been the superficial one whether one or two boards were expedient. Rather it was whether the Board of Directors, the body charged with the responsibility for the academic affairs of the institution, *whose constituency of orthodox men was the one guarantee, in a time of inclusivism and drift, that the Faculty would also be orthodox,* was to be maintained in control. Since the question was fundamentally one of personnel and principles rather than of outward organization and expediency, even at this point the Princeton tradition was preserved more assuredly at Westminster through a single Board than at Princeton with its two Boards until 1929 and a single inclusivist Board thereafter. For though, as ensuing events were to disclose, mistakes were made in the organization of the board, there was present in the minds of Machen and many of his associates the profound conviction that only through the utmost vigilance and circumspection in the election of members to the Board could there be any hope of preserving a sound organization. This estimate also forms the background for the tradition that one or two members of the Faculty should be included within the membership of the Board's nominating committee.

A particular advantage of Westminster's organization was that members of the Board and Faculty did not necessarily have to be recruited from a single denomination. Since the Seminary emerged from and was directed mainly towards a concrete historical situation in the Presbyterian Church in the U. S. A., these persons were for the most part members of that body. But from the first a number of trustees were chosen from other denominations, thus emphasizing the more catholic ministry of the institution. And as noted above it proved possible to disregard the boundaries of the Presbyterian Church in establishing the strongest possible Faculty without requiring a necessary change of ecclesiastical affiliation.

When the Seminary opened there was an enrollment of fifty students, who were about equally divided between the three regular classes. This total was gratifying in the circumstances. For the time had been short, there was little or no prospect of the granting of advanced degrees, and the graduates might jeopardize their hopes of ecclesiastical opportunity. Most of the fifty students were Presbyterians but others were welcomed in accordance with Machen's words in his opening address.

That the Seminary opened its doors a few weeks before the calamitous Wall Street crash of 1929 was not without significant effects upon its outward prosperity. Considering the catastrophic effects of the depression which ensued one might well wonder that the young institution, without capital assets of any kind and faced with the necessity of raising large sums of money every year, even survived. That it did do so is due to the extraordinary self-sacrifice of many devout people. Machen himself and members of his family including especially his mother gave very liberally. But there were great numbers of others who responded to the appeals that were regularly sent out. During those early years much of the stability of the Seminary must be credited to the inspiring leadership provided by Dr. Frank H. Stevenson as president of the Board of Trustees. Due to declining health he had retired from his post as pastor of the Covenant Presbyterian Church of Cincinnati to take an active part in the struggle at Princeton, and he gave unstintingly of himself to the new cause until his untimely death in 1934. His letters and articles were eloquent and stirring calls to sacrifice in the cause of truth. And in the councils of the Seminary as in his many contacts his contagiously fervent spirit made a deep and favorable impression on all. The loyalty and generosity of Mrs. Stevenson during these years and afterward were both typical of, and an example to, many god-fearing women who undergirded the work of the Seminary with their prayers and gifts.

INCREASING BURDENS

Although Machen had been living a strenuous life for many years there was a quickening of the tempo with the inception of Westminster, and he was engaged in carrying out an almost incredible program of service. That he accomplished all that he did is explicable at all only because of his astonishing mental and physical energies and the sheer singleness of purpose with which he devoted himself to his labors. Although he had hoped to see more of his mother because of the proximity of Baltimore, the visits were few and very brief. And although he delighted to entertain the students at "checker club" parties in his new apartment, and to be host to members of the Faculty circle, he found that his engagements reduced such pleasures to rather rare occasions. He loved his teaching and gave that first place. And since he was now undertaking several courses for the first time, including the major course on Gospel History and many new electives, he could not, even if his standards of scholarship had permitted, neglect this central task. His writing of *The Virgin Birth of Christ* had marked a climactic event in his work as scholar and author, but many strenuous hours had to be given to proof-reading and preparation of indexes before it appeared early in 1930.

He continued to be in demand as a preacher and speaker on special occasions, and it was a rare Sunday when he was not out of town on such an engagement. Most of his energies not spent in academic and scholarly labors, however, were employed in connection with the promotion of the Seminary. One of the most crucial tasks of that first year was the formulation of the Charter and Constitution of the Seminary, and as a member of the sub-committee to which the drafting of this document was committed a large share of this task fell upon him. In connection with the incorporation of the Seminary and the formal adoption of the Charter and Constitution, which took place in the spring of 1930, another decision of far-reaching significance concerned the determination of the constituency of the Board of 21 which took the place of the Committee of 15. Machen of course was also deeply involved in this matter.

During the course of the year it had gradually become apparent that *The Presbyterian* would be lost to the cause of Westminster and a militant testimony on the ecclesiastical front. Though Dr. Craig, the editor, owned a substantial block of stock adding up to many thousands of dollars of personal investment, it appeared that the majority of stock was owned by persons favorable to the reorganization of Princeton, and early in 1930 Dr. Craig was forced out of his position. Machen and Stevenson among others recognized how indispensable a new organ would be to the cause, and urged Craig to begin a new paper. This led to the establishment of *Christianity Today,* of which Craig, Machen and Mr. James F. Shrader, a lawyer, and a member of the Westminster Board, were the incorporators. Machen not only supported the new paper very liberally with financial gifts but also was one of the principal contributors to its pages for more than five years.

Machen's actions and attitudes at this juncture again disclose the basic makeup of the man. One factor was that of intense loyalty to Dr. Craig as a man who had stood valiantly for the truth and had suffered because of it. Consequently he protested in the most vigorous terms when, contrary to his expressed will, his name continued for a time to appear on the letterhead of *The Presbyterian.* And he likewise felt that persons who actively co-operated with *The Presbyterian* after its treatment of Craig and the victory gained for its mediating policy were not worthy of complete confidence, and that their presence on the Board of Westminster would constitute a threat to its security. On the other hand, his support of Craig was not a mere matter of personal regard for later, in 1935, when it appeared that *Christianity Today* would no longer support what Machen regarded as a consistent policy of reform within the Church, he felt compelled to sever his connection with it, and was instrumental in establishing *The Presbyterian Guardian.* Rare indeed are such persons who, though delighting in personal friendships, yet are able consistently to follow the course of principle. More pliable and pragmatic persons found it virtually impossible to understand a character like Machen's.

THE VIRGIN BIRTH OF CHRIST

On the eve of the appearance of Machen's big book his mother could not hide her excitement and gratification. On Feb. 13th, the 56th anniversary of her wedding, she expressed the hope that he had now seen his new book, and that she would be able to share the triumph before long. "It is a triumph over many obstacles, over interruptions innumerable, attacks of enemies and perfidy of friends, over petty demands and over grand and overmastering claims of absorbing duties."

Though the date of publication was delayed until March 13th, he had a few copies about a month earlier. In sending one off to his mother, he urged her not to attempt to read "this terrific book all through." On Feb. 17 she wrote to tell of her joy at receiving the book:

> What a wonderful day is this for me—my beloved Son, I was all alone—about noon—when I opened the package and held in my hand the Book of my dreams, the fulfillment of my hopes! I took it in—the pretty cover, the outside inscription, the good clear print, the satisfactory size, the lightness to hold. Then the loving inscription, the nice title-page—and when I turned that—oh, wonder!—the dedication to Mother. Here the tears of joy came. I was overwhelmed, not having expected this crowning tribute. I know the book is especially my own for many reasons; but I had had my two dedications and I thought that this one would have been for some close friend. I am glad and I thank my dear boy. I am proud to have a son to whom God has given the will and the ability to write a book on this great theme. I read the Introduction, dipped around here and there and then settled on the Chapter on Inherent Credibility. But I am going back now to the very first, and read, mark, learn and inwardly digest . . . Then later I made a very earnest and special prayer of thanksgiving that the ambition of my life should have been thus satisfied; and then for blessing upon your Book! God grant that this book may have the success it richly deserves. How it has gone on growing from a few twigs into a stately tree all amid the strife of tongues and the slings and arrows of those who privily shoot at the upright in heart!

And in reply to his advice concerning her reading of the book, she wrote on the 23rd:

> I should think I *would* read every word of *The Virgin Birth,* my Book! I am already reading it in my slow, painstaking way, with great profit and delight and a thankful pride in being uplifted and instructed by my own son. I got a little confused over the first chapter, feeling very ignorant among the many primitive writers and the confusion of tongues. Yet I came out of it with a well-attested conviction that a "firm belief in the Virgin Birth extended back to the early years of the Second Century." The second chapter (the Birth Narratives) is very rich and beautiful. I am pleased

with myself for understanding so well the Greek character of the Prologue. The whole is very fine and convincing and I like especially the passage on The Holy Spirit, p. 56. The third and fourth chapters are most interesting and touching—it has been good for my soul to go over so carefully all those wonderful events—the good Simeon, the Visitation, the Hymns, the Shepherds. What is more wonderful than to be led by my own son's hand over this way of privilege and miracle, now in my old age when I need it so much.

I love the allusions here and there to the researches of "the present writer" alongside of Harnack and Zimmerman and the rest. And our footsteps are to be found all the way along in the memory of various articles as they came out. So many years leading up to this Book! I remember how proud I was of Harnack's review of your two articles in the Literaturzeitung...

The silence of Mary is very sacred, very touching. Yet, though she pondered in her heart all the solemn and momentous things that had come to her (and perhaps made a hymn about them); yet, when she visited Elizabeth, if ever, her reserve would naturally have been broken. A woman in her state, full of unuttered thoughts on her miraculous destiny, when visiting an older woman, trusted and beloved, would have poured out her soul. So one would think. And that is what she did.

This is about all I have read—about one-fourth of the book. It has been my great joy during this rather trying time, for I have had unbroken days of headache since Feb. 12, with only little letups some days. I have simply seized the lucid intervals.

Machen's replies to these observations were of course full of his profound gratification and affection. With regard to her reflections on the dedication he asked: "But indeed to whom else could it possibly have been dedicated, except to the one who believes in the book so much more than the author has done and has never failed in her loving encouragement?" And he spoke of his thrill and amazement at her reading of the early chapters, and added, "I am glad that my Mother is one of those who has intellect enough to tackle even so tough a nut."

A few weeks later as she neared its close she wrote again of her estimate of the book:

I am anticipating pleasure in the final chapter, after I finish the Pagan Derivation. I laughed just now when, after the statement of Gressmann's extraordinary theory, you offer your reader "a slight pause to get his breath." For I had just gasped for air myself. I think you have written an exhaustive treatise, and I cannot think there is much more for anybody to say on the subject. You have throughout been fair and courteous to your opponents even while probing their fallacies. I am not able tonight to tell you how the beautiful and luminous passages of your precious Book have stirred your Mother's heart. I must seem to you to have taken a long time with the reading. But, in the first place, I have read very thoroughly, looking up references and keeping my Bible open beside me. And then I have had to seize my lucid intervals for reading. I have been very stupid and draggy, after growing sleepy, and your book is not one to read when groggy with sleep.

THE PASSING OF MRS. MACHEN

In view of the large place which Mrs. Machen has occupied in these pages as the biographer has sought to suggest something of the wonderfully loving and significant relationship between them, one must record with sorrow the fact that it came to an end on October 13, 1931 when she passed away in her 83rd year. Never of robust health she had yet been a person of great intellectual and spiritual strength, and these inward forces seemed to command such physical strength as she ordinarily required. Finally, however, toward the end of the summer of 1931, following a return from a speaking engagement in California, it became apparent to Machen that an extraordinary debility had overtaken her. On August 28th he wrote with alarm to his brother Arthur of the gravity of her condition as manifested, in part, in anemia, but especially in weakness and acute shortness of breath. She nevertheless undertook the journey from Seal Harbor to Baltimore toward the end of September hopeful of improvement which never materialized. Machen was all solicitude as he kept in intimate touch with developments, and his letters were if possible even more affectionate than his love-letters had been through the years. His letter on Sept. 27th began as follows:

My dearest Mother:

A telegram from Arly, sent at my request to Gorham, New Hampshire, told me of your arrival, and I have received today a good letter from him. I had some thought of running down to Baltimore to spend Sunday, but a severe cold put a stop to that plan. It would not do at all to add to your troubles by bringing any cold-germs into 217.

My dearest Mother, you were wonderfully precious to me this summer, and it rends my heart to think of all the suffering that you are passing through. I do hope and pray that measures may be found for the speedy relief of your distress. Through it all you are so amazingly sweet and dear. May you be given strength to bear this suffering and emerge from it speedily to the joy of those who love you! Except for your suffering I did so enjoy being with you this summer. Even now I am running over in my mind all the ways in which, despite your suffering, you cheered me up and kept me in the right way. What a great thing it must be to think, as you have a right to do, of the immeasurable blessing that one has been to others! . . .

Many duties await me. I do not see how in the world I am going to do all that I have to do. But at least it is fruitful work. It looks as though we are going to have a greatly increased enrollment at the Seminary.

May God bless the measures for your speedy recovery, my dearest Mother! I long for better news. Needless to say, *you* must not even think of writing. Arly will keep me informed.

On the 6th of October she undertook a brief letter which was to be her last in the remarkable series of more than a thousand that had passed between them for some thirty years. Her handwriting had remained extraordinarily clear and firm except for this very last message. In it she spoke of her joy in his last letter, of her disappointing breakdown upon arrival at her home in Baltimore and the "obstruction and oppression of breath" which did not seem to improve. In the midst of all her weakness and discomfort her thoughts were still with him and his work:

I hope your cold is better and that you are getting along with your work, Mother is feeble but she is with Dassie every step. I love to remember our prayers together. Mr. Kirk has twice offered a prayer with me. I was grateful but the prayer was too laudatory of me to be spread before the Lord. God bless you!

Mother

Machen was to write one more letter to her, on the 11th:

It gave me a tremendous thrill to get a letter from my dearest Mother written with her own hand. And what a wonderfully sweet letter it was! I don't believe I have ever had a letter, even among the unsurpassed series of letters that I have received from you, my dearest Mother, letters which have been the comfort and strength of my life—I don't believe I ever had one which was quite so precious as this, although that is certainly saying a good deal. Even amid all the suffering and weakness you are a wonderful letter-writer; but the biggest reason of all why you are such a wonderful letter-writer is that you are such a wonderful person—the best and wisest that I ever knew.

All the same, I don't want you to write until it becomes easy enough for you to do it without overtaxing yourself. Arly has been very good about giving me the news.

My heart aches when I think of your suffering. May God bless the measures that are being taken for your recovery, and may you soon have relief! . . . It has been a great grief to me not to get down to see you. I had treasured the hope of going tomorrow, but, alas, it is not to be. My duties here have simply swamped me.

There was however to be no relief or recovery, and two days later she had gone. He had however been called to her bedside and had been with her on the last day. It was characteristic of Machen that when he returned to his duties at the Seminary he did not indulge in comment upon the overwhelming grief that had overtaken him. But something of his emotion of those days, as well as of his personal relationships with the students of the Seminary, has been preserved in a letter he wrote as, on October 15, following the funeral, he traveled westward to keep a speaking engagement, and acknowledged their expression of sympathy:

EN ROUTE
MANHATTAN LIMITED
PENNSYLVANIA RAILROAD

October 15, 1931

Mr. John Paul Clelland
President, The Student Association
Westminster Theological Seminary
Dear Mr. Clelland.

I have sat here for a long time with a perfectly blank sheet of paper in front of me, thinking of the beautiful flowers that came from the student body of Westminster Seminary and trying to find words to express what is in my heart. The thing that I want to say is so utterly simple, and yet I know that when I try to say it by the cold media of pen and paper I shall be tempted to tear up whatever I may write. Despite all I can do I am so afraid that it will seem like one note of thanks among other notes of thanks, when as a matter of fact my whole soul is in it.

When I sat at the service yesterday afternoon in the old home where I was born, it was the thought of the comrades in Westminster Seminary which gave the most comfort; and to these comrades not only the Faculty but also the students belong. I think that is the most wonderful thing about our little company. Somehow I cannot think of myself as a "teacher" in the midst of "students" when I am with Westminster men; rather do we seem to be above all brethren and learners together as we study God's Word. With some of you I am already united by ties of affection formed by one year or two years of fellowship together in labor, in testimony and in prayer; but to save my life I cannot think even of the men of the entering class as in any real sense strangers. Knowing as I do the motives that have brought you to us I feel somehow that we are more closely united already than would be possible by whole years of the only kind of friendship that the world knows. And I knew when I received your tribute yesterday that with it went true affection of the heart. God give us all, during the years of the Seminary course, and throughout all our lives, an ever-deepening fellowship with one another in Christ!

My mother said to me, on the last day of her life, that it seemed to her somehow to be "like Sunday." I thought at first that she meant that her sons were with her as sometimes used to be the case on Sundays. But it appeared that she meant something deeper than that. It was a day when she had had some relief from the pain of labored breathing; and "Sunday"—the old Sunday which the world regards as a day of irksome restraint—was to her the highest symbol of rest and peace. Then, in the evening, when pain came upon her again, she said: "My Sunday is over." But she was wrong. According to the blessed words of the Epistle to the Hebrews, it had just begun. She entered very soon into the sabbath rest that remaineth for the people of God.

There is no bitterness in it. All the bitterness was borne once for all by Christ upon the Cross, and that is the thing that really matters. My Mother seems—to me at least—to have been the wisest and best human being I ever knew. But the thing that I really longed to hear in the moment of her parting from me was that she had been bought by the precious blood of Christ. That comfort had been given me by you men of Westminster Seminary, and because it could be given to me and to others, Westminster Seminary is not just one theological seminary among others but a true brotherhood that the world can never make to be afraid.

With heartfelt affection and gratitude to you and to all the brethren, I am

Cordially yours,
J. Gresham Machen

24

FOREIGN MISSIONS IN THE BALANCE

With the publication of *Rethinking Missions* late in the year 1932, a new and climactic phase of the doctrinal struggle that engaged Machen's powers was opened up. Even more incandescent than the flaming twenties, it struck with something of the force of lightning after a period of stillness.

In the earlier developments there was nothing quite so explosive. Although the fall of Princeton had been a crushing defeat, it had been forecast by the trend of events for a number of years. The establishment of Westminster had been a significant counter movement and its early success was somewhat indicative of the fact that the larger struggle was not over. Neverthless, in view of the precedent of independent Union Seminary of New York there apparently was no effective way of thwarting its ministry. Attacks upon it consequently had been rather oblique. Meanwhile comfort was taken in the prediction that the Seminary could hardly last. Moreover, however successful Westminster might become, its activities could hardly arouse the Church as a whole. Traditionally, at any rate, the cause of theological education was rather remote from the daily concerns of most church members.

The new phase of the conflict, on the other hand, could not be cheerily dismissed. For it concerned a matter close to the heart of most Christians: the subject of the proclamation of the gospel in foreign lands in obedience to the great commission. And in view of the colossal proportions this aspect of ecclesiastical life had assumed, church officials were bound to be sensitive to any development that might directly threaten the success of the official program.

BEFORE THE STORM

Before the new storm broke, however, there was, following the establishment of Westminster, a kind of lull. And this brief interlude at the turn of the decade offers an occasion to recall some of the other activities which engaged Machen's attention in this period.

Following the death of his mother, Machen felt free, as he had not for many years, to accept engagements which took him away from the United States. Yielding to the urgently repeated invitation of the Bible League of Great Britain he made a journey to Europe in the summer of 1932. After delivering three lectures at their annual meeting on "The Importance of Christian Scholarship," he undertook a strenuous speaking tour lasting nearly a month. There were notable opportunities in England, Scotland, Ireland and Wales as well as two addresses in Paris where he spoke in French under the auspices of the Union des Chretiens Evangeliques.

Machen then returned to the mountains of Switzerland for his first extensive vacation in many years. It was hardly less strenuous than his speaking tour had been, however, for he was constantly in the mountains, and his successes included nothing short of ascents of the Matterhorn and the Dent Blanche!! Something of his exhilaration in these exploits later came to expression in his paper on "Mountains and Why We Love Them."

This period is also marked off from the climactic years by Machen's own delightful autobiographical essay entitled, "Christianity in Conflict." which appeared in Volume I of the series *American Contemporary Theology*, edited by Vergilius Ferm. Reviewing in inimitable fashion the impact made by his parents and his teachers, he spoke briefly of his career at Princeton, and concluded with a statement of faith, in which he stressed especially his great hope for Westminster Seminary and the cause it represented. His outlook upon his Church's future was generally pessimistic, but he did not yet foresee the crisis that lay just ahead. To this period belongs also a number of other noteworthy activities. Among his contributions to *Christianity Today*, in addition especially to his articles of ecclesiastical moment, was the series of "Notes on Biblical Exposition," devoted to a vivid and penetrating treatment of the Epistle to the Galatians. Beginning with the Jan. 1931 issue they continued for just over two years when regrettably, due largely to the pressure of other duties, they were broken off with the treatment of Gal. 3:10-14. In 1932 there also appeared a second, revised edition of *The Virgin Birth of Christ* which took account of the significant evaluations it had received in reviews and articles. Reviews from his pen appeared in the *American Journal of Philology* and *The Evangelical Quarterly*, and articles in *The Forum* and *The Evangelical Student*. The article in *The Forum* (March, 1931) was entitled, "Christianity and Liberty, A Challenge to the Modern Mind," and expressed in an eloquent way the theme that in a world characterized by loss of liberty, and a tendency to the drabness of standardization of life, men should find escape "in the high adventure of the Christian religion." A notable address on the subject, "The Responsibility of the Church in our New Age," was delivered before the American Academy of Political and Social Science in 1932.

There was therefore a ceaseless flow of activities throughout this period. Bereavement and heartache might come, but healing medicine was dispensed by the challenge of seizing opportunities of bearing witness to the truth as well as by the performance of routine duties.

EARLY INTEREST IN MISSIONS

It was not the publication of *Rethinking Missions*, it is well to remind ourselves, that first centered Machen's attention upon foreign missions. His father and mother, responsive Christians that they were, took such an active and intelligent interest in this aspect of the work of the church, that he must have been impressed with its significance from the earliest days that he was instructed in the message of the Bible. At the Seminary, moreover, he came to number among his most intimate friends some who eventually served as missionaries—Jim Brown and Updegraaf, for example—and he was overwhelmed with emotion, as they sailed for foreign lands, at the impact of the constraining love of Christ which moved them to answer this call. And his files bring to light scores of letters reflecting his keenly sympathetic interest, throughout his career, in the labors of missionaries in various parts of the world.

When the modernist-fundamentalist controversy broke out in the twenties, various evidences of defection from the cause of the Gospel came to his attention and disturbed him as they did the Christian Church generally. As has been observed above, he took occasion in his books on Christianity, in considering its application to the current problems of the Church, to call into question the propriety of the support of the missionary agencies in the absence of evidence of complete allegiance to the Gospel. These frank comments led to protests on the part of various ecclesiastical leaders like Robert E. Speer and J. Ross Stevenson, and considerable correspondence on the subject developed.

Robert E. Speer, senior secretary of the Board of Foreign Missions, had been an inspiring figure, and Machen was one who had come to identify him with the cause of evangelicalism in its most appealing form. He acknowledged that Speer had influenced his own life in a salutary way. To his great sorrow, however, this missionary leader had come to be aligned with the minority forces in the Princeton Board of Directors, and at the Assembly of 1927 had contributed by his moderatorship to the creation of an atmosphere of evasion of the doctrinal issues of the hour. Distressingly also Speer's books began to disclose that he had developed an uncritical attitude toward modern viewpoints at root opposed to the message of the Bible, and that on this background he also took a complacent attitude toward modernism as that had emerged in the Presbyterian Church. In a review published in *Christianity Today,* in October, 1931, of Speer's book, *Some Living Issues,* Machen had had occasion to point this out. Paying tribute to his high spiritual gifts and rare eloquence, he nevertheless showed that Speer's position oftentimes appeared to be a kind of synthesis of evangelical and liberal viewpoints, and resulted in a palliative attitude as to the modern ecclesiastical situation. In a later evaluation of Speer and his book on *The Finality of Christianity,* Machen paid tribute to Speer's "truly amazing power over the hearts and minds of men," and spoke of the strong prejudice in Speer's favor with which he had begun.

> From my student days on I stood under the spell of his eloquence; I admired him with all my soul; I agreed with what he said. But during the past fifteen years or so I have been obliged to reverse this attitude. . . The change has not been due to any personal likes or dislikes, but it has been due to the stern impulsion of the facts. The plain fact is that in the great issue of the day between Modernism and Christianity in the Presbyterian Church, Dr. Speer is standing for a palliative, middle-of-the-road, evasive policy, which is in some ways a greater menace to the souls of men than any clear-cut Modernism could be.

But, said Machen, Speer's failure to work for and support the reformation of the work of foreign missions was the chief obstacle to its success, and this lack could be traced to the confusion in his mind regarding many basic aspects of the Bible and its message.

RETHINKING MISSIONS

The book *Rethinking Missions* owed its origin to "a laymen's inquiry after one hundred years," which was privately sponsored and financed. Although unofficial therefore, and not necessarily representative of opinion in the churches, it had been prepared for by the generally liberal or latitudinarian spirit which had developed in the course of the fifty or more preceding years. *The Christian Century* reviewed the volume sympathetically, though acknowledging that "the report has burst like a thunderclap on a great portion of the American church," and that "mission boards and other forms of institutionalized religion are having a bad time trying to find some way of dealing with it." *The Presbyterian Banner* and *The Presbyterian Advance,* though reporting some unfavorable reactions, adopted a very calm and respectful attitude. Pearl Buck, herself a missionary under the Presbyterian Board, on the eve of its publication, hailed the book with enthusiasm in an article in *The Christian Century.*

> The book presents a masterly statement of religion in its place in life, and of Christianity in its place in religion. The first three chapters are the finest exposition of religion I have ever read. . .
>
> I think this is the only book I have ever read which seems to me literally true in its every observation and right in its every conclusion. . . If Christians take this book seriously at all, I foresee possibly the greatest missionary impetus that we have known for centuries. What do I not see—what possibilities for showing forth Christ, at last as he truly is, to the world!

And pleading for a new attitude towards missions and a new appraisal of the success of the missionary, she said:

> Let the sole question about that missionary be whether or not he is beloved in the community, whether the people see any use in his being among them, whether or not the way he has lived there has conveyed anything to the people about Christ—not mind you, whether or not he has *preached,* for that is of no value, but whether by the way he has lived he has conveyed anything. If he has not, then let him be returned to his own country. . . .
>
> But above all, let the spread of the spirit of Christ be rather by mode of life than preaching. I am weary unto death with this incessant preaching. It deadens all thought, it confuses all issues, it is producing in our Chinese church a horde of hypocrites and in our theological seminaries a body of Chinese ministers which makes one despair for the future.

In an article in *Harper's Magazine* for Jan. 1933 entitled, "Is There a Case for Foreign Missions?" she indicated even more clearly her repudiation of the traditional, or as she called it the magical, conception of Christianity and missions. Her complete indifference to the gospel of Christ, understood as the glad tidings of what Christ had done on behalf of sinners by his life and death, came to unambiguous expression:

> Even though it is proved in some future time that there never lived an actual Christ and what we think of as Christ should some day be found as the essence of men's dreams of simplest and beautiful goodness, would I be willing to have that personification of dreams pass out of men's minds? . . . . Others live it also, many who have never heard the name of Christ; but to know the meaning of

> Christ's life, to know how he lived and died, is an inestimable support and help.

And in *The Cosmopolitan* for May, 1933, she said:

> If there existed mind or minds, dreams, hopes, imaginations, sensitive enough to the human soul and all its needs, perceptive enough to receive such heavenly imprint on the spirit as to be able to conceive a personality like Christ's and portray him for us with matchless simplicity as he is portrayed, then Christ lived and lives, whether He was once one body and one soul, or whether He is the essence of men's highest dreams.

Dr. Macartney spoke out strongly against *Rethinking Missions* in a sermon preached on January 8, 1933, an excerpt of which was mimeographed for publicity purposes. Entitling this statement "Renouncing Missions" or "Modernism Unmasked," he declared that the inquiry commission, while concluding that missions ought to continue, propose what "sounds like a complete repudiation of historic and evangelical Christianity.'" Underscoring the statement of the report that we are "to look forward, not to the destruction of those religions, but to their continued coexistence with Christianity, each stimulating the other in growth towards the ultimate goal, unity in the completest religious truth," Macartney observed that Christianity thus appeared as just one of the numerous religions of the world. The Name of Christ on this view would no longer be the only name given under Heaven among men whereby we must be saved. Nevertheless Macartney was thankful for the confirmation which the report gave as to the issue facing the churches, an issue to which they had appeared to be largely blind or indifferent at the time of the Fosdick controversy:

> They have scattered the fog; torn off from the face of Modernism its mask and its disguise, so that he who runs may now know that there is an irreconcilable difference between the Christianity of the Scriptures, of the Apostles, and of the ages, and that vague and inchoate collection of human thoughts and fancies which has been masquerading as a new and higher interpretation of Christianity. "Choose ye this day whom ye would serve!"

MACHEN'S ANALYSIS

Early in January Machen also undertook a thorough analysis of the report and of its evaluation on the part of the Board of Foreign Missions. With regard to the book, he said that it constitutes from beginning to end an attack upon the historic Christian Faith. It presents as the aim of missions that of *seeking* truth together with adherents of other religions rather than that of *presenting* the truth which God has supernaturally recorded in the Bible. "The relation between religions," it says, "must take increasingly hereafter the form of a common search for truth" (p. 47). It deprecates the distinction between Christians and non-Christians (pp. 58, 141); it belittles the Bible and inveighs against Christian doctrine (pp. 103, 102f., and *passim*); it dismisses the doctrine of eternal punishment as a doctrine antiquated even in Christendom (p. 19); it presents Jesus as a great religious Teacher and Example, as Christianity's "highest expression of religious life," but certainly not as very God of very God: it belittles evangelism, definite conversions, open profession of faith in Christ, membership in the Christian Church (p. 277), and substitutes "the dissemination of spiritual influences" (p. 100) and "the permeation of the community with Christian ideals and principles" (p. 164) for the new birth.

More disquieting than the Report itself however was the attitude of the Board toward it as disclosed by its action on Nov. 21, 1932. Since previously the Board had welcomed the inquiry, and two of its members were members of the body which appointed the Appraisal Commission, the Presbyterian Church had a right to expect an unequivocal evaluation of the Report when its contents became known. Instead, however, it failed to utter any ringing disapproval of its central position and contented itself with a vague statement concerning its loyalty to the evangelical basis of the missionary enterprise. Disquieting also was the consideration that the candidate secretary, whose function was that of interviewing candidates for foreign service, and either encouraging them or discouraging them in their plans, was a signer of the Auburn *Affirmation*, and apparently enjoyed the confidence of the Board.

This elaborate memorandum was dated Jan. 7, 1933, and formed the background for the proposed overture which Machen brought forward at the January meeting of the Presbytery of New Brunswick with a view to action at the April meeting. This overture read as follows:

THE PRESBYTERY OF NEW BRUNSWICK RESPECTFULLY OVERTURES THE GENERAL ASSEMBLY OF 1933,

1. To take care to elect to positions on the Board of Foreign Missions only persons who are fully aware of the danger in which the Church stands and who are determined to insist upon such

verities as the full truthfulness of Scripture, the virgin birth of our Lord, His substitutionary death as a sacrifice to satisfy Divine justice, His bodily resurrection and His miracles, as being essential to the Word of God and our Standards and as being necessary to the message which every missionary under our Church shall proclaim,

2. To instruct the Board of Foreign Missions that no one who denies the absolute necessity of acceptance of such verities by every candidate for the ministry can possibly be regarded as competent to occupy the position of Candidate Secretary,

3. To instruct the Board of Foreign Missions to take care lest, by the wording of the application blanks for information from candidates and from those who are asked to express opinions about them, or in any other way, the impression be produced that tolerance of opposing views or ability to progress in spiritual truth, or the like, is more important than an unswerving faithfulness in the proclamation of the gospel as it is contained in the Word of God and an utter unwillingness to make common cause with any other gospel whether it goes under the name of Christ or not,

4. To warn the Board of the great danger that lurks in union enterprises at home as well as abroad, in view of the widespread error in our day.

In his characteristic thoroughness and concern for objectivity, and disregard of personal expense, Machen prepared in support of his proposed overture a printed booklet of 110 pages entitled *Modernism and the Board of Foreign Missions.* It included several matters in addition to those already mentioned, including an extensive communication from the Hon. Arie Kok, Chancellor of the Dutch Legation in Peking, a devout evangelical who had been a warm supporter and close observer of Christian missions in China for many years.

THE PEARL BUCK CASE

Perhaps the most striking new feature of the pamphlet, however, was its presentation of the case of Mrs. J. Lossing (Pearl) Buck in its implications for the overture. There were those who understood this as a personal and rather unworthy attack upon Mrs. Buck, but that was not Machen's view nor that of Mrs. Buck herself as their personal correspondence bears out. In this connection, one may recall the tribute Mrs. Buck was to pay Machen at the time of his death, as published in *The New Republic* of Jan. 20, 1937, which discloses that she admired him more than "the princes of the church" who "play their church politics and trim their sails to every wind." She wrote:

> I admired Dr. Machen very much while I disagreed with him on every point. And we had much the same fate. I was kicked out of the back door of the church and he was kicked out of the front one. He retaliated by establishing a church of his own. The mother church was called the Presbyterian Church of the United States of America, but he gave his church a bigger name—the Presbyterian Church of America. Of course what he did not realize was that he would have had to compromise with this opinion or that, or more impossible still to him, with a majority opinion, and he would have had to break again with them all. One might say death was merciful to him, except I have an idea he enjoyed his wars.
>
> The man was admirable. He never gave in one inch to anyone.

Machen's criticism of Mrs. Buck was actually a criticism of the Board because it retained on its list of missionaries one who took up a position of open conflict with the official doctrinal standards of the Church, and thus gave proof that it could not retain the confidence of persons who desired to support faithful Christian missionaries.

The Buck case received great prominence because of her distinction as an author of *The Good Earth* and other successful novels. In its issue of May 6, 1933 *The Literary Digest,* for example, carried a page and a half story under the page-wide heading "Mrs. Buck Under Fire As a 'Heretic'," accompanied by photographs of Mrs. Buck and Machen. Under the former was the caption, "She Believes in Christ Whether He actually lived or not. But no creeds are needed says Mrs. Pearl S. Buck, famous missionary and novelist, and she is accused of heresy." Under the latter were the words, "A Stern Calvinist Dr. J. Gresham Machen will carry his fight against Mrs. Buck and the Presbyterian Board of Foreign Missions to 'the people of the Church'."

After the charges were made, the Board followed a policy of hesitation. Even *The Christian Century* stated editorially that "the difference between the statements regarding Mrs. Pearl S. Buck made to the press by Dr. Robert E. Speer and Dr. Cleland B. McAfee, secretaries of the Presbyterian mission board, indicates that the board finds itself in the unhappy position of having taken hold of a buzz-saw." While Speer admitted that she was under scrutiny McAfee assured the public that "we do not take this case so seriously as do some people." In defending a tolerant policy the *Century* described Mrs. Buck as "one of the very small number of missionaries who have been able to mediate understanding and good will between different cultures." It was considered unthinkable that Dr. Speer and the Presbyterian Church "would attempt to discipline Mrs. Buck for her views on this dogma" (the damnation of the heathen who die without personal confession of faith in Christ). Considerable discomfiture appeared among the spokesmen for the Board, including, besides the secretaries, Dr. Erdman, and they sought to minimize the significance of Machen's charges. Finally, however, they summoned her to appear before the Board. But Mrs. Buck refused and forthwith resigned. The Board accepted her resignation "with regret." This qualification was also debated. On the one hand the claim was made that this was another evidence of the Board's equivocation on the doctrinal issue; the defense, on the other hand, was that it signified only a concern to act in a good spirit. Mrs. Buck's own evaluation of the matter has been noted above.

THE TRENTON DEBATE

When Machen and Speer met on the same platform in the Fourth Presbyterian Church of Trenton on April 11, 1933, there was a widespread recognition that issues of the greatest historical significance were hanging in the balance. A large audience was present including, besides the members of the Presbytery, many ministers and laymen from the Eastern sector of the Church. Among these the Faculty and student bodies of Princeton and Westminster Seminaries were well represented. There was an atmosphere of suppressed excitement as these giants of intellect and eloquence clashed and the momentous nature of the decision of the day was contemplated. No one who was present that day could ever forget it. And it may still come to life through the report that has been preserved in the April, 1933, number of *Christianity Today*. Machen disclaimed the power of eloquence, and he was usually a man of simple, straightforward speech, never given to meretricious rhetoric or orator's bombast. But when he was afire with the passion of his profound convictions his speech took on an eloquence of the most impressive kind. As the staff correspondent (H. McAllister Griffiths) described it, Machen

> completely captured the attention and imagination of his audience. A deathly silence hushed the church, full as it was. Men's ears were straining to catch every syllable. Like some great figure of days gone by,—a Knox, a Luther or an Edwards, the speaker's face was composed and serene, lit as with a divine certainty and conviction. Here was true eloquence,—not the eloquence of the facile phrase and the sonorous period, but the eloquence of deep smoldering moral earnestness that now blazed up like a consuming fire and now flashed downward like a shining sword. Eloquence as art faded from men's minds in the presence of eloquence as truth.

Machen summed up the argument of his pamphlet effectively, but chose to dwell at length upon the criterion of truth by which the Board and the broader issue were to be judged. For Machen this criterion was "solely the blessed book which lies open before us on this pulpit." And so it was necessary to reject the appeal of Buchmanism to "changed lives" or experience, likewise "the mind of Christ" understood as the combined or common mind of Christians, and the so-called "spirit of Christ." Accordingly, Machen closed his address with an insistence that the Word of God should be acknowledged. As reported in *Christianity Today,*

> Dr. Machen ended his address with an appeal of such strength and lofty thought that the reporter was simply unable to catch all the words. And even if he had all the words no printed page could ever convey the power, dignity and tenderness that were mingled together. It was an appeal to return to the power of the Word of God. Here is God's truth: His Holy Book. It was a joy to speak for that Book,—to testify to the Christ of the Bible, against the whole current of the age that held the minds of men so rigidly in its embrace of death. He was glad to have spoken a word for Christ, to call men to return from the wisdom of the world to His wisdom. For this wisdom we thank God, and may He raise up men and women who will go forth and not be ashamed to carry it to the ends of the earth.

To Machen's deep disappointment, and that of many in the audience, Speer chose not to reply to Machen's argument. Instead he read word for word a prepared statement in which he defended the Board. His statement criticized Machen's overture for singling out the Board of Foreign Missions, appealed to previous actions of the General Assembly as having vindicated the Board, took the position that the Board could not sit in judgment upon its candidate secretary since he was a minister in good and regular standing in the Church, and claimed that at most there were only two missionaries of whose doctrinal disloyalty there was any knowledge. Thus the doctrinal issues raised by Machen's argument and by the background of defection as reflected in the Auburn *Affirmation* were evaded. And rather than responding to Machen's appeal to make the Bible the criterion of judgment Speer stated in effect that his own general confidence in the missionary enterprise, and that of the Church both past and present, should suffice to assure the Presbytery of its faithfulness. Obviously there could be no interest in reforming the missionary work of the Church where there was no awareness of a need of reforming the Church as a whole.

When the vote was put the overture was defeated rather decisively, and thereupon a motion of confidence in the Board prevailed. Thus Machen lost a battle, but the victory of the Board was a costly one. It may have appealed effectively to the prevailing peace-at-any-price mood of the day, but the disquietude of many with regard to the Board's unsoundness was not allayed. When it was announced in various papers including *Christianity Today* and *The Sunday School Times* that Machen would make his pamphlet available to inquirers, thousands upon thousands responded, and thus his case against the Board was widely publicized. Moreover, the overture was to enjoy a different fortune in a number of other presbyteries, including the Presbytery of Philadelphia, where it was adopted by a vote of 57 to 16. Thus the issue was sure to come before the Assembly about to convene in Columbus.

THE COLUMBUS ASSEMBLY

The Assembly of 1933, however, was no more a reform assembly than the several that had preceded it, and it gave the Board of Foreign Missions and its personnel "whole-hearted, unequivocal, enthusiastic and affectionate commendation." A valiant effort was made indeed by a minority of the Assembly's committee of review, consisting of Rev. Robert S. Marsden of Middletown, Pennsylvania, and Mr. Peter Stam, Jr., an elder, to arrest the course of declension. Their minority report recorded with a profound sense of sorrow and regret their conviction that the criticisms contained in Machen's *Modernism and the Board of Foreign Missions* were substantiated in fact, and declared that the equivocal policy of the Board was ethically indefensible. It further called upon the Assembly to deplore the acts and policies of the Board which had seriously impaired the confidence of thousands of loyal and earnest Presbyterians and asked the Assembly to express its loyalty to the Gospel in unambiguous terms. Finally, in order to take the first practical step to make this pledge effective and thus to re-establish confidence, the Committee nominated a slate of conservative persons for election to the class of 1936. This final feature of the minority report disclosed that the conservatives were not to be put off with piously sounding resolutions; they insisted on action that would make perfectly plain that a course of reformation had been adopted.

Just how seriously this proposal was meant no doubt escaped the Assembly at the time, content as it was to follow the path of inclusivism. How it carried water on both shoulders is disclosed pointedly in its treatment of *Rethinking Missions*. It seemed to be concerned to satisfy the critics of the Report in stating that the Assembly does "definitely repudiate any and all theological statements and implications in that volume which are not in essential agreement with the doctrinal position of the Church." But this said nothing! One might still favor the book if he regarded it as being in complete agreement with the theological position of the Church. This was borne out later when it was observed that a member of the Appraisal Commission, on record therefore as supporting its radical position, had been a member of the assembly committee which had recommended this declaration!

The temper of the Assembly was also disclosed in a deliverance on the subject of the method of expressing criticism which was generally recognized as having Machen and his associates in view. The main thrust of this statement was to the effect that criticisms of representatives of the Board should be made only before established church courts. There was also the charge that the current criticism was largely concerned with suspicion of motives.

As a matter of fact Machen had scrupulously avoided personalities. His criticism had been fully documented, but his marshalling of facts had been substantially ignored. The other point, however, was one that possessed more plausibility, and since Machen was called upon on various occasions to indicate why he did not initiate heresy trials rather than engage in a general exposure of the unfaithfulness of certain agencies, it is important to note his position on this matter. Eventually at least, if not in the earlier phases of his ecclesiastical struggle, Machen came to recognize the propriety and wisdom of seeking to bring heretics in general, and signers of the Auburn *Affirmation* in particular, to trial. He was fully sympathetic, for example, with the effort made in the Philadelphia Presbytery in that direction in the year 1935. He was profoundly convinced, however, that the pressing of heresy charges was not necessarily the only or primary duty of a faithful Presbyterian in a time of unbelief. It might prove quite impractical in certain cases to bring a person to trial, and yet his published views might indicate to the Church at large that he was not a person who was qualified to undertake a special responsibility on behalf of the Church. With regard to members of the Board of Foreign Missions, for example, Machen's position was that they were not immune from criticism. No man had an inherent right to be a member of the Board, and the Church should choose no one without particular assurance of his qualifications. And in holding that the members *had tolerated Modernism*, he held that their disqualification had been demonstrated altogether apart from the question whether they could be proved to be heretics in their personal beliefs.

THE INDEPENDENT BOARD

When the Assembly failed to take measures to assure the Church that its policies and work would be brought into conformity with the Constitution of the Church, the early formation of an independent Board of Foreign Missions was announced at Columbus, on behalf of Machen and himself, by H. McAllister Griffiths. Fifteen ministers, five ruling elders and five women were listed as having agreed to serve on the projected board. And it was stated that it would meet for organization in Philadelphia on June 27th. Commenting editorially upon its formation, *Christianity Today* stated:

> The decision of the General Assembly in accepting the majority report of the Committee on Foreign Missions, expressing confidence in the Board, placed squarely before conservatives in the Church an inevitable choice. Could they continue to recommend for support a Board against which the evidence had piled so high? The action of a General Assembly that was never in possession of the facts in the case could not quiet the consciences of those who knew what the facts were, and who knew them to be true.
>
> The choice made was therefore based upon a requirement of principle, not of mere tactics or expediency. No people believe more passionately in the work of Foreign Missions, and believe it must go on, than those who protest against modernism in the policies of the old Board. And if the old Board had by its policies forfeited its true Presbyterian spiritual heritage, then those who held without equivocation or compromise to the glorious faith once for all delivered unto the saints had no alternative but to establish their own agency. The formation of a new Board was therefore announced at Columbus, but only after an earnest effort to reform the old Board had broken itself upon the adamant walls of ecclesiastical bureaucracy.

The new Board continued through the summer with temporary officers but a considerable amount of preliminary work was undertaken which made it possible for it to launch out upon its marked course in the fall. At the October meeting Machen was elected president. One of the most fruitful steps taken was the election of Charles J. Woodbridge, a missionary under the Presbyterian Board to the French Cameroun, West Africa, to the position of general secretary. Mr. Woodbridge, a graduate of Princeton Seminary in the class of 1927, had studied for a year at Berlin and Marburg, and had served four years as a pastor in Flushing, N. Y. As a volunteer for missionary service, he followed in the footsteps of his father who had served in China for forty-four years. Much of the Board's success in its early years may be attributed to the inspiring and efficient services of Mr. Woodbridge as he labored in close conjunction with Machen and the other leaders.

Meanwhile, however, the warning clouds of storms ahead had begun to appear. At its fall meeting the Presbytery of New Brunswick, over the vigorous protest of Machen, Caspar Wistar Hodge and others, amended its rules so as to require ministers seeking entrance in its membership and candidates seeking licensure or ordination to pledge support to the authorized Boards and agencies. Machen entered an elaborate protest in which he showed that such requirements were unconstitutional, (1) as setting up requirements of ministers and candidates which could become mandatory only by amendment of the Form of Government, and (2) as contravening the Presbyterian principle that support of the Church and its work must be on a free-will basis rather than a tax.

Soon thereafter the far-reaching question of the constitutionality of the Independent Board was raised. As reported in *Christianity Today* for Nov. 1933, Dr. John McDowell, moderator of the 1933 Assembly, was raising this question in his country-wide tours. Taking account of a statement released for publication by Dr. McDowell, Mr. Murray Forst Thompson, a member of the Pennsylvania Bar, and treasurer of the new Board, undertook a defense of its constitutionality. This was published in the December, 1933 issue of *Christianity Today,* and later in pamphlet form, under the title "Have the Organizers of the Independent Board for Presbyterian Foreign Missions Violated the Law of the Presbyterian Church in the U. S. A.?" His argument involved four basic propositions: (1) the law of the Church is to be found in the Bible and the Constitution, and loyalty to the Church does not therefore necessarily carry with it loyalty to any and all phases of the work of the Church regardless of their character; (2) there is nothing in this law forbidding the establishment of an Independent Board, which as a faithful steward will maintain missions to which Bible-believing Christians can contribute; (3) Church judicatories have no power to pass laws "binding the conscience" and penalizing those who conduct or support the Independent Board; and (4) the law of the Church expressly permits members to designate their gifts for Christian benevolences other than those controlled by Boards and Agencies of the Church.

Another phase of this battle developed when Machen sought to be transferred to the Presbytery of Philadelphia. Since the reorganization of Princeton the atmosphere in the Presbytery of New Brunswick had become less congenial, and it seemed that transfer to Philadelphia would mean that his labors as a presbyter would be more fruitful as well as more convenient. He was regularly dismissed and was received in Philadelphia on March 5, 1934 by a vote of 79 to 48. In connection with discussion of the motion there had been attempts to question Machen concerning his attitude toward the Board of Foreign Missions and his relation to the Independent Board, but the moderator ruled such questions out of order, and this ruling was not appealed from. Nevertheless, forty-four members of the Presbytery soon filed a notice of complaint with the Stated Clerk of Presbytery against Machen's reception, and this was later formally presented to the Presbytery and carried to the Synod of Pennsylvania. It was maintained that this complaint served as a stay in the case, and that Machen's reception was not finally and officially consummated. This matter remained in a confused state for some time. Although Machen did not acknowledge the legality of the stay, he nevertheless did not refuse to deal with the Presbytery of New Brunswick when they initiated action against him in the course of the year.

THE 1934 MANDATE

As the 1934 Assembly approached it became evident that the issue of the Independent Board had become the burning question before the Church. In response to a request by Dr. John McDowell, Machen and certain associates conferred on May 3rd with him and Dr. Lewis S. Mudge, the Stated Clerk of the Assembly, who indicated that they were acting in their capacity as members of the Administrative Committee of the General Council. To the complete surprise of Machen and his associates these officials intimated that they had come to the position that the Independent Board was unconstitutional, and that members thereof were violating their ordination or membership vows or both. They further expressed the hope that assurances would be given that the organization and operation of the Independent board would be discontinued. A memorandum summing up this position was placed in Machen's hands.

How far these officials had gone in their efforts to deal drastically with the Independent Board appears further from the consideration that an elaborate 43-page printed document entitled, *Studies of The Constitution of The Presbyterian Church in the U. S. A.*, devoted to this issue, was ready for the commissioners to the 1934 Assembly when it convened at Cleveland. It maintained in substance that churches were not free to devote their missionary offerings to independent agencies, and contained the following astonishing sentence:

A church member or an individual church that will not give to promote the officially authorized missionary program of the Presbyterian Church is in exactly the same position with reference to the Constitution of the Church as a church member or an individual church that would refuse to take part in the celebration of the Lord's Supper or any other of the prescribed ordinances of the denomination as set forth in Chapter VII of the Form of Government.

At the Assembly not only these studies but a deliverance relating specifically to the Independent Board, which had also been prepared by the General Council, was passed. In brief the latter demanded that the Independent Board desist from functioning, called upon all Presbyterian members to sever their connections with it and declared that refusal to do so and continuance of membership would be considered a disorderly and disloyal act on their part and subject them to the discipline of the Church. And Presbyteries were ordered to proceed with appropriate action in cases where the directives of the Assembly had not been obeyed.

Both at the Assembly, within the severe limits imposed upon discussion, and immediately afterward there was a loud cry of protest and alarm at this tyrannical action. Mr. H. W. Fry of the Philadelphia *Evening Bulletin* wired Machen for a statement in which he asked particularly whether this meant a new denomination. To this Machen replied by wire:

ACTION OF GENERAL ASSEMBLY YESTERDAY ATTACKING INDEPENDENT BOARD FOR PRESBYTERIAN FOREIGN MISSIONS DOES NOT NECESSARILY MEAN NEW DENOMINATION BECAUSE ACTION IS QUITE CONTRARY TO THE CONSTITUTION OF THE PRESBYTERIAN CHURCH IN THE U. S. A. AND IS THEREFORE INVALID. I SHALL OF COURSE NOT OBEY ANY SUCH ORDER AND SHALL CONTINUE TO BE A MEMBER OF THE INDEPENDENT BOARD. THE MEANING OF THE ASSEMBLY'S ACTION IS THAT EVERY OFFICER AND MEMBER OF THE PRESBYTERIAN CHURCH IN THE U. S. A. IS ORDERED BY THE GENERAL ASSEMBLY EITHER TO SUPPORT THE OFFICIAL BOARD, WHICH IS CARRYING ON MODERNIST PROPAGANDA, OR ELSE TO SEPARATE FROM ALL MISSIONARY ENDEAVOR STOP NO CHRISTIAN MAN CAN DO EITHER OF THESE TWO THINGS WITHOUT BEING DISLOYAL TO CHRIST

STOP WE MAY ULTIMATELY BE PUT OUT OF THE PRESBYTERIAN CHURCH IN THE U S A STOP BUT THE SPREAD OF THE GOSPEL THAT WE PREACH WILL NOT THEREBY BE CHECKED STOP NOW AS ALWAYS IT REMAINS TRUE THAT THE WORD OF GOD IS NOT BOUND.

Dr. Macartney, who had not consented to serve on the Independent Board, prepared for *The Presbyterian* (the issue of July 19) a rousing call to action, entitled "Presbyterians, Awake!" He declared:

I am one of those who believes that our last General Assembly, through "the frailty inseparable from humanity," erred grievously, deeply and dangerously in the action which it took towards those who are associated with the Independent Board for Presbyterian Foreign Missions. I am not a member of that Board, nor did I take any part in the organization of it. But the action of the General Assembly in dealing with this Board affects me and every other Presbyterian minister, and every officer and communicant of the Presbyterian Church, because it involves questions of conscience and liberty in the Presbyterian Church under its Constitution. . .

The action of the General Assembly, leaving out for a moment all questions as to the Constitution, was in its spirit and tone harsh, severe, unscriptural and un-Presbyterian. It savors more of a papal bull than of the deliberations of the General Assembly of a free Protesant Church. . . It has not been the custom in past ages for Presbyterians to be frightened or intimated or suppressed by such threats or condemnatory measures. Indeed, it has been the glory of our Church that its members have ever claimed liberty of conscience under the Constitution and under the Scriptures, and have scorned and denied every attempt to put them in ecclesiastical irons.

The action of the General Assembly was unjust and unconstitutional in that it amounted to a sentence upon ministers and laymen within the Church without a hearing and without a trial . . . violates the constitutional liberties of churches, sessions and individuals in the matter of their contributions to the work of Christ's kingdom . . . would compel sessions and individual members to contribute to a regularly established board or agency of the Church even when, in their opinion, such board or agency was not faithful to the Gospel, to the Scriptures, and to the Constitution of the Church . . . would unlawfully bind the conscience of those

> who feel that they cannot contribute through the boards of the church . . . in effect amends the Constitution by adding to the subscription vows of candidates for licensure and ordination a vow to support the boards of the Church.
>
> Can it be possible that this unspeakable position has been declared and defended within our Presbyterian Church? . . Is it possible that the morale of the Presbyterian Church has sunk so low that it will bow to this unjust and unconstitutional decree?
>
> The Assembly's severe act will not win contributions to the Board of Foreign Missions, but, on the contrary, will alienate many contributors. You cannot bludgeon Presbyterians into giving to any cause. The Christian method of giving is cheerfully, freely, from the heart, not in answer to an ukase of the General Assembly . . . The act of the General Assembly, if an attempt is made to enforce it in the Presbyteries, will sow the dragon's teeth of strife, and will result in contention and bitterness in the ecclesiastical courts, and also in the civil courts.
>
> Are godly men to be harried, disciplined, censured, persecuted, because they have banded together as Presbyterians to do a good work and to give the Gospel to the heathen? God forbid! It is unthinkable!
>
> If we are to enter upon an era of inquisition and persecution, is it not strange that the ones singled out for trial and discipline should be those ministers and laymen who love the Holy Gospel of our Lord Jesus Christ and desire to give it, uncorrupted and unchanged, to a lost and perishing world? Presbyterians, awake!

There were other articles in *Christianity Today, The Presbyterian* and elsewhere in support of the position of the Independent Board. *The Presbyterian,* speaking editorially on June 21, predicted optimistically that it was doubtful that any presbytery "would press any individual very hard for his connection with it."

That this optimism was ill-founded soon appeared. *The Presbyterian Banner* and *The Presbyterian Advance* vigorously supported the Assembly. And Dr. W. B. Pugh, who was to succeed Dr. Mudge as Stated Clerk, answered Macartney in *The Presbyterian* for Sept. 6 and 13, contending that "Presbyterians Are Awake!" Moreover, as early as June 13, 1934 Dr. Mudge initiated correspondence with the members of the Independent Board and with the clerks of their Presbyteries directing attention to the action of the Assembly.

The Presbytery of New Brunswick moved with apparent patience but with inexorable certainty in fulfilling the requirement of the Assembly. Several months were taken up with preliminary inquiries in which Machen steadfastly persisted in his expression of his intention of remaining on the Independent Board. A proposed interview with the Presbytery's committee of preliminary investigation did not materialize because Machen insisted that there should be a stenographic record of such a conference, but he consented to produce a detailed statement of his position, and this was presented in printed form shortly before the Presbytery was to meet in December. Following a summary statement of the historical developments, he formulated his position in the following forthright terms:

BRIEF STATEMENT OF MY POSITION

Having been ordered by the General Assembly of the Presbyterian Church in the U. S. A., to sever my connection with The Independent Board for Presbyterian Foreign Missions, I desire to say, very respectfully:

I. I cannot obey the order.

A. Obedience to the order in the way demanded by the General Assembly would involve support of a propaganda that is contrary to the gospel of Christ.

B. Obedience to the order in the way demanded by the General Assembly would involve substitution of a human authority for the authority of the Word of God.

C. Obedience to the order in the way demanded by the General Assembly would mean acquiescence in the principle that support of the benevolences of the Church is not a matter of free-will but the payment of a tax enforced by penalties.

D. All three of the above mentioned course of conduct are forbidden by the Bible, and therefore I cannot engage in any of them. I cannot, no matter what any human authority bids me to, support a propaganda that is contrary to the gospel of Christ; I cannot substitute a human authority for the authority of the Word of God, and I cannot regard support of the benevolences of the Church as a tax enforced by penalties, but must continue to regard them as a matter of free-will and a thing with regard to which a man is responsible to God alone.

II. Though disobeying an order of the General Assembly, I have a full right to remain in the Presbyterian Church in the U. S. A. because I am in accord with the constitution of that Church and can appeal from the General Assembly to the Constitution.

In the more than eighty pages of text that followed he then proceeded to support his position in detail, and developed the second main proposition under the following heads:

A. The Constitution is above the General Assembly: and the General Assembly is consequently just as much subject to the Constitution as is the humblest member of the Church.

B. The action of the 1934 General Assembly in the matter of the Independent Board for Presbyterian Foreign Missions is contrary to the Constitution of the Presbyterian Church in the U.S.A.

This latter proposition was supported at length under eight propositions, in the course of which he underscored one of the basic erroneous presuppositions of the action of the General Assembly:

4. The General Assembly's action confuses mere pronouncements with decisions arrived at by process (in this case, judicial process). It encourages the impression that a mere pronouncement against The Independent Board for Presbyterian Foreign Missions has the force that a decision against The Independent Board in a judicial case would have. In effect, it amounts to the condemnation of the members of the Independent Board for Presbyterian Foreign Missions without a trial.

The far-reaching effect of this presupposition was to appear most clearly when the presbyteries concerned adopted it, and consequently, though going through the form of a trial, actually served only as executioners of the deliverance of the Assembly.

AN AMAZING TRIAL

The Presbytery convened on December 20th at Trenton and, on the background of the recommendations of its investigating committee, appointed a judicial commission of seven members to try Machen on the following charges:

With the violation of his ordination vows; with his disapproval of the government and discipline of the Presbyterian Church; with renouncing and disobeying the rules and lawful authority of the Church; with advocating rebellious defiance against the lawful authority of the Church; with refusal to sever his connection with "the Independent Board for Presbyterian Foreign Missions" as directed by the General Assembly; with not being zealous and faithful in maintaining the peace of the church; with contempt of and rebellion against his superiors in the church in their lawful counsels, commands and corrections; with breach of his lawful promises; with refusing subjection to his brethren in the Lord.

This formidable list of charges might easily give the impression that Machen was charged and possibly guilty of a long series of transgressions of the law of God. (To the present time of writing, ministers against whom the same charges were filed, and who were adjudged guilty, have been publicly denounced as having been guilty of the most serious moral offences, which have seemed the more heinous because they have not been specified). The plain fact is, however, that *all of the charges had in view only a single alleged offense, namely, disobedience to the order of the General Assembly regarding membership and activity in The Independent Board.* If Machen had been willing to resign his membership, the charges would immediately have been dropped, as the report of the investigating committee specifically stated. Moreover, the specifications filed by the prosecuting committee bear out this fact. Except for a vague specification to the effect that certain ministers were ready to testify that Machen had greatly disturbed the peace of the Church, they all concerned his membership in the Independent Board. It is also noteworthy that the same specifications were repeated for each charge. Appeal was also made to Exodus 20:7, 12, 15, 16 as interpreted in the subordinate standards, and thus transgression of the law of God was charged. But all the heaping up of charges and specifications could not disguise the fact that the issue reduced itself solely to that of membership in the Independent Board.

That Machen was actually to be brought to trial for his refusal to obey an order of the General Assembly was generally viewed as an astonishing development in spite of the stormy character of Machen's career. Even the secular press gave it prominent place in its columns. The New York *Times,* for example, reported it in a lengthy article commencing on page 1 under the headline, "Presbytery To Try Machen As Rebel."

The trial itself took place at a series of sessions during February and March, 1935. First of all the defense unsuccessfully challenged the right of various members of the judicial commission to sit in judgment. Dr. J. Cordie Culp, the moderator, was a signer of the Auburn *Affirmation;* Dr. John E. Kuizenga was a member of the Princeton Faculty, and in view of the recent Princeton history hardly an objective judge. Thereupon the question of jurisdiction was argued but once again the defendant's position was not sustained. But these reverses were nothing compared with that which developed at the third session when the commission, following Machen's solemnly entered plea of "Not Guilty" to all the charges, ruled that it would not admit evidence bearing on several crucial matters. It would not accept or hear any arguments concerned with the Auburn *Affirmation,* with the question of the soundness of the Board of Foreign Missions, or with the history of the Princeton-Westminster controversy, and thus it ruled out much of the argument that Machen was prepared to present in defense of his position. But these rulings were still mild compared with the amazing ruling that *it could not accept or regard any arguments questioning the legality of the Assembly's mandate. Thus with one stroke Machen was denied the right of having his day in court to prove that the order which he disobeyed was an unlawful order.* It remains almost incredible that a Presbyterian court should thus have flouted the most elementary principles of justice. That it happened can only be attributed to a shocking disregard of the basic Protestant principles that God alone is Lord of the conscience and that the Scriptures are the only infallible rule of faith and practice by which all controversies are to be judged.

THE VERDICT

As a matter of course Machen thus was not accorded an opportunity of defense. And so the verdict of "Guilty" rendered on March 29 could be foreseen. The judgment was that he should be suspended from the ministry. Appeal was taken to the Synod and ultimately to the General Assembly, but both Synod and Assembly (the Syracuse Assembly of 1936) rejected the appeal. And so one of the most extraordinary developments in modern church history came to pass.

There was widespread astonishment at the nature and results of the trial. Albert C. Dieffenbach, the astute Unitarian editor of the column "Religion Today" in the Boston *Evening Transcript*, reviewed the case and its historical background at great length under the heading, "The Amazing Trial of J. Gresham Machen."

> Strangest of all church trials in modern times is that which has just convicted Prof. J. Gresham Machen of disobedience to the authorities of the Presbyterian Church. . . Here is a man of distinction in scholarship and of unquestioned devoutness who for twenty years and more has declared that those who control the power of his communion have repudiated the authentic and official Presbyterian faith in favor of a modernistic emasculation of the pure Gospel of the Bible and the Reformation. It is a dramatic situation, extraordinary for its utter reversal of the usual situation in a judicial doctrinal conflict. It amounts virtually to this: one man is declaring that, in administrative effect, his whole church has become heretical.

Dr. Daniel Russell, moderator of the Presbytery of New York, gave out a statement which was published in the metropolitan press, criticizing the verdict and declaring that the representation that no doctrinal issue was at stake was untrue, since "there are doctrinal matters that run into the heart of the entire problem." And he deplored the fact that Machen was not permitted to discuss them in his defense. In *Christianity Today*, Dr. Craig also insisted that it was a case impossible to judge without taking doctrinal matters into consideration.

> Is it not a doctrinal question to ask whether the authority of the General Assembly is superior to that of the Word of God? Are doctrinal matters not involved when it is asked whether the Board of Foreign Missions is pursuing a policy friendly to the Modernist Auburn Affirmation? . . The cry "the issue is administrative not doctrinal" is the same false cry that was raised in the Princeton Seminary case and even more misleading in this instance than in the former.

Analyzing the trial in the Christian Reformed *Banner* Professor R. B. Kuiper, writing on the background of his own firsthand observations of a large part of the proceedings, denounced the trial from several points of view:

> The Machen trial is a notable revelation of the intolerance of so-called liberalism and its abettors. . . Un-Presbyterian leaders are refusing to tolerate a good Presbyterian in the Presbyterian ministry.
>
> The Machen trial affords a striking revelation of the destructive influence of liberalism and liberal leanings on Christian ethics. . . Here was a minister on trial with his very ecclesiastical life at stake. Might it not be expected that the court would grant him every possible opportunity of defense? Surely the court would lean backward to give the defendant a square deal. Did it? It leaned far forward to deprive him of a square deal. It deliberately destroyed his defense beforehand.

Macartney was to sum up the reaction of many devout Presbyterians following the Syracuse decision, when he spoke of the action as "the saddest tragedy which has befallen the Presbyterian Church in the United States of America in half a century." And he added:

> The suspension of Dr. Machen will cause astonishment and sorrow to thousands of earnest believers in the Presbyterian Church and in all churches.
>
> Only once in a generation or two does such a man as Dr. Machen arise in the church. His ability has shed renown upon our church and his suspension will weaken its witness to the truth. It is our church which will suffer by the suspension. No church, in this day of revealed religion, can afford to lose believers in the gospel like Dr. Machen.

25

THE CLOSING SCENE

In this concluding chapter farewell is taken from J. Gresham Machen as his sudden death on January 1, 1937 is memorialized. So many intimate details of his life have been reviewed and analyzed in the foregoing chapters that, hopefully, a rather accurate estimate of the man has been gained. At least a few new strokes remain however to be added as the concluding months of his life are surveyed. The consideration that Machen was centrally involved in the formation of a new Presbyterian Church is sufficient to draw attention to this period even if the treatment of it must be marked by brevity. My principal aim in any case has been not so much to depict in detail the history of the institutions with whose beginnings Machen's name was prominently associated as to set forth their background in order that the leading historical factors and motive forces might be illumined.

A NEW CHURCH?

The possibility of the eventuation of a separation from the Presbyterian Church in the U. S. A. was in view for many years as the strenuous efforts at reformation seemed be of little or no avail. If Machen had yielded to the course calculated to give him the utmost personal happiness and ease, he would long before have left the Presbyterian Church. Added to the coldness or hostility with which his reformatory labors were generally greeted was the bitter and depressing experience of being made the object of abuse and slander. But considerations of principle restrained him from precipitate action. Machen did not share the widespread depreciation of the doctrine of the visible Church which had found expression among many fundamentalists who remained in the organized churches or had come to more consistent expression in contemporary undenominationalism. Nor did he hold to independency. He was nothing more nor less than a Presbyterian. Moreover, as a minister in the Presbyterian Church his zeal to uphold the Constitution was second to none. Indeed to a large extent the issue of the day, as he viewed it, was whether the Constitution was to be maintained. Accordingly, his was not a sense of estrangement from or slackening of loyalty to historic Presbyterianism. Not he but those who were proving unfaithful to their vows, he felt, should have taken the honest course of leaving the Church. Schism, moreover, and for the same basic reasons of principle, was abhorrent to him. On one occasion he spoke of it as "a very heinous sin." Separation from a Church could be countenanced only if it was demonstrated that that organization had abandoned the authority of the Word of God for another authority, only, that is, if it proved thereby that it was not really a Church of Jesus Christ. Under such circumstances, however, it would virtually be an act of schism to remain, for then one would be separating oneself from the true Church of Jesus Christ.

Following the mandate of 1934, and the evidence that the ecclesiastical princes were ruthlessly going to carry through judicial process, it became very doubtful indeed that it would prove even possible to remain within the Presbyterian Church. And this tendency reached an astonishing climax when the members of the Independent Board were denied a day in court when they might appeal to the Bible and the Constitution of the Church in justification of their actions. The ecclesastical courts might solemnly convene in the name of Jesus Christ, and might cite Scripture in drafting charges and specifications, but if the accused were to be denied the right of seeking to establish the conviction that the order of an Assembly was contrary to the Word of Christ, as well as to specific provisions of the subordinate standards, such professions would be vanity and mockery.

Moreover, in purely arbitrary and tyrannical fashion the Constitution was being virtually set at naught to bolster the maintenance of the status quo when candidates for the ministry (who did not yet enjoy the favored status of ministers) were subjected to pressure to promise implicit obedience to and support of the official program of the Church regardless of its character. If space permitted a number of pages might well be devoted to the valiant stand made by many of these young men. Graduates of Westminster Seminary were being singled out for special treatment, and thus the official policy came to be recognized as a studied effort to crush the new Seminary in an oblique fashion.

That this analysis is not exaggerated appears most strikingly from a "directive," sent by Dr. Lewis S. Mudge, the Stated Clerk, to the Presbytery of Baltimore, containing the following:

> If and when any students from Westminster Seminary come before your Presbytery, they should be informed that the Presbytery will neither license or ordain them until they have given a written pledge that they will support the official agencies of the Church

> as a part of their pledge of loyalty to the government and discipline of the Church.

Incidentally this statement discloses how far the Presbyterian officialdom was from understanding the historic significance of the vow relating to church government. The approval pledged meant a commitment to the principles of Presbyterian church government, and the submission to the specific church bodies was specifically qualified as a submission *in the Lord,* that is in subordination to the Lord's revealed will and allowing of appeal from human or ecclesiastical actions to the Lord of the conscience.

THE COVENANT UNION

In this atmosphere of tyranny preparations were made for eventualities through the organization of the Constitutional Covenant Union on June 27, 1935. As the central features of its Constitution it adopted articles on *Purpose* and *Pledge* which precisely delineated its character. On the background of a reference to the occasion of its formation in the "increasing dominance" of Modernism in the Presbyterian Church in the U. S. A., as disclosed by several developments including the 1934 mandate, it stated:

> The purpose of this Covenant Union shall be to defend and maintain the Constitution of the Presbyterian Church in the U. S. A.,—that is, to defend (1) the Word of God upon which the Constitution is based, (2) the full, glorious system of revealed truth contained in the Confession of Faith and Catechisms, commonly called (to distinguish it from various forms of error) the "Reformed Faith," and (3) the truly Scriptural principles of Presbyterian Church government guaranteeing the Christian's freedom from implicit obedience to any human councils and courts and recognizing instead, in the high Biblical sense, the authority of God.

Then followed the *Pledge* which served to demonstrate that the commitment to Presbyterianism was not in word merely:

> We, the members of this Covenant Union, are resolved, in accordance with God's Word, and in humble reliance upon His grace, to maintain the Constitution of the Presbyterian Church in the U. S. A., (1) making every effort to bring about a reform of the existing church organization, and to restore the Church's clear and glorious Christian testimony, which Modernism and indifferentism have now so grievously silenced, but (2) if such ef-

> ports fail and in particular if the tyrannical policy of the present majority triumphs, holding ourselves ready to perpetuate the true Presbyterian Church in the U. S. A., regardless of cost.

This was not the language or program of schismatics! Machen was not an officer of this organization but of course was a prime mover in it.

It was about this time that it became clear that many who had been reckoned among the conservatives in the Church, and even some who had taken a courageous and self-sacrificial part in the great Presbyterian conflict of the preceding years, came to the determination that they would not go along in the course marked out especially by the *Pledge* of the Covenant Union. Next perhaps to the temporizing of many conservative Princeton Directors following the 1928 Assembly there is no sadder development that is recorded in this narrative. To Machen at any rate it was a blow that brought intense pain and heartbreak. Most distressing of all was the fact that Dr. Craig, stalwart of stalwarts among the Directors in the Princeton struggle, and later Drs. Allis and Macartney, committed themselves to a policy which could not but be regarded by Machen as a shrinking back from the consequences of a forthright course. The severity and relentlessness with which the action against members of the Independent Board had been undertaken had evidently compelled many to realize for the first time that the ultimate outcome of the dynamic reformatory movement might be separation, and they began to wonder whether they were going to find themselves where they wanted to be.

Dr. Craig himself, though at first a member of the Independent Board and a supporter of it in *Christianity Today,* changed his approach. While not modifying his vigorous dissent from such actions as the issuance of the 1934 mandate, he began to question the wisdom of the Independent Board and justified the designation of gifts as a proper policy for those who were not ready to contribute to the Independent Board. This appeared in the September 1935 issue of *Christianity Today.*

Even more indicative of the inwardness of Craig's position was the fact that in the same issue, editorializing on the formation of the Covenant Union, he offered as objections to it that

> we question whether said Union will prove effective in securing united action on the part of all those within the Presbyterian Church in the U. S. A., who are opposed to Modernism and indifferentism. We question whether any very large proportion of sound Presbyterian ministers, elders and lay people will want to join it.

Dr. Craig was right in predicting that people would not join the Union in large numbers. But he did appear to be abandoning the fight in terms of sheer commitment to principle when he appealed to an estimate of probable outcome, and when he voiced objections of this kind rather than seeking to rally members of the Church for a forthright stand. In the course of the editorial his position was somewhat illumined by his plea for a more inclusive organization of conservatives who might undertake the fulfillment of the *Purpose* of the Union but without the burden of its *Pledge*:

> While in our opinion one of the planks of that platform should commit its supporters to the defense of the members of the Independent Board against the unchristian and unconstitutional mandate of the 1934 Assembly, we are persuaded that it must be broad enough to provide seats for many who think that the formation of the Independent Board was unwise or premature, and even for some who think its formation of questionable constitutionality.

This attitude, which seemed to add up to a "stay in at all costs" policy, was basically present in the 1935-36 conflict within Westminster Seminary as the result of which Dr. Allis of the Faculty and Dr. Macartney and several Trustees resigned. In this connection one of the arguments used most persistently was that the Independent Board was having harmful effects upon Westminster Seminary, affecting as it had the ecclesiastical life of professors and students and threatening to close the doors to future opportunity. To a person like Machen, on the other hand, such an argument could not in the nature of the case be allowed to be regulative of the policy or program. To him the issue was much simpler and clear cut: there was only the path of consistent, militant witness and action regardless of consequences — *or* that of compromise.

EVALUATION

This story is written by one whose choice was that of Machen's position as the strong, valiant one of sheer devotion to principle, though without the claim that apart from Machen's powerful enunciation of principles and constraining example his way would necessarily have been followed. Judged in terms of the Constitution of the Church as well as traditional Presbyterian policy the formation of the Independent Board was legal. The methods pursued in the effort to suppress it and to discipline its members were emphatically highhanded and unconstitutional. In refusing to give its members a day in court a shocking travesty of justice was enacted.

It must be admitted that there was an element of abnormality about the formation of an Independent Board since under ordinary circumstances the missions program would be conducted by official agencies of the Church. But these were abnormal times, and the bold and explosive action of the organizers of this Board, if it is to be fairly evaluated, must be understood in the context of the historical situation. It was basically an extraordinary act in a time of crisis, when it became imperative that unusual measures should be taken if the gospel in its purity was to be preached in fulfillment of the divine command. It was also a heroic movement for reformation in an hour when it was still hoped that it would be possible to remain within the Church, and that the Church might still be awakened to realize her jeopardy. The times were times of crisis, when the moment of final decision was at hand but not unmistakably present, when a life and death battle for the supremacy of the Word of God was engaging the soldiers of Christ almost to the breaking point. Let the casual observer of such a momentous struggle take care not to restrict his vision to questions of regularity and normality!

Reflecting further upon that complex situation, however, one cannot fail to face the question why so many true and noble men like Craig and Allis and Macartney came to dissociate themselves from Machen. The basic reason in the judgment of the biographer is that they occupied an essentially weaker and more inconsistent position. But may there not have been secondary factors of some significance, factors in the sphere of personal relationships? Though of the conviction that if such men had followed Machen, they would have taken a stronger position in terms of principle, and one that would have been far more fruitful for the advancement of the Reformed Faith than the one they came to follow, my impression is that Machen might possibly have taken more time to persuade his comrades in years of battle of the necessity of taking the measures he came to take. No one indeed did take greater pains to set forth his position so that none could misunderstand and in general to persuade men to join with him. Moreover, before the formation of the Independent Board was announced there was correspondence and consultation by telephone with these and other leaders. One finds it difficult to escape the conclusion, however, that further conferences were desirable and perhaps a meeting of conservative leaders, before the announcement was made of its formation. The actions of the 1933 Assembly seemed to signal the hour to strike, but it must have seemed somewhat precipitate especially to certain of the older ministers. About this time Machen came to associate with himself a number of rather youthful men who lacked the background common to pastors and others of long experience. Unfortunately Dr. Frank H. Stevenson was not at all well and became less and less active until his early death the following year. Considering, on the one hand, his deep appreciation of and loyalty to Machen, and, on the other, his charm, capacity for making friends and dealing with difficult practical situations, it is likely that, could he have been more active, he would have been able to soothe over ruffled feelings and to resist centrifugal forces.

Machen himself was a man with great capacity for friendship and one who was generous to a fault in consideration of others. But along with his strength as a man to whom political expediency and craft were entirely foreign went a kind of generalship which was satisfied to state and expound principles and objectives and then simply appealed to men to follow them. Since he penetrated easily and quickly to the depths of issues, and could not bring himself to seek to commit men to himself personally, an impression of impatience with those who did not immediately agree was sometimes given. But this fault was not one of conceit or irritability for Machen submerged his own personal interests in his complete devotion to the cause of truth as he understood it. It is possible therefore that Machen contributed somewhat to the lack of harmony among the older Presbyterian leaders.

A certain confirmation of this analysis is provided by the observation that later on Machen came to be disillusioned with regard to several members of the Independent Board who seemed not to have shared his sense of its commitment to distinctively Presbyterian missions and gave various evidences of a tendency to independency in church government. His deep disquietude with regard to this Board during the months immediately preceding his death may have made Machen himself wonder at times whether due caution had been exercised in its formation. As in the case of the Seminary it was again proved that not all who were willing to stand vigorously against Modernism were thereby shown to be qualified to provide leadership in organizations established on a Presbyterian or Reformed platform.

THE PRESBYTERIAN GUARDIAN

One of the costly consequences of the split with Craig was that a new organ had to be established to take the place of *Christianity Today* as the spokesman for the viewpoint of the Covenant Union. Without an organ Machen felt that a cause was dumb. It was in the final analysis more indispensable than anything else. Accordingly, as he had previously given vigorous and generous support to *The Presbyterian* and *Christianity Today,* he now threw himself heart and soul into the formation of a new paper. Though it was published as the organ of the Covenant Union, it was virtually Machen's creation and responsibility. Almost single-handedly Machen underwrote its financial support. It was called *The Presbyterian Guardian,* a name which Machen had much preferred to *Christianity Today* when that paper was founded, because it forthrightly indicated that it was committed to historic Presbyterianism as distinguished from a vaguer or more inclusive evangelicalism. H. McAllister Griffiths, who had been Managing Editor of *Christianity Today* and who had resigned due to the differences that developed with Craig, became Editor. Thomas R. Birch began his association with the paper in a promotional capacity.

Machen himself, though scrupulously keeping hands off so far as editorial decisions were concerned, undertook a series of one-page articles under the general rubric, "The Changing Scene and the Unchanging Word." These articles were marked by Machen's characteristically lucid and persuasive style, but also are memorable because of the pithy and pungent manner in which topics of current moment were discussed. Later on, in mid-summer 1936, when Griffiths resigned, Machen became senior editor, and transferred his activity to the editorial page. Frequently the exigencies of the day required editorials of two and more pages as crucial issues in the church arose. Together with the "Unchanging Scene" essays they comprise immensely interesting and effective exhibitions of Machen's thought and activity during the final year and a half of his life.

The Guardian served admirably from the date of its first issue (October 7, 1935) until the Syracuse tragedy in May, 1936, to keep people in touch with the swiftly rushing current of ecclesiastical events —the Independent Board and other trials, new evidences of Modernism in the official agencies, the progress of the new foreign missions movement—and sharply illumined the deeper significance of what was taking place. When the dreadful, though hardly unexpected, blow fell, therefore, men were prepared for action. The First Annual Convention of the Constitutional Covenant Union had been called for June 11-14 in Philadelphia to deal with the existing situation. The Purpose and Pledge of the organization's constitution did not allow doubt as to the course that would be followed if and when the worst happened. And thus the annual convention almost automatically became the organizing meeting of a new church.

THE PRESBYTERIAN CHURCH OF AMERICA

The decisive step in the formation of the Church was taken on June 11, 1936 when the following resolutions were adopted:

> In order to continue what we believe to be the true spiritual succession of the Presbyterian Church in the U. S. A., which we hold to have been abandoned by the present organization of that body, and to make clear to all the world that we have no connection with the organization bearing that name, we, a company of ministers and ruling elders, having been removed from that organization in contravention as we believe, of its constitution, or having severed our connection with that organization, or hereby solemnly declaring that we do sever our connection with it, or coming as ministers or ruling elders from other ecclesiastical bodies holding the Reformed Faith, do hereby associate ourselves together with all Christian people who do and will adhere to us, in a body to be known and styled as the Presbyterian Church of America.
>
> We, a company of ministers and ruling elders do hereby in our own name, in the name of those who have adhered to us, and by the warrant and authority of the Lord Jesus Christ constitute ourselves a General Assembly of the Presbyterian Church of America.

At this Assembly Machen was chosen moderator. At its concluding service he preached a notable sermon entitled "The Church of God" on the text Acts 20:28, a stirring utterance which served to set the tone of the new Church and its mission on the highest possible plane. Through the action of the Covenant Union in its closing moments *The Presbyterian Guardian* with its assets and liabilities (the liabilities, at least the financial ones, predominated) to a Company in which Paul Woolley and Murray Forst Thompson were associated with Machen. Thus the pattern of an independent press was established at the beginning of the new denomination's life. In the first issue published under its new ownership Machen's column was devoted to the theme, "A True Presbyterian Church at Last." It was an article in which he reviewed briefly the long, painful struggle from 1920 onward which had resulted finally in the triumph of unbelief and sin. In that struggle many terrible sins had been committed by those who sought reform. "What a fearful sin of omission it was, for example, that an effort was not made in 1924, in every single presbytery in which any of us stood, to bring the Auburn Affirmationists to trial!" Nevertheless, on the whole, a faithful effort had been made to bring about a return from Modernism and indifferentism to the Bible and the Constitution in keeping with the solemn ordination pledge requiring us to be "zealous and faithful in maintaining the truths of the gospel and the purity and peace of the Church, whatever persecution or opposition may arise unto us on that account." The dominant mood of the article, however, was one of relief and joy:

On Thursday, June 11, 1936, the hopes of many long years were realized. We became members, at last, of a true Presbyterian Church; we recovered, at last, the blessing of true Christian fellowship. What a joyous moment it was! How the long years of struggle seemed to sink into nothingness compared with the peace and joy that filled our hearts!

To the world, indeed, it might seem to have been not a happy moment but a sad one. Separation from the church of one's fathers; a desperate struggle ahead, with a tiny little group facing the hostility of the visible church—what possible joy or comfort can be found in such things as these?

Yet to us it was a happy and a blessed moment despite all. You see, we do not look upon these matters as the world looks upon them. We ground our hopes not upon numbers nor upon wealth but upon the exceeding great and precious promises of God. If our opponents despise us as being but a tiny little group, we remember the words of Scripture: "There is no restraint to the Lord, to save by many or by few." If we are tempted to be discouraged because of our lack of material resources, we say, again in the words of Scripture: "Not by might, nor by power, but by my spirit, saith the Lord of hosts." . . .

With what lively hope does our gaze turn now to the future! At last true evangelism can go forward without the shackle of compromising associations. The fields are white to the harvest. The evangelists are ready to be sent. Who will give the funds needed to send them out with their message of peace?

The hostility of the Presbyterian Church in the U. S. A. was to express itself in an unexpected fashion when before many months had passed the infant church was prosecuted in a civil suit to compel a change in the name of the denomination. The new body desired only to be known as Presbyterian, and not as a peculiar brand of the same. And it felt assured as to the legality of the name "Presbyterian Church of America" since other Presbyterian Churches, including the Presbyterian Church in the U. S. (the Southern Presbyterian Church, so-called), were distinguished from the Northern Church only by minor geographical variations. Ultimately, however, the name had to be abandoned and the Church became known as the Orthodox Presbyterian Church, a name which had the merit of underscoring its resolve to stand faithfully for the historic Presbyterianism of the Westminster doctrinal standards.

A TRULY PRESBYTERIAN CHURCH?

There were other problems, however, which were far more disturbing than this attack from without. These concerned the question whether the Church would be in fact as well as in profession a true Presbyterian Church. To some extent the dangers in this regard had been foreseen in view of the failure of many devout evangelicals who were opposed to Modernism to grasp the meaning of the constitutional commitment of Presbyterianism to the Reformed Faith. Alarmed at this situation and hoping to correct the evil before it was too late, it had been determined after careful deliberation that it was necessary to apprise the adherents of the movement of the line that marked off Presbyterianism from various current views. In response to this need Professor John Murray undertook the preparation of a series of articles under the general heading, "The Reformed Faith and Modern Substitutes," which appeared in *The Presbyterian Guardian,* beginning with the issue of Dec. 16, 1935. In these articles Mr. Murray showed that not only Arminianism but also "Modern Dispensationalism" of the Scofield Bible type were contrary to the Reformed Faith and the Bible.

The question whether the new body would be distinctly Reformed was raised in another manner at the very first General Assembly in connection with the decision as to the precise form in which the Westminster Standards would be adopted. Machen and his most intimate associates were determined once for all to get free from the mediating 1903 amendments, and though the final decision was postponed until the Second Assembly, called to meet in November, 1936, the Committee on the Constitution was specifically authorized at the first Assembly to propose the elimination of these amendments. Major articles by Machen and others appeared in the *Guardian* in support of this view. The final decision in November, 1936, was in agreement with this position. It is indicative of the situation that had developed, however, that the Rev. Carl McIntire and others led a vigorous fight against this proposal at the time. Their contention was not that these amendments were necessarily to be kept intact but rather that in the interest of maintaining "the spiritual succession" of the Presbyterian Church in the U. S. A., they should be considered after the new Church had begun. To the others the appeal to spiritual succession could not in the nature of the case be decisive. If that were taken as a determining voice in matters of faith and life, it might frequently result in the maintenance of beliefs and practices which had developed in the period of gradual declension in which Modernism had taken root. To a Church that stood for the Word of God, and desired therefore to eliminate all compromising features from its faith and practice, there could be no temporizing in the fundamental matter of the truth or error of its doctrinal standards.

Essentially the same issue was at stake in connection with other matters that were raised from this same quarter. In connection with Professor Murray's evaluation of modern dispensationalism the subject of premillennialism as such had not been raised. It was recognized that the traditional liberty granted to this point of view would continue to be maintained. There were pre-millenarians, however, who were restive under this criticism of Modern Dispensationalism, and held that their "eschatological liberty" was being put in jeopardy. And when Professor Kuiper reported in a story about the new Church, published in the Christian Reformed *Banner*, that, in connection with the examination of candidates for ordination at the First Assembly, "it would have warmed the cockles of the heart of any Christian Reformed minister to hear how closely they were questioned about the two errors which are so extremely prevalent among American fundamentalists, Arminianism and the Dispensationalism of the Scofield Bible," and that "the Assembly wanted to make sure that these prospective ministers were not tainted with such anti-reformed heresies," Mr. McIntire, who had initiated the publication of *The Christian Beacon*, attacked Kuiper charging that he had designated premillennialism as a heresy. When Kuiper asked that a reply to this misrepresentation be published in *The Beacon*, the editor refused. Machen was deeply grieved at this, partly because he felt that suspicion and injustice with regard to Kuiper and the cause resulted, but also because it seemed to him a matter of elementary journalistic ethics that Kuiper's reply should have been printed, and that without delay. Machen dealt with this and related matters at considerable length in the *Guardian*, and the pertinent documents were printed in full in its news columns.

J. Oliver Buswell, Jr., president of Wheaton College, a member of the Independent Board who had been tried by his presbytery, and who had been honored with the moderatorship of the Second Assembly, shared Mr. McIntire's outlook to a large degree. Shortly before Machen's death Buswell submitted to him an extensive critique of Westminster Seminary which Machen never found opportunity of answering, though he did discuss it at length with his colleagues. Machen thus came to realize that not only the infant Church but the Seminary itself, and its stand for the Reformed Faith, were being threatened. The charges made against the Seminary included the issue of dispensationalism but in addition its view of Apologetics, its conception of evangelism, and its attitude toward "the separated life." Machen had absolutely no sympathy with this criticism, in fact, he felt that the integrity of the witness of the cause to the Reformed Faith was in danger of being undermined. This estimate was confirmed as he saw a common pattern unfold in the councils of the Independent Board and among a minority in the New Church.

This was the background which led shortly after Machen's death to a certain realignment of forces. Dr. MacRae, assistant professor of Old Testament resigned from the Seminary charging "alien control" had developed and repeating various features of Dr. Buswell's indictment. And at the Third General Assembly, when they failed to secure approval of the Independent Board, which had ousted Machen from its presidency, and were unsuccessful in securing the adoption by the Assembly of a total abstinence resolution, they withdrew to form the Bible Presbyterian Synod. Soon thereafter Faith Theological Seminary was established with Dr. MacRae as its president. Meanwhile, several members of the Independent Board who agreed with Machen's strong Presbyterian emphasis resigned. The details of this significant development take us beyond the scope of this narrative, but they are fully documented in *The Presbyterian Guardian* for those who are interested to evaluate them.

The Seminary and the cause as a whole suffered as a result of the impact made by this division, especially because of distorted and unfounded representations as to its position and practices. But it survived these and other adversities to remain a monument to Machen's valiant and unswerving stand for the supremacy of Scripture. The Reformed Faith on this view is not a mantle which may be laid aside at pleasure but is nothing short of Christianity come into its own, and therefore the message which must be proclaimed and handed down without diminuation, impairment or obstruction.

It is hardly a wonder that Machen was virtually crushed under the burden of the anxieties and labors that were present day and night during the last months of his life. Besides the multiplicity of activities of which mention has previously been made—teaching and administrative functions, preaching and speaking and the "care of all the churches," the mountains of correspondence and countless meetings and conferences—he had assumed the demanding responsibility of speaking regularly on the radio week after week during the winter months, beginning early in 1935. In the midst of his dreadfully crowded schedule it involved the sheerest toil to prepare these messages. They were however very well received, and a considerable portion of them have been published in two volumes *The Christian Faith in the Modern World* and *The Christian View of Man*. Machen's hope was that he might be enabled to publish at least four such books which might serve as a popular treatment of Christian Doctrine. They disclose his intense and increasing interest in the systematic exposition of the Reformed Faith, and have been used since their publication with great edification by countless readers who have rejoiced in his marvelous gifts as an expositor.

FAITHFUL UNTO DEATH

If Machen had not been given a sturdy physical constitution to accompany his magnificent mind, he would not have been able to undertake the half of what he lived to do. He was not a giant—only five feet, eight inches—and in later years he had become perhaps slightly overweight—about 180 lbs. as compared with 150 ten or so years before his death. But there was nothing flabby about him as any one who tried to keep pace with him when he walked up the street soon realized. During the last summer of his life he had managed to get away to the Canadian Rockies for a little climbing. He seemed to his associates to look somewhat drawn when they saw him first in the fall. Had he perhaps engaged in somewhat too strenuous exercise considering his fifty-five years? Perhaps not, although his too infrequent opportunities of recreation did not form the ideal background for such vigorous activity. As the year drew to its close, however, it seemed at times that he was deadly tired. And no doubt all of his anxieties with regard to the course and future of the movement with which he was associated as the acknowledged leader gave him many sleepless nights. But he was not one to pamper himself, and there was no one of sufficient influence to constrain him to curtail his program to any significant degree.

And so during the brief recess from academic teaching at the Christmas vacation he fulfilled an engagement to speak in a number of churches in North Dakota at the invitation of their pastor, the Rev. Samuel J. Allen. Taking account of his cold and his evident need of a rest, members of his immediate family in Baltimore urged him to cancel the engagement, but Machen was unwilling to disappoint Allen and the churches to which he ministered. Leaving the moderate climate of Philadelphia he arrived in the frigid—twenty below zero—temperature of Bismarck, North Dakota. Though admitting, in an offhand way, that he had been ill during the night, he declared on that Tuesday morning that he was ready to do anything that would help the cause. So a trip to Carson and Leith was proposed and undertaken. Evidently his condition grew steadily worse as he rode along through the bitter weather. On the outward journey he kept saying, as the Rev. S. J. Allen later reported, "You are not seeing Dassie at his best; I'm not like this very often." But his conversation centered upon the Reformed Faith and his hopes for Westminster and *The Presbyterian Guardian*. At Leith during his speech "he was hampered by a cough that made it appear as though he were troubled with asthma . . . Nevertheless, he went straight through without one single complaint or excuse." Mr. Allen's account now continues:

> Almost immediately after his talk he was stricken with pleurisy. He could not walk up the steps by himself. The pain was intense. He was in agony. From Leith to Bismarck (75 miles) he groaned with pain and had a terrible thirst. Sometimes he thought he was going to die. More than once he cried out about his thirst. I offered to stop but he said, "We can't do it. Wait until we get to Bismarck." At one time he cried, "I can't make it, I can't make it"; then he would say, "I can't die now, I have so much work to do." This was the saddest and most grievous trip I ever made. . . At last, after what seemed an age, we arrived in Bismarck about 7:17 P. M. He had to be helped from my car to his room. At first he wouldn't consent to the calling of a doctor, but the pain was so intense that he finally yielded on the point.

Although the doctor advised hospitalization at once, Machen insisted on going through with his evening engagement in Bismarck. After he had been bound about his chest, he felt some relief and insisted that he was "fit as a fiddle." And so he carried through his appointment in his usual impressive manner and answered questions for fifteen minutes afterward. He was now again close to collapse, but was delighted that he had been able to put across his message without persons in the audience being the wiser. Now his great concern was to get back to Philadelphia, and on Wednesday morning he was all dressed and ready to depart when the doctor, taking account of his condition and his intense pain, absolutely refused to permit him to go. The diagnosis at first was pleurisy and he was constrained to enter the Roman Catholic hospital. In the hope of relieving the minds of his brother and his family in Baltimore and the colleagues in Philadelphia, he sent telegrams with the message that there was no cause for alarm.

But he grew steadily worse and by Thursday the diagnosis was pneumonia. His breathing was so difficult and in general his condition so distressing that he realized that he was gravely ill. But as the sisters who attended him testified, "He was all spirit." His mind was on the cause as it centered in Philadelphia and he sent off several telegrams. He also wrote out a substantial check to cover certain *Guardian* bills that were about to fall due. The nurses felt that he should be using all of his waning energies in resisting the disease.

On New Year's Eve Mr. Allen called briefly and offered prayer. And then Machen told him of a vision he had had of being in heaven: "Sam, it was glorious, it was glorious." And a little later, "Sam, isn't the Reformed Faith grand?" The following day he was largely unconscious, but there were intervals when his mind was thoroughly alert. In one of those periods he dictated a telegram to his colleague John Murray which was his final word: "I'm so thankful for active obedience of Christ. No hope without it." And so he died at about 7:30 P. M. on January 1, 1937.

The reference to the active obedience of Christ finds its background in a sermon on that theme which he had preached over the radio on December 20th. Previously he had been discussing the doctrine with Murray, as he occasionally did other topics with which he dealt. And now that he realized that he was about to pass over the river into the eternal city, he bore testimony to the confidence that he reposed in the substitutionary atonement of Christ. And so he gave expression to the conviction that he had assurance not only of remission of sin and its penalty but also of being accepted as perfectly obedient and righteous, and so an heir of eternal life, because of the perfect obedience of Christ to the divine will. And it was most characteristic of Machen that, even in his agony, he wanted to express his exultant faith to one who shared it with him in rich measure. His eyes were upon Christ as his living hope. But he was also virtually thanking his colleague for his contribution to the appreciation of that doctrine as they had discussed it together on the basis of the Word of God.

His body was returned to Philadelphia where on January 5 a service was held at the Spruce Street Baptist Church. Immediately afterward it was carried to his native Baltimore and was interred in Greenmount Cemetery adjoining the graves of his father and mother.

His associates and friends were overwhelmed with sorrow. But there was also determination that he should not have died in vain. Though his great heart had stopped beating and his steadying hand would no longer be felt, his example of uncalculating devotion to truth and duty remained. For many it remains fresh and fragrant to the very present day. May these pages help to arouse in a generation that did not know him a bright vision of the significance of a life that came to be marked by steadfast faith in the Crucified One and by complete abandon in commitment to the service of God. As his favorite hymn expresses it,

> Were the whole realm of nature mine,
> That were a present far too small;
> Love so amazing, so divine,
> Demands my soul, my life, my all.

Notes and References

Index

NOTES AND REFERENCES

Key to Abbreviations:

CT — *Christianity Today*
DAB — *Dictionary of American Biography*
PG — *The Presbyterian Guardian*
Pn. — *The Presbyterian*
PTR — *The Princeton Theological Review*
WIC — *What Is Christianity?* Edited by the author.

CHAPTER I

Page 17 — The name J. Gresham Machen, and especially the maternal family name Gresham, is frequently mispronounced. At the request of the publisher of *The Literary Digest,* Machen wrote at some length on the subject, and on the background of this information the magazine in its issue of July 14, 1934 carried the following key over the name of the lexicographer Frank H. Vizetelly: "*gress' am,* not *gresh' am; may' chen,* not *may' ken.*" The chief pitfall in the pronouncing of the name, as Machen said, is in the drawing of the "s" and "h" together in Gresham. The "h" is silent as in "Markham" or "Badham."

Page 18 — The memorial volumes are *Letters of Arthur W. Machen with Biographical Sketch,* compiled by Arthur W. Machen, Jr.; *Stories and Articles by Arthur W. Machen,* collected by Arthur W. Machen, Jr., (Baltimore, 1917); and *Testimonials to the Life and Character of John Jones Gresham* [by Minnie Gresham Machen] (Baltimore, 1892). All were privately printed.

Pages 29f. — Edwin Mims, *Sidney Lanier* (Houghton Mifflin, 1905), p. 20.

Page 33 — An article from the pen of Mrs. Machen on "The Faculty of 1865" was published in *The Wesleyan Alumnae,* May, 1931, pp. 52ff.

Pages 33f. — *The Atlanta Journal* article appeared on Jan. 7, 1932.

Page 34 — On Baltimore the following are of special interest: *Baltimore. Its History and Its People* (Baltimore, 1912), edited by E. C. Hill; M. Janvier, *Baltimore in the Eighties and Nineties* (Roebuck, 1933); *Maryland. A Guide to the Old Line South* (P.W.A., 1940); Hamilton Owens, *Baltimore on the Chesapeake* (Doubleday, Doran, 1941); C. Hirschfield, *Baltimore,* 1870-1900 (Johns Hopkins University Press, 1941).

Page 35 — On Johns Hopkins University see especially Daniel Coit Gilman, *The Launching of A University* (Dodd, Mead, 1906); Fabian Franklin, *Life of Daniel Coit Gilman* (Dodd, Mead, 1910); W. Carson Ryan, *Studies in Early Graduate Education* (Carnegie Foundation, 1939); Abraham Flexner, *Daniel Coit Gilman* (Harcourt, Brace, 1946); and many issues of the *Johns Hopkins Alumni Magazine.*

Pages 35ff. — "The Ode to the University" and other poems of Lanier are quoted by permission from the *Collected Works of Sidney Lanier* (Johns Hopkins University Press, 1945), Vol. I, edited by C. R. Anderson. The poem addressed to Mrs. Bird, written on Jan 14, 1878, appears in a somewhat different text in L. Lorenz, *The Life of Sidney Lanier* (Coward, McCann, 1935): "love wants" for "lonely wastes." The letters of Lanier are also quoted by permission, and appear in *Collected Works,* Vol. VII-X, edited by C. R. Anderson and A. H. Starke,

Page 36 — An obituary of Mrs. Bird, written by Mrs. Machen, was published in *The Presbyterian of the South* on Mar. 30, 1910.

Page 38 — Edwin Mims, *op. cit.,* contains an account of Mrs. Machen's personal impressions of Lanier.

CHAPTER II

Page 50 — The quotations from Gildersleeve are from *Essays and Studies* (Johns Hopkins Press, 1890), preface: *The Creed of the Old South* (Johns Hopkins Press, 1915), p. 51; *Hellas and Hesperia* (Henry Holt, 1909), pp. 16, 19.

Page 52f. — The quotations concerning Gildersleeve are from Paul Shorey, "The American Scholar and Gentleman," (*Johns Hopkins Alumni Magazine*, Jan. 1925), an address delivered at the Gildersleeve Memorial Meeting; Abraham Flexner, *Daniel Coit Gilman* (Harcourt, Brace, 1946), pp. 67f. The latter is quoted by special permission. On Gildersleeve see also DAB and the *Cambridge History of American Literature*.

Page 53 — The letter of protest was addressed to Professor M. I. Pupin, chairman of the executive committee, under date of Nov. 6, 1925.

CHAPTER III

Pages 61ff. — On Princeton Seminary see *Princeton Seminary Centennial* Volume (De Vinne Press, 1912), pp. 350, 364f., 349f., 565; the *Charles Hodge Semi-centennial* volume (1872); pp. 52, 46; *The Presbyterian and Reformed Review* and PTR; *Princeton Seminary Bulletin;* and the catalogues of the Seminary. Other significant works are the biographies of Archibald Alexander, Samuel Miller, Joseph A. Alexander and Charles Hodge and *A. A. Hodge, In Memoriam* (1887) and C. A. Salmond, *Princetoniana* (1888).

Page 65 — The estimate of Patton's university administration follows essentially DAB. A somewhat different evaluation is found in Thomas Jefferson Wertenbaker, *Princeton*, 1746-1896 (Princeton University Press, 1946). On Patton see also *The Great Presbyterian Conflict. Patton vs. Swing* (Chicago, 1874); Francis L. Patton, *Fundamental Christianity* (Macmillan, 1926). The citation of Dean West was published in his *Presentations for Honorary Degrees in Princeton University*, 1905-1925 (Princeton, 1929), pp. 43f.

Pages 66ff. — On Warfield see also Patton in PTR, 1921; C. W. Hodge, Jr. in PTR, 1922; Samuel G. Craig in B B. Warfield, *Biblical and Theological Studies* (Presby. and Refd. Pub. Co., 1952), pp. xi-xlvii.

CHAPTER IV

Page 72 — Dr. Vos' sermon to which reference is made was later published in a volume of sermons entitled *Grace and Glory* (Eerdmans, 1922), pp. 89-104. The text was John 20:16 and the title "Rabboni!"

Page 75f. — James B. Brown, "A Young Man at Princeton," in PG, Aug. 25, 1940, p. 51.

CHAPTER V

Page 106 — The Browning reference is evidently to *Christmas Eve*, XIV and XV.

CHAPTER IX

Pages 170f. — A popular series of expository studies on Galatians, which nevertheless serves to illustrate Machen's gifts as an exegete and expositor, was published in CT, Jan. 1931 - Feb. 1933. Unfortunately the series does not carry one beyond Gal. 3:14.

Page 176 — Warfield's address was published in *Calvin as a Theologian and Calvinism Today* (*Philadelphia*, 1909).

CHAPTER X

Pages 203ff. -- This work was published under the title, *A Rapid Survey of the Literature and History of New Testament Times* (Presbyterian Board of Publication 1914 and 1915), and remains a useful survey. There were two forms, a teacher's manual and a student's textbook.

With James Oscar Boyd he later undertook *A Brief Bible History* (Westminster Press, 1921), a book belonging to the same category. For some unknown reason this work is not mentioned in his own list of his writings, for example in "Christianity in Conflict" (in *Contemporary Theology,* Vol. I, Round Table Press, 1932). But he did sometimes express the hope of preparing a revised edition of the earlier work.

CHAPTER XI

Page 213 — Dr. Mackay's estimate was published in *Princeton Seminary Bulletin,* Jan., 1940, pp. 1f.

CHAPTER XII

Page 243 — Shorey, *op. cit.*, pp. 149f.

Pages 244f. — John Adam Cramb, *Germany and England* (London, 1914). Reprints were also published in America.

CHAPTER XVI

Page 334 — Not unconnected with the impact made by Machen's book on Paul is the fact that at the June, 1922, commencement of Hampden-Sydney College he was awarded the honorary degree of doctor of divinity. His honorary Litt.D. degree was awarded by Wheaton College in 1928.

CHAPTER XVII

Page 336 — S. G. Cole, *The History of Fundamentalism* (Richard Smith, 1931) surveys the development of fundamentalism in somewhat broader perspective and from a different point of view.

Pages 337f. — The quotations relating to Machen's attitude toward fundamentalism are from his article, "What Fundamentalism Stands For Now," (*N. Y. Times* for June 21, 1925; republished in WIC) and his Statement of Nov. 23, 1926, submitted to the committee of investigation of Princeton, p. 37.

Page 339 — On developments in the Orient see, besides the articles and notices in the weekly papers, the article, "Modernism in China," by W. H. Griffith Thomas in PTR, Oct. 1921, pp. 630ff.

Page 348 — The Lippmann quotation is from *A Preface to Morals* (Macmillan, 1926), p. 32, and is used by permission.

CHAPTER XVIII

Pages 357f. — The sermon on "The Present Issue in the Church" is republished in *God Transcendent* (Eerdmans, 1949), pp. 40ff. There it appears as the fifth in a group of eight sermons known to have been preached in the sequence given while Machen was Stated Supply in Princeton. Some judgment of his preaching at that time can also be formed from the book *What is Faith?* (1925), which utilized considerable sermonic materials presented during that year of preaching

Page 370 — The comment on Dr. Fosdick's letter appeared in Pn. Oct. 23, 1924; the debate regarding Fosdick, under the title, "Is the Teaching of Dr. Fosdick Opposed to the Christian Religion?" in *The World Work* for Dec. 13, 1924; and the review of *The Modern Use of the Bible* in PTR, Jan. 1925.

Page 370 — Other articles from this period on the issues of the day included "Dr. Merrill and The World's Work" (Pn., Feb. 7, 1924); "Dr. Xenos and the Present Issue in the Church" (Pn., May 22, 1924); "Christian Fellowship and World-wide Conflict" (Pn., Nov. 24, 1924); "Honesty and Freedom in the Christian Ministry" (*Moody Monthly,* Mar. 1924); "Rupert Hughes and the Christian Religion," a reply to an article "Why I Quit Going to Church" in the *Cosmopolitan,* Oct. 1924 (*Sunday School Times,* Nov. 8, 1924)

CHAPTER XIX

Pages 371ff. — Primary sources for this chapter include Machen's *Statement and Appended Documents* (Printed, not published Nov. 23, 1926) and *Additional Statement* (Dec. 18, 1926), which were submitted to the Committee of Investigation.

Page 377 — Machen's later evaluation of the League of Evangelical Students appears in an article in PG, Dec. 1935.

CHAPTER XX

Page 395 — The article, "My Idea of God," was published in the *Women's Home Companion* for Dec. 1925 and was later incorporated in the book of the same title, edited by Joseph Fort Newton (Little, Brown, 1926). Machen also participated in a symposium review of the book in *Unity,* March 28, 1927. Other articles utilized in *What is Faith?* include "Religion and Fact," in *The Real Issue* (organ of the Philadelphia Society of Princeton University), April 15, 1924; "Faith and Knowledge," a paper read at the Fourth Biennial Meeting of Theological Seminaries and Colleges in the United States and Canada, held in June, 1923, and published in its *Bulletin,* Aug. 1924; "The God of the Early Christians," an article published in PTR, Oct. 1924; "The Biblical Teacher and Biblical Facts," in *Christian Education,* Dec. 1924, republished in the *Sunday School Times* for Dec. 27, 1925 and (in German translation) in *Kirchenzeitung* for May 5, 1925.

Page 401 — An important statement of Machen's view of science appeared in PTR, Jan. 1926 under the title, "The Relation of Religion to Science and Philosophy."

Page 404 — Other utterances on the subject of education include two addresses on "The Necessity of the Christian School" and "The Christian School, the Hope of America" delivered before the National Union of Christian Schools in 1933 and 1934 respectively and published in the proceedings of the Union, and "Shall We Have Christian Schools?", his final editorial published in PG, Jan. 9, 1937. The address on "The Necessity of the Christian School" has been republished in WIC. Of interest also is Machen's article on "Teacher Oaths" in PG for Jan. 6, 1936.

Page 405 — On the Child Labor Amendment the following communications and articles may be noted: Letters to the *N. Y. Times* (Nov. 17, 1924), *N. Y. Herald Tribune* (Nov. 19, 1924), *The New Republic*: "Child Labor and Liberty," (Dec. 3, 1924); an article "The So-called Child Labor Amendment" in Pn. for Jan. 22, 1925; a Reply in the Christian Reformed *Banner* for Jan. 4, 1935; an editorial in PG, Dec. 26, 1936.

Page 408 — Letters on various public questions appeared in the *N. Y. Herald Tribune* on Dec. 10, 1924; Dec. 7, 1925; Feb. 10, 1926; April 19, 1296; Dec. 28, 1930.

CHAPTER XXI

Pages 409ff. — Machen's copy of "The Transcript of the Hearings of the General Assembly's Special Committee to Visit Princeton Seminary" has been the chief source for this chapter.

Pages 409f. — Lipscomb's appraisal was published in Pn. on Sept. 9, 1926.

Page 423 — A different appraisal of the Princeton struggle, including especially the investigation, appears in the biography of J. M. T. Finney, *A Surgeon's Life* (Putnams, 1940). Dr. Finney was a Director in the minority group, and writes admittedly from the standpoint of intimate friendship for and support of Drs. Erdman and Stevenson. His recollections are shown to be inaccurate at at least one point when he states that he himself was a member of the Assembly's investigating committee. He was rather a member of a Director's committee of six which sought to work out a compromise.

Page 424 — A portion of the manuscript used for the Smyth Lectures was published in PTR in Oct., 1927. As evidence of further contacts with the Southern Church about this time mention may be made of two articles contributed to the *Union Seminary Review*: "What is the Gospel?" in Jan., 1927, and "Forty Years of N. T. Research" in Oct., 1928.

Page 425 — The Bible League Lectures of 1927 were on the theme, "Is the Bible Right About Jesus?" They were republished in WIC.

CHAPTER XXII

Pages 432f. — In addition to *A Plea For Fair Play* and the reply to Mr. Jessup Machen wrote an article on "The Gist of the Princeton Question" for Pn., May 17, 1928.

Page 434 — The summary and selective nature of this portion of the narrative has not permitted adequate notice of the writing of other notable defenders of the conservative position, including especially Dr. Samuel G. Craig. editor of *The Presbyterian,* and Dr. Frank H. Stevenson. Among the latter's brilliant essays was a pamphlet published in 1928 under the title, *A Pastor Looks At Princeton.*

Page 438 — A later appraisal of the Christian Reformed Church appeared in Machen's column in PG, July 20, 1936.

Page 441 — Among the legal opinions on the questions involved in the reorganization of Princeton mention may be made of those prepared by Humes, Buck & Smith of New York on Feb. 4, 1928; Armstrong, Machen & Allen of Baltimore on May 1, 1928; and Lindabury, DePue & Faulks of Newark on May 17, 1928. Professor W. P. Armstrong also prepared a pamphlet on *Certain Legal Aspects of the Proposal to Amend the Charter* on May 12, 1928.

CHAPTER XXIII

Page 455 — Machen's opening address is republished in WIC. Other memorable utterances concerning the background and origins of Westminster appear in the issues of CT, 1930-34. Special mention may be made of C. E. Macartney, "Protestantism's Tomorrow" (the first commencement address), May, 1930; F. H. Stevenson, "Samuel G. Craig" (May, 1933); and S. G. Craig, "Westminster Seminary and the Reformed Faith" (the fifth commencement address), Oct. and Nov., 1934.

Pages 462ff. — *The Virgin Birth of Christ* was reviewed even more extensively and at least as favorably as his other books. Some ninety reviews in magazines and newspapers of several countries have been preserved, many written by the most distinguished theologians of the day. In the space available at best a bare summary of a few could have been given. and in this case (since a choice was inevitable)it has seemed better to present instead Mrs. Machen's own response to the book.

CHAPTER XXIV

Page 470 — The lectures on "The Importance of Christian Scholarship" and "Mountains and Why We Love Them" have been republished in WIC.

Pages 472ff. — Various aspects of the developments related in this chapter are treated in considerably greater detail in *The Presbyterian Conflict* by Edwin H. Rian (Eerdmans, 1940).

No account is taken here of the issue that developed in connection with a plan to unite The Presbyterian and United Presbyterian Churches, although Machen devoted considerable attention to it. Several articles on this and other phases of the ecclesiastical struggle were published in CT and PG. See also Rian, *op. cit.*

CHAPTER XXV

Pages 495f. — On the Covenant Union see Machen's discussion in PG, Nov. 18. 1935, various articles in PG about this period, and Rian, *op. cit.*

Pages 500ff. — The beginnings of the new Presbyterian Church and its early fortunes are reported in detail in PG, beginning with the issue of June 22, 1936. Machen's editorial utterances during this period frequently dealt with the basic questions before the Church.

Pages 506ff. — S. J. Allen, "The Last Battle of Dr. Machen" in PG, Jan. 23, 1937.

Page 508 — The sermon on "The Active Obedience of Christ" has been republished in *God Transcendent.* See also John Murray, "Dr. Machen's Hope and the Active Obedience of Christ" in PG. Jan. 23, 1937. The Jan. 23 issue of PG was a Memorial Number and contains several other articles relating to Machen; the issue of Feb. 13 contains numerous tributes to him at the time of his death.

Index